D1711860

RODNEY D. JOHNSON

*Federal Reserve Bank of Philadelphia
and Temple University*

BERNARD R. SISKIN

Temple University

QUANTITATIVE TECHNIQUES FOR BUSINESS DECISIONS

PRENTICE-HALL, INC., Englewood Cliffs, New Jersey

Library of Congress Cataloging in Publication Data

JOHNSON, RODNEY D

    Quantitative techniques for business decisions.
      1. Decision-making   Mathematical models.   2. Op-
erations research.   3. Business   Data processing.
I. Siskin, Bernard R., joint author.
II. Title.
HD69.D4J63   658'4'03   75-31845
ISBN 0-13-746990-X

To Our Patient Wives

Carolyn and Barbara

10 9 8 7 6 5 4 3 2 1

Printed in the United States of America

PRENTICE-HALL INTERNATIONAL, INC., *London*
PRENTICE-HALL OF AUSTRALIA PTY. LTD., *Sydney*
PRENTICE-HALL OF CANADA, LTD., *Toronto*
PRENTICE-HALL OF INDIA PRIVATE LIMITED, *New Delhi*
PRENTICE-HALL OF JAPAN, INC., *Tokyo*
PRENTICE-HALL OF SOUTH-EAST ASIA PRIVATE LIMITED, *Singapore*

contents

II
OPTIMIZATION MODELS

III
ANALYSIS MODELS

preface

To an ever-increasing extent, modern management is adopting and applying quantitative techniques to aid in the process of decision making. The intelligent use of the appropriate tools can reduce an otherwise highly complex problem to one of manageable dimensions. The collection of these techniques has become loosely known as "decision theory," although there certainly is no such thing as an integrated theory of how to make decisions. Nevertheless, one would seriously underestimate the ultimate impact these methods are going to have if they are viewed as nothing more than a handful of tools that are sometimes used to solve particular types of problems. Indeed, there is a growing body of opinion that believes that the greatest impact of the quantitative approach will not be in the area of problem solving, but will rather be on problem formulation. It will radically alter the way managers think about their problems—how they size them up, gain new insights, relate them to other problems, communicate with other people about them, and gather information for solving them. Thus quantitative analysis could have a profound effect on the "art" of management.

At present, seat-of-the-pants, reactive managerial styles are already on the wane, and increased emphasis is being placed on "scientific" analysis and planning. Up-to-date experience is still invaluable, but it must be used with greater discipline. Analysis is now more rigorous, and computers permit more alternatives to be analyzed in greater depth. But, most important, formal planning is being used as a basis for action, not merely for *pro forma* exercises. On a higher and more conceptual level, quantitative analysis is facilitating communication where it never existed before. When a problem has been stated quantitatively, one can often see that it is structurally similar to other problems (perhaps from completely different areas) which, on the surface, appear to be quite different. And once a common structure has been identified, insights and predictions can be transferred from one situation to another; the quantitative approach can actually foster communication.

Thus it is not necessary—or even desirable—for modern managers to be skilled practitioners of quantitative analysis. But they frequently lack even the ability to recognize the right tool or data when they see them, let alone the ability to focus on the basic structure of a problem rather than its situational uniqueness. Yet they must be able to do so if they are to do more than generate elegant nonsense. Managers must learn what the various tools are designed to do and what the limits of their capabilities are. They must be able to understand what staff specialists are attempting to achieve by a particular analysis and to discuss the appropriateness of alternative procedures sensibly (which also requires the development of additional vocabulary). They must fully understand the variables a model will and will not consider and be able to evaluate whether the relationships among the variables are sensible. Managers cannot use an analytical tool wisely unless they fully comprehend the underlying assumptions, what the analysis achieves, what compromises the model makes with reality, and how its conclusions are to be adapted to changing circumstances and intangible considerations. All of this requires a more thorough knowledge of operations than of mathematics.

In anticipation of the dramatic changes that are even now gaining momentum and to help today's manager prepare himself for the new roles he must fill in the future, this book is written to acquaint the manager with the more important and commonly used quantitative techniques. The book is designed to develop a familiarity with the application of these techniques (as opposed to the development of their underlying theory) and has three primary objectives. One is to provide an introduction to the availability and use of these techniques. A second is to maximize the value of the informational content of the final solution. The third, related to the first two, is to alert the manager to the assumptions inherent in the procedure and the resulting limitations. The presentation stresses practical applications of the methods introduced, with both uses and limitations, and the level of mathematical rigor used in the development is kept to an absolute minimum. (It should not be inferred, however, that because the book is not very mathematically demanding that it is not intellectually demanding; most readers who are new to the field of operations research will find the book challenging —but hopefully also stimulating and rewarding.) By requiring minimal mathematical sophistication it is hoped that the reader will not become absorbed in the mathematics of the technique and lose sight of its potential usefulness and limitations in decision making. Some of the methods discussed also enable the manager to systematically and rationally incorporate his personal judgment or subjective feelings into the decision process.

We would like to thank the following people for their comments and help: Professor Gilbert Gordon (Bernard Baruch College); Professor Rocco Carzo, Jr. (Temple University); Professor Robert Childress (University of Southern California); Professor Richard H. Haase (Drexel University);

Professor Charles L. Hubbard (Georgia State University); Professor Fred E. Kindig; Professor Charles H. Kriebel (Carnegie-Mellon University); Professor Henry W. Nace; and especially Professor Mildred Massey (California State University).

We would like to express special gratitude to Professor Michael Bommer, a former colleague now at the Clarkson Institute of Technology, Professor John F. Fleuck of Temple University, and Professor Ronald Gulezian of the University of Delaware for reading portions of the manuscript and offering valuable suggestions. Comments by numerous others, including some of our students, have also been useful. A special debt is due to Ms. Bernna Berkowitz and Ms. Ruth Williams, who have patiently typed and retyped the bulk of the book. The ultimate responsibility for the final content of the book must, of course, rest with the authors.

1
introduction

From its executive suite on Manhattan's Park Avenue to its mines and smelters in the Peruvian Andes, the buzzword these days among managers and operations men at Cerro de Pasco Corp. is "optimization." With the aid of a complex mathematical management science technique called linear programming (LP), and a farsighted young management consultant, the subsidiary of Cerro Corp. has come up with a computerized working "optimization" model of its entire zinc business. Results in just six months indicate that the model may yield a big payoff in profitability.

This reference to the profitable application of a well-known quantitative method to a practical business problem is the lead paragraph from an article in *Business Week*.[1] The article then proceeds to describe the formulation and use of the model and indicates the safeguards that were taken to ensure the reliability of the model. The benefits of using such an optimization model are illustrated in the following excerpt.[2]

First, the computer is fed a host of "variables" that have a direct bearing on profits: metal prices, labor and transportation costs, capital and raw material costs. Also fed in are various limiting factors, or constraints, including the amounts of ore or metal concentrates available, and the rates at which C de P plants can turn out relatively crude zinc concentrates or refined products such as metallic zinc, cadmium, and sulfuric acid.
The intricate relationships between all the variables and constraints are expressed in a set of algebraic equations which make up the actual LP model for the computer. The model of Cerro de Pasco's zinc operations, which the company calls its zinc circuit, contains some 370 variables and more than 150 equations. What comes out of the computer is a simplified printout in lan-

---

[1] "A Computer Model To Upgrade Zinc Profits," *Business Week* (August 26, 1972), p. 74.

[2] *Ibid.*

guage that tells management, at a glance, how much of the company's wide variety of zinc concentrates it should ship overseas and what it should refine further in its own plants for optimum profits.

The zinc model, like other LP optimizing models, is valuable in other ways. If conditions suddenly change—if, for instance, metals prices fall by 2¢, or if there is a wildcat strike or a 10% jump in transportation costs—Cerro de Pasco can immediately determine the best strategy for adjusting its zinc operations at a minimum cost. In minutes, the computer can grind out a new optimal plan to improve or double-check a seat-of-the-pants decision.

THE USE OF MODELS

Linear programming (presented later in Chapters 5, 6, and 7) is a widely used decision-making tool. Despite their widespread application, however, linear programming models cannot be used to solve all kinds of problems. Applications generally are limited to problems where the interrelationships among the major variables are known and the variables themselves can be expressed quantitatively and controlled. Not all problems can be so clearly specified, but fortunately many different quantitative techniques are available to aid in the process of decision making. Each technique is especially well suited to solve particular types of problems. The intelligent use of the appropriate tools can reduce an otherwise highly complex problem to one of manageable dimensions. The collection of these techniques has become loosely known as "decision theory," although there certainly is no such thing as an integrated theory of how to make decisions. There are instead a number of different methods available, and the practitioner must be able to select the method that is best suited for the problem he is attempting to solve.

Following the 1969 baseball and football seasons, the New York Mets won the World Series and the New York Jets won the Super Bowl. Donn Clendennon and Joe Namath were voted the outstanding players for their respective teams. But probably neither of the New York teams would have been victorious if Joe Namath had played center field for the Mets and Donn Clendennon had quarterbacked the Jets. Both of these individuals are outstanding athletes, but their special talents would be wasted in a position for which they were not adapted. In a less obvious way, the potential benefits of quantitative methods can be wasted—or made harmful—if they are applied in the wrong situations. One of the primary objectives of this book is to introduce the reader to the availability and proper use of a wide variety of quantitative techniques. As a very minimum, one should be able to recognize a situation where a particular method would be applicable and go elsewhere to seek assistance. Although the attainment of this minimal level of competence does not require a thorough understanding of the theory underlying each technique, it does necessitate the formulation of a few problems and the performance of the computations necessary to reach a solution. Ample opportunity to acquire such practice and insights will be provided in the remainder of this book.

The reader should not infer that the available assortment of quantitative techniques represents a decision-making panacea for the previously harassed manager. Mathematical or optimization models can be useful aids to the decision-making process, but the degree of usefulness can be limited by the quality of the implementation of the technique being employed. "Optimization" can refer either to minimization, as in the case of costs, time, distance, material, etc., or maximization, as in the case of profits, sales, productivity, etc. The solution of an optimization model will dictate the "optimal" decision. The solution of some models is prescribed by a sequence of operations that are to be precisely followed. It is frequently necessary to repeat the sequence of operations, called an *algorithm*, several times. The execution of one complete sequence of operations is called an *iteration*. A solution is obtained with each iteration, but the solution is continually improved until, with the final iteration, an optimal solution is finally achieved.

In some situations, it is not possible to construct an optimization model, but a mathematical model representing the actual decision situation still can be used to advantage. Models can be used on a "what if" basis to explore the possible future consequences of decisions that might be made today. For example, a model could be used to predict what would happen, given various future outcomes, if a firm changes its capital structure or dividend policy, adds a new warehouse or manufacturing plant, alters its product mix or marketing strategy, and so on. The ability to explore the possible consequences of alternative courses of action can enable a manager to consider a wider range of alternatives while identifying and focusing his attention on those factors that are most critical to the success or failure of a particular project.

A model, by the way, is not something fabricated from wood or plastic. A model is a system of mathematical equations that is formulated in such a way as reasonably to depict the structure of the problem and the relationships among the relevant variables. An optimization model can be solved to obtain directly the strategy that will lead to the desired objective. Experiments can be performed on a "what if" model to ascertain the possible consequences of alternative strategies. The results of these experiments can then be evaluated to determine which strategy is most consistent with a desired objective.

Of course, to the extent that a particular model is not a reasonable approximation of reality, the value of the model's output is diminished. A useful model must identify the factors that can influence the course of a particular decision and determine how these factors interact to produce departures from the expected or desired outcome. Any model must make certain assumptions about the structure of the underlying problem; no system of equations can produce useful results if it consists entirely of unknowns. The key to successful model building is to represent the decision situation as accurately as possible and, in particular, not to compromise the critical elements of the problem. To use the best possible model, and therefore to get the best possible answers, it is helpful to have an awareness of what types of models are available and the types of problems to which they generally are applied. This book presents a survey of many of the more widely used models, illustrates their implementation, and discusses the usefulness and limitations of the output of these models.

SOME ADDITIONAL BENEFITS

A not insignificant benefit of achieving some degree of proficiency with quantitative methods is evidenced by the way problems are perceived and formulated. It is not possible to get by with loose and sloppy thinking. The problem must be well defined before it can be formulated into some structural framework. All relevant factors and the interrelationships among them must be specified clearly and precisely. These requirements impose a need for rigor and discipline that may seem burdensome until the necessary tools are adequately developed. It eventually will become evident that mathematical skills by themselves are insufficient; the major demand is for a comprehensive understanding of the operational setting in which a manager must operate and make decisions.

Once they are mastered, the proper tools can systematically account for many different factors and help the decision maker reach his desired objective more efficiently. Thus he can react more rapidly and decisively in an increasingly dynamic and quickly changing world. He can have the freedom to use his imagination and explore fully a wider variety of possible courses of action. He will be able to move faster, with better perspective, and with greater confidence in his personal judgments and evaluations than he did before.[3]

Experts in the area of quantitative methods, generally operating under the label of management science or operations research people, frequently are criticized for developing their own special vocabulary, complete with specialized terminology, acronyms, and other bits of conversational shorthand. Such jargon allegedly results in a barrier between the expert and the decision maker that renders the quantitative tools next to useless. Undoubtedly, these accusations sometimes are true. In other cases, the accuser may be (thinly) masking his own insecurity and fear of the unknown. In the long run, however, it is necessary for both sides to develop the skills necessary to overcome any communications gap; again, success should bring its own reward. Consider the following:[4]

On a higher and more conceptual level, quantitative analysis is facilitating communication where it never existed before. When a problem has been stated quantitatively, one can often see that it is structurally similar to other problems (perhaps problems in completely different areas) which on the

---

[3] Some of the methods to be covered in this book formally enable the decision-maker to rationally and systematically incorporate his personal judgment or subjective feelings into the decision process.

[4] Robert H. Hayes, "Qualitative Insights from Quantitative Methods," *Harvard Business Review*, July–August, 1969, p. 109.

surface appear to be quite different. And once a common structure has been identified, insights and predictions can be transferred from one situation to another, and the quantitative approach can actually increase communication.

Thus, once one burrows beneath specialized terminology and different measurement units, apparent differences tend to disappear and the structural similarity of many problems becomes evident. For example, the problems of allocating production resources (either materials, production time, or labor) so as to maximize profits or minimize costs, investing limited funds among competing capital investment proposals to maximize total return, and spreading an advertising budget over various types of media to maximize sales all can be solved within the same basic framework as the zinc circuit model discussed above.

The ability to derive maximum value from the informational content of the final solution of some quantitative model is another primary objective of this book. Another related objective is to develop an awareness of the assumptions inherent in any particular technique and an appreciation of the importance of the resulting limitations.[5] The development of interpretative skills will enable the businessman to determine the effect of various departures from the optimal solution prescribed by the model. The alert manager who is able to detect subtle changes as they occur will be able to fine tune his decisions with the intelligent use of his data outputs. Thus he can raise the "art of management" to the higher levels of excellence that are becoming more necessary in an increasingly dynamic business environment. Of course, if he is using a model that assumes a linear relationship between two primary variables that in reality vary exponentially with one another, his efforts might amount to little more than an exercise in elegant nonsense. We can see, then, that it is becoming a management responsibility to be able to use a vast array of quantitative methods competently and confidently.

This book will hopefully lay the foundation for building competence and confidence. Although these qualities are achieved and refined only by successful application in the field, it is necessary first to become acquainted with the potential usefulness, limitations, and format of various techniques, as we shall do in the chapters that follow.

[5] These abilities become more important as the growing availability of computers, remote access terminals, and canned computer routines increases the potential for the misapplication of various techniques.

I
THEORY

2
probability
concepts

Many of the decision models presented in this text allow for decisions to be made under conditions of uncertainty. Uncertainty means that decisions must be made before we know which one from a set of possible future events will exist. The possible events are called states of nature, and in decision making under uncertainty we must choose a course of action before we know the true state of nature that will occur. Consider the problem of deciding whether to purchase a certain stock. The price may go up or down or stay the same. Clearly, if we know in advance what the true state of nature will be, there is no decision problem. Unfortunately, as every investor knows, we are forced to decide whether or not to buy without perfect information about the future. However, if we are to make rational decisions in the face of uncertainty, the prerequisite is that we have some *measure of the likelihood of occurrence* of each possible state of nature. Such a measure is called probability.

DEFINITION

Probability can not be easily defined any more than we can easily define space, time, or value. Nevertheless, we speak in terms of measuring probability just as we measure time or space.

Probability is a measure of relative likelihood of occurrence measured on a scale from 0 to 1. The extremes of the scale are clearly defined. A probability of 1 means that the event is an absolute certainty to occur, whereas a probability of 0 means the event can *not* possibly occur. Life, of course, is not as simple as 0 and 1 probabilities, and we must deal with probabilities between 0 and 1. Probability is a relative measure of likelihood; hence the closer to 1 the probability, the more likely the event is to occur.

An event with a probability of 0.6 is more likely to occur than an event with a probability of 0.3. In fact, it is twice as likely to occur.

What exactly do we mean, however, when we say a probability of 0.65 or 0.21? In decision making, probabilities are defined as relative frequencies. The proportion of times that an event occurs over a large number of observations is called its relative frequency of occurrence. That is, if in the past 50 years 50 percent of all Caucasian males of age 25 in good health lived to age 65, we would say the probability of a 25-year-old male Caucasian in good health living to at least 65 is 0.50. Since 0.50 is exactly in the middle of the probability scale, this would indicate that it is equally likely that he will live to 65 as that he will die before reaching age 65. More precisely, probability refers to the percentage frequency of occurrence in the long run. When an executive says the probability for success of a given product is 0.80, he means that among a large number of similar products marketed in similar ways and under similar circumstances, on the average 4 out of 5 will succeed and 1 out of 5 will fail.[1] When we quote a probability for the occurrence of an event we thus refer to what will happen in the long run in a large number of similar events.

Probability having been defined, two essential questions remain:

1. How do we assign numerical values of probabilities?
2. How do we use known probabilities to calculate others?

Let us turn our attention to the first question.

SAMPLE SPACE AND RANDOM VARIABLES

The first step in assigning probabilities is to list or define all the possible outcomes or states of nature. Such a list is called a *sample space*. The only conditions that must be met in constructing the sample space are that the events listed in the sample space be exhaustive (i.e., all possible outcomes should be accounted for) and mutually exclusive (i.e., there should be no overlap in the listing of events in the sample space).

There are many different ways that the events in the sample space can be listed. The only constraint in devising the list is that every point in the sample space must correspond to a single event in the list. This does not mean that an event may not be assigned to represent more than one outcome; only that each outcome indicates a specific event. For example, if we are considering two stocks *A* and *B*, the sample space would consist of four events:[2]

[*A* and *B* up in price, *A* up and *B* down, *A* down and *B* up, *A* down and *B* down]

---

[1] The term *odds* comes directly from probability. If the odds *for* some event are 4 to **1**, there are 4 chances for vs. 1 against, so the odds *against* the event are 1 to 4. Hence, an event with probability 0.30 would have odds 3 to 7 for and 7 to 3 against its occurring.

[2] Assume for simplicity that the stocks must either go up or go down.

Note that the list covers all possibilities and that each event represents a unique outcome. Consider the incorrect alternative listing [*A* up, *A* down, *B* up, *B* down]. This listing of the sample space is incorrect because each event is not mutually exclusive. That is, the events *A* up and *B* up are not unique, and they could occur simultaneously.

The sample space presented here is finite, but sample spaces can be infinite. Consider the sample space of the experiment "flipping a coin until a head appears." The possible outcomes would be [H, TH, TTH, TTTH, ...]. In theory we could flip forever before a head appears. When we are dealing with an infinite sample space, it obviously is not possible actually to list all outcomes. In such a situation we simply indicate a rule that determines which events are in the sample space, such as: Let X = number of flips until a head appears. Then the sample space consists of X being all positive integers, $X = 1, 2, 3, \ldots$.

Such a rule for indicating the sample space, used commonly not only for infinite but also for finite sample spaces, hinges on the use of a *random variable*. The random variable in the above illustration is X. A random variable is a function that assigns numerical values to every element in the sample space. Distinction should be drawn between the random variable denoting possible outcomes and the value of the random variable indicating the actual outcome that occurred. Probability theory is concerned with measuring the likelihood of the various possible values of the random variable occurring. If we roll a single die, the outcomes or sample space could be indicated using any of the following random variables:

a. $X = 1, 2, 3, 4, 5, 6$ (face of die)

b. $X = \begin{cases} 0, \text{ if die even} \\ 1, \text{ if die odd} \end{cases}$

c. $X = \begin{cases} 0, \text{ if die is less than 4} \\ 1, \text{ if die is greater than or equal to 4} \end{cases}$

All three alternative random variable assignments cover every possible outcome, and each numerical value represents a unique set of outcomes. The random variable definition used in practice would depend upon the particular problem to be solved.

The random variables presented in the above illustration are discrete random variables; that is, the values that X can assume are specific values within a range. Random variables are called continuous if they can take on any value within a range rather than only specific values. For example, if X equals the diameter of a pipe that can have any value between 2 in. and 4 in., then $2 \leq X \leq 4$ in. The distinction between a discrete and continuous random variable is important, since we shall handle the mechanics (but not the concept) of probability assignments differently for each case.

The reader should not become confused with the concept of continuity and the reality of continuity. In the real world everything is made discrete because of man's limitations in measurement. For example, time is listed in hours, minutes, and seconds, or maybe as detailed as hundredths of a second.

We normally see time listed as 12:01, 12:02, 12:03, etc. However, time is a continuous measure, and theoretically time could be measured to units of one-billionth of a second or less. In classifying a variable as discrete or continuous, we deal in the theoretical abstract and not with the limitations of our ability to measure in a continuous fashion.

Having defined the sample space, or, more commonly, the appropriate random variable, we now can address the problem of assigning probability values to each element in the sample space or to each value of the random variable.

ASSIGNING PROBABILITIES

The assignment of probabilities is often the most important task in decision making under uncertainty, since the ultimate decision is founded upon the probabilities initially assigned. Unfortunately, the assignment is often the most difficult task in the decision process.

When one is assigning probabilities, there are certain rules that must be followed. A probability cannot be less than zero or greater than one, and the sum of all the probabilities assigned to each element in the sample space must be exactly one. Although these basic rules must be followed, they do not really restrict the composition of alternative probability assignments.

What constitutes the "best" assignment can only be judged in light of what seems best to depict reality. For example, consider the random variable

$$X = 0, 1$$

the number of heads in a flip of a coin. Let possible alternative assignments be as given in Exhibit 2–1.

Exhibit 2–1   Hypothetical Probability Assignments

	Alternatives	
	1	**2**
X	**Probability**	**Probability**
0	$\frac{1}{2}$	0
1	$\frac{1}{2}$	1

If we have a fair coin, assignment 1 best represents reality; in the long run the proportion of heads ($X = 1$) will be 0.50. However, if we have a two-headed coin, assignment 2 will be more realistic, since every flip will yield a head.

There are three conceptual methods of assignment:

1. Subjective
2. A priori
3. Empirical

A *subjective probability* assignment is when the probabilities are assigned by *personal judgment*. When a mutual fund manager assigns the probability 0.80 to the event that a certain stock will go up, he is saying that he feels four out of five times the same stock in the same situation would go up. Obviously, there is a very good chance that two persons could assign different subjective probabilities to the same sample space. It is the fact that different people assign different subjective probabilities concerning stock movements which makes buyers and sellers in the stock market. How realistic the subjective assignments are clearly depends upon the expertise of the person assigning the probabilities. When decision-making models are based on subjective probabilities, the resultant "optimal" decision is best only for the persons who assigned the probabilities (or persons who would assign identical values). The "optimal" decision model then determines the most rational decision for that individual based on his probability assessment and is truly optimal only if his assessment is correct. A priori and empirical assignments, on the other hand, are objective methods of assigning probabilities that are replicable among all decision makers.

An *a priori probability* is assigned by calculating the ratio of the number of ways in which a given outcome can occur to the total number of possible outcomes. Thus the probability of rolling the number 5 in a single roll of a die is $\frac{1}{6}$, and the probability of rolling an even number is $\frac{3}{6}$. The establishment of these probabilities conforms precisely to the definition. There are exactly six possible ways a die can fall, and of these, one satisfies the condition of being the number five, and three satisfy the condition of being an even number. In a like manner, we can establish a large number of simple probabilities, provided that we know in advance the total number of possible outcomes and the number of these outcomes that satisfy a given condition. In using this method, the outcomes of the experiment must consider the simplest events that can occur. The basic underlying assumption in using this procedure is that every possible outcome is *equally likely to occur*. The probability of $\frac{1}{6}$ of rolling a five with a single die implies that the die is a perfect, homogeneous cube rolled in a completely random fashion.

It is not difficult to conceive of situations where a priori assignments of probability lead to ridiculous conclusions. Consider the insurance underwriter's problem of assigning a probability to the event that a Caucasian of age 25 will live to age 26. There are two possible outcomes, he lives or he dies, one of which satisfies the given condition, but obviously the probability assignment $\frac{1}{2}$ is not in keeping with reality. In such cases probabilities can be assigned by the empirical method.

The *empirical approach* defines a probability as the relative frequency of occurrence of a given event over an infinite number of occurrences. Obviously, in practice we can observe only a finite (though perhaps very large) number of cases and calculate the relative frequency of the event in question. It must be recognized that the probability so calculated is only an approximation of the "true" probability. This generally is not a serious difficulty, especially if the number of observations is large. Generally, the relative frequency of an event tends to converge quickly to the "true" probability.

A more serious problem is that since we look at outcomes over a fixed period of time and for a specific physical location, the results are restricted in time and space. Consider the following two common applications of empirical probability assignments. (a) In assigning the probability of death at any age we use life tables. Life tables are constructed by examining the death records in the United States over a period of past time. For instance, for all Caucasians in the United States who reached age 25 in the early 1900's, 10 percent died before reaching age 35. Thus we assign the probability 0.9 to the event that a Caucasian citizen of the United States age 25 will live to 35. Clearly, to the extent that over time medical and nutritional improvements have increased life expectancy, this probability assignment will underestimate the true probabilities of the event for a person aged 25 today. (b) Suppose, in developing an inventory model, we need to know the probabilities associated with product demand. Our assignments must be based on *past* and *present* empirical information. To the extent that future conditions are not a reflection of the past, the assignments will be unrealistic.

MEAN AND VARIANCE OF RANDOM VARIABLE

Once we have defined our random variable of interest and assigned probabilities to each random variable, we have what is called a probability distribution. Exhibit 2–2 illustrates a probability distribution for the sample space of the number of stock transactions by a broker on a given day, where x is the random variable representing the number of transactions. Often

Exhibit 2–2   Probability Distribution for Number of Stock Transactions by a Broker on a Given Day

Random Variable x: Number of Transactions	Probability Distribution $f(x)$
6	0.1
7	0.2
8	0.2
9	0.2
10	0.2
11	0.1

probability distributions are presented in a derived form called a *cumulative probability distribution*, and denoted by $F(x)$ (note the capital F rather than small f). In a cumulative distribution $F(a)$ is the probability that the random variable x takes on a value less than or equal to a. Exhibit 2–3 gives the cumulative distribution for Exhibit 2–2.

Exhibit 2–3   Cumulative Probability Distribution for Number
of Stock Transactions by a Broker on a Given Day

x: Number of Transactions a	Cumulative Probability Distribution $F(x)[p(x \le a)]$
6	0.1
7	0.3
8	0.5
9	0.7
10	0.9
11	1.0

Random variables and their associated probability distributions are often described by two summary statistics, their mean or expected value and their variance.

The mean and expected value of a random variable are conceptually and numerically the same but usually denoted by different symbols. The symbol $E(x)$ represents the expected value of x and μ the mean. The two symbols are completely interchangeable, since they both represent identical computations and numerical answers. For simplicity, we shall refer only to the expected value. The expected value of the random variable is the average value of x that would occur if we were to average an infinite number of outcomes of x. In other words, it is the average value of x in the long run. The expected value of x is calculated by weighting each value of x by its probability and summing over all values:[3]

$$E(x) = \sum_{i=x}^{n} x_i p(x_i)$$

where x_i is the ith value x can take on. For our example

$$E(x) = (6)(0.1) + (7)(0.2) + (8)(0.2) + (9)(0.2) + (10)(0.2) + (11)(0.1)$$
$$= 8.5$$

This result means that in the long run the broker would average 8.5 transactions per day.

The expected value of a random variable in itself is not adequate to present a view of how the random variable actually behaves. Consider the two random variables given in Exhibit 2–4. They both have the same expected value but represent quite different patterns of outcomes. The expected value of x is not a very typical outcome. Only 20 percent of the time will a 5 occur and 40 percent of the time x will be two units away from its expected

---

[3] This formula is correct for only discrete random variables. If the random variable is continuous, we must use calculus and take the integral over the whole range of values rather than sum over all values. While the mathematics of calculation are different the concept is identical. The same is true for the calculation of the variance of the random variable.

Exhibit 2–4 Two Distinct Random Variables with Identical Means

x	$f(x)$	$x \cdot f(x)$	y	$f(y)$	$y \cdot f(y)$
3	0.2	0.6	3	0.01	0.03
4	0.2	0.8	4	0.05	0.20
5	0.2	1.0	5	0.88	4.40
6	0.2	1.2	6	0.05	0.30
7	0.2	1.4	7	0.01	0.07
		$E(x) = \overline{5.0}$			$E(y) = \overline{5.00}$

value. On the other hand, y will equal its expected value 88 percent of the time and will be two units away only 2 percent of the time. What is needed is a measure describing how "typical" the expected value really is on any trial or, more precisely, a measure of the dispersion of x about its expected value. Such a measure is the variance of x, denoted by σ_x^2.

The variance of x is defined as the sum of the squared deviations of x from the expected value weighted by their probability.

$$\sigma_x^2 = \sum_{i=1}^{n} (x_i - E(x))^2 p(x_i)$$

For convenience of calculation the above expression can be expanded and regrouped, yielding

$$\sigma_x^2 = \sum x_i^2 p(x_i) - [E(x)]^2 \qquad (2\text{--}1)$$

Using equation (2–1), we calculate the variance of x and y in Exhibit 2–4 as

$$\sigma_x^2 = (3)^2(0.2) + (4)^2(0.2) + (5)^2(0.2)$$
$$+ (6)^2(0.2) + (7)^2(0.2) - (5)^2$$
$$= 2$$

and

$$\sigma_y^2 = (3)^2(0.01) + (4)^2(0.05) + (5)^2(0.88)$$
$$+ (6)^2(0.05) + (7)^2(0.01) - (5)^2$$
$$= 0.18$$

As is to be expected, the variance of y is considerably less than the variance of x. This result indicates that the outcomes of y are more closely clustered about the expected value than are the outcomes of x.

Often, rather than reporting or using the variance, we give the corresponding standard deviation of x. The standard deviation of x is simply the square root of the variance of x and accordingly is denoted σ_x. It should be noted that in order to calculate the standard deviation one must first calculate the variance and then take the square root.[4]

[4] The reader is reminded that $\sqrt{a^2 + b^2} \neq a + b$; i.e., $\sqrt{3^2 + 4^2} \neq 7$, but $\sqrt{25} = 5$.

Chebyshev's Inequality

The importance of the mean and variance as descriptors of a probability distribution can be seen from the fact that given only the mean and variance of a random variable we are able to put a limit on the probability that an item will fall outside a specific interval centered around the expected value. This follows from a theorem called Chebyshev's Inequality:

$$P(|x - E(x)| > k\sigma) \leq \frac{1}{k^2}$$

Thus if $E(X) = 20$ and $\sigma_x = 5$, it follows that the probability of x being greater than 30 or less than 10 is less than $\frac{1}{4}$.

$$P(|x - E(x)| > 10) \leq \frac{1}{2^2} = \frac{1}{4}$$

since 30 or 10 represents 2σ units from the expected value of x.

Although Chebyshev's theorem demonstrates the power of $E(x)$ and σ^2 as summary statistics, it is not generally useful in practice because the probability bound calculated is too large. That is, the actual probability is considerably less than the bound calculated by the theorem. For example, if we were interested in the probability that x exceeds its expected value by more than 5 rather than 10, we would get

$$P(|x - E(x)| > 5) \leq \frac{1}{1^2} = 1$$

which is a useless result, since the probability of any event must be less than or equal to one.

LINEAR COMBINATIONS OF A RANDOM VARIABLE

New random variables are sometimes created that are linear combinations of another random variable. Such linear combinations are in the form of $z = a + bx$, where a and b are constants and x is a random variable. For instance, suppose that x equals the number of items sold per day of a perishable item, such as pie. The pie sells for 70¢ (b) and 10 pies are produced each day at a cost of $3.00 ($-a$). Then $z = -3.00 + 0.70(x)$ represents the daily profit (or loss). Although we could construct a probability distribution for z and calculate its expected value and variance, it is not necessary, since z is a sole function of x and its expected value and variance can be mathematically related to x:

$$E(a + bx) = a + bE(x)$$

and

$$\sigma^2_{a+bx} = b^2\sigma^2_x$$

For our illustration

$$E(z) = -3.00 + 0.70E(x)$$

and

$$\sigma^2_z = 0.49\sigma^2_x$$

PROBABILITY DISTRIBUTIONS

Fortunately, it is not always necessary to calculate probabilities specifically for every outcome in the sample space. For many commonly encountered problems, mathematical rules or formulas exist that assign probabilities to the values of the random variables. Such rules are called *probability functions* or *distributions*, and we shall denote them as $f(x)$. There are numerous probability distributions, each fitting a particular type or class of problems. Once the appropriate probability distribution is chosen, the specific numerical values obtained vary, depending only on the values of the parameters of the distribution.[5] Usually a distribution has only one or two parameters. Thus instead of having to assign probabilities to every element in a sample space, we find that the task narrows to selecting the appropriate assignment rule (probability distribution) and assigning values to the few parameters.

While the choice of a probability distribution can be made on the basis of the type or class of problem, the values of the parameters generally will be different for every problem. Since the actual probabilities assigned depend on the parameter values, care must be exercised in assigning values to the parameters. Usually the true values of the parameters are unknown and must be estimated by either examining empirical evidence or subjective estimate. Much of statistical theory deals with the problem of the best way to estimate the parameters.

Probability distributions can be categorized into two types, discrete or continuous, depending upon whether the random variable is discrete or continuous. There is a distinct difference in usage of the two types of distributions. For discrete probability distributions, $f(x)$ evaluated at $x = a$ represents probability that $x = a$. If the probability distribution is continuous, the problem is not so simple. We must use calculus (or tables that have already done the calculus for us) to find the probabilities given $f(x)$.[6]

---

[5] Parameters are certain values associated with the conditions of the experiment or conditions of the population from which events will occur. For example, the true percentage of defective items produced by a machine, the long term average demand for a product, or the true average life of a product are parameters.

[6] The cumulative distribution $F(x)$, however, can be evaluated as a discrete distribution by simply evaluating the function numerically.

Let us consider the simple case of drawing two items from the daily output of some machine and let x = number of defective items. The probability distribution is given by

$$f(x) = (2 - |1 - x|)P^x(1 - P)^{2-x} \qquad x = 0, 1, 2$$

where P is the parameter giving the average percentage of defective items produced by the machine. Since x is discrete, we assign a value to the parameter P and evaluate $f(x)$ at 0, 1, and 2, to get the probabilities that x = 0, 1, and 2, respectively.

Exhibit 2–5   Probabilities of x, for Various Values of P

	Probability of x		
x	$P = 0.1$	$P = 0.5$	$P = 0.9$
0	0.81	0.25	0.01
1	0.18	0.50	0.18
2	0.01	0.25	0.81

As Exhibit 2–5 depicts, the problem of assigning probabilities is reduced to defining $f(x)$ and assigning a value to the parameter P. We should also realize that the probability distribution above is appropriate for many other problems than the one specifically used above. For example, if $P = 0.5$, x could represent the number of heads in two flips of a coin, or if $P = \frac{1}{6}$, x could represent the number of 6's in two rolls of a die.

Volumes have been written describing the various probability distributions, their properties, and the types of problems for which they are appropriate. A few of the most commonly used distributions are presented in this chapter.

PROBABILITY DISTRIBUTIONS—DISCRETE

Binomial

The most common discrete probability distribution is the binomial distribution. The binomial distribution has theoretical justification for situations where there are repeated trials of an experiment for which only one of two mutually exclusive outcomes can result on each trial. There are many situations that have outcomes that are naturally dichotomous, such as: an item is defective or nondefective; a coin is heads or tails; a stock price goes up in price or it does not go up in price; an answer is right or wrong. In addition, almost any variable can be reduced to two mutually exclusive outcomes by classifying the outcome simply as having the characteristic of interest or as not having the characteristic of interest. For instance, if we are interested in the number of sevens that will occur in continued rolling of a pair of dice, we can classify each outcome of a roll as "seven" or "not seven."

Since each outcome of a trial results in one of two mutually exclusive outcomes, it is common terminology to refer to one class of outcomes as a *success* and the other as a *failure*. These terms are simply labels and have no relationship to the usual meaning of the words "success" and "failure." The choice of which outcome is labeled success and which failure often is arbitrary.

The theoretical conditions for which the binomial distribution is appropriate are

1. Each trial results in an outcome that can be classified into one of two mutually exclusive categories: e.g., "success" or "failure."
2. The probability of "success" is the same for all trials.
3. The outcome of any particular trial is independent of the outcome(s) of any other trial(s).

The random variable of interest in the binomial probability distribution is

$$x = \text{number of "successes" in } n \text{ trials.}$$

The binomial probability distribution is given by[7]

$$f(x) = \binom{n}{x} p^x (1 - p)^{n-x} \tag{2-2}$$

where

$$n = \text{number of trials}$$

$$p = \text{probability of "success" on a trial}$$

The parameters of the binomial distribution are n and p. Clearly, knowledge of p truly defines the probability of x, since n is known by definition of the problem.

The expected value of x, or mean of x, is np and the variance of x is $np(1 - p)$. The value of the binomial distribution function for various values of n and p are widely available in tables. This text contains a binomial probability table (see Appendix F–1) and a cumulative binomial table (see Appendix F–2). In the noncumulative table, the values given under each value of x, n, and p give the probability of getting exactly x "successes" in n trials, where the probability of success on any individual trial is p. In the cumulative table, the values given represent the probabilities of getting at least ($\geq$)x "successes" in n trials when the probability of "success" on any trial equals p. For example, if p $= 0.40$ and n $= 12$, $P(x = 4) = 0.231$, $P(x \geq 10) = 0.0028$, and $P(x \leq 9) = 0.9972[1 - P(x \geq 10)]$. Note that

---

[7] Those not familiar with the combinatorial notation $\binom{n}{x}$ are referred to Appendix C for a review of this and rules of counting in general.

the $P(x = 7)$, given p = 0.65 and n = 10, is equal to $P(y = 3)$ where $y = n - x$ (the identical outcome), given p = 0.35 and n = 10. Thus the tables are constructed for values of p only up to 0.50.

Rather than use x, the number of "successes" in n trials, as the random variable, the equivalent random variable $\bar{p}$, the proportion of "successes" in n trials, is often used. The symbol $\bar{p}$, of course, simply equals x/n, and any binomial probability problem can be expressed equivalently in terms of x or $\bar{p}$.

It is not difficult to think of situations where the use of the binomial probability distribution is appropriate: the probability of five heads in ten flips of a fair coin; the probability of black's occurring in roulette five times out of six; the probability that 15 out of 100 items, produced by a machine whose process produces 10 percent defective on the average, will be defective; the probability that at most 10 percent of the life insurance policies written by an insurance company on persons aged 32 will result in claims. Moreover, there are situations where the binomial, although it is not the theoretically exact distribution to use, nevertheless can be used as a good approximation. For example, such cases occur when we are sampling a small fraction of a large population without replacement.[8]

Negative Binomial

The basic theoretical conditions underlying the binomial distribution also underlie the negative binomial distribution. The basic difference between the two distributions hinges on the probability question they ask. In the negative binomial distribution the random variable is

$$x = \text{the trial that the kth "success" occurs.}$$

Whereas in the binomial distribution we fixed the number of trials and asked about the probability of getting x "successes," in the negative binomial we fix the number of "successes" as k and ask for the probability that it will take exactly x trials for the k successes to occur. (This obviously implies that the kth "success" occurs exactly on the xth trial.)

The negative binomial probability function is

$$f(x) = \binom{x-1}{k-1} p^k (1 - p)^{x-k} \qquad x = k, k + 1, \ldots \qquad (2\text{--}3)$$

where

$$k = \text{number of successes}$$

$$p = \text{probability of "success" on any trial}$$

[8] In such cases the trials are not independent and the exact distribution is called hypergeometric. However, because the sampling fraction is small (n/N), the value of p on each trial normally changes so slightly that the binomial distribution yields an excellent approximation. The reason for using the binomial approximation is simply that values for the hypergeometric distribution are not widely available in tables and it is cumbersome to deal with computationally.

The parameters of the negative binomial are k and p; since k is defined by the question asked, p actually delineates the probability distribution.

The expected value or mean of the negative binomial variable x is $k(1 - p)/p$, and its variance is $k(1 - p)/p^2$.

The negative binomial distribution is often used in problems involving queueing and replacement theory.

Poisson Probability Distribution

The Poisson probability distribution plays an important role in queueing models, risk models, inventory models, and replacement models. Experience has shown that the Poisson probability distribution is good for computing probabilities associated with x "occurrences" in a given time period or specified area.[9] For example, the number of defects in a yard of material, the number of arrivals at a service counter during a given hour, the number of machine failures in a given week, or the number of accidents within a company in a given month. The Poisson random variable is

x = number of occurrences of a given event during a given interval.

The interval may be time, distance, area, etc.

The Poisson probability distribution is

$$f(x) = \frac{e^{-\lambda}\lambda^x}{x!} \qquad x = 0, 1, 2, \ldots \qquad (2\text{--}4)$$

where

λ = average number of occurrences per specified interval

The only parameter of the Poisson distribution is λ, the average number per interval.[10] The expected value of the Poisson random variable is λ and its variance is also λ.

Underlying the Poisson model is the assumption that if there are on the average λ occurrences per interval t, then there are on the average $k\lambda$ occurrences per interval kt. Thus if x, the number of arrivals at a service counter in *a given hour*, has a Poisson distribution with $\lambda = 5$, then y, the number of arrivals at a service counter in a given *8-hour day*, has the Poisson with $\lambda = 40$ (8×5).

---

[9] Unlike the binomial distribution, the Poisson can not be deduced on purely theoretical grounds based on the conditions of the experiment. It must be assumed based on experience with similar experiments and justified empirically.

[10] λ must be determined empirically. Unlike p in the binomial, it never can be deduced theoretically.

The Poisson distribution is well tabled. This text contains two tables, the Poisson distribution (Appendix F–3) and the cumulative Poisson distribution (Appendix F–4), for selected values of λ. In the noncumulative table the value given represents the probability of exactly x occurrences in a given interval when on the average λ occur per interval. In the cumulative table the value given represents the probability of at most $(\leq)x$ occurrences in a given interval when on the average λ occur per interval.

CONTINUOUS DISTRIBUTIONS

Exponential

In the negative binomial distribution, we asked for the probability that the kth success will occur exactly on the x trial. In the exponential distribution, we ask the analogous question in the Poisson model: What is the probability that it will take x trials before the first occurrence? Unlike the negative binomial, the exponential deals only with the first success. In the exponential, however, we are dealing with length of time or distance, so x is a continuous variable that takes on any value between zero and positive infinity. In this context, the exponential distribution plays an important role in queueing, reliability, and replacement models. Although the exponential distribution can theoretically be developed in the above context, the distribution does often seem to satisfy many other empirical situations, such as the probability of dollar loss in an accident.

The exponential probability distribution is given by

$$f(x) = \mu e^{-\mu x} \qquad \mu \geq 0 \tag{2-5}$$

where

μ = the average length of the interval between two occurrences.

μ is the only parameter of the exponential distribution.[11]
The expected value or mean of the exponential is $1/\mu$, and its variance is $1/\mu^2$.
The (less than) cumulative distribution of the exponential is

$$F(x) = 1 - e^{-\mu x}$$

Thus, for example, the probability that x would be less than or equal to 2 is $1 - e^{-2\mu}$. Appendix F–5 contains values of $e^{-\mu x}$ for selected values of μx.

---

[11] This definition of μ is consistent with the Poisson model.

Normal Distribution

By far the most important and frequently used continuous probability distribution is the normal distribution. The normal distribution, although it theoretically can be derived as the limiting form of many discrete distributions, derives its importance primarily from the fact that it empirically fits many types of physical phenomena, such as weight of men, length of machine parts, demand for certain products, sales of certain products, etc. More importantly, as proved by the central limit theorem, it is generally the appropriate distribution to describe probabilistically the link between the sample results and the population from which the sample is drawn. Hence the normal distribution is of great importance in inferential statistics.

The normal probability distribution is given by

$$f(x) = \left(\frac{1}{\sqrt{2\pi}\,\sigma} \right) e^{-(1/2)[(x-\mu)^2/\sigma^2]} \qquad -\infty \leq x \leq +\infty \qquad (2\text{–}6)$$

where

$$\mu = \text{the mean of the distribution}$$

$$\sigma^2 = \text{the variance}$$

The normal distribution is clearly defined by two parameters, μ and σ^2. The normal distribution is graphically illustrated in Illustration 2–1.

The characteristics of the normal distribution are

1. It is a symmetric distribution about the mean; that is, it is equally likely that x would be greater than two units above the mean as less than two units below the mean.
2. The mean μ defines where the peak of the curve occurs.
3. The variance σ^2 defines the spread of the curve.

The characteristics referred to in points 2 and 3 are illustrated in Illustrations 2–2 and 2–3.

Since the normal distribution is for a continuous random variable (i.e., the random variable x can take on an infinite number of values within a specified range), the probability of any single exact value occurring necessarily must be zero (i.e., $P(x = a) = 0$). Instead, we find the probability

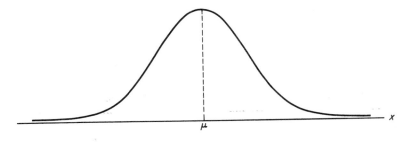

Illustration 2–1

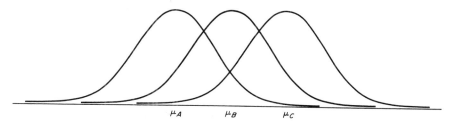

Illustration 2–2   Normal Distributions with Different Means and Equal Variances

of an occurrence within a range of values. In order to find the probability that x is between a and b, we must use calculus. The integral of the normal distribution [Eq. (2–6)] from a to b would yield the proper probability. Taking the integral between a and b is equivalent to finding the area under the normal curve between a and b. The normal distribution is used so frequently, however, that, rather than having to evaluate an integral every time we want a probability, the corresponding area under the normal curve has been extensively tabled. Clearly, it would be impossible to prepare tables of areas under the curve for every conceivable normal distribution defined by some μ and σ^2 combination. Fortunately, however, it is necessary to prepare only one table giving the area under the curve for a standard normal variable. A standard normal variable, denoted as z, is a normal variable with $\mu = 0$ and $\sigma^2 = 1$. This convention is convenient, since every probability to be calculated for a normal variable with mean μ and variance σ^2 can be converted to an equivalent problem for a standard normal variable. This transformation can be accomplished by subtracting the mean and dividing by the standard deviation. For example, if x follows a normal distribution with $\mu = 10$ and $\sigma = 5$, then the question $P(x > 20)$ can be transformed to the equivalent question in terms of z:

$$P(x > 20) = P\left(\frac{x - \mu}{\sigma} > \frac{20 - 10}{5}\right) = P(z > 2)$$

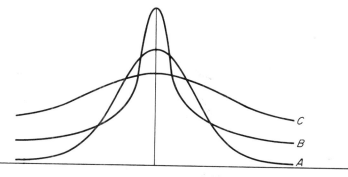

Illustration 2–3   Normal Distributions with Equal Means and Different Variances
[Var (a) < Var (b) < Var (c)]

Once the probability question is transformed to the equivalent question about z, we need only look up the answer in the standard normal tables. The text contains a table of standard normal probabilities in Appendix F-6. The value given in the table under Z represents

$$P(0 \leq z \leq Z)$$

If we recall that the total area under the curve is 1, and the curve is symmetric about the mean 0, so that

$$P(-Z \leq z \leq 0) = P(0 \leq z \leq Z)$$

and

$$P(z \leq 0) = P(z \geq 0) = 0.5$$

simple subtraction and/or addition using the values in the table will produce any probability in question. For example:

$$P(z \leq 1.3) = 0.9032$$
$$P(z \leq -1.25) = 1 - 0.8944$$
$$= 0.1056$$
$$P(z \geq 1.64) = 1 - 0.9495$$
$$= 0.0505$$
$$P(z \geq -0.95) = 0.8289$$
$$P(0.50 \leq z \leq 1.50) = 0.9332 - 0.6915$$
$$= 0.2417$$
$$P(-1.47 \leq z \leq 0.70) = 0.7580 - (1 - 0.9292)$$
$$= 0.7580 - 0.0708 = 0.6872$$

As mentioned previously, the normal distribution is the limiting distribution of many discrete distributions, the binomial and Poisson being two of them. In this context, for large n in the binomial case or large λ in the Poisson case, the normal distribution can be used as a good approximation for the respective discrete distributions. The main advantage of approximating through use of the normal distribution is that, for large n and λ, the discrete distributions are not well tabled. Thus the normal distribution is much easier to use computationally. In order to use the normal approximations, all we have to know are the two normal parameters, μ and σ^2. The mean and variance for the binomial and Poisson distribution were given previously.

RULES OF PROBABILITY

Once we have assigned (or determined a method for assigning) probabilities to the events in the sample space, there exists a body of rules that allows us to calculate the probability of events which represent combinations of events in the sample space, the probability of one and/or another event's occurring, events occurring jointly, or one event's occurring given that another event has occurred. The rules are grounded in mathematical logic, so that given the initial assignment of probabilities to the elements in the sample space, there exists a "correct" answer for the probability of the event or events in question. Of course, the correctness of the answer in terms of the corresponding reality of the situation depends upon the reality of the initial assignment of probabilities.

Complimentary Events

One rule of probability states that if the probability of the occurrence of event A is $P(A)$, the probability that it will not occur is $1 - P(A)$. This agrees with our definition of probability. If the probability that *at least one* item is sold on a given day is 0.6, then the compliment, the probability that *none* is sold, is $(1 - 0.6) = 0.4$. In other words, 60 percent of the time at least one item will be sold, while 40 percent of the time none will be sold.

Another rule of probability refers to special kinds of events, events that are mutually exclusive. Two or more events are said to be *mutually exclusive if the occurrence of one precludes the occurrence of the other(s)*. If we toss a coin, heads and tails are mutually exclusive, since we can get one or the other but *never both*. Similarly, the events demand equals 1, 2, 3, or 4 on a given day are mutually exclusive events. On the other hand, having potatoes or rice with a dinner are not mutually exclusive, since a person can have both.[12] In other words, when events are mutually exclusive, it means that the occurrence of one event prohibits the occurrence of the other(s).

Special Rule of Addition

If A and B are mutually exclusive, then $P(A \text{ or } B) = P(A) + P(B)$. That is, if two events A and B are mutually exclusive, the probability that either event (but not both) will occur equals the sum of their individual probabilities.

If the probability of getting a head in one flip of a coin is $\frac{1}{2}$, and the probability of getting a tail is $\frac{1}{2}$, then $P(A \text{ or } B) = (P[H]) + (P[T]) = \frac{1}{2} + \frac{1}{2} = 1$.

If the probability that a person in New York has an annual income of under \$8500 is 0.54, and the probability that he has an income over \$10,000 is 0.18, then the probability that his income is under \$8500 *or* over \$10,000 is $0.54 + 0.18 = 0.72$.

---

[12] The term "or," unless specified otherwise, normally is interpreted to mean and/or (that is, one or the other or both), where at least one of the events, but possibly both, is to occur.

The special rule of addition can be generalized to apply to more than two *mutually exclusive events* $A_1, A_2, \ldots, A_k$; the probability that one of them will occur is $P(A_1 \text{ or } A_2 \text{ or } \ldots \text{ or } A_k) = P(A_1) + P(A_2) + \ldots + P(A_k)$. The probability that a person will receive an A in a course is 0.10, a B = 0.20, a C = 0.50, a D = 0.10, and an F = 0.10. These are mutually exclusive events, and the probability that he will pass is

$$P(A \text{ or } B \text{ or } C \text{ or } D) = 0.10 + 0.20 + 0.50 + 0.10 = 0.9$$

General Rule of Addition

Now let us consider the case where the two events are not mutually exclusive. Suppose we roll a pair of dice, one green and one red. If A represents the outcome "The green die equals 1," and B the outcome "The red die equals 1," then how do we calculate the probability that A or B equals 1? The question is interpreted as "and/or," meaning that we are satisfied if either the green die or red die is one or if both dice are 1 (i.e., at least one die is equal to 1). Clearly, the events A and B are not mutually exclusive, since the outcome (1, 1) is possible. Exhibit 2–6 lists the sample space for this experiment.

Exhibit 2–6 Sample Space for Rolling a Pair of Die (Green die, Red die)

	Event A					
Event B	−1, 1	1, 2	1, 3	1, 4	1, 5	1, 6
2, 1	2, 2	2, 3	2, 4	2, 5	2, 6
3, 1	3, 2	3, 3	3, 4	3, 5	3, 6
4, 1	4, 2	4, 3	4, 4	4, 5	4, 6
5, 1	5, 2	5, 3	5, 4	5, 5	5, 6
6, 1	6, 2	6, 3	6, 4	6, 5	6, 6

The first column is all the possible outcomes that represent event A, while the first row is all the possible outcomes that represent event B. The probability of A is $\frac{1}{6}$, since A represents six out of the equally probable 36 outcomes. Similarly, $P(B) = \frac{1}{6}$. The outcome (1, 1) is the joint outcome of A *and* B; thus the joint probability of $P(A \text{ and } B) = \frac{1}{36}$. To calculate the $P(A \text{ and/or } B)$ by simply adding $P(A)$ and $P(B)$ *double counts* the joint outcome (1, 1). It is counted as one of the outcomes in calculating $P(A)$ and is also counted as one of the outcomes in calculating $P(B)$. Hence, we must correct for double counting, and the probability of the green die and/or the red die being 1 is equal to $\frac{1}{6} + \frac{1}{6} - \frac{1}{36} = \frac{11}{36}$. The general rule is, therefore,

$$P(A \text{ and /or } B) = P(A) + P(B) - P(A \text{ and } B)$$

Of course, if A and B are mutually exclusive, then $P(A \text{ and } B) = 0$, and the general rule reduces to the previous special addition formula.

Independent versus Dependent

Before we formulate a rule for calculating the joint probability $P(A$ and $B)$, let us first explain what is meant by *independent* and *dependent* events.

Two or more events are said to be independent if the occurrence or non-occurrence of one in no way influences or affects the probability of occurrence or nonoccurrence of any of the others.

If A and B stand for getting heads in two successive flips of a coin, then A and B are independent. The outcome of the second flip is in no way affected by what happens in the first flip.

Similarly, if A stands for your having a checking account, and B stands for your having read *Gone with the Wind*, it is difficult to see how these two events can possibly be dependent. Obviously, if two events are mutually exclusive, they are also dependent; by definition, the occurrence of one precludes the occurrence of the other.

Whether events are independent is often clear from examination of the events in question. However, in many cases it is not self-evident, and the question of independence may itself be of prime interest. Consider the events having a checking account at a bank and having a loan account at the same bank. It may be that having a checking account at the bank increases the probability that the person would also have a loan account. This has practical implications, for if this is true, then it would make sense to advertise loan programs to your checking account clients, since these persons may be your best prospective clients.

One approach to the problem is to *assume* independence or dependence. Clearly, the correctness of the resultant probability analysis depends upon the truth of the assumption. In practice we often assume independence, and compare the *calculated* resultant probabilities with the *actual frequencies* of outcomes and compare the two to infer whether the assumption of independence is warranted.[13]

If two events are independent, the probability that both will occur is given by the following rule.

Special Rule of Multiplication

If A and B are independent, then $P(A$ and $B) = P(A) \cdot P(B)$. This formula tells us that the probability of the occurrence of two independent events equals the product of their individual probabilities.

Applying the above formula to the game of "heads or tails," we find that the probability of getting heads in *each* of two flips of a balanced coin is the probability of getting heads on the first *multiplied* by the probability of getting a head on the second flip, or $\frac{1}{2} \cdot \frac{1}{2} = \frac{1}{4}$. If the probability that a person 30 years or older (who is interviewed in a survey) has completed four years of college is 0.07, and the probability that he is less than six feet tall is

---

[13] For formal statistical testing of the assumption of independence, the student should refer to the section on contingency table analysis in any of the basic statistics texts.

0.80, then the probability that he is less than six feet tall *and* has completed four years of college is $(0.07) \cdot (0.80) = 0.056$.

The special rule of multiplication can easily be extended to more than two independent events. Given k independent events, $A_1, A_2, \ldots, A_k$ the probability that all will occur is

$$P(A_1 \text{ and } A_2 \text{ and } \ldots A_k) = P(A_1) \cdot P(A_2) \ldots P(A_k)$$

For instance, the probability of getting five heads in a row with a balanced coin is $\frac{1}{2} \cdot \frac{1}{2} \cdot \frac{1}{2} \cdot \frac{1}{2} \cdot \frac{1}{2} = \frac{1}{32}$.

Conditional Probability Rule

A very important concept of probability especially useful in decision making is that of a conditional probability. The probability that event B will take place provided that event A has taken place (is taking place, or will positively take place) is called the conditional probability of B relative to A. Symbolically, it is written as $P(B/A)$.

The meaning of any probability depends upon the group or population of elements to which the discussion is directed. In other words, the probability of any event is conditional upon the definition of elements or sample space in which we are interested.

To discuss the concept of a conditional probability in somewhat more detail, let us consider the following problem. Suppose that there are 100 male executives, all of whom are candidates for the presidency of a large corporation, with each having a probability of 0.01 of being selected for the job. Some of these candidates are over 55 years old and some are younger, some are college graduates and some are not, with the exact breakdown as given in Exhibit 2–7.

Exhibit 2–7

	A Over 55	B Under 55	Total
C—College graduate	52	26	78
N—Not a college graduate	15	7	22
Total	67	33	100

If we let A represent the event that the person selected is over 55 and C the event that he is a college graduate, we have

$$P(A) = \frac{52 + 15}{100} = \frac{67}{100} = 0.67$$

and

$$P(C) = \frac{52 + 26}{100} = 0.78$$

by virtue of the assumption that each candidate has an equal chance of being selected. It follows that the probability of not being a college graduate is equal to $1 - 0.78 = 0.22$, and the probability of being under 55 is $1 - 0.67 = 0.33$.

Let us suppose that for some reason the selection is now restricted to college graduates. This means that we have restricted the sample space of possible candidates—to only those with college degrees. The reduced number of choices or outcomes that we are now interested in is 78, and assuming that these 78 outcomes are still equally likely, we obtain

$$P(A/C) = \frac{52}{78} = 0.667$$

Had the selection been restricted to persons who are under 55, event B, and had we been interested in $P(NC/B)$, the probability that the person selected is not a college graduate *given* he is under 55, we would have obtained $P(NC/B) = \frac{7}{33}$ (assuming that each of the 33 possible outcomes in the reduced denominator is still equally likely).

This rule for conditional probability can be written

$$P(A/B) = \frac{P(A \text{ and } B)}{P(B)}$$

This formula gives the proportion of the probability of event B which occurs with A. If we relate this to the a priori probability definition, we have

$$P(A/B) = \frac{\text{number of ways } A \text{ and } B \text{ occur together}}{\text{number of ways } B \text{ occurs in total}}$$

General Multiplication Rule

By simply cross multiplying the general conditional probability rule, we get the general multiplication rule for joint probabilities.[14]

$$P(A \text{ and } B) = P(B)P(A/B)$$

or

$$P(A \text{ and } B) = P(A)P(B/A)$$

since

$$P(B/A) = \frac{P(A \text{ and } B)}{P(A)}$$

---

[14] Although both rules yield the same result for a particular problem, the use of one is often much easier than the other. Which of the two rules is easier to use is usually obvious from the natural order of the events.

Suppose that an urn contains four white balls and three red balls. We select two balls and are interested in the probability that the first is white (event A) and the second is red (event B). Using the multiplication rule, we would get $(\frac{4}{7})(\frac{3}{6}) = \frac{2}{7}$; i.e., on the first selection there are 7 balls, 4 of which are white, while on the second selection there are only 6 balls left (since we took out a white ball on the first draw) of which 3 are red. In this example, the outcome of event A clearly affects the probability of B. Thus A and B are dependent events. Suppose, however, that after selecting the ball and noting its color, we return it to the urn before selecting the second ball. In such a situation the probability of the second ball's being red would be $\frac{3}{7}$, regardless of the color of the first ball. Events A and B would be independent; hence $P(B/A) = P(B)$, since conditioning on the first event A has no effect on the probability of B. As we see, when the events are independent the general multiplication rule reduces to the special case given previously.

The general rule of multiplication can easily be extended to three or more events. If k events, $A_1, A_2, \ldots, A_k$, are given, the probability that *all k* events will occur is

$$P(A_1 \text{ and } A_2 \text{ and } \ldots \text{ and } A_k)$$

$$= P(A_1)P(A_2/A_1)P(A_3/A_1A_2) \ldots P(A_k/A_1 \ldots A_{k-1})$$

Examples of Combinations of Rules

Although we have discussed each rule separately, this is not to imply that the rules can not be used in combination to solve a problem. Recall the problem with the 4 white balls and 3 red balls. Suppose we seek the probability that we get a red ball *and* a white ball but we do not care about the order in which the balls are drawn. Then the $P(\text{red } and \text{ white}) =$

$P([\text{red on the first } and \text{ white on the second}] \ or$

$$[\text{white on the first } and \text{ red on the second}])$$

Now using the special addition rule (since the two joint events are mutually exclusive), we get

$$P(\text{red } and \text{ white}) = P(\text{red first } and \text{ white second})$$

$$+ P(\text{white first } and \text{ red second})$$

Each of the joint probabilities in turn can be solved by using the general multiplication rule. Hence

$$P(\text{red and white}) = P(\text{red first})P(\text{white second/red first})$$

$$+ P(\text{white first})P(\text{red second/white first})$$

$$= (\tfrac{3}{7})(\tfrac{4}{6}) + (\tfrac{4}{7})(\tfrac{3}{6}) = \tfrac{4}{7}$$

As this example illustrates, one of the most important parts of solving a probability problem is clearly defining specifically what events satisfy the ultimate event in question.

Let us consider another example. A patch test for the disease tuberculosis is developed with the following properties: If you have TB, the test will show positive 99 percent of the time, i.e., $P(P/\text{TB}) = 0.99$, while if you do not have TB, the test incorrectly shows positive 10 percent of the time, i.e., $P(P/\text{N.TB}) = 0.10$. If we assume that only 1 percent of the population has TB, i.e., $P(\text{TB}) = 0.01$ and conversely $P(\text{N.TB}) = 0.99$, what is the probability that the test will show positive on a randomly selected person? The first step is to ask ourselves what the event positive outcome really consists of. Positive means [the person has TB *and* shows positive] *or* [the person does not have TB *and* shows positive]. That is,

$$P(P) = P([\text{TB } and \text{ } P] \text{ } or \text{ } [\text{N.TB } and \text{ } P])$$

As before, using first the special addition rule (since a person can not both have TB and not have TB; thus the two events are mutually exclusive) and then the general multiplication rule, we find

$$P(P) = P(\text{TB})P(P/\text{TB}) + P(\text{N.TB})P(P/\text{N.TB})$$
$$= (0.01)(0.99) + (0.99)(0.10)$$
$$= 0.1089$$

Bayes' Rule

In the last example, the probability that is of most interest is the conditional probability that, given a test shows positive, the person actually has TB, i.e., $P(\text{TB}/P)$. To solve, we can initially set the problem into the rule for conditional probabilities.

$$P(\text{TB}/P) = \frac{P(\text{TB and } P)}{P(P)}$$

However, as we just saw, the denominator $P(P)$ has to be expanded to be calculated. Thus we have

$$P(\text{TB}/P) = \frac{P(\text{TB and } P)}{P(\text{TB})P(P/\text{TB}) + P(\text{N.TB})P(P/\text{N.TB})}$$

The joint probability in the numerator is found by using the general joint probability rule to get

$$P(\text{TB}/P) = \frac{P(\text{TB})P(P/\text{TB})}{P(\text{TB})P(P/\text{TB}) + P(\text{N.TB})P(P/\text{N.TB})}$$

Note the choice of which rule to use in the numerator was guided by the fact that $P(P/TB)$ is known, while $P(TB/P)$ is what we are solving for. Plugging in the appropriate probabilities, we can now find our answer.

$$P(TB/P) = \frac{(0.01)(0.99)}{(0.01)(0.99) + (0.99)(0.10)} = 0.09$$

This expanded form of the conditional probability rule is called Bayes' rule, after the mathematician Bayes who developed it. In general Bayes' rule can be written

$$(PA_i/B) = \frac{P(A_i)P(B/A_i)}{\sum\limits_{i=1}^{n} P(A_i)P(B/A_i)}$$

where $A_1, \ldots, A_n$ is the set of possible outcomes if B is given.

Bayes' rule can best be solved using tabular analysis. For example, suppose a production process produces light bulbs that are 10 percent defective. Each item is inspected before being shipped, but the inspector will incorrectly classify an item 10 percent of the time. (Only items classified good are shipped.) What proportion of items shipped are defective? In other words, what is the conditional probability of an item's being defective, if it is given that it has been classified as good? The basic data can be structured as in Exhibit 2–8, since there are only two possible outcomes for an item, good or defective. Prior to inspection 90 percent are good and 10 percent are defective. Given an item is good, it is correctly classified as good 90 percent of the time, and given an item is defective, it is incorrectly classified as good 10 percent of the time.

Exhibit 2–8 Information Necessary for Solution of Bayes' Rule, Presented in Tabular Form

A_i Possible Outcomes	$P(A_i)$ Probability of Outcome	$P(B/A_i)$ P(Classified Good/Outcome)
A_1: Item good	0.9	0.9
A_2: Item defective	0.1	0.1

We want to find P(defective/classified good), or $P(A_2/B)$. The first step is to multiply each element in column 2 by its respective element in column 3, as shown in Exhibit 2–9. Each element in the new column (column 4) represents a joint probability, which is one of the terms in the numerator of the foregoing equation representing Bayes' rule. Thus each element represents the probability of the row's outcome and B, and the sum of the column values equals the value of the denominator. Finally, division of the individual column entry by the column sum represents the conditional probability $P(A_i/B)$. Hence $\frac{81}{82}$ or 98.8 percent of the items shipped (and therefore classified good) will be good, and conversely $\frac{1}{82}$ or 1.2 percent will be defective.

Exhibit 2–9 Tabular Solution of Bayes' Rule

A_i	$P(A_i)$	$P(B/A_i)$	$P(A_i \text{ and } B)$ or $P(A_i)P(B/A_i)$	$P(A_i/B)$
A_1: Item good	0.9	0.9	0.81	$\frac{81}{82} = P(\text{G/shipped})$
A_2: Item defective	0.1	0.1	$\underline{0.01}$	$\frac{1}{82} = P(\text{D/shipped})$
			$0.82 = P(B)$	

Bayes' rule is of special interest because it gives us a mechanism to revise our initial probability estimates, given new information. Consider the situation where we feel that the probability a stock is a good buy is 0.4. That is, our *prior* (before new information) probabilities are $P(\text{good buy}) = 0.4$ and $P(\text{bad buy}) = 0.6$. Now an investment service that has a record of being right 80 percent of the time recommends purchase of the stock. What then should be our revised or posterior (after new information) probability that the stock is a good buy, i.e., $P(\text{good buy/invest service recommendation})$? Using the Bayesian tabular analysis, we find that the revised or posterior probabilities are $\frac{32}{44}$ that the stock is a good buy and, conversely, $\frac{12}{44}$ that it is a bad buy.

Exhibit 2–10 Tabular Analysis of Example

A_i	$P(A_i)$	$P(B/A_i)$	$P(A_i)P(B/A_i)$	$P(A_i/B)$
A_1: Good buy	0.4	0.8	0.32	$\frac{32}{44}$
A_2: Bad buy	0.6	0.2	$\underline{0.12}$	$\frac{12}{44}$
			0.44	

In analyzing the use of Bayes' rule to revise prior probability estimates in light of new information, the following relationship should be noted. The stronger the initial prior probabilities, the less effect the new information has on changing the probabilities. Conversely, the more conclusive the new information, the greater the impact on the revised probabilities. For example, if the prior probabilities are 0.01 and 0.99 for a good buy and a bad buy, respectively, the revised probabilities would be $\frac{792}{794}$ and $\frac{2}{794}$, respectively. If the investment service is right 99 percent of the time, the revised probabilities would be $\frac{198}{201}$ and $\frac{3}{201}$, respectively. (The reader should calculate these probabilities to make sure that he knows how to use Bayes' rule.)

PROBLEMS

1. A firm studied the differences in attitude toward its company by sex. Attitudes were classified into three groups: (1) favorable, (2) neutral, and (3) unfavorable. Describe the sample space.

2. A sales forecaster predicts that sales will increase, remain the same, or decrease during the next year. After one year, the actual sales results will be classified into one of these three categories.
   a. Describe the sample space, including all possible combinations of predictions and results.
   b. How many of the sample points have correctly predicted sales?

3. A family has two children. Assume that the probability of a boy is $\frac{1}{2}$.
   a. Find the probability of two boys.
   b. Find the conditional probability of two boys, given that one of the children is a boy.

4. A company studied the differences based on salary of their employees' opinions of a new proposal, and found that 300 of its 400 employees with salaries of less than \$15,000 were in favor of the proposal, and a total of 200 were opposed. There are 600 employees in the company.
   a. How many of the employees have incomes of at least \$15,000, and how many of these favor the proposal?
   b. Find the probability that an employee selected at random favors the proposal
   c. Given that an employee favors the proposal, what is the probability that his income is $\geq \$15,000$?

5. Based on an analysis of the previous year's business, it is estimated that 100 people enter a certain store on Tuesday, 150 on Wednesday, and 120 on Thursday. The probabilities that these customers will make at least one purchase are 0.7, 0.8, and 0.75, respectively.
   a. Find the probability that a customer who entered the store on one of these days made at least one purchase.
   b. Given that a purchase was made on one of these three days, find the conditional probability that the purchase was *not* made on Wednesday.

6. Consider again the situation where we are examining two stocks, A and B. As before, assume that the stocks must go either up or down. The probability that stock A goes up is 0.6, stock B, 0.7.
   a. Find the probability that both stocks go up.
   b. Find the probability that exactly one stock goes up.
   c. Find the probability that at least one stock goes up.
   d. If we did not assume that the stocks must go either up or down, how do you think the previous probabilities would change?

7. Two friends are taking a course in statistics. Assume that both have a probability of $\frac{1}{2}$ of receiving a grade of B or better.
   a. What is the probability that both will receive grades of at least B?
   b. What is the probability that both will receive grades less than B?
   c. What is the probability that one will receive at least a B?

8. The probability that a personnel manager interviews an unacceptable candidate is $\frac{1}{3}$; an acceptable candidate, $\frac{1}{2}$; and a superior candidate, $\frac{5}{6}$. What is the probability that neither of the next two candidates he interviews is unacceptable?

9. The brakes of a new car can be rated as either poor, fair, or good. Denote the ratings as P, F, or G. Describe in words the following events.
   a. $P[\text{P or F}]$
   b. $P[\text{F or G}]$
   c. $P[\text{P and G}]$

10. Which of the following are incorrect statements?
 a. $P[A] = 0.1$
 b. $P[B] = 0$
 c. $P[C] = 1$
 d. $P[D] = 1.2$

11. Let P denote profit. $P[P < \$15,000] = 0.5$ and $P[10,000 < P > 30,000] = 0.35$. What additional information is needed to find $P[P \geq 30,000]$?

12. Which of the following events are mutually exclusive?
 a. A is the event of accepting a full-time job with Company A, and B is the event of accepting a full-time job with Company B.
 b. R is the event of rejecting a full-time job with Company R, and S is the event of rejecting a full-time job with Company S.
 c. Y is the event of being less than 21 years old, and P is the event of being president of a large corporation.

13. Which of the following events are independent?
 a. A is the event of being 25 years old, and C is the event of attending college.
 b. W is the event of graduating from high school on the west coast, and E is the event of attending college on the east coast.
 c. T is the event that it will be 70° at sometime tomorrow, and Y is the event that the temperature will reach 95° at sometime during next year.

14. A pair of dice have been thrown.
 Let A be the event that one die is a 3 or 4.
 Let B be the event that the other die is a 4 or 5.
 Let C be the event that the sum of the dice is an 8.
 Let D be the event that the sum of the dice is a 9.
 True or false?
 a. A and B are mutually exclusive.
 b. A and B are independent.
 c. C and A are independent.
 d. D and A are independent.

15. If A and B are independent, show that $P[A/B] = P[A]$.

16. One real estate agent offers another a bet of $5.00 against $1.00 that he will not be able to sell a house to his first client of the day. For this to be a fair bet, what must the probability of selling the house be? If the same bet was offered for the last client of the day, what should the probability of selling the house be for a fair bet?

17. A stockbroker predicts that the odds are 2 to 1 that a certain stock will go up during the next week, and 1 to 3 that the value will stay the same. What is the probability that the value of the stock will go down during the next week?

18. A firm has found that a test for an irregular heartbeat administered after an executive has been inactive is not very effective. If the test showed positive, the probability of an irregular heartbeat was 30 percent, i.e., Pr [IRREG H.B/P] = 0.3. For this reason, it has been decided to test executives for an irregular heartbeat after moderate activity. The probability of an irregular heartbeat is 20 percent. When the test is administered after moderate activity, it has the following properties; i.e., P (P/REG H.B.) = 0.3 and P (P/IRREG H.B.) = 0.7.
 a. Using Bayes' rule, find P[IRREG H.B/P].
 b. Compare P[IRREG H.B/P] for both tests.
 c. Can you state which test is better? Why or why not?

19. A firm uses a personality test to aid in the selection of management trainees. During the past year, 70 percent of all persons accepted as management trainees achieved a rating of "satisfactory"; the remainder were "unsatisfactory." Of these rated as "satisfactory," 85 percent had acceptable scores on the personality test; of those rated unsatisfactory, 35 percent had acceptable scores. Using Bayes' rule, find the probability that an applicant would be a "satisfactory" management trainee, given an acceptable score on the personality test.

20. Assume that in a very large lot of similar articles produced by a manufacturer, nine-tenths are known to be perfect and one-tenth is known to be defective. If ten of these articles are selected at random and tested, what is the probability of getting exactly three (3) defectives, at most three (3) defectives, and at least three (3) defectives?

21. Suppose that 12 dice are thrown simultaneously. Each 5 or 6 spot appearing is considered to be a success. What is the probability that no more than two successes will occur?

22. A process produces 20 percent defectives. If a person samples 10 items, what is the probability
    a. That exactly two will be defective?
    b. That exactly eight will be good?
    c. That more than three will be defective?
    d. That at most four will be defective?

23. Assume that phone calls during any hour between 9:00 and 5:00 any day of the week to the firm of Ajax, Ajax, and Brillo have a Poisson distribution with mean 3.
    a. What is the probability that in a specific hour more than four calls will be received?
    b. What is the probability that in a specific hour less than two calls will be received *or* more than four calls?
    c. What is the probability that on a given work day less than 20 calls will be received? (Set up but do *not* work out numerical answer.)

24. Let z be a standard normal variable. Find
    a. $P(z \geq 2)$
    b. $P(z < 1)$
    c. $P(z > -1.23)$
    d. $P(z < -0.67)$
    e. $P(+1.01 \leq z < 1.11)$
    f. $P(1.01 < z < 1.11)$
    g. $P(-1.03 \leq z \leq +2.22)$
    h. $P(z = 1.03)$

25. Solve
    a. $P(z > 1.61)$
    b. $P(z \leq -0.86)$
    c. $P(z < -0.86)$
    d. $P(0.41 \leq z \leq 1.50)$
    e. $P(z < 1.46)$

26. If I draw a sample of 100 items from a normal distribution, within what accuracy can I estimate μ, with 95 percent probability?

27. Algar Power has capacity of 1,000,000 kilowatts per hour. If demand in a given hour is normally distributed with a mean of 900,000 and a standard deviation of 100,000,
    a. What is the probability of an overload (demand > capacity) in the given hour?
    b. How would you go about calculating the probability of no overload in a given day?

28. Let x = the number of bombs hitting target on a given bombing raid by one plane. x has a Poisson distribution with mean 2. Suppose 10 planes fly the mission. What is the probability that no bombs hit the target?

29. A certain type of rope breaks under a pressure of 2000 psi 10 percent of the time. If you test five ropes at 2000 psi, what is the probability that exactly one will break?

30. From the historical data of accounts payable, we know the probability that a new customer will be a bad debt is 0.10.
  a. What is the probability that in 400 new accounts there will be fewer than 35 bad accounts? (Set up but do *not* work out arithmetic.)
  b. Use an approximation to find the probability asked for in a.

31. The number of visible particles per cubic centimeter seen in a dusty gas in using an ultramicroscope is distributed according to the Poisson distribution with a mean of 5. What is the probability that a cubic centimeter of this gas will contain exactly three visible particles?

32. Is the following function a probability distribution? Explain.

$$f(x) = \frac{x}{8} \quad \text{for } x = 1, 2, 3, 4$$

$$f(x) = 0 \quad \text{elsewhere}$$

33. In an industrial complex the average number of fatal accidents per month is one-half. The number of accidents per month is adequately described by a Poisson distribution. What is the probability that four months will pass without a fatal accident?

34. If the probability of an item produced by a certain machine being defective is 0.2, what is the probability that the first defective produced will be the ninth item? That the third will be the ninth item?

35. If the probability that any customer entering the store will purchase an item is 0.2, what is the probability
  a. That one of the next 5 customers will purchase?
  b. That at least one of the next five customers will purchase?
  c. That the first customer to purchase is the fifth one to enter the store?
  d. That the second customer to purchase is the fifth one to enter the store?

36. Given the following probability distribution,

x	f(x)
0	$\frac{1}{8}$
1	$\frac{2}{8}$
2	$\frac{3}{8}$
3	$\frac{2}{8}$

calculate the expected value of x, its variance, and standard deviation.

37. If $E(x) = 15$ and $\sigma_x^2 = 5$, find
  a. $E(10x)$
  b. $E(ax)$
  c. σ_x
  d. σ_{5x}^2
  e. $E(5x - 3)$
  f. $\sigma_{(5x-3)}^2$

3

decision strategies,
utility,
and game theory

When a decision maker has access to all information that would be relevant to a particular problem, and he can accurately predict the outcome of each alternative action available to him, he is said to be operating under conditions of certainty. The model he constructs to help analyze the problem is called a *deterministic model*. For example, a commuter might evaluate alternative routes for driving between his home and office based on minimizing total mileage or the number of traffic signals encountered. A wrong decision would have to be attributed either to excessively difficult computations or errors in the original formulation of the problem.

It frequently is necessary to make decisions when any one of several different outcomes could possibly occur following the selection of a particular course of action. These decisions are said to be made under conditions of risk or uncertainty.[1] In some cases, all possible outcomes of a particular course of action cannot be specified. In other cases, perhaps all outcomes can be specified but nothing is known about the relative likelihood of each one's occurring. Most quantitative techniques cannot be employed to analyze these situations. Formal analysis of a decision that can result in any one of several different consequences requires that each consequence and its associated probability of occurrence can be specified.

DECISION STRATEGIES

We shall be concerned in this chapter with formulating strategies for making decisions under uncertainty. Models that are constructed to represent such

[1] Some people draw a technical distinction between the terms risk and uncertainty, There is not a consensus on how or whether to differentiate, however, and in this book the two terms will be used interchangeably.

problems are called *probabilistic models*. Since a multiplicity of outcomes can result from the choice of a particular action, the decision maker in effect is forced to gamble. Regardless of the quality of the analysis upon which the decision is based, the decision may turn out, after the fact, to have been wrong. No strategy will consistently lead to objectively correct decisions. Thus a strategy for making decisions under uncertainty cannot be formulated until we first specify what we mean by a "best" decision. While a "best" decision might mean different things to different people, we should at least devise a strategy that is consistent with the individual decision maker's personal judgment and preferences. Several different strategies are frequently used.

The Minimax/Maximin and Minimax Regret Principles

We shall identify actions that can be taken by the decision maker with numbers and events that can occur following the selection of an action with letters. The outcome of a particular action depends on the event that occurs. Thus the problem portrayed in Exhibit 3–1 contains four possible actions and three events. The event that occurs is assumed to be independent of the action that is taken. For example, the possibility (event) of having a fire is not affected by our decision (action) of whether or not to purchase fire insurance. Exhibit 3–1 is called a *conditional payoff table*. It specifies the payoff that will occur for each event *given* the specification of a particular action. Thus, from Exhibit 3–1, if action 3 is selected and event *B* occurs, the outcome is a gain of $8. This outcome of $8 is called a conditional payoff; i.e., it is conditional on selecting action 3 and having event *B* occur.

Exhibit 3–1   Conditional Payoff Table

Event	Actions			
	1	2	3	4
A	$5	− $2	$3	$7
B	7	0	8	10
C	6	− 4	2	8

There is no doubt as to the best decision in this problem. Regardless of which event occurs, the best outcome is associated with action 4. Thus action 4 dominates the others and is the one we would select. The solution is not always so apparent, however. For example, consider the problem in Exhibit 3–2. If event *D* occurs, our best decision would have been action 1. Action 3 would have been best if *E* occurs, and 2 would have been best if *F* occurs. But we do not know which event will occur at the time we must make a decision.

Exhibit 3-2   Conditional Payoff Table

	Actions			
Event	1	2	3	4
D	$9	$7	$3	$6
E	7	2	8	5
F	6	11	1	7

One possible strategy would be to select that action that would *maxi*mize our *mini*mum gain, or payoff. This is the *maximin* principle, which is the basis for a conservative decision strategy. The decision maker is behaving as though nature—or whoever or whatever else determines which event is going to occur—is acting against him and will choose the most adverse event possible given the action that he has selected. The worst possible outcomes for actions 1, 2, 3, and 4 are, respectively, $6, $2, $1, and $5. According to the maximin criterion, therefore, action 1 would be selected. That is, the worst possible outcomes for actions 2, 3, and 4 are less desirable than the worst possible outcome for action 1.[2]

The maximin strategy is appropriate only when the conditional payoff represents gains. If the "payoffs" are costs or losses, maximizing the minimum cost is clearly never a good strategy. A similar conservative decision strategy as maximin, however, can be formulated from the opposite perspective. That is, rather than maximize the minimum gain, the decision maker could select the action that would *mini*mize the *maxi*mum loss (or cost). Such a decision strategy is called *minimax*. Clearly minimax and maximin are conceptually the same conservative strategy of assuming that nature will choose the most adverse event possible given the action that has been selected. The only difference is that in maximin the outcomes are gains and in minimax they are costs (or losses).

Sometimes the blind application of decision rules such as the maximin or minimax criteria can lead to poor decisions. Suppose, for example, an investor is trying to decide whether to invest in a bond or a stock. The percentage returns on these two alternative investments, conditional on one of two possible states of the economy (E_1 or E_2) occurring, are given in Exhibit 3-3. The maximin principle would lead to investment in the bond, but this would not be a good decision unless the investor felt strongly that economic conditions E_2 were in fact going to occur.

Exhibit 3-3   Investment Returns

	Bonds	Stock
E_1	8%	20%
E_2	8%	7%

[2] A gambler or someone who expected nature to respond benevolently might select action 2 based on the maximax principle—maximize the maximum possible gain.

An alternative decision strategy could be based on the criterion of *mini*mizing the decision maker's *max*imum "regret," or loss. This is called the *minimax regret* principle. It assumes nature is neutral but that the decision-maker wants to minimize his possible discomfort from thinking of "what might have been." Suppose we select action 2 in Exhibit 3–2 and event *D* occurs. Our gain, or payoff, of $7 is $2 less than what would have been realized if action 1 had been selected. With the advantage of hindsight, therefore, we could claim to have suffered a $2 opportunity loss from not selecting the best action *given the event that occurred.* Each outcome could be represented by a conditional opportunity loss equal to the payoff corresponding to the best action that could have been taken given the occurrence of a particular event minus the conditional payoff of the alternative action being considered. A conditional loss table is given in Exhibit 3–4. Notice that the conditional opportunity loss of the best action for each possible event is zero and the conditional opportunity losses of all other actions for the same event are equal to their respective payoffs subtracted from the payoff for the best action. If we want to minimize our maximum potential loss, we would now select action 4.

Exhibit 3–4   Conditional Loss Table

| | | Actions | | |
Event	1	2	3	4
D	$0	$2	$6	$3
E	1	6	0	3
F	5	0	10	4

Expected Values

It is generally more appropriate to regard nature as being neutral as opposed to malevolent (or benevolent). An event will not be selected in response to our decision. In fact, the probability of each event's occurring will not be affected by the choice of a particular action. We should, therefore, devise a decision strategy that, based on the neutrality of nature, will maximize benefits in the long run. Selecting the action with the largest expected value is such a strategy. The expected value is a weighted average of the conditional values. The weights are the probabilities of each conditional value actually being received. Thus the expected value of a given action is the average outcome that would occur if the same action were repeated a large number of times under identical circumstances. An example of the calculation of an expected value is given in Exhibit 3–5.

Exhibit 3–5 Calculation of Expected Value

Event	Probability	Conditional Value	Expected Value
X	0.2	$10	$ 2
Y	0.5	14	7
Z	0.3	20	6
	1.0	Expected Value =	$15

It should be obvious that no alternative action could provide greater total payoffs in the long run than the action with the highest expected value. (This is not to deny that alternative actions may, after the fact, have been superior *for some* trials.) It is also true, however, that applying the maximum expected value criterion to nonrepetitive decisions is the strategy that will maximize the expected total payoffs to the firm in the long run. Any other strategy may result in occasional spectacular gains, but it will be a suboptimal strategy over a prolonged period of time.[3]

Expected Payoff Tables

The following problem is a simple example of the use of payoff tables and expected values to determine the best action. Assume that a merchant can buy an item for $7.00 and sell it for $10.50. The probabilities of a daily demand for "less than 5," 5, 6, 7, 8, 9, 10, and "more than 10" items are, respectively, 0, 0.05, 0.15, 0.30, 0.25, 0.15, 0.10, and 0. (These probabilities may be subjective, or they may be based on past records.) Any unsold items must be scrapped at the end of the day and have no salvage value. The merchant wants to know how many items he should stock at the beginning of each business day.

Our objective is to find which action (amount stocked) leads to the optimum outcome (highest expected value). We shall consider stocking only 5 through 10 items, inclusive, since there is zero probability of demand for any other number of items. Given the number of items stocked S and the number demanded D, we can express the conditional payoff as follows:

$$\text{Conditional payoff} = \begin{cases} 10.50D - 7.00S, & \text{if } S > D \\ 3.50S, & \text{if } S \leq D \end{cases}$$

The entries in the conditional payoff table given in Exhibit 3–6 follow directly from the formulation. Notice that conditional payoffs are calculated on a strict cash basis. Foregone opportunities from demands exceeding supply are not considered.

---

[3] We assume at this point that the amounts involved are not large enough to significantly alter day-to-day operations. This assumption will be relaxed later in the chapter when the concept of utility is introduced.

Exhibit 3–6   Conditional Payoff Table

Event (demand)	Probability of Event's Occurring	Actions (number stocked)					
		5	6	7	8	9	10
5	0.05	$17.50	$10.50	$ 3.50	− $ 3.50	− $10.50	− $17.50
6	0.15	17.50	21.00	14.00	7.00	0	− 7.00
7	0.30	17.50	21.00	24.50	17.50	10.50	3.50
8	0.25	17.50	21.00	24.50	28.00	21.00	14.00
9	0.15	17.50	21.00	24.50	28.00	31.50	24.50
10	0.10	17.50	21.00	24.50	28.00	31.50	35.00
	1.00						

The next step is to find the expected payoff for each possible action. The expected payoff for any given action is obtained by summing the products of each conditional outcome and its associated probability of occurring. These individual products and their sum for each action are given in Exhibit 3–7. The computations in the exhibit indicate that the merchant's best strategy is to stock 7 items per day. This strategy would give him an expected daily payoff of $21.875. Stocking any other number of items would give a lower expected payoff.

Exhibit 3–7   Expected Payoff Table

Event (demand)	Probability of Event's Occurring	Actions (number stocked)					
		5	6	7	8	9	10
5	0.05	$0.875	$0.525	$0.175	− $0.175	− $0.525	− $0.875
6	0.15	2.625	3.150	2.100	1.050	0	− 1.050
7	0.30	5.250	6.300	7.350	5.250	3.150	1.050
8	0.25	4.375	5.250	6.125	7.000	5.250	3.500
9	0.15	2.625	3.150	3.675	4.200	4.725	3.675
10	0.10	1.750	2.100	2.450	2.800	3.150	3.500
Expected Payoff =		$17.500	$20.475	$21.875	$20.125	$15.750	$9.800

Expected Loss Tables

The same decision can be reached by means of a loss analysis. If the merchant overstocks, he suffers a loss of $7.00 on each unsold item. If he understocks, he suffers an opportunity loss of $3.50 on each item he could have sold if he had ordered a sufficient supply. Notice that both cash and opportunity losses are considered in a loss analysis. The conditional loss for each action-event combination can be expressed as follows:

$$\text{Conditional loss} = \begin{cases} 7.00(S - D), & \text{if } S \geq D \\ 3.50(D - S), & \text{if } S < D \end{cases}$$

The conditional loss table is given in Exhibit 3–8. Notice that the conditional loss table can also be obtained directly from the conditional payoff table in Exhibit 3–6. First find the highest conditional payoff corresponding to each event. This payoff, in turn, corresponds to the best action that could have been taken given a particular event had occurred. Then subtract all other payoffs in an event row from the optimal one. This procedure will yield the same numbers that are contained in Exhibit 3–8. Losses are incurred either by understocking or overstocking. The diagonal of zero losses represents the ideal situation where the number of items stocked equals the number demanded.

Exhibit 3–8 Conditional Loss Table

Event (demand)	Probability of Event's Occurring	Actions (number stocked)					
		5	6	7	8	9	10
5	0.05	$ 0	$ 7.00	$14.00	$21.00	$28.00	$35.00
6	0.15	3.50	0	7.00	14.00	21.00	28.00
7	0.30	7.00	3.50	0	7.00	14.00	21.00
8	0.25	10.50	7.00	3.50	0	7.00	14.00
9	0.15	14.00	10.50	7.00	3.50	0	7.00
10	0.10	17.50	14.00	10.50	7.00	3.50	0

An expected loss can be calculated for each possible action by using the same procedure that was employed to calculate expected payoffs. An expected loss table is presented in Exhibit 3–9. Our decision criterion is now to select that action with the minimum expected loss. This criterion leads us again to select the action "stock 7 items."

Exhibit 3–9 Expected Loss Table

Event (demand)	Probability of Event's Occurring	Actions (number stocked)					
		5	6	7	8	9	10
5	0.05	$ 0	$0.350	$0.700	$1.050	$1.400	$1.750
6	0.15	0.525	0	1.050	2.100	3.150	4.200
7	0.30	2.100	1.050	0	2.100	4.200	6.300
8	0.25	2.625	1.750	0.875	0	1.750	3.500
9	0.15	2.100	1.575	1.050	0.525	0	1.050
10	0.10	1.750	1.400	1.050	0.700	0.350	0
	Expected Loss =	9.100	6.125	4.725	6.475	10.850	16.800

Expected Value of Perfect Information (EVPI)

The expected opportunity loss of the best action, stock 7 items, is $4.725. This is the smallest possible expected loss we can achieve, and it results from the decision that 7 items are to be stocked each day even though demand will be for more or less than 7 items 70 percent of the time. This expected loss could be eliminated only if we knew in advance what each day's demand was going to be, so just the right number of items would be stocked. Since this information is not available, the minimum expected daily loss can be thought of as the *cost of uncertainty*.

The cost of uncertainty in our problem is $4.725 and, in the absence of additional information about daily demand, is an irreducible cost. Suppose that somehow we are able to determine in advance the number of items that will be demanded on the following day. Given the availability of this perfect information, we would always order so that the number of items stocked would equal demand and there would never be a loss from understocking or overstocking. We would order 5 items and have a payoff of $17.50 five percent of the time; we would order 6 items and have a payoff of $21.00 fifteen percent of the time; etc. The expected, or average, daily payoff under conditions of certainty would be $26.60, as shown in Exhibit 3–10. In other

Exhibit 3–10   Expected Daily Payoff under Conditions of Certainty

Daily Demand	Probability	Conditional Payoff	Expected Payoff
5	0.05	$17.50	$0.875
6	0.15	21.00	3.150
7	0.30	24.50	7.350
8	0.25	28.00	7.000
9	0.15	31.50	4.725
10	0.10	35.00	3.500

Expected Daily Payoff = $26.600

words, the average daily profit over a long period of time would be $26.60 if perfect advance information were available on daily demand. In the absence of this perfect information, the expected daily payoff is $21.875. The difference between these amounts is the *expected value of prefect information* (EVPI). This means that the merchant could pay up to a maximum of $26.60 − $21.875 = $4.725 per day to obtain a perfect forecast of the following day's demand. The $4.725 represents the increase in expected daily payoff that could be achieved if perfect demand information was available.

Notice that the EVPI is equal to the cost of uncertainty. They represent the same quantity interpreted in slightly different ways. It should also be noticed that the sum of the expected payoff and the expected loss is $26.60 for all alternative actions. (The reader should reason out for himself why this relationship holds.)

The EVPI can be used as a quick check of the advisability of sampling to obtain additional information. If the cost of sampling is in excess of the EVPI, it clearly would not be worthwhile. If sample information can be obtained very inexpensively, and if it would greatly improve our ability to forecast daily demand, we would definitely want to proceed. But if the cost of taking a sample is relatively expensive (although less than the EVPI) and/or the potential value of sample information is questionable, a more formal analysis would have to be conducted to calculate the expected value of sample information.[4]

Suppose, however, that the merchant decides to stock 8 items per day instead of the optimal 7. The expected daily loss of this action is $6.475. The merchant is using a suboptimal strategy and is therefore incurring a higher expected loss than is necessary. The difference between this expected loss and the cost of uncertainty is called the *cost of irrationality*. The cost of irrationality is $6.475 − $4.725 = $1.750. This is the amount of the *additional* expected daily loss, over and above the cost of uncertainty, incurred by the merchant as a result of his choice of a suboptimal, or irrational, action.

From the expected payoff table in Exhibit 3–7, the expected payoff of stocking 7 items is $21.875. This is the highest daily expected payoff that can be achieved. A decision to stock any number of items other than 7 will result in a lower expected daily payoff. For example, the expected payoff from the action "stock 8" is $20.125. The difference in the two payoff values is $21.872 − $20.125 = $1.75, which is again the cost of irrationality. This relationship will always occur; i.e., the cost of irrationality is equal to both the increase in the expected loss and the decrease in the expected payoff that results from selecting a suboptimal action. Thus the cost of irrationality of the action "stock 9 items" is $10.850 − $4.725 = $21.875 − $15.750 = $6.125.

Critical Ratio

The above example illustrates the basic concepts that are involved in using expected value as a criterion for decision making under uncertainty. In more complex problems, however, a very large number of supply and demand levels may be possible. The large number of alternative actions would make an analysis through a payoff or loss table a cumbersome means of solution. Fortunately, a solution can be obtained very readily if the unit costs of understocking and overstocking remain constant regardless of the differential between supply and demand. Let the cost of understocking be k_u per unit and the cost of overstocking be k_o per unit.

Suppose that the amount supplied is increased from $n − 1$ to n units. The probability that this nth unit is demanded is equal to the probability that total demand equals or exceeds n units, $P(D \geq n)$. Similarly, the probability that this nth unit will not be demanded is $P(D < n)$. Thus, for the additional nth unit, the expected loss of understocking is

$$k_u \cdot P(D \geq n) = k_u[1 − P(D < n)],$$

and the expected loss of overstocking is

$$k_o \cdot P(D < n)$$

---

[4] The procedure for calculating the expected value of sample information is given in Chapter 4. Sampling techniques are discussed in Chapter 20.

An additional unit should be stocked if the expected loss of overstocking is less than the expected loss of understocking, or if

$$k_o \cdot P(D < n) < k_u[1 - P(D < n)]$$

This inequality can be rewritten to show that an additional unit should be stocked if

$$P(D < n) < \frac{k_u}{k_u + k_o}$$

This result gives the critical ratio (CR), which can be defined as the percentile in the demand distribution that corresponds to the best action (i.e., the optimal number of items to stock). The critical ratio is calculated according to Eq. (3–1).

$$CR = \frac{k_u}{k_u + k_o} \qquad (3\text{–}1)$$

In our example, $k_u = \$3.50$ and $k_o = \$7.00$. Therefore,

$$CR = \frac{3.50}{3.50 + 7.00} = \frac{3.50}{10.50} \approx 0.29$$

The 29th percentile in the probability distribution of demand corresponds to 7 items. We have again obtained the result that the best action is to stock 7 items.

The critical ratio increases with the cost of understocking and decreases with the cost of overstocking. The higher the critical ratio, the greater the number of items that should be stocked. Thus, for example, an increase in the cost of understocking would cause an upward shift in the number of items stocked. Similarly, an increase in the cost of overstocking would result in a reduction in the number of items stocked.

Finally, we should emphasize that the critical ratio approach applies only to special types of problems. Specifically, it applies only to problems involving stocking decisions for "perishable" items, such as fresh fruits and vegetables, newspapers, etc. This approach is not appropriate when inventory items can be carried forward for use in future periods or when the costs of over- or understocking are not strictly linear.

Example

Let us now consider a slightly more complex and interesting example. A businessman has two independent investments available to him, but does not have the capital to undertake both of them simultaneously. He can choose to take A first and then stop, or if A is successful then take B, or vice versa. The probability of success on A is 0.7, while for B it is 0.4. Both investments require an initial capital outlay of $2000, and both return nothing if the venture is unsuccessful. Investment A will return \$3000 (over cost) if it is successful, whereas successful completion of B will return \$5000 (over cost). Using expected monetary value as a decision criterion, decide the best strategy the businessman can take.

The first step is to identify all possible actions and events. There are five alternative actions: (a) do nothing (denoted by 0); (b) accept A and then stop, regardless of the outcome $(A, 0)$; (c) accept B and then stop, regardless of the outcome $(B, 0)$; (d) accept A and, if successful, then accept B (A, B); (e) accept B and, if successful, then accept A (B, A). There are four possible events that can occur: (a) both A and B will be successful (AB); (b) A will be successful, but not B $(A\bar{B})$; (c) B will be successful, but not A $(\bar{A}B)$; (d) neither A nor B will be successful $(\bar{A}\bar{B})$.

The next step is to calculate the conditional payoffs for each action-event combination. The conditional payoff table is given in Exhibit 3–11.

Exhibit 3–11   Conditional Payoff Table

Event	Probability[a]	0	A, 0	B, 0	A, B	B, A
AB	0.28	\$0	\$3000	\$5000	\$8000	\$8000
$A\bar{B}$	0.42	0	3000	−2000	1000	−2000
$\bar{A}B$	0.12	0	−2000	5000	−2000	3000
$\bar{A}\bar{B}$	0.18	0	−2000	−2000	−2000	−2000
	1.00					

[a] For a review of the concepts used to obtain these probability figures, see Chapter 2.

The final step in calculating the expected payoffs is shown in Exhibit 3–12.

Exhibit 3–12   Expected Payoff Table

Event	Probability	0	A, 0	B, 0	A, B	B, A
AB	0.28	\$0	\$ 840	\$1400	\$2240	\$2240
$A\bar{B}$	0.42	0	1260	−840	420	−840
$\bar{A}B$	0.12	0	−240	600	−240	360
$\bar{A}\bar{B}$	0.18	0	−360	−360	−360	−360
Expected Payoff =		\$0	\$1500	\$ 800	\$2060	\$1400

The optimal strategy, accept A and, if successful, then accept B, has an expected payoff of \$2060. Conditional and expected loss tables, indicating the same optimal strategy, are given in Exhibits 3–13 and 3–14. (As a review, the reader should see that the cost of uncertainty and the EVPI = \$2040; the cost of irrationality for the action B, A is \$660; etc.)

Exhibit 3–13   Conditional Loss Table

Event	Probability	0	A, 0	B, 0	A, B	B, A
				Action		
AB	0.28	$8000	$5000	$3000	$ 0	$ 0
$A\bar{B}$	0.42	3000	0	5000	2000	5000
$\bar{A}B$	0.12	5000	7000	0	7000	2000
$\bar{A}\bar{B}$	0.18	0	2000	2000	2000	2000
	1.00					

Exhibit 3-14   Expected Loss Table

Event	Probability	0	A, 0	B, 0	A, B	B, A
				Action		
AB	0.28	$2240	$1400	$ 840	$ 0	$ 0
$A\bar{B}$	0.42	1260	0	2100	840	2100
$\bar{A}B$	0.12	600	840	0	840	240
$\bar{A}\bar{B}$	0.18	0	360	360	360	360
	Expected Loss = $4100	$2600	$3300	$2040	$2700	

UTILITY THEORY

The discussion so far has argued that the decision maker should base his choices on the criterion of maximizing expected monetary value. He should prefer a 50–50 chance of receiving one dollar or nothing to the certain receipt of forty cents. Not infrequently, however, the selection of an alternative other than the one that maximizes expected monetary value can be justified as purely rational behavior. For example, how many of us would choose a 50–50 chance of receiving $1,000,000 or nothing in favor of a certain $400,000? Or suppose you had to choose between a 50–50 chance of gaining $1,000,000 or losing $500,000 and receiving a certain $200,000? We would probably choose the sure thing in either case, even though we would be choosing the alternative with the smaller expected monetary value. Since both choices would be consistent with normal and rational behavior, our decision theory must be extended if it is to accurately explain and predict observed behavior.

The concept that we shall use to describe an individual's behavior when choosing between risky alternatives is called *utility theory*. In essence, this concept proposes that an individual makes decisions so as to maximize the value of his own personal utility, or the satisfaction he enjoys from fulfilling his personal human wants. Utility is personal in that it reflects the desirability of some article or service to an individual. The degree of desirability, or utility, of some object can vary from individual to individual. Some individuals place a high value on works of art, others on flashy cars, others on travel, etc. Their personal utility schedules reflect these preferences. Utility is obviously descriptive as opposed to normative, and it does not have the ethical connotation of distinguishing between social and economic "desirability." That is, it does not imply what ought to be desired; it does indicate the extent to which something is desired.

The concept of utility can also be applied to the desirability of alternative investment opportunities. This would explain why different individuals could reasonably make different choices when faced with the same situation. As described below, a relationship between utility and monetary value can be derived for each individual. This relationship is called a utility curve or a utility function, and its shape reflects the individual's attitude about assuming risk. Utility is measured in arbitrary units called *utiles*. Any convenient scale can be used, because only relative utilities have any meaning. *Absolute utility cannot be measured.*[5]

Utility is perhaps best understood through the notion of decreasing marginal utility. For example, if an individual is able to increase his total consumption, his total utility will increase as well. Utility will increase at a decreasing rate, however; particularly when large quantities of the commodity being considered are involved, the added utility from the last extra unit of some commodity will be less than that added by the preceding unit. This notion is consistent with observance of risk averse behavior. The first $X received in income or as return on investment generally will have greater utility than the receipt of a second $X. Similarly, the loss of $X probably would result in "disutility" greater than the utility that would be received from a gain of $X.

Construction of Utility Curves

Let us now illustrate the process through which an individual's utility curve could be derived. Suppose Mr. A is *indifferent* between a 50–50 chance of receiving $1,000,000 or nothing and a certain $350,000. (If the certainty amount is less than $350,000, he would prefer to gamble; if the certainty amount is greater than $350,000, he would prefer the sure thing.) We can arbitrarily assign $0 a value of 0 utiles and $1,000,000 a value of 100 utiles. (Remember that utility has relevance only in a relative sense. Therefore, absolute values can be assigned in any arbitrary and convenient way.) Then, given Mr. A's expressed indifference amounts, $350,000 would have a value of $0.5(0) + 0.5(100) = 50$ utiles. It follows that if he is indifferent between a 50–50 chance of receiving $350,000 or nothing and a certain $150,000, the

---

[5] The term "cardinal utility" is used when each alternative can be assigned an explicit relative numerical value. Ordinal utility refers to the preferential ranking of alternatives without any numerical measures. Measures of cardinal utility are developed in the following discussion.

utility value of $150,000 would be 0.5(0) + 0.5(50) = 25 utiles. If he is indifferent between a 50–50 chance of receiving $350,000 or $1,000,000 and $550,000 with certainty, the utility of $550,000 would be 0.5(50) + 0.5(100) = 75 utiles. The determination of several other indifference points would enable us to plot the indifference curve shown in Illustration 3–1. Notice that points for negative dollar amounts have also been determined.

Interpretation of Utility Curves

Once an individual's utility curve is determined, we should be able to predict his choices from sets of risky alternatives. He should make decisions so as to maximize his utility. In addition to his utility curve, we again need to know the return that results from each outcome and the probability of each outcome's occurring. (The probability assignments can be determined objectively or based on personal and subjective judgments.)

Let us illustrate the use of utility curves with the following example. Mr. A must choose between two alternatives. One will return $200,000 with a probability of 0.4 or $500,000 with a probability of 0.6, while the other has a 50–50 chance of returning either $900,000 or nothing. The expected

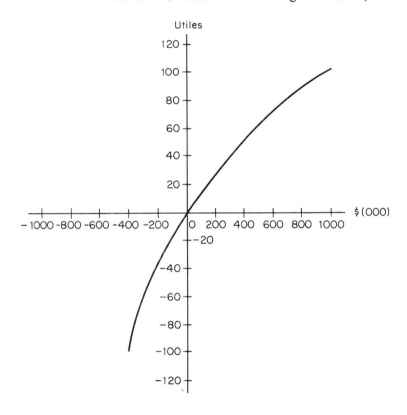

Ilustration 3–1 Utility Curve

utility of the first alternative, based on utility values read from Illustration 3–1, is 0.4(25) + 0.6(65) = 49 utiles. The expected utility of the second is 0.5(95) + 0.5(0) = 42.5 utiles. We would predict that Mr. A would prefer the first alternative over the second, since the first alternative has the higher expected utility.

Let us consider another example. Mr. A can receive $450,000 with certainty or he can select an investment that will return $200,000 with a probability of 0.3, $500,000 with a probability of 0.4, or $900,000 with a probability of 0.3. The utility of the first alternative, 55 utiles, can be read directly from the curve in Illustration 3–1. The expected utility of the second alternative is 0.3(25) + 0.4(65) + 0.3(95) = 62 utiles. We would, therefore, expect Mr. A to select the second alternative.

Notice that, on the basis of the objective of maximizing expected utility, we predicted in the first example above that Mr. A would choose the alternative with the lower expected monetary value, while in the second example we predicted that he would choose the one with the higher expected monetary value. This emphasizes that we are postulating behavior to be consistent with expected utility, and not necessarily with expected monetary value. Perhaps we should also reemphasize that utility has meaning only in a relative sense. There is no such thing as absolute utility. The vertical axis depicting utility in Illustration 3–1 could be multiplied by any positive number, or some constant could be added to or subtracted from it, and our predictions would not be altered.

Risk Aversion

Most investors, whether they be corporate managers purchasing operating assets or individual or institutional investors purchasing securities, tend to reflect risk aversion in their investment decisions. Like Mr. A, they are willing to accept a lower expected monetary value for greater certainty of the final outcome. The degree of aversion to risk is generally related to the amounts at stake. We may gamble boldly when only a few dollars are at stake but become very conservative when large sums of money are involved. And "large sums of money" means different things to a corner dry cleaning proprietor and to General Motors.

Aversion to risk is therefore related to a decreasing marginal utility for money. The utility we would receive from our first million dollars is generally greater than the additional utility we would enjoy from our second million. Stated differently, if we have only recently joined the millionaire's club, the utility of gaining a second million would not equal the disutility of losing our first. The more we have, the less we are hurt by small losses and the less we benefit from small gains. Decreasing marginal utility explains the shape of the curve in Illustration 3–1. Marginal utility is measured by the slope of the curve at any given point (see Appendix E). Since the slope decreases as the dollar amount decreases, the curve reflects decreasing marginal utility and risk aversion.

The three utility curves drawn in Illustration 3–2 indicate the three possible attitudes toward risk. These three curves are drawn with the two initial reference points O and P. The individual with utility curve *I* is, like Mr. A, a risk averter. The individual depicted by curve II is risk neutral. Notice that a risk neutral individual will always make decisions consistent with maximizing expected monetary value, because his utility varies linearly with monetary value. Curve III represents a gambler, a person who prefers risk. His marginal utility for additional money is increasing. The typical investor displays risk aversion rather than risk preference. An occasional person might have a strong inclination to take risks, or a company may need a minimum amount of money to avoid bankruptcy and management will take any project that has even a remote possibility of providing the necessary cash. These are examples of unusual individuals or situations, however.

Although risk preference is not observed frequently, risk neutrality is a fairly common occurrence. In fact, unless the amounts of money involved are substantial enough to seriously affect the continued operation of the firm or household, one could argue that all decisions should be made in accordance with risk neutrality; i.e., according to the objective of maximizing expected monetary value. This argument would be based on the fact that some projects will turn out better than expected and some worse, but these will average out and in the long run this policy will maximize the total value of the firm. Of course, as indicated above, exceptions must be made when the stakes are

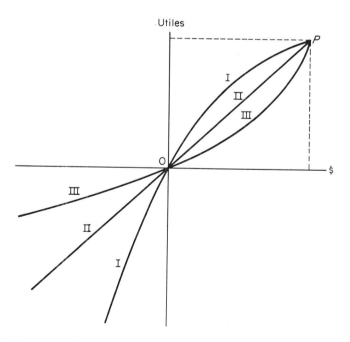

Illustration 3–2 Utility Curves

substantial enough to interfere with the continued normal operations of the enterprise.

Individual Utility Curves

Several attempts have been made to construct personal utility curves, similar to those in Illustrations 3–1 and 3–2, for corporate managers and investors. These efforts have yielded two results that are particularly noteworthy, and both suggest that too much conservatism is frequently used by those in positions of decision-making responsibility. Mr. A is typical. Notice how his utility curve, drawn in Illustration 3–1, falls off sharply when negative amounts of money (i.e., losses) are involved. This indicates that Mr. A would strongly bias his judgment against a project that had any possibility of an adverse outcome, regardless of how attractive the project might be on a more objective expected monetary value bias. Such behavior would clearly be costly to a large firm inhabited by many Mr. A's.

The second observation is related to the first. A company with annual sales of several billion dollars should be risk neutral with respect to a $500,000 project. Any other strategy would not be in the best long-term interests of the company. But suppose you are a manager administering a department with an annual budget of $500,000. Surely your judgment would be conditioned by the thought of having your personal performance rating determined largely by the success of one project. You would approach it with a high degree of caution, and your behavior would be quite common. There is evidence that corporate managers' utility curves seem to relate more closely to the amounts with which they are accustomed to dealing than to the size of their company.[6] If such risk-avoiding behavior is prevalent, perhaps the control mechanisms used to motivate and direct behavior should somehow be modified to encourage greater risk taking.

Perhaps a concluding comment is in order on the uses of utility theory. It certainly provides a framework within which we can explain observed decision-making behavior. We could also make a strong case for the normative use of utility theory; i.e., in indicating how people should behave when reacting to risky situations. We could perhaps also claim to be able approximately to *predict how* people will actually behave.

It is not necessary for individuals to understand the mathematical and graphical representation of utility curves for them to behave consistently with the objective of maximizing their utility as measured by some predetermined utility function. If it is true that people are rational and consistent when making decisions under uncertainty, then utility theory will be useful for describing and explaining behavior. If utility theory does have some predictive capabilities, a firm could determine "risk profiles" for all its managers in decision-making positions and perhaps discover managerial ten-

---

[6] Ralph O. Swalm, "Utility Theory—Insights into Risk Taking," *Harvard Business Review,* November–December, 1966, pp. 123–36.

dencies and characteristics that would not otherwise be apparent. The key is to establish consistent patterns of response to risky situations. The delegation of decision-making authority should possibly be changed and, over the long run, attempts should be made to modify behavior to make it consistent with corporate objectives.

GAME THEORY

The maximization of expected value has been advocated as the optimal decision strategy when the outcome of a decision is to be determined by some neutral factor. In other words, the probability distribution of possible outcomes is independent of what course of action is pursued. In some situations, however, the response to an action is determined by an intelligent and well-informed adversary. Labor-management relations, political battles, military maneuvers, competitive marketing, and financial negotiations are examples of situations that might be characterized by one party trying to maximize his over-all welfare at the expense of some similarly inclined opponent.

Game theory has evolved as a mathematical process for formally developing optimal strategies for dealing with these types of competitive situations. Since many decisions are made in a hostile or competitive environment, it would seem that game theory would have wide applicability. Applications have been limited to date, however, because the theory is not advanced enough to handle the complexity of most situations. Nevertheless, the basic concepts of game theory, including the formulation of the problem, the establishment of decision criteria, and the development of decision strategies, are worth studying for their contribution to logical decision-making concepts.

There are various types of games. One distinction is between two-person games and three-or-more-person games. As the names imply, the former type involves only two adversaries or players while the latter type involves three or more. Most of the research to date has been based on two-person games. Both the fascination and the complexity of three-or-more-person games are illustrated in the following passage:[7]

The three-man coalition game can be played as an auction with one seller and two buyers. The seller has a reserve price of, say, $10 on the object to be sold. The first buyer is willing to go to not more than $15; the second buyer to not more than $20. Clearly the second buyer being the stronger will get the object. Ordinarily he is expected to get it for something over $15. But suppose the second buyer approaches the first and makes a deal to eliminate competitive bidding. He can then get the object for something over $10. The deal, however, requires a division of the spoils. The second, stronger buyer

[7] "The 'Game' of Business," reprinted from *Strategy in Poker, Business and War* by John McDonald, illustrated by Robert Osborn, by permission of W. W. Norton and Company, Inc. © 1950 by John McDonald and Robert Osborn, pp 244–45.

must pay the first, weaker buyer something for making the coalition. That payment must be enough to yield the second buyer the "best" profit, and yet enough to ensure that his partner will remain in the coalition: two maximums which must be resolved. For another, rival deal is possible—in game theory but not in classical economics—namely this: The seller may cross the market and break up the coalition by paying something to the second buyer to restore the bidding and thereby push the selling price back above $15. Thus each two-man game in this three-man game is under the influence of the other possible two-man games, in arriving at the distribution payment.

In the theory of games a number of solutions, i.e., distribution schemes, are possible, some of which are enforceable and therefore dominate others. In classical theory the weaker buyer gets nothing; in game theory he gets a bribe, and the bribe will be expressed in the price. Here the difference between classical economics and game theory can be shown with simple numbers. In classical theory the price is between $15 and $20 (all going to the seller). In game theory it is between $10 and $20, depending on the bargaining ability of the players.

Most games are also of the zero-sum game variety. Zero-sum means that one player wins what the other loses, so that the sum of their net winnings is zero. The game represents a closed system. Thus two individuals matching dimes would be engaging in a two-person-zero-sum game.

As an interesting example of a possible nonzero-sum game, consider the market for the popular mobile campers. Winnebago has been one of the more successful of several relatively small companies that have participated in the growth of this market. What happens to Winnebago if General Motors, with all its marketing muscle, moves strongly into this field? Winnebago's share of the market would probably decline, but, because of the large increase in total advertising that would follow GM's entry, the size of the total market should grow. Thus the net effect on Winnebago's total sales is unclear. In either event, this would be an example of a nonzero-sum game.

Development of Strategies

The remainder of the discussion will be based on two-person-zero-sum games and the development of optimal decision strategies. The term *strategy*, as used in game theory, refers to a comprehensive plan of action. The strategy can be good or bad; all that is required is that it be complete and cover all possibilities. When the total number of possible strategies can be counted, the game is called a finite game. When there are an unlimited number of strategies, it is called an infinite game. The solution of infinite games requires the use of advanced mathematical techniques (and they are not very practical in the real world), so we shall restrict our attention to finite games.

We shall label the two competing players Black and Red. We shall initially assume that Black has two alternative strategies and Red has three. The payoffs that would result from each strategy are shown in Exhibit 3–15.

Exhibit 3–15   Game Matrix

		RED 1	RED 2	RED 3
BLACK	A	$6	$4	$7
	B	4	3	4

This array of numbers, which is really a payoff table, is generally called a game matrix. The entries in the matrix are based on the convention that a positive number represents a gain for Black and a loss for Red while a negative number indicates just the opposite. The strategies that should be used in this game are obvious. Black would employ strategy A because, regardless of what his opponent does, it is superior to strategy B. For similar reasons, Red would use strategy 2. Any other strategy would result in a larger payoff to Black and therefore a larger loss for Red. If both players use their optimal strategies, Red will have to pay $4 to Black. The *value* of the game is therefore $4, and Black should pay $4 to Red prior to playing the game to make it a fair game. (A fair game is one in which neither player starts with a distinct advantage over the other.)

Saddle Points

Not all games contain dominant strategies, so it is not always obvious what each player should do. The game matrix presented in Exhibit 3–16, where

Exhibit 3–16   Game Matrix

		RED 1	RED 2	RED 3	Row Minimum
	A	$2	−$2	$7	−$2
BLACK	B	4	−1	−3	−3
	C	1	0	3	0 =
	Column Maximum	4	0 =	7	

each player has three possible strategies, is an example. Black could choose strategy A, which could result in a payoff of $7. His intelligent opponent, however, might respond with strategy 2 and inflict a loss of $2 on Black. If he selected strategy B, Black could receive a payoff of $4 but could also suffer a loss of $3. If strategy C is selected, Black cannot lose anything and can possibly gain. Black, therefore, could attempt to *maximize* his *minimum* gain, or employ the maximin criterion (described earlier in the chapter), when choosing a strategy. He would, therefore, choose strategy C. Red, on the other hand, could try to *mini*mize his *maxi*mum loss, or use the minimax criterion. On the basis of this criterion, he would use strategy 2. If this combination of strategies is used, there is no gain or loss for either player. The value of the game is zero, and the game is a fair one.

This same result can be obtained through a different line of reasoning. The reader might wonder why the players would not occasionally "go for broke," i.e., Black pick strategy A in the hope that Red will pick 3, or Red pick strategy 3 in the hope that Black will pick B. The reason that these strategies would not normally be selected is that the hopes they are based on are groundless. This can be demonstrated by analyzing the game matrix.

Red would never use strategy 1 since, for him, it is dominated by strategy 2. Therefore his options are restricted to strategies 2 and 3. Black also would recognize this situation and as a result the game matrix would be effectively reduced by the dismissal of column 1. This, however, means that row C would dominate row B for Black and therefore it would be irrational for Red to choose C in the hope that Black will select B. After eliminating column 1 and row B, column 2 would now dominate column 3 for Red. Red would disregard column C and it would be groundless for Black to select A in the hope of getting a $7 gain. Since Red has eliminated columns 1 and 3, he will play column 2. Knowing this, Black has no rational alternative to playing row C. Finally, notice that even if Red deduces that Black will select row C, there still is no incentive for him to switch from column 2.

In some games, Black's maximin and Red's minimax values will not be found in the same row-column position. When they are, as in this example, the position corresponding to a minimum in its row and a maximum in its column is called a *saddle point*. The initial solution is a stable one; i.e., there is no advantage to either player from changing strategies, so Black would use his maximin strategy exclusively, and Red his minimax.

Mixed Strategies

Suppose that Red and Black are faced with the game matrix presented in Exhibit 3–17. The maximin strategy for Black is C and the minimax strategy for Red is 3. The maximin and minimax values are not the same, so the game has no saddle point. The lower value of the game is 0 and the upper value is 3.

Exhibit 3–17 Game Matrix

		RED			
		1	**2**	**3**	**Row Minimum**
BLACK	A	−$2	$5	$3	−$2
	B	−3	1	2	−3
	C	4	0	1	0 =
	Column Maximum	4	5	3 =	

The initial solution of this game is not a stable one. Suppose that both players begin the game using the strategies found above. Black would win $1 from Red on each trial. Red would quickly detect Black's strategy, however, and switch to strategy 2, where his loss would be zero. Black, who is also intelligent and rational, would counter by switching to strategy A and gaining $5 from Red. Red, in turn, could move to strategy 1 and gain $2 from Black. This shifting of strategies could continue indefinitely. Notice that the shifting results from each player's using one strategy until the other player adjusts. When one player's strategy is predictable, the other can exploit it to his advantage.

The only time a player cannot capitalize on his opponent's strategy is when he does not know in advance which strategy will be employed. Thus the only rational policy in a game without a saddle point is to use a *mixed strategy*. That is, Black, for example, should use some optimal combination of "pure" strategies A, B, and C. One of the pure, or original, strategies would be used each time the game is played. The selection of a particular pure strategy for a given trial would be determined by a random process based on a probability distribution specified by the mixed strategy. Thus a mixed strategy would indicate the relative frequency with which each pure strategy would be used over a large number of trials. Only one pure strategy is used at a time, however; a combination of pure strategies cannot be used for an individual trial. For example, Black could use strategies A, B, and C each one-third of the time or he could use A one-half of the time and B and C each one-fourth of the time. There would be two possible mixed strategies. Given the probability distribution, the selection of a pure strategy for the upcoming trial must be based on some random process, or the opponent could determine the selection pattern and use it to his advantage.

The final job is to determine the probability distributions Black and Red should use for selecting pure strategies. Notice that strategy A dominates strategy B in the game matrix contained in Exhibit 3–16. Black would, therefore, ignore B and use only strategies A and C. Suppose that he uses A and C with probabilities of p and $1 - p$, respectively. As long as one of the players is restricted to two pure strategies, a graphical solution for the optimal value of p can readily be obtained.[8] Black's "conditional expected payoff," given the strategy to be used by Red, is given below:[9]

Strategy Used by Red	Black's Conditional Expected Payoffs
1	$p(-2) + (1 - p)4 = -6p + 4$
2	$p(5) + (1 - p)0 = 5p$
3	$p(3) + (1 - p)1 = 2p + 1$

[8] For more complicated games, where each player can use three or more strategies, linear programming (see Chapters 5, 6, and 7) can be used to obtain a solution.

[9] The term "conditional expected payoff" may seem a bit ambiguous, although it accurately describes the payoffs involved. The payoffs are based on Black's mixed strategy (thus they are expected values) and the use of a particular strategy by Red (thus they are conditional values).

These payoffs, expressed as a function of p, are graphed in Illustration 3–3.

If Black initially lets $p = p_1$, and Red uses strategy 1, the expected payoff will be EP_1, as shown by point R in Illustration 3–3. Red eventually will determine this mixed strategy, however, and will respond by using strategy 2. The resulting payoff to Black will be reduced to EP_2 (point S). Given Red's ability to adjust, Black should pick the mixed strategy that will maximize his minimum expected payoff irrespective of the strategy used by Red. In other words, he should again use the maximin criterion. The maximin point is T; regardless of the strategy used by Red, Black's minimum expected payoff is EP_3. The optimal value of p, $p = p^*$, is determined by the interaction of lines 1 and 3. Solving, we get $-6p + 4 = 2p + 1$ and $p^* = \frac{3}{8}$. The optimal mixed strategy for Black is to use pure strategy A three-eighths of the time and pure strategy C five-eighths of the time. The expected payoff from this strategy is $-6(\frac{3}{8}) + 4 = -\frac{18}{8} + \frac{32}{8} = \frac{14}{8} = \frac{7}{4}$ (or $2(\frac{3}{8}) + 1 = \frac{7}{4}$).

The optimal mixed strategy for Red is determined from the minimax criterion. If Red uses strategies 1, 2, and 3 with probabilities q_1, q_2,

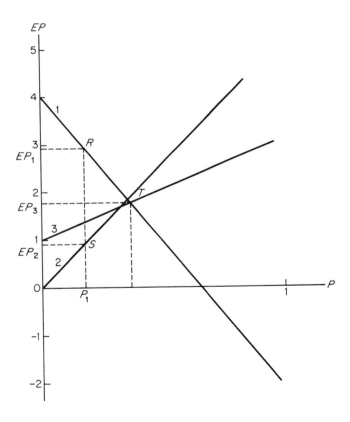

Illustration 3–3 Black's Conditional Expected Payoffs

and q_3, respectively, the expected payoff of the game can be written as follows:

$$EP = q_1(-6p + 4) + q_2(5p) + q_3(2p + 1)$$

If Black follows his optimal mixed strategy of setting $p = \frac{5}{8}$, the expected payoff is

$$EP = q_1(\tfrac{7}{4}) + q_2(\tfrac{15}{8}) + q_3(\tfrac{7}{4})$$

If Red wants to minimize his maximum expected loss, he should not use strategy 2. This is because it has a higher conditional expected payoff than strategies 1 and 3. Thus $q_2 = 0$, EP $= q_1(\tfrac{7}{4}) + q_3(\tfrac{7}{4})$, and $q_1 + q_3 = 1$. It now may appear that the choice of strategies for Red is arbitrary, since the expected payoff is $\frac{7}{4}$ whether he uses 1 or 3 exclusively or some combination of the two. If he is careless, however, Black can adjust his mixed strategy and increase his expected payoff. Remember that the above expected values are based on the use of a particular strategy by Black. There is an optimum mixed strategy for Red that will minimize his maximum expected loss at $\frac{7}{4}$. That is, Red wants a mixed strategy that will result in an expected loss of $\frac{7}{4}$— and no more—regardless of the mixed strategy used by Black. Thus it should follow that, *for any value of p,*

$$q_1(-6p + 4) + q_3(2p + 1) = \tfrac{7}{4}$$

To solve for two unknowns q_1 and q_3, we need a system of two independent equations. We can obtain them by arbitrarily assuming any two values of p, since the equation should hold for *all* values of p between 0 and 1 inclusive. Suppose we choose $p = 0$ and $p = 1$. Then

$$p = 0: \qquad 4q_1 + q_3 = \tfrac{7}{4}$$
$$p = 1: \quad -2q_1 + 3q_3 = \tfrac{7}{4}$$

and $q_1^* = \frac{1}{4}$ and $q_3^* = \frac{3}{4}$.

The optimal mixed strategy for Red is to randomly employ strategy 1 and strategy 3, respectively, one-fourth and three-fourths of the time. This will result in an expected loss to Red equal to the expected payoff to Black of $\frac{7}{4}$. The value of the game is now $\frac{7}{4}$ and the solution, based on the optimal mixed strategies of Red and Black, is stable.

SUMMARY

While the techniques discussed in this chapter can be used directly for decision-making purposes, the general concept of maximization of expected value underlies many of the more elaborate decision-making models to be considered in the remainder of the book. Decisions to be made under conditions of uncertainty generally can be analyzed by utilizing a model developed from a probability distribution/expected value framework. Thus a thorough understanding of basic probability concepts and decision strategies is essential for realizing maximum benefit from most of the material to follow.

In this chapter, strategies were formulated for making single decisions based on current conditions. Although mixed strategies were discussed for some game situations, the underlying assumption of stable conditions (or more appropriately a stable probability distribution) was implicit throughout the chapter. There are cases, however, where today's decisions might affect tomorrow's options or where the outcome of today's decisions might be affected by future circumstances that could differ markedly from today's. The expected value concept will be extended to deal with sequential decisions and the additional consideration of time-dependent variables in the following chapter.

PROBLEMS

1. A business man has three alternative actions he can take, each of which can be followed by any of four possible events. The conditional payoffs for each action-event combination are given below.

	Actions		
Event	1	2	3
A	4	−2	7
B	0	6	3
C	−5	9	2
D	3	−1	4

   a. Which action should he take based on the maximin criterion?
   b. Which action should he take based on the minimax regret criterion?
   c. Which action should he take based on the criterion of maximizing expected value? (Assume that all events have equal probabilities of occurring.)

2. a. If you are to receive $1 for each dot that shows following the roll of a die, what is the expected payoff?
   b. What is the expected number of heads that would result from 25 flips of a fair coin?
   c. What are the probabilities of the expected values calculated in a and b above actually occurring? How do you explain this result?

3. A company is considering an expansion of its current plant. The required investment should return 12 percent if business conditions remain unchanged. If there is a recession, however, it will return 3 percent. Alternatively, a safe return of 6 percent can be realized by investing the money in government bonds. What would the probability of a recession have to be in order to make the two investments have the same expected value? What would the return on the expansion have to be if the probability of a recession is 0.4? 0.75? (If there is a recession, the return on the expansion would remain 3 percent.)

4. a. Construct a conditional loss table from the conditional payoffs given above in Problem 1.

b. Given $P(A) = 0.2$, $P(B) = 0.4$, $P(C) = 0.3$, and $P(D) = 0.1$ [where $P(A) =$ probability of event A occurring, etc.], calculate the expected payoff and expected loss of each action. Which action should be chosen?

c. Calculate the cost of uncertainty and the expected value of perfect information.

d. Calculate the cost of irrationality for each action. Can the cost of irrationality ever be negative?

5. A group of students raises money each year by selling souvenirs outside the stadium after the Super Bowl. They can buy any of three different batches of souvenirs from a supplier. Batch 1 contains mostly Team A items, Batch 2 contains mostly Team N items, and Batch 3 is equally divided. Their sales are largely dependent on which team wins the game. A conditional payoff table is given below:

	Batch 1	Batch 2	Batch 3
Team A wins	$1200	$800	$ 300
Team N wins	250	700	1100

a. Construct a conditional payoff table and a conditional loss table.

b. The experts predict that the probability of Team A's winning is 0.6. Which batch should the students buy? What are the expected payoff and the expected loss of the best action?

c. What is the cost of uncertainty?

d. What is the cost of irrationality for each of the three possible acts?

6. The owner of a large suburban nursery is trying to decide how many acres of available land to allocate to a popular type of shrub. Each acre costs $500 to plant, maintain, and market. The shrubs can be sold for $800 an acre, but any that are not sold at the end of the growing season are worthless. The owner's estimated demand distribution is given below.

Acres	P (Demand)	Acres	P (Demand)
5	0.05	12	0.10
6	0.05	13	0.10
7	0.05	14	0.05
8	0.10	15	0.05
9	0.10	16	0.05
10	0.10	17	0.05
11	0.15		1.00

a. Use the critical ratio to find the number of acres that should be planted to maximize expected value.

b. What is the expected value of the best decision?

c. For $400, the owner can survey the area builders and landscapers to get a better estimate of potential demand. Do you think this information is worth obtaining?

d. Repeat a, b, and c, assuming that there is an additional goodwill cost from future lost profits of $150 for every acre's shrubs that are demanded but were not planted.

7. An investment company is considering making an investment in one of two currently available mutually exclusive alternatives. Investment A costs $5000 and will return $8000 one month from now if there is not a tax increase announced; if a tax increase is announced during the month, only $4000 will be returned. Investment B costs $6000, and will return $12,000 if there is no announcement, $3000 if there is. If there is no announcement the company knows of another opportunity that will be available at the end of the one-month period. This new alternative will cost $2500 and return $4000 with a probability of 0.7, $2000 with a probability of 0.3. The probability assigned to the announcement of a tax increase during the one-month period is 0.2. Ignore taxes and present value considerations.
   a. Use a payoff table to show the alternatives open to the company.
   b. Identify and give the expected payoff of the best strategy the company could take, using expected monetary value.

8. Rework Problem 4, using the utility curve drawn below.

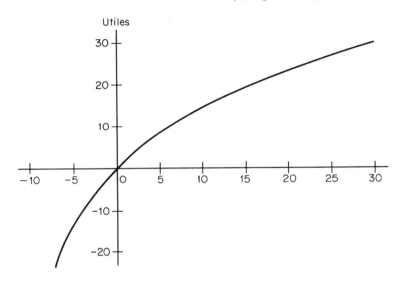

9. Explain the significance of the shape of the above indifference curve. What risk attitudes does it portray? Explain how different decisions might be made depending on whether expected monetary value or expected utility is used as a decision criterion.

10. For each of the following game matrices, find the optimal strategy for each player. What is the saddle point and the value of each game? Are the games fair?

(a)
Green

		1	2	3
	A	3	-3	-1
Yellow	B	0	4	-2
	C	1	3	0

(b)
Blue

		1	2	3
	A	-4	-3	4
White	B	6	-2	3
	C	5	-4	-5

11. For each of the following game matrices, use the graphical procedure outlined in the chapter to determine the optimal mixed strategy for each player.

		(a) Purple		
		1	**2**	**3**
Brown	A	3	-2	1
	B	4	0	-2
	C	2	-4	0

		(b) Gray		
		1	**2**	**3**
Gold	A	-2	3	4
	B	2	0	3
	C	5	-1	2

12. Candidates X and Y are competing for election to the Senate, and X is attempting to increase his total votes at the expense of Y. The strategies available to each candidate involve newspaper, radio, or television advertising. The increases in votes available to Candidate X, given various combinations of strategies, are given below. (Assume that this is a zero-sum game, i.e., any gain by X is equal to the amount lost by Y.) Determine the optimal strategy that should be used by candidate X during the duration of the campaign. How many votes should X gain by following this strategy?

		Candidate Y		
	Strategies	Newspapers	Radio	Television
Candidate X	Newspapers	300,000	200,000	100,000
	Radio	600,000	500,000	400,000
	Television	300,000	400,000	600,000

13. Does it seem reasonable that the situation described in Problem 12 would, in reailty, be a zero-sum game? Discuss.

4

decision trees
and dynamic
programming

The alternative courses of action that will be available in the future are frequently determined by the decisions that are made today. Sometimes the interrelationships between current and future actions are known, so strategies can be devised that will lead to an optimum sequence of decisions. Future decisions will be based on future events, certainly, but a well-devised strategy will indicate which action should be taken given the event (or sequence of events) that has occurred in the past.

A situation may require a series of actions, and there can be several different sequences, or strategies, that can be followed. For example, the introduction of a new product or a new manufacturing process may require the construction of new plant facilities. The size of plant that will be needed will depend on the success of the new product or process. Three alternatives initially are open to the firm. A large plant can be constructed immediately, a small plant can be constructed, or the firm can decide to maintain the status quo and do nothing. The construction of a small plant would be a cautious decision. If future events indicate that it is justified, larger facilities could be provided by an expansion of the small plant.

A similar problem could be involved in marketing a new product. A strong national marketing effort could be undertaken immediately. Alternatively, the product could be test marketed in one or more regions and, if successful, brought out nationally at a later date. Or the firm could decide not to market the product at all. If cost figures and probability estimates of future demand are available, decision trees can be utilized in solving these problems. Decision trees can also be applied to optimum sample size problems. Decision tree techniques will be developed in the first section of this chapter.

Other types of problems involve the selection of an optimal time for taking some particular action or the optimal allocation of resources, production, etc. For example, a company may want to know whether it should call an outstanding bond issue now or wait until some future period. An investor trying to decide whether to exercise a warrant now or to continue to hold the option is facing a similar problem. The introduction of a new product or advertising campaign also can present the need to make a decision on timing. Multiperiod or multilocation allocation problems also have dynamic characteristics. These and similar problems are amenable to solution by dynamic programming. This technique will be discussed in the last section of the chapter.

DECISION TREES

A decision tree is a network representation of sequences of action-event combinations that are available to the decision maker. Each possible sequence of decisions and consequences is shown by a different path through the tree. Although some of the problems that are solved through the use of decision trees are very complex, the fundamental solution techniques are relatively straightforward. In fact, one of the major advantages of decision trees is that the problem is structured clearly. This enables the problem of solving for the optimum strategy to be attacked systematically and logically.

Just about any problem that can be solved by using decision trees can also be solved with payoff tables (Chapter 3). The two techniques have much in common. Payoff tables generally are used when only one decision must be made, however (or where the same situation—and therefore decision—is to be repeated), whereas decision trees are used most often when a series of decisions must be made over time. Payoff tables quickly become unwieldy when used for the latter type of problem. To illustrate the similarity of the two techniques, we shall solve a problem presented in terms of a payoff table in Chapter 3 using the decision tree approach.

Investment Problem

The problem concerns a businessman who has two independent investments available to him, but he lacks the capital to undertake both of them simultaneously. He can choose to take A first and then stop, or if A is successful then take B, or vice versa. The probability of success on A is 0.7, while for B it is 0.4. Both investments require an initial capital outlay of $2000, and both return nothing if the venture is unsuccessful. A will return $3000 (over cost) if it is successful, and successful completion of B will return $5000 (over cost).

Identify Strategies

Five alternative strategies are available: (a) do nothing; (b) accept A and then stop regardless of the outcome; (c) accept B and then stop regardless of the outcome; (d) accept A and, if successful, then accept B; (e) accept B and, if successful, then accept A.

Each individual strategy was analyzed in the payoff table solution. In a decision tree, however, each decision, including components of an over-all strategy, is analyzed individually. A decision tree depicting the above problem is presented in Illustration 4–1. Notice that the tree consists of alternating action-event areas. The action area represents a time of decision for the decision maker. The event area that follows indicates the various consequences that can follow the action that is taken. For obvious reasons, these areas are also frequently called areas of choice and chance. The probabilities of success or failure are shown on the tree following actions that can result in these two outcomes.

Solution Procedure

A solution is obtained by working backwards through the tree; i.e., from right to left. This is sometimes called the "rollback" method. We assume that we have reached various decision points in the tree and then solve for the optimum decision *conditional* on having reached the decision point being analyzed. Once we have analyzed one decision point, we can move backwards along the path and analyze the preceding decision point. The preceding decision point is analyzed in terms of both its immediate possible outcomes and the expected consequences of subsequent decisions. We can illustrate the procedure by solving the above problem. For reference purposes, each decision point in Illustration 4–1 has been identified with a circled number. We shall evaluate decision 3 first. This point is reached after successful investment in B. We now must decide whether to stop or to accept A. The

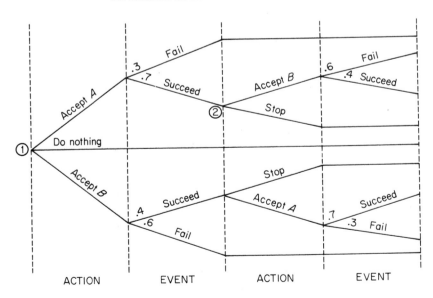

Illustration 4–1   Decision Tree for Investment Problem

expected values of these two alternatives are given in Exhibit 4–1.[1] The expected value of stopping is $0, and the expected value of accepting A is $1500. Based on the criterion of maximizing expected value, our decision would be to accept A *conditional* on the successful completion of B. We shall, therefore, assign a value of $1500 to the position corresponding to decision 3.

Exhibit 4–1   Evaluation of Decision Point 3

1. Accept A

Outcome	Probability	Conditional Value	Expected Value
Success	0.7	$3000	$2100
Failure	0.3	− 2000	− 600
			$1500

2. Stop

Expected value = $0

We shall next evaluate decision 2. The alternative actions and their expected values are given in Exhibit 4-2. Based on the calculated expected values, the best decision would be to accept B. Thus the value of successfully investing in A and being in a position to accept B is $800. We reflect this potential expected gain by assigning a value of $800 to the position corresponding to decision point 2.

Exhibit 4–2   Evaluation of Decision Point 2

1. Accept B

Outcome	Probability	Conditional Value	Expected Value
Success	0.4	$5000	$2000
Failure	0.6	− 2000	− 1200
			$ 800

2. Stop

Expected value = $0

At this point, we have made two conditional decisions. We know that A should be accepted following successful investment in B and that B should be accepted following successful investment in A. The final step is to decide

[1] We shall evaluate the examples in this chapter using the criterion of maximizing expected monetary value. The utility concept is applicable but, in order not to obscure the presentation, will not be used. For similar reasons, we shall not discount the cash flows.

whether to first accept A, first accept B, or do nothing. These choices are shown at decision point 1 in Illustration 4–1. The expected values of these three alternatives are shown in Exhibit 4–3. The procedure is similar to that

Exhibit 4–3   Evaluation of Decision Point 1

1. Accept A

Outcome	Probability	Conditional Value	Expected Value
Success	0.7	$3000 + 800	$2660
Failure	0.3	− 2000	− 600
			$2060

2. Accept B

Outcome	Probability	Conditional Value	Expected Value
Success	0.4	$5000 + 1500	$2600
Failure	0.6	−2000	− 1200
			$1400

3. Do nothing

Expected value = $0

used before, but one additional factor must now be considered. Successful completion of A brings an immediate cash benefit of $3000 *plus* the opportunity to undertake investment B. The expected value of accepting investment B is $800, so the total payoff of successfully investing in A is $3000 plus $800, for a total of $3800. Likewise, if B is accepted first and is successful, the total payoff is $6500. This amount consists of $5000, the immediate and direct benefit, plus $1500, the expected value of being able to continue and accept A.

Based on the computations in Exhibit 4–3, the best initial decision is to accept A. The best over-all strategy is to accept A and, if successful, then to accept B. The path through the tree that corresponds to this strategy has an expected value of $2060. This is the same result obtained in the payoff table solution presented in Exhibits 3–10 and 3–11. The reader should compare the expected payoffs calculated in Exhibit 3–11 with the results obtained in Exhibits 4–1, 4–2, and 4–3 to verify for himself the equivalence of the two procedures.

This example clearly illustrates the usefulness of the rollback procedure. Although most problems are much more complicated than the one discussed above, the use of the decision tree approach enables a final solution to be obtained from the systematic solution of a series of small, individual subproblems. The computations become more time-consuming than difficult as the size and complexity of the decision tree grows.

Inventor Problem

Our second example concerns an inventor who is trying to decide whether or not to invest the $15,000 that is required to develop a new process for treating industrial wastes. If he proceeds, there is a 60 percent chance his process will be successful. If he does succeed, he can apply for a patent. This would cost $5000 and would have a 50–50 chance of being approved. If the process is successful, and regardless of any patent decisions, the inventor then has the choice of using the process himself or selling the rights. The process is expected to be profitable for a period of four years. His profits from these alternatives would, of course, be affected by the availability of a patent. In addition, there is some uncertainty concerning the amount of annual proceeds that will be generated by the process. Government assistance, in the form of tax rebates, subsidies, etc., could make a substantial, moderate, or light contribution to annual profits. The conditional proceeds from these alternatives are given in Exhibit 4–4.

Exhibit 4–4 Conditional Payoffs

1. Proceeds if rights to process are sold

Patent approved	$40,000
Patent denied	25,000
Patent not applied for	30,000

2. Annual cash flow if process retained

Government Assistance	Probability	Patent Status		
		Approved	Denied	No Application
Substantial	0.3	$15,000	$7,000	$11,000
Moderate	0.4	10,000	5,500	8,000
Light	0.3	6,000	3,000	5,000

The decision tree for this problem is drawn in Illustration 4–2. Notice that this decision tree has three action-event sequences, as compared to two for the previous example. The decision points are again identified by circled reference numbers. Points 3, 4, and 5 are evaluated in Exhibit 4–5. If we again use the criterion of maximizing expected value,[2] we can compare the figures in Exhibits 4–4 and 4–5 and see that the rights to the process should be retained and used if the patent is approved or if a patent is *not* applied for, but if the patent *is* applied for and denied the rights should be sold. We should assign values of $41,200, $25,000, and $32,000 to points 3, 4, and 5, respectively.

---

[2] We shall concentrate on the decision tree analysis and not use present value figures. In actuality, however, the analysis should be performed in terms of discounted cash flows (see Chapter 12).

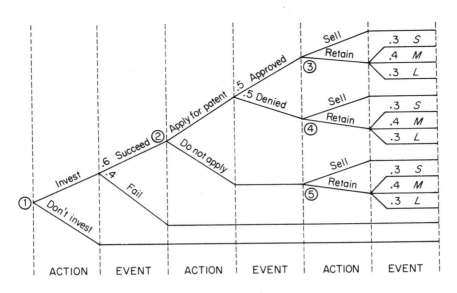

Illustration 4–2 Decision Tree for Inventor Problem

Exhibit 4–5 Evaluation of Decision Points 3, 4, and 5

1. Expected annual return if process retained

Government Assistance	Probability	Expected Values		
		Point 3	Point 4	Point 5
Substantial	0.3	$4,500	$2,100	$3,300
Moderate	0.4	4,000	2,200	3,200
Light	0.3	1,800	900	1,500
		$10,300	$5,200	$8,000

2. Expected four-year return if process retained

Point 3: 4(10,300) = $41,200
Point 4: 4(5,200) = $20,800
Point 5: 4(8,000) = $32,000

Decision point 2 is evaluated in Exhibit 4–6. Notice that the expected values calculated above for points 3 and 4 are the conditional values when the alternative of applying for the patent is being analyzed. The expected value of applying for the patent, net of the application cost, is less than the expected value of not applying. The inventor should choose not to apply, therefore, and we assign a value of $32,000 to point 2. Notice that points 2 and 5 now have equivalent values. This is because we have just shown that a shift to point 5 should occur automatically if the inventor finds himself at point 2.

74

Exhibit 4–6   Evaluation of Decision Point 2

1. Apply for patent

Event	Probability	Conditional Value	Expected Value
Approved	0.5	$41,200	$20,600
Denied	0.5	25,000	12,500
			$33,100

$$\text{— Cost of Application} \quad 5,000$$
$$\text{Net expected value} = \$28,100$$

2. Do not apply

Expected value = $32,000

The final decision, at point 1, is whether the inventor should invest $15,000 to develop his new process. (Remember that it has already been decided not to apply for a patent and not to sell the rights to the process if the process is developed and it proves successful.) The computations for this decision are presented in Exhibit 4–7. The expected value of developing the process, $4,200, is greater than zero, the expected value of not developing the process. The inventor should, therefore, develop the process. To summarize our final decision and complete strategy, the investor should invest $15,000 to develop the process; if the process is successful, he should forego a patent application but retain the rights to the process and use it himself.

Exhibit 4–7   Evaluation of Decision Point 1

1. Develop process

Event	Probability	Conditional Return	Expected Return
Succeed	0.6	$32,000	$19,200
Fail	0.4	0	0
			$19,200

$$\text{— Cost of development} \quad 15,000$$
$$\text{Expected value of developing process} = \$\ 4,200$$

2. Do not develop process

Expected value = $0

EVSI Problem

Decision trees also can be used to determine the expected value of sample information (EVSI), which was discussed in Chapter 3.[3] Consider the

---

[3] This type of analysis is practical only if the number of sample observations is small. If the number of sample units is large, the analysis becomes cumbersome and would be done by systematic numerical methods. Several canned computer programs exist for certain types of such analyses.

following example. A publishing firm is contemplating the publication of a new novel. If the novel is a success, the firm can expect to earn one million dollars over the next five years; if a failure, it will lose a quarter of a million dollars over the next five years. After reading the book, the publisher feels that there is a 0.3 probability of the novel's being a success. The publisher can send the manuscript to a professional critic for his opinion. The critic's opinion is equivalent to obtaining sample information. The critic's fee is $2000. If the novel will be a success, the probability that the critic will like it is 0.5. If the novel will be a failure, the probability the critic will like it is 0.2. The publisher must decide whether to hire the professional critic or make the decision based solely on his own judgment.

The decision tree for this problem is drawn in Illustration 4–3. Although decision point 1, the initial decision in the tree, is the decision of immediate interest, we shall again work backwards through the tree. Let us start by examining decision point 2, where we are following the path of not hiring the critic and relying on the publisher's judgment. Thus we must use the publisher's subjective probability assessments of success and failure. As Exhibit 4–8 shows, solely on the basis of the publisher's appraisal, we would publish the novel and expect to make $125,000.

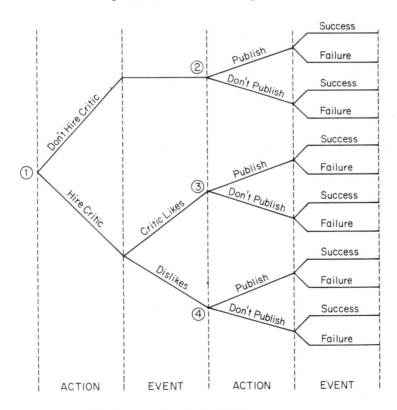

Illustration 4–3   Decision Tree for EVSI Problem

Exhibit 4–8 Evaluation of Decision Point 2

1. Publish

Outcome	Prior Probability	Conditional Value	Expected Value
Success	0.3	$1,000,000	$300,000
Failure	0.7	− 250,000	− 175,000
			$125,000

2. Do not publish

Expected value = $0

Now let us consider decision point 3. At this point we have hired the critic, and he has recommended publishing the book. Hence, we must now adjust the publisher's prior probabilities by the new sample information gained from the critic. This is accomplished by using Bayesian probability analysis. (Readers not familiar with Bayesian probability theory are referred to Chapter 2.) Exhibit 4–9 presents the calculations of the revised *posterior*

Exhibit 4–9 Bayesian Posterior Probability Calculation

Outcome	(1) Prior Probability	(2) Probability of Critic's Liking	(3) (1) × (2)	(1) × (2)/Σ[(1) × (2)] Posterior Probabilities
Success	0.3	0.5	0.15	0.68
Failure	0.7	0.1	0.07	0.32
			0.22	

probabilities of success and failure, given that the critic has responded favorably. Using the new revised *posterior* probabilities of success and failure to evaluate decision point 3, we find that if the critic likes the novel we should publish it. The expected value calculations are shown in Exhibit 4–10.

Exhibit 4–10 Evaluation of Decision Point 3

1. Publish

Outcome	Probability	Conditional Value	Expected Value
Success	0.68	$1,000,000	$680,000
Failure	0.32	− 250,000	− 80,000
			$600,000

2. Do not publish

Expected value = $0

The same logic is used to evaluate decision point 4. As Exhibits 4–11 and 4–12 illustrate, if the critic responds unfavorably the best decision is not to publish the book.

Exhibit 4–11   Bayesian Posterior Probability Analysis

Outcome	(1) Prior Probability	(2) Probability of Critic not Liking	(3) (1) × (2)	Posterior Probability
Success	0.3	0.5	0.15	0.19
Failure	0.7	0.9	0.63	0.81
			0.78	

Exhibit 4–12   Evaluation of Decision Point 4

1. Publish

Outcome	Probability	Conditional Value	Expected Value
Success	0.19	$1,000,000	$190,000
Failure	0.81	− 250,000	− 202,500
			− 12,500

2. Do not publish

Expected value = $0

Now we are ready to analyze decision point 1, i.e., should we or should we not hire a critic. If we do not hire the critic, then we would publish the novel and our expected return would be $125,000. If we do hire the critic and if he likes the novel, we should publish it and our expected return would be $132,000. *If* he does not like it, we should not publish it and our expected return would be $0. Clearly, our decision and expected return depend on what the critic would decide, which at this point is unknown. However, we do know the unconditional probabilities that the critic will respond favorably or unfavorably. (Again, readers not familiar with Bayesian analysis are urged to read carefully the relevant material in Chapter 2.) Thus we can use these probabilities to calculate the expected return if we hire the critic.

$$(0.22)(600,000) + 0.78)(\$0) = \$132,000$$

Comparing the expected return from hiring the critic ($132,000) to the expected return from not hiring the critic ($125,000), we see that the expected gain from obtaining the sample information from the critic is $7000. The difference between the expected value with sampling and the expected value without sampling is called the *expected value of sampling information* (EVSI).

Since the cost of obtaining the sample information, the critic's fee, is $2000, the *expected net gain* from sampling (ENG) is $5000 (ENG = EVSI − cost of obtaining sample data), and the proper decision is to hire the critic and abide by his decision on publishing.

The concept of EVSI and ENG can obviously be extended. We could consider the ENG from hiring two, three, or four or more critics. The optimal number of critics (i.e., the optimal sample size) would be that number which maximizes the expected net gain. It should be noted that the calculation of the expected net gain from sampling depends heavily on the initial prior probabilities. Since no sample information is available, these probabilities usually are based on the decision maker's subjective or personal evaluation. Hence different decision makers may choose different "optimal" sample sizes. As a general guideline, the stronger the initial or prior belief, the less value sample information will have to the decision maker. For instance, if the publisher had felt the probability of success was 0.9, the critic's opinion would not have swayed him, and the expected value of sample information would be $0 and the expected net gain would be −$2000. On the other hand, the more reliable a predictor the sample information is, the larger will be the expected value of sample information and the expected net gain. For example, if the critic was never wrong, the expected value of sample information would be $175,000[4] and the expected net gain would be $173,000. (The reader is referred to Problem 4, where he is asked to prove the last example.)

The decision tree technique is similar to the more general method of dynamic programming. Many dynamic programming problems are solved by a procedure called "backward induction," which is a fancy way of saying that a solution is obtained by starting at the end of the problem and working backwards. Thus the rollback technique used to solve decision tree problems is a form of backward induction. The general characteristics and method of solution of dynamic programming problems will be discussed in the remainder of the chapter.

DYNAMIC PROGRAMMING

Dynamic programming problems are characterized by the need for a series of interrelated decisions. The objective of the dynamic programming technique is to find a combination of decisions that will optimize some appropriate measure of effectiveness. For example, it might be desirable to specify a series of marketing decisions that will maximize total sales, a series of production decisions that will minimize total costs, etc. Whereas decision trees are used for problems that are probabilistic in nature, dynamic programming is an "under certainty," or deterministic, procedure where all relevant information is known.

A dynamic programming problem can thus be divided into a number of stages, where a decision must be made at each stage. The decision made at

---

[4] This, of course, is the expected value of perfect information. (See Chapter 3.)

each stage influences the next. In fact, the decision made at each stage must take into account its effect not only on the next stage, but also on the entire subsequent sequence of stages. Dynamic programming provides a systematic procedure whereby, starting with the last stage of the problem and working backward, one makes an optimal decision for each stage of the problem. The inputs for the last stage are the outputs of the preceding stage. Thus if, by working backwards, the effectiveness of each stage is optimized, the resulting sequence of decisions will give an optimal solution to the problem.[5] This is only a general procedure for formulating and solving a problem, however. There is not a formal mathematical algorithm for solving dynamic programming problems, such as is available for some of the other types of problems discussed in this book. The specific elements of dynamic programming problems can vary. Therefore, we shall present a series of examples illustrating the application of the fundamental procedures.

National Sales Manager Problem

A national sales manager, based in New York City, is in San Francisco to attend a series of marketing seminars. In the process of returning to New York, he wants to stop in one city in each of three intervening sales districts to discuss what he has learned at the seminars. He wants to arrange his visits with the objective of minimizing total travel costs. The possible routes he can take are diagrammed in Illustration 4–4. The fare between any two cities in adjoining districts is indicated in Exhibit 4–13 and it is also shown in the illustration.

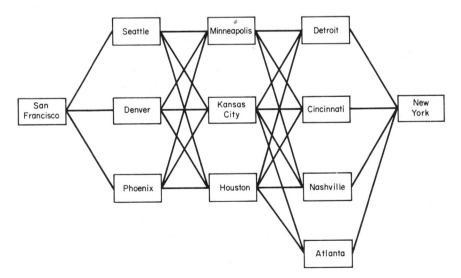

Illustration 4–4   Diagram for Sales Manager Problem

[5] Dynamic programming problems also can be solved by working forward; i.e., starting with the first stage and working forward to the last stage. Only the backward procedure will be discussed in this chapter, however.

Exhibit 4–13 Travel Costs for Sales Manager Problem

	To
From	**New York**
Detroit	$40
Cincinnati	45
Nashville	50
Atlanta	60

	To			
From	**Detroit**	**Cincinnati**	**Nashville**	**Atlanta**
Minneapolis	$40	$45	$60	$75
Kansas City	60	45	65	75
Houston	80	70	60	45

	To		
From	**Minneapolis**	**Kansas City**	**Houston**
Seattle	$60	$70	$75
Denver	60	40	55
Phoenix	70	45	40

	To		
From	**Seattle**	**Denver**	**Phoenix**
San Francisco	$55	$45	$35

There are 36 alternative paths that can be taken. Thus it is desirable to obtain a solution without having to resort to complete enumeration; i.e., specifying each path and calculating total travel cost. One alternative approach would be to take the cheapest possible flight between two successive districts. The cheapest flight out of San Francisco is to Phoenix; the cheapest out of Phoenix is to Houston. From there, this route would proceed through Atlanta and on to New York. The total travel cost would be $180.

Taking the best alternative at each successive stage of the problem will not necessarily result in the optimal over-all path, however. This is because the choice of a more expensive flight at one stage may allow a more than offsetting saving at a later stage. The optimum path from San Francisco to New York can systematically be determined by a procedure known as backward induction. This procedure starts by solving a small portion of the problem and, by gradually enlarging the portion of the problem accounted for in the solution, eventually arriving at an optimal solution. The optimal solution at each stage of the problem is based on the optimal solution from the preceding stage. That is, the next decision is optimal given the optimal policy already prescribed by the preceding decisions.

There are four stages in this problem. Each stage corresponds to the flight from a city in one district to a city in the next. Thus a decision must be made at each stage: What city should the sales manager visit next? Because the problem is solved by working backwards, Stage 1 will correspond to the flight into New York. Stage 4 will then correspond to the flight out of San Francisco. If the sales manager is in Detroit, Cincinnati, Nashville, or Atlanta, he has no decision to make. The optimal solution for Stage 1, the choice of a flight into New York, is trivial, since there is only one route available from each of these cities to New York. Suppose, at Stage 2, he is in Minneapolis. He can stop at any of the above cities en route to New York. If he decides to visit Detroit, Cincinnati, Nashville, or Atlanta his total remaining travel costs will be, respectively, $80, $90, $110, and $135. Thus his best choice would be to go to Detroit and then to New York. Similarly, if he is in Kansas City in Stage 2, he should next stop in Cincinnati and then go on to New York, for a minimum total remaining travel cost of $90. If he is in Houston, his fares for the remainder of the trip will be minimized at $105 if he goes from there to Atlanta.

These optimal Stage 2 solutions are utilized when one is finding the best routes out of Stage 3 cities. The reader should verify that the optimal path from Seattle would be through Minneapolis (cost = $140). He should go through Kansas City if he is coming from Denver (for a cost of $130) or Phoenix ($135).

On the basis of these Stage 3 solutions, he should leave San Francisco and head for Phoenix. His over-all optimal route would be San Francisco-Phoenix-Kansas City-Cincinnati-New York. Total air fare would be $170. For the reader's convenience, these successive solutions are summarized in Exhibit 4-14 [6]

Exhibit 4–14   Summary of National Sales Manager Problem

1. Solution to Stage 1

Leaving	Going to	Total Accumulated Cost
Detroit	New York	$40
Cincinnati	New York	45
Nashville	New York	50
Atlanta	New York	60

2. Solution to Stage 2

Leaving	Going to	Total Accumulated Cost
Minneapolis	Detroit	$80
Kansas City	Cincinnati	90
Houston	Atlanta	105

[6] This same procedure can be used to find the critical path through the PERT and CPM networks discussed in Chapter 10.

Exhibit 4–14 continued

3. Solution to Stage 3

Leaving	Going to	Total Accumulated Cost
Seattle	Minneapolis	$140
Denver	Kansas City	130
Phoenix	Kansas City	135

4. Solution to Stage 4

Leaving	Going to	Total Accumulated Cost
San Francisco	Phoenix	$170

OPTIMAL PATH: San Francisco-Phoenix-Kansas City-Cincinnati-New York

Teller Assignment Problem

A bank's personnel director has just hired seven new tellers. Each teller is to be assigned to one of four different branches. The addition of new tellers to a branch will increase service to customers and result in more business and an increase in the annual earnings, although the effect on earnings of additional tellers is uneven among branches. Exhibit 4–15 gives the increase in annual earnings that would be realized at each branch if various numbers of the new tellers were assigned to it. If the personnel director's objective is to maximize the aggregate increase in earnings from all four branches, how many tellers should be assigned to each branch?

Exhibit 4–15 New Tellers and Increases in Branch Earnings ($000)

Number of New Tellers	Branch			
	A	B	C	D
0	$0	$0	$0	$0
1	5	4	7	2
2	9	7	10	6
3	11	9	12	8
4	13	11	14	10
5	15	14	16	11
6	16	16	18	12
7	17	16	18	12

    Although there is no fixed sequence in which decisions must be made, this problem can be formulated and solved by using a dynamic programming approach.[7] The four branches can be viewed as the four stages of the problem. We shall arbitrarily designate Branch D as Stage 1, Branch C as Stage 2, Branch B as Stage 3, and Branch A as Stage 4. The state of the problem at

[7] This problem may appear to be amenable to solution by marginal analysis. This procedure will not always work, however, and in fact fails to give an optimal solution to this problem.

any given point is given by the number of tellers still left to be assigned to a branch.

The method of solution is fairly straightforward. We shall begin with Stage 1 and proceed, step by step, to Stage 4. In the following solution, T_i^* refers to the total number of tellers to be assigned at stage i. The symbol T_A^* gives the optimal number to assign to Branch A, T_B^* gives the optimal number to assign to Branch B, and so on. The symbol AE is the aggregate additional earnings that would be realized annually by the branches from the corresponding allocation of tellers. The Stage 1 solution is again a trivial one. In this problem, it consists of the assignment to tellers in Branch D.

Solution to Stage 1:

T_1^*	T_D^*	$AE(\$000)$
0	0	0
1	1	2
2	2	6
3	3	8
4	4	10
5	5	11
6	6	12
7	6, 7	12

Notice that there is a tie for T_D^* when $T_1^* = 7$. This is because increasing the number of tellers at Branch D from 6 to 7 has no effect on the branch's annual earnings.

Branch C enters the solution as we move to Stage 2. The objective now is to obtain an optimal allocation of tellers between Branches C and D. Two interesting things are observed in this solution. As T_2^* increases from 2 to 3, notice that T_D^* increases by 2 and T_C^* decreases by 1. This shift is caused by the large increase in earnings achieved by Branch D when the number of tellers assigned to it increased from 1 to 2.[8] When $T_2^* = 5$ and 7, the optimal allocations are not unique. The extra teller can be assigned to either branch with the same increase in additional earnings.

Solution to Stage 2:

T_2^*	T_D^*	T_C^*	$AE\ (\$000)$
0	0	0	0
1	0	1	7
2	0	2	10
3	2	1	13
4	2	2	16
5	2, 3	3, 2	18
6	3	3	20
7	3, 4	4, 3	22

[8] This example also illustrates the hazards of using marginal analysis.

The Stage 2 solution gives the optimal number of tellers to be assigned to Branches C and D for various values of T_2^*. We can use this information to obtain the Stage 3 solution. At Stage 3, Branch B is brought into the solution. We can let $T_2^* = T_D^* + T_C^*$ from the Stage 2 solution, and treat the Stage 3 solution as an allocation between Branch B and Stage 2. Notice that there are again ties when $T_3^* = 3$ and 7.

Solution to Stage 3:

T_3^*	T_2^*	T_B^*	AE ($000)
0	0	0	0
1	1	0	7
2	1	1	11
3	1, 2	2, 1	14
4	2	2	17
5	3	2	20
6	4	2	23
7	4, 5	3, 2	25

This solution tells us that when $T_3^* = 6$, $T_2^* = 4$, and $T_B^* = 2$. From the Stage 2 solution, we can find that if $T_2^* = 4$, the optimal allocation is $T_D^* = 2$ and $T_C^* = 2$.

This same approach can be used to obtain a solution to Stage 4, where Branch A is introduced. We define $T_3^* = T_D^* + T_C^* + T_B^*$ and proceed as above. In the final optimal solution, $T_3^* = 5$ and $T_A^* = 2$. From the Stage 3 solution, $T_2^* = 3$ and $T_B^* = 2$ if $T_3^* = 5$. And from the Stage 2

Solution to Stage 4:

T_4^*	T_3^*	T_A^*	AE ($000)
0	0	0	0
1	1	0	7
2	1	1	12
3	1, 2	2,1	16
4	2	2	20
5	3	2	23
6	4	2	26
7	5	2	29

solution, $T_D^* = 2$ and $T_C^* = 1$ if $T_2^* = 3$. Thus the dynamic programming solution has found that two tellers should be assigned to Branches A, B, and D and one should be assigned to Branch C. The annual increase in aggregate earnings from this optimal allocation is $29,000.

Production Smoothing Problem

The basic concepts of dynamic programming sometimes can be applied to obtain a solution from a system of equations that are formulated to represent the problem. Thus a tabular approach would not be necessary (although the use of differential calculus is necessary).[9] We shall present a very simple example to illustrate the basic procedures that are involved in obtaining an analytic solution.[10]

A small plant is required to provide 12 units of some product in period 1 and 18 units in period 2. It has no inventory at the beginning of period 1 and should not have any inventory at the end of period 2. In other words, it should produce just enough to satisfy total demand over the two periods. The production costs for any period are X^2, where X is the number of units produced during the period. The inventory carrying costs are $4I$, where I is the number of units carried in inventory from one period to the next. The problem is to determine how many units should be produced in each period in order to minimize total production and inventory costs.

The total cost (TC) equation is

$$TC = X_1^2 + X_2^2 + 4(X_1 - 12)$$

where X_1 is the number of units produced in period 1 and X_2 is the number produced in period 2. Thus the first two terms on the right-hand side of the TC equation are the production costs for periods 1 and 2, respectively. The third term is the inventory carrying cost incurred during period 2. The number of units carried in inventory during the second period can be denoted by I_2 (where $I_2 = X_1 - 12$) and the TC equation can be rewritten as

$$TC = X_1^2 + X_2^2 + 4I_2$$

It follows that the number of units produced during the second period must be the requirement for the period minus the beginning inventory; i.e., $X_2 = 18 - I_2$. The cost incurred during the period 2, C_2, can be written in terms of I_2 as follows:

$$C_2 = X_2^2 + 4I_2 = (18 - I_2)^2 + 4I_2$$

The cost incurred during period 1 is simply $C_1 = X_1^2$. The TC cost equation can now be written

$$TC = C_1 + C_2 = X_1^2 + (18 - I_2)^2 + 4I_2$$

Substituting $I_2 = X_1 - 12$, we can express the TC as a function of X_1:

$$TC = X_1^2 + [18 - (X_1 - 12)]^2 + 4(X_1 - 12)$$

---

[9] Those readers without a knowledge of calculus may refer to Appendix E or skip this section without a loss of continuity.

[10] One shortcoming of this method is that it will not necessarily yield an integer or a nonnegative solution.

Simplifying, we have

$$TC = 2X_1^2 - 56X_1 + 852$$

TC is minimized when $X_1 = 14$.[11]

Since $X_1 + X_2 = 30$, it follows that $X_2 = 16$ units. Thus the optimum production schedule would be to produce 14 units in period 1 and 16 units in period 2. Two units would be carried in inventory from period 1 to period 2.

Financial Applications

Individual and institutional investors and corporate financial managers generally are concerned with multiperiod financial instruments. Economic changes (in, e.g., interest rates, tax rates, tariffs, inventory levels, government spending, etc.) have varying effects upon different types of financial instruments. The administration of a portfolio or a capital structure is more of a dynamic problem than a static one. Thus there are many financial applications of dynamic programming.

Dynamic programming can be used to time a call for the redemption of outstanding bonds as part of a refunding operation. It can be used to time a call to force the conversion of outstanding convertible debentures. An investor can use dynamic programming to determine whether voluntarily to convert a convertible security or exercise a warrant or to continue holding the instrument he now has. Some equipment replacement problems can be formulated as dynamic programming problems.

A rigorous solution to these problems requires the specification of fairly sophisticated financial inputs (such as the distribution of future stock price changes) and a thorough understanding of financial instruments. This would take us beyond the intended scope of the book and would really be a diversion from the areas of primary interest. Nevertheless, by pointing out areas where dynamic programming can be applied, we hope that the reader will gain a better appreciation and understanding of the usefulness of this technique.

---

[11] The value of X_1 that minimizes total cost can be determined by setting the first derivative of TC with respect to X_1 equal to zero and solving for X_1. (This procedure is discussed in Appendix E.)

$$\frac{dTC}{dX_1} = 4X_1 - 56$$

$$X_1 = 14$$

The second derivative is positive $\left(\frac{d^2TC}{dX_1^2} = 4\right)$, indicating that total cost has been minimized (again, see Appendix E).

PROBLEMS

1. Rework Problem 7 from Chapter 3, using decision trees.

2. Specify a marketing or production problem where decision trees can be used to obtain a solution. Lay out the tree you would use to represent your problem, being sure to carefully label each branch.

3. The Pear Recording Co. has just discovered a new musical group, the Quantitatives, and is considering offering them a five-year recording contract. If a contract is offered, Pear then has to decide whether to promote the group immediately on a national level or to introduce them initially in a limited number of selected cities and then, if warranted, go to a national effort after one year. Market acceptance can be classified as heavy, moderate, or light. Pear's annual profits, conditional on strategy and market acceptance, are given below. Notice that a heavy acceptance in a limited market will provide an opportunity for imitator groups to copy Quantitative's style and reduce Pear's profit in the last four years. A joint probability distribution of market acceptance is also given.

Annual Profits ($000)

Marketing Strategy	Market Acceptance	Period 1 (first year)	Period 2 (last 4 years)
Immediate	Heavy	$1500	$1500
national	Moderate	800	800
promotion	Light	−200	−200
Limited	Heavy	520	300
promotion	Moderate	360	360
only	Light	120	120
Limited,	Heavy	—	1200
national	Moderate	—	660
after 1 year	Light	—	−420

- -

	Period 1			
Period 2	Heavy	Moderate	Light	
Heavy	0.2	0.1	0	0.3
Moderate	0.1	0.2	0.1	0.4
Light	0	0.1	0.2	0.3
	0.3	0.4	0.3	

a. Draw a decision tree to represent the problem.

b. Using the criterion of maximizing expected monetary value, what marketing strategy should Pear use?

c. Rework b, assuming that it would cost $400,000 to undertake an immediate national promotion, $150,000 for a limited effort, and $350,000 to go from a limited to a national basis after one year. All other cost items are accounted for in the annual profit figures given above.

4. Refer to the EVSI problem in the chapter. Suppose that the critic can always predict accurately the success or failure of a new model. Show that the EVSI is $175,000.

5. Refer to the EVSI problem in the chapter. Suppose that additional critics are available at a fee of $2000 each. What is the optimal number of critics that the publisher should hire? Fully explain your decision criterion.

6. Briefly discuss three marketing applications of dynamic programming. Select one and outline the procedures you would follow to obtain a solution.

7. Given the following network and transition matrices:

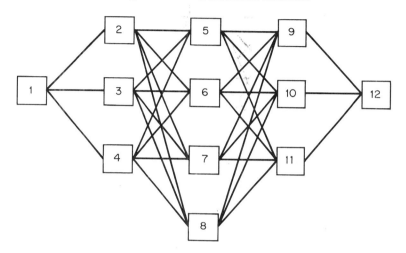

	To		
From	**2**	**3**	**4**
1	$5	$3	$6

	To			
From	**5**	**6**	**7**	**8**
2	$4	$3	$7	$7
3	5	5	3	4
4	7	4	6	3

	To		
From	**9**	**10**	**11**
5	$7	$ 6	$9
6	6	7	6
7	8	9	6
8	8	10	8

	To
From	**12**
9	$ 9
10	12
11	8

a. Determine the least-cost route from 1 to 12.
b. Determine the highest-cost route from 1 to 12.

8. A salesman has secured 10 tickets for an all-star baseball game. He will keep one himself and give the remaining nine away to various people he calls on in five different companies.

Number of Tickets	Company				
	A	B	C	D	E
0	0	0	0	0	0
1	8	7	10	9	8
2	15	14	18	17	16
3	22	21	25	25	23
4	28	26	32	31	30
5	34	31	38	37	36
6	40	36	44	43	42
7	45	41	48	48	48
8	50	45	52	53	53
9	54	49	55	57	57

a. Suppose that the above numbers represent the additional expenses he would have to incur (transportation, dinner, etc.) for a particular allocation of tickets. How many tickets should he distribute within each company so as to minimize his total additional expenses?

b. Suppose the above numbers represent the additional truckloads of orders he would receive over the coming year from a particular allocation of tickets. How many tickets should he distribute within each company so as to maximize his total additional orders?

9. Production costs for one period are X^2, where X is the number of units produced during the period. Inventory carrying costs are $4I$, where I is the number of units carried in inventory from one period to the next.

If 16 units are required in period 1 and 24 units are required in period 2, and there is no beginning or ending inventory allowed except between the two periods, what production schedule should be followed to minimize total costs?

II
OPTIMIZATION MODELS

5

linear
programming:
graphical analysis

Linear programming (LP) is one of the most common and useful planning and analysis tools used by the operating practitioner.[1] Although many different types of problems can be solved by using LP techniques, they all must share certain common characteristics. Like all models, the LP model requires that certain assumptions be made concerning the real world it is attempting to describe. The principal characteristic of problems that can be readily adapted to a LP model is linearity. That is, the problem to be solved is formulated entirely in terms of linear equations and inequalities. Thus the value of a LP solution depends largely on the validity of the assumption of linear relationships.

Linear programming refers to a technique for the formulation and solution of problems in which some linear function of two or more variables is to be optimized subject to a set of linear constraints, at least one of which must be expressed as an inequality. The linear function that is to be optimized is referred to as the *objective function*. Optimization can refer to either maximization or minimization. For example, the objective may be to maximize a profit function or to minimize a cost function. The variables contained in the objective function are referred to as *activity variables* or, alternatively, as *decision variables*, because the solution specifies the level of activity (e.g., the number of units produced of some product) for each variable represented in the objective function. A solution can specify zero production of some variables, but negative variable values obviously can

---

[1] While the examples in this chapter are based on production type problems, it should be emphasized that linear programming techniques can be applied to a wide range of areas and types of problems.

not be permitted in the solution of an LP problem, because it is impossible to produce a negative number of units of some product.[2] Each linear constraint must contain all or some of the activity variables contained in the objective function, but cannot contain any variable not included in the objective function. Each variable in the objective function must be included in at least one constraint. Constraints are simply algebraic statements which, for maximization problems, generally specify the limited availability of resources—time, labor, materials, money, etc.—while, for minimization problems, they usually establish minimum quality or composition requirements. Consider the former type of problem. There is a cost corresponding to each activity variable in each constraint, where the cost represents the marginal amount of the total resource available that is consumed when the activity variable level is increased by one unit. For example, the production of one additional unit of activity variable X_1 may require the consumption of 6 pounds of raw material and 7 minutes of machine time.

As indicated above, the solution of a maximization LP problem is constrained by the fact that the activity levels specified for each variable in the solution cannot consume more than the total amount of resource available for each group of activities. In other words, a solution cannot require the utilization of resources in excess of available raw materials, machine and labor time, budgetary limitations, etc. On the other hand, it is not required that all available resources be utilized in an optimal solution. In fact, the solution of a complex LP problem almost invariably results in some idle, or slack, capacity for some of the constraints.

AN EXAMPLE PROBLEM

As an example of a maximization LP problem, consider a small department of a printing company which makes two grades of wall posters. The better quality poster sells for $2.50, and the poorer quality poster for $1.50. Paper costs $0.75 for each of the better quality posters and only $0.25 for each of the poorer quality posters. Because of the poorer quality paper, however, the less expensive poster requires two minutes of printing time, while the more expensive one requires only one minute. The department is allocated $150 per day for paper. There are 480 minutes of printing time available daily, and each minute that is used is estimated to cost the company $0.25. In addition, the department incurs fixed daily costs of $125, which are not affected by the quantity or quality of posters produced. Management wants to know how many of each type of poster to produce in order to maximize daily profits. We will let X_1 denote the number of better quality posters produced and X_2 the number of poorer quality posters.

---

[2] LP problems that allow negative values can be formulated, but the general solution procedures developed to date do not allow negative values.

This problem can be solved by using a LP graphical procedure. The department's daily profits, total revenue minus total costs, can be expressed as

$$Z' = 2.50X_1 + 1.50X_2 - 1.00X_1 - 0.75X_2 - 125$$
$$= 1.50X_1 + 0.75X_2 - 125$$

where Z' represents daily profit. Variables X_1 and X_2 represent activity (or decision) variables. If the department's objective is to maximize daily profits, it would set X_1 and X_2 so as to maximize Z'. But note that the fixed daily cost of \$125 remains constant regardless of the values of X_1 and X_2. Therefore, we can accomplish the same objective by simply maximizing $Z = 1.50X_1 + 0.75X_2$. Since 1.50 and 0.75 represent the unit contributions for X_1 and X_2, respectively, we can define Z to be total daily contribution.[3]

The department cannot produce unlimited amounts of X_1 and X_2. It must, rather, seek to maximize Z by selecting the optimal values of X_1 and X_2 from all values that are feasible. Not all combinations of X_1 and X_2 values are feasible because of the constraints imposed by the paper budget and printing time limitations. We are also restricted to nonnegative values of X_1 and X_2. On the basis of these considerations, we can restate the problem as follows:

Maximize the objective function

$$Z = 1.50X_1 + 0.75X_2$$

subject to the constraints

1. $0.75X_1 + 0.25X_2 \leq 150$ paper budget
2. $X_1 + 2X_2 \leq 480$ printing time
3. $X_1 \geq 0$
4. $X_2 \geq 0$

The problem is illustrated graphically in Illustration 5–1. The points $OABC$ enclose an area that is called the *set of feasible solutions*. Only combinations of X_1 and X_2 that are within or on the boundary of $OABC$ represent feasible solutions, because any solution outside this area would violate one or more of the four constraints. The objective of the decision maker is to select from among the set of feasible solutions that combination of X_1 and X_2 that would maximize the objective function.

Solution by Trial and Error

As a first method of solution, let us successively assume different values for Z. That is, we can assume different values of Z and check to see whether they

---

[3] The unit contribution is the selling price minus the variable cost per unit.

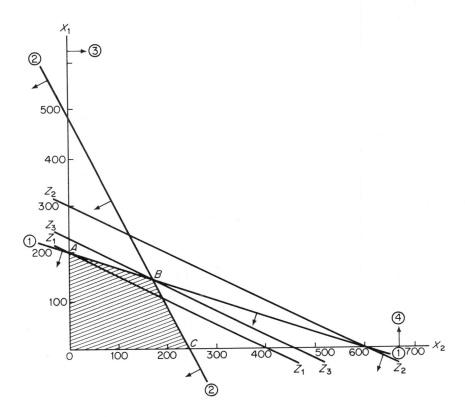

Illustration 5–1

violate either constraint. The largest possible value of Z that satisfies both constraints is the maximum value of the objective function. We can then find the optimum values of X_1 and X_2 that correspond to this value of Z. For example, in our first trial Z_1 is assumed to have a value of $300 and the objective function (denoted by Z_1) is plotted in Illustration 5–1.[4] Any X_1, X_2 combination on line Z_1 and within or on $OABC$ would provide a feasible solution. None of these equivalent solutions would be optimal, however, since there are other feasible solutions within or on $OABC$ that would produce a higher value of Z. Let us, therefore, assume Z_2 equal to $450 and plot it in Illustration 5–1. (It should be noticed that lines Z_1 and Z_2 are parallel with different intercepts.) No feasible solution lies along line Z_2, so our second selection was of an unattainably large value of Z. Suppose we revise our value downward and assume Z_3 equal to $342. When Z_3 is plotted, the corner point B lies directly on it. Any value of Z greater than $342 would, therefore, not have a corresponding feasible solution. Any value

---

[4] When $Z = 300, the objective function becomes $300 = 1.50X_1 + 0.75X_2$. This equation can be rewritten as $X_1 = 200 - 0.50X_2$. Thus line Z_1 has an intercept of 200 and a slope of -0.50. Changing the value of Z will shift the intercept but will not affect the slope.

96

of Z less than \$342 would have multiple corresponding feasible solutions, but none of them would be optimal. Thus Z can be increased until it reaches \$342. The corresponding solution would be point B, where $X_1 = 144$ units and $X_2 = 168$ units.

An important principle of LP is now evident: An optimal solution will (almost) always be at a corner point of the set of feasible solutions. The optimal solution will always be unique except for rare cases where the slope of a constraint line equals the slope of the objective function, in which case all feasible solutions along the constraint line will be optimal; but even then the corner-point solutions will always be included in the set of equivalent optimal solutions.

Solution by Evaluating Corner Points

This principle suggests a second method of solution which, although it also is basically a trial-and-error approach, generally is more efficient. We can solve for Z, using the values of X_1 and X_2 that are found at each corner point. Whichever of these solutions yields the highest value of Z is the optimal solution. Enumeration according to this rule, performed in Exhibit 5–1, shows that the optimal solution is B and the optimal value of Z is \$342.

Exhibit 5–1

Corner Point	X_1	X_2	Z
O	0	0	0
A	200	0	300
B	144	168	342
C	0	240	180

The optimal solution to the problem utilizes fully the available paper budget and printing time. Suppose we temporarily redefine $Z = 1.75X_1 + 0.50X_2$, however, by assuming different revenue and cost figures. The optimal solution is now point A, where 200 units of X_1 and 0 units of X_2 are produced. This solution utilizes all the paper budget, but results in more than half (280 minutes) of the available printing time being unused. Note that the optimal solution may intuitively be considered a wasteful solution because so much of the available printing time is not utilized. X_1 is now much more profitable than X_2, however, and X_1 requires a greater proportion of the paper budget and a smaller proportion of the printing budget. Increasing production of X_1 results in exhausting the paper budget before all the available printing time has been utilized.

ADDING AN ADDITIONAL CONSTRAINT

We have so far implicitly assumed unlimited demand for whatever posters are produced. We could introduce the additional constraint that there exists a

98

Optimization
Models

maximum daily demand of 100 units for X_1 and then rewrite the original problem:

Maximize $Z = 1.50X_1 + 0.75X_2$

subject to
(1) $0.75X_1 + 0.25X_2 \leq 150$ — paper budget
(2) $X_1 + 2X_2 \leq 480$ — printing time
(3) $X_1 \leq 100$ — demand
(4) $X_1 \geq 0$
(5) $X_2 \geq 0$

We now have a new set of feasible solutions $OEDC$, as shown in Illustration 5–2. Note that the new constraint 3 dominates (i.e., is more restrictive than) constraint 1, the paper budget constraint. The new optimal solution is at point E, where $X_1 = 100$, $X_2 = 190$, and $Z = \$292.50$. At point E, all available printing time is utilized and the maximum daily demand for X_1 is met, but \$40.25 of the paper budget is unused.

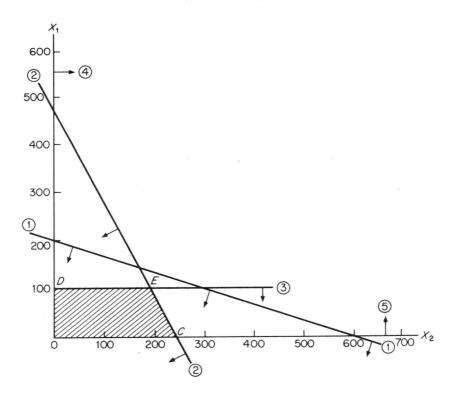

Illustration 5–2

SOLUTION BY ANALYSIS OF ECONOMIC TRADE-OFFS

Let us now return to our original problem, as portrayed in Illustration 5–1, and consider a third method of solution. This method, based on the economic trade-offs involved in getting from one corner-point solution to the next, provides some background for the procedures to be discussed in the following chapter. Assume that our initial solution is the origin, or point O, where both X_1 and X_2 equal zero. From point O we can move to either of corner points A or C. Movement to either would improve our solution, but moving toward A (or increasing X_1) gives a contribution of $1.50 per unit, whereas moving toward C (or increasing X_2) gives a contribution of only $0.75 per unit. Let us, therefore, increase X_1 as much as possible, moving us to our second solution point A, where $X_1 = 200$ units and $X_2 = 0$. Note that X_1 could be increased to 480 units and still satisfy constraint 2, but constraint 1 would be violated. Constraint 1 is satisfied when $X_1 = 200$ units, although slack capacity for constraint 2 then results. It is a general rule that a solution is restricted by the tightest constraint.

The next question is whether we can further improve our solution by moving from A to B. The answer requires some careful reasoning. Movement from A to B is accomplished by moving along the constraint line 1 corresponding to the paper budget. Because of the differences in costs between the better and poorer quality paper ($0.75 and $0.25, respectively), the sacrifice of one unit of X_1 means that three additional units of X_2 can be produced (as long as constraint 2 is not violated). The sacrifice of one unit of X_1 means that contribution of $1.50 is lost, but because three units of X_2 are received in exchange, contribution of $2.25 (3 × $0.75) is gained for a net gain per unit of X_1 sacrificed of $0.75 ($2.25 − $1.50). Since there is a net gain in contribution from moving from A to B, movement in that direction will improve our solution. We shall continue to move from A to the right along constraint line 1 until we reach point B. Further movement beyond B would result in the violation of constraint 2 and thus is not permitted. At point B, $X_1 = 144$ units and $X_2 = 168$ units. Note that the reduction in X_1 of 56 units is exactly one-third of the new level of X_2, as it should be. We found above that a net gain in contribution of $0.75 was realized for every unit of X_1 sacrificed. Since X_1 was decreased by 56 units, we should have a net gain in total contribution of 56($0.75), or $42, which can be added to the $300 total contribution at point A to give $342 total contribution at point B. The total contribution can also be obtained from the objective function, where $Z = 1.50(144) + 0.75(168) = 342$.

Further substitution of X_2 for X_1 would have to be accomplished by moving along constraint line 2 from B to C. Sacrifice of one unit of X_1 along this line will allow the production of only one-half additional unit of X_2 (X_2 requires twice as much printing time as X_1). Thus $1.50 contribution will be lost and $\frac{1}{2}$($0.75) will be gained, for a net loss of $1.50 − $0.375 or $1.125 per unit. Since these economic trade-offs would worsen our solution, we stop at our optimal point B. (Note that when the constraint limiting total demand for X_1 was added above, the optimal solution was $X_1 = 100$, $X_2 = 190$, and $Z = \$292.50$. This solution represents a reduction in X_1 of 44 units from the previous solution, and an increase in X_2 of $\frac{1}{2}(44)$ or 22 units. The reduction in daily total contribution is $\$342.00 - \$292.50 = \$49.50 = 44 \times \$1.125$.)[5]

A MINIMIZATION PROBLEM

As a brief example of a minimization problem, suppose we have the following:

Minimize $\quad K = 6Y_1 + 8Y_2$

subject to (1) $4Y_1 + 3Y_2 \geq 120$
            (2) $3Y_1 + 6Y_2 \geq 120$
            (3) $Y_1 \geq 0$
            (4) $Y_2 \geq 0$

The constraints are graphed in Illustration 5–3. The set of feasible solutions consists of all points on or above and to the right of *RST*. Again,

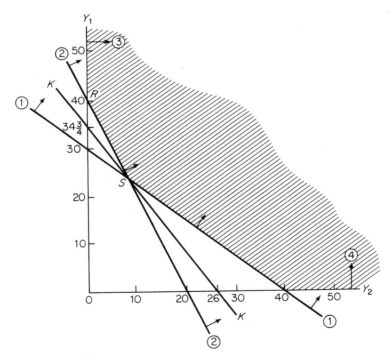

Illustration 5–3

[5] The reader should use this method of solution to verify that $X_1 = 200$ units and $X_2 = 0$ when $Z = 1.75X_1 + 0.50X_2$.

the optimal solution will occur at a vertex of the lines bounding the set of feasible solutions. As shown in Exhibit 5–2, the optimal solution occurs at point S, where K is minimized at 208. (The objective function when $K = 208$ is shown in Illustration 5–3 as line K–K.)

Exhibit 5–2

Corner Point	Y_1	Y_2	K
R	40	0	240
S	24	8	208
T	0	40	320

ADDING AN ADDITIONAL PRODUCT

The procedures given in this chapter are adequate only for the simplest of problems. For example, suppose that our original example is expanded to include an intermediate quality poster that provides unit contribution of $1.25, uses paper that costs $0.50, and consumes one minute of printing time. The expanded problem can be summarized as follows, where X_3 represents the intermediate quality poster:

Maximize $\quad Z = 1.50X_1 + 0.75X_2 + 1.25X_3$

subject to
(1) $0.75X_1 + 0.25X_2 + 0.50X_3 \leq 150$
(2) $X_1 + 2X_2 + X_3 \leq 480$
(3) $X_1 \geq 0$
(4) $X_2 \geq 0$
(5) $X_3 \geq 0$

With such a minor expansion of the problem a graphical solution is still possible but perhaps impractical. If the problem were expanded further to include a fourth possible product, a graphical solution would become impossible to obtain. A solution can be obtained by complete enumeration of all possible corner points, however. Feasible vertices can be obtained by setting the above five inequalities to equalities and then solving sets of three equations, eliminating solutions which do not satisfy all the constraints. (Sets of three equations are solved because the problem now has three decision variables. A unique solution requires that three independent equations be solved simultaneously.) The solution is given in Exhibit 5–3. The optimal value of the objective function is now $390, obtained by producing 0 units of X_1, 120 units of X_2, and 240 units of X_3. It should be obvious that the previous solution could not be worsened by the introduction of X_3. At worst, zero production of X_3 would be specified, and the solution would remain as before.

Exhibit 5–3

Constraints	X_1	X_2	X_3	Value of Objective Function	Constraint Violated
1, 2, 3	0	120	240	390	
1, 2, 4	−360	0	840	Infeasible Solution	3
1, 2, 5	144	168	0	342	
1, 3, 4	0	0	300	375	
1, 3, 5	0	600	0	Infeasible Solution	2
1, 4, 5	200	0	0	300	
2, 3, 4	0	0	480	Infeasible Solution	1
2, 3, 5	0	240	0	180	
2, 4, 5	480	0	0	Infeasible Solution	1
3, 4, 5	0	0	0	0	

The addition of yet another product or another constraint would begin to make complete enumeration an inefficient method of solution. Certainly for much more complex problems a more efficient procedure must be used. Such a procedure is given in the next chapter.

Finally, perhaps a caveat is in order before we proceed to the next chapter. Our objective so far has been to introduce the general characteristics of LP problems without the distractions of unnecessary complications. Real life problems can be much more complex than the examples given in this chapter, and the reader is cautioned against drawing rash generalizations about the scope and format of LP problems. For example, the maximization problems discussed so far have had constraints of the "less than or equal to" type, while the minimization problem had "greater than or equal to" constraints. In the original formulation of many real-life problems, constraints of both types might be included. Techniques for solving more complex problems will be given in the next chapter.

PROBLEMS

1. Maximize $Z = 2X_1 + 3X_2$
   subject to the following constraints:
   (1) $3X_1 + 4X_2 \leq 120$
   (2) $2X_1 + X_2 \leq 60$
   (3) $X_1 \geq 0$
   (4) $X_2 \geq 0$

2. Minimize $Z = 5X_1 + 4X_2$
   subject to the following constraints:
   (1) $4X_1 + X_2 \geq 80$
   (2) $2X_1 + 3X_2 \geq 90$
   (3) $X_1 \geq 0$
   (4) $X_2 \geq 0$

3. Minimize $Z = 2X_1 + 3X_2$
   subject to the following constraints:
   (1) $2X_1 + X_2 \geq 10$
   (2) $3X_1 + 4X_2 \geq 30$
   (3) $X_1 \geq 0$
   (4) $X_2 \geq 0$

4. Graph the following constraints and explain the significance of each.
   (1) $2X_1 + X_2 \leq 18$
   (2) $X_1 + X_2 \leq 12$
   (3) $4X_1 + 3X_2 \leq 42$
   (4) $2X_1 + 3X_2 \leq 36$
   (5) $X_1 \geq 0$
   (6) $X_2 \geq 0$

5. A publisher sells a hardcover edition of a textbook for $9.00 and a paperback edition of the same text for $5.00. Costs to the publisher are $7.00 and $3.60 per book, respectively, in addition to weekly fixed costs of $1200. Both types require 5 minutes of printing time, although the hardcover requires 10 minutes binding time and the paperback requires only 2 minutes. Both the printing and binding operations have 4800 minutes available each week.

   a. How many of each type of book should be produced in order to maximize profits?

   b. What if technological improvements reduce the required printing time to only 4 minutes for the paperback? Explain the changes you find in your optimal solution.

   c. Assume that a deluxe hardcover is also to be published. It will sell for $15.00, will cost $12.00, and will require 8 minutes of printing time and 12 minutes of binding time. (Ignore the information given in b.) Now how many of each type of book should be produced? Would it ever be possible for a positive number of all three types of books to be produced in an optimal solution? Why?

6. A new type of lawn fertilizer is to be marketed in bales which must weigh at least 150 pounds. Each bale is to be a combination of two components, A and B. Component A is used in two-pound units, which cost $3.25 each. Component B is used in three-pound units, which cost $2.50 each. In addition, each bale must contain at least 10 pounds (160 ounces) of Grenoble Green, a new miracle lawn product. Each unit of A contains 4 ounces of Grenoble Green and each unit of B contains 2 ounces.

   a. How much of each component should go into each bale to minimize total cost?

   b. How much will each bale cost?

   c. How much will each bale weigh?

   d. How much Grenoble Green will each bale contain?

6

simplex method

The simplex method is a systematic step-by-step (or iterative) computational procedure for solving LP problems. The algorithm starts with an initial corner-point solution and progresses to an optimal corner-point solution by the systematic application of simple rules at each step. Thus the simplex method works in exactly the same way as the third method of graphical solution (by analysis of economic trade-offs) presented in the preceding chapter (although the simplex method can handle much more complex problems).

The procedures for working through the simplex algorithm will be presented in this chapter. The first method to be presented will develop an appreciation for exactly what the simplex procedure is doing and why, and will help with the interpretation of the final results. The analogous steps in the graphical solution also will be indicated. The second method to be presented is more efficient computationally than the first, although both produce identical numerical results.

PROPERTIES OF SIMPLEX SOLUTIONS

Before we proceed to the method of solution, the properties of basic feasible solutions and slack variables will be discussed. Let us begin by giving a *temporary* definition of a basic feasible solution. In a LP problem with n decision variables and m ($m \leq n$) linearly independent constraints,[1] a *basic feasible solution* is any feasible solution in which $n - m$ or more of the

[1] The symbol m is the number of "capacity" constraints. The constraints specifying that each decision variable must have a nonnegative value are *not* included.

decision variables have values equal to zero.[2] The decision variables that have nonzero values are called *basic variables*, and the decision variables that have zero values are called *nonbasic variables*. Remember that no decision variables can have negative values.

Any optimal solution will be a basic feasible solution. This is an important, but perhaps anti-intuitive, rule. This rule means that if we are considering a problem with five products and only two constraints, we shall produce *at most* two products in our optimal solution, and *at least* three products will not be produced at all. In other words, we will never produce more products in an optimal solution than we have constraints.

The validity of this rule can be understood if we think about what is required in order to obtain algebraic solutions to find the corner points in a *n* product, *m* constraint problem. Notice that, in every case, at least one of the decision variables has a zero value in the three-product, two-constraint problem enumerated in Exhibit 5–3. You might also visualize the graphical solution of a two-product, one-constraint problem. In order to obtain a corner-point solution, you would have to produce all of one product or all of the other; you could not obtain a corner-point solution (and therefore not an optimal solution) by producing some combination of both.

Slack Variables

The concept of slack variables is also important. A *slack variable* can be added to each constraint to account for the unused amount of the total available capacity. The addition of slack variables converts the original "less than or equal to" inequality constraints into strict equalities, or equations. We can add slack variables and rewrite the problem discussed in the previous chapter as

Maximize $Z = 1.50X_1 + 0.75X_2 + 0X_3 + 0X_4$

subject to
(1) $0.75X_1 + 0.25X_2 + X_3 = 150$ paper budget
(2) $X_1 + 2X_2 + X_4 = 480$ printing time
(3) $X_1 \geq 0$
(4) $X_2 \geq 0$
(5) $X_3 \geq 0$
(6) $X_4 \geq 0$

Slack variable X_3 represents one dollar, or, more generally, one unit, of the available paper budget. Slack variable X_4 represents one minute, or one unit, of the available printing time. If a slack variable has a nonzero value, there is some unused capacity in the constraint associated with that slack variable. For example, assume that $X_4 = 100$. This means that 380 minutes of the available printing time is being utilized (i.e., $X_1 + 2X_2 = 380$) and the

---

[2] Note that *m* cannot be greater than *n*, because there cannot be more *linearly independent constraints* than there are decision variables.

remaining 100 minutes is idle, or *slack*, capacity. Thus, $X_1 + 2X_2 + X_4 = 380 + 100 = 480$, the total available capacity. Likewise, if $X_3 = 30$, $30 of the paper budget is not being used. It follows that $0.75X_1 + 0.25X_2 = 120$, and $120 + 30 = 150$. Obviously, the (marginal) unit contribution of a slack variable is zero. This is indicated in the objective function.

Basic Feasible Solution Redefined

Once slack variables have been introduced, and the inequality constraints have been changed to equalities, we can proceed with the simplex solution to our problem. We must first find an initial basic feasible solution. We can also now replace our temporary definition of a basic feasible solution with a permanent one. Before the introduction of slack variables, a basic feasible solution was said to contain $n - m$ *or more* of the decision variables with values of zero. Suppose, for example, that there are eight decision variables ($n = 8$) and five constraints ($m = 5$). *At least three* of the decision variables must, therefore, have values of zero. If exactly three have zero values and five have nonzero values, there would be no unused capacity in any of the five constraints. If four decision variables have zero values and four have nonzero values, there would be unused capacity in one of the constraints. If five have zero values and three have nonzero values, there would be unused capacity in two of the constraints, and so on. In the last example, where two constraints have excess capacity, two slack variables would have nonzero values. If we now define the set of decision variables to include *not only product* variables, as before, *but also slack* variables, we can redefine a basic feasible solution to be a feasible solution containing *exactly* $n - m$ decision variables with values of zero, and m decision variables with nonzero values. Thus, in the above examples, each basic solution contained five decision variables with nonzero values. These basic solutions consisted of five product variables; four product variables and one slack variable; and three product variables and two slack variables, respectively.

OBTAINING A SIMPLEX SOLUTION

If there are m constraints, there will be m slack variables.[3] Since there must also be m decision variables with nonzero values in any basic feasible solution, it is convenient to use the slack variables as the basic variables (i.e., having nonzero values) and the product variables as the nonbasic variables (i.e., having zero values) for the initial solution. In our example problem, the basic variables would be $X_3 = 150$ and $X_4 = 480$ and the nonbasic variables would be $X_1 = X_2 = 0$. This is equivalent to starting from the origin in a graphical solution.

[3] This statement is accurate based on the development thus far. As will be seen later in more complex examples, these m variables can be slack, artificial (to be defined later), or even product variables. The above statement applies to problems where all constraints are of the "less than or equal to" type.

Improving the Initial Solution

The next step is to express all the nonbasic variables as linear equivalent combinations of the basic variables. The production of one unit of X_1 requires the consumption of 0.75 units (dollars) of the paper budget and 1.0 unit (minute) of the available printing time. Since X_3 represents one unit of the paper budget and X_4 represents one unit of printing time, we can express one unit of X_1 as the equivalent of 0.75 units of X_3 and 1.0 unit of X_4; i.e., $X_1 \equiv 0.75X_3 + X_4$. Likewise, $X_2 \equiv 0.25X_3 + 2X_4$. For completeness, we could also say $X_3 \equiv 1 \cdot X_3 + 0 \cdot X_4$ and $X_4 \equiv 0 \cdot X_3$ and $1 \cdot X_4$.

We thus see that the production of one unit of X_1 would decrease the level of X_3 by 0.75 units and the level of X_4 by 1.0 unit. The production of one unit of X_2 would decrease the level of X_3 by 0.25 unit and the level of X_4 by 2.0 units. We can, therefore, determine whether the production of any of the nonbasic variables would yield greater contribution than its equivalent linear combination of basic variables. For example, the production of one unit of X_1 would provide a contribution of \$1.50. The contribution of the units of X_3 and X_4 that would be sacrificed would have a value of zero. Therefore, the "net" contribution of producing one unit of X_1 would be \$1.50. Algebraically, the net contribution is $1.50(1) - 0(0.75) - 0(1) = 1.50$. Similarly, the net contribution of $X_2 = 0.75(1) - 0(0.25) - 0(2) = 0.75$.

The Iterative Process

Since these net contributions are positive, we can improve our solution (i.e., increase the total contribution) by producing more of X_1 and X_2 and less of X_3 and X_4. At this point we must introduce the iterative nature of the simplex method. Remember that there must always be exactly m nonzero variables in a basic feasible solution. Therefore, we must increase the production of *either X_1 or X_2* to a positive level, but not both. It is also necessary to increase the level of X_1 or X_2 to the point where either X_3 or X_4 goes to zero. Our new basic solution will, therefore, consist of one product variable and one slack variable, for the required total of two decision variables. Failure to force one of the slack variables to a zero value would leave three basic variables, which would automatically preclude an optimal solution.

One iteration in the simplex method consists of completely replacing one of the basic variables from the previous solution with a nonbasic variable from the previous solution. An efficient rule to follow is to enter that variable which has the largest net contribution. Applying this rule, we shall enter X_1 into our solution and eliminate either X_3 or X_4.[4]

The problems of which variable to remove from the solution and what the level of X_1 should now be are related. Suppose, for example, it arbitrarily is decided to eliminate X_4. The production of one unit of X_1 requires the

---

[4] When two or more variables tie for the largest net contribution, the choice of which one to bring in is arbitrary. While theoretical complications arise in such a situation, there generally is not a practical problem to worry about.

reduction of X_4 by one unit. Since $X_4 = 480$ in the previous solution, it follows that X_1 must equal 480 in the new solution. But since the production of one unit of X_1 consumes 0.75 dollar of the paper budget, the production of 480 units of X_1 requires 0.75(480) = \$360 for the paper budget. Only \$150 is available, and X_3 cannot equal $-\$210$ (as constraint 5 would be violated), so X_1 cannot completely replace X_4.

The other alternative is to see if X_1 can completely replace X_3. Since one unit of X_1 consumes 0.75 unit of X_3, and X_3 has a value of 150, the new value of X_1 would be 150/0.75 = 200 and the new value of X_3 would be zero. If $X_1 = 200$, 200(1) = 200 minutes of printing time would be consumed. The remaining 280 minutes would be idle time, so the new value of X_4 would be 280. We have, therefore, arrived at a new solution where $X_1 = 200$, $X_4 = 280$, $X_2 = X_3 = 0$. As a general rule, remove the variable that results in the *smallest positive value* for the new basic variable. This ensures that no other constraints will be violated.[5] Or, in other words, we want to increase X_1 to as large a value as possible, but increasing X_1 affects X_3 and X_4. We therefore increase X_1 until either X_3 or X_4 is forced to zero and drops out of production. (At this point the struggling reader might find it instructive to return to Chapter 5 and follow the corresponding steps of the above iteration through the graphical solution.) The total contribution is now $Z = 1.50(200) + 0.75(0) + 0(0) + 0(280) = \$300$.

Completing the New Solution

Given the new solution, it is again necessary to express all of the nonbasic variables as linear combinations of the basic variables. This can be accomplished by algebraically restating the linear equivalent combinations from the previous solution in terms of the new basic variables X_1 and X_4. Previously we had

$$X_1 \equiv 0.75X_3 + X_4 \qquad \text{(a)}$$
$$X_2 \equiv 0.25X_3 + 2X_4 \qquad \text{(b)}$$
$$X_3 \equiv X_3 + 0X_4 \qquad \text{(c)}$$
$$X_4 \equiv 0X_3 + X_4 \qquad \text{(d)}$$

By using the same techniques used to solve simultaneous equations (linear combinations and multiples of the original equations), we can perform the following operations:

$$
\begin{aligned}
3X_2 &\equiv 0.75X_3 + 6X_4 & 3 \cdot \text{(b)} \\
- X_1 &\equiv 0.75X_3 + X_4 & \text{(a)} \\
\hline
3X_2 - X_1 &\equiv 5X_4 & 3 \cdot \text{(b)} - \text{(a)} \\
3X_2 &\equiv X_1 + 5X_4 & 3 \cdot \text{(b)} - \text{(a)} \\
X_2 &\equiv \tfrac{1}{3}X_1 + \tfrac{5}{3}X_4 & (\tfrac{1}{3})[3\text{(b)} - \text{(a)}] = \text{(b}')
\end{aligned}
$$

[5] In practice, when a tie results, the choice of which variable to remove can be treated as arbitrary. When the procedure requires division by zero, treat the quotient as a very large number so that the variable will remain in the solution. Negative numbers do not count because the value of the new basic variable must be positive.

Substituting (b′) in (b) and solving for X_3, we obtain

$$\tfrac{1}{3}X_1 + \tfrac{5}{3}X_4 \equiv \tfrac{1}{4}X_3 + 2X_4$$
$$\tfrac{1}{4}X_3 \equiv \tfrac{1}{3}X_1 - \tfrac{1}{3}X_4$$
$$X_3 \equiv \tfrac{4}{3}X_1 - \tfrac{4}{3}X_4 \qquad \text{(c′)}$$

The total set of new linear equivalent combinations will be

$$X_1 \equiv X_1 + 0X_4 \qquad \text{(a′)}$$
$$X_2 \equiv \tfrac{1}{3}X_1 + \tfrac{5}{3}X_4 \qquad \text{(b′)}$$
$$X_3 \equiv \tfrac{4}{3}X_1 - \tfrac{4}{3}X_4 \qquad \text{(c′)}$$
$$X_4 \equiv 0X_1 + X_4 \qquad \text{(d′)}$$

To make sure the significance of these linear combinations is understood, let us consider (b′) in more detail. From the original problem it is seen that one unit of X_1 required 0.75 dollar of the paper budget and 1 minute of printing time, or, in terms of slack variables, $X_1 \equiv 0.75X_3 + X_4$. In terms of slack variables, $X_2 \equiv 0.25X_3 + 2X_4$. Equality (b′), which gives the number of units of X_1 and X_4 that would be sacrificed to produce one unit of X_2, can also be written in terms of slack variables. Thus, if the production of X_1 is decreased by $\tfrac{1}{3}$ unit,

$$X_2 \equiv 0.25X_3 + 2X_4 \equiv \tfrac{1}{3}X_1 + \tfrac{5}{3}X_4 \equiv \tfrac{1}{3}(0.75X_3 + X_4) + \tfrac{5}{3}X_4$$
$$\equiv (0.25X_3 + \tfrac{1}{3}X_4) + \tfrac{5}{3}X_4 \equiv 0.25X_3 + 2X_4$$

it is also necessary to reduce X_4 by $\tfrac{5}{3}$ units to provide sufficient printing time to produce one extra unit of X_2. Notice that, from (c′), if X_3 is increased by one unit, X_1 is *decreased* by $\tfrac{4}{3}$ units and X_4 is *increased* by $\tfrac{4}{3}$ units (an increase is indicated by the negative coefficient).

Improving the New Solution

Once the equivalent combinations (a′), (b′), (c′), and (d′) have been obtained, we can compute the net contributions of the nonbasic variables to see whether the solution can be further improved. The net contribution of $X_2 = 0.75 - \tfrac{1}{3}(1.50) - \tfrac{5}{3}(0) = 0.25$. The net contribution of $X_3 = 0 - \tfrac{4}{3}(1.50) + \tfrac{4}{3}(0) = -2.00$. The solution would therefore be improved by increasing the production of X_2 and worsened by increasing X_3 (so that reducing the paper budget by one dollar would result in lost contribution of two dollars). Variable X_2 will therefore enter the solution as a basic variable and X_4 will be removed. Equality (b′) can be used to show that X_4, and not X_1, will become a nonbasic variable if, from the previous solution, $X_1 = 200$ and $X_4 = 280$. If $X_1 = 0$, $X_2 = 200/\tfrac{1}{3} = 600$; if $X_4 = 0$, $X_2 = 280/\tfrac{5}{3} = 168$. As in the previous iteration, X_2 must assume the lowest possible value. Since $168 < 600$, $X_2 = 168$ and $X_4 = 0$. Again referring to (b′), we see that an increase of one unit of X_2 requires a decrease of $\tfrac{1}{3}$ unit of X_1. Thus if X_2 is now equal to 168 units, the level of X_1 must be reduced by $\tfrac{1}{3}(168) = 56$

units. In the new solution (corresponding to point B in Illustration 5–1), $X_1 = 200 - 56 = 144$, $X_2 = 168$, $X_3 = X_4 = 0$.

The net contribution of X_2 was determined to be $0.25 per unit. Since 168 units of X_2 were added to the solution, total contribution should now be the previous solution's contribution of $300 plus $0.25(168) = 42$, or $342. This figure can be verified by plugging the new activity levels into the objective function.

$$Z = 144(1.50) + 168(0.75) + 0(0) + 0(0)$$
$$= 216 + 126 + 0 + 0$$
$$= \$342$$

Repeating the Iterative Process

The nonbasic variables could again be expressed as linear equivalent combinations of the basic variables and their net contributions could be found. The reader should satisfy himself that $X_3 \equiv \frac{8}{5}X_1 - \frac{4}{5}X_2$ and $X_4 \equiv -\frac{1}{5}X_1 + \frac{3}{5}X_2$ and that the net contributions of X_1 and X_2 are $-\$1.80$ and $-\$0.15$, respectively. Since the net contributions of both nonbasic variables are negative, the current solution cannot be improved and an optimal solution has therefore been obtained. The problem is finished.

AN ALTERNATIVE SOLUTION PROCEDURE

The preceding method of solution was presented so that the basic principles of LP and, in particular, the informational content of the final solution can be better understood. The required computations quickly become unwieldy, however, as the problem becomes more complex. Fortunately, a more efficient procedure is available which has the additional advantage of being readily adaptable to computer solution. We shall introduce the new procedure by again reworking the (hopefully now familiar) problem solved above. Then a larger and more complex example will also be presented.

Let us again use the slack variables as our initial basic solution. A tabular summary of this initial solution is presented below in Exhibit 6–1.

Exhibit 6–1

Unit contribution =		1.50	0.75	0	0	
Basic variables are	Decision variables are	X_1	X_2	X_3	X_4	
X_3		0.75	0.25	1	0	$X_3 = 150$
X_4		1	2	0	1	$X_4 = 480$
Net contribution =		1.50	0.75	0	0	Total contribution = 0

The linear equivalent combinations of the decision variables in terms of the basic variables are now read downwards in the four primary vertical columns. Thus we again see that $X_1 \equiv 0.75X_3 + X_4$, etc. The unit contributions are given in the top row and the net contributions are given in the bottom row. The numerical values of the basic values are given in the right-hand column and the total contribution is given in the bottom right-hand corner. Since the same basic format is used for all solutions, it is not necessary to keep repeating the extensive labels. Thus we can further condense the above summary, as shown in Exhibit 6–2. This *tableau*, as it is called, contains all

Exhibit 6–2

		1.50	0.75	0	0	
		X_1	X_2	X_3	X_4	
(1a)	X_3	0.75	0.25	1	0	150
(1b)	X_4	1	2	0	1	480
(1c)	NC	1.50	0.75	0	0	0

the information we need to solve the problem. A check of the net contribution row reveals positive numbers, which means that our initial solution can be improved. We shall again select X_1, the variable with the largest positive net contribution, to be included in our next basic feasible solution. If we remove X_3, X_1 will equal $150/0.75 = 200$; if we remove X_4, X_1 will equal $480/1 = 480$. To avoid violating any constraints, the variable that results in the smallest value of X_1 is removed. Therefore, X_1 replaces X_3 in our next solution. The next solution is represented by a tableau similar to Exhibit 6–2. In fact, each sequential solution in our iterative process is represented by a separate tableau (although, because the unit contributions do not change, the top row of the initial solution is usually not carried over to succeeding solutions).

Because it is necessary that $X_1 \equiv X_1 + 0X_4$ and $X_4 \equiv 0X_1 + X_4$, we know what some of the entries in the new tableau must be. We also have found previously that the net contribution of each basic variable is zero. These values are entered in Exhibit 6–3. The remainder of the tableau can be

Exhibit 6–3

		X_1	X_2	X_3	X_4
(2a)	X_1	1			0
(2b)	X_4	0			1
(2c)	NC	0			0

filled in by performing simple row operations on Exhibit 6–2 so as to obtain the required entries in Exhibit 6–3. For example, to get a 1 in the X_1-X_1 position (denoting row-column) of the new tableau, row (1a) can be divided by 0.75 to obtain row (2a). The remaining rows in the second tableau can be

Exhibit 6–4

		X_1	X_2	X_3	X_4	
(2a)	X_1	1	$\frac{1}{3}$	$\frac{4}{3}$	0	200
(2b)	X_4	0			1	
(2c)	NC	0			0	

obtained by subtracting an appropriate multiple of the newly obtained row corresponding to the new basic variable from the same rows in the preceding tableau. (This is not as bad as it sounds.) For example, we know a zero must go in the X_4-X_1 position of row (2b). The X_4-X_1 position of (1b) contains a 1. We can, therefore, obtain (2b) directly by subtracting row (2a) from row (1b).

(1b)	1	2	0	1	480
$-$(2a)	1	$\frac{1}{3}$	$\frac{4}{3}$	0	200
(2b)	0	$\frac{5}{3}$	$-\frac{4}{3}$	1	280

Similarly, a zero is needed in the first position of the net contribution row (2c). This position has a value of 1.50 in row (1c). We can, therefore, obtain row (2c) by multiplying row (2a) by 1.50 and subtracting the result from row (1c). (Notice that the total contribution entry is included.)

(1c)	1.50	0.75	0	0	0
$-1.50 \times$ (2a)	1.50	0.50	2.00	0	300
(2c)	0	0.25	-2.00	0	-300

Once rows (2b) and (2c) are complete, the second tableau is finished. The final product is shown as Exhibit 6–5. The basic variables in this solution

Exhibit 6–5

		X_1	X_2	X_3	X_4	
(2a)	X_1	1	$\frac{1}{3}$	$\frac{4}{3}$	0	200
(2b)	X_4	0	$\frac{5}{3}$	$-\frac{4}{3}$	1	280
	NC	0	0.25	-2.00	0	-300

are $X_1 = 200$ and $X_4 = 280$. The total contribution is \$300. (The negative value in the tableau is due to the procedure being used. This value will always be negative or zero. Thus the total contribution is simply the absolute value of the negative amount shown in the tableau.) Variable X_2 has a positive net contribution. Therefore, the solution can be improved by making X_2 a basic variable. Variable X_4 will be removed, since $280/\frac{5}{3} = 168$ is less than $200/\frac{1}{3} = 600$.

In the new solution, X_2 replaces X_4. The X_2 row of the third tableau [row (3b) of Exhibit 6–3] can be obtained by multiplying row (2b) by $\frac{3}{5}$.

$$(3b) = \tfrac{3}{5}\cdot(2b) = 0 \quad \underset{=}{1} \quad -\tfrac{4}{5} \quad \tfrac{3}{5} \quad 168$$

Row (3a) is obtained by multiplying (3b) by $\frac{1}{3}$ and subtracting the product from (2a).

(2a)	1	$\tfrac{1}{3}$	$\tfrac{4}{3}$	0	200
$-\tfrac{1}{3}\cdot$(3b)	0	$\tfrac{1}{3}$	$-\tfrac{4}{15}$	$\tfrac{1}{5}$	56
(3a)	1	0	$\tfrac{8}{5}$	$-\tfrac{1}{5}$	144

Row (3c) is obtained by multiplying (3b) by $\frac{1}{4}$ and subtracting the product from (2c). This solution is summarized in Exhibit 6–6.

(2c)	0	0.25	-2.00	0	-300
$-\tfrac{1}{4}\cdot$(3b)	0	$\tfrac{1}{4}$	$-\tfrac{1}{5}$	$\tfrac{3}{20}$	42
	0	0	-1.80	-0.15	-342

Exhibit 6–6

		X_1	X_2	X_3	X_4	
(3a)	X_1	1	0	$\tfrac{8}{5}$	$-\tfrac{1}{5}$	144
(3b)	X_2	0	1	$-\tfrac{4}{5}$	$\tfrac{3}{5}$	168
(3c)	NC	0	0	-1.80	-0.15	-342

All the net contribution values for this solution are zero or negative; therefore, we have reached an optimal solution. The optimal solution is achieved by producing 144 units of X_1 and 168 units of X_2. The resulting total contribution would be \$342. Any other combination of our decision variables will result in an inferior solution.

We shall now present three problems that are more complex than the one discussed above. Each problem will be presented and put into a LP framework. Initial solutions will be specified, and the substitutions made at each iteration will be indicated. Complete solutions will be presented, with the exception of the intermediate row operations. The reader should work through each iteration to make sure that he can perform the required computations.

REVISED POSTER PROBLEM

Additional factors can be introduced to complicate our previous example. As in Chapter 5, a maximum demand for X_1 of 100 units can be specified. In addition, some of the printing work can now be subcontracted. Subcontracted units cost $0.10 more than those printed by the firm, so unit contributions would be $0.10 less. The firm is responsible for supplying paper to the subcontractor, although the paper budget has been increased to $250.

This revised problem can be formulated as follows:

Maximize $\quad Z = 1.50X_1 + 0.75X_2 + 1.40X_1' + 0.65X_2'$

subject to
(1) $0.75X_1 + 0.25X_2 + 0.75X_1' + 0.25X_2' \le 250 \qquad$ paper
(2) $X_1 + 2X_2 \le 480 \qquad$ printing
(3) $X_1 + X_1' \le 100 \qquad$ demand
(4) $X_1 \ge 0$
(5) $X_2 \ge 0$
(6) $X_1' \ge 0$
(7) $X_2' \ge 0$

In the above equation and inequalities, X_1' and X_2' represent units of X_1 and X_2, respectively, where the printing has been subcontracted. The initial solution and subsequent iterations are presented below in Exhibits 6–7 through 6–11. Variables X_3, X_4, and X_5 are the slack variables. (Notice

Exhibit 6–7

	X_1	X_2	X_1'	X_2'	X_3	X_4	X_5	
X_3	0.75	0.25	0.75	0.25	1	0	0	250
X_4	1	2	0	0	0	0	0	480
X_5	1	0	1	0	0	0	1	100
NC	1.50	0.75	1.40	0.65	0	0	0	0

that there are now three constraints. Therefore, a basic solution must contain three decision variables.)

Exhibit 6–8 First Iteration: X_1 Replaces X_5

	X_1	X_2	X_1'	X_2'	X_3	X_4	X_5	
X_3	0	0.25	0	0.25	1	0	-0.75	175
X_4	0	2	-1	0	0	1	-1	380
X_1	1	0	1	0	0	0	1	100
NC	0	0.75	-0.10	0.65	0	0	-1.50	-150

Exhibit 6–9 Second Iteration: X_2 Replaces X_4

	X_1	X_2	X_1'	X_2'	X_3	X_4	X_5	
X_3	0	0	0.125	0.25	1	-0.125	-0.625	127.5
X_2	0	1	-0.5	0	0	0.5	-0.5	190
X_1	1	0	1	0	0	0	1	100
NC	0	0	0.275	0.65	0	-0.375	-1.125	-292.5

Exhibit 6–10 Third Iteration: X_2' Replaces X_3

	X_1	X_2	X_1'	X_2'	X_3	X_4	X_5	
X_2'	0	0	0.5	1	4	-0.5	-2.5	510
X_2	0	1	-0.5	0	0	0.5	-0.5	190
X_1	1	0	1	0	0	0	1	100
NC	0	0	-0.05	0	-2.60	-0.05	0.5	-624

Exhibit 6–11 Fourth Iteration: X_5 Replaces X_1

	X_1	X_2	X_1'	X_2'	X_3	X_4	X_5	
X_2'	2.5	0	3	1	4	-0.5	0	760
X_2	0.5	1	0	0	0	0.5	0	240
X_5	1	0	1	0	0	0	1	100
NC	-0.50	0	-0.55	0	-2.60	-0.05	0	-674

According to the optimal solution, 240 units of X_2 and 760 units of X_2' should be produced. That is, the firm should print 240 units of the low-quality poster and subcontract the printing of 760 more. The objective function would have a value of $674.

No units of X_1 or X_1' should be produced. Neither variable appears in the final set of basic variables. This same result is reflected by the value of X_5 in the optimal solution. X_5 is the slack variable for the high-quality poster demand constraint. The slack variable has a value of 100 units, which means that it has absorbed the total capacity of this constraint.

PORTFOLIO PROBLEM

An investor wants to allocate his portfolio among five different types of securities. These securities are identified in Exhibit 6–12. Their expected returns, denoted by $E(R)$, and standard deviations of expected return, denoted by σ, are also given.

Exhibit 6–12   Return-Risk Characteristics

Type of Security	Proportion	E(R)	σ
Speculative stock	X_1	14%	10%
Mutual fund	X_2	10%	5%
Blue chip stock	X_3	8%	4%
Long-term bond	X_4	7%	2%
Bank savings account	X_5	5%	0%

The investor's objective is to maximize his expected return, although the realization of this objective must be conditioned by the existence of several constraints. As indicated in Exhibit 6–12, X_1 represents the proportion of his total portfolio invested in speculative stocks; X_2 represents the proportion invested in mutual funds; etc. He obviously cannot allocate more than 100 percent of his total portfolio; i.e.,

$$\sum_{i=1}^{5} X_i \leq 1.0$$

He is also unwilling to hold a portfolio with a combined standard deviation in excess of 6 percent. In addition to this restriction on total variability of return, he feels that, to keep his ulcer under control, the proportion invested in speculative stocks must be limited to 0.4. Finally, he cannot invest negative amounts in any type of security.[6] The problem can be summarized as follows:

$$\text{Maximize} \quad Z = 14X_1 + 10X_2 + 8X_3 + 7X_4 + 5X_5$$

subject to
(1) $X_1 + X_2 + X_3 + X_4 + X_5 \leq 1$ total funds
(2)[7] $10X_1 + 5X_2 + 4X_3 + 2X_4 + 0X_5 \leq 6$ total risk
(3) $X_1 \leq 0.4$ speculative stock
(4) $X_1 \geq 0$
(5) $X_2 \geq 0$
(6) $X_3 \geq 0$
(7) $X_4 \geq 0$
(8) $X_5 \geq 0$

The slack variables again are used as the initial basic solution. The initial solution and the iterations leading to the optimal solution are presented in the tableaus below (Exhibits 6–13 through 6–16).

Exhibit 6–13 Initial Solution

	X_1	X_2	X_3	X_4	X_5	X_6	X_7	X_8	
X_6	1	1	1	1	1	1	0	0	1
X_7	10	5	4	2	0	0	1	0	6
X_8	1	0	0	0	0	0	0	1	0.4
NC	14	10	8	7	5	0	0	0	0

Exhibit 6–14 First Iteration: X_1 Replaces X_8

	X_1	X_2	X_3	X_4	X_5	X_6	X_7	X_8	
X_6	0	1	1	1	1	1	0	−1	0.6
X_7	0	5	4	2	0	0	1	−10	2
X_1	1	0	0	0	0	0	0	1	0.4
NC	0	10	8	7	5	0	0	−14	−5.6

[6] This restriction means he cannot, for example, borrow from the bank (a negative X_5) to increase his investment in other types of securities.

[7] This equation assumes that the variability of returns for all securities is perfectly positively correlated (see Chapter 13). This constraint is simply a weighted average of the standard deviations of the components of the portfolio.

Exhibit 6–15   Second Iteration: X_2 Replaces X_7

	X_1	X_2	X_3	X_4	X_5	X_6	X_7	X_8	
X_6	0	0	0.2	0.6	1	1	−0.2	1	0.2
X_2	0	1	0.8	0.4	0	0	0.2	−2	0.4
X_1	1	0	0	0	0	0	0	1	0.4
NC	0	0	0	3	5	0	−2	6	−9.6

Exhibit 6–16   Third Iteration: X_8 Replaces X_6

	X_1	X_2	X_3	X_4	X_5	X_6	X_7	X_8	
X_8	0	0	0.2	0.6	1	1	−0.2	1	0.2
X_2	0	1	1.2	1.6	2	2	−0.2	0	0.8
X_1	1	0	−0.2	−0.6	−1	−1	0.2	0	0.2
NC	0	0	−1.2	−0.6	−1	−6	−0.8	0	−10.8

The optimal portfolio should consist of 20 percent speculative stocks and 80 percent mutual funds. The other three types of securities should not be included. The expected return from this portfolio would be 10.8 percent. X_7, the slack variable for the total risk constraint, is not a basic variable in the final optimal solution. We therefore know that the standard deviation of the expected return of the optimal portfolio is 6 percent (the maximum permitted by the total risk constraint). Another constraint specified a maximum value of X_1 of 0.4, although a value of 0.2 is specified for X_1 in the final solution. The difference is accounted for by X_8, the associated slack variable.

A MINIMIZATION PROBLEM

The constraints in the examples discussed so far have all been in the form of "less than or equal to" inequalities. It is possible that some constraints could be equalities or in the form of "greater than or equal to" inequalities. There would be no slack variable in the former case, and a negative slack would be required in the latter case. This would preclude the use of the slack variables as an initial basic solution. There are several alternative methods for obtaining an initial solution. The most convenient one involves the introduction of *artificial variables*. One artificial variable would be added to each constraint that is not in "less than or equal to" form. These variables are used solely as a convenient means of finding an initial solution, and have no physical significance in the sense that slack variables do. Each artificial variable could be assigned a *large* negative unit contribution in the objective function to ensure that it would not appear in the final optimal solution.

The optimal solution could be the one that minimizes, rather than maximizes, the objective function. For example, many problems are formulated to minimize total cost. Most minimization problems, such as the one presented in Chapter 5, have "greater than or equal to" constraints as discussed above. One way to handle minimization problems is to reverse most of the steps outlined in the chapter for the basic simplex procedure. The variable with the largest *negative* net contribution should be entered into the basic solution, and the optimal solution would be reached when all net contribution values are zero or positive. A second procedure would be to multiply the objective function by -1 and then proceed as usual. Multiplication by -1 would convert a minimization problem to a maximization problem.

To illustrate the use of artificial variables in a simple example, let us solve the following minimization problem.

Minimize $Z = 3X_1 + 2X_2$

subject to (1) $X_1 + X_2 \geq 10$
(2) $2X_1 + 3X_2 \geq 24$
(3) $X_1 \geq 0$
(4) $X_2 \geq 0$

Notice that, to remove the inequalities of the first two constraints, slack variables must be introduced with negative coefficients. Thus these slack variables cannot serve as the initial basic solution. We therefore add an artificial variable, with a positive unity coefficient, to each constraint to obtain an initial feasible solution. Since this is a minimization problem, each artificial variable must be assigned a large positive unit contribution in the objective function to ensure that it will not appear in the final solution.

The slack variables are X_4 and X_6. The artificial variables are X_3 and X_5. The artificial variables are each assigned an arbitrary unit contribution of 20. With these additions, the problem can be rewritten as follows:

Minimize $3X_1 + 2X_2 + 20X_3 + 0X_4 + 20X_5 + 0X_6$

subject to (1) $X_1 + X_2 + X_3 - X_4 = 10$
(2) $2X_1 + 3X_2 + X_5 - X_6 = 24$
(3) $X_1 \geq 0$
(4) $X_2 \geq 0$
(5) $X_3 \geq 0$
(6) $X_4 \geq 0$
(7) $X_5 \geq 0$
(8) $X_6 \geq 0$

Using the artificial variables as the initial solution, the initial tableau is given below in Exhibit 6–17. Notice that when the initial solution includes artificial variables, rather than consisting entirely of slack variables, the initial value of the objective function is not equal to zero. However, since the value of the objective function is based on the values arbitrarily assigned to the artificial variables, the initial value is meaningless. Moreover, the value of the objective function will be meaningless as long as an artificial variable is contained in the basic solution.

Exhibit 6–17   Initial Solution

	X_1	X_2	X_3	X_4	X_5	X_6	
X_3	1	1	1	−1	0	0	10
X_5	2	3	0	0	1	−1	24
NC	−57	−78	0	20	0	20	−680

X_2 replaces X_5 in the second iteration. The second and third tableaus are given in Exhibits 6–18 and 6–19.

Exhibit 6–18   First Iteration: X_2 Replaces X_5

	X_1	X_2	X_3	X_4	X_5	X_6	
X_3	$\frac{1}{3}$	0	1	−1	$-\frac{1}{3}$	$\frac{1}{3}$	2
X_2	$\frac{2}{3}$	1	0	0	$\frac{1}{3}$	$-\frac{1}{3}$	8
NC	−5	0	0	20	26	−6	−56

Exhibit 6–19   Second Iteration: X_6 Replaces X_3

	X_1	X_2	X_3	X_4	X_5	X_6	
X_6	1	0	3	−3	−1	1	6
X_2	1	1	1	−1	0	0	10
NC	1	0	18	2	20	0	−20

In the optimal solution, all nonbasic variables have *positive* net contribution values. The value of the objective function is 20. $X_2 = 10$, $X_6 = 6$, and $X_1 = X_3 = X_4 = X_5 = 0$.

RESTRICTIVE ASSUMPTIONS

The optimal solution given in Exhibit 6–16 is unique. This is because the net contribution values for all the nonbasic variables were negative. If any had had a positive value, the solution could have been improved by introducing that variable into the set of basic variables to completely replace another variable. Bringing in a variable with a negative net contribution, however, would worsen the solution. If a nonbasic variable has a zero net contribution, it could be substituted for one of the basic variables with no net effect on the value of the objective function. In this case, we could obtain an optimal solution, but it would not be unique.

There are certain situations where the general simplex procedures outlined above will break down, although these are more of a theoretical than a practical problem. Some of these situations result in a condition known as *degeneracy*. Degeneracy can occur when there is a tie between two or more variables for removal from the basic solution. In other words, a nonbasic variable could be substituted for more than one basic variable. While theoretically this could result in the computations becoming entrapped in a perpetual loop, there is no known case of such cycling occurring in actual problems. Any arbitrary but systematic rule, such as choosing the first variable from those involved in the tie, should handle any problems satisfactorily.

Finally, after developing the LP computational techniques in this and the preceding chapter and before discussing the interpretations of the final solution in the next, we should make a few brief comments on the mathematical assumptions and restrictions that affect the applicability of this widely used model. The fact that an actual situation must be represented by a system of linear equations is, of course, of major importance.[8] This means that inputs and outputs are assumed to be strictly proportional to one another. For example, doubling the input will double the output, and doubling the output will double the contribution. It also ignores the possibility of interactions among different activities. In other words, it makes no difference whether activities are performed separately or simultaneously. If activities are not proportional and additive, the system is not truly linear (although a LP model might still be a good approximation).

No decision variable can have a negative value. Thus caution must be exercised when one is structuring problems involving borrowing or dipping into inventories. The final solution can be expressed in terms of fractions of units. This may or may not be an actual possibility. When it is not, integer programming (see Chapter 8) can be used. Finally, notice that the data are assumed to be known with certainty. The model is deterministic rather than probabilistic. Special techniques must be used when the parameters are not known.

There obviously will be few problems that fit perfectly into a LP framework. Nevertheless, LP models have valuable and widespread applicability. The burden is on the user to recognize a situation that can be reasonably represented by a LP model, correctly formulate and solve the

[8] Quadratic programming involves the optimization of a quadratic objective function subject to a set of linear constraints. The algorithm for solving these problems is much more complicated than the simplex algorithm.

problem, and accurately interpret the final results. He must be satisfied that the required assumptions and approximations do not distort the problem to the extent that the final solution is misleading or unreliable.

PROBLEMS

1. Solve Problem 1 at the end of Chapter 5, using the simplex method.
2. Solve Problem 5 at the end of Chapter 5, using the simplex method.
3. The Steinem Corporation manufactures dress-up dolls for little girls. Final assembly of the dolls is accomplished by a small group of trained workers. Due to space limitations, the working group may not exceed ten in number. The firm's operating budget allows $6750 per month as salary for the group.

   A certain amount of discrimination is evidenced by the fact that the firm pays men in the group $750 per month, while women doing the same work receive $600. However, previous experience has indicated that a man will produce about $1500 in "value added" per month, while a woman worker adds only $1350. If the firm wants to maximize the value added by the group, how many men and how many women should be included?

4. Solve the following problem using the simplex method.

   Maximize $Z = 10X_1 + 7X_2 + 12X_3 + 9X_4$

   subject to $3X_1 + X_2 + 4X_3 + 2X_4 \leq 120$
   $X_2 + 2X_3 \leq 80$
   $2X_1 + 2X_2 + 3X_4 \leq 90$
   $X_1, X_2, X_3, X_4 \geq 0$

5. A contractor is laying out plans for a suburban development that will be built on a 60-acre plot of ground. He can build four variations of his classic Ticky Tacky model. The basic model is a three-bedroom house on a leveled $\frac{1}{4}$-acre lot. It would take 10 man-days to complete and would return a profit of $3000. The same house on a wooded lot would take 12 man-days to build and would earn the contractor an extra $1000. He could build a four-bedroom version on a barren $\frac{1}{2}$-acre lot in 12 man-days that would earn him $4500. The larger house could be built on a wooded lot in 15 man-days and would return $5500. He has 18 workers available, and he estimates that the weather will allow 150 working days before the development must be completed. He also feels that, because of pressure from the surrounding community, he should not strip the trees from more than 100 lots.
   a. Formulate the objective function and constraints. Clearly label each constraint.
   b. If his objective is to maximize his total profit, how many of each variation should the contractor plan to build? What will be his total profit?
   c. What effect does the community pressure have on the contractor's plans?
6. Using the information in Problem 5, assume that the decision of how many houses to build now rests with a municipal planning committee (which will also bow to community pressure regarding wooded lots). The basic house will yield annual tax revenues of $700. On a wooded lot, it will yield $800. The four-bedroom model will result in $1000 in tax revenues on a leveled lot and $1100 on a wooded lot.
   a. If the objective now is to maximize tax revenues, how many of each house will be built?

b. What will be total tax revenues and the contractor's total profit?
c. What is the effect of community pressure?
d. Discuss any differences in your answers to parts a, b, and c of Problems 5 and 6.

7. Rework Problem 6 from Chapter 5, using the simplex method.

8. Solve the following problem, using the simplex method.

Maximize $Z = X_1 + 3X_2 + X_3$

subject to $4X_1 + 6X_2 \leq 120$
$X_1 + 4X_3 \leq 100$
$3X_2 + 2X_3 \leq 90$
$X_2 \leq 40$
$X_1, X_2, X_3 \geq 0$

9. Solve the following problem, using the simplex method.

Maximize $Z = 4X_1 + 2X_2 + 5X_3 + 2X_4$

subject to $2X_1 + 3X_2 + X_3 \leq 150$
$3X_1 + 2X_3 + 4X_4 \leq 120$
$X_1 + 2X_2 + 2X_3 \geq 50$
$X_1, X_2, X_3, X_4 \geq 0$

10. Solve the following problem, using the simplex method.

Minimize $Z = X_1 + 3X_2 + 4X_3$

subject to $2X_1 + 4X_2 + 3X_3 \geq 60$
$3X_1 + 2X_2 + X_3 \geq 60$
$2X_1 + X_2 + 3X_3 \leq 90$
$X_1, X_2, X_3 \geq 0$

7
interpretation
of results:
final tableau
and dual

A great deal more information is contained in the final solution of a LP problem than the specification of how many units of each product should be produced or what proportion of each type of security should be included in a portfolio. Brief references to some of the information contained in the final tableau were made in the previous chapter, but they were limited and largely incidental. In the first section of this chapter, we shall analyze more fully the informational content of the final solution. In the second section, we shall examine the dual formulation of a LP problem.

INTERPRETATION OF FINAL TABLEAU

A thorough understanding of the concept of equivalent linear combinations of activities that was developed in Chapter 6 is fundamental to gaining maximum benefit from a final simplex solution. These equivalent combinations specify the trade-offs that should be made if, for some reason, we are forced to deviate from the optimal solution. They also allow us to find the effect these deviations would have on the value of the objective function.

Revised Poster Problem

Let us return to the modified poster problem that was presented in Chapter 6 and see what additional information we can glean from the final solution.

For convenience, the problem is repeated below.

Maximize $Z = 1.50X_1 + 0.75X_2 + 1.40X_1' + 0.65X_2' + 0X_3 + 0X_4 + 0X_5$

subject to
(1) $0.75X_1 + 0.25X_2 + 0.75X_1' + 0.25X_2' \leq 250$ paper

(2) $X_1 + 2X_2 \leq 480$ printing

(3) $X_1 + X_1' \leq 100$ demand

(4) $X_1 \geq 0$

(5) $X_2 \geq 0$

(6) $X_1' \geq 0$

(7) $X_2' \geq 0$

The variables X_1 and X_2 represent, respectively, the number of high- and low-quality posters that are produced and X_1' and X_2' represent, respectively, high- and low-quality posters where the printing has been subcontracted. The final simplex tableau is

Exhibit 7–1

	X_1	X_2	X_1'	X_2'	X_3	X_4	X_5	
X_2'	2.5	0	3	1	4	−0.5	0	760
X_2	0.5	1	0	0	0	0.5	0	240
X_5	1	0	1	0	0	0	1	100
NC	−0.50	0	−0.55	0	−2.60	−0.05	0	−674

Variables X_3, X_4, and X_5 are the slack variables for the paper, printing, and demand constraints, respectively. From this solution, we know immediately that 240 units of X_2, 760 units of X_2', and no units of X_1 or X_1' should be produced. X_3 and X_4 are nonbasic variables, so the paper budget and printing capacity both are being fully utilized. There is no slack. X_5, the slack variable for the quality poster demand constraint, is equal to 100 units. This is consistent with the result that no units of X_1 or X_1' should be produced in an optimal solution. The value of the objective function is $674. The fact that all the nonbasic variables have negative net contribution values tells us that the solution is optimal and unique.

Deviations from Optimal Solution

The information from the final solution is read easily from the tableau, is consistent, and seems complete. What happens, however, if we are forced to deviate from the final solution? Suppose it is necessary to produce some of the nonbasic variables, or some of the constraints are changed? Is it then necessary to reformulate and resolve the problem? The answer generally is "No." As indicated above, a full comprehension of the trade-offs prescribed by the final tableau will enable us to answer these questions in most cases. The exceptions will be indicated later in the discussion.

Production of a Nonbasic Variable

Let us briefly review what is meant by linear equivalent combinations of activities. In Chapter 6 we found that, at each iteration, it was necessary to express each of the nonbasic activities as a linear combination of the basic activities. From the above tableau, it is seen that $X_1 \equiv 2.5X_2' + 0.5X_2 + X_5$. The inputs required to produce one unit of X_1 are equivalent to the combined inputs necessary to produce 2.5 units of X_2', 0.5 unit of X_2, and 1 unit of X_5.[1] Furthermore, this equality specifies the trade-offs that should be made if it were necessary to produce one unit of X_1. The production of the other basic variables should be reduced accordingly.

We can now examine these trade-offs in terms of the original constraints. One high-quality poster requires three times as much of the paper budget as one low-quality poster. When X_1 is increased by one, X_2' and X_2 are decreased by a total of $2.5 + 0.5 = 3$. This gives the required 1-to-3 paper budget trade-off. A high-quality poster consumes only half the printing time that a low-quality poster consumes. Thus the production of one unit of X_1 requires the sacrifice of only 0.5 unit of X_2. (X_2' consumes none of the available printing time, because the printing of a unit of X_2' is subcontracted.) There is a one-to-one trade-off between X_1 and X_5. But remember that X_5 is the slack variable for the high-quality poster demand constraint. Increasing actual production by one unit must necessarily reduce the associated slack variable by one unit.

Once these trade-offs are known, the net contribution values follow immediately.[2] X_1 has a unit contribution of \$1.50. The gain resulting from the production of one unit of X_1 would be countered, however, by the necessary decreases in the basic variables. The unit contributions of the basic variables are \$0.65 for X_2', \$0.75 for X_2, and \$0 for X_5. These values can be obtained directly from the objective function. Thus the net contribution of X_1 is computed as follows:

$$\text{NC of } X_1: 1.50 - 2.5(0.65) - 0.5(0.75) - 1(0) = -0.50$$

The same procedure is used to compute the net contributions of the other nonbasic variables.[3]

$$\text{NC of } X_1': 1.40 - 3(0.65) - 0(0.75) - 1(0) = -0.55$$

$$\text{NC of } X_3: 0 - 4(0.65) - 0(0.75) - 0(0) = -2.60$$

$$\text{NC of } X_4: 0 - (-0.5)(0.65) - (0.5)(0.75) - 0(0) = -0.05$$

---

[1] For purposes of discussion, we shall refer to a reduction in the slack of some constraint as "production" of the associated slack variable.

[2] These net contribution values are given various names by different writers. For example, they are also commonly referred to as shadow prices or imputed prices. We should perhaps mention that they are *not* related to traditional accounting prices, but they are the same as the economist's marginal cost concept.

[3] Clearly, the net contribution of each basic variable must be zero.

These trade-offs would be maintained proportionately if it were necessary to increase a nonbasic variable by more than one unit. Suppose, for example, ten high-quality posters are required for display purposes in retail stores. This simple request creates several problems. First of all, should the company or the subcontractor do the printing for these ten quality posters? That is, should 10 units of X_1 or X_1' be produced? The net contribution values tell us that the production of each unit of X_1 will decrease the value of the objective function by \$0.50, whereas producing a unit of X_1' will force a decrease of \$0.55. The least expensive alternative should be chosen, so 10 units of X_1 should be produced. (The printing will not be subcontracted.) The objective function will decline by 10(\$0.50), or \$5.00. The new value will be \$674 − 5 = \$669. If X_1 is increased by 10 units, something else must decrease to make the required inputs available. The trade-offs are simply 10 times what was specified for a one-unit increase in X_1. X_2' should decrease by 10(2.5) = 25 units, X_2 should decrease by 10(0.5) = 5 units, and X_5 should decrease by 10(1) = 10 units. The new optimal solution (given the additional constraint that $X_1 + X_1' = 10$) is $X_1 = 10$, $X_2 = 240 − 5 = 235$, $X_2' = 760 − 25 = 735$, $X_5 = 100 − 10 = 90$, and $X_1' = X_3 = X_4 = 0$. This new solution is obtained directly from the old one, and it is not necessary to rework the problem.

Change in Available Capacity

The quality control department wants the printing machine shut down for 20 minutes a day for cleaning, adjusting, and other routine maintenance. This would be equivalent to reducing the available printing capacity or, alternatively, to increasing the slack capacity by 20 minutes. When the capacity limit of any constraint is changed, the effect on the final solution can be ascertained by looking at the associated slack variable. Thus, the effect of the quality control department's request is analyzed by setting $X_4 = 20$. The value of the objective function would decrease by 20(0.05) = \$1.00, to \$673. The value of X_2' would *increase* (notice the negative sign in the tableau) by 20(0.05) = 10 units to 770, the value of X_2 would decrease by 20(0.5) = 10 units to 230, and the value of X_5 would not change.

Notice in the original printing time constraint that each low-quality poster consumes 2 minutes of printing time. Reducing the capacity by 20 minutes would, therefore, reduce production by 10 units. This decline in production would in turn create some slack in the paper budget, although this slack could be utilized by subcontracting the printing. Thus the net effect of the maintenance time requirement is to shift the printing of 10 low-quality posters from the firm to the subcontractor. The unit contribution of subcontracted posters is \$0.10 less than if the firm did the printing. Ten posters at \$0.10 each gives the \$1.00 decline in the value of the objective function. We see, then, that the changes specified by the final solution are consistent with the initial statement of the problem.

Constraint limits can be increased as well as decreased, and the basic analytical concepts remain the same. Suppose a worker will put in one hour of overtime at the printing machine. The cost to the firm for this additional 60 minutes of printing capacity would be $5.00. Should the firm retain the worker for the extra hour or not? We again look at X_4, the printing time slack variable, to obtain an answer. Just as a reduction in capacity (or an increase in slack) will decrease the value of the objective function by $0.05 per minute lost, a gain in capacity will increase the value of the objective function by $0.05 per minute gained. If an additional 60 minutes are available, the total increase in the objective function is 60(0.05) = $3.00. If it would cost $5.00 to realize a gain of $3.00, the firm should not accept the overtime offer. If the hourly cost is in excess of $3.00, the offer should be rejected.

Management feels that the $250 paper budget was set rather arbitrarily, and they are currently considering changing it. Should they increase it or decrease it? We must look at X_3, the slack variable associated with the paper budget constraint. If the budget (or capacity) is decreased by $1.00 (or one unit), the value of the objective function will decrease by $2.60. On the other hand, if the budget is increased by $1.00, the value of the objective function will increase by $2.60. This clearly would be an attractive trade-off.

If the budget is increased by $1.00, the production of X_2' (low-quality posters with the printing subcontracted) would be increased by 4 units. (Notice that the paper for each low-quality poster costs $0.25). The unit contribution of each unit of X_2' is $0.65. Thus the net contribution is 4(0.65) = $2.60 per dollar added to the budget.

On the basis of the original formulation of the problem, there would be no limit on the amount by which the paper budget could be increased. Every additional dollar would mean four more subcontracted low-quality posters. In reality, however, there would probably be constraints resulting from limited market demand, limited subcontracting capacity, and limited funds with which to increase the budget. Suppose the most binding of these possible constraints would be a total daily market demand for low-quality posters of no more than 1200 posters. You should see that the paper budget should be increased by $50, and the production of X_2' should be increased by 200 units.

Need To Resolve Problem

There are occasions when it is necessary to deviate from the optimal solution and the final simplex solution will not provide the optimal trade-offs. Suppose, on one particular day, it is necessary to produce 270 high-quality posters and the printing must be done by the subcontractor. In other words, it is necessary to set $X_1' = 270$ units. According to the final tableau, the effect on the original basic variables would be to decrease X_2' by 270(3) = 810 units, X_2 by 270(0) = 0 units, and X_5 by 270(1) = 270 units. The value of the objective function would be decreased by 270(0.55) = $148.50. These changes are impossible, however, because they would result in a value of $X_2' = -50$ units and a value of $X_5 = -170$. No variable can have a negative value. In this case, a new constraint of $X_1' = 270$ would have to be added to the original problem and the problem would have to be resolved. Whenever the indicated trade-offs result in the negative value, it is necessary to reformulate and resolve the problem.

Sensitivity Analysis and Parametric Programming

The analysis performed above is an example of sensitivity analysis, a procedure for determining the ranges of values the parameters of the problem can assume without affecting the net contribution values. For example, we found above that setting $X_1 = 90$ units resulted in a value of $X_2' = -30$ units. Since this would be an impossible occurrence, it would be necessary to restate and resolve the problem.

The change in X_2' ($\Delta X_2'$) will be three times the change in X_1' ($3\Delta X_1'$). Thus the maximum possible $\Delta X_1'$ that would not require restating and resolving the problem would be $3\Delta X_1' = 240$ units (the value of X_2' in the original solution). If $\Delta X_1' = 80$, X_2' will be reduced to zero. Sensitivity analysis uses these techniques for analyzing activity and resource trade-offs to determine the changes in constraints, numbers of units produced, and prices that are possible without necessitating a complete restructuring of the problem.

While sensitivity analysis focuses on the ranges of parameter values within which deviations from the optimal solution can be examined without affecting the net contribution values, parametric programming is used to examine deviations from the optimal solution as the amount of available resources varies over a wide range. Parametric programming might be used, for example, to determine the changes in a net contribution value as the available capacity for a given constraint is varied.

The difference between these techniques can be illustrated through a simple example. We found above that a $1.00 increase in the paper budget resulted in a net contribution of $2.60. Assuming that the total daily market demand for low-quality posters would not exceed 1200 posters, it was calculated that the paper budget should be increased by $50 and the production of X_2' should be increased by 200 units. This change would increase the total contribution by $2.60(50) = \$130$.

The above analysis was performed using sensitivity analysis. Management might reasonably wonder, however, about the effect of raising the paper budget by more than $50. Since the unit contribution value for the paper budget would change, this would be a job for parametric programming. Suppose the paper budget is to be increased by $51. After a $50 increase, $X_2 = 240$, $X_2' = 960$, and any further increases in production would have to be for either X_1 or X_1'. Since all internal printing capacity is being utilized, X_1 will remain zero and any increases will be for X_1'.

The unit contribution of X_1' is $1.40 for the original specification of the problem and each unit requires only $0.75 of the paper budget. Thus $1.00 of additional paper budget will allow $\frac{4}{3}(1.40) - 1.00 = $1.86\frac{2}{3} - 1.00 = $0.86\frac{2}{3}$. This result tells us it would be worthwhile for management to increase the paper budget sufficiently to allow the production of 100 units of X_1' (enough to satisfy maximum daily demand). In this revised solution, $X_1 = 0$, $X_1' = 100$, $X_2 = 240$, $X_2' = 960$, the paper budget would be $375 ($250 + 50 + 75), and the total contribution would be $891.67 ($675 + 130 + 86.67).

Portfolio Problem

We shall now examine the final tableau of the portfolio problem presented in Chapter 6. The problem was

Maximize $Z = 14X_1 + 10X_2 + 8X_3 + 7X_4 + 5X_5$

subject to
(1) $X_1 + X_2 + X_3 + X_4 + X_5 \leq 1$ total portfolio
(2) $10X_1 + 5X_2 + 4X_3 + 2X_4 + 0X_5 \leq 6$ total risk
(3) $X_1 \leq 0.4$ speculative stock
(4) $X_1 \geq 0$
(5) $X_2 \geq 0$
(6) $X_3 \geq 0$
(7) $X_4 \geq 0$
(8) $X_5 \geq 0$
X_1 = proportion invested in speculative stocks
X_2 = proportion invested in mutual funds
X_3 = proportion invested in blue chip stocks
X_4 = proportion invested in long-term bonds
X_5 = proportion invested in bank savings account

The coefficient of each variable in the objective function gives the expected percentage return from the associated type of security. The coefficients of the total risk constraint are the standard deviations of the expected returns of each type of security. The problem is to allocate the portfolio among the various types of securities so as to maximize the objective function while satisfying all the constraints.

The optimal simplex solution is presented in Exhibit 7–2.

Exhibit 7–2

	X_1	X_2	X_3	X_4	X_5	X_6	X_7	X_8	
X_8	0	0	0.2	0.6	1	1	-0.2	1	0.2
X_2	0	1	1.2	1.6	2	2	-0.2	0	0.8
X_1	1	0	-0.2	-0.6	-1	-1	0.2	0	0.2
NC	0	0	-1.2	-0.6	-1	-6	-0.8	0	-10.8

This solution indicates that 20 percent of the portfolio should be invested in speculative stocks and 80 percent in mutual funds. The expected return is 10.8 percent. X_7, the slack variable associated with the total risk constraint, is a nonbasic variable. It therefore has a value of 0, and the standard deviation of the expected return of the optimal portfolio is 6 percent.

On the basis of the equivalent linear combinations of activities given in the above tableau, you should be able to verify the net contribution values for each nonbasic variable. We gave detailed explanations of the effects of deviations from the optimal solution of the poster problem. For the portfolio problem, we shall identify a change from the final solution and indicate the effect it would have. Explanations will be less detailed than for the previous example, although you should be able to understand and duplicate the results that are presented. The following changes are not treated cumulatively.

In order to obtain a desired loan, it is necessary to maintain 10 percent of the portfolio in a savings account with the bank. This means that $X_5 = 0.1$. The new values of the original basic variables are $X_8 = 0.2 - 1(0.1) = 0.1$; $X_2 = 0.8 - 2(0.1) = 0.6$; $X_1 = 0.2 - (-1)(0.1) = 0.3$. The new value of the objective function is $10.8 - (1)(0.1) = 10.7$ percent.

The investor desires to spread his portfolio over both fixed and variable income securities. He wants to know what would happen if he allocated 20 percent of his portfolio to long-term bonds. The composition of the new portfolio would be as follows: $X_4 = 0.2$; $X_8 = 0.2 - 0.6(0.2) = 0.08$; $X_2 = 0.8 - 1.6(0.2) = 0.48$; $X_1 = 0.2 - (-0.6)(0.2) = 0.32$. The value of the objective function would be $10.8 - 0.6(0.2) = 10.68$ percent.

Some investment analysts might feel that blue chip stocks could help the investor balance his portfolio almost as well as long-term bonds, and the former have the advantage of a higher expected return. If he put 20 percent of his portfolio into blue chips, however, his overall expected return would be $10.8 - 1.2(0.2) = 10.56$ percent. This is a lower expected return than he would have with the same proportion invested in long-term bonds. (Why, in spite of their lower expected return, do long-term bonds perform better in his investor's portfolio than blue chip stocks? Compare the risk of the two types of securities.)

The problem was formulated in terms of a percentage distribution within the portfolio rather than in terms of the total number of dollars available. What should the investor do if he suddenly receives some extra cash that he can add to his portfolio? The answer is simply to invest the additional money so as to maintain the same proportions as the original portfolio.

The investor feels that perhaps he was too conservative in limiting his overall standard deviation of return to 6 percent, and is thinking about increasing his maximum acceptable risk to 7 percent. To see the effect this change would have, we must look at X_7, the slack variable of the total risk constraint. His new portfolio would be constructed as follows: $X_8 = 0.2 - 0.2(1) = 0;$[4] $X_2 = 0.8 - 0.2(1) = 0.6$; $X_1 = 0.2 + 0.2(1) = 0.4$. The new value of the objective function would be $10.8 + 0.8(1) = 11.6$ percent.

---

[4] Notice that an increase in total risk to a value greater than 7 percent would drive the value of X_8 to a negative value. This is not permissible, so the problem would have to be resolved.

The investor's wife looks at his original guide lines, and is horrified at the possibility of having 40 percent of their portfolio in speculative stocks. She reminds him that he is not as young as he used to be, and that he must start looking ahead to his retirement. He agrees, and sets a maximum limit on X_1 of 25 percent. How does this affect the final solution? It does not. Only 20 percent of his portfolio was originally allocated to X_1 anyway. So the only change in the final solution is to decrease X_8, the associated slack variable, from 0.20 to 0.05. All other values remain unchanged.

THE DUAL PROBLEM

For every LP problem, there exists another LP problem with a very distinct relationship to it. The original problem, such as the ones we have been discussing in this and the preceding chapters, is called the *primal*. The associated problem is called the *dual*. When solving a primal problem we might, for example, want a solution that will specify the production levels of various products that would maximize total profit (or total contribution).

The problem could alternatively be formulated in its dual form, where we would minimize the cost of resources used in the solution. The combination of production levels that maximizes total profit is also the solution that minimizes the total cost of resources utilized in production.

The solution to the dual problem does not contain any information that could not be obtained from the solution to the primal. A thorough understanding of the material in the first section of this chapter is sufficient for a complete analysis of a LP problem. The dual formulation, however, attacks the problem from a different perspective than the primal and emphasizes different relationships. The solution to the primal gives activity or production levels for the product and slack variables. The net contribution values are more or less by-products of the primal solution. These net contributions also are referred to as *shadow prices*, *imputed prices*, or *dual evaluators*. The label "dual evaluators" refers to the fact that the solution to the dual directly yields the values of additional units of resources or capacity. Thus the net contribution values yielded by the primal solution are the decision variables found directly by the dual solution, and vice versa. The relationship between the primal and the dual will be discussed more thoroughly with the example presented in the following pages.

It does not matter how the problem is originally formulated. The dual of a minimization problem is a maximization problem. The dual of a maximization problem is a minimization problem. The dual of a dual is the primal. The dual is obtained by transposing rows and columns of coefficients, reversing the inequalities, and reversing the direction of the objective function; i.e., minimize instead of maximize, or vice versa. There must be one variable in the dual problem for each constraint in the primal and one constraint in the dual for each variable in the primal (excluding slack variables).

Original Poster Problem

Let us return to the original poster problem, which was initially introduced in Chapter 3, to illustrate the relationship between the primal and the dual. The original (or primal) problem is restated below:

Maximize $Z = 1.50X_1 + 0.75X_2$

subject to·
(1) $0.75X_1 + 0.25X_2 \leq 150$ paper budget
(2) $X_1 + 2X_2 \leq 480$ printing time
(3) $X_1 \geq 0$
(4) $X_2 \geq 0$

The optimal solution is to produce 144 units of X_1 and 168 units of X_2. The value of the objective function is $342.
     The problem can alternatively be stated in its dual form. Let

U_1 = value of one unit of paper budget
U_2 = value of one unit of printing time
y = value of total resources used

The dual problem is

Minimize $y = 150U_1 + 480U_2$

subject to
(1) $0.75U_1 + U_2 \geq 1.50$ value of resources for one X_1
(2) $0.25U_1 + 2U_2 \geq 0.75$ value of resources for one X_2
(3) $U_1 \geq 0$
(4) $U_2 \geq 0$

     The dual problem is portrayed graphically in Illustration 7–1. The optimal solution is at corner point B, as shown in Exhibit 7–1. At the optimal

Exhibit 7–1   Evaluation of Corner-point Solutions

Corner Point	U_1	U_2	y
A	0	1.50	720
B	1.80	0.15	342
C	3.00	0	450

solution, $U_1 = \$1.80$ and $U_2 = \$0.15$. The value of the objective function is $342, which is the same value that was obtained in the solution to the primal. This result should always occur. The maximum (minimum) value of the objective function of the primal problem will equal the minimum (maximum) value of the objective function of the dual.

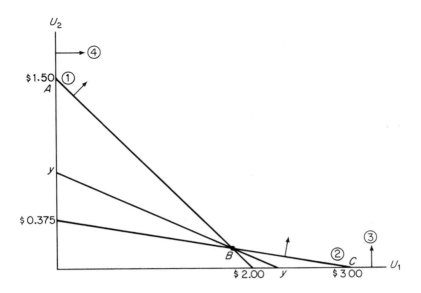

Illustration 7–1 Graphical Solution of Dual Poster Problem

Other results also show a consistent relationship between the primal and the dual. The solution to the dual gives the costs of the two resources (paper and printing) that will minimize the total value of resources used. The values that are obtained for U_1 and U_2 are identical to the net contribution values of the slack variables associated with the paper and printing constraints, respectively.[5]

Just as the primal specifies an optimal production schedule and, through the net contribution values, indicates the value of each resource, so does the dual specify a set of prices that, in turn, indicates the optimal production schedule. Suppose we specify two slack variables, U_3 and U_4, so that constraints (1) and (2) above could be rewritten:

(1') $0.75U_1 + U_2 - U_3 = 1.50$
(2') $0.25U_1 + 2U_2 - U_4 = 0.75$

After adjusting for the negative signs, we can express U_1 and U_2 as linear equivalent combinations of U_3 and U_4.

$$-U_1 \equiv 0.75U_3 + 0.25U_4$$
$$-U_2 \equiv U_3 + 2U_4$$

---

[5] For this reason, and as indicated above, the net contribution values are also sometimes called the *dual evaluators*.

134

In the final solution, U_3 and U_4 are nonbasic variables and U_1 and U_2 are basic variables. Rewriting the above equalities, we can express the nonbasic variables as linear equivalent combinations of the basic variables.

$$U_3 = -\tfrac{8}{5}U_1 + \tfrac{1}{5}U_2$$
$$U_4 = \tfrac{4}{5}U_1 - \tfrac{3}{5}U_2$$

From these equivalent combinations, the net contribution values of U_3 and U_4 can be obtained.

NC of U_3: $0 + \tfrac{8}{5}(150) - \tfrac{1}{5}(480) = 144$
NC of U_4: $0 - \tfrac{4}{5}(150) + \tfrac{3}{5}(480) = 168$

Not coincidentally, these net contribution values are identical with the optimal values of X_1 and X_2 obtained in the solution to the primal problem. Thus the solution to the dual problem provides a convenient interpretation of the primal. The major difference is one of perspective and the choice of which relationships are to be formally emphasized.

PROBLEMS

1. On the basis of the tableau below, answer the following questions (clearly show all work):

	85 X_1	60 X_2	70 X_3	160 X_4	140 X_5	130 X_6	0 X_7	0 X_8	0 X_9	0 X_{10}	
X_7	0	0	0	$-\frac{1}{3}$	$-\frac{1}{3}$	0	1	$-\frac{2}{3}$	$-\frac{2}{3}$	$-\frac{1}{2}$	66.67
X_1	1	0	0	$\frac{8}{3}$	0	0	0	$\frac{1}{3}$	0	0	200
X_2	0	1	0	0	$\frac{8}{3}$	0	0	0	$\frac{1}{3}$	0	66.67
X_3	0	0	1	0	0	0	0	0	0	$\frac{1}{4}$	200
NC	0	0		$-66\frac{2}{3}$	-45		0	$-28\frac{1}{3}$	-20	$-17\frac{1}{2}$	

a. Complete the tableau.
b. Is the solution optimal? Why?
c. How many product variables are there? How many constraints?
d. What are the values of all variables and the objective function?
e. What happens to the value of the objective function if you lose 50 units of capacity in machine 1? If you lose 75 units of capacity?
f. What is the value of an additional unit of capacity on machine 3?
g. What is the value of an additional 150 units of capacity on machine 3?
h. Suppose you have to produce three units of product 4 to meet a contractual obligation. What is the new value of the objective function, and what are the new variable values?
i. Suppose the unit contribution of product 5 increases from 140 to 180. What changes, if any, would you propose in the composition of the above solution?

2. The following is a computer printout from a linear programming problem.

	10	14	8	0	0	0	
	X_1	X_2	X_3	X_4	X_5	X_6	
X_2	2	1	0	$\frac{5}{2}$	0	-2	2000
X_3	-1	0	1	-3	0		100
X_5	1	0	0	20	1	10	200
NC		0	0	-11		-4	

    a. What is the value of the objective function in the above solution?
    b. Complete the tableau. Is this an optimum solution? Why or why not? Very briefly give the reasoning behind your answer.
    c. On the basis of the above solution:
        i. What are the new variable values, and what is the new value of the objective function if five units of X_1 are produced?
        ii. What are the new variable values, and what is the value of the objective function if 10 more units of capacity are made available on the machine corresponding to the first constraint?

3. The final tableau of a simplex maximization problem (primal) is given below.

	0.40	0.28	0.32	0.72	0.64	0.60	0	0	0	0	
	X_1	X_2	X_3	X_4	X_5	X_6	X_7	X_8	X_9	X_{10}	
X_7	0	0	0	$\frac{1}{200}$	$\frac{1}{200}$	$\frac{1}{300}$	1	$-\frac{1}{2}$	$-\frac{1}{2}$	$-\frac{1}{3}$	150
X_1	1	0	0	$\frac{5}{2}$	0	0	0	50	0	0	35,000
X_2	0	0	0	0	$\frac{5}{2}$	0	0	0	50	0	5000
X_3	0	0	1	0	0	$\frac{8}{3}$	0	0	0	$\frac{100}{3}$	30,000
NC	0	0	0	-0.28	-0.06	$-\frac{76}{3}$	0	-20	-14	$-\frac{32}{3}$	$-25,000$

    a. Indicate the value of all variables and the objective function for the optimal solution to the primal problem.
    b. Indicate the value of all variables and the objective function for the optimal solution to the dual problem.

4. Set up the portfolio problem discussed in the chapter in its dual form. Discuss the meaning of all variables, constraints, and the objective function.

5. A partial simplex tableau is given below.

	2	3	1	0	0	0	0	
	X_1	X_2	X_3	X_4	X_5	X_6	X_7	
X_2		1	0	$\frac{1}{6}$	0	0	0	20
X_5	3	0	0	1	1	-2	0	40
X_3	$-\frac{1}{2}$	0	1		0	$\frac{1}{2}$	0	15
X_7	$-\frac{1}{3}$	0	0	$-\frac{1}{6}$	0	0		20
NC	$\frac{3}{2}$	0	0	$-\frac{1}{4}$			0	

a. Complete the tableau.

b. Is the solution optimal? Why?

c. How many product variables are there? How many constraints?

d. What are the values of all variables and the objective function? How are these values interpreted?

e. What happens to the values of the objective function and the product and slack variables if 10 units of X_1 are produced?

f. Repeat e, except for 15 units of X_1.

g. What is the value of an additional unit of capacity on machine 2? On machine 3?

h. What is the value of 20 additional units of capacity on machine 2? Of 60 additional units of capacity?

i. What would happen to the solution if capacity on machine 4 is reduced by 10 units? By 30 units?

j. What would happen to the solution if a market survey indicated that the demand for product 3 will not exceed ten units? What adjustments would be made?

8

integer
programming

It is not required that the decision variables in the solution of a LP problem be integers. Thus it is possible—in fact, probable—that the optimal solution will involve fractional values. It is not difficult to think of many cases where fractional solutions are unrealistic because the units are not divisible. One approach is to round off the linear programming solution to the nearest integers that do not violate the set of constraints. Simply rounding off the linear programming solution may lead to the optimal integer solution, although there is no guarantee that it will. In cases where the numbers of units are small, the optimal integer solution may be drastically different from the rounded linear programming solution.

Consider the following case:

Maximize $Z = 30X_1 + 130X_2$

subject to $X_1 + 4X_3 \leq 11$
$X_1, X_2 \geq 0$ and integer

If the integer constraint is ignored, examining the corner points ($X_1 = 0$, $X_2 = 2\frac{3}{4}$, and $X_1 = 11$, $X_2 = 0$) yields the optimal linear programming solution of $X_1 = 0$, $X_2 = 2\frac{3}{4}$, and $Z = 357.5$. Rounding the noninteger X_2 would yield the integer solution $X_1 = 0$, $X_2 = 2$, and $Z = 260$. (Notice that in rounding we must round down so that our new solution does not violate the constraint.) However, if we were to examine all the feasible integer solutions, we would find that the integer solution $X_1 = 3$, $X_2 = 2$ yields a Z value of 350.0, which is the optimal integer solution.[1] (In practice

---

[1] In this simple problem the optimal integer solution can be found by inspection, but in more complex problems that is usually impossible.

138

so large a percentage difference in the rounded solution and the optimal integer solution usually occurs only when the units of X are small.)

In this chapter we shall discuss a technique known as *integer programming* which will determine the optimal integer solution. It should be obvious that the value of the objective function from the integer programming solution must be less than or equal to that resulting from using linear programming, since all feasible integer solutions are considered in linear programming. Thus we can calculate the possible savings from employing integer programming, rather than rounding the linear programming solution, by subtracting the Z value of the rounded solution from the Z value of the optimal linear programming solution. Since the integer technique is more complex than linear programming, we may choose simply to use the rounded linear programming solution if the potential savings are insignificant.

INTEGER PROGRAMMING ALGORITHM

The integer programming algorithm is an extension of the LP algorithm. We initially ignore the integer constraints and solve the problem using the linear programming simplex method. If the solution is all integer, we are finished. If the solution is not all integer, we add a new constraint to the problem such that the new set of feasible solutions includes all the original feasible integer solutions but does not include the optimal noninteger solution initially found. This new constraint is called a *cut*. We then solve the revised problem using the simplex method and see if we get an integer solution. If not, we add another cut and repeat the process until an integer solution is found. Since we never eliminate any feasible integer solutions from consideration when we add cuts, the integer solution ultimately found must be optimal.

Let us graphically illustrate the procedure using the previous example. The original noninteger solution is shown in Illustration 8–1 as point A. The set of all feasible integer and noninteger solutions is represented by the area below and to the left of the constraint line. Now suppose we add the constraint $X_1 \leq 2$, which reduces the feasible set of solutions to the shaded area. None of the feasible solutions that are eliminated (the unshaded area below and to the left of constraint line segment AB and above the cut) contain integer solutions. Thus the new set of feasible solutions contains all the possible integer solutions of the old problem. Examining the corner points of the new problem leads to the optimal integer solution $X_1 = 2$, $X_2 = 3$ (point B).

In reviewing the procedure for integer programming we see that the only difference from linear programming is that we iteratively add new constraints to the problem. In effect, integer programming is nothing more than the repeated use of the linear programming simplex method. Now let us turn our attention to how we determine what new constraint to add.

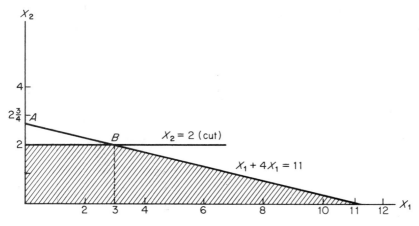

Illustration 8–1   Graphic Solution to Integer Programming

Determining the Cut

To show how we determine the cut or new constraint, let us consider the following integer programming problem.

Maximize $Z = 3X_1 + 4X_2$

subject to   (1) $X_1 + X_2 \leq 4$ (1)
          (2) $\frac{3}{5}X_1 + X_2 \leq 3$ (2)
          (3) $X_1, X_2 \geq 0$ and integer

The method we shall use to determine the cut requires that all the coefficients in the original constraints be integers. This can easily be accomplished by multiplying any constraint by the smallest positive integer that will make all the coefficients integers. In our case we must multiply constraint (2) by 5 and rewrite it as

$$3X_1 + 5X_2 \leq 15 \qquad (2')$$

Solving the problem using the simplex method yields the final tableau given in Exhibit 8–1. The optimal solution ($X_1 = \frac{5}{2}$ and $X_2 = \frac{3}{2}$) is non-integer, so we must find a cut (i.e., new constraint) to add to the problem.

Exhibit 8–1   First Optimal Linear Programming Solution

	X_1	X_2	X_3	X_4	
X_1	1	0	$\frac{5}{2}$	$-\frac{1}{2}$	$\frac{5}{2}$
X_2	0	1	$-\frac{3}{2}$	$\frac{1}{2}$	$\frac{3}{2}$
NC	0	0	$-\frac{3}{2}$	$-\frac{1}{2}$	$-\frac{27}{2}$

Although both X values are noninteger, we can add only one cut at a time. The procedure is to add one constraint, solve the restated problem by using the simplex method, then add another constraint if necessary to obtain another solution, and repeat this process as many times as necessary. To find the cut we arbitrarily choose one of the noninteger X's contained in the optimal solution. In this case let us select X_2. Now let us examine the row in the simplex table corresponding to the noninteger value we selected. We can rewrite the row in terms of only its fractional part F. Any number N can be written as an integer I plus a fraction F. That is, $N = I + F$, *where F is always positive.* For example,

$$\tfrac{3}{2} = 1 + \tfrac{1}{2}$$

$$-\tfrac{1}{6} = -1 + \tfrac{5}{6}$$

Rewriting the row in terms of its fractional part yields

	X_1	X_2	X_3	X_4	
X_2	0	0	$\tfrac{1}{2}$	$\tfrac{1}{2}$	$\tfrac{1}{2}$

This leads us directly to our cut,

$$-\tfrac{1}{2}X_3 - \tfrac{1}{2}X_4 \le -\tfrac{1}{2}$$

In general if we let

$f_i = $ the fractional part of the value in the simplex table under variable X_i in the row corresponding to the noninteger X

and

$F = $ the fractional part of the solution value of the selected noninteger X

then the cut is

$$-\sum f_i X_i \le -F$$

Adding a New Constraint

While the new constraint gives us a new linear programming problem to solve, we fortunately do not have to start the simplex procedure from the beginning again. It is possible simply to slide the new constraint into the simplex table and continue from there. This technique gives results that are equivalent to resolving the problem with a new constraint introduced at the beginning. The procedure for adding the constraint is straightforward. We must first add a new row and a new column to the old simplex table. The new column represents the new slack variable from the additional constraint and would have a 1 in the new column and 0 elsewhere. The new row represents the new constraint and would have $-f_i$ in each X_i column and $-F$ in the solution column. In effect, the new row would be the negative of the row of the non-integer X_i selected, written in terms of its fractional part only. The revised simplex tableau with the new constraint added for the example problem is presented as Exhibit 8–2.

Exhibit 8–2   Revised Simplex with Cut Added

	X_1	X_2	X_3	X_4	X_5	
X_1	1	0	$\frac{5}{2}$	$-\frac{1}{2}$	0	$\frac{5}{2}$
X_2	0	1	$-\frac{3}{2}$	$\frac{1}{2}$	0	$\frac{3}{2}$
X_5	0	0	$-\frac{1}{2}$	$-\frac{1}{2}$	1	$-\frac{1}{2}$ infeasible
NC	0	0	$-\frac{3}{2}$	$-\frac{1}{2}$	0	$-\frac{27}{2}$

cut: $-\frac{1}{2}X_3 - \frac{1}{2}X_4 \leq -\frac{1}{2}$

The solution of the revised tableau is infeasible, since the new slack variable enters with a negative value. Thus before the normal simplex procedure can be used, the revised tableau must be corrected. This can be done by taking X_5 out of the solution and bringing in a new basic variable. In order to find a candidate to bring into the solution, we examine all the negative elements in the X_5 row and select that which, when divided by its corresponding NC value, has the *smallest absolute value*. In our example, we select X_4 to enter, since $|-\frac{1}{2}/\frac{1}{2}| < |-\frac{1}{2}/\frac{3}{2}|$. Having selected the variable to enter the solution, we use normal simplex procedures for bringing a new variable into the solution. The resultant tableau will be feasible, but not necessarily optimal. In our example, we see in Exhibit 8–3 that the revised tableau is optimal and, moreover, integer.

Exhibit 8–3   Revised Simplex Corrected for Infeasibility

	X_1	X_2	X_3	X_4	X_5	
X_1	1	0	3	0	-1	3
X_2	0	1	-2	0	1	1
X_4	0	0	1	1	-2	1
NC	0	0	-1	0	-1	-13

In summary, the integer programming procedure is

1. Solve, using linear programming and ignoring the integer constraints.
2. If solution is integer, problem is solved; if it is not all integer, select one of the noninteger solution values.
3. Using the selected noninteger X, construct a new constraint (cut) and slide it into the simplex tableau.
4. Correct the revised simplex for infeasibility by removing the new slack variable from the solution.
5. Solve for the optimal linear programming solution, using the simplex method.
6. Repeat steps 2–5 until an optimal integer solution is found.

CAPITAL BUDGETING AS AN INTEGER PROGRAMMING PROBLEM

So far we have discussed integer programming as a tool to solve problems in the linear programming structure where the units are in reality non-divisible. However, there are many practical problems that can realistically be structured only as integer programming problems. Such problems revolve around the introduction of a 0, 1 integer variable representing a yes/no choice. One such case that we shall examine is the use of integer programming to structure capital budgeting problems, where the alternative decisions are to invest or not to invest.

Suppose a firm has D_i dollars to invest in year i, where $i = 1, \ldots, t$. There are n different projects that are competing for these funds. Suppose project j requires an investment of d_{ji} dollars in year i. Let P_j be the present value of all future returns from project j. Moreover, let us assume that a project must either be undertaken in year 1 or not undertaken at all. The objective is to maximize the sum of the present value of all future projects within the capital constraints. If we let $X_j = 0$ if project j is not undertaken and 1 if project j is undertaken, then we can structure the problem as the following integer programming problem:

Maximize $\quad Z = \sum_{j=1}^{n} P_j X_j$

subject to $\qquad$ (1) $\sum_{j=1}^{n} d_{j1} X_j \leq D_1$

$\qquad$ (2) $\sum_{j=1}^{n} d_{j2} X_j \leq D_2$

$\qquad$ $\vdots$

$\qquad$ (t) $\sum_{j=1}^{n} d_{jt} X_j \leq D_t$

$\qquad$ (t + 1) $\quad X_j \leq 1$ for all j

$\qquad$ (t + 2) $\quad X_j \geq 0$ and integer for all j

The objective function would then be the sum of the present values of all projects undertaken, since X_j would be 1 if undertaken and 0 if not undertaken.[2] Constraints (1) through (t) would be the budget constraints, since $\sum_j d_{ji}X_j$ would represent the total cost in year i for all projects undertaken. Constraints (t + 1) and (t + 2) indicate that X_j must be 0 or 1.

Exhibit 8-4   Capital Budgeting Problem

| Project | Needed Dollar Investment | | | Present Value of Expected Profits |
	Year 1	Year 2	Year 3	
1	500	425	300	500
2	700	300	200	550
3	200	50	0	100
4	300	100	0	150
Total dollars available to invest	900	500	300	

Consider the following numerical example given in Exhibit 8-4. The problem could be structured as follows:

Maximize $Z = 500X_1 + 550X_2 + 100X_3 + 150X_4$

subject to   (1) $500X_1 + 700X_2 + 200X_3 + 300X_4 \leq 900$
(2) $425X_1 + 300X_2 + 50X_3 + 100X_4 \leq 500$
(3) $300X_1 + 200X_2 \leq 300$
(4) $X_1 \leq 1$
(5) $X_2 \leq 1$
(6) $X_3 \leq 1$
(7) $X_4 \leq 1$
   $X_1, X_2, X_3, X_4 \geq 0$ and integer

Generalizations of the above procedure can be used to incorporate added dimensions encountered in real-world problems. For example, there may be manpower constraints associated with undertaking each project. If we let M_k = the manpower available in period k and M_{jk} = the manpower requirement of project j in period k, we can take into account the manpower requirements by annexing the constraints

$$\sum_{j=1}^{n} M_{jk}X_j < M_k \qquad k = 1, \ldots, t$$

[2] See Appendix A for an introduction to the concept of present value and Chapter 12 for a thorough discussion of capital budgeting techniques.

The problem could also be extended to allow projects to be started in different time periods and to make capital available for investment in any given time period dependent on revenues generated by projects undertaken in previous time periods.[3] However, it should be noted that when integer programming is used, the objective function will always be to maximize expected profits and hence, the decision process does not consider the risk involved with investment (see Chapter 13).

SUMMARY

The technique discussed in this chapter is only one of a variety of methods that have been developed to efficiently solve an integer programming problem. The one given here is not the best in terms of efficiency of solution, but it is one of the easier methods to understand. The primary purpose of presenting this algorithm is to acquaint the reader with the concept of integer programming and to present one approach for solution. A thorough discussion of various methods is beyond the scope of this text; the reader who is interested in pursuing this topic further should examine more advanced texts.

PROBLEMS

1. Explain the following statement: In effect, integer programming is nothing more than continuous repetitions of the linear programming simplex method.

2. What is a cut? What must be done before deciding whether a cut is necessary?

3. Write each constant as the sum of an integer and a positive fraction less than one.

$$\tfrac{7}{2}, \tfrac{5}{6}, -\tfrac{7}{4}, -\tfrac{2}{3}$$

4. Explain the procedure for adding a new constraint.

5. Describe the procedure for determining a cut.

6. Determine the cut given the following noninteger optimal solution.

	X_1	X_2	X_3	X_4	
X_1	1	0	$\tfrac{3}{2}$	1	4
X_2	0	1	$\tfrac{3}{4}$	$1\tfrac{1}{2}$	$3\tfrac{1}{2}$
NC	0	0	$-1\tfrac{1}{4}$	$-1\tfrac{1}{2}$	15

[3] For an extensive discussion the reader is referred to Martin Weingartner, *Mathematical Programming and the Analysis of Capital Budgeting Problems* (Englewood Cliffs, N.J.: Prentice-Hall, Inc., 1963).

7. Solve the following problem, using integer programming.

Maximize $\qquad Z = 2X_1 + 6X_2$

subject to $\quad 3X_1 + 20X_2 \leq 50$

$$X_1 \leq 8$$

$$X_1, X_2 \geq 0$$

8. Consider the following investment data:

Project	Needed Dollar Investment			Present Value of Expected Return
	Year 1	Year 2	Year 3	
1	600	450	300	550
2	750	450	250	600
3	200	50	0	125
4	250	100	0	150
Total dollars available to invest	1000	600	300	

a. Formulate as an integer program problem with the objective function and all constraints.

b. Solve part a.

9. Let M_k = the manpower available in period k and M_{jk} = the manpower requirement of project in period k. Write the manpower constraint.

10. Why is the optimal solution with integer programming less than or equal to that resulting from linear programming?

9

transportation and assignment problems

TRANSPORTATION PROBLEM

A commonly encountered problem is that of determining the minimum cost for allocating a product from several supply sources to several destinations. Such problems, when costs of allocation are linear, are amenable to solution by a special algorithm called the *transportation algorithm*. The transportation algorithm is a specialized application of the more general linear programming simplex algorithm. The steps for solving a transportation problem are

1. Structure the problem into the transportation framework.
2. Find an initial solution.
3. Move from the initial solution to the optimal solution, using the iterative transportation algorithm.

Structure of the Problem

The basic structure of a problem that lends itself to solution by the transportation algorithm is presented in Exhibit 9–1. The solution we are seeking is the minimum cost for the allocation of identical or interchangeable items from n different sources to fulfill the requirements at m various locations. The amount available from source i is a_i and is indicated in the last column, while the amount required by destination j is b_j and is indicated in the last row. Note that a necessary condition for solution is that $\sum_{i=1}^{m} a_i = \sum_{j=1}^{m} b_j$, that is, the total amount available from the various sources must equal the total amount required at the various destinations. If there is an inbalance between sources and requirements, the difference can be accounted for through the introduction of a slack variable.

The allocation of an item from any source to any destination has an associated cost, denoted by c_{ij}. The costs used in the analysis represent the least expensive acceptable method of allocating one item from each source to each destination. The appropriate least expensive cost is not necessarily the lowest dollar method of allocation. Factors such as reliability and speed must be considered and trade-offs made. Thus the appropriate costs represent the unit costs for those methods that management has chosen for allocation.

It is required that the costs associated with allocation be linear. That is, if it costs $10 to transport five items from source i to destination j, it must cost $20 to transport ten items. The unit cost is constant regardless of the amount shipped. In practice, however, we often find that the unit cost is not constant as required in the transportation problem. We are familiar with volume discounts, and, in transportation especially, the unit cost of shipping a full carload is normally considerably less than that of shipping a partially filled car. If destination requirements permit, this problem can be handled by considering each item as a full-car shipment. If this is not possible, then theoretically the transportation algorithm is not appropriate. Nevertheless, if the unit cost does not vary by large amounts, the average unit cost can be used in the transportation algorithm to give a good approximation of the minimum cost allocation pattern.

Exhibit 9–1   General Structure of Transportation Problem

Destination

Supply Source	1	2	. . .	m	Supply
1	C_{11}	C_{12}	. . .	C_{1m}	a_1
2	C_{12}	C_{22}	. . .	C_{2m}	a_2
. . .	. . .	. . .	. . .	. . .	. . .
n	C_{n1}	C_{n2}	. . .	C_{nm}	a_n
Demand	b_1	b_2	. . .	b_m	$\sum a_i = \sum b_j$

The general structure presented in Exhibit 9–1 contains all the data that are necessary for solving the transportation problem. Before discussing the method of solution, let us consider some examples that can be structured in the transportation framework.

Example 9–1   Basic Transportation Problem: Roy Toy Problem

The Roy Toy Company has three plants from which orders from their five wholesale outlets are filled. The orders are placed three times a year—March, June, and September. The capacity and unit costs of each plant are given in Exhibit 9–2. The September orders from each of the stores are given in Exhibit 9–3. The costs for shipping a unit of toys from each plant to each store are given in Exhibit 9–4. This information is all that is required. The problem can readily be structured into the transportation framework, as illustrated in Exhibit 9–5.

Exhibit 9–2   Roy Toy Plant Capacities

Plant	Unit Cost	Capacities
1	12	45
2	14	70
3	15	125
		240

Exhibit 9–3   Roy Toy Order 8/30

Stores	Order Sizes
1	10
2	20
3	30
4	80
5	100
	240

Exhibit 9–4   Roy Toy Minimum Shipment Costs (in dollars)

	Store				
Warehouse	1	2	3	4	5
1	7	10	5	4	12
2	3	2	0	9	1
3	8	13	11	6	14

149

Exhibit 9–5   Roy Toy Problem in Transportation Framework

Store

Plant	1	2	3	4	5	Capacity
1	7	10	5	4	12	45
2	3	2	0	9	1	70
3	8	13	11	6	14	125
Store requirements	10	20	30	80	100	240

Example 9–2   Surplus Supply

Now let us consider a slightly more complex situation. Suppose that the September orders are as in Exhibit 9–6 rather than as in Exhibit 9–3. In this situation the capacity (supply) exceeds the orders (demand). There is a surplus capacity of 20 units. In order to structure a problem for solution in the transportation framework, it is necessary for the supply to equal the demand. This requirement is met by creating a dummy destination that has a demand equal to the surplus supply. For this problem we have to add a dummy sixth store whose order is 20 units. Any entry in the extra column represents unused capacity of the plant in the respective row. The cost associated with shipment from any source to the dummy destination is clearly 0, since it costs nothing not to produce and ship.

Moreover, since there is surplus capacity, and all plants will not be producing at full capacity, the problem becomes not merely to find the minimum cost of shipment, but rather to find the minimum cost method of allocating both production and shipment. Thus the appropriate costs become the total costs of producing and shipping an item from supply source i to destination j. The new cost matrix consists of the transportation cost matrix with the cost of production of supply source i added to each shipping cost in row i.

The revised problem can be structured in the transportation framework as shown in Exhibit 9–7. It should be noted that the revised costs for the dummy destination remain 0. Furthermore, it should be recognized that the costs of production are important only if there is a surplus, so that allocation of production is part of the decision problem.

Exhibit 9–6   First Revised Roy Toy Orders 8/30

Store	Order Sizes
1	10
2	20
3	30
4	70
5	90
	220

Exhibit 9–7   Surplus Roy Toy Problem in Transportation Framework

			Store				
Plant	1	2	3	4	5	6	Capacity
1	19	22	17	16	24	0	45
2	17	16	14	23	15	0	70
3	23	28	26	21	29	0	125
Orders	10	20	30	70	90	20	240

Example 9–3   Shortage

In the last example there was surplus capacity. Let us now examine the situation where a supply shortage exists. Suppose the orders from the store were as given in Exhibit 9–8. We now have a shortage of supply of 25 units. Since, to obtain a solution, it is required that supply equal demand, we have to create a dummy supply source whose capacity equals the amount of shortage. This requires creating a fourth dummy plant whose supply is 25 units. In the solution the shipments appearing in the dummy row would represent the amount of shortage of each order for the column in which it appears. The appropriate costs associated with the dummy supply source represent the costs associated with not fulfilling that particular store's order. In practice, it is usually assumed that it is equally costly to short each destination. If this assumption is appropriate, the costs can arbitrarily be set at any constant.

Suppose we assume that it is equally costly to short stores 2, 3, 4, and 5, but that it is a necessity to fulfill the order from store 1. We could arbitrarily assign a cost of 1 to cells (4, 2), (4, 3), (4, 4), and (4, 5). Cell (4, 1) would be treated in one of two ways. If we are solving by hand, the easiest method is simply to cross out the cell so that no entry can be made to it (since an entry in that cell would represent the shortage for store 1). If we are solving by digital computer, we can simply place an extremely large cost, say 140, or 10 times the largest actual cost. This would preclude this cell from appearing in the final solution and would thus have the same effect as crossing out the cell.

Since there are no production decisions to be made, the appropriate costs for the remaining cells would be those associated with the transportation costs. Exhibit 9–9 presents the problem in the transportation framework.

Exhibit 9–8   Second Revised Roy Toy Orders 8/30

Store	Order Sizes
1	20
2	25
3	30
4	90
5	110
	275

Exhibit 9–9   Shortage Roy Toy Problem in Transportation Framework

Store

Plants	1	2	3	4	5	Capac-ity
1	7	10	5	4	12	45
2	3	2	0	9	1	70
3	8	13	11	6	14	125
4	1	1	1	1	1	25
Orders	20	25	30	90	110	275

Example 9-4   Production Scheduling

In Example 9–2, the transportation problem was modeled for solving simultaneously for the optimal transportation and production decision. Now let us consider a situation where the transportation framework can be used to structure a problem which has nothing to do with transportation.

Polyform Inc., a manufacturing concern, produces a lamp called the Lotus. The sales of the lamp are subject to monthly fluctuations, with some month's demand exceeding the month's regular production capacity. To meet the demand in the high-volume months, the firm can work overtime and/or overproduce in the low-volume months and accumulate an inventory for the high-volume months. The projected demands for the product during the first few months of the year are given in Exhibit 9–10.

Exhibit 9-10   Projected Demand for Lotus Lamp

Month	Projected Sales (in thousands)
January	6
February	8
March	12
April	18
	44

The production facility can produce 10,000 lamps a month without overtime and 18,000 lamps with overtime. However, it costs $5.20 to produce a lamp on the overtime shift compared to $3.80 on the regular shift.

Inventory carrying costs are $1.00 per month per lamp. For simplicity, we shall assume this to be a constant cost regardless of when during the month a lamp is produced. Thus a lamp made in February and sold in March would incur $1.00 in inventory carrying costs regardless of when it was made in February or when it was sold in March. The problem is to determine a production schedule so that storage charges are balanced against overtime charges in such a way as to minimize the total production and inventory carrying costs.

Let us first consider our supply sources. Each of the four monthly regular shifts can supply 10,000 units and the four overtime shifts can supply 8000 units each. The destinations are the four months; the requirements are the demand for each month. Thus the total requirements are 44,000 and the total supply is 72,000 lamps, resulting in a surplus supply of 28,000. Entries in the excess supply column indicate the amount of unused production capacity for the respective shift. This problem, structured in the transportation framework, is presented in Exhibit 9–11. Notice that certain cells represent impossible events. For example, it is impossible to produce on regular shift in March to meet February's demand. Thus those cells are crossed out.

153

Destination

Supply	Jan.	Feb.	March	April	Un-used Capac-ity	Capac-ity
Regular Jan.	3.80	4.80	5.80	6.80	0	10
Overtime Jan.	5.20	6.20	7.20	8.20	0	8
Regular Feb.	✕	3.80	4.80	5.80	0	10
Overtime Feb.	✕	5.20	6.20	7.20	0	8
Regular March	✕	✕	3.80	4.80	0	10
Overtime March	✕	✕	5.20	6.20	0	8
Regular April	✕	✕	✕	3.80	0	10
Overtime April	✕	✕	✕	5.20	0	8
Orders	6	8	12	18	28	72

Now all that is left is to calculate the costs for the remaining cells. This is a simple task. For the rows representing regular shifts, the cost of producing the item to be sold in the same month is $3.80. The cost increases by $1.00 for each month later that it is sold due to storage charges. For overtime shifts the unit cost would be $1.40 higher.

Finding an Initial Solution

The first step in solving the transportation problem after it has been structured is to find an initial solution. If we denote an allocation from supply source i to destination j (cell i, j) by X_{ij}, an initial solution can be defined as a set of X_{ij}'s such that $\sum_{j=1}^{m} X_{ij} = a_i$ for all i and $\sum_{i=1}^{n} X_{ij} = b_j$ for all j. That is, all the supply is allocated to meet all the demand requirements. Once this initial solution is found, the transportation algorithm can be used to find the minimum cost solution.

Since the transportation algorithm moves in a stepwise fashion toward the optimal solution, it is advantageous for the initial solution to be as close to the optimal solution as possible so as to reduce the number of iterations required to reach the optimal solution. Unfortunately, the difficulty of finding an initial solution increases as we try to improve its efficiency. While there are numerous methods for finding an initial solution, we shall restrict our attention to the row minima and the penalties method. The row minima is relatively an easy procedure. The penalties method, while more complex than the row minima method, is also much more efficient. In fact, in many cases the penalties method leads directly to the optimal solution. First, we shall describe the row minima procedure.

Row Minima Rule Begin by choosing the minimum cost in row one. Suppose that it occurs in column r. Set $X_{1r} = \min(a_1, b_r)$. If $X_{1r} = a_1$ (i.e., $a_1 < b_r$), cross off row one and move to row two. If $X_{1r} = b_r$ (i.e., $a_1 > b_r$), cross off column r and determine the next lowest cost in row one. Assume that it occurs in column s. Set $X_{1s} = \min(a_1 - b_r, b_s)$. Continue in this way until the first row total is exhausted. When the requirement of the first row is satisfied, cross off row one and repeat the above procedure for row two. Continue until the last row constraint is satisfied. Whenever a minimum cost within a row is *not* unique, make an arbitrary choice among the minima. In the event that a row constraint, say row k, and a column constraint are satisfied simultaneously, cross off only the column. Then find the next lowest cost in row k, and set $X_{k,s} = 0$, where s is the column with the next lowest cost. Then cross off row k, and move on to row $k + 1$. (This is an example of degeneracy, which will be explained later.)

We can use this method to find an initial solution for the Roy Toy problem presented in Exhibit 9–5. The lowest cost in the first row is in column 4. The minimum of the row and column total is the row value of 45, so we make $X_{14} = 45$ and move to the second row. The minimum cost here is in column 3, so we make $X_{13} = 30$ and cross out column 3. The next lowest cost in row 2 is in column 5, and we can complete the row requirement by making $X_{25} = 40$. Continuing in this fashion, we reach the initial solution as presented in Exhibit 9–12.

Exhibit 9–12   Row Minima Initial Solution to Roy Toy Problem

Store

Warehouse	1	2	3	4	5	Inventory
1				45		45
2			30		40	70
3	10	20		35	60	125
Orders	10	20	30	80	100	240

The cost of this solution is

$$(4)(45) + (0)(30) + (1)(40) + (8)(10) + (13)(20) + (6)(35) + (14)(60) = \$1610$$

The row minima procedure clearly does not always give the lowest column cost. Consider column 2, for example. Instead of using the second row cost of 2, we used the considerably higher cost of 13 in the third row. Since we must make an allocation to at least one cell of each row and column, it clearly would be preferable to consider both row and column costs simultaneously. Thus the penalties method is more efficient, because it is based on the minimum opportunity loss for *not* using the *lowest cost* in both each column and each row. The procedure for the penalties method is as follows.

Penalties Method

1. Compute a penalty for each row and column. The penalties are the difference between the lowest cost in the row (column) and the second lowest cost in the row (column).
2. Find the largest penalty and the corresponding least cost cell for that column or row and allocate as much as possible to that cell (the minimum of the row or column total). In case of ties make an arbitrary choice.
3. Eliminate any row or column that was completely satisfied by the entry in step 2 or reduce any partially filled column or row by the entry in step 2.[1]
4. Continue steps 1, 2, and 3 until a solution is reached.

Now let us reconsider the Roy Toy problem, using the penalties method to find an initial solution. As shown in Exhibit 9–13A, the largest penalty

Exhibit 9–13A Penalties Matrix, Roy Toy Problem

	Store						
Plant	**1**	**2**	**3**	**4**	**5**	**Capacity**	**Penalties**
1	7	10	5	4	12	45	1
2	3	2	0	9	1 70	70	1
3	8	13	11	6	14	125	2
Orders	10	20	30	80	100	240	
Penalties	4	8	5	2	11		

[1] It is possible for an allocation to satisfy simultaneously the row and column. This indicates degeneracy, which is discussed later, but does not alter this procedure. Simply cross out both the column and row and continue.

is associated with column 5 and the lowest column cost is in row 2. Thus we set $X_{25} = 70$, which exhausts the supply of row 2. Next we eliminate row 2, reduce the requirement of column 5 by 70 to 30, and recompute the new penalties for our reduced matrix as shown in Exhibit 9–13B. Now the highest penalty is associated with column 3. Exhibit 9–13C shows the new reduced penalty matrix after column 3 has been eliminated, and Exhibit 9–13D gives the final solution. The cost of the final initial solution is

$$(10)(15) + (5)(30) + (1)(70) + (8)(10) + (13)(5) + (6)(80) + (14)(30) = \$1415$$

a reduction of 195 over the row minima method. In fact, as we shall see in the proceeding sections, this initial solution is the optimal solution.

Exhibit 9–13B First Reduced Penalty Matrix

Plant	1	2	3	4	5	Capacity	Penalties
			Store				
1	7	10	5 / 30	4	12	45	1
3	8	13	11	6	14	125	2
Orders	10	20	30	80	30		
Penalties	1	3	6	2	2		

Exhibit 9–13C Second Reduced Penalty Matrix

Plant	1	2	3	4	Capacity	Penalties
		Store				
1	7	10 / 15	4	12	15	3
3	8	13	6	14	125	2
Orders	10	20	80	30		
Penalties	1	3	2	2		

Exhibit 9–13D Penalties Method Initial Solution to Roy Toy Problem

Store

Plant	1	2	3	4	5	Capacity
1		15	30			45
2					70	70
3	10	5		80	30	125
Order		20	30	80	100	

Degeneracy

Once we have an initial solution, we are ready to use the transportation algorithm to move to the optimal, provided that the initial solution is not degenerate. A solution is *degenerate* if the number of filled cells is less than the number of rows plus the number of columns minus one $(n + m - 1)$. In both previous cases, degeneracy did not exist, since the problem had three rows and five columns, and the number of filled cells was 7. If degeneracy occurs, it can easily be remedied by using the *perturbation technique*. Simply select an empty cell and place ε in it and add ε to the corresponding row and column totals.[2] Epsilon (ε) represents an arbitrarily small number. This new solution is not degenerate. When one is solving by hand, it is easy to carry along the ε's, although it is necessary that $\varepsilon < X_{ij}$ for all $X_{ij} > 0$. It is never necessary to determine ε explicitly. In the final solution, of course, $\varepsilon = 0$. (If a digital computer is used, set ε at a very small number so that it can be eliminated by truncating the last few digits to the right of the decimal.) It should be noted that although degeneracy is most prevalent in the initial solution it can also occur at some subsequent iteration and can be handled in the same way.

Transportation Algorithm

Once we have structured the problem and found an initial nondegenerate solution, we are ready to solve for the optimal solution. Let us refer back to the initial solution for the Roy Toy problem presented in Exhibit 9–12. The cost of the solution was 1610. There are eight empty cells representing eight paths of shipment we have not used. Let us examine the feasibility of using cell (1, 1). We do this by calculating the change in total cost resulting from

---

[2] This assumes the number of filled cells in one shot. If we are more than one short. simply place enough ε's in cells so that the number of filled cells including ε's is $n + m - 1$,

shipping one unit from supply source 1 to destination 1. First, we must recognize that to increase cell (1, 1) by one unit means that we must reduce a cell in row 1 and a cell in column 1 by one unit each in order to keep the row and column sums correct. Moreover, for each reduction in a new row and column we must increase an entry in that row and column to keep the row and column sums constant. For cell (1, 1), the *path of change* is as follows: Increase cell (1, 1); decrease cell (3, 1); increase cell (3, 4); decrease cell (1, 4) (see Exhibit 9–14). Note that in constructing the path of change we use only cells with positive entries (with the exception of the cell under evaluation). We can now use the path of change and respective costs to calculate the change in total cost resulting when one unit is assigned to cell (1, 1) [where $\Delta_{i,j}$ is defined as the change in total cost from using cell (i, j) for one unit].

$$\Delta_{1,1} = 7 - 8 - 4 + 6 = +1$$

Exhibit 9–14   Path of Change Cell (1, 1)

	1	2	3	4	5
1	+			45−	
2			30		40
3	10−	20		35+	60

Thus the use of supply source 1 to ship to destination 1 would result in an increase in total cost of \$1.00 per unit shipped, and hence would not be profitable. Let us next examine cell (1, 2). If we let $C_{i,j}$ equal the cost of shipping 1 item from i to j, the path of change would be

$$C_{1,2} - C_{3,2} + C_{3,4} - C_{1,4}$$

and $\Delta_{1,2}$ would be

$$\Delta_{1,2} = 10 - 13 + 6 - 4 = -1$$

Thus we can improve our solution (decrease total cost) by \$1.00 for each unit shipped from source 1 to destination 2. We can similarly evaluate the possible use of each cell to improve our solution. Exhibit 9–15 presents the path of change and resultant impact on total costs for each empty cell. The solution can be improved by using cells (1, 2), (1, 3), or (3, 3). Since the largest unit improvement results from using cell (1, 3), that is the one we shall use. The largest amount we can shift to cell (1, 3) is the minimum amount in the negative cells in the path of change; i.e., min $(X_{23}; X_{35}; X_{14})$, which is 30.

This rule follows from the fact that each unit shipped via the new cell will reduce the transportation cost of our solution. Thus we continue to increase the number of units shipped through the new cell until the value of one of the negative cells in the path of change is driven to zero. Just as in the simpler technique, each new solution is obtained by one variable completely replacing another in the solution.

Exhibit 9–15 Path of Change and Impact on Total Costs

c_{ij}	Path of Change	Δ_{ij}
1, 1	$C_{1,1} - C_{1,3} + C_{3,4} - C_{1,4}$	$+1$
1, 2	$C_{1,2} - C_{3,2} + C_{3,4} - C_{1,4}$	-1
1, 3	$C_{1,3} - C_{2,3} + C_{2,5} - C_{3,5} + C_{3,4} - C_{1,4}$	-6
1, 5	$C_{1,5} - C_{3,5} + C_{3,4} - C_{1,4}$	0
2, 1	$C_{2,1} - C_{3,1} + C_{3,5} - C_{2,5}$	$+8$
2, 2	$C_{2,2} - C_{3,2} + C_{3,5} - C_{2,5}$	$+2$
2, 4	$C_{2,4} - C_{3,4} + C_{3,5} + C_{2,5}$	$+16$
3, 3	$C_{3,3} - C_{3,5} + C_{2,5} - C_{2,3}$	-2

Thus we get our improved solution by letting $X_{13} = 30$ units, increasing X_{25} and X_{34} by 30, and decreasing X_{23}, X_{35}, and X_{14} by 30. The new solution is presented in Exhibit 9–16. Note that the negative cell that had the constraining amount that could be shifted, $C_{2,3}$, becomes 0 in the new solution. The new solution has $n + m - 1$ filled cells and is therefore nondegenerate. If, however, there had been a tie for the minimum among the negative cells when the shift was made, both cells would have become 0 and the new solution would have been degenerate. This would present no real problem. We would place ε in some empty cell (and add ε to the appropriate row and column) if the current solution were not optimal, so as to eliminate degeneracy in the new solution.

Exhibit 9–16 First Improved Solution to Roy Toy Problem

Plant	1	2	3	4	5	Capacity
1			30	15		45
2					70	70
3	10	20		65	30	125
Order	10	20	30	80	100	240

Store

After making the shift, we now have a new solution and, if necessary, we can repeat the same procedure to improve that solution. Thus the steps of the transportation algorithm are

1. For any solution, calculate $\Delta_{i,j}$ for each empty cell.
2. **a.** If all $\Delta_{i,j}$'s are nonnegative, the solution is optimal and we are finished.
   b. If any $\Delta_{i,j}$ is negative, the solution is not optimal and we proceed.
3. Select the cell with the most negative $\Delta_{i,j}$ and calculate the minimum X_{ij} in the negative cells in the path of change. Increase all the positive cells by that amount and decrease all the negative cells by that amount. (If there is a tie among the negative cells for the minimim X_{ij}, arbitrarily add ε to one of the negative cells and the respective column and row total to correct for the resulting degeneracy.)
4. Repeat steps 1–3 until an optimal solution is found.

The meaning of a 0 unit cost change is of special interest. This means that we could use this cell to create a new solution, and the cost of the new solution would be identical with that of the old solution. Thus, if in our final iteration we have all positive unit cost changes except for one zero unit cost change, the solution we have found is optimal but not unique. Another solution using the cell with the zero $\Delta_{i,j}$ which yields the same minimum cost can be found.

An Efficient Method for Calculating $\Delta_{i,j}$ Fortunately, a simpler procedure exists to evaluate the unit cost change for each cell that does not require calculating the path of change for each cell. The procedure is as follows:

1. Assign to the first row the arbitrary value $U_1 = 1$.
2. For each column in the first row that has an entry, assign the column a value denoted V_j, such that $U_1 + V_j = C_{1,j}$.
3. For each column assigned a number in step 2, find the filled cells in that column. For each filled cell (i, j) assign a number U_i to row i such that $U_i + V_j = C_{i,j}$.
4. For each row in step 3 where a U value was assigned, find the filled cells in that row. For each filled cell (i, j) assign a number V_j to the column j such that $U_i + V_j = C_{i,j}$.
5. Repeat steps 3 and 4 until each row and column has been assigned a number.
6. The unit change in cost for each empty cell is then calculated as

$$\Delta_{ij} = C_{i,j} - (U_i + V_j)$$

The tableau employed in using the U_i, V_j method is presented in Exhibit 9–17.

Exhibit 9–17 Transportation Algorithm Tableau

U_i \ V_j	V_1	V_2	V_3	V_4	V_5	Supply
U_1						a_1
U_2		C_{ij} $\;U_i + V_j$ $\;\;X_{ij}$ $\;\Delta_{ij}$				a_2
U_3						a_3
Requirement	b_1	b_2	b_3	b_4	b_5	

Reconsider the Roy Toy problem and its initial solution given in Exhibit 9–12. Now let us use the transportation algorithm employing the U_i, V_j procedure for calculating the $\Delta_{i,j}$'s. We first set $U_1 = 1$. Then since column 4 is filled in row 1, we set $V_4 = C_{1,4} - U_i = 4 - 1 = 3$. Now since row 3 in column 4 is filled, we set $U_3 = C_{3,4} - V_4 = 6 - 3 = 3$. Continuing, we obtain the U_i and V_j values shown in Exhibit 9–18A. The largest negative $\Delta_{i,j}$ appears in cell (1, 3) so we create a new solution using that cell. The new value of X_{13} is 30, the min (X_{23}, X_{35}, X_{14}). The path of change is shown in the exhibit and the new solution is shown in Exhibit 9–18B. This new solution will be (6)(30), or \$180, less than the previous solution, since we save \$6 for each unit of X_{13} we use.

Exhibit 9–18A Solution of Roy Toy Problem Using Transportation Algorithm, (Δ_{ij}'s computed by U_i, V_j Method)

U_i \ V_j	5	10	10	3	11	a_i
1	7 6 1	10 11 −1	5 11 + (−6)	4 4 45− 0	12 12 0	45
−10	3 −5 8	2 0 2	0 0 (30−) 0	9 −7 16	1 1 40+ 0	70
3	8 8 10 0	13 13 20 0	11 13 −2	6 6 35+ 0	14 14 60− 0	125
b_j	10	20	30	80	100	240

Exhibit 9–18B

U_i \ V_J	5	10	4	3	11	a_i
1	7 6 1	10 +11 (−1)	5 5 30 0	4 4 (15−) 0	12 12 0	45
−10	3 −5 8	2 0 2	0 −6 6	9 −7 16	1 1 70 0	70
3	8 8 10 0	13 13 20− 0	11 7 4	6 6 65+ 0	14 14 30 0	125
b_J	10	20	30	80	100	240

Repeating the procedure on the new solution results in filling cell (1, 2) at a level of 15 units. (The constraining negative X_{ij} is circled, and the path of change is shown.) Exhibit 9–18C gives the new solution, which is $(1) \cdot (15)$ or \$15, cheaper than the previous solution. Examining the solution presented in Exhibit 9–18C, we find that all the $\Delta_{i,j} > 0$, so this solution is optimal. The cost of the final solution is

$$(10)(15) + (5)(30) + (1)(70) + (8)(10) + (13)(5) + (6)(80) + (14)(30) = \$1415$$

Exhibit 9–18C

U_i \ V_J	4	9	4	2	10	a_i
1	7 5 2	10 10 15 0	5 5 30 0	4 3 1	12 11 1	45
−9	33 −5 8	2 0 2	0 −5 5	9 −7 16	1 1 70 0	70
4	8 8 10 0	13 13 5 0	11 8 3	6 6 80 0	14 14 30 0	125
b_J	10	20	30	80	100	240

Maximizing

In some cases, problems can be structured into the basic transportation frame-work, where C_{ij} is profit instead of a cost. The objective is to maximize profit rather than to minimize costs. Such problems can be solved by using the transportation algorithm with only slight modification. Instead of select-ing the largest negative $\Delta_{i,j}$ to determine which cell to fill to improve the solution, select the largest positive $\Delta_{i,j}$. This is because $\Delta_{i,j}$ would now represent the unit change in profit rather than unit change in cost. Thus in the optimal solution all $\Delta_{i,j}$ would be negative or zero. Similarly, fill the cell with the largest $C_{i,j}$ rather than the one with the smallest $C_{i,j}$ when finding an initial solution using the row minima method. When using the penalties method, compute the penalties as the difference between the largest and second largest $C_{i,j}$ in each row and column.

ASSIGNMENT PROBLEM

Consider the problem of assigning n facilities to n tasks in such a way as to minimize some over-all measure. Some examples of such problems would be assigning men to tasks to minimize total time spent, assigning production lines to product lines to minimize total production cost, assigning men to ser-vice calls (where it is assumed that service men work only one call per day, so routing between calls is not considered) to minimize total transportation costs, or matching flights with return flights so as to minimize the time airline crews spend on the ground away from home.

Suppose that we have four men available and four jobs to be done. Each man is capable of doing any job but, due to their individual talents, it takes them different amounts of time to do each job. The problem is how to assign the men to the jobs in such a way as to minimize the total time spent on the jobs. This problem can be structured in the transportation framework with the men being the supply sources, the jobs the destination, the $C_{i,j}$'s the time it takes man i to perform job j, and all $a_i = b_j = 1$.[3] However, when we attempt to find an initial solution it becomes obvious that we need to fill only four cells and our solution is completely degenerate ($n + m - 1 = 7$). Thus solution by the transportation algorithm becomes very inefficient as many iterations will simply shift around the three needed ε's, so that the optimal solution will not be immediately recognized.

Fortunately, such degenerate transportation problems, differentiated as assignment problems, can be solved easily by hand with a special procedure known as the *assignment algorithm*.

Assignment Algorithm

Consider the following trivial cost matrix for an assignment problem in which there are three persons assigned to three jobs (Exhibit 9–19).

---

[3] In the normal transportation problem all $X_{ij} \geq 0$, while here, since we must assign exactly one man to one job, all $X_{ij} = 0$ or 1. However, it can be shown that if $a_i = b_i = 1$, in the optimal solution all $X_{ij} = 0$ or 1.

Exhibit 9–19   Trivial Cost Matrix

	Task		
Person	1	2	3
1	5	[1]	6
2	[2]	7	5
3	6	3	[2]

The solution to this problem is obvious (solution is shown by boxing the appropriate assignments), since the boxed cells represent the smallest costs in each column and row. Consider now the case where the solution is not so obvious, since the smallest cost for each task is in the same row (e.g., Exhibit 9–20). The cost matrix can be altered to make the solution obvious by employing the fact that we can add or subtract any constant from every element of a row or column without changing the decision problem. (Recall the discussion in Chapter 3 on the use of opportunity loss tables and payoff tables. It was clear that only the relative differences are important in the decision problem.)

Exhibit 9–20   Cost Matrix Assignment Problem

	Task		
Person	1	2	3
1	13	12	10
2	7	4	6
3	19	20	21

Suppose, therefore, that we subtract the lowest element in each row from all the elements in that row, so each revised cost represents the opportunity loss from not using the lowest element in each row. The results make the optimal assignments clear, since the boxed assignments yield a zero opportunity loss, as seen in Exhibit 9–21. Suppose, however, instead of first

Exhibit 9–21   Row Reduced Matrices of Exhibit 9–20

Person	1	2	3	Subtracted from Each Row
1	3	2	[0]	10
2	3	[0]	2	4
3	[0]	1	2	19

computing the row opportunity costs, we had computed the column opportunity costs by subtracting the lowest cost in each column from each element in each row. This alteration (shown in Exhibit 9–22a) would not make our solution clear. We then could compute the row opportunity costs for our reduced matrix, and the optimal solution would become evident, since an assignment would exist that has zero opportunity cost (Exhibit 9–22b).

Exhibit 9–22   Reduced Matrix of Exhibit 9–19

	(a) Task				(b) Task			
Person	1	2	3	Person	1	2	3	Subtracted
1	6	8	4	1	2	4	[0]	4
2	0	0	0	2	0	[0]	0	0
3	12	16	15	3	[0]	4	3	12
Subtracted	7	4	6					

The assignment procedure is thus simply to add and to subtract constants to the cost entries of the rows and columns until we have reduced the matrix to the point where a solution exists with zero opportunity cost. The resultant matrix must contain a set of zeros such that no two zeros in the set occur in the same row or column. The assignments corresponding to the cells of the set of zeros is, therefore, the optimal assignment.

Solution Procedure   An efficient procedure exists for reducing the original cost matrix to a reduced cost matrix that contains a set of zeros such that an optimal solution can readily be found. The procedure is as follows.

1. Subtract from each row the lowest cost in the row.
2. From the new cost matrix subtract from each column the lowest cost in the column.
3. Start with column 1 and see if it has only one zero entry. If it does, box it, and cross out all other zeros that occur in the row of the boxed zero. Move to column 2 and see if it has only one zero entry that has not been crossed out. If it does, box it and cross out all other zeros that are in the row. Continue the procedure across all columns.
4. Start with the first row that does not have a boxed zero and see if it has only one zero entry. If it does, box that zero and cross out all other zeros that occur in that column. Move to the next row that does not have a boxed zero and repeat the process.
5. If any zeros remain that have not been boxed or crossed out, use trial and error to box the maximum number of additional zeros. (Remember that only one boxed zero can occur in any row or column.)

6. If the number of boxed zeros equals the number of rows, the optimal solution is given by the boxed zeros. If not, continue.

7. a. Mark all rows that have a boxed zero.

   b. Mark all columns that have zeros (boxed or unboxed) in unmarked rows.

   c. Remove the row marks from all rows that have boxed zeros in the newly marked columns.

   d. Repeat steps b and c until no new rows or columns can be marked.

   e. Draw a line through each marked row and through each marked column.

8. Select the minimum value left uncovered by a line and subtract that value from all values uncovered and add that value to each element that is covered by two lines. (This is equivalent to subtracting that value from every column in which an uncovered element occurs and adding that value to every row. So in effect we continue simply to add and subtract constants from each row and column.)

9. Repeat steps 3–8 until the optimal solution is found.

Exhibits 9–23(a–h) illustrate the step-by-step use of the procedure. The cost of the optimal solution is 15. The reader should notice that the optimal solution to this problem is not unique. Another set of zeros exists that has only one zero in each row and column. The reader should derive this set and show that the cost of this alternative solution is also 15.

Exhibit 9–23

Original Cost Matrix (a)

	1	2	3	4	5
1	5	12	3	6	2
2	5	7	6	5	4
3	4	4	3	2	1
4	5	3	8	6	9
5	6	1	3	7	4

After Step 1 (b)

	1	2	3	4	5
1	3	10	1	4	0
2	1	3	2	1	0
3	3	3	2	1	0
4	2	0	5	3	6
5	5	0	2	6	3

After Step 2 (c)

	1	2	3	4	5
1	2	10	0	3	0
2	0	3	1	0	0
3	2	3	1	0	0
4	1	0	4	2	6
5	4	0	1	5	3

After Step 3 (d)

	1	2	3	4	5
1	2	10	[0]	3	⊠
2	[0]	3	1	⊠	⊠
3	2	3	1	[0]	⊠
4	1	0	4	2	6.
5	4	0	1	5	3

Exhibit 9–23

After Step 4
(e)

	1	2	3	4	5
1	2	10	[0]	3	X
2	[0]	3	1	X	X
3	1	3	1	[0]	X
4	1	[0]	4	2	6
5	4	X	1	5	3

After Step 5
(f)

	1	3	4	5	5
1	2	10	[0]	3	0
2	[0]	3	1	0	0
3	1	3	1	[0]	0
4	1	[0]	4	2	6
5	4	0	1	5	3

After Step 7
(g)

	1	2	3	4	5
1	2	10	[0]	3	X
2	[0]	3	1	0	X
3	1	3	1	[0]	X
4	1	0	4	2	6
5	4	0	11	5	3

After Step 8
An Optimal Solution
(h)

	1	2	3	4	5
1	2	11	(0)	3	0
2	0	4	1	(0)	0
3	1	4	1	0	(0)
4	(0)	0	3	1	5
5	3	(0)	10	4	2

Special Problems

In certain cases, modifications must be made in order to structure a problem so that it can be solved by the assignment algorithm.

One such case would be where the number of rows does not equal the number of columns. In this case, it would be necessary to add dummy rows or columns. If we add dummy columns (tasks), the costs would reflect the costs of not using each facility. If we add dummy rows (facility), the costs would have to reflect the costs associated with not completing each task. In practice, it is usually assumed that this cost is equal for each task or facility, and a constant (usually 0) is assigned to elements in the row or column.

Another special problem occurs when not every facility can be assigned to every task. This can easily be taken into account by simply crossing out the appropriate cell(s) and not considering it (them) in the calculations. If we are using a computer, we can accomplish the same end by assigning an extremely large cost to the appropriate cell(s).

A common problem is the case where we want to maximize rather than minimize. In this case, the cost matrix would represent a profit matrix. The maximization problem can be handled very easily by converting the profit matrix into an opportunity loss matrix (see Chapter 3). Then minimizing the opportunity loss is equivalent to maximizing profit. For simplicity, rather than subtracting the maximum value from each individual row or column, we subtract the largest element in the matrix from all the other elements. This is possible since we can add or subtract any constant from each row or column without altering the basic problem.

The reader should verify for himself that we can convert the new cost matrix derived in Exhibit 9–24 to the appropriate row or column opportunity loss table by simply subtracting the smallest element in each row or column from all the elements in the row or column.

Exhibit 9–24 Example of Maximization Conversion to Assignment Minimization Problem

Profit Matrix				(Cost) Matrix		
8	6	3	subtract	0	2	5
2	5	1	$\xrightarrow{\quad}$	6	3	7
4	6	2	8	4	2	6

PROBLEMS

1. Referring to Exhibit 9–1, describe in words
   a. a_n
   b. b_m
   c. $\sum a_i = \sum b_j$
   d. c_{nm}
2. Referring to Exhibit 9–5, give the value of
   a. a_2
   b. b_3
   c. c_{15}
3. What is meant by linear costs? Is the assumption of linear costs reasonable for all transportation problems?
4. Consider the following transportation framework:

Store

Plants	1	2	3	4	Capacity
1	18	20	17	0	55
2	22	12	11	0	45
Orders	25	35	30	10	100

a. Does this transportation framework represent a surplus supply or a supply shortage?

b. What does column 4 represent and why is it used?

5. The following tables give plant capacities, orders, and minimum shipment costs.

Plant Capacities

Plant	Unit Cost	Capacities
1	15	40
2	10	60
		100

Orders

Stores	Order Sizes
1	25
2	30
3	45
	100

Minimum Shipment Costs (in dollars)

Warehouse	(store) 1	2	3
1	6	5	8
2	10	2	4

Use this information to form a problem in the transportation framework.

6. Suppose the orders in Problem 5 are revised as follows:

Revised Orders

Stores	Order Sizes
1	30
2	35
3	45
	110

Form the revised transportation framework.

7. What is the problem in determining a production schedule using the transportation framework for a product whose demand is not constant?

8. Referring to Exhibit 9–11, explain the meaning of an x entry in
  a. c_{11}, c_{12}, c_{14}
  b. c_{62}
9. In a transportation problem, all the supply is allocated to meet all the demand requirements. Express this statement in mathematical terms.
10. Why is the penalty method more efficient than the row minima rule?
11. Given the transportation framework

		Store			
Plants	1	2	3	4	Capacity
1	2	17	0	11	20
2	3	4	16	14	30
3	12	8	6	7	50
Orders	10	20	30	40	100

find an initial solution and its cost by using
  a. Row minima rule
  b. Penalties method
12. Is this solution degenerate?

	1	2	3	4	
1	20		30		50
2		40	30		70
3	10			70	80
	30	40	60	70	200

13. What are the steps of the transportation algorithm?
14. Referring to Exhibits 9–14 and 9–15, construct the path of change for cell (1, 5) and calculate Δ_{15}. What does the value of Δ_{15} mean?
15. Using Exhibit 9–18B, calculate $\Delta_{1,2}$ using the path of change and compare it to the value obtained by using the U_i, V_j method.

16.

Store

Plants	1	2	3	4	Capacity
1	5	8	1	6	50
2	10	12	4	2	100
Orders	20	30	40	60	150

    a. Find an initial solution using the row minima rule, and then solve by using the transportation algorithm employing the U_i, V_j procedure.

    b. Find an initial solution using the penalties method, and then solve by using the transportation algorithm employing the U_i, V_j procedure.

17. Consider the problem of assigning men to service calls in the context of a transportation problem.

    a. What are the supply sources?

    b. What are the destinations?

    c. What are the costs?

17. Discuss the general relationship between the transportation problem and the assignment problem.

18. Why aren't assignment problems solved by the transportation algorithm?

19. Solve the following assignment problem, where four persons are assigned to four jobs.

Job

Person	1	2	3	4
1	3	5	11	4
2	2	1	6	9
3	8	10	2	7
4	10	6	1	5

10
CPM–PERT

PERT (Program Evaluation and Review Technique) and CPM (Critical Path Method) are used as decision-making aids and tools for analyzing and administering large, complex projects. Projects that best lend themselves to analysis by these techniques consist of many specific independent jobs that generally must be performed in some technological sequence. When the success of a complicated project depends on the scheduled completion of each of its component activities, and when a delay in one job can create delays in several others, the managerial requirements can become as complex —and as important—as the technological requirements. The basic scheduling of these projects can present a seemingly impossible task, to say nothing of the problem of determining an "optimal" schedule.

A project is represented by a diagram, or network, in a PERT or CPM analysis, with each individual activity contributing one element to the diagram. The analytical techniques then draw on elements of dynamic programming, linear programming, and probability theory to plan and control the most efficient sequence of activities. Some examples of undertakings that are readily amenable to PERT or CPM analysis are space and defense projects, residential and industrial construction, research and development, advertising campaigns, computer installations, the erection of stadiums and bridges, manufacturing, etc.

PERT is used for the analysis of complex, nonrepetitive jobs. Since the project to be performed is unique, and there are no historical data to draw from, often only subjective estimates of the times required to complete various components of the over-all job will be available. Nevertheless, these subjective estimates can be used to maintain effective and continuous control over the project, to schedule and budget time so as to avoid delays and meet deadlines, and to obtain probability estimates of realizing various completion dates. CPM is a variation of PERT. It is used for repetitive jobs where some historical cost data are available. Whereas PERT is primarily time-oriented, CPM recognizes cost as well as time. Although many variations are used, and most applications involve very complex projects, the basic concepts of these two techniques are presented below.

PERT

"Activity" and "event" are two words that have very specific meanings when used in a PERT problem. *Activity* refers to the actual performance of some job. Thus pouring a foundation, raking the lawn, attaching a door, and reading the directions are examples of activities. An *event* refers to the starting or the completion of some activity. Foundation started, lawn raked, door attached, and directions started are examples of events. Activities represent the actual performance of a job, so they also require the consumption of a certain amount of time. An event, on the other hand, does not consume time.

Since there is no past experience on which to base estimates of the time required to complete each activity, subjective estimates must be made based on any related experience that is appropriate. Three time estimates are necessary for each activity. These are optimistic, most likely, and pessimistic time estimates, and are denoted by a, m, and b, respectively. Technically, the optimistic and pessimistic estimates represent times that have probabilities of only 1 in 100 of being reached or exceeded. The most likely estimate is the one that has the highest probability of being the actual required time.

PERT calculations involving estimated completion times for *individual activities* are based on the beta probability distribution. The beta distribution is continuous and unimodal, has finite variance, and can be skewed to either the left or right. These properties make the beta distribution ideally suited for use in PERT analysis. The mode of the distribution is the most likely estimate. If the most likely estimate is closer to the optimistic than the pessimistic time estimate (i.e., m is closer to a than to b), the distribution is skewed to the right. If the most likely estimate is closer to the pessimistic than the optimistic time estimate (i.e., m is closer to b than to a), the distribution is skewed to the left. Thus the beta distribution has the important attribute of allowing the most likely estimate the freedom to move between the optimistic and pessimistic estimates. For any activity, the distribution of completion times can be skewed in either direction or symmetrical. Finally, the amount of uncertainty contained in the time estimates can be calculated for a beta distribution. Examples of various time estimate distributions are shown in Illustration 10–1.

Expected Completion Time

The expected time required to complete an activity, $E(t)$, is a weighted average of the three time estimates. The optimistic and pessimistic estimates are each given a weight of 1, and the most likely estimate is given a weight of 4. The formula for $E(t)$ is given in Eq. (10–1).

$$E(t) = \frac{a + 4m + b}{6} \qquad (10\text{--}1)$$

$E(t)$ is the mean of the distribution of possible activity completion times. Thus it is a point estimate that is approximately equal to the average completion time that would be calculated if the same activity were performed a large number of times. But in reality the activity is performed only once, and chances are the actual completion time will be either greater than or less than the expected.

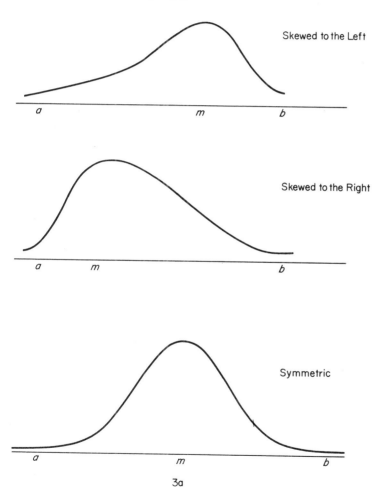

Illustration 10–1   Distributions of PERT Time Estimates

Variance

The larger the dispersion of the probability distribution, the greater will be the probable deviation from the expected time. The variance (discussed in Chapter 2) is a measure of the dispersion of a distribution. The variance of the distribution of possible activity completion times, σ_t^2, is given by Eq. (10–2).[1]

$$\sigma_t^2 = \left(\frac{b - a}{6}\right)^2 \tag{10–2}$$

As an example of the use of time estimates, consider an activity where $a = 4$ weeks, $m = 6$ weeks, and $b = 10$ weeks.[2] The expected time to complete this activity is $E(t) = [4 + 4(6) + 10]/6 = \frac{38}{6} = 6\frac{1}{3}$ weeks. The variance of the distribution of completion times is

$$\sigma_t^2 = \left(\frac{10 - 4}{6}\right)^2 = \left(\frac{6}{6}\right)^2 = 1 \text{ week}$$

PERT Network

Many of the activities in a PERT network must be performed in a definite sequential order. Some activities must be performed in series, and some must be performed in parallel, whereas others may be completely independent of one another. For example, the foundation of a house must be poured before the frame can be erected, both the wiring and the plumbing should be installed before the walls are plastered, while the installation of the windows is not at all dependent on when the doors are hung. Activities that must be completed prior to the start of another activity and must immediately precede it, are called *predecessor activities*. Activities that cannot be started until one or more other activities are completed, and immediately succeed them, are called *successor activities*. When all of the individual activities from an overall project are laid out diagrammatically in their proper and logical sequence, the result is a PERT network.

A PERT network indicates the flow of activities that is necessary for the completion of a project. Thus it establishes the interrelationships between activities and events. We shall generally discuss the sequential paths through a PERT network in terms of activities, although the reader should remember the distinction between activities and events. An *event* refers to the starting or the completion of an activity. Thus the event "the foundation has been poured" must occur before the event "erection of frame started" or the activity "the erection of the frame" can occur.

[1] The standard deviation is the square root of the variance. Therefore $\sigma_t = \dfrac{b - a}{6}$.

[2] Projects analyzed with the PERT technique are usually fairly complex and their completion generally involves an extended period of time. Therefore a week is the most commonly used unit measure of time, although days, months, or any other appropriate measure also could be used.

Let us now construct a simple PERT network and see how it is used. The first column in Exhibit 10–1 lists the 13 activities contained in the project, and the second column lists the predecessor activities. This is sufficient information to allow us to draw the network, as in Illustration 10–2. When one is drawing a network, events are represented by circles and activities are represented by arrows which indicate the direction of the work flow.

The network clearly indicates the sequence in which activities must be performed. The line corresponding to the performance of a particular activity is called an activity line. Thus the line indicated by E represents activity E. The network shows that F and G are predecessor activities to J, while G and H are successor activities to D. The flow of activities proceeds from left to right.

Exhibit 10–1   Data for Construction of PERT Network

Activity	Predecessor Activity	a*	m*	b*	E(t)*	σ_t^2
A	—	5	9	13	9	$(\frac{8}{6})^2$
B	—	8	11	17	$11\frac{1}{2}$	$(\frac{9}{6})^2$
C	A	3	4	5	4	$(\frac{2}{6})^2$
D	A	7	10	12	$9\frac{5}{6}$	$(\frac{5}{6})^2$
E	B	4	6	10	$6\frac{1}{3}$	$(\frac{6}{6})^2$
F	C	7	9	12	$9\frac{1}{6}$	$(\frac{5}{6})^2$
G	D	2	5	6	$4\frac{2}{3}$	$(\frac{4}{6})^2$
H	D	6	9	10	$8\frac{2}{3}$	$(\frac{4}{6})^2$
I	E	9	13	16	$12\frac{5}{6}$	$(\frac{7}{6})^2$
J	F, G	1	4	5	$3\frac{2}{3}$	$(\frac{4}{6})^2$
K	H, I	4	6	9	$6\frac{1}{6}$	$(\frac{5}{6})^2$
L	E	8	11	15	$11\frac{1}{6}$	$(\frac{7}{6})^2$
M	J, K	5	7	11	$7\frac{1}{3}$	$(\frac{6}{6})^2$

* Time estimates are given in weeks.

The a, m, and b columns of Exhibit 10–1 give the optimistic, most likely, and pessimistic time estimates for each activity. A weighted average of these three estimates is calculated according to Eq. (10–1) to give $E(t)$, the expected time required to complete each activity. The expected time for each activity is given in Exhibit 10–1 and also is shown in parentheses along its corresponding activity line in Illustration 10–2.

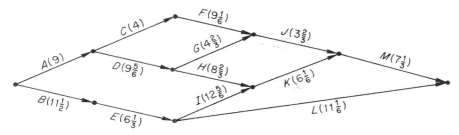

Illustration 10–2   PERT Network

Earliest Starting Time

Once the expected times are calculated for each activity, we can find the times at which we can expect to reach certain events. These expected times are indicated by T_E, and they represent the shortest possible time period that will be required [based on $E(t)$ estimates] to reach a certain *event*. We shall find T_E values based on events corresponding to the *beginning* of activities. Thus the event corresponding to "start activity E" cannot occur until B is completed. Since the expected time for the completion of B is $11\frac{1}{2}$ weeks, the earliest possible time that E can be started is $11\frac{1}{2}$ weeks after work has commenced on the entire project. You should see that the value of T_E is 9 weeks

Exhibit 10–2   Earliest Start, Latest Start, and Slack Time

Event: Start of Activity	T_E	T_L	$T_L - T_E$
A	0	$3\frac{1}{6}$	$3\frac{1}{6}$
B	0	0	0
C	9	20	11
D	9	$12\frac{1}{6}$	$3\frac{1}{6}$
E	$11\frac{1}{2}$	$11\frac{1}{2}$	0
F	13	24	11
G	$18\frac{5}{6}$	$28\frac{1}{2}$	$9\frac{2}{3}$
H	$18\frac{5}{6}$	22	$3\frac{1}{6}$
I	$17\frac{5}{6}$	$17\frac{5}{6}$	0
J	$23\frac{1}{2}$	$33\frac{1}{6}$	$9\frac{2}{3}$
K	$30\frac{2}{3}$	$30\frac{2}{3}$	0
L	$17\frac{5}{6}$	33	$15\frac{1}{6}$
M	$36\frac{5}{6}$	$36\frac{5}{6}$	0
Project completed	$44\frac{1}{6}$	$44\frac{1}{6}$	0

for starting both activities C and D. The T_E for the start of activity F is 13 weeks. The T_E for the start of J is $22\frac{1}{6}$ weeks if we follow path ACF. Notice that G is also a predecessor activity to J, however, and it will take $23\frac{1}{2}$ weeks to complete the sequence of activities ADG. Since T_E represents the *earliest* possible time at which we can start a new activity, and since *all* predecessor activities must be completed before their successor activities can be started, the correct value of T_E for the event "start activity J" is $23\frac{1}{2}$ weeks. As a general rule, when there are multiple paths leading to the same event, the earliest possible time we can expect to reach that event is determined by the longest time-consuming path leading to it. The value of T_E is given in Exhibit 10–2 for all events, including the event "project completed." You should be sure you understand the process by which each value of T_E is determined.

Critical Path

There are many paths that must be completed before an entire project is finished. Although they are all important, one of them is of primary interest to us. We would like to know which path, going from the start to the finish of the project, will take the longest time to complete. This path determines the earliest possible completion date of the project, and is called the *critical path*. The critical path for the network in Illustration 10–2 is *BEIKM* and, as shown in Exhibit 10–2, takes an expected time of $44\frac{1}{6}$ weeks to complete. Notice that a delay in any activity along the critical path will delay the completion of the entire project. Thus the project managers should be particularly concerned that these activities proceed on schedule.

While great pains may be taken to avoid delays of activities along the critical path, it is possible that other activities can suffer delays with no adverse effects on the project's total completion time. In fact, if it is known that the completion of some activities can be safely delayed, it may be possible temporarily to shift resources from them to activities along the critical path that are in danger of not being completed on schedule.

Latest Starting Time

To help the project manager maintain control over the progress of the entire project, and to be able effectively to shift resources when necessary without prolonging the project's completion time, it is desirable to know the latest possible date at which a given activity can be started while still keeping the project on schedule. (Notice that the time at which a particular activity can be started coincides with the completion of *all* predecessor activities.) The latest possible starting time for an activity will be denoted by T_L. T_L can most readily be obtained by working backwards through the PERT network.

The entire project is scheduled to be completed in $44\frac{1}{6}$ weeks. Activity M has an expected completion time of $7\frac{1}{3}$ weeks. Therefore, it must be started no later than $36\frac{5}{6}$ weeks after the project is started, or the completion date will be delayed. The expected time to complete activity L is $11\frac{1}{6}$ weeks. Therefore, it must be started within 33 weeks ($44\frac{1}{6}$ less $11\frac{1}{6}$ weeks) after the project is started, and T_L for activity L is 33 weeks. Activity D must be completed in time to allow for the completion of activities G, J, and M. These latter three activities have a total expected completion time of $4\frac{2}{3} + 3\frac{2}{3} + 7\frac{1}{3} = 15\frac{2}{3}$ weeks. But D must also be finished in time for H, K, and M to be completed, which will require an expected time of $8\frac{2}{3} + 6\frac{1}{6} + 7\frac{1}{3} = 22\frac{1}{6}$ weeks. If it is not to delay completion of the entire project, D must be finished in sufficient time to allow for the completion of *all* succeeding paths. Activity D has an expected completion time of $9\frac{5}{6}$ weeks, and activities H, K, and M are expected to require a total of $22\frac{1}{6}$ weeks; therefore, D must be started no later than $44\frac{1}{6} - 22\frac{1}{6} - 9\frac{5}{6} = 12\frac{1}{6}$ weeks after the project is initiated. Or, $T_L = 12\frac{1}{6}$ weeks for activity D. Thus if multiple paths follow the completion of a given activity, and different T_L values can be found for each, the smallest is the correct value of T_L for that activity; i.e., the smallest value specifies the latest time at which the activity can be started without delaying the project.

Slack Time

The difference between T_L, the latest time at which an activity can be started, and T_E, the earliest time at which it can be started, is called the activity's *slack time*. For example, if $T_L = 12$ weeks and $T_E = 8$ weeks, the activity has a slack time of 4 weeks. Slack times measure the amount of leeway the project manager has in starting or completing different activities, and are useful to him if he has to shift resources from one activity to another. A large slack time indicates an excess of resources that can be temporarily directed to potential trouble areas. The slack time for each activity in our example is given in Exhibit 10–2. Notice that the slack time for any activity along the critical path is zero. This again indicates that a delay in any of these activities will delay completion of the project.

We have so far based the discussion on the assumption that the project will be completed in a period of time equivalent to the *expected* time required to complete all activities along the critical path. This is $44\frac{1}{6}$ weeks in our example. Suppose, however, that a contract has been signed that specifies completion in 41 weeks. An initial PERT network analysis would show negative slack for some activities (B, E, I, K, and M), zero slack for some (A, C, and H), and positive slack for the others (C, F, G, J, and L). (The new slack times would be those given in Exhibit 10–2 minus $3\frac{1}{6}$ weeks.) On the basis of this analysis, resources could be reallocated from those activities with positive slack to those with negative or zero slack. This illustrates the value of this technique in helping management efficiently coordinate the assignment of limited resources to the many interrelated activities that must be completed on schedule if the completion of the project itself is not to be delayed.[3]

Probability of Achieving Specified Completion Times

The expected time to complete the project is obtained by summing the expected times required to complete each activity [obtained from the three subjective time estimates for each activity according to Eq. (10–1)] along the critical path. We do not know for certain, however, that any activity will be completed in exactly its expected time, and it would be highly unlikely that *all* activities would be completed in exactly their expected times. The expected time is the *average* time that would be required to complete the activity if it were performed a large number of times. Any one trial could require more or less than the expected time. Similarly, the time required actually to complete the project could require more or less time than was expected. Given this uncertainty, it would be useful to have *estimates* of the probability of completing the project within a specified period of time (remember that this probability is based on the initial time estimates).

[3] Under Secretary of Defense McNamara, all large Department of Defense contract bids were required to be submitted on a PERT basis. It was felt that such bids would be more thoroughly prepared and realistic. The National Aeronautics and Space Administration had similar requirements.

Suppose, for example, we wanted to know the probability of completing the project in our example within 41 weeks. The expected completion time is $44\frac{1}{6}$ weeks. To obtain a probability estimate, we need to know something about the dispersion of the distribution of actual completion times around the expected completion time. The variability of any one activity can be measured by the variance, which is calculated according to Eq. (10–2). The value of the variance for each activity is given in Exhibit 10–1. The variance of the critical path σ_{cp}^2 is the sum of the variances of each activity along the critical path. Thus $\sigma_{cp}^2 = (\frac{9}{6})^2 + (\frac{6}{6})^2 + (\frac{7}{6})^2 + (\frac{5}{6})^2 + (\frac{6}{6})^2 = 6.31$. The standard deviation is the square root of the variance, so $\sigma_{cp} = \sqrt{6.31} = 2.51$.[4]

The first step in determining the probability of completing the project within 41 weeks is to calculate the Z value, or the number of standard deviations between T_c and T_E.[5]

$$Z = \frac{T_c - T_E}{\sigma_{cp}} = \frac{44 - 41.17}{2.51} = \frac{-3.17}{2.51} = -1.26$$

The next step is to use the calculated Z value to find the desired probability from Exhibit F–1 in Appendix F. We find that the probability of completing the project within 41 weeks is 0.10.[6]

We could also find the probability of finishing within any other period of time, such as 48 weeks. The procedure is the same.

$$Z = \frac{48 - 44.17}{2.51} = 1.53$$

and the corresponding probability is 0.94.

The probability calculations are based on the assumption that the distribution of project completion times is normal. This assumption, in turn, is based on the central limit theorem. The central limit theorem, as applied here, says that the distribution of completion times along any path should approach normality as the number of individual activities along that path gets very large. Thus, even though the distributions for individual activities

---

[4] This procedure implicitly assumes that all activities are independent; i.e., that a factor affecting the time required to complete one activity will not affect the time required to complete any other activity. If, however, weather or economic conditions would similarly affect several different activities, they would not be independent, and the assumption of independence would be inappropriate.

[5] See Chapter 2 for a detailed discussion of this procedure.

[6] It is possible that the probability of completing all activities along the critical path within a given time period would be greater than the probability of completing some other path through the network within the same period. This is possible because different activity variances are encountered along different paths. Thus an extremely large variance for some activity not along the critical path could affect the probability of completing the project within a specified period of time.

can be highly skewed in one direction or the other, these deviations from normality should tend to even themselves out over a sufficient number of activities. Although the central limit theorem may not apply in a simple problem like the example discussed above, it would be valid for a more realistic—and therefore much more complex—problem with a far greater number of activities.

The procedure used to find the variance of the critical path assumed that the distributions for each activity were independent of those for all other activities. In other words, a delay in activity I, for whatever reason, would not change the probability of a delay in activity K. If there is some degree of positive dependence, where some common factor(s) may cause delays in both activities, the variance along the critical path would be underestimated and the probability calculations would be biased.

Finally, it should be recognized that the quality of a PERT network analysis can be no better than the quality of the three initial time estimates for each activity. All subsequent computations are based on these estimates. Every possible effort should be made, therefore, to obtain estimates from the most experienced and reliable sources available. On the other hand, even if the subjective time estimates turn out to be very inaccurate, the detailing of a PERT analysis forces the logical consideration of all segments of the network. In large, one time projects, often carried out under severe time and other pressures, there is considerable opportunity for sloppiness. A planning procedure that will minimize these opportunities is valuable even if the time estimates are unreliable.

CPM

CPM is closely related to PERT. There are two major differences between the two techniques. First, CPM directly introduces the concept of cost into the analysis. PERT indirectly accounts for cost if we assume that cost is related to time. A reduction in time should be a proxy for a reduction in cost. This relationship would generally be very crude, however, for it recognizes neither the amount of the reduction (we must assume that a reduction of two weeks results in exactly twice the cost savings as a reduction of one week) nor the activity in which the reduction was realized (so we must assume equal cost savings for all activities from the same time reduction). CPM is much more explicit about cost-time relationships for individual activities.

In addition to the time estimates, costs must be assigned to each activity on the CPM network. The cost assignments are activity oriented and are not concerned with unit time periods. Thus each activity represents a cost center, and the assignments cut across accounting periods and traditional organizational boundaries. Once obtained, these estimates are used to schedule resources so that the over-all project is completed based on an optimum mix of time and cost requirements.

A second distinction between CPM and PERT is that more reliable data are available on which to base time estimates when CPM is used. CPM is used for repetitive jobs, whereas PERT is used for nonrepetitive jobs. CPM would be used for planning residential construction, while PERT could be used to plan the assembly of a space platform. Therefore, historical cost information can be used for a CPM analysis of a project.

Two time estimates and two cost estimates are specified for each activity in a CPM network. One of the time estimates corresponds to the "most likely" estimate in a PERT analysis. This time estimate, and its related cost estimate, are called the *normal time and cost estimates.* The other time and cost estimates are called *crash estimates.* The normal estimates indicate what the time and cost requirements would be expected to be under ordinary circumstances. The crash estimates reflect expectations based on an all-out effort to complete the project in the shortest possible time. They would reflect such factors as overtime pay, the costs of hiring additional personnel or extra shifts, different efficiencies under different working conditions, etc.

Data for a simplified CPM problem are given in Exhibit 10–3. Let us also assume that the project has fixed costs of $100 per day. The first step is to draw a diagram of the project and, using the normal time estimates, determine the critical path. The CPM network is drawn in Illustration 10–3. The critical path is *ADEH* and should be completed in 24 days. (Slack times can be computed and used in the same way as in a PERT analysis.)

Exhibit 10–3   Data for CPM Problem

Activity	Predecessor Activity	Normal Time (days)	Normal Cost	Crash Time (days)	Crash Cost	Crash Cost per day
A	—	8	$450	7	$490	$40
B	—	6	400	4	490	45
C	B	5	300	4	350	50
D	A	4	500	3	585	85
E	C, D	7	475	5	625	75
F	A	8	600	6	740	70
G	B	2	150	2	150	—
H	E, F	5	350	4	420	70
		Total =	$3225		$3850	

Suppose that we want to shorten the period of time required to complete the project. One possible approach would be to put all activities on a crash basis. This procedure would be both extremely expensive and unnecessary. One of the primary purposes of a CPM analysis is to determine where a reduction in time can be achieved with the minimum increase in costs. There is obviously nothing to be gained by crashing activities *B, C,* or *F.* The project's completion time can be reduced only by crashing some activity on the critical path. If we wanted to reduce the completion time from 24 days to

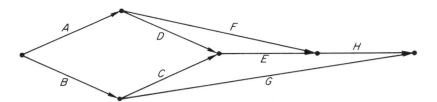

Illustration 10–3   CPM Network

23 days, we could crash any of activities *A*, *D*, *E*, or *H*. The most logical choice, however, is the one that can be accomplished at least cost. The last column in Exhibit 10–3 gives the per day cost of crashing each activity.[7] The least expensive alternative is to crash activity *A* at a cost of $40.

Suppose we now want to reduce further the project completion time to 22 days. We have already crashed *A*, so it will not provide any additional time savings. The next best alternative is to crash activity *H* at a cost of $70. (For the reader's convenience, a summary of these sequential crash strategies is presented in Exhibit 10–4).

Exhibit 10–4   Optimal Crash Strategies

Change in Project Completion Time	Crash Strategy	Cost	New Critical Path(s)
24 days to 23 days	Crash *A*	$40	*ADEH*
23 days to 22 days	Crash *H*	70	*ADEH*
22 days to 21 days	Crash *E*	75	*ADEH, BCEH*
21 days to 20 days	Crash *E*	75	*ADEH, BCEH*
20 days to 19 days	Crash *B* and *D*	130	*ADEH, BCEH*

Either *D* or *E* will have to be crashed if the project is to be completed in 21 days. Since *E* costs less per day to crash than *D*, our choice would be *E*. Notice that the critical path is no longer unique. Path *ADEH* and path *BCEH* both now require 21 days to complete. Any further reduction in the project's completion time would require that both of these paths be reduced.

Activity *E* can be crashed again, and paths *ADEH* and *BCEH* would both be shortened to 20 days. These two paths remain critical. Activities *A*, *E*, and *H* now have been crashed to their shortest possible completion times. Activity *D* could be crashed, and the original critical path now could be performed in 19 days, but the project would still require 20 days. To

[7] When a crash program will reduce an activity's completion time by more than one day, we assume a linear time-cost relationship. For example, activity *F* can be completed in six days, rather than eight, for an additional cost of $140. We assume a cost of $70 per day, and we assume that we can crash to save either one or two days.

reduce the total project time to 19 days, either *B* or *C* would have to be crashed simultaneously with *D*. The least expensive choice would be *B*. Crashing both *B* and *D*, at a total cost of $130, would enable the project to be completed in 19 days.

At this point, all activities along path *ADEH* are being performed in the shortest possible time. Thus, even though other activities could still be crashed, there would be no reason for doing so because there is no way that the completion time for the entire project can be reduced from 19 days. Crashing all the activities indicated in Exhibit 10–4 would be the least expensive strategy for completing the project in the shortest possible time.

Suppose, however, that the objective is to complete the project at minimum total cost. Total cost includes normal costs, crash costs, and fixed costs of $100 for each day spent on the project. The trade-offs are quite apparent. If the cost of crashing to reduce total completion time by one day is less than the daily fixed charge of $100, we should crash. Daily reductions up to 20 days result in net savings. The shorter completion time from 20 to 19 days, however, costs $130 and saves only $100, for a net loss of $30. Therefore, the optimum—in terms of minimum total cost—number of days in which to complete the project is 20. Total cost figures for the possible completion times are given in Exhibit 10–5. The trade-offs between crash costs and daily fixed costs should be evident.

Exhibit 10–5 Time-cost Trade-offs

Type of Costs	Completion Time (days)					
	24	23	22	21	20	19
Normal costs	$3225	$3225	$3225	$3225	$3225	$3225
Crash costs	0	40	110	185	260	390
Daily fixed costs	2400	2300	2200	2100	2000	1900
Total costs	$5625	$5565	$5535	$5510	$5485	$5515

This short example indicates the potential usefulness of CPM analysis. Work schedules can be efficiently planned, and bottlenecks can be avoided. The project manager should be able to maintain better control over all aspects of the project. In particular, he is able to identify and exploit the most economical cost-time trade-offs. In the example, the minimum completion time for the project was 19 days. By using a CPM analysis, selected activities were crashed at a total cost of $390 and the minimum completion period was realized. The crude strategy of crashing all activities would not complete the project any sooner, but would require total crash costs of $625 (see Exhibit 10–3).

PROBLEMS

1. A project consisting of six independent activities is to be analyzed by using PERT. The following information is given (time estimates are in days):

Activity	Predecessor Activities	a	m	b
A	—	3	4	5
B	—	2	2	2
C	A	1	3	5
D	B, C	0	4	14
E	D	1	2	3
F	A	2	9	10

a. Diagram the project and indicate its critical path.
b. What is the expected time to complete the project?
c. What is the probability that the project will be completed in 14 days or less?

2. A project is comprised of eight independent activities. Diagram the project and identify its critical path. What is the expected time to complete the project? What is the probability of completing the project in 20 weeks or less? Time estimates (in weeks) are as follows:

Activity	Predecessor Activities	a	m	b
A	—	1	3	5
B	—	2	3	4
C	—	3	4	5
D	A	2	9	10
E	C	4	5	6
F	B, D, E	5	6	13
G	A	2	4	6
H	C	0	3	6

3. A team of chemists is planning to undertake an applied research and development project to test a formula for a new synthetic material. The project can be separated into twelve distinct steps. The relationships among the steps and PERT time estimates are given below (time estimates are in weeks).

Activity	Predecessor Activity	a	m	b
A	—	2	2	2
B	—	1	3	7
C	A	4	7	8
D	A	3	5	7
E	B	2	6	9
F	B	5	9	11
G	C, D	3	6	8
H	E	2	6	9
I	C, D	3	5	8
J	G, H	1	3	4
K	F	4	8	11
L	J, K	2	5	7

a. Diagram the research development project and indicate its critical path.
b. Indicate the earliest and latest completion times and the slack time for each activity.
c. What is the expected time to complete the project?
d. What is the probability of completing the project in 26 weeks or less? In 23 weeks or less? In 25 weeks *or more*?

4. An electronics firm has signed a contract to install an instrument landing device at the local airport. The complete installation can be broken down into fourteen separate activities. Each activity (labeled *A* through *N*), its predecessor activities, normal times and cost, and crash time and cost are given below. The contract specifies that the installation will be completed within 18 days. There is a penalty of $100 per day beyond the specified completion time.

Activity	Predecessor Activities	Normal Time (days)	Normal Cost	Crash Time (days)	Crash Cost
A	—	3	$320	2	$360
B	—	5	550	4	500
C	—	6	575	4	700
D	*A*	7	750	5	850
E	*A*	4	420	3	490
F	*B, D*	2	180	2	180
G	*C*	4	425	4	485
H	*A*	8	850	5	1060
I	*C*	5	475	4	535
J	*C*	7	675	5	735
K	*E, F, G*	4	400	3	440
L	*H, I*	6	650	4	750
M	*L*	3	280	2	335
N	*J, K*	5	525	4	575

a. What is the normal time to complete the installation?
b. What is the shortest possible time for completion of the installation?
c. What is the most economical period of time in which to schedule the installation?
d. What is the minimum total cost (installation plus penalty)?

5. A construction project is composed of nine independent activities. The first three can start independently; the fourth and fifth require completion of the third; the sixth requires completion of both the second and the fourth; the seventh and ninth require completion of the first; and the eighth requires completion of the fifth, sixth, and seventh.

Normal times (in weeks) and direct costs for the nine activities are, respectively: 2, $100; 4, 200; 3, 200; 6, 280; 8, 500; 5, 450; 10, 1200; 6, 575; 15, 2200. Crash times (in weeks) and direct costs are, respectively: 2, $100; 3, 250; 3, 200; 4, 400; 6, 650; 4, 475; 8, 1500; 5, 625; 12, 2575. Assume that the project has a fixed cost of $250 per week.

a. What is the normal time to complete the project?
b. What is the shortest possible time for completion of the project?
c. In how many days should the project be completed in order to minimize total (i.e., direct plus fixed) costs?
d. What is the minimum cost?

11

inventory models, cash balances, and replacement models

With the growing availability of electronic data processing systems, the application of optimization models to various types of management problems increasingly has become part of many firms' general operating procedures. Some problems can be controlled entirely by mathematically programmed models, while others benefit from the application of these techniques at least at some stages. In a self-reinforcing cycle, the increased acceptance and capability to implement these models has stimulated the development of still more varied and sophisticated models.

The more elaborate models are also more complex and specialized. Our objective in this chapter is to acquaint the reader with a few of the more basic and general models. Once mastered, these basic models can be adapted to fit the structure of a particular problem (if the basic model is appropriate for the problem to begin with) given its special requirements.

First we will discuss fixed and variable demand situations where reordering during the period is not possible. Then we will assume that reordering is possible and develop the well-known economic order quantity model, one of the most basic and widely used optimization models. The restrictive assumptions of this model will be discussed, and more complex variations of the original formulation will be developed. An adaptation of the economic order quantity is then applied to the problem of controlling cash balances. Finally, we shall develop a model for the optimal timing of the replacement of capital assets. It should be noted that the inventory and cash management models are similar, and they are developed under the assumption of conditions of certainty. The replacement model is conceptually a different technique and is developed for conditions of uncertainty.

In this section we are concerned with the very restrictive situation where reorders cannot be placed during the period to replenish the supply of inventory. A level of inventory adequate to last the entire period must be placed at the beginning of the period. The only decision to be made is how many units should be ordered; it is not necessary to be concerned with the timing of an order or with how many orders should be placed during the period.

Stable Demand

The number of units to be acquired at the beginning of the period will depend on the aggregate demand expected during the period and the costs of over- and under-stocking. The simplest case would be where there is a known stable demand from period to period. If the demand for one period is known and stable over time, this same number of units would be acquired at the beginning of each period. The beginning inventory would be consumed during the period, and there would never be an excess or a shortage of inventory at the end of the period.

Variable Demand

The ideal situation of a known stable demand will seldom occur in the real world. In most cases, the required level of inventory will vary from period to period. When demand is variable, however, there may or may not be advance knowledge about the number of units to be required in the upcoming period. The inventory ordering policy to be followed will depend on whether or not perfect information about the next period's demand is available.

With Perfect Information Although demand might vary from period to period, there are certain situations where the level of demand for the next period might be known in advance. For example, the manager of a restaurant's banquet facilities could require advance specification of the number of dinners to prepare, or a university could order basketball uniforms only after the number of players to be on the team has been determined. Order size decisions for these situations would be almost as simple as for the stable demand case. We would always place an order equal to the number of units to be demanded in the next period. While the order quantity might vary from one period to the next, there would be neither an excess inventory nor a shortage at the end of any given period.

Without Perfect Information The owners of a small newspaper stand or flower shop might know from historical data what the probability distribution of daily demand will be, but they would not know in advance what the demand would be from day to day. But if we assume that yesterday's news-papers or yesterday's cut flowers cannot be sold today, both of these small entrepreneurs must make a daily inventory order quantity decision. If we assume that daily demand will follow the historical probability distribution, that changes in successive days' demand are independent, and that the costs of over-stocking and under-stocking can be estimated, the payoff and loss table techniques discussed in Chapter 3 (where several inventory examples are presented) can be applied. The optimal inventory policy will be to order a fixed number of units each day so that, even though actual demand will vary from day to day, the long-run average daily profits will be maximized.

INVENTORY CONTROL WITH REORDERING

There are three categories of costs associated with an inventory policy with reordering: (a) the costs of ordering inventory, (b) the costs of carrying items in inventory, and (c) the costs associated with stockouts, or running out of inventory. In the basic system, an inventory policy is specified by the order quantity and order point. The order quantity indicates how many units should be procured when an order is placed. The order point gives the level of existing inventory at which an order should be placed. An increase in the order quantity will decrease the number of orders placed during a given period of time but will increase the average number of units in inventory, and thus will decrease the period's total ordering costs and increase total carrying costs. Similarly, an increase in the order point will increase the period's average inventory level and total carrying costs but will decrease the costs resulting from stockouts. (Increasing the order quantity will decrease the number of orders placed during a period, thus tending to decrease the costs resulting from stockouts. In practice, however, the order quantity's effect on stockouts is minor in relation to the effect of the order point.) In establishing an efficient over-all inventory policy, the specification of the order quantity focuses on the trade-off between ordering and carrying costs while the specification of the order point focuses on the trade-off between carrying and stockout costs. That is, the objective of the firm is to minimize the total cost of meeting its inventory requirements.

EOQ MODEL

The economic order quantity (EOQ) model can be used to calculate the optimal quantity to specify in the over-all inventory policy. One of the most widely known and used quantitative models, the EOQ model initially was derived for use in inventory control systems. The same basic model was obtained independently by several different researchers during the 1920's. The combined forces of increased business size, keener competitive pressures, and a growing appreciation for scientific decision aids have resulted in widespread applications of this basic formulation. We shall develop the fundamental

191

Inventory
Models, Cash
Balances, and
Replacement
Models

equations as applied to inventory control in the first section of this chapter, and shall then apply the same concepts to the area of cash management in a later section.

Inventories are shown on the assets side of the balance sheet, and they require an investment of capital, as do buildings, trucks, and machinery. All assets must compete for limited capital funds, and they should justify the firm's commitment to them. Although the carrying of inventories is unavoidable, it should be recognized that inventories are not "operating" assets. That is, they do not directly produce output, which could in turn be transformed into revenues, in the sense that a press or an automatic welder would produce marketable products. Therefore, the firm would like to minimize as much as prudently possible its investment in the nonoperating asset of inventories.[1]

Since inventories do not produce revenues, the firm can accomplish the above objective by minimizing the cost of meeting its inventory requirements. The EOQ formula gives the optimum order size that will minimize the related total inventory costs.[2] While this formula has received widespread application, its use is limited by the fact that it is based on certain restricting assumptions concerning inventory procurement, usage, and ordering costs. (Thus there also is ample opportunity for misapplication of the EOQ formula.)

The major assumptions underlying the EOQ formula are the following: (a) The total inventory requirement for some specified period of time is known in advance; (b) inventory consumption (through direct sale or use in the production process) occurs uniformly during the period; (c) lead time for filling orders is known with certainty. Notice that these assumptions prescribe the ideal conditions in which no buffer, or safety, inventory stock must be maintained, since all relevant information is known with certainty.

Before deriving the EOQ formula, we need to define the following terms:

k_o = fixed cost of placing an order[3]
k_c = cost of carrying one unit in inventory for one period[4]
R = total inventory requirement for one period
Q = number of units specified in each order
n = number of orders placed per period

---

[1] It is probably not coincidental that several research efforts on inventory control systems were made simultaneously during the 1920's. The "inventory depression" of 1921, which was brought on by excessive accumulations of inventories, made the need abundantly clear. Even today, changes in inventory levels are considered to be leading indicators of economic changes.

[2] Our discussion will concentrate on purchases of inventory items from outside suppliers. The same basic concepts apply to the problem of scheduling internal production, however.

[3] Only direct, or out-of-pocket, costs are relevant. Allocated costs should not be considered. Relevant costs would include telephone expenses, costs of processing the necessary paper work, transportation, etc. Items such as allocated overhead should be ignored.

[4] Relevant portions of carrying cost include insurance, financing, storage space, etc.

The firm's inventory level is assumed to follow a time pattern as indicated in Illustration 11–1. Q units are available at the beginning of the period. They are used continuously and linearly until the initial supply is exhausted, at which time a new shipment of Q items is received. This cycle is repeated n times during the period.

If R is the total inventory requirement for the period and Q is the number of units received with each order, then $R/Q = n$, the number of orders placed during the period. The total ordering cost (TOC) during the period is the number of orders times the cost of placing an order, as given in Eq. (11–1).

$$\text{TOC} = k_o \cdot n = k_o \cdot \frac{R}{Q} \qquad (11\text{–}1)$$

From Illustration 11–1, it can be seen that the average inventory held during the period is $Q/2$. The total carrying cost (TCC), given in Eq. (11–2), is the average inventory times the unit carrying cost.

$$\text{TCC} = \frac{Q}{2} \cdot k_c \qquad (11\text{–}2)$$

The sum of these two costs is the total inventory cost (TIC).

$$\text{TIC} = \text{TOC} + \text{TCC} = k_o \cdot \frac{R}{Q} + \frac{Q}{2} \cdot k_c \qquad (11\text{–}3)$$

These costs are shown graphically in Illustration 11–2. The total ordering cost varies inversely with Q, because increases in the order quantity decrease the total number of orders that are required during the period. The total carrying cost varies directly with Q, however, because increases in the order quantity result in a larger average inventory. From small order

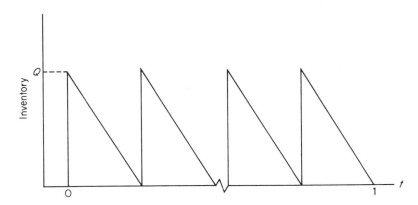

Illustration 11–1   Pattern of Inventory Levels

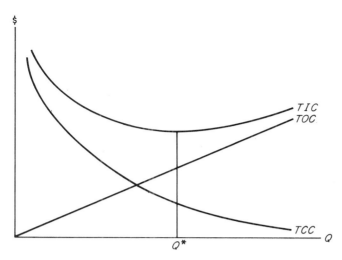

Illustration 11–2   Order Quantity—Cost Curves

quantities, increases in Q result in reductions in TOC that more than offset the simultaneous increases in TCC. As Q gets larger, however, further increases eventually result in increases in TCC that more than offset the cost reduction in TOC. Thus the total inventory cost first decreases with increases in Q, but the reduction gradually decreases until the curve turns upward and TIC increases with Q.

Total inventory costs are minimized at the point in Illustration 11–2 where the TIC curve levels off and starts to increase. The optimum, or economic, order quantity can readily be obtained by setting the first derivative of Eq. (11–3) equal to zero and solving for Q (see Appendix E for a review of the required calculus operations).

$$\frac{d\text{TIC}}{dQ} = -\frac{k_o R}{Q^2} + \frac{k_c}{2} = 0$$

$$Q^2 = \frac{2k_o R}{k_c}$$

$$Q^* = \sqrt{\frac{2k_o R}{k_c}} \tag{11-4}$$

Equation (11–4) is the EOQ formula. Q^* is the number of units that should be specified in each order so as to minimize total inventory costs for the period.[5]

---

[5] The second derivative,

$$\frac{d\text{TIC}^2}{d^2 Q} = \frac{2k_o \cdot R}{Q^3}$$

is positive. Thus Eq. (11–4) specifies a minimum point on the TIC curve (see Appendix E).

Once Q^* is determined, we can also find the optimal number of orders to be placed per period. Since $n = R/Q$, $n^* = R/Q^*$. Therefore,

$$n^* = R \bigg/ \sqrt{\frac{2k_o \cdot R}{k_c}} = \sqrt{\frac{R \cdot k_c}{2k_o}} \qquad (11\text{--}5)$$

Notice that Eqs. (11–4) and (11–5) are redundant. We can find n^* if we know Q^*, and vice versa. If k_o, k_c, and R are given, either Q or n can serve as the decision variable, although Q generally is used.

Equation (11–4) is consistent with what we would logically expect. The economic order quantity Q^* increases with increases in the cost of placing an order and with the total requirement for the period, and decreases with increases in the unit carrying cost. The formula specifies the exact nature of the relationship, however. If k_c increases by a factor of 9, Q^* should decrease by a factor of 3. The EOQ formula also specifies that Q^* should increase with the square root of R. This latter result indicates the existence of economy of scale opportunities in the administration of inventory programs.[6]

Example

Let us now consider a numerical example of the use of Eqs. (11–4) and (11–5). Suppose $k_o = \$1.20$, $k_c = \$4.00$, and $R = 6000$ units. From Eq. (11–4),

$$Q^* = \sqrt{\frac{2(1.20)(6000)}{4.00}} = 60 \text{ units}$$

From Eq. (11–5),

$$n^* = \sqrt{\frac{6000(4.00)}{2(1.20)}} = 100$$

These results tell us that the optimal plan for meeting total inventory requirements of 6000 units is to place 100 orders of 60 units each. The total inventory cost that would be incurred during the period under this plan can be obtained from Eq. (11–3). $\text{TIC} = 1.20(\frac{600}{60}) + \frac{60}{2}(4.00) = 120 + 120 = \$240$.

Suppose that we increase k_o by a factor of four to \$4.80. The optimal EOQ should increase by the square root of 4, or by a factor of 2. From Eq. (11–4),

$$Q^* = \sqrt{\frac{2(4.80)(6000)}{4.00}} = 120 \text{ units}$$

The reader should verify to himself that, if all other parameters remain unchanged, $Q^* = 30$ units if $R = 1500$ units; $Q^* = 180$ units if $R = 54,000$ units; $Q^* = 120$ units if $k_c = \$1.00$; $Q^* = 30$ units if $k_c = \$16.00$.

---

[6] If Eq. (11–4) is substituted in Eq. (11–3), we get the result that $\text{TIC} = \sqrt{2Rk_ok_c}$. Thus TIC increases with the square root of R (or less than proportionately with R).

195

Inventory
Models, Cash
Balances, and
Replacement
Models

Equation (11–4) is an EOQ formula based on a highly simplified set of assumptions. The same basic concepts would be used to derive a new EOQ formula if we were to relax the restrictive assumptions and develop a more realistic and complex model. In some cases the step toward greater realism will make the computations and the final formula considerably more complicated, although in other cases the introduction of additional factors will have little or no effect.

Variable Ordering Costs

Let us consider one of the latter cases. We may expect that at least a portion of the cost of fulfilling an order will vary with the number of units involved. We can designate k_v to represent the variable cost of ordering one unit. Then the total cost of placing an order will be $k_o + k_v \cdot Q$. The cost of placing n orders during the period will be

$$n(k_o + k_v \cdot Q) = \frac{R}{Q}(k_o + k_v \cdot Q) = \frac{R}{Q} \cdot k_o + R \cdot k_v$$

We can derive the EOQ formula as follows:

$$\text{TIC} = k_o \cdot \frac{R}{Q} + k_v \cdot R + \frac{Q}{2} \cdot k_c$$

$$\frac{d\,\text{TIC}}{dQ} = -\frac{k_o \cdot R}{Q^2} + \frac{k_c}{2} = 0$$

$$Q^* = \sqrt{\frac{2k_o \cdot R}{k_c}}$$

This new EOQ formula does not even contain k_v. In fact, it is exactly the same as Eq. (11–4). The reason is obvious when we reexamine the above total inventory cost equation. Total variable ordering costs are equal to $k_v \cdot R$. Since, under any plan, R units must be ordered during the period, the total variable costs incurred during the period will not change as we change the value of Q. Therefore, k_v will not affect our final results.

Quantity Discounts

Other complications are not disposed of quite so easily. For example, quantity discounts are frequently used to encourage buyers to order in larger quantities. The unit purchase price would now vary inversely with the size of the order, and this variable unit cost must be included in the computation of the optimum EOQ. (A constant unit price would not have to be considered for the same reason that k_v did not affect our final results.)

Let us consider an example. Suppose $k_o = \$10.00$, $k_c = \$8.00$, $R = 49{,}000$ units, and the unit purchase price schedule is as given in Exhibit 11–1. This problem is not as difficult as it first appears if we approach it

Exhibit 11-1   Quantity—Purchase Price Schedule

Quantity Ordered	Discount	Unit Purchase Price
1– 99	—	$8.00
100–249	2%	7.84
250–499	4%	7.68
500 or more	5%	7.60

carefully and logically. All that is required is to analyze the trade-off between total inventory costs and total purchasing costs. The first step is to ignore temporarily the possibility of quantity discounts and use Eqs. (11–4) and (11–5). Solving, we find $Q^* = 350$ units and $n^* = 140$ orders. Any deviation from Q^*—ordering more or less than 350 units—will increase total inventory costs (see TIC curve in Illustration 11–2). Furthermore, a reduction in the quantity ordered to less than 250 units will also increase total purchasing costs. We can, therefore, eliminate this possibility from further consideration. On the other hand, total purchasing costs will be decreased if we increase the quantity ordered to 500 units or more. We should immediately realize that no more than 500 units would be ordered. Ordering in excess of 500 units would result in further increases in total inventory costs while yielding no additional reductions in total purchasing costs. Therefore, our only two rational alternatives are either (a) to place 140 orders of 350 units each at a unit purchase price of $7.68, or (b) to place 98 orders of 500 units each at a unit purchase price of $7.60. From Eq. (11–3), we can find the total inventory cost to be $2800 for the first alternative and $2980 for the second. Thus additional inventory costs of $180 are incurred when the individual order quantity is increased from 350 to 500 units. A corresponding benefit of a reduction of $0.08 in the unit purchase price would also be received, however. The decrease in total purchasing costs for the period would be $0.08(49,000) = $3920. Since this savings is substantially greater than the increase in inventory costs, the optimum policy would be to place 98 orders for 500 units each.

Gradual Receipt of Orders

We have assumed so far that all orders are filled instantaneously in one shipment. In many actual situations, however, several partial shipments are received or the supplies come gradually over a period of time. Thus inventory is being consumed at the same time it is being received, but the level of inventory is accumulating because the inventory is being received at a faster rate than it is being used. Inventory does not arrive during the full period, so the inventory level gradually increases when shipments are being received and then declines during the remainder of the period after receipts stop. The resulting time pattern of inventory levels is shown graphically in Illustration 11–3.

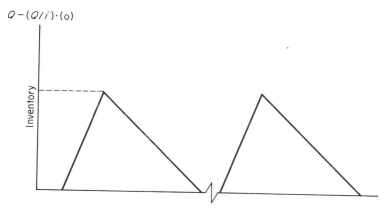

$Q - (Q/i) \cdot (o)$

Inventory

Illustration 11–3 Pattern of Inventory Levels with Gradual Receipt of Orders

We will assume that inventory shipments are received at a uniform daily rate of i units per day, that inventory is used at the daily rate of o units per day, and that $i > o$. If the order quantity is Q, it will take Q/i days for the entire order to be filled and $(Q/i) \cdot (o)$ gives the number of units of inventory consumed during the time that the order is being filled. It follows that, whereas Q units is the largest inventory level that will be reached when orders are filled instantaneously, the largest inventory level with gradual shipments will be $Q - (Q/i) \cdot (o)$.

If we assume that the average inventory level is roughly half the maximum level, the average inventory will be $\frac{1}{2}[Q - (Q/i) \cdot (o)]$ and the inventory carrying costs for the period will be $\frac{1}{2}[Q - (Q/i) \cdot (o)] \cdot k_c$ or

$$\tfrac{1}{2}Q \left[1 - \frac{o}{i} \right] \cdot k_c$$

The total ordering costs will be $(R/Q) \cdot k_o$ and the total inventory costs will be the sum of the carrying and ordering costs, or

$$\text{TIC} = \tfrac{1}{2}Q \left[1 - \frac{o}{i} \right] \cdot k_c + \frac{R}{Q} \cdot k_o$$

Solving for the value of Q that minimizes TIC gives the following result:

$$Q^* = \sqrt{\frac{2Rk_o}{k_c(1 - o/i)}}$$

This result is the EOQ formula derived earlier with the $(1 - o/i)$ term entered in the denominator. The order quantity will be larger if receipt is not instantaneous, which is what we should expect. If o is relatively large or if i

is relatively small, Q will be higher than if o is relatively small or if i is relatively large. The latter case would approximate the instantaneous receipt case and, at the extreme, the term $1 - o/i$ would approach $1 - 0$.

A Production Example

The above result can be applied readily to a situation where inventory is produced at some uniform rate i rather than purchased and k_o is the setup cost for a production run rather than the cost of placing an order. With these two changes in notation, Q^* gives the optimum size of a production run. For example, if $R = 500$ units, $i_o = \$50.00$, $k_c = \$5.00$, $o = 20$ units per day, and $i = 10$ units per day, we obtain the following:

$$Q^* = \sqrt{\frac{2(500)(50)}{10(1 - 10/20)}} = 10,000 = 100$$

The optimum production run size is 100 units and there should be five production runs during the period.

Order Point

The assumption of a known constant lead time for filling orders makes the specification of the order point a trivial problem. In general terms, the order point would be the product of the units demanded per period and the number of periods required to fill an order. For example, if daily demand is ten units and it will take four days to fill an order, the order point would be 40 units. This order point would result in a zero inventory level being reached just as the new shipment is received. A lower order point would cause stockouts and a higher order point would result in carrying a higher average inventory than would be necessary.

The specification of an order point is more difficult when demand and the time required to fill an order are unknown. One approach is simply to estimate an average daily demand and lead time and add a "reasonable" safety stock to the order point obtained from the above procedure. If assumptions can be made about the probability distributions of daily demand and lead time, sophisticated formulas can be derived which will specify an optimum order point. (The development of these formulas is beyond the scope of this book. The interested reader is referred to any advanced text on inventory control.) If the data do not conform to a well-known distribution but the probability distributions for demand and lead time can be estimated, the technique of simulation can be used to obtain an efficient order point and order quantity. (The use of simulation to solve an inventory problem is demonstrated in Chapter 16.)

ABC Classification Technique

Another problem area is deciding when it is worthwhile to pursue an EOQ analysis and when it is not. We have so far presented the discussion in terms

199

Inventory
Models, Cash
Balances, and
Replacement
Models

of units of a single item. It is not at all unusual, however, for a firm to maintain inventories of several hundred different items. For most of these items, it would probably cost more to implement a detailed inventory control system than would slight deviations from some optimal inventory policy. It is, therefore, prudent to develop a sound classification procedure to distinguish those items which justify close attention from those which do not.

It has been found that a typical manufacturing company may have a large percentage of its dollar value of inventory tied up in a relatively small percentage of the number of different items that it maintains in stock. These are the A classification items shown in Exhibit 11–2. The C items represent a large percentage of the number of items in stock but a small percentage of the dollar inventory value. The B items are somewhere in between. This system is referred to as the ABC classification procedure.

Exhibit 11–2   Representative Distribution of Inventory Items and Value

Classification	Number of Items	Inventory Value
A	15%	75%
B	25%	15%
C	60%	10%

The A classification items tend to be either high-volume or high-unit-cost items. An inventory control system should be directed toward these items, because this is where the major economies can be achieved. An elaborate system developed for C classification items would probably cost more to design, implement, and run than it could ever generate in savings. Less elaborate procedures should be used for these items.

When we are deciding how closely to monitor inventory levels of different items, it is also important to determine how important an item is to the sales or production efforts, the type of demand distribution, the possibility of obsolescence, and other related factors. Proper recognition of these factors, including the dollar value of each inventory item, will lead to a sound method of classification and record keeping. And this identification and analysis of inventory items is an essential first step toward an effective inventory control system.

EOQ as a Range

As should be obvious by now, an effective inventory control system may be required to account for a wide variety of factors. The resulting model can become quite rigorous and sophisticated. In turn, the proper use of the final formulas requires a thorough understanding of the concepts and assumptions from which they were derived. Otherwise, an elegant model can lead to excessive and consistent suboptimization when it is put into actual use.

For example, in an earlier example (k_o = \$1.20, k_c = \$4.00, R = 6000 units) we found Q^* = 60 units and n^* = 100 orders. Suppose, however, that our supplier normally ships in standard lots of 75 units. Accepting his standard lot represents a 25-percent departure from our calculated optimal order quantity. Should we insist on following an "optimal" policy, or should we acquiesce and maintain the goodwill of our supplier? Perhaps some comparative cost figures will help us decide. The total inventory cost for the period [from Eq. (11–3)] is \$240 if we rigidly adhere to the EOQ formula. If we place 80 orders of 75 units each, total inventory cost increases to \$244. Thus the difference in total costs for the entire period is only \$4. Knowing this, we would most likely order in standard lots of 75 units each.

Assumptions of EOQ Model

The above example illustrates an important, but frequently overlooked, property of EOQ calculations. They allow more flexibility than is generally realized. It has been argued that the EOQ should be interpreted as a range of quantities, rather than a specific quantity.[7] Fairly wide deviations from the calculated EOQ may produce only relatively small increases in total inventory costs. Therefore, the ordering quantity generally can be adjusted to convenient levels without serious increases in costs.

It is also important to remember that EOQ formulas are based on assumptions that sometimes take severe liberties when approximating reality. In the derivation of Eqs. (11–4) and (11–5), several important assumptions were made. We assumed a uniform rate of consumption of inventory over time, although usage might actually be lumpy and subject to seasonal variations. The total inventory requirements for a period were assumed known. A constant unit carrying cost was used. The assumption that orders could be filled immediately, with a constant lead time, or at a uniform rate, allowed us the luxury of not having to maintain a safety stock. If these and other assumptions do not reasonably represent the conditions under which the firm actually operates, the resulting formulas will be of little or no value. In fact, they may do more harm than good.

There are several alternatives open to the firm when it is trying to establish an inventory control system in a fairly complex situation. In some cases it may be possible to develop a complicated but realistic model from which a reliable EOQ formula can be derived. In many cases, however, alternative approaches are preferable. Suppose that inventory usage is not uniform and the total requirement for a period is not known, but a probability distribution of the inventory requirement for some subperiod, such as a day, can be estimated. The length of time that will be required to fill an order is not known, but we can again estimate a probability distribution of lead times. We would now have to cope with the possibility of stockouts, and would probably want to carry some safety stock. Two decision variables

---

[7] See Arthur Snyder, "Principles of Inventory Management," *The Financial Executive* (April 1964), pp. 13–21.

would now be required, rather than just one: We must specify when an order is to be placed as well as the order quantity. Many sophisticated models have appeared in the literature offering solutions to specific types of situations. It is possible, however, that the most efficient way of approaching this problem is to simulate different inventory policies and, by systematic trial and error, to arrive at a least cost solution.[8] The techniques of simulation will be described and illustrated in Chapter 16 and their application to an inventory problem will be presented.

CASH BALANCES

The use of the inventory model is not restricted to controlling levels of supplies, raw materials, etc. In fact, we could argue that the major limitation in the application of this approach is one's creativity and imagination. One well-known application that is closely related to the control of physical inventory stocks involves the control of idle cash balances held by the firm.[9]

Our objective is to determine the relationship between transactions demands for cash and the level of interest rates. (We are concerned only with the balances that the firm will have to maintain to meet its actual cash obligations. We shall not be concerned with cash balances held for precautionary and speculative motives.) The model should show that, above some minimum, the higher the interest rate, the more economical of cash balances transactors will be. This in no way implies uncertainty concerning the level of interest rates. The emphasis is simply on the cost of transfers between cash and interest-bearing assets and the yield level of these assets.[10]

We shall assume that bonds represent the alternative asset in which transaction balances might be held. Bonds and cash are the same in all but two respects: Bonds are not a medium of payment, and bonds bear an interest rate. We shall further assume that there is no risk of default on the bonds or of a change in the level of interest rates.

Basic Problem

Suppose that an individual (or a firm) receives $\$Y$ at time $t = 0$. This receipt is then dispersed in a steady stream, so he has a zero balance at the end of the

---

[8] There is a model, known as the square root approximation of the Poisson distribution, that can be used to establish an acceptable level of safety stock. This formula is based on the observed relationship between the Poisson distribution and fluctuations in average industrial demand patterns. The more abnormal the demand patterns for the item(s) being analyzed, the less applicable is this formula.

[9] Most of this section is based on an article by William J. Baumol, "The Transactions Demand for Cash: An Inventory Theoretic Approach," *Quarterly Journal of Economics* (November 1952).

[10] The model to be developed is typically applied to a situation where cash disbursements must be made over a period of time from a single receipt. The same basic techniques can be used when a series of receipts are to be received, followed by a lump sum or a pattern of disbursements.

period, $t = 1$. His transactions balance during the period is shown in Illustration 11–4. This balance consists of some combination of cash and bonds.[11]

Transactions costs include both fixed and variable components. The fixed component will be denoted by a and the variable cost per dollar by b. Therefore, a transaction of X between cash and bonds will cost $(a + bX)$. The interest rate per period will be denoted by r.

These are two relevant costs that must be considered. One is transactions costs. The greater the number of transactions between cash and bonds, the greater will be total transactions costs. There is also an opportunity cost r of holding cash. This is the interest income foregone by holding transactions balances in the form of cash rather than bonds. The greater the average cash balance held during the period, the greater will be the opportunity cost.

Determining Withdrawals Only

Let us first consider the simple case where the Y received at $t = 0$ is entirely in bonds. The individual's only problem is to determine the amount of each transfer from bonds to cash. Each withdrawal will be denoted by C. If Y in bonds is initially received, and withdrawals of C are made at regular intervals, the number of withdrawals will be Y/C. Therefore, total transactions costs will be $(Y/C)(a + b \cdot C)$. As shown in Illustration 11–4, a withdrawal of C is made, a smooth and continuous stream of cash disbursement is made until the cash balance is down to zero, and then another withdrawal of C is made. This cycle is repeated several times during the period. The average

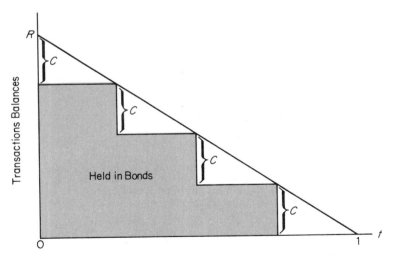

Illustration 11–4   Composition of Transactions Balances over Time

[11] The objective of maximizing interest revenue requires that all conversions from cash into bonds should occur at time $t = 0$ and that a transaction from bonds into cash should not occur until the cash balance is zero.

203

Inventory
Models, Cash
Balances, and
Replacement
Models

cash balance held during the period is $C/2$. Thus the opportunity cost of holding cash rather than bonds is $(C/2) \cdot r$. The total cost during the period, which is the sum of transactions and opportunity costs, is given in Eq. (11–6). Notice the similarity to Eq. (11–3).

$$\text{Total Cost} = \frac{Y}{C}(a + bc) + \frac{C}{2} \cdot r = \frac{Y \cdot a}{C} + b \cdot Y + \frac{C}{2} \cdot r \quad (11\text{-}6)$$

Transactions costs vary inversely with C, and opportunity costs vary directly with C. Y is analogous to R; C to Q; a to k_o; b to k_v; r to k_c. Similarly, we want to solve for the value of C that will minimize total cost. The formula for C^* is given in Eq. (11–7). Again note the strong similarity to Eq. (11–4).

$$\frac{d\text{TC}}{dC} = -\frac{Ya}{C^2} + \frac{r}{2} = 0$$

$$C^* = \sqrt{\frac{2Y \cdot a}{r}} \quad (11\text{-}7)$$

Equation (11–7) tells us that the size of the cash withdrawal should increase with the square roots of Y and a and decrease with the square root of r. The directions of the changes are as we would intuitively anticipate. The formula specifies the exact form of the relationship, however.[12]

Determining Investment and Withdrawals

Let us now turn to the more complicated case where the $\$Y$ is received in the form of cash. The individual must now determine the amount to be withheld in cash, the amount to be invested in bonds, and the optimum amount of each cash withdrawal. The time pattern of transactions is shown in Illustration 11–5.

Of the Y dollars received, let B be invested in bonds and the remainder, call it K, be withheld in cash. Thus $K = Y - B$. The K dollars initially withheld will meet transactions needs for the proportion of the total period equal to $(Y - B)/Y$. The average cash balance held during this portion of the total period is $K/2 = (Y - B)/2$. The effective interest rate for this portion of the period is $r \cdot (Y - B)/Y$. Therefore the cost of withholding K and investing B is

$$\frac{Y - B}{2} \cdot r \cdot \frac{Y - B}{Y} + a + b \cdot B$$

---

[12] Equation (11–7) can be rewritten in exponential form as $C^* = (2Y \cdot a)^{1/2}(r)^{-1/2}$. Students of economics will recognize the exponents as measures of elasticity. C^* measures the demand for money, and Y, a, and r are variables that influence demand.

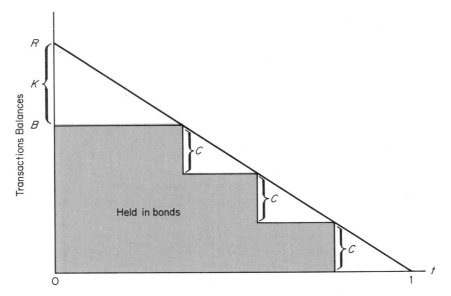

Illustration 11-5 Composition of Transactions Balances over Time

Transactions needs for the remainder of the period will be met by making equal cash withdrawals of C dollars each. Illustration 11-5 shows the portions of the total transations balance that are allocated to bonds and cash during the period.

The average cash balance for the remainder of the period will be $C/2$ and the effective interest rate will be $r \cdot (B/Y)$. The number of cash withdrawals will be B/C. The cost of obtaining cash for the remainder of the period will be

$$\frac{C}{2} \cdot r \cdot \frac{B}{Y} + (a + b \cdot C)\frac{B}{C}$$

Differentiating the sum of the above two cost equations with respect to B and setting the result equal to 0 gives

$$\frac{Y - B}{Y} \cdot r + b + \frac{C \cdot r}{2Y} + \frac{a}{C} + b = 0$$

This result can be rewritten in the form

$$K = Y - B = \frac{C}{2} + \frac{a \cdot Y}{C \cdot r} + \frac{Y(2b)}{r} \qquad (11\text{-}8)$$

Again differentiating the total cost, this time with respect to C, and setting the result equal to 0 gives

$$\frac{r \cdot B}{2Y} - \frac{a \cdot B}{C^2} = 0$$

204

205

Inventory
Models, Cash
Balances, and
Replacement
Models

From this equation we can solve for the optimum value of C.

$$C^* = \sqrt{\frac{2Y \cdot a}{r}} \tag{11-9}$$

From Eq. (11–9) and the middle term on the right-hand side of Eq. (11–8), we can obtain

$$\frac{a \cdot Y}{C \cdot r} = \frac{2a \cdot Y}{2C \cdot r} = \frac{C^2}{2C} = \frac{C}{2}$$

This result enables us to simplify Eq. (11–8).

$$K^* = Y - B = \frac{C}{2} + \frac{C}{2} + \frac{Y(2b)}{r} = C + \frac{Y(2b)}{r} \tag{11-8a}$$

The quantity Y is given, so once we have solved for K the value of B is automatically determined. With the derivation of Eqs. (11–9) and (11–8a), the entire problem is solved. K^* dollars should initially be withheld, $B^* (= Y - K^*)$ dollars should be invested in bonds, and transfers from bonds to cash of C^* dollars should be made whenever the cash balance reaches a zero level.

Equations (11–9) and (11–7) are equivalent. Therefore, the size of the optimal cash withdrawal is the same as before. The amount that should initially be withheld in cash is equal to C^*, the amount of a regular withdrawal, plus $Y(2b)/r$. The latter term has a straightforward economic interpretation. Every dollar making the complete cycle of cash to bonds and back to cash will incur a variable transactions cost of $2b$. Interest revenue, however, depends on how long the dollar stays in bonds. It is worthwhile to buy bonds only if they can be held long enough that interest earnings exceed $2b$. Or, since the maximum time period equals 1, r must exceed $2b$. Thus the minimum time bonds must be held in order to break even is $2b/r$. Holding bonds beyond this point, so far as transactions need permits, will result in interest earnings that are pure gains. An investment held for a shorter length of time would cost more to execute than it could earn. K^* is therefore equal to $(2b/r) \cdot Y$ plus C^*, the amount of a regular cash withdrawal.[13]

The cash balances model is subject to the same limitations as the regular inventory model derived in the first section of the chapter. The comments made there apply equally here. Of course, more complex models and the possibility of utilizing simulation techniques are available for

---

[13] Notice that $(2b \cdot Y)/r$ allows for variable transactions costs, while the optimum regular withdrawal C^* reflects the fixed portion of transactions cost.

monitoring cash balances just as they are for controlling inventory stocks. The two problems have much in common.

REPLACEMENT MODELS

The replacement of capital equipment usually occurs for one of four reasons: (1) Newly developed equipment makes current equipment technologically obsolete; (2) equipment becomes unusable and must be replaced; (3) it is economically advantageous to replace deteriorating equipment, since its cost increases steadily with age; (4) it is economically advantageous to replace equipment in anticipation of costly failure, the probability of which increases over time. The latter two situations are discussed in the following sections.

Replacement of a Deteriorating Asset

Most capital equipment deteriorates with age or usage, resulting in increased expenditures for operating costs[14] and/or decreases in the value of the equipment and/or decreases in the productivity of the equipment. Decreases in the productivity of equipment can be treated as a cost. For example, a machine produces 20,000 items per year when new, but only 18,000 items in its second year of use. If the item sells for $1 and the material and sales costs are $0.30, then the cost of productivity loss is $1400 ($0.70 × 2000). Typically these costs tend to increase over time at an increasing rate.[15]

Similarly, as the equipment ages its resale or salvage value decreases. Hence the real capital cost of the equipment, depreciation, also increases over time. In this discussion, we shall use an economic concept of depreciation rather than the more familiar accounting one. Depreciation is defined to be purchase price minus resale value.[16] However, unlike operating costs, the amount of additional depreciation declines each year. As anyone who has purchased a new automobile knows, the greatest amount of depreciation occurs at the time of purchase. Thus we have two relevant costs, one (operating and productivity losses[17]) whose average cost is increasing over time and one (depreciation) whose average cost is decreasing over time. Thus, if we assume that we shall have need for the equipment for an indefinite period, it is logical that we should keep the equipment for that period of time which minimizes its average cost. Illustration 11–6 shows the relevant cost curves and the optimal replacement time.

[14] Operating costs are all costs involved in running the equipment, including repairs and maintenance.

[15] Occasionally the first year's operating costs will be disproportionately high due to start-up costs, but after the start-up period the costs usually will monotonically increase.

[16] If the replacement equipment cost is different from the initial purchase price, the new repurchase price should be substituted in calculating depreciation.

[17] Decreases in productivity losses can be lumped with operating costs since they possess the same functional characteristics.

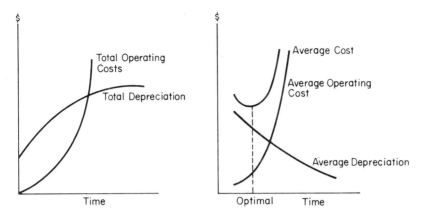

Illustration 11–6   Cost Curves and Graphic Solution for Deteriorating Asset Replacement Problem

Example

Consider the following example. Roca Cola Inc. uses a bottling machine that cost $50,000 when new. Exhibit 11–3 presents estimates of the expected operating costs per year, the annual expected production of the bottler (measured in thousands of cases) per year, and the salvage value of the machine. The wholesale price for a case less cost of sales and materials is $1.00. Using this data we can now compute the relevant costs and the average cost of the bottler per year. As shown in Exhibit 11–4, the optimal replacement policy is to purchase a new bottling machine at the end of every third year.[18]

Exhibit 11–3   Data Associated with Age of Bottling Machine

Age	1	2	3	4	5
Operating costs	7,000	8,000	10,000	14,000	20,000
Production (in cases)	208,000	208,000	200,000	190,000	175,000
Salvage value	30,000	19,000	15,000	12,000	10,000

[18] This example assumes that an integer number of years is accurate enough for practical purposes. In practice, treating real time periods as discrete intervals is usually adequate. However, with the use of calculus, the integer assumption can be dropped. You would calculate $C(t)$, the continuous function yielding the total cost of the equipment as a function of time. Hence

$$\int_0^t \frac{C(t)\,dt}{T}$$

gives the average cost curve as a function of time, denoted by $Ac(t)$. Thus to find the minimum of the average cost curve with respect to T we solve $d\,AC(t)/dT = 0$ for t.

Exhibit 11–4 Calculation of Average Cost of Capital Equipment

Age	1	2	3	4	5
Total operating costs	7,000	15,000	25,000	39,000	59,000
Total production loss costs	0	0	8,000	18,000	33,000
Depreciation	20,000	31,000	35,000	38,000	40,000
Total cost	27,000	46,000	68,000	95,000	132,000
Average cost	27,000	23,000	22,667	23,750	26,400

Assumptions

The replacement model presented assumes that we have use for the equipment indefinitely and at the time of purchase we can accurately estimate depreciation and operating costs. Clearly the model will yield results only as good as our cost estimates. Moreover, increases or decreases in the repurchase cost can alter the optimal replacement period. An incentive, such as the investment tax credit for new capital equipment, has the effect of decreasing depreciation[19] and thus reducing the replacement period, while an increase in the price of new equipment would have the reverse effect. It is necessary, therefore, to constantly review the replacement decision as new information becomes available. If the need for the capital equipment is only for fixed time periods, the model can still be used but with certain adjustments. In calculating the average cost, we calculate it over the total fixed time period. We would then select the replacement period which minimizes the average cost over the time period the equipment is needed.

Preventive Replacement

The deterioration of some types of equipment does not result in increased operating costs or in decreased productivity. Consider a light bulb, which either shines or does not shine. The effect of age is simply to increase the probability that it will burn out. A possible replacement policy for such equipment could be to replace it when it fails. However, in many cases the cost of failure of the equipment may dwarf the cost of replacement. Consider the obvious case of electrical equipment in an airplane. The equipment may cost a few thousand dollars to replace, but if it fails when the plane is in the air the cost could be the aircraft and many lives. Clearly, it would make sense to replace the equipment *before* it fails if it would greatly decrease the probability of failure. Less dramatic situations also call for preventive replacement. A conveyor belt on an assembly line of a bottling company may cost only $50 and may take fifteen minutes to replace. However, in fifteen minutes 250 cases worth $1.20 each can be produced. The probability of the belt's breaking increases with age and usage. When the

[19] Remember we are talking about repurchase price — resale price, not normal accounting depreciation.

209

Inventory
Models, Cash
Balances, and
Replacement
Models

probability of breaking becomes high, it makes economic sense to replace the belt during nonproduction hours before it breaks to avoid the cost of failure.

General Model

Let us now determine how we can find an optimal replacement policy. In order to do this we shall define the following terms.

C_R = cost of replacement

C_F = cost of failure (including replacement cost)

p_t = probability that an item will fail in time period t, if it has not failed previously

P_t = probability that an item will *not* fail during or before time period t. $[P_t = (P_{t-1})(1 - p_t)$, i.e., the probability that it did not fail during or before time period $(t - 1)$, times the probability that it does not fail during time period t.]

The optimal replacement policy is to replace the item every T time periods if it has not failed sooner, so that the expected cost per time period is minimized. In order to find the replacement period T that yields the minimum average cost, we first must compute the expected cost for any selected replacement time period T. If T is our replacement period, the maximum life of any item is T. However, some will fail prior to T and will have to be replaced earlier. Thus the expected or average life of the item U_T would be

$$U_T = \sum_{t=1}^{T-1} tP_{t-1} p_t + T(1 - P_{T-1}) \qquad (11\text{--}10)$$

Equation (11–10) can be calculated more readily by

$$U_T = 1 + \sum_{t=1}^{T-1} P_t$$

If the expected life of the equipment is U_T under replacement period T, then in the long run, on the average over an arbitrarily fixed period of time k, we would use k/U_T pieces of equipment. Recall that the probability that any piece of equipment will *not* fail prior to replacement at time period T[20] is P_{T-1}; it follows that of the k/U_T pieces of equipment we would expect $(P_{T-1})(k/U_T)$ to be replaced before failure and the remaining $(1 - P_{T-1})$ proportion of the k/U_T pieces of equipment to fail prior to replacement. Thus the expected cost for the period k would be given by Eq. (11–11).

$$\frac{k(1 - P_{T-1})C_F}{U_T} + \frac{kP_{T-1}C_R}{U_T} \qquad (11\text{--}11)$$

[20] Replacement is assumed to occur at the beginning of the time period.

Dividing by the number of periods yields the expected cost per period for replacement policy T,

$$AC(T) = \frac{(1 - P_{T-1})C_F + P_{T-1}C_R}{U_T} \qquad (11\text{--}12)$$

Hence the value of T that minimizes Eq. (11–12) is the optimal replacement policy.

For example, if the expected life of the equipment under a preventive replacement policy of replacing all equipment when it is 25 days old is 20 days, U_T, then in a 100-day period k we would, on the average, use five pieces of equipment, k/U_T. Now if the probability of a piece of equipment's lasting until the twenty-fifth day is $0.8(P_{T-1})$, then we would expect four pieces to be replaced prior to failure $[(k/U_T)(1 - P_{T-1})]$. Thus the expected cost of this policy would be $(1)C_F + (4)C_R$, and the expected average cost per day would be $(C_F + 4C_R)/100$.

Since Eq. (11–12) gives us the average cost for a preventive replacement policy of time T, to find the optimal replacement period T all we need to do is calculate the average cost for each possible T and select that T which minimizes the expected average cost. [It should be noted that k cancels out of Eq. (14–12), so no arbitrary time period need actually be selected.]

Example

To illustrate this procedure let us reconsider the conveyer belt problem. The cost of replacement C_R is \$51.75 if 15 minutes of labor is worth \$1.75. The cost of failure C_F is \$351.75, resulting from \$300 in lost production and \$51.75 for replacement. Exhibit 11–5 presents p_t and P_t and the calculations of

Exhibit 11–5 Probabilities and Calculation of Average Expected Cost for Preventive Replacement Policies

Weeks	1	2	3	4	5
p_t	0.01	0.05	0.10	0.15	0.25
P_t	0.990	0.941	0.847	0.720	0.540
U_t	1	1.990	2.931	3.778	4.498
$(1 - P_{T-1})C_F + P_{T-1}C_R$	51.75	54.75	69.45	97.65	135.75
$AC(t)$	51.75	27.51	23.70	25.85	30.18

average cost corresponding to the replacement policy for each time period.

The minimum average expected cost is reached in time period 3. Thus the optimal replacement policy is to replace any belt that has been in use for three weeks.

As in all models, the results are only as good as the data that go into the model. In most situations the estimates of the costs of replacement and failure should be fairly easily and accurately obtainable. The difficult problem in practice usually is estimating the probabilities of equipment failure.

211

Inventory
Models, Cash
Balances, and
Replacement
Models

PROBLEMS

1. Why are two decision parameters required for an inventory policy with reordering, while only one decision parameter is necessary with no reordering?

2. Discuss the cost trade-offs that are involved when the order point and order quantity are varied.

3. The requirement for a particular inventory item is 10,000 units per period. The ordering cost is $4.00 and the carrying cost is $2.00.
   a. What is the economic order quantity?
   b. What is the optimal number of orders per period?
   c. What is the total inventory cost for the period?
   d. Rework a, b, and c, assuming the requirement for the period has doubled. Compare your results.
   e. Rework a, b, and c, assuming that the carrying cost has doubled. Compare your results.
   f. Rework a, b, and c, assuming that both the ordering cost and carrying cost have doubled. Compare your results.
   g. Increase the optimal order quantity computed in a by 25 percent and find the total inventory cost for the period. Compare this cost with your answer to c. What conclusions do you draw?

4. Assume that 10 percent of the order quantity is to be maintained at all times as a safety stock. Derive a new EOQ formula that allows for this additional requirement. Compare this new formula with Eq. (11–4).

5. Discuss at least three problems to which the basic inventory model could be applied. Indicate any asumptions that you are forced to make. Formulate a simple model for one of the problems you have discussed.

6. An inventory item has a unit cost of $5.00. The usage requirement is 180,000 units per period, the ordering cost is $4.00, and the carrying cost is $9.00.
   a. What is the economic order quantity?
   b. What is the optimal number of orders per period?
   c. What is the total inventory cost for the period?
   d. Assume the supplier offers a 5 percent discount on the cost of each unit if orders are for round lots of 1000 units each. Should the offer be accepted?
   e. What is the minimum percentage discount that would make it economical to order in round lots of 1000 units each?

7. A corporation needs 4,000 units of rolled paper during the upcoming period. The corporation uses 14 rolls a day and the supplier can make delivery at the rate of 50 rolls a day. Ordering costs are $18.00 per order and carrying costs are $20.00 per roll.
   a. What is the economic order quantity?
   b. How many orders will be placed during the period?
   c. What is the total inventory cost during the period?
   d. Answer a, b, and c under the assumption that the supplier can fill any order in just one shipment. Compare your answers and discuss the differences.

8. If the lead time between placing an order and receiving shipment is expected to be 4 days and a firm uses an average of 15 units a day, what would be the minimum order point? Why might the order point be higher? What factors would influence how much higher than the minimum amount calculated above the order point should be set?

9. A large corporation collects outstanding receivables at the end of each month. This money is then available to be invested in short-term securities at the beginning of the next month. The cash manager is currently beginning a 30-day month (assume that all days are working days) with $10,000,000 on hand. All

of this money will be spent, more or less uniformly, during the month. He can invest some of this money in Treasury Bills, which would yield 0.625 percent if held for one month. The cost of investing in Bills is 0.125 percent of the amount invested. The same cost is incurred when Bills are transferred back to cash. In addition, a fixed cost of $50 is incurred with each transaction from cash to Bills or from Bills to cash.

a. How much should the cash manager initially invest in Bills, and how much should he withhold in cash?

b. How much should he transfer from Bills to cash each time he makes a withdrawal?

c. What is his net gain during the month if he follows this optimal policy?

10. Abbott Trucking maintains a fleet of 10 delivery trucks. A truck costs $5000. From past history it has constructed the following cost information.

Age of Truck	1	2	3	4	5	6
Operating costs (per year)	600	700	810	1350	2000	3800
Salvage value	3100	2000	1500	1300	1200	1100

a. What is the optimal replacement period?

b. After five new trucks have been purchased, the cost of trucks increases to $6100. When should they replace these five trucks?

c. After five new trucks have been purchased, the cost of trucks decreases to $4000. When should they replace these five trucks?

d. If the average revenue per year from a truck is $5000, what is the average net return per truck?

11. Resook Inc., a machine shop firm, has made a comprehensive study of lathe bits. A bit costs $6 to replace. If a bit breaks on a job, the production loss is estimated to be $29. In the past the life of a bit has been as given in the following table.

Jobs	Proportion of Bits Used on Job Breaking
1	0.01
2	0.03
3	0.09
4	0.13
5	0.25
6	0.55
7	0.95

After how many jobs should a firm replace a bit that has not broken?

12

evaluation
of capital
investments

This chapter will present various decision criteria that can be used to evaluate capital investment proposals. Some decisions may require the acceptance or rejection of individual investment proposals, whereas others may require the choice of one from a set of mutually exclusive proposals. It is necessary to develop (a) consistent and unambiguous decision criteria, (b) a procedure to deal efficiently and optimally with the problem of capital rationing, and (c) methods for incorporating adjustments for risk into the decision process.

ACCRUAL AND CASH ACCOUNTING

Most accounting statements are based on the accrual method, where the accountant attempts to match revenues and expenses by allocating portions of an item's actual cash cost or revenue to different accounting periods. Expenses are recognized on the books when the benefit from an asset is enjoyed and not when the actual expenditure is made; revenue is recognized when it is earned and not when the cash is received. For example, if a three-year insurance policy is paid for immediately, one-third of the total cost will be recognized and charged against annual income in each of the next three years.

Assume that a machine with an estimated ten-year life is purchased with an immediate cash outlay of $10,000. No expense is recognized at the time the expenditure is made. The machine is capitalized (entered as an asset on the balance sheet), and depreciation is then charged against annual income over the following ten-year period. Other items that would be treated on an accrual basis are bond discounts and premiums, intangibles (such as goodwill or patents), and revenue (on a percentage of completion basis, for example) under long-term contracts.

The accrual method does not recognize the actual timing of expenditures and receipts of cash. But most capital budgeting problems are solved on the basis of when actual cash flows occur, and not on the basis of when revenues and expenses are recognized through accounting book entries. Therefore, the solution of capital budgeting problems generally requires an adjustment from an accrual to a cash basis.

It is also imperative that the problem be analyzed by using appropriate cash flow figures. Some investments increase revenues, while others decrease costs, but both types increase earnings. Opportunity costs are the relevant costs for the solution of a capital budgeting problem. The appropriate question is, "What cash flows will change as a result of a decision to invest?" Cash flows that change are relevant; those that remain unchanged are not relevant. Thus it is inappropriate to include allocated fixed overhead expenses in a capital budgeting analysis. It is appropriate to consider a required addition to inventories as an additional cash outflow.

Needless to say, the estimation of future cash flows is subject to uncertainties and is by far the most difficult part of an actual capital budgeting problem. Nevertheless, since these estimates require inputs from such diverse areas as the marketing, accounting, and production and engineering departments, and since the procedures and degree of uncertainty vary from firm to firm and from project to project, no systematic methodology will (or can) be formulated for estimating cash flows. We shall, therefore, take the estimated cash flows as given and focus our attention on the next step in the decision process, that of evaluating proposed capital investments. (Techniques for adjusting for risk will be discussed in the last section of this chapter.)

Initial Cash Outlay

The first step in solving a capital budgeting problem is to find the initial cash outlay required to undertake the proposed project. The machine in the above example costs $10,000. It is possible that this is the required outlay, although it is more likely that additional complicating factors must be taken into account. For example, the new machine may have freight and installation costs of $800 and $1400, respectively. Less obvious, but equally important, are any required increases in working capital. If the machine is to manufacture a new product, it will presumably be necessary for the firm to purchase and maintain additional inventory to support the production of the machine. As the new units are produced and sold, any credit sales will lead to an increase in accounts receivable. It is important to recognize that an investment to increase current assets requires a cash outlay, just as does an investment to increase fixed assets.

Another possibility is that the machine is being purchased to replace an older one. If so, there will probably be a salvage value and a tax gain or loss that will also affect the required outlay. Assume, for example, that the old machine has an estimated remaining economic life of ten years, a current market value of $4000, and a remaining book value of $3000, and that the appropriate marginal corporate income tax rate is 40 percent.[1] The net proceeds from the disposal of the old machine is then the market value of $4000 minus the 40 percent tax on the $1000 gain over book value, or $4000 − 0.40(1000) = $3600.[2]

If we include the freight and installation costs (and assume there are no increases in working capital), the total cost of the new machine is $12,200. But if we adjust for the net proceeds from disposal of the old, the initial cash outlay required to purchase the new machine is $12,200 − 3600 = $8600.

Annual Cash Inflows

Assume that the purchase of the new machine will yield the same output as the old, but that greater efficiencies will reduce operating costs by $2500 per year. This savings results in a $2500 annual increase in earnings before depreciation and taxes (EBDT). Depreciation is *increased* by $920 per year, if we assume straight-line depreciation. ($1220 per year on the new machine minus the $300 per year that would be available if the new machine is rejected and the old one retained. It is the *change* in the annual depreciation expense resulting from a decision to invest that is the relevant amount.) The additional EBDT minus the additional depreciation leaves earnings before taxes (EBT), and if taxes are then subtracted we are left with earnings after taxes (EAT). EAT is the reported earnings on the income statement, but it includes a noncash deduction for depreciation. Thus the annual depreciation can be added to the reported EAT to find the annual cash flow. The above discussion is summarized in Exhibit 12–1, which clearly shows the difference between the accrual and cash concepts.

Exhibit 12–1   Annual Cash Flow from Proposed Machine

	Accrual Basis		Cash Basis	Without Depreciation
Additional EBDT		$2500	$2500	$2500
Additional Depreciation:				
New machine	1220			
− Old machine	300			
		920		0
Additional EBT		1580		2500
− Additional Taxes		632	632	1000
Additional EAT		948		1500
+ Additional Depreciation		920		0
Additional Cash Flow		$1868	$1868	$1500

[1] A 40 percent marginal tax rate is assumed throughout this chapter.

[2] The gain (market value minus book value) is taxed at the 40 percent rate, unless the market value exceeds the original purchase price. Then the gain over and above original cost is taxed as a capital gain. If the book value exceeds market value, there is a loss that results in a tax saving. The procedure is the same as above, with the appropriate change in sign.

The third "Without Depreciation" column is added to Exhibit 12–1 to highlight the effect of depreciation on cash flows. The tax payment is $368 greater without depreciation than with depreciation. This amount is 40 percent of the $920 additional depreciation, illustrating that depreciation acts as a tax shield. Notice that the cash flow is $368 greater with depreciation than without, so the greater cash flow is a direct result of the reduction in taxes.[3]

A Comprehensive Example

Let us take the above example and add some complications. Assume that acceptance of the new machine will necessitate an additional investment in working capital of $400, that the old machine has a remaining economic life of five years rather than ten, and that the new machine will have an estimated salvage value at the end of ten years of $2200. The solution incorporating these new assumptions is given in Exhibit 12–2.

Exhibit 12–2 Initial Outlay for New Machine

Purchase price	$10,000
Freight	800
Installation	1,400
Additional working capital	400
Total	12,600
Less proceeds from disposal of old	3,600
Initial Outlay	$9,000

Annual Net Cash Flows

	Years 1–5	Years 6–9	Year 10
EBDT	$2500	$2500	$2500
− Depreciation			
New	1000	1000	1000
Old	600	0	0
	400	1000	1000
EBT	2100	1500	1500
− Taxes	840	600	600
EAT	1260	900	900
+ Depreciation	400	1000	1000
+ Salvage value	0	0	2200
+ Release of working capital	0	0	400
Net Cash Flow	$1660	$1900	$4500

The old machine is depreciated over five years, so the difference in years 6–10 is the full amount of annual depreciation for the new machine.

---

[3] Notice that depreciation increases the cash flow only if earnings are otherwise high enough that the additional depreciation can reduce the total tax liability. Depreciation is not a direct source of cash; it serves only as a tax shield.

(The difficult problem presented by the fact that the old and new machines now have different economic lives, so that they would have to be replaced at different points in time, is ignored.) The new machine is depreciated down to its estimated salvage value at the end of 10 years. Then the salvage value (with no tax adjustment, since market value will equal book value) and the released investment in working capital are added to the cash flow for year 10. The investment in working capital is not depreciated. The same amount is invested and then released 10 years later, amounting to a 10-year investment at a zero rate of return (i.e., $400 is invested now and $400 is returned 10 years later).

METHODS OF EVALUATING CAPITAL INVESTMENTS

There are four methods of evaluating capital investments that are generally covered in discussions of capital budgeting. These are (a) average (or accounting) rate of return, (b) payback, (c) net present value (and profitability index), and (d) internal rate of return.[4] The latter two methods employ discounting techniques (see Appendix A), whereas the former two do not. The mechanics of calculation and the usefulness and limitations of each measure are discussed in this section. In addition, a fifth method, terminal value, is also introduced. This last method is gaining increased acceptance and popularity among (normative, at least) writers on the topic of capital budgeting. It will be seen in succeeding sections that terminal value is a useful method for resolving certain problems encountered with the more traditionally used methods (c) and (d) above. In all examples, it is assumed that projected cash flow and income figures are known with certainty. Risk is not considered until the last section of this chapter.

Average Rate Return

Of all the methods that are used to evaluate capital investments, average rate of return is the only one that is based on accounting (or accrual) concepts of income and investment rather than on actual cash flows. The average rate of return is intended to measure the annual rate of return over the life of an investment. The calculated rate is compared to a minimum required cutoff rate for an accept-reject decision. Obviously, the higher the average rate of return, the more attractive the investment. The average rate of return is found by dividing average income by average investment.[5] The method of calculation will be illustrated using Example Problem 12–1.

---

[4] When the term "rate of return" is used in the literature, with no descriptive or identifying adjective, the writer is generally referring to the *internal* rate of return as it is defined in this chapter.

[5] A variation of this measure, obtained by dividing average income by the total initial investment, is also sometimes used.

Example Problem 12–1

Purchase price of new machine = initial outlay = $10,000
Estimated life = 5 years, salvage value = 0, straight line depreciation
Marginal tax rate = 40 percent

	Years 1, 2, 3	Years 4, 5
EBDT	$5000	$4000
− Depreciation	2000	2000
EBT	3000	2000
− Taxes	1200	800
EAT	1800	1200
+ Depreciation	2000	2000
Cash Flow	$3800	$3200

Average income is a weighted average of the annual reported income (EAT) over the five-year period. Thus

$$\text{Average income} = \frac{3(\$1800) + 2(\$1200)}{3 + 2} = \frac{\$7800}{5} = \$1560$$

The average investment is the average of the book value of the asset over its depreciable life. After one year the machine would have a book value of $8000, after two years $6000, etc., until the book value would be written to zero at the end of the fifth year. The average book value would, therefore, be $\frac{1}{2}(\$10,000) = \$5000$, and the average rate of return would be $\frac{1560}{5000} = 31.2$ percent.

The procedure for finding the average investment can perhaps be understood more clearly by reference to Illustration 12–1. The book value of

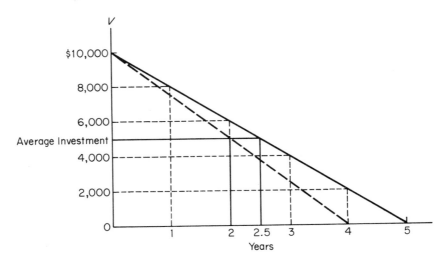

Illustration 12–1 Book Value versus Time

the machine V is shown as a function of time.[6] The average investment is clearly $\frac{1}{2}(\$10,000)$. Note that the average investment would be the same whether the machine was depreciated over four years (as shown by the dashed line), eight years, ten years, etc.

This simple and straightforward procedure must be modified somewhat as the problem becomes more complex. Consider, for example, Example Problem 12–2, which is Example Problem 12–1 with a salvage value and an investment in additional working capital added.

Example Problem 12–2

Purchase price of new machine		$= \$10,000$
Additional investment in working capital	$=$	3,000
Initial outlay		$= \$13,000$

Estimated life $= 5$ years, salvage value $= \$2000$, straight line depreciation
Marginal tax rate $= 40$ percent

	Years 1, 2, 3	Year 4	Year 5
EBDT	$5000	$4000	$4000
− Depreciation	1600	1600	1600
EBT	3400	2400	2400
− Taxes	1360	960	960
EAT	2040	1440	1440
+ Depreciation	1600	1600	1600
+ Salvage value	0	0	2000
+ Release of working capital	0	0	3000
Cash Flow	$3640	$3040	$8040

$$\text{Average income} = \frac{3(\$2040) + 2(\$1440)}{3 + 2} = \frac{\$9000}{5} = \$1800$$

As seen in Illustration 12–2, the average investment is the working capital plus the salvage value plus one-half the amount to be depreciated. Numerically, average investment $= \$3000 + \$2000 + \frac{1}{2}(\$10,000 - \$2000) = \$9000$. The average rate of return then equals $\$1800/\$9000 = 20$ percent.

Payback

The payback period is the number of years required for the investment to generate enough cash to cover the initial investment. The shorter the payback period, the better the investment is supposed to be. A firm may establish a maximum payback period for acceptable investment proposals. In Example Problem 12–1 the initial cash outlay was $10,000. Total accumulated cash flow was $7600 after two years and $11,400 after three years. Thus sometime during the third year the payback period was reached. A total of $2400 ($10,000 − $7600) must be realized in the third year to reach the

---

[6] It is assumed that the machine is depreciated smoothly over each year rather than periodically. Thus the graph is linear rather than a step function. Since most corporations pay taxes quarterly, this simplifying assumption involves little error.

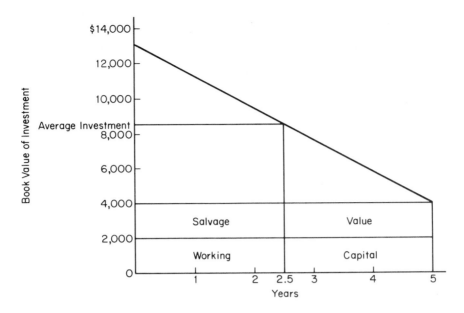

Illustration 12–2 Book Value versus Time

payback period. If we make the reasonable assumption that cash generated from operations is realized continuously and linearly throughout the year, the payback period is 2.632 ($2 + \frac{2400}{3800}$) years. In Example Problem 12–2, 3($3640) = $10,920 has been received by the end of the third year, which is $2080 ($13,000 − $10,920) short of the payback period. Thus the payback period is $3 + \frac{2080}{3040}$ = 3.684 years.

Criticisms of Payback and Average Rate of Return

There are two major criticisms of the payback criterion: (a) It does not consider the full life of the investment and (b) it does not take into account the pattern of cash flows (or the time value of money). These two shortcomings are readily evident from the (admittedly exaggerated) examples in Exhibit 12–3. Strict application of the payback criterion would rank R over S, although it is obvious that S is far superior to R. R and T are ranked equally, although if $400 were preferred in year 1 rather than year 2 (as it should be), T is preferable to R.

Payback is generally advocated because it is simple to apply, stresses liquidity, and, by emphasizing the rapid return of cash, is biased against risky investments. Payback is certainly simpler to apply than are the other methods considered in this chapter. But the projection of cash flows consumes most of the time, effort, and expense in analyzing an investment opportunity, and the additional effort required to use more reliable decision criteria is relatively minor. It will be seen that, if liquidity and risk are im-

220

portant considerations, the discount rate to be used in the following methods can be increased to give greater weight to rapid recovery of cash without also introducing the other shortcomings of the payback criterion.[7]

Exhibit 12–3

	Cash Flow		
Year	R	S	T
0	− $1000	− $1000	− $1000
1	400	400	800
2	400	400	0
3	400	300	400
4	400	1000	400
5	400	1000	400
Payback (years)	$2\frac{1}{2}$	$2\frac{2}{3}$	$2\frac{1}{2}$

The average rate of return criterion considers the entire life of the investment, so it is not open to one of the criticisms leveled against payback. It is open to the related criticisms of not using cash flows and of not considering the time value of money. Suppose, for example, that some accelerated form of depreciation were used in Example Problem 12–1. EAT would be less in years 1 and 2 and greater in years 4 and 5 than in the original problem, although the total earnings over the five-year period would be the same in either case. So regardless of the pattern of reported earnings, average income would be the same. (Note that the use of accelerated depreciation would reduce the average investment, so that the average rate of return would increase.[8]) But the pattern of cash flows will change in the opposite direction from EAT; i.e., cash flows will be greater in the earlier years and less in the later years, although the total cash generated over the life of the investment will be the same. Any decision criterion that fails fully to reflect this widely acknowledged advantage of accelerated depreciation would seem to be seriously deficient.

We now turn to an examination of net present value (NPV), internal rate of return (IRR), and terminal value (TV). All three of these methods use discounting (or compounding) techniques and, *if used correctly*, should give the same ranking to alternative investment proposals and lead to the same decisions.[9]

[7] Discounted payback has recently become popular. Under this method, the payback period is the length of time required for discounted future cash flows to cover the initial investment. This method is obviously more conservative than the one described above.

[8] If the measure obtained by dividing average income by the total initial investment is used, switching to an accelerated form of depreciation would have absolutely no effect on the calculated average rate of return.

[9] See Appendix A for a discussion of the use of present value tables.

The net present value method evaluates investment alternatives relative to a minimum required rate of return which distinguishes between acceptable and unacceptable proposals. This minimum acceptance rate will be called the cost of capital (CC). The CC is designated the minimum required rate of return for the acceptance of any investment proposal and is (vaguely but conveniently) defined as the rate of return expected by the suppliers of the firm's capital.

Suppose, for example, a firm with a CC of 15 percent is considering the purchase of the machine described in Example Problem 12–1. The present value of the future cash inflows resulting from the purchase of the machine is $(3.352)(\$3200) + (2.283)(\$600) = \$12,096.20$. Thus if the firm paid exactly $12,096.20 for the machine, a rate of return of exactly 15 percent (equal to the discount rate) would be earned on the investment. Since the machine can be purchased for only $10,000, the actual rate of return would be in excess of 15 percent, and the proposal should be accepted.

This simple example illustrates the NPV criteria. The NPV is defined as the discounted value of all future cash flows resulting from an investment minus the initial outlay required to undertake the investment. Thus the NPV of the above example is $\$12,096.20 - \$10,000.00 = \$2096.20$. The decision criterion is to accept an investment if the NPV is positive and reject it if it is negative. It will be demonstrated in the next section that the proper choice from a set of mutually exclusive alternatives is to choose the one with the highest NPV, regardless of whether the initial outlays are the same.[10]

The NPV of the machine described in Example Problem 12–2 is $(2.283)(\$3640) + (0.572)(\$3040) + 0.497(\$8040) - \$13,000 = \$14,044.88 - \$13,000 = \$1044.88$. This figure is positive, and the investment is acceptable. If the required outlay were $15,000, the NPV would be $-\$955.12$, and the investment would be unacceptable.

The profitability index (PI) performs the same function as the NPV when an accept-reject decision is required for an individual proposal. The PI is defined as the discounted value of all future cash flows divided by (rather than minus) the initial outlay. Thus if the NPV is positive, the PI will be greater than one, and the investment will be accepted. If the NPV is negative, the PI will be less than one, and the investment will be rejected. The PI's of Example Problems 12–1 and 12–2 are $12,096.20/10,000 = 1.21$ and $14,044.88/13,000 = 1.08$, respectively. Both are greater than one, and therefore both would be acceptable as individual investments.

If a choice had to be made between two different machines based on the figures from Example Problems 12–1 and 12–2, the former would be chosen because it has the greater NPV ($2096.20 > $1044.88). The PI's would give the same ranking in this case, but the PI cannot be used as a consistently

---

[10] We are assuming in this and the next two sections that the firm has sufficient capital to undertake any acceptable investment. The problem of capital rationing will be considered later in this chapter.

reliable criterion for choosing between alternatives, whereas the NPV can (again it is assumed that we are not in a capital rationing situation). For example, if the machine in Example Problem 12–1 required an outlay of $11,100, it would have a lower NPV and a higher PI than the machine described in Example Problem 12–2. It will be demonstrated later in the chapter that NPV is the correct decision criterion to use.

Internal Rate of Return

The IRR criterion compares a project's rate of return with the CC. If the IRR exceeds the CC, the project is acceptable, and if the IRR is less than the CC, the project is unacceptable. We have already established the fact that the rate of return exceeds the CC if the NPV is positive, and vice versa, so we should always get consistent results when using NPV and IRR. There is a preference in practice for using IRR criterion, because we are generally more comfortable thinking in terms of percentage returns rather than an absolute number such as NPV. Furthermore, the IRR method delays the need for formal specification of the discount rate.

The IRR is generally more difficult to calculate than NPV because, with rare exceptions, a trial and error procedure is necessary.[11] The IRR is the discount rate that equates the present value of all future cash flows with the initial outlay (i.e., makes NPV = 0). In Example Problem 12–1 we know that the IRR must be greater than 15 percent, because the NPV at the CC is positive. To illustrate the trial and error procedure, let us first try a discount rate of 20 percent: $(2.991)(\$3200) + (2.106)(\$600) = \$10,834.80$. If the firm were to pay exactly $10,834.80 for the machine, the rate of return would be exactly 20 percent. But the required investment is only $10,000, so the actual rate of return must be greater than 20 percent. Let us next try 25 percent: $(2.689)(\$3200) + (1.952)(\$600) = \$9776.00$ is less than $10,000. Twenty-five percent is too high, so we drop down and try 24 percent: $(2.745)(\$3200) + (1.981)(\$600) = \$10,572.60$. Thus the IRR is between 24 and 25 percent. By interpolating, we find the IRR = 24.72 percent.[12] By a similar trial and error procedure, we can find the IRR in Example Problem 12–2 to be 19.95 percent.[13]

As was mentioned previously, a trial and error procedure is not always necessary. Trial and error is not necessary when the future cash flows are in

[11] Most financial packages for computer systems provide easy-to-use programs that calculate the IRR. Nevertheless, the user should know the significance and any possible limitations of the number printed out by the computer.

[12]
$$\begin{array}{ll} 24.0 & 10,572.60 \\ X & 10,000.00 \\ 25.0 & 9,776.00 \end{array} \qquad X = 24.00 + \frac{572.60}{796.60} = 24.72 \text{ percent}$$

[13] Try 20%: $(2.106)(\$3640) + (0.482)(\$3040) + (0.402)(\$8040) = \$12,363.20$
Try 18%: $(2.176)(\$3640) + (0.576)(\$3040) + (0.437)(\$8040) = \$13,014.76$

$$\begin{array}{ll} 18.00 & 12,363.20 \\ X & 13,000.00 \\ 20.00 & 13,014.76 \end{array} \qquad X = 18.00 + \frac{636.80}{651.56}(2) = 19.95 \text{ percent}$$

the form of either one lump sum payment or a uniform annuity. For example, suppose that $5650 is paid for the receipt of $1000 at the end of each of the next ten years. To find the IRR, we want to discount back the future cash receipts so that they equal the initial outlay; i.e., we want $1000 × (discount factor) = $5650. But this equation is satisfied only if the discount factor = $\frac{5650}{1000}$ = 5.650. Given that the annuity is for ten years, we can find from Exhibit A4 that the IRR is exactly 12 percent.

Similarly, suppose that an outlay of $37 is made, with $100 to be received five years later. To find the IRR, $100 × (discount factor) must equal $37, and the discount factor must be $\frac{37}{100}$ = 0.370. From Exhibit A3, we can find that the IRR is 22 percent.

The above procedure suggests a way to make the solution of problems requiring trial and error more efficient. Consider, for example, the four investments in Exhibit 12–4. The IRR of W (25 percent) can be easily found.

Exhibit 12–4

Year	Cash Flows			
	W	**X**	**Y**	**Z**
0	− $3329	− $3329	− $3329	− $3329
1	1000	1100	1200	900
2	1000	1100	1200	900
3	1000	1100	1200	900
4	1000	1100	1200	900
5	1000	900	800	1100
6	1000	900	800	1100
7	1000	900	800	1100
8	1000	900	800	1100

While the others cannot be determined quite so readily, it should be obvious that the IRR of X has to be somewhat above 25 percent, the IRR of Y has to be even higher than that of X, and the IRR of Z has to be less than 25 percent. Thus, to the extent that an uneven stream of cash flows can be smoothed and approximated with an annuity, we can *approximate* the true rate of return to initiate our trial and error procedure. Furthermore, by noticing whether the cash flows in the early years are increased or decreased by the smoothing, we can tell whether our approximation will understate or overstate the true rate of return and adjust our first guess accordingly. A little practice greatly reduces the number of trials usually needed to arrive at a final solution.

Finally, we found a higher IRR for the machine in Example Problem 12–1 than we did for the one in Example Problem 12–2. This result is consistent with the ranking we found using NPV. Using either criterion, we would choose the first in preference to the second if such a choice were necessary. In most cases the same ranking will be obtained by using either criterion, but, as will be seen shortly, not always. It will be shown that, when the two methods give contradictory rankings, NPV is generally more reliable than IRR.

Terminal Value

The TV method is similar to NPV except that, rather than discounting future cash flows to find their present value, they are compounded to find the future value to which they will accumulate. The investment can then be analyzed as though only a single cash inflow (equal to the TV) is to be received at the end of the life of the project. Suppose, for example, that an investment of $100 will return $70 at the end of each of the next two years and that the $70 received at the end of the first year can be reinvested during the second year at a rate of return of 20 percent. At the end of the second year a total of $154 [70(1 + 0.20) + 70] will be available. Thus the above investment is equivalent to investing $100 and receiving $154 two years later; the $154 is the TV of the investment. The TV method is primarily useful for comparing mutually exclusive investment alternatives. The application of this method will be illustrated in the following section.

CONTRADICTIONS BETWEEN NPV AND IRR[14]

There are two types of situations where the NPV and IRR criteria can lead to contradictory rankings between mutually exclusive investment alternatives. These are when there are differences in the amounts of the initial outlays and when investments with substantially different time horizons or cash flow patterns are being compared.

Differences in Initial Outlays

The net present value and IRR criteria, calculated as in the preceding section, give contradictory results when applied to the mutually exclusive investments A and B described in Exhibit 12–5. Investment A has the higher IRR, while B has the higher NPV. Why the apparent contradiction between what should be two consistent methods? How can this contradiction be resolved? Answers are easily obtained by redefining the problem in terms of the incremental investment I_1. (The incremental investment is obtained from the

Exhibit 12–5

Year	A	B	$I_1 = B - A$
0	−$100	−$200	−$100
1	60	100	40
2	60	100	40
3	60	100	40
4	60	100	40
NPV	$90.20	$117.00	$26.80
IRR	47.3%	34.9%	21.7%

[14] The examples used in this section are based on Rodney D. Johnson and Richard H. Klein, "A Further Note on the Analysis of Capital Budgeting Expenditures," *Mississippi Valley Journal of Business and Economics*, Fall 1973, pp. 74–87.

differences in the initial outlay and future cash flows between the less expensive of two mutually exclusive investments and the one requiring the larger initial outlay. Thus in our example the incremental investment $I_1 = B - A$.[15]) The ranking of A and B now depends solely on an evaluation of I_1.[16] Rewriting $I_1 = B - A$ as $B = A + I_1$, we can see that if I_1 is determined to be a desirable investment we would prefer B to A; if I_1 is unacceptable, we would prefer A to B. Since I_1 has a positive NPV and an IRR greater than the CC, it is an acceptable investment and B is preferable to A. How can we now justify this choice consistently in terms of both NPV and IRR?

The initial solution obtained by using the NPV criterion was correct. Since, by definition, $B = A + I_1$, it follows that $\text{NPV}_B = \text{NPV}_A + \text{NPV}_{I_1}$. (Note that \$117.00 = \$90.20 + \$26.80.) If $\text{NPV}_{I_1} < 0$, $\text{NPV}_A > \text{NPV}_B$; if $\text{NPV}_{I_1} > 0$, $\text{NPV}_B > \text{NPV}_A$. Thus, as a general rule, choose the investment with the larger initial outlay if the incremental investment has a positive NPV; if the NPV is negative, choose the investment with the smaller initial outlay.

We must next determine why the initial ranking given by IRR was wrong and find a way to reformulate the problem so IRR will give a correct solution. Think of B as being composed of two separate investments, A and I_1. Investment A requires an outlay of \$100 and returns \$60 at the end of each of the next four years, for an IRR of 47.3 percent. Investment I_1 also requires an outlay of \$100, but returns only \$40 at the end of each of the next four years, for an IRR of 21.7 percent. When the second \$100 investment is added to the first, the over-all rate of return is reduced from the initial 47.3 percent to 34.9 percent. Thus B has a lower IRR than A simply because I_1 has a lower IRR than A. But to properly solve the problem in terms of IRR, the relevant comparison is between the IRR of I_1 and the CC. Since the IRR of I_1 exceeds the CC, I_1 is an attractive investment and B is therefore preferred to A.

It is perhaps more clearly evident that B is preferable to A when the comparison is made based on equivalent initial outlays. Investment B, defined as A plus I_1, consists of \$100 invested at 47.3 percent and a second \$100 invested at 21.7 percent. Investment A consists of \$100 invested at 47.3 percent; the second \$100 would presumably be invested at the CC of 10 percent. When compared on these terms, B is clearly preferable.

A consistently correct ranking of two mutually exclusive investments using IRR criteria can be obtained only by finding the IRR of the incremental investment. Note that if the IRR of the incremental investment is greater than the CC, its NPV must be positive. We will, therefore, never

---

[15] The examples used in this chapter assume that there are never more than two mutually exclusive investments. The same procedure can be used for any number, however, by defining sequential incremental investments and making pairwise comparisons.

[16] This incremental approach gives only the proper ranking of two investments. It is not sufficient if it is possible that both investments might be rejected.

have contradictory results using NPV and IRR if the problem is formulated in terms of the incremental investment.

Differences in Time Horizons

Investments C and D, described in Exhibit 12–6, are ranked differently by NPV and IRR criteria even though their initial outlays are the same. In this case, the contradiction arises because the two investments cover different periods of time. To make them comparable, they must both be considered over the same time period. In order to perform this comparison an assumption must be made about the rate at which the $150 received at the end of year 2 in C can be reinvested for the next three years. It is because of this problem of reinvestment rates that the contradiction between NPV and IRR occurs. The NPV method implicitly assumes reinvestment at the CC; the IRR method, however, implicitly assumes reinvestment at the rate of return that the project was earning up to the point of reinvestment (22.5 percent in this example). If it can be assumed that the CC (i.e., the reinvestment rate) will remain constant over the next five years, the problem is solved. The NPV method makes the correct assumption and therefore gives the correct ranking.

Exhibit 12–6

| | **Cash Flows** | | |
Year	C	D	$I_2 = D - C$
0	− $100	− $100	$0
1	0	0	0
2	150	0	150
3	0	0	0
4	0	0	0
5	0	240	240
NPV	$23.90	$49.04	—
IRR	22.5%	19.1%	17%

However, what if it cannot be reasonably assumed that the CC will remain constant? One of two different approaches can be used. In the first, a variation of the incremental investment approach can be used to obtain $I_2 = D - C$. This formulation tells us that accepting D is equivalent to accepting C and reinvesting the $150 received at the end of year 2 so that it will accumulate to $240 at the end of year 5. If $150(1 + i)^3 = 240$, where i is the reinvestment rate, i is then equal to 17 percent.[17] Our decision rule can therefore be stated as: Accept C if the anticipated reinvestment rate exceeds 17 percent; otherwise accept D. (Notice that IRR, which assumed reinvestment at 22.5 percent, ranked C higher; NPV, which assumed reinvestment at 10 percent, ranked D higher.)

---

[17] If $150(1 + i)^3 = 240$, $1/[(1 + i)^3] = 150/240 = 0.625$. Then, from Exhibit A3, $i = 17$ percent.

The above method avoids the need for an explicit assumption about reinvestment rates by finding an indifference or cutoff rate. A second procedure, based on the TV method, can incorporate into the analysis any explicit assumptions about reinvestment rates that management wants to make. The TV of a project is the future value of all cash flows compounded to the end of the time horizon being considered. The project can then be analyzed as though only a single cash inflow (the TV) is to be realized at the end of its life. If i is the assumed reinvestment rate, the TV of C, TV_C, is $150(1 + i)^3$. If $i = 10$ percent (the CC), then, over the appropriate five-year horizon,

$$NPV_C = \frac{150(1 + 0.10)^3}{(1 + 0.10)^5} - 100 = \frac{150}{(1 + 0.10)^2} - 100 = \$23.90$$

Thus it is seen that NPV implicitly assumes reinvestment at the CC. Letting r be the IRR and assuming reinvestment at 22.5 percent, we have $TV_C = 150(1 + 0.225)^3$, and the IRR of C (again over the five-year horizon) is the value of r that satisfies the equation $TV_C/(1 + r)^5 = 100$; $r = 22.5$ percent. Thus it is seen that IRR implicitly assumes reinvestment at the IRR calculated for the project prior to the point of reinvestment.

Assume that management feels that the $150 received at the end of year 2 in C could be reinvested for the next three years at an annual rate of 12 percent. Then $TV_C = \$150(1 + 0.12)^3 = \$200.74$. Since $TV_D = \$240 > TV_C$, D is preferable to C. (This result is consistent with the previous method, since 12 percent is less than the 17 percent indifference reinvestment rate calculated above.) The same ranking can also be obtained by using NPV and IRR once it is recognized that the reinvestment rate for any period is also the appropriate discount rate.

$$NPV_C = \frac{150(1 + 0.12)^3}{(1 + 0.10)^2(1 + 0.12)^3} - 100$$

$$= \frac{TV_C}{(1 + 0.10)^2(1 + 0.12)^3} - 100$$

$$= \$23.90$$

$$NPV_D = \frac{240}{(1 + 0.10)^2(1 + 0.12)^3} - 100$$

$$= \frac{TV_D}{(1 + 0.10)^2(1 + 0.12)^3} - 100$$

$$= \$51.15$$

$$IRR_C: \frac{150(1 + 0.12)^3}{(1 + r)^5} = \frac{TV_C}{(1 + r)^5} = 100; \qquad r = 15.0 \text{ percent}$$

$$IRR_D: \frac{240}{(1 + r)^5} = \frac{TV_D}{(1 + r)^5} = 100; \qquad r = 19.1 \text{ percent}$$

Notice that $NPV_C < NPV_D$ and $IRR_C < IRR_D$ only if $TV_C < TV_D$. Once a problem is correctly specified in terms of TV, all three methods should give consistent rankings.[18]

A Digression on TV

Since the popular use of the TV concept is relatively new compared to NPV and IRR, let us digress and further explore the use of this method. It is not necessary to assume one constant reinvestment rate, for example. The same procedure can be used to accommodate any assumed pattern of reinvestment rates. In the example in Exhibit 12–7, a reinvestment rate of 10 percent is assumed in year 2 with a drop to 8 percent in years 3 and 4. (It is assumed for simplicity that cash flows are realized at the end of each year and that reinvestment occurs for consecutive one-year periods only.)

Exhibit 12–7

Year	Years to End of Project	Cash Flow	Reinvestment Rate	Compound Factor Until End of Project	Terminal Value
1	3	$5000	—	1.283[a]	$6415
2	2	5000	10%	1.166[b]	5830
3	1	4000	8%	1.080[c]	4320
4	0	4000	8%	—	4000
					$20,565

Required initial investment = $11,000.

[a] Compound factor at 10 percent for 1 year, 8 percent for 2 years.
[b] Compound factor at 8 percent for 2 years.
[c] Compound factor at 8 percent for 1 year.

The traditional method of finding the IRR is to solve the following equation for r:

$$\frac{5000}{(1+r)} + \frac{5000}{(1+r)^2} + \frac{4000}{(1+r)^3} + \frac{4000}{(1+r)^4} = 11,000$$

The value of r that satisfies the equation is 24.4 percent. But, as we have shown, this method of calculation of the IRR implicitly assumes that cash flows generated in years 1, 2, and 3 are reinvested through the end of year 4 at 24.4 percent.

In the example we have explicitly assumed much more modest reinvestment rates. They can be incorporated into the calculation of the IRR

[18] NPV and TV will always yield consistent results. If the initial outlays are different, however (as they typically would be), the IRR ranking should be formulated in terms of an incremental approach.

of return by first finding the TV and then solving the following equation
for r:

$$\frac{20{,}565}{(1 + r)^4} = 11{,}000$$

where r is equal to 16.9 percent. Thus the (implicit or explicit) assumptions made about reinvestment rates in the method of calculation of the IRR can make a substantial difference in the result. It would seem that the latter method of calculation would be more appropriate for decision-making purposes than the former.

MULTIPLE RATES OF RETURN

Suppose an amount A_0 is invested with future cash returns of A_1 and A_2 to occur one and two years later, respectively. The IRR of the investment is the value of r that satisfies the equation

$$\frac{A_1}{1 + r} + \frac{A_2}{(1 + r)^2} = A_0, \quad \text{or} \quad \frac{A_2}{(1 + r)^2} + \frac{A_1}{1 + r} - A_0 = 0$$

Letting $X = 1/(1 + r)$, we have $A_2 X^2 + A_1 X - A_0 = 0$, a simple quadratic equation. Since a quadratic equation has two roots, there are two values of X, and therefore two values of r, that satisfy the equation. More generally, an investment generating cash flows for n years can be written as an n-degree equation and will therefore have n solutions. Fortunately, there is usually only one relevant solution. In Illustration 12–3A, for example, there are two roots but only the positive one, r^*, is of any significance to us. Occasionally, however, we have a situation as in Illustration 12–3B where there are two positive roots, r' and r''; i.e., there is no unique positive IRR. The latter case can occur only when there are multiple sign reversals of the project's cash flows. For example, an initial outlay (negative cash flow) would generally be followed by positive cash flows. If, however, a negative

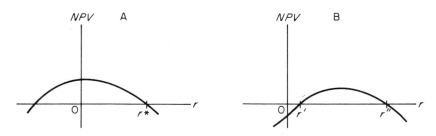

Illustration 12–3

cash flow followed a positive cash flow, a situation such as Illustration 12–3B could occur.[19]

A classic example of a situation where multiple rates of return are possible is given in Exhibit 12–8.[20] An oil field will continue to produce for the next two years, yielding $5000 per year (denoted by E). However, a new and more efficient pump would drain the field in only one year, yielding $10,000 in year 1 and nothing in year 2 (denoted by F). Variable X represents the cost of the new pump and I_3 is the appropriate investment to evaluate.

Exhibit 12–8

Year	Cash Flows			X	IRR	
	E	F	$I_3 = F - E$			
0	0	$-X$	$-X$	$450	11.1%	900%
1	5000	10,000	5000	800	25%,	400%
2	5000	0	-5000	1050	42.9%,	233%
				1200	66.7%,	150%
				1250	100%	

A seemingly paradoxical situation exists where the IRR of I_3 appears to increase with increases in the initial outlay. As shown in Exhibit 12–8, an IRR of 11.1 percent can be calculated if the outlay is $450; an IRR of 25 percent can be calculated if the outlay is $800; an IRR of 42.9 percent can be calculated if the outlay is $1050; and so on. Actually, this apparent paradox can be explained by reference to Illustration 12–4.

If the outlay X is $450 and a zero percent discount rate is used, the NPV of I_3 is $-$450. As the discount rate is increased in Stage 1, the negative cash flow at the end of year 2 is discounted more heavily than the positive cash flow at the end of year 1, and the NPV increases. In Stage 2, however, the negative flow in year 2 has been heavily discounted and further increases in the discount rate will primarily affect the positive flow in year 1. The positive flow in year 1 becomes dominated by the negative initial outlay. The NPV will decrease, and will continue to decrease until the discounted value of the flows in years 1 and 2 will both approach zero and the NPV will asymptotically approach $-$450. Raising the purchase price simply lowers the intercept on the graph, increasing the lower root and decreasing the higher one. (The upper and lower roots converge as the purchase price is increased until, at a price of $1250, there is one double root. A purchase price greater than $1250 will yield imaginary roots.)

[19] Illustration 12–3B depicts a two-year investment with two positive roots. It is also mathematically possible for two imaginary roots to exist, so there would be no real IRR for the investment. Interestingly, since imaginary roots occur in conjugate pairs, an investment covering three years would have three roots, at least one of which must be real. Thus an investment covering an even number of years may have no real roots (IRR), while an investment covering an odd number of years must have at least one real solution.

[20] This example is similar to one presented by Ezra Solomon, "The Arithmetic of Capital Budgeting Decisions," *Journal of Business* (April 1956), pp. 124–28.

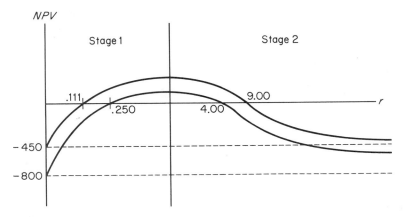

NPV

Stage 1   Stage 2

.111
.250   4.00   9.00   r

−450

−800

Illustration 12–4

What is the correct method for evaluating an investment of this type? Actually, there are several alternative procedures. One obvious way is to use NPV. If a CC of 10 percent is used, Illustration 12–4 shows that the NPV is negative for an outlay of $450 or more (and the greater the outlay, the more negative the NPV), so the proposal would be rejected. If the required outlay is $300, NPV $= -5000(0.826) + 5000(0.909) - 300 = \$113$, and the project would be accepted.

An alternative method would be to find the TV of the investment, where we assume reinvestment at the CC of 10 percent. If we again assume that the outlay is $300, TV $= -300(1 + 0.10)^3 + 500(1 + 0.10) - 5000 = \$137$. Since the TV is positive, we would accept the proposal. The NPV and TV methods should always give consistent results.[21] Using the same TV concept, we can also find the true IRR of the investment. The relevant question is, "What is it worth now to receive $5000 in one year rather than in two?" If we assume reinvestment at 10 percent, an additional $500 would be available at the end of year 2. Thus the problem of finding the IRR reduces to

$$-300 + \frac{500}{(1 + r)^2} = 0, \qquad r = 28.9 \text{ percent[22]}$$

CAPITAL RATIONING

It was assumed in the previous sections that the firm had sufficient capital to undertake any and all investments that were acceptable under the established

[21] This method can be used to find the maximum amount that could be paid for the new pump, a CC of 10 percent being assumed. Letting $X =$ the maximum price of the new pump, we have $-X(1 + 0.10)^2 + 5000(1 + 0.10) - 5000 = 0$. Solving, we find $X = \$413$ (which is also equal to the purchase price of $300 plus the NPV of $113 in the above example; note also that $\$113(1 + 0.10)^2 = \$137$, the TV of the project).

[22] At the break-even cost of $413 calculated in footnote 21, $1/[(1 + r)^2] = 413/500 = 0.826$, the present value factor of a single sum of 10 percent for two years.

criteria. In this section we shall assume that the total investment required to undertake all individually acceptable investments exceeds the amount of funds available for capital expenditures. Thus the available capital must be rationed among competing investment alternatives. The objective is to select that group of investments which maximizes the over-all return. This objective generally is accomplished by ranking investments according to the profitability index and then selecting investments with sequentially decreasing profitability indices until the entire capital budget has been allocated.[23]

Suppose that a total of $600 is available to undertake capital investments. Available investments are given in Exhibit 12–9. Investment A_{MB} is mutually exclusive with B_{MA}, and J_{MK} is mutually exclusive with K_{MJ}. All other investments are independent. Investments will be ranked according to decreasing PI and then, in the first solution presented, selected in a two-step procedure. The profitability index is now used as a ranking device rather than NPV because only a limited amount of capital is available. The objective is to maximize net present value *per dollar of investment*. Ranking by PI accomplishes this objective.

Exhibit 12–9

	Year					NPV	IRR	PI
	0	1	2	3	4			
A_{MB}	−$100	$60	$60	$60	$60	90.20	47.3%	1.902
B_{MA}	−200	100	100	100	100	117.00	34.9%	1.585
G	−150	100	100	100	100	167.00	56.3%	2.113
H	−50	25	25	25	25	29.25	34.9%	1.585
J_{MK}	−100	55	55	55	55	74.35	41.2%	1.744
K_{MJ}	−200	85	85	85	85	69.45	25.2%	1.347
L	−100	35	35	35	35	10.95	15.0%	1.110
M	−100	120	0	0	0	9.08	20.0%	1.091
N	−100	0	0	0	0	36.60	19.0%	1.366
$I_1 = B_{MA} - A_{MB}$	−100	40	40	40	40	26.80	21.7%	1.268
$I_4 = K_{MJ} - J_{MK}$	−100	30	30	30	30	−4.90	7.7%	0.951

Initially assume that all investments are independent. In order, investments G, A_{MB}, J_{MK}, B_{MA}, and H will be selected, requiring exactly the $600 available. But A_{MB} and B_{MA} are not independent; acceptance of one precludes acceptance of the other. We shall, therefore, proceed by first comparing mutually exclusive investments and selecting the highest ranking one

---

[23] This procedure does not cope with the problem of discontinuities. Discontinuity problems arise when, for example, the budget is almost completely allocated and the addition of one large investment may preclude the acceptance of two smaller investments which are, in combination, more profitable than the one large one. There is no known systematic way of handling this problem.

from each set; thus A_{MB} dominates B_{MA} and J_{MK} dominates K_{MJ}.[24] We next select from all remaining investments, treating them as independent. The capital budget of \$600 would now be used to undertake G, A_{MB}, J_{MK}, H, N, and L. The pattern of cash flows from this group is given below:

Year	0	1	2	3	4
Total Cash Flow	−600	275	275	275	475

However, this procedure will not always lead to an optimal solution. It is not necessary to prespecify which mutually exclusive investment dominates the other; it is instead possible to specify a procedure that will automatically make the optimal choice. We can proceed as above, except that we shall add I_1 $(B_{MA} - A_{MB})$ and I_4 $(K_{MJ} - J_{MK})$ to the list of available investments. Investment I_1 is superior to L, so the new optimal group of investments would be G, A_{MB}, J_{MK}, H, N, and I_1. Since $A_{MB} + I_1 = B_{MA}$, the solution has really specified that B_{MA} should replace A_{MB} and I_1, and the optimal group of investments is now G, J_{MK}, H, N, and B_{MA}. The pattern of cash flows from this group is slightly superior to the pattern from the first solution obtained above:

Year	0	1	2	3	4
Total Cash Flow	−600	280	280	280	480

The steps in selecting a group of investments under conditions of capital rationing are, therefore, as follows:

1. See if any proposals are mutually exclusive. If some are, treat the one requiring the smallest initial outlay and the incremental investment as independent and include them both in the next step.
2. Rank all investments according to decreasing PI. Choose from the top of the list until the amount available for investment has been allocated (abstracting from the problem of discontinuities discussed above).
3. If a mutually exclusive investment and the corresponding incremental investment are both included, replace them both with the larger incremental investment. If only the smaller mutually exclusive investment is included, and the incremental is not, the optimal solution has already been reached. If only the incremental investment is included, and the smaller mutually exclusive proposal is not, replace both the smaller and the incremental with the larger and repeat step 2.

[24] This procedure is the method of solution suggested in J. Lorie and L. J. Savage, "Three Problems in Rationing Capital," *Journal of Business* (October, 1955), pp. 229–39. Lorie and Savage also present a general methodology which is conceptually the same as the one that follows. They extend the analysis, however, and present a general solution for capital rationing of investments that require cash outlays beyond the initial period.

Adherence to this procedure will always result in the selection of an optimal group of investments.[25] Finally, notice that, for reasons discussed previously in this chapter, an optimal solution will not always be obtained if investments are ranked according to IRR rather than PI.

CONSIDERATIONS OF RISK

Management cannot be expected to have the same degree of confidence in estimated future cash flows for different projects. For example, estimates based on a long-term service contract would be more accurate than estimates based on the market potential for a newly developed product. Likewise, estimates for the next few years can be made more confidently than estimates of cash flows several years in the future. Thus it is desirable to be able to reflect a project's riskiness in the present value calculations. There are two methods of explicitly incorporating risk into the analysis of an individual investment alternative which are traditionally discussed in the literature. The mechanics of these two methods will be briefly described in this section. A more complex discussion of risk will be presented in the following chapter.

Risk-Adjusted Discount Rate

The risk-adjusted discount rate is probably the only one of the two suggested methods that is seriously used in practice. Its greater popularity stems from the fact that it is both easier to use and easier to understand. To find the risk-adjusted discount rate, we add a premium reflecting the level of risk of the project being analyzed to a risk-free rate. The risk-free rate is simply the rate that would be used to evaluate risk-free proposals; i.e., proposals for which all cash flows can be predicted with absolute certainty. The value of the premium to be added will, of course, be determined by the degree of risk (i.e., the degree of uncertainty of projected cash flows) of the project being evaluated. Thus, for example, a risk premium of 6 percent may be added to a risk-free rate of 8 percent, so the project will be evaluated on the basis of a discount rate of 14 percent. Note that this procedure allows two mutually exclusive proposals of different risk to be compared on the basis of two different, but respectively appropriate, discount rates. It is also possible to vary the risk premium as cash flows are projected farther into the future.[26]

Certainty-Equivalents

The certainty-equivalent method of adjusting for risk is based on the concept of utility, which is developed in Chapter 3. This method requires the subjec-

---

[25] A recent article advocates ranking according to TV, with results consistent with those above. See William H. Jean, "Terminal Value or Present Value in Capital Budgeting Programs," *Journal of Financial and Quantitative Analysis* (January, 1971), pp. 649–52.

[26] Occasionally the total cash flow is divided into two parts, one resulting from operations and the other from depreciation charges. Since the former may be considerably more uncertain than the latter, the former may be discounted at a higher rate.

tive determination of a cash flow that management can conceptually receive with certainty. The difference between that amount and the actual estimated, but uncertain, amount should not matter. The greater the uncertainty (or risk) of the estimates of future cash flows, the smaller should be the indifference certainty cash flow. Once we obtain a certainty-equivalent cash flow for each year of a proposed investment's life, we can discount these cash flows, using a risk-free discount rate. Thus, rather than increase the discount rate to decrease the present value of a risky cash flow estimate, we first reduce the cash flow estimate itself to a certainty-equivalent.

PROBLEMS

1. Find the NPV (assuming a CC of 10 percent) and IRR of the investments given in Exhibits 12–3 and 12–4.
2. Assuming reinvestment at the CC of 10 percent, what is the true IRR of investment C in Exhibit 12–6?
3. Assuming reinvestment at 20 percent in years 3 through 5 for investment C in Exhibit 12–6, use both NPV and IRR criteria to show that C is preferable to D.
4. Refer to the investment in a new pump described in Exhibit 12–8. If the cost of the new pump is $500, explain how it is possible for the investment to be unacceptable if the CC = 10 percent but favorable if the CC = 20 percent.
5. Depreciation is sometimes referred to as a "source of cash," although accounting purists object to this usage. Why? Discuss the role of depreciation as a source of cash.
6. The Watson Company is switching from straight-line to accelerated depreciation. How will this affect their (a) reported profits and cash flows each year and in total over the entire life of an investment and (b) evaluation of investment alternatives based on present value procedures? How would their evaluation of investment alternatives be affected if the firm used *average* rate of return as a decision criterion?
7. A machine originally costing $8000 is fully depreciated, although it still has an estimated useful physical life of eight or more years. It has no salvage value at present. The department head proposes the purchase of a new machine to replace the old one. Its full cost, including freight and installation, will be $12,000. Its expected economic life is eight years, at the end of which time it will have no salvage value. The plant engineer estimates that labor, material, and other direct costs of operation will be reduced by $5400 per year (before taxes) during each of the first four years the machine is in use, and by $5000 during each of the last four years. Income taxes are expected to be at a rate of 50 percent. Each question below should be considered independently.
   a. Determine each of the following:
      (1) Payback period
      (2) Average rate of return
      (3) Internal rate of return
   b. Assume that X dollars additional working capital were required to support the investment discussed in part a of this question. This money will be returned during the last year of the investment. Discuss the effects of this on the rate of return calculated in part a(3) (no further calculations are necessary).
   c. What weaknesses are present in payback and average rate of return criteria as methods to rank alternative investment proposals?

8. The Forbes Company is considering the purchase of a machine tool to replace an obsolete one. The machine being used for the operation has a tax book value of zero, although it is in good working order and will last, physically, for the next ten years. However, the proposed machine will perform the operation so much more efficiently that Forbes Company engineers estimate that labor, material, and other direct costs of the operation will be reduced $4000 a year if the proposed machine is installed. The proposed machine costs $16,000, delivered and installed. Its economic life is estimated to be ten years, with zero salvage value. The company expects to earn 12 percent on its investment after taxes. The tax rate is 40 percent.

    a. Should Forbes buy the machine?

    b. Assume that the tax book value of the old machine is $5000, that the annual depreciation charge is $500, and that it has a sale value of $3000. How do these assumptions affect your answer?

9. A firm is considering the purchase of either Machine *S* or Machine *T*. The following information is available (assume straight-line depreciation):

	Machine *S*	Machine *T*
Cost of new machine	$5000	$5000
Additional working capital	0	2000
Transportation and installation	0	2000
Economic life of new machine	5 years	5 years
Salvage value of new machine	$0	$2000
Market value of old machine	0	0
Book value of old machine	0	2000
Remaining life of old machine	5	2
Corporate tax rate	40%	40%
Cost of capital	12%	12%
Annual cash savings before depreciation and taxes with purchase of new machine	$2000	$2000

    a. Calculate for both *S* and *T*:

        (1) Initial cash outlay
        (2) Annual net cash flow
        (3) Payback
        (4) Average rate of return
        (5) Net present value
        (6) Profitability index
        (7) Internal rate of return

    b. On the basis of the above calculations, which machine is more desirable? Why?

10. A company is considering replacing existing equipment by a more efficient unit. The cost of removing the old machine is $700, but it can then be sold immediately for $1800. Its book value is still $600 with an estimated five years remaining before it is fully depreciated. The new machine will cost $8000, with miscellaneous installation and break-in costs of $1100. It will be fully depreciated, on a straight-line basis, in five years. Anticipated annual net income before taxes and depreciation attributable to the new investment is estimated at $5000 per annum for the next three years and $4000 per annum for the following two years. The company paid a consultant a fee of $300 to advise them concerning the technical qualities of the proposed new equipment. (Assume corporate income tax rate of 40 percent and cost of capital of 12 percent.)

    a. What is the initial outlay?

    b. What are the annual net cash benefits?

c. What is the internal rate of return?
d. What is the net present value?
e. Would you purchase the new unit? Why?

11. The Eastern Corp. is using a computer whose original cost was $30,000. The computer is being depreciated on a straight-line basis over its ten-year life to a $2000 estimated salvage value. The machine is now 5 years old and has a current market (salvage) value of $6000.

Management is contemplating the purchase of a new computer whose cost is $35,000 and whose estimated salvage value after an estimated five-year life is $6000. Expected annual savings before depreciation and taxes from the new computer are $11,000. The new computer will be depreciated on a straight-line basis over its five-year life. The firm's cost of capital is 12 percent. Assume a 40 percent tax rate on profits and capital gains and losses.

a. Evaluate the proposed new computer according to:
  (1) Payback
  (2) Average rate of return
  (3) Net present value
  (4) Internal rate of return
b. What action would you suggest; i.e., should Eastern purchase the new computer or not?

12. Two mutually exclusive projects have projected cash flows as follows:

	X	Y
0	−$15,000	−$15,000
1	3,000	0
2	10,000	0
3	10,000	0
4	10,000	50,000

a. Assuming that the CC of 10 percent is expected to remain constant over the next several years and given a tax rate of 40 percent, determine for each project:
  (1) Average rate of return
  (2) Payback
  (3) Terminal value
  (4) Net present value
  (5) Profitability index
  (6) Internal rate of return
b. Which project would you select, and why?

13. Two conflicting proposals of equal risk have been made for the purchase of new equipment. The data on each are given below:

	Proposal A	Proposal B
Net cash outlay	$9000	$7500
Salvage value	0	0
Estimated life	5 years	5 years

Net cash benefits before depreciation and taxes

Years 1–3	$4500	$3500
Years 4 and 5	3500	3000

Assume straight-line depreciation and a corporate income tax of 40 percent. The CC is 10 percent.

a. Rank the proposals (and explain any contradictions) in terms of
   (1) Average rate of return
   (2) Payback
   (3) Net present value
   (4) Profitability index
   (5) Internal rate of return

b. Recompute the above, assuming $1500 salvage value and $2000 additional working capital requirements for proposal a.

c. Recompute a, assuming that sum-of-the-years digits depreciation is used.

14. As a rising young executive with a growing family, you are faced with a problem. You expect to be located in the same city for at least the next ten years. You can either buy a small home now for $28,000 and add an addition in five years for an estimated $12,000, or you can buy a larger house now for $35,000. The large house would require greater heating and tax expense of $400 per year. Assume that after the enlargement of the small house in five years, annual expenses would be the same for either house. You feel that you can prudently invest your money and earn an annual rate of return of 8 percent over the next several years. Based on financial considerations only, what would be your wisest course of action?

15. The following ten investment opportunities are available to the Constraint Corp. All projects are independent except L_{MM} and M_{ML}, which are mutually exclusive, as are Q_{MR} and R_{MQ}. Assume a CC of 15 percent.

	Year				
	0	**1**	**2**	**3**	**4**
J	− $1000	$500	$500	$500	$500
K	− 500	200	200	200	200
L_{MM}	− 1000	350	350	350	350
M_{ML}	− 1500	700	700	700	700
N	− 1000	400	400	400	400
O	− 1000	0	0	0	2500
P	− 800	350	350	350	350
Q_{MR}	− 1000	450	450	450	450
R_{MQ}	− 1500	660	660	660	660
S	− 1000	1300	0	0	0

a. On the basis of rankings according to PI, which groups of investments should be selected, given the following amounts available for investment?
   (1) $3500
   (2) $4300
   (3) $4500
   (4) $5300
   (5) $5500
   (6) $6500

b. Same as a, except rankings are based on IRR. What differences do you observe in your results? What basis for ranking seems preferable? Why?

III

ANALYSIS MODELS

13

measurement
and analysis
of risk

Many financial decisions are based on single point estimates of future cash flows or percentage rates of return. Thus they generally do not reflect the varying degrees of risk with which the estimates and resulting decisions are made. For example, consider three different investments requiring equal initial outlays, one returning $1000 with certainty, a second with a 50 percent chance of returning $500 and a 50 percent chance of returning $1500, and a third with a 50 percent chance of losing $500 and a 50 percent chance of returning $2500. All three investments have an expected value of $1000, yet most decision makers would clearly not be indifferent if forced to choose one of the three alternatives. Under the typical situation of risk aversion, the first alternative would be the most desirable and the third would be the least desirable. (See Chapter 3 for a discussion of attitudes about risk and utility theory.) The desirability ranking of these three investments would be inversely related to the amount of variation in possible final outcomes. Since the expected values of the above investments are insufficient to make meaningful comparisons, it is necessary that we obtain quantitative measures of the riskiness of each investment.

The combination of both expected return and risk measures will greatly improve our decision-making efficiency. In the above example we could distinguish among investments with equivalent expected returns by choosing the one with the least risk. Similarly, for a given amount of risk, we would choose the investment with the highest expected return.

MEASURES OF RISK

We can initially think of the risk of an investment as being determined by the variability of its possible returns. As stated above, the greater the variability of possible returns, the greater the risk. One frequently used measure of risk, and one that has the virtues of both being easy to find and having a certain amount of statistical validity, is the range. The range specifies the interval from the highest possible outcome to the lowest. Thus if a particular action could result in outcomes as high as 30 and as low as 7, the range of possible outcomes would be 24. If two different actions both have expected outcomes (or values) of 15, but one has a range of 24 and the other a range of 11, the former would be considered riskier than the latter. One shortcoming of the range is the fact that it is affected by extremely high or low values. To preclude any bias that might be introduced by extreme values, the interquartile range could be used. The interquartile range is the range of values in the second and third quartiles of all observations. In other words, the highest 25 percent and the lowest 25 percent of all observations are ignored, and the range is determined for those observations that are left.

Variance and Standard Deviation

Another measure of risk, and one that is especially important in theoretical considerations, is the variance σ^2 (or its square root, σ, the standard deviation). The variance is calculated by taking the average of the squared deviations from the mean (or expected value). Thus

$$\sigma^2 = \sum_{i=1}^{n} \frac{(X_i - \mu)^2}{n} \tag{13-1}$$

where X_i represents the different returns that can actually occur, μ represents the expected value, and n is the number of possible outcomes. The variance of expected return for the above three investments would be, respectively,

$$\frac{(1000 - 1000)^2}{1} = 0$$

$$\frac{(500 - 1000)^2 + (1500 - 1000)^2}{2} = \frac{500,000}{2} = 250,000$$

$$\frac{(-500 - 1000)^2 + (2500 - 1000)^2}{2} = \frac{4,500,000}{2} = 2,250,000$$

When, as frequently will be the case, there is a probability distribution of possible returns, Eq. (13–1) can be modified as follows:

$$\sigma^2 = \sum_{i=1}^{n} f_i(X_i - \mu)^2 \tag{13-2}$$

where f_i gives the relative frequency or probability of each individual outcome. Using Eq. (13–2) to calculate the variance for the last two of the above investments, we would get $0.5(500 - 1000)^2 + 0.5(1500 - 1000)^2 = 250,000$ and $0.5(-500 - 1000)^2 + 0.5(2500 - 1000)^2 = 2,250,000$, numerically the same results we obtained using Eq. (13–1).

As will be seen in the following section, the variance has certain statistical properties that make it a very useful measure of risk. For some purposes, however, the special properties of the standard deviation may make it a more useful measure. In particular, we can use the standard deviation to calculate a range within which the actual return can be expected to fall with a certain probability.

If the distribution of possible returns is reasonably normal, we know that the actual return should be within (plus or minus) one standard deviation from the mean (or expected return) with a probability of about 0.68; the probability of being within two standard deviations of the mean is about 0.95; the probability of being within three standard deviations of the mean is about 0.99, and so on. Even if the distribution has no discernible shape or pattern, Chebychev's inequality (see Chapter 2) can be employed to obtain a range within which the actual return should fall with a given probability.

Variance and standard deviation may seem to be unnecessarily complex concepts. If we want to obtain a measure of risk, and risk is a function of the variability of returns, it would seem that we could simply sum the individual deviations from the mean and divide by the number of observations. The major difficulty with this measure is that, because deviations occur on both sides of the mean, positive and negative fluctuations will cancel one another out. Thus we could not discriminate between relatively safe investments and others with widely fluctuating returns. In fact, since deviations on either side of the mean must cancel out exactly, the expression $\sum_{i=1}^{n} (X_i - \mu)/n$ will always have a value of zero for any investment.

Some measure is needed that will prevent positive and negative deviations from cancelling one another out. There are two obvious procedures. One is to average the absolute values of the deviations (and thus to ignore signs) and the other is to average the squares of the individual deviations. The latter procedure, which yields the variance, has statistical properties that make it much more useful than the former. We shall, therefore, use the variance (or the standard deviation) as our primary measure of risk, although we shall see that it may occasionally need to be supplemented or modified.

The use of the variance or standard deviation of expected return as a measure of risk implicitly assumes that a large variability well in excess of the expected value contributes to the riskiness of an asset in the same way as variability considerably below the expected value. It seems more reasonable, however, that only variability on the downward side of the expected return would affect an asset's riskiness. As a decision maker, you are primarily concerned with the possibility of failure to achieve the target objective. Thus variability and risk may not necessarily imply the same thing, so we need to explore other measures of risk.

Minimum Return Criterion

First of all, variability by itself cannot be used as a measure of risk unless investments of equal expected return are being compared. If the expected returns are not equal, risk depends not only on variability, but also on the expected return from which the variation will occur. For example, consider investments X and Y in Exhibit 13–1, where the distributions of possible returns are assumed to be normal. While Y has a larger standard deviation of expected return, it is difficult to consider it the riskier investment. If, for example, a minimum return of 10 percent is considered critical, Y would be considered less risky because it would have a much smaller probability of yielding a return less than 10 percent than would X. In fact, Exhibit 13–1

Exhibit 13–1   Variability of Return for Investments X and Y

	X	Y
Expected return	12.00%	17.00%
Standard deviation	2.00%	3.00%
$P(r \geq 10\%)$	0.84	0.99
r' so that $P(r \geq r') = 0.90$	9.44%	13.16%
r' so that $P(r \geq r') = 0.95$	8.71%	12.06%
r' so that $P(r \geq r') = 0.99$	7.34%	10.01%

shows that, for almost any positive minimum return specified, project Y has a greater probability of exceeding it than does X. Thus it is clear that at least two parameters describing the possible returns from an investment are necessary for effective decision making. Neither the expected return nor some measure of the variability of expected return is adequate by itself, but in combination the two usually provide a satisfactory return-risk description of a proposed investment project.

Semi-Variance

While the variance of expected returns is the most commonly used measure of risk, there are other measures that are more consistent with the general notion that risk reflects the likelihood of receiving a return below—rather than above—the expected or some other minimum critical return. For example, the semi-variance is calculated according to Eqs. (13–1) or (13–2), except that only deviations below the mean are included in the calculations. Deviations below the mean are squared and summed, while deviations above the mean are treated as though they had values of zero. Consider investments R, S, and T described in Exhibit 13–2. All three have the same expected return. Investment R has the largest variance. While S and T have the same variance, probably few decision makers would be indifferent between the two. Despite the fact that S and T have the same return-risk parameters (expected return and variance), T, with its possibility of lower returns, would probably be considered less desirable. This preference for S in a world dominated by risk-averters is reflected by the semi-variances. Because it exposes the investor to less downside risk potential, S has a lower semi-variance than T. (Note that the semi-variance for R is exactly half the variance. This is because the distribution of possible returns for R is perfectly symmetric.)

Exhibit 13–2 Return-risk Parameters

		Probability of Return		
	Return	R	S	T
	0.07	0.1	0.0	0.1
	0.08	0.1	0.0	0.1
	0.09	0.2	0.6	0.1
	0.10	0.2	0.1	0.1
	0.11	0.2	0.1	0.6
	0.12	0.1	0.1	0.0
	0.13	0.1	0.1	0.0
Expected return		0.10	0.10	0.10
Variance		0.00030	0.00020	0.00020
Semi-variance		0.00015	0.00006	0.00014
Skewness		0	+	−

Equations (13–1) and (13–2) can also be used to calculate a measure of risk similar to the semi-variance where some critical minimum return is used rather than the expected return. Suppose, for example, that a return less than 9 percent is considered to be particularly undesirable. Measures of risk could, therefore, be obtained for the above investments by using the sum of the squared deviations below 9 percent. The calculated risk value for S would now be zero, while R and T would have identical nonzero values.

Skewness

Additional information about the variability of returns can be obtained by calculating the skewness of the distribution of possible returns. Skewness measures the extent to which the distribution is not symmetric. A distribution that is perfectly symmetric will have a skewness of zero. The distribution of returns for investment P, drawn as a continuous distribution in Illustration 13–1, is nonsymmetric due to the small possibility of an extremely low return. This distribution is said to be positively skewed, or skewed to the right. Conversely, the distribution for investment Q is negatively skewed, or skewed to the left. Again, since decision makers normally tend to be risk averters, P would probably be preferred to Q in spite of the fact that their expected returns and variances are the same.[1] In general, it seems reasonable that

---

[1] Notice that skewness and semi-variance should yield reasonably consistent results. Project S in the preceding example had the smallest semi-variance and was positively skewed, while T had a larger semi-variance and was negatively skewed.

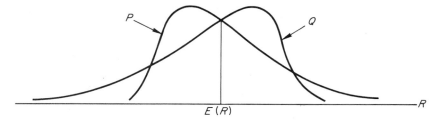

Illustration 13–1   Return Distributions for Securities *P* and *Q*

positive skewness would be considered desirable and negative skewness would be considered undesirable. Thus the degree of risk of a particular investment would be positively related to its variance and negatively related to its skewness.

In spite of the intuitive appeal of such measures as semi-variance and skewness, the empirical evidence regarding their relative importance has yielded mixed results. In some studies these or related measures have been found to be very important, whereas in others they have appeared to be totally insignificant. This latter finding is of some comfort to theoreticians who are drawn to the nice statistical properties of the variance. Almost all descriptions of the return distribution of an investment are based on two basic parameters, the mean and the variance.

There may be some justification for using mean-variance descriptions beyond mere statistical convenience. For example, if an investment's final return is affected by a large number of different factors, the resulting return distribution should be reasonably normal, regardless of the shape of the distributions of the component parts.[2] Also, skewness would be more easily diversified away and therefore less relevant in a portfolio context than variance would be. Finally, as was noted above, the variance would always be twice the semi-variance for a symmetric distribution, and both measures would give the same rankings. Thus while the empirical results regarding different measures of risk have been inconclusive, we shall proceed, assuming that the expected return and variance provide a reasonable description of a proposed investment.[3]

ANALYSIS OF RISK

The variance of the distribution of expected returns is an appropriate measure of risk for a single investment only when it is to be held by itself. In the usual

[2] This follows from what is known as the central limit theorem. For details on this very important theorem in statistics, see any standard statistics text.

[3] Perhaps as disturbing as our incomplete description of the return distribution is our implicit assumption that the investor is concerned only with the expected *monetary* return. Investments in antiques or works of art might produce returns that cannot be expressed quantitatively in dollar terms.

case it will be held in combination with a group of other assets; i.e., it will be one component of a portfolio. The preceding discussion must be extended to account for risk in a portfolio context. An asset that would be judged undesirably risky if it were to be held singly might be considered an attractive addition to a particular portfolio.

A portfolio can contain real estate, equipment and supplies, machinery, rolling stock, patents and licenses, etc., as well as jewels, works of art, antiques, stocks and bonds, etc. Thus the following discussion is relevant to the portfolio of assets held by a firm. For purposes of convenience, and since most of the previous work on portfolio theory has evolved from the capital markets area, we shall refer to the components of a portfolio as *securities*. The use of this term should not narrow one's perspective, however. A very broad and diverse range of assets can be given the common label of securities and held together as a portfolio.

To describe the concepts involved in a reconsideration of risk in a portfolio context, we shall start with a very simple case in which two securities A and B are to be combined to form a portfolio. Let us start with the extreme assumption that A and B are perfectly correlated; i.e., if the return on A changes, the return on B will change linearly with it. Assume that some proportion X_A of the amount available for investment is invested in security A while the proportion $X_B (= 1 - X_A)$ is invested in security B. Then the expected return from the combined securities $E(R_c)$ would be

$$E(R_c) = X_A \cdot E(R_A) + X_B \cdot E(R_B) \qquad (13-3)$$

simply a weighted average of the expected returns for A and B. The variance of the expected return would be

$$\sigma_c^2 = X_A^2 \sigma_A^2 + X_B^2 \sigma_B^2 + 2X_A X_B \text{ cov}_{AB} \qquad (13-4)$$

where cov_{AB} = the covariance of A and B. The covariance is equal to the correlation coefficient between A and B (denoted ρ_{AB}) times the product of the standard deviations for A and B, i.e., $\text{cov}_{AB} = \rho_{AB} \cdot \sigma_A \cdot \sigma_B$. Since we are assuming perfect correlation between A and B ($\rho_{AB} = 1$), $\text{cov}_{AB} = \sigma_A \cdot \sigma_B$, and Eq. (13-4) becomes *for this special case*

$$\sigma_c^2 = X_A^2 \sigma_A^2 + X_B^2 \sigma_B^2 + 2X_A X_B \sigma_A \sigma_B \qquad (13-4')$$

or

$$\sigma_c^2 = (X_A \sigma_A + X_B \sigma_B)^2$$

Taking the square root of both sides of (13-4'), we see that the standard deviation of the combined securities is simply a weighted average of the standard deviations of A and B. Thus the return-risk characteristics of various combinations of A and B can be drawn as the straight line AB in Illustration 13-2.

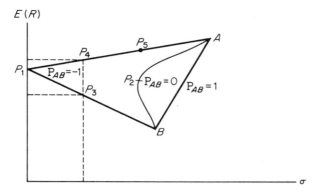

Illustration 13–2 Return-Risk Characteristics of Combinations of Securities *A* and *B*

Let us now consider the opposite extreme, where there is perfect negative correlation between *A* and *B*; i.e., $\rho_{AB} = -1$. The expected return and variance of the return would again be given by Eqs. (13–3) and (13–4), respectively. But now, since we are assuming negative correlation, the third term on the right-hand side of Eq. (13–4) is negative. Thus this term deducts from the over-all variability of return, and the equation expressing the total risk for the combination of securities *A* and *B* becomes

$$\sigma_c^2 = X_A^2 \sigma_A^2 + X_B^2 \sigma_B^2 - 2X_A X_B \sigma_A \sigma_B$$

or   (13–4″)

$$\sigma_c^2 = (X_A \sigma_A - X_B \sigma_B)^2$$

If we now take the square root of both sides of Eq. (13–4″), substitute $X_B = 1 - X_A$, and set the right-hand side equal to zero (so total risk is equal to zero), X_A can be found as a function of σ_A and σ_B.

$$\sigma_c = X_A \sigma_A - X_B \sigma_B = X_A \sigma_A - (1 - X_A)\sigma_B = 0$$

$$X_A \sigma_A - \sigma_B + X_A \sigma_B = 0$$

$$X_A = \frac{\sigma_B}{\sigma_A + \sigma_B}$$

Similarly, $X_B = \sigma_A/(\sigma_A + \sigma_B)$ and $X_A + X_B = (\sigma_A + \sigma_B)/(\sigma_A + \sigma_B) = 1$, as required.

We can now make some interesting observations concerning the nature of risk in a portfolio context. Assume that an investor who is an extreme risk averter is asked to construct a portfolio consisting of some combination of securities *A* and *B*. His objective in selecting a portfolio is to minimize risk. Since, as shown in Illustration 13–2, *B* has less risk than *A*, he may reject *A* completely and invest 100 percent of his available funds in *B*. Such a decision would be inefficient, however, since the investor would be over-looking the possibility of diversification. The kinked line AP_1B represents the return-risk characteristics of various combinations of A and B given $\rho_{AB} = -1$. Investing exclusively in B is clearly inferior to the portfolio represented by point P_1. At P_1, where $X_A = \sigma_B/(\sigma_A + \sigma_B)$, total risk is zero because the variability of returns for A and B completely offset one another. This would certainly be optimal for an extreme risk averter.

Furthermore, $X_A = \sigma_B/(\sigma_A + \sigma_B)$ would be the *minimum* proportion invested in security A regardless of an individual investor's preferences for risk. The portfolio along line segment AP_1 dominates the portfolio along line segment P_1B. For example, suppose that an investor chose a combination of A and B that resulted in the portfolio indicated by P_3 in Illustration 13–2. He could increase his expected return without incurring any additional risk by increasing X_A and decreasing X_B until he obtained the portfolio corresponding to P_4. Similarly, any other portfolio along P_1B is dominated by a portfolio on AP_1. Line segment AP_1 thus represents what is called the *set of efficient portfolios*. For any given portfolio along AP_1, there is no other attainable portfolio with a greater expected return for a given amount of risk or with less risk for the same expected return.

Once the set of efficient portfolios is defined, the final problem is one of portfolio selection. Different investors will have different optimum portfolios along AP_1, depending upon the shapes of their individual return-risk utility curves (see Chapter 3). An investor who wants to minimize risk will choose P_1. Another investor who wants to maximize expected return, regardless of risk, will choose A. Yet a third investor, falling between these two extremes, may select P_4 if the combination of A and B represented by this portfolio represents the optimal return-risk trade-off *for him*. Notice that any increase in expected return, such as moving from P_4 to P_5, can be accomplished only at the expense of greater risk exposure. As long as the utility of the additional return more than offsets the disutility of the additional risk, an investor should continue to move from left to right along AP_1 (i.e., increase X_A and decrease X_B). When the trade-off is no longer favorable, the investor has reached his optimum portfolio.

It is highly unusual to find two securities whose returns are perfectly positively or negatively correlated. The correlation coefficient is typically between $+1$ and -1 and, in most cases, it is positive. If the returns from two securities are perfectly independent, the correlation coefficient is zero and the third term on the right-hand side of Eq. (13–4) is equal to zero. Thus, given $\rho_{AB} = 0$, we find that the combined variance is given by

$$\sigma_c^2 = X_A^2\sigma_A^2 + X_B^2\sigma_B^2 \qquad (13\text{–}4''')$$

The return-risk characteristics of different combinations of two completely independent securities is given by curve AP_2B in Illustration 13–2. One section of the curve (AP_2) again dominates another section (P_2B). Portfolio P_2 represents the least risky attainable portfolio. The proportion of available funds invested in A for portfolio P_2 is $X_A = \sigma_B^2/(\sigma_A^2 + \sigma_B^2)$ [so the proportion invested in B must equal $X_B = \sigma_A^2/(\sigma_A^2 + \sigma_B^2)$].[4] This value of X_A would thus represent the minimum proportion of available funds invested in X_A for an efficient portfolio. For example, if $\sigma_A^2 = 6$ percent, $\sigma_B^2 = 4$ percent, $E(R_A) = 14$ percent, and $E(R_B) = 9$ percent, we could find for all efficient portfolios:

$$X_{A_{min}} = \frac{6}{4 + 6} = 0.6$$

$$X_{B_{max}} = \frac{4}{4 + 6} = 0.4$$

$$\sigma_{c_{min}}^2 = 0.36(6) + 0.16(4) = 2.80 \text{ percent}$$

$$E(R_c)_{min} = 0.6(14) + 0.4(9) = 12.0 \text{ percent}$$

If the proportion invested in A is increased, so that $X_A = 0.7$, we would have

$$\sigma_c^2 = 0.49(6) + 0.09(4) = 3.30 \text{ percent}$$

$$E(R_c) = 0.7(14) + 0.4(9) = 13.4 \text{ percent}$$

We again observe that the expected return on the portfolio can be increased only by also increasing the degree of risk.

We have seen that the principle of diversification is dependent upon interaction between the expected returns of our two securities A and B. This interaction has been measured by the correlation coefficient, ρ_{AB}. If $\rho_{AB} = 1$, no diversification is possible. If $\rho_{AB} = -1$, it is possible to diversify away all of the total risk. Between these two extremes some, but not total, diversification is possible. The lower the correlation coefficient (going from $\rho_{AB} = +1$ to $\rho_{AB} = -1$), the greater is the degree of diversification that can be achieved.

If we extend our example beyond a simple two-security portfolio, the same basic principles apply, although the degree of complexity increases rapidly. It is first necessary to determine the expected return and the variance of expected return for each security, plus the degree of interaction of each

---

[4] $\sigma_c^2 = X_A^2 \sigma_A^2 + (1 - X_A)^2 \sigma_B^2 = X_A^2 \sigma_A^2 + \sigma_B^2 - 2X_A \sigma_B^2 + X_A^2 \sigma_B^2$. These proportions can be verified through the use of basic differential calculus. We can minimize σ_c^2 by setting the derivative with respect to X_A equal to zero and solving for X_A.

$$\frac{d\sigma_c^2}{dX_A} = 2X_A \sigma_A^2 - 2\sigma_B^2 + 2X_A \sigma_B^2 = 0$$

$$X_A = \frac{\sigma_B^2}{\sigma_A^2 + \sigma_B^2}$$

The second-order conditions for minimization are also met.

$$\frac{d^2\sigma_c^2}{dX_A^2} = 2\sigma_A^2 + 2\sigma_B^2 > 0$$

security with *every other security* being considered (i.e., find the covariance or the correlation coefficients). Next, it is necessary to calculate the risk and return of every possible portfolio combination and then to find the efficient frontier. Finally, given an individual investor's (or group of investors') return-risk preferences, the optimal portfolio can be selected from the efficient frontier. If an individual (or a mutual fund) wanted to construct a portfolio restricted to stocks listed on the New York Stock Exchange, the human and computer expense of determining and processing the required data would be prohibitive. If the eligibility list is expanded to include other listed and over-the-counter stocks, the problem becomes even more prohibitive. We clearly need a simplified procedure that will still reflect interactions among different securities while considerably reducing the required computations.

Fortunately, a straightforward and reasonably efficient approach is available. The underlying concept is that the relative fluctuations of two securities do not depend on the characteristics of these two securities alone. It is more likely that they would both respond to some basic underlying influence that would systematically affect all securities to a greater or lesser extent. For example, we may find that we can measure the responsiveness of an individual security's return to a change in the return of some market index, such as the Standard and Poor's 500 or the Dow Jones Industrials. A portion of a security's return variability will be associated with the market, and the remainder will be independent of the market. Thus, letting ρ_{im} represent the correlation coefficient between the ith security and the market, we can express the total variability of return of security i, σ_i^2, as

$$\sigma_i^2 = \rho_{im}\sigma_i^2 + \sigma_i^2 - \rho_{im}\sigma_i^2$$

or

$$\sigma_i^2 = \rho_{im}\sigma_i^2 + (1 - \rho_{im})\sigma_i^2 \qquad (13\text{--}5)$$

The first term on the right-hand side of Eq. (13–5) represents the proportion of total variability that is attributable to a relationship with the market; i.e., *the systematic risk*. The second term represents the remaining risk, that which is independent of market movements and is therefore called *unsystematic risk*. Since systematic risk linearly affects all securities, it is not amenable to diversification. Unsystematic risk, consisting of return fluctuations that are uncorrelated with the market, are diversifiable. Therefore, systematic risk is also called *undiversifiable risk*; unsystematic risk is also called *diversifiable risk*. For decision-making purposes, only the systematic portion of total variability should be relevant. If $\rho_{im} = 1$, systematic risk $= \sigma_i^2$ and unsystematic risk $= 0$. If $\rho_{im} = 0$, systematic risk $= 0$ and unsystematic risk $= \sigma_i^2$. If $\rho_{im} = -1$, systematic risk is *negative* $(-\sigma_i^2)$, indicating that fluctuations in the return of this security *systematically offset* fluctuations in the market, thereby directly decreasing risk by reducing the combined fluctuations.

A convenient and more practical alternative to Eq. (13–5) is to express the expected return on the ith security as a function of the expected market return (e.g., the return from an appropriately weighted portfolio consisting of all stocks in the Standard and Poor's 500 Index).

$$E(R_i) = R_f + \beta_i[E(R_m) - R_f]$$
$$= R_f(1 - \beta_i) + \beta_i[E(R_m)] \tag{13-6}$$

In Eq. (13–6), $E(R_i)$ and $E(R_m)$ refer to the expected returns on security i and the market, respectively. R_f represents a riskless, or pure, return. Any return in excess of R_f is a compensation for the systematic risk incurred by the investor. If Eq. (13–6) is rewritten as $E(R_i) - R_f = \beta_i[E(R_m) - R_f]$, the term $E(R_i) - R_f$ gives the risk premium contained in the total return of security i. β_i is a coefficient that can be determined through simple regression techniques. β_i measures the responsiveness of the return on security i to a given percentage change in the market return. For example, if $\beta_i = 1.2$, a 1 percent increase in R_m will mean a 1.2 percent increase in R_i; a 2.5 percent decrease in R_m will mean a 3.0 percent decrease in R_i; and so on. If β_i is positive, R_i responds positively to R_m (i.e., ρ_{im} is positive). If β_i is equal to zero, R_i is independent of $R_m(\rho_{im} = 0)$. If β_i is positive and equal to 1, changes in R_i and R_m will be equal. If β_i is greater than 1, fluctuations in R_i will be greater than fluctuations in R_m, and vice versa if β_i is less than 1. Thus β_i, which measures the magnitude of the variations in return of security i relative to the market, is a measure of the (undiversifiable) risk of that security.[5] The greater the value of β, the greater the risk. Notice that the size of the risk premium defined above is a positive function of β.

Equation (13–8) represents what is commonly known as the market model, based on expected returns. For the ex post case, the equation can be rewritten as

$$R_i = R_f + \beta_i(R_m - R_f) + \varepsilon_i \tag{13-7}$$

Not all of the changes in R_i are going to be related to changes in R_m. In other words, some of the risk of security i will be unsystematic—or diversifiable. The ε_i term in Eq. (13–7) (generally referred to as a *random error term*) allows for the unsystematic risk of security i. Assume, for example, $\beta_i = 1$ and $E(R_m) = 10$ percent. The predicted value of R_i, or $E(R_i)$, would also be 10 percent. The actual value of R_m could be 10 percent, although the actual value of R_i could be 8 percent or 13 percent (or any other reasonable value). If $R_i = 8$ percent, $\varepsilon_i = -2$ percent; if $R_i = 13$ percent, $\varepsilon_i = 3$ percent. ε_i thus allows for the (likely) possibility that the actual and

[5] In terms of the statistical concepts used above, we can define β_i as follows:

$$\beta_i = \frac{\text{cov}_{im}}{\sigma_m^2} = \frac{\rho_{im}\sigma_i\sigma_m}{\sigma_m^2}$$

predicted (or expected) values of R_i will not be equal. The only requirement of Eq. (13–7) is that the expected, or average, value of ε_i be zero. In other words, it is required that, on the average, positive and negative values of ε_i occur in reasonable balance so as to cancel one another out.

Unsystematic risk may be the major component of the total variability of return for some securities. But since the risk is unsystematic and has an expected value of zero, the random movements from the predicted return for a group of well-diversified securities should fairly well cancel each other out. Thus the sum of the unsystematic components should be approximately zero for an effectively diversified portfolio. The objective of diversification is to eliminate aggregate unsystematic risk.

Only systematic risk remains for a well-diversified portfolio, and β_i is the relevant measure of a security's risk. If X_i represents the proportion of available funds invested in security i, the return on the total portfolio is a weighted average of the return of each component security as given by Eq. (13–7). The unsystematic risk of the portfolio is a weighted average of the summed ε_i terms for each security, as shown in Eq. (13–8). R_p = the return on the portfolio, n is the number of securities in the portfolio, and it is required that $X_i \geq 0$ and $\sum X_i = 1$.

$$R_P = \sum_{i=1}^{n} X_i R_i = \sum_{i=1}^{n} X_i R_f (1 - \beta_i) + \sum_{i=1}^{n} X_i \beta_i R_m + \sum_{i=1}^{n} X_i \varepsilon_i \quad (13\text{–}8)$$

If it is assumed that $\sum X_i \varepsilon_i \cong 0$,[6] the riskiness of the portfolio is given by $\beta_p = \sum X_i \beta_i$ (notice how a large negative β would reduce total risk). A portfolio should be constructed so that β_p has a value consistent with the risk preferences of the holder(s) of the portfolio. A high value of β_p means greater risk than a low value of β_p. Finally, notice that effective diversification means $\sum X_i \varepsilon_i = 0$; it *does not* imply that $\sum X_i \beta_i = 1$. A value of β_p greater than or less than 1 could be reasonable, depending upon the portfolio holder's risk preferences.

PROBLEMS

1. Given the following probability distribution of returns for project X, calculate the expected return, variance, standard deviation, and semi-variance.

R:	0.09	0.10	0.11	0.12	0.13	0.14	0.15	0.16
$P(R)$:	0.10	0.10	0.10	0.10	0.10	0.20	0.10	0.20

[6] It has been found that, for the "average" common stock, unsystematic risk, as reflected in the random error term, accounts for approximately 60 percent of total variability. In a well-constructed portfolio, the contribution of unsystematic risk to total variability is typically reduced to less than 10 percent.

2. Express the expected return and variance of expected return for a three-security portfolio, using equations similar to Eqs. (13–3) and (13–4).

3. The expected return and variance are given below for securities E and F. Notice that E has both the higher expected return and the lower variance.

	E	F
$E(R)$	16%	12%
σ^2	4%	6%

"Diverting part of one's funds from E to F will lower the expected return. It will also be increasing the proportion invested in the higher-risk security. Therefore, the optimal portfolio, regardless of one's risk preferences, would be to invest exclusively in E." Discuss this statement.

4. How will the set of efficient portfolios obtained by using expected return-standard deviation parameters (as in Illustration 13–2) differ from the set of efficient portfolios obtained by using expected return-variance parameters?

5. Given the following values of ρ_{EF} for Problem 3 above, determine the maximum proportion that should be invested in security F to obtain an efficient portfolio.
   a. $\rho_{EF} = +1$
   b. $\rho_{EF} = 0$
   c. $\rho_{EF} = -1$
   d. $\rho_{EF} = -0.5$

6. Assume that σ_B is greater than σ_A. Then gains from diversification are possible only if ρ_{AB} is less than σ_A/σ_B. That is, unless the condition $\rho_{AB} < \sigma_A/\sigma_B$ is met, the optimal value of X_A will be 1, *regardless* of the risk preferences of the investor. Prove this result.

7. The possible one-year returns for four securities, conditional on the state of the economy one year hence, are given below. Each state has an equal probability of occurring; i.e., the probability of each occurring $= \frac{1}{4}$. Assume that the cost per share of each security is the same. Also assume that you are a risk averter.

		State		
Security	1	2	3	4
A	$7\frac{1}{2}\%$	$12\frac{1}{2}\%$	$17\frac{1}{2}\%$	$22\frac{1}{2}\%$
B	$-7\frac{1}{2}$	$7\frac{1}{2}$	$22\frac{1}{2}$	$37\frac{1}{2}$
C	$22\frac{1}{2}$	$17\frac{1}{2}$	$12\frac{1}{2}$	$7\frac{1}{2}$
D	$37\frac{1}{2}$	$22\frac{1}{2}$	$7\frac{1}{2}$	$-7\frac{1}{2}$

a. Calculate the expected return for each security.
b. You can buy one share of one of the above securities. Rank them in descending order according to your personal preferences.
c. What would you do if you could buy any two shares that you choose (one each of two different securities or two shares of any one)?
d. What would you do if you had to buy one share of each of any three of the above securities (or, of which security would you *not* want a share)?

8. You own 12 shares of a widely diversified mutual fund M. The expected return per share, given the state of the economy, would be

	1	2	3	4
M	0%	10%	20%	30%

If each state of the economy has an equal probability of occurring,

   a. What is your expected return per share from M?
   b. Express the returns of securities A, B, C, and D in Problem 7 as a function of the return on M; e.g., in the form $R_A = R_f (1 - \beta_A) + \beta_A R_m$.
   c. Suppose that you could buy any combination of five shares of A, B, C, and/or D to hold in combination with your 12 shares of M. What would you buy?
   d. Same as c, except that you can now buy any combination of eight shares.
   e. Same as c, except that you can now buy any combination of nine shares.

9. Assume that you are a mutual fund manager. You feel that a long upward trend in security prices is about to be reversed. What significance would this have on the average β values of securities you would want to be holding in your portfolio?

10. The manager of fund K holds securities with an average β value of 0.8 and recently earned a 12 percent return on his portfolio. The manager of fund L holds securities with an average β value of 1.3 and earned a 13 percent return over the same period. How would you rank the performance of the two fund managers?

14

Markov processes

In this chapter we shall discuss a useful mathematical model for analyzing a process over time. The mathematical representation and analysis of how a random variable changes over time is often an important part of many decision models for inventory, queueing, replacement, and other problems.

A crucial element of all models under uncertainty is the analysis of the probability of certain random variables being in particular stages at some given point in time. For example, in inventory models we deal with the probability of demand being at a specific level at some given point in time. In queueing models, we are concerned with the probability of having X arrivals occur during some specified interval of time.

In many situations the variable of interest is time-sequenced; i.e., it changes from one state to another over time. Thus we can think of demand for a product as being represented by a sequence of random variables $X_1, X_2, \ldots, X_t, \ldots$, where X_t represents the level of demand at time period t and X_{t-j} represents the level of demand at time period $t-j$. Technically, any time-sequenced set of random variables, where X_t represents a measurable characteristic of interest at time t, is called a *stochastic process*. Analysis of a stochastic process is of practical interest only in cases where the probability of X being in a certain state in time period t depends on where it was in some time period(s) prior to t.[1] Obviously, if the state of X in time period t is totally independent of the chain of events prior to t, the stochastic aspects of the variable are of no real interest. However, when there is *some* pattern to the change in the state of X from period to period, analysis of the stochastic process may be important to a full description and analysis of the problem.

---

[1] There is interest, however, in ascertaining whether a process is or is not independent of a chain of past events.

Analysis of both the short-term and long-term patterns of change of stochastic processes over time can be of interest to the decision maker. When one is analyzing the short-term pattern of change, interest would center on both the actual resultant changes of the variable over time and the underlying pattern of change. The first is clearly of value in forecasting future values of the variable. The second can be extremely valuable in determining and evaluating management decisions intended to affect the value of the variable over time.

Consider the following stochastic process representing a customer's brand preference where there are three competitive brands. Let $X_1, X_2, \ldots, X_t, \ldots$, represent the sequence of customers' brand purchases over time. Of interest for sales forecasting would be the proportion of customers purchasing a given brand in time period $t + 1$, *given* prior purchasing history. The probabilities of switching from brand to brand, however, should also be of interest to the marketing department as a guide to identifying potential customers on the basis of previous purchasing history and in directing and evaluating promotional efforts toward attracting these potential customers. Suppose that recent analysis has shown that customers with a certain purchasing history have a 50 percent chance of switching in the next period to brand A. Suppose also that a large promotional effort is made to convert these people to brand A, which results in 50 percent of these people switching to brand A. On the basis of the analysis of the stochastic process, we would conclude that the advertising effort was ineffective. Without an analysis of the stochastic process we might wrongly believe the advertising effort was successful, attributing the 50 percent switch of customers to the promotional efforts when, in fact, this switch probably would have occurred anyway.

The long-term properties of the process deal with the *steady-state* probabilities[2] that the variable will be in given states after a long series of transitions. Besides representing the equilibrium state of the process, these probabilities also represent the expected proportion of time that the variable will be in each state. The steady state probabilities are the ones most frequently used in optimizing a model. For example, a fixed inventory policy can be devised so that there are constant opportunity costs associated with each possible state of the random variable demand at any point in time. If we then select the strategy that minimizes opportunity costs, using the steady state probabilities for the probability distribution of demand, it would be the strategy which has the minimum actual (long-run) average cost per unit time.

FIRST-ORDER MARKOV PROCESS

There are many stochastic processes that have been analyzed and found to be well suited for actual applications. The following discussion will be

[2] It should be noted that steady-state probabilities do not exist for all stochastic processes.

restricted to only one particular type of stochastic process, the first-order Markov process. The conditions under which a first-order Markov process is appropriate are the following:

1. At any point in time, X_t can take on only a finite number of mutually exclusive and exhaustive values. The finite set of values represents the possible states of the system.

2. The conditional probabilities of moving from one state to another (or remaining in the same state) are independent of past transitions. Such a system is said to have no memory. This means that at any point in time the probability of moving from state i to state j, denoted by P_{ij}, is the same, regardless of the path taken to reach state i. Hence it does not matter whether the variable was in state i for the last 30 time periods or whether it just entered state i for the first time—the probability of moving from state i to j in the next time period is the same. The conditional probabilities of moving from one state to another or remaining in the same state in a single time period are called *transition probabilities*.

3. The transition probablities P_{ij} are the same at any point in time. Moreover, the probability that a variable in state i will wind up in state j after exactly n future time periods or transitions will be the same at any point in time. These probabilities are denoted by P_{ij}^n and are called *n-step transition probabilities*.[3]

4. At the initial point of time of study, there exists a set of probabilities that the variable is in any state. These are denoted by P_i. For example, suppose that there are four possible states and at t_0, the variable is in state 2; then the initial probabilities are $P_1 = 0$, $P_2 = 1$, $P_3 = 0$, and $P_4 = 0$. Alternatively, suppose that the four states represent consumer purchases of a product of one of four competitive brands, and we know that at t_0, market shares of the four products are 10 percent, 30 percent, 50 percent, and 10 percent, respectively. Then the initial probabilities would be $P_1 = 0.10$, $P_2 = 0.30$, $P_3 = 0.50$, and $P_4 = 0.10$.

EXAMPLES OF MARKOV PROCESSES

First-order Markov processes have been found to have many real-life applications. They have been used to study the replacement pattern of machines and personnel, the brand loyalty and switching pattern of consumers, inventory stock over time, and breakdown patterns of equipment.

The application of the first-order Markov process cannot usually be justified on theoretical grounds alone. Empirical evidence from studying a system over time is usually needed to test the goodness of fit of the model. In fact, the situation often is such that, on theoretical grounds, the first-order Markov is not an appropriate model but empirically it seems to approximate the actual pattern of outcomes over time quite well. In particular, conditions 2 and 3 require the most scrutiny.

In applying stochastic processes in real life, two alternative approaches are generally used. In the first method we first study the characteristics of the

---

[3] First-step transition probabilities are simply the transition probabilities noted in condition 2. The superscript 1 and the term "first step" are usually deleted in reference.

situation generating the data. Based on this analysis we then hypothesize the particular type of stochastic process we believe best represents the situation. In effect we have assumed a model, which, if right, should generate data whose pattern is very similar to the actual pattern of the data. To get actual values from the particular type of stochastic process model chosen we need to know certain parameters of the model. Thus we next collect empirical data to estimate the parameters and to see if the assumed model really does generate data similar to the actual data. Then, if we are satisfied that the model does describe the situation, we can use the stochastic process model we have chosen and the estimate of its parameters to predict what will occur in the future or analyze the past and present. If not we could try other particular types of stochastic processes and repeat the procedure.

The second approach is to look at the empirical data first. Then after examining the pattern of the data, choose a model, estimate the parameters, and test the model. Assuming the model is satisfactory, we would use it for prediction and analysis. The problem of estimating the parameters and testing the goodness of the model are statistical problems beyond the scope of this text. The interested reader is referred to the statistics literature.

Let us consider the problem of studying brand switching over time. It would seem highly unlikely that a consumer's future brand purchases would, in fact, be affected only by his last purchase. It would seem that a consumer who purchased brand A 10 times in a row would be more likely to purchase brand A than a consumer who recently purchased brand A for the first time. However, studies have shown that the first-order Markov process has approximated reality quite well when applied to studying *groups* of consumer behavior. This is probably due to the fact that, when groups of consumers are studied at any point in time, the past patterns of behavior of persons who have currently and those who have consistently purchased brand A "averages out" so that historical purchasing patterns are not of significance. It should be realized, however, that, although such a model may predict and analyze the purchasing patterns of groups of consumers, it would be inappropriate for predicting and analyzing an individual consumer's pattern.

The third condition of a first-order Markov, that the transition probabilities are stationary, is one for which the system must be carefully examined. In brand-switching problems it should be evident that a large amount of marketing effort is intended to alter the transition probabilities. Major advertising campaigns are often planned to entice consumers who currently are using a certain brand to try the advertiser's brand. In effect, the major purpose of such advertising is to increase the transition probability associated with switching from that brand to the advertiser's brand. Although this would not necessarily mean the first-order Markov could not be used, it would clearly limit the length of projection into the future which would be relevant. However, if this limitation is recognized, short-term predictions and analysis of the switching patterns using the first-order Markov may be quite successful and useful.

ANALYSIS OF FIRST-ORDER MARKOV PROCESS

Transition Probabilities

The first step in any analysis of a first-order Markov process is the construction of the transition probabilities. In order to estimate the transition probabilities, detailed data on individual changes over time are required. For the brand-switching problem, suppose that the only data available are a time series of data representing the market shares over time (such as given in Exhibit 14–1). The data are insufficient because we do not know the actual

Exhibit 14–1 Insufficient Data for Estimating Transition Probabilities for Brand-Switching Problem

Market Shares of Products (%)

	Time Period					
Products	1	2	3	4	5	6
A	30	25	31	32	30	32
B	40	45	34	40	40	38
C	30	30	35	28	30	32

changes from one state (brand) to another over time. Having only aggregate data, we are unable to determine, for example, how brand B went from 40 percent in period 1 to 45 percent in period 2. It is impossible to tell whether all its customers remained loyal and only A's customers switched, or whether some of B's customers switched but this was offset by switches from A and C customers, or whether some other combination of events resulted in the change in market share. Since transition probabilities represent the probability of switching from one particular state to another, detailed sample information on individual patterns over time, such as that given in Exhibit 14–2, is needed to estimate transition probabilities.

Exhibit 14–2 Sufficient Data for Estimating Transition Probabilities for Brand-Switching Problem

Average Period Switches

	To		
	A	B	C
From A	120	60	38
B	55	155	63
C	40	55	180

From the data given in Exhibit 14–2, estimates of the transition probabilities would be (where P_{11} = purchase of A in period 1 and purchase of A in period 2; P_{13} = purchase of A in period 1 and purchase of C in period 2; P_{23} = purchase of B in period 1 and purchase of C in period 2; and so on):

$$P_{11} = \frac{120}{218} = 0.551$$
$$P_{12} = \frac{60}{218} = 0.275$$
$$P_{13} = \frac{38}{218} = 0.174$$
$$P_{21} = \frac{55}{273} = 0.201$$
$$P_{22} = \frac{155}{273} = 0.568$$
$$P_{23} = \frac{63}{273} = 0.231$$
$$P_{31} = \frac{40}{275} = 0.145$$
$$P_{32} = \frac{55}{275} = 0.200$$
$$P_{33} = \frac{180}{275} = 0.655$$

Transition probabilities are usually presented in a matrix form as given in Exhibit 14–3, where the i, j element represents the transition probability p_{ij} (the probability of moving from state i to state j). For example, the circled element in the matrix represents the probability or proportion of customers currently using brand A who are expected to switch in the *next* time period to brand B.

Exhibit 14–3 Transition Matrix for Brand-
Switching Problem

$$P = \begin{bmatrix} 0.551 & 0.275 & 0.174 \\ 0.201 & 0.568 & 0.231 \\ 0.145 & 0.200 & 0.655 \end{bmatrix}$$

Useful management information is contained in the transition matrix. Examination of the resultant transition matrix pinpoints the brand's effectiveness in keeping its customers and to whom and from whom switches are taking place. By looking at the competing products and advertising, analysis should yield insights into the strengths and weaknesses of the product and its advertising.

Short-Term Forecasts

Given that we have estimates of the transition probabilities, let us examine how these may be used for short-term forecasting. Suppose that in the initial time period market shares are distributed 40 percent, 30 percent, and 30 percent for brands A, B, and C, respectively, so we can expect that, out of every 10,000 consumers, 4000 will be using product A; 3000, product B; and 3000, product C. Now let us predict what the market shares will be in the next time period. We shall first estimate the number of consumers A will have in the next time period. Of the 4000 current A customers, 55.1 percent, or 2204, will continue to use A. In addition, 20.1 percent, or 603, of the current

B customers will switch to A, and 14.5 percent, or 435, of the current C customers will switch to A, yielding a total predicted number of 3242 customers for A, or a market share of 32.42 percent. In general, the prediction of the percentage or number of elements in state i in the next period is

$$P_i P_{ii} + \sum_{\substack{j=1 \\ j \neq i}}^{n} P_j P_{ji} = \sum_{j=1}^{n} P_j P_{ji} \tag{14-1}$$

Using Eq. (14–1), we find that it follows that the estimated market shares would be

Brand $A = (0.4)(0.551) + (0.3)(0.201) + (0.3)(0.145) = 32.42$ percent

Brand $B = (0.4)(0.275) + (0.3)(0.568) + (0.3)(0.200) = 34.04$ percent

Brand $C = (0.4)(0.174) + (0.3)(0.231) + (0.3)(0.655) = 33.54$ percent

If we simply repeat the process, using the new estimates for the market shares in the next time period and the transition probabilities, we obtain the estimate of the market shares two periods hence. Iteratively we thus could predict n periods ahead.[4]

n-step Probabilities

A problem related to predicting n periods ahead is finding the probability that an item currently in state i will be in state j n periods hence. As mentioned previously, such probabilities are called n-step probabilities and are denoted by P_{ij}^n. Let us first consider how we could calculate the second-step probability P_{ij}^2. If we are in state i at time t_0, we can move to any state in the first period as long as we move from there to state j in the second period. Clearly, the sum of the probabilities of the paths taken through all possible k states in the first period to state j in the second period equals P_{ij}^2.

Period: initial   first   second

State: i $\rightarrow$ k $\rightarrow$ j

Thus the desired probability would be

$$P_{ij}^2 = \sum_{k=1}^{n} P_{ik} P_{kj}$$

[4] Those who know matrix algebra will realize that this is equivalent to the matrix multiplication n-step forecast

$$p^n = p_1 p^n$$

For example, the probability that a customer currently using brand A will be using brand C two periods hence is

$$P_{13}^2 = P_{11}P_{13} + P_{12}P_{23} + P_{13}P_{33}$$
$$= (0.551)(0.174) + (0.275)(0.231) + (0.174)(0.655) = 0.237$$

To calculate the third-step probability P_{ij}^3, it would follow that the item can go from initial state i to any state l in period 1, to any state k in period 2, and from k to j in the third period.

$$
\begin{array}{cccc}
\text{initial} & \text{first} & \text{second} & \text{third} \\
i & \rightarrow \quad l & \rightarrow \quad k & \rightarrow \quad j
\end{array}
$$

The first two steps, however, represent second-step probabilities. Thus

$$P_{ij}^3 = \sum_{k=1}^{n} P_{ik}^2 P_{ij}$$

For the brand switching example,

$$P_{13}^3 = P_{11}^2 P_{13} + P_{12}^2 P_{23} + P_{13}^2 P_{33}$$
$$= (0.384)(0.174) + (0.302)(0.231) + (0.237)(0.655) = 0.292$$

where

$$
\begin{aligned}
P_{11}^2 &= P_{11}P_{11} + P_{12}P_{21} + P_{13}P_{31} = 0.384 \\
P_{12}^2 &= P_{11}P_{12} + P_{12}P_{21} + P_{13}P_{32} = 0.302 \\
P_{13}^2 &= P_{11}P_{13} + P_{12}P_{23} + P_{13}P_{33} = 0.237
\end{aligned}
$$

and

Using the same logic, we see that it follows that the n-step probabilities can be calculated by using the general formula (14–2).[5]

$$P_{ij}^n = \sum_{k=1}^{n} P_{ik}^{n-1} P_{kj} \tag{14–2}$$

STEADY STATE PROBABILITIES

As mentioned previously in optimization models, the long-term properties of the first-order Markov process are of special interest; that is, the probability of finding an item in state j after a large number of transitions has

[5] Those readers familiar with matrix algebra should recognize the n-step probabilities as simply the transition matrix raised to the nth power.

taken place. For example, the twentieth-step probability matrix for the brand-switching problem is given below.

$$P^{20} = \begin{bmatrix} 0.273 & 0.349 & 0.378 \\ 0.273 & 0.349 & 0.378 \\ 0.273 & 0.349 & 0.378 \end{bmatrix}$$

The probabilities in each column are identical, indicating that the probability of being in a certain state after 20 periods is independent of the initial state. This means that regardless of what the market shares were initially, after twenty periods we would predict the shares to be 27.3 percent, 34.9 percent, and 37.8 percent, respectively, for brands A, B, and C. Moreover, we would estimate the same for all future periods. These probabilities thus represent the steady-state probabilities. It should be realized that this does *not* mean that transitions will not take place after 20 periods, or that every consumer will settle into a single brand. Rather, it means that the pattern of switching by individual consumers will be such that the resultant proportion of items in each state will remain constant.

Let us discuss briefly the interpretation of the steady state probabilities when we are studying a single item over time. The above interpretation is meaningful for large number of items, but it could be confusing when applied to a single item that at any period can be in only one state. In this situation the steady state probabilities specify the exact *proportion of time* that the item will spend in each state over the long run. That is, if we were dealing with a single customer, we could conclude that over a long period of time 27.3 percent of the time he would purchase brand A, 34.9 percent of the time brand B, and 37.8 percent of the time brand C.

The calculation of the steady state probabilities comes directly from the property of the long-run concept. If we denote the steady state probabilities as Π_i, $i = 1, 2, \ldots, n$, then we know that the transition matrix must be such that the resultant proportions in each state remain constant or equal to the set of Π_i's again. Let us focus on the proportion of items in state 1. If we have reached equilibrium or steady state, then Π_1 is the proportion in state 1. In the next period, it follows from the transition matrix that the proportion in state 1 would be

$$\Pi_1 P_{11} + \Pi_2 P_{21} + \cdots + \Pi_n P_{n1}$$

But from the concept of steady state it is clear that this must equal Π_1. Hence the steady state probabilities must satisfy the set of equations

$$\Pi_i = \sum_{j=1}^{n} \Pi_j P_{ji} \quad \text{for all } i$$

and

$$\sum \Pi_i = 1$$

This gives us $n + 1$ equations and n unknowns. It can be shown, however, that one of the equations in the first set is redundant. Hence, any one of the first n equations can be eliminated arbitrarily, leaving n linearly independent equations and n unknowns. Methods for solving n simultaneous equations are well known and, while solution of a set of n equations may be quite tedious by hand, the steady state probabilities can be computed easily with the aid of high-speed digital computers.

Calculating the steady state probabilities for our brand-switching problem would entail solving the following set of three simultaneous equations.

$$\Pi_1 = 0.551\Pi_1 + 0.201\Pi_2 + 0.145\Pi_3$$

$$\Pi_2 = 0.275\Pi_1 + 0.568\Pi_2 + 0.200\Pi_3$$

and

$$1 = \Pi_1 + \Pi_2 + \Pi_3$$

where the third equation ($\Pi_3 = 0.174\Pi_1 + 0.231\Pi_2 + 0.655\Pi_3$) is the one arbitrarily chosen to be deleted. Solving these three equations would yield the following solution:

$$\Pi_1 = 0.273$$

$$\Pi_2 = 0.349$$

$$\Pi_3 = 0.378$$

DECISION MAKING USE OF STEADY STATE PROBABILITIES

Consider the following problem. A manufacturing company has a certain piece of equipment that is inspected at the end of each day and classified as "just overhauled," "good," "fair," or "inoperative." If the item is inoperative it is overhauled, a procedure that takes one day. Let us denote the four classifications as states 1, 2, 3, and 4, respectively. Assume that the working condition of the equipment follows a first order Markov process with the following transition matrix:

$$P = \begin{vmatrix} 0 & \frac{3}{4} & \frac{1}{4} & 0 \\ 0 & \frac{1}{2} & \frac{1}{2} & 0 \\ 0 & 0 & \frac{1}{2} & \frac{1}{2} \\ 1 & 0 & 0 & 0 \end{vmatrix}$$

The transition matrix can be interpreted as indicating that three-fourths of the time a just overhauled machine is in good condition after a day's use and one-fourth of the time it is in fair condition after a day's use. A machine that is in good condition has an equal chance of still being in good condition or being in fair condition after a day's use, while a machine in fair condition has a 50–50 chance of being in fair or inoperative condition after a day's use. An inoperative machine will be overhauled the next day, so that at the end of the day it will have been just overhauled. Suppose it costs $125 to overhaul a machine (including lost time), on the average, and $75 in production is lost if a machine is found inoperative.

Using the steady state probabilities, we can compute the expected per day cost of maintenance, since the steady state probabilities represent the proportion of time that the machine will be in each state in the long run. Solving for the steady state probabilities requires solving the following simultaneous equations:

$$\Pi_1 = \Pi_4$$
$$\Pi_2 = \tfrac{3}{4}\Pi_1 + \tfrac{1}{2}\Pi_2$$
$$\Pi_3 = \tfrac{1}{2}\Pi_2 + \tfrac{1}{2}\Pi_3$$
$$\Pi_4 = \tfrac{1}{2}\Pi_3$$

and

$$\Pi_1 + \Pi_2 + \Pi_3 + \Pi_4 = 1$$

Solving yields the following probabilities:

$$\Pi_1 = \tfrac{2}{11}$$
$$\Pi_2 = \tfrac{4}{11}$$
$$\Pi_3 = \tfrac{3}{11}$$
$$\Pi_4 = \tfrac{2}{11}$$

Thus, on the average, two out of every 11 days the machine will be overhauled, three out of every 11 days it will be in good condition, four out of every 11 days in fair condition, and two out of every 11 days it will be found inoperative at the end of the day. Thus the average cost per day of maintenance will be

$$(\tfrac{2}{11})(125) + (\tfrac{2}{11})(75) = \$36.36$$

Now suppose that management wants to consider overhauling the machine whenever it is in fair condition, eliminating the possibility of the machine's becoming inoperative. The revised transition matrix would be

$$P = \begin{bmatrix} 0 & \tfrac{3}{4} & \tfrac{1}{4} \\ 0 & \tfrac{1}{2} & \tfrac{1}{2} \\ 1 & 0 & 0 \end{bmatrix}$$

and the resultant steady state probabilities would now satisfy the equations:

$$\Pi_1 = \Pi_3$$
$$\Pi_2 = \tfrac{3}{4}\Pi_1 + \tfrac{1}{2}\Pi_2$$
$$\Pi_3 = \tfrac{1}{2}\Pi_2 + \tfrac{1}{2}\Pi_3$$

and

$$\Pi_1 + \Pi_2 + \Pi_3 = 1$$

The steady state probabilities would be

$$\Pi_1 = \tfrac{2}{7}$$

$$\Pi_2 = \tfrac{3}{7}$$

and

$$\Pi_3 = \tfrac{2}{7}$$

The resultant expected maintenance cost per day would be

$$(\tfrac{2}{7})(125) = \$35.71$$

Comparing this with the previous result, we see that the suggested new maintenance policy is better than the old one by 65 cents per day on the average.

Let us reconsider the brand-switching example. Suppose that the producers of brand A are considering two alternative marketing strategies. One is aimed at attracting brand C customers while also reducing the loss of its customers to brand C. Under this strategy, it is assumed that it can increase the probability of a customer switching from C to A by 0.10 and reduce the probability of a customer switching from C to A by 0.10. The objective would be a resultant transition matrix as in Exhibit 14-4.

Exhibit 14-4 Revised Transition Matrix 1 under Strategy 1

$$\begin{bmatrix} 0.651 & 0.275 & 0.074 \\ 0.201 & 0.568 & 0.231 \\ 0.245 & 0.200 & 0.555 \end{bmatrix}$$

The second marketing strategy is aimed at brand B with similar goals, as illustrated in the projected transition matrix given in Exhibit 14-5.

Exhibit 14-5 Revised Transition Matrix under Strategy 2

$$\begin{bmatrix} 0.651 & 0.175 & 0.174 \\ 0.301 & 0.468 & 0.231 \\ 0.145 & 0.200 & 0.655 \end{bmatrix}$$

To evaluate the efficacy of each strategy, it is necessary first to calculate the immediate estimated effect of each strategy. Strategy 1 would result in a market share in the next time period of 36.42 percent for brand A, while strategy 2 would result in an identical market share for A.[6] Let us now examine the long-term implications of the two alternative strategies. Strategy 1 would result in the steady state market share for A of 38.5 percent, while

---

[6] A's share under strategy 1 = (0.40)(0.651) + (0.30)(0.201) + (0.30)(0.245) = 0.3642.
 A's share under strategy 2 = (0.40)(0.651) + (0.30)(0.301) + (0.30)(0.145) = 0.3642.

strategy 2 would result in A's share being 40.2 percent.[7] Strategy 2 obviously is better.

The examples cited above are illustrations of using the calculation of the steady state probabilities as aids to management decisions. The common denominator of these examples is that management in effect had some control over the transition probability matrix. Even when management has no control over the transition matrix, however, the use of the Markov process to make short- and long-range forecasts can be an invaluable aid to decision makers in planning.

FURTHER CONSIDERATION

In this chapter we have dealt with only one mathematical model for describing the movement of a process over time. Although it is a frequently used model and a fairly simple one to use, it clearly will not fit all real-life situations. There are a multitude of other mathematical models available to describe a process over time. A whole class of higher-order Markov processes exists (i.e., second-, third-, fourth-order Markov processes, etc.) which allow for the transition probabilities to be dependent on the later part of the path taken to reach the current state. The order represents the length of memory. That is, in a second-order Markov the probability of moving from state i to j in time period t depends on only what happened one time period previously, i.e., the path of the item in $t - 2$ which resulted in its being in state j in $t - 1$.

Besides Markov processes, a multitude of totally different stochastic models exist. Choosing a model that will adequately fit the data is often a difficult and challenging task, but a very important one. The model describing the process over time is often a crucial input in many situations. The correctness of the results from any optimization model depends on the correctness of the data inputs.

PROBLEMS

1. Define the following terms.
   a. Time-sequenced random variable

[7] Under strategy 1 we solve the following set of simultaneous equations to find Π_1.

$$0.651\Pi_1 + 0.201\Pi_2 + 0.245\Pi_3 = \Pi_1$$
$$0.275\Pi_1 + 0.568\Pi_2 + 0.200\Pi_3 = \Pi_2$$
$$0.074\Pi_1 + 0.231\Pi_2 + 0.555\Pi_3 = \Pi_3$$
$$\Pi_1 + \Pi_2 + \Pi_3 = 1$$

Under strategy 2 we solve the following set of simultaneous equations fo find Π_2.

$$0.651\Pi_1 + 0.175\Pi_2 + 0.174\Pi_3 = \Pi_1$$
$$0.301\Pi_1 + 0.468\Pi_2 + 0.231\Pi_3 = \Pi_2$$
$$0.445\Pi_1 + 0.200\Pi_2 + 0.655\Pi_3 = \Pi_3$$
$$\Pi_1 + \Pi_2 + \Pi_3 = 1$$

b. Stochastic process

c. Transition probability

2. What do the following represent?

   a. Xt

   b. X_{t-j}

   c. P_{ij}^h

3. Under what conditions is a stochastic process a first-order Markov process?

4. Does the problem of inventory stock over time meet the conditions of a first-order Markov process? Explain your answer.

5. Suppose a machine can be in one of two states: (a) running, or (b) under repair. The data on changes over time is given below.

	Average Period Switches	
	To	
	a	**b**
From a	270	30
b	60	90

P_{12} = running in period 1 and under repair in period 2. Find the transition matrix.

6. The results of a manual dexterity training procedure leads to the following probability matrix that describes the pattern of "correct" and "incorrect" responses.

	Correct	**Incorrect**
Correct	0.9	0.1
Incorrect	0.2	0.8

If the probability of the initial response being correct is 60 percent, what is the probability that the next response will be correct?

7. With reference to Exhibit 14–3, what is P_{11}^3?

8. What is meant by steady state probabilities? Find the steady state probabilities for this transition matrix.

$$P = \begin{vmatrix} 0.4 & 0.5 & 0.1 \\ 0.2 & 0.3 & 0.5 \\ 0.6 & 0.1 & 0.3 \end{vmatrix}$$

9. Consider the following transition matrix for brand-switching.

$$\begin{vmatrix} 0.50 & 0.15 & 0.35 \\ 0.20 & 0.55 & 0.25 \\ 0.25 & 0.30 & 0.45 \end{vmatrix}$$

The manufacturers of brand C are considering a marketing strategy to attract brand B customers. It is estimated that this strategy will: (a) increase probability of customers' switch from B to C by 0.20, (b) decrease probability of customers' switch from C to B by 0.10, and (c) decrease probability of customers' switch from A to C by 0.25. Should the new strategy be used?

15

queueing theory
and applications

The word *queue* refers to waiting in line. The next surest thing to death and taxes is that most people will spend part of their lives waiting in line for some service. The concept of waiting can be viewed in a broader sense than just people waiting in line. Any person or object can become a customer for some service and in the process have to wait for service. People wait at supermarkets for their groceries to be checked out; airplanes wait at airports for clear runways to take-off; broken machines wait idle for a repairman; students frequently wait in horrendous lines at registration time. We all have our favorite examples of inconveniences caused by regularly having to wait in line.

THE QUEUEING PROBLEM

In theory, almost all waiting lines could be eliminated by increasing the facilities for service. It is always possible to add more checkout counters at the supermarket, build more runways, or hire more repairmen or registration workers. The expansion of facilities, however, costs money. On the other hand, there generally is a cost that can be assigned to waiting. An idle machine does not produce; a plane waiting at a runway for take-off uses fuel and, more importantly, irritates customers, who may choose a different airline or mode of transportation next time; long lines at supermarket checkout counters is one of the reasons convenient but high-priced, quick-service grocery chains are in existence; memories of long registration lines, attributed to inefficiency and/or indifference toward students, could affect the reactions of alumni to appeals for contributions.

In sum, there are two costs: those associated with the servicing facilities and those associated with having the customer wait for service. Decision makers are faced with the problem that actions tend to reduce one at the expense of increasing the other. The cost of facilities can be viewed from two perspectives, the cost of adding a new facility for service and, if it is given that a set of facilities already exists, the cost associated with a facility being idle. These costs we usually are able to calculate. The costs of waiting similarly can be divided into two types of costs: those directly associated with waiting, such as the cost of fuel while waiting for a clear runway, and those indirectly associated with waiting, such as the cost of lost business because of disenchantment with waiting. The direct costs of waiting are usually readily measurable. The indirect costs are clearly more difficult to measure. The short-term loss of business, that is, customers who turn away because the line is too long, can sometimes be estimated by on-the-spot observation. The longer-range effect this has on his returning, however, is more difficult to assess and often requires experimentation or surveying.

Consider the case of a large retailer's phone order department. It can put in x number of lines and hire y number of operators at a known cost. The more facilities it puts in for customer service (at greater total cost), the less likely it will be that a customer will have to wait because of a busy signal. On the other side, the immediate cost of waiting is evident but not so easily computed. Every time a customer does not eventually place an order as the result of a busy signal, sales are lost. The longer-term impact is even more difficult to evaluate. The problem is to determine how many customers refrain from ordering in the future because of the expectation of having to wait, regardless of whether or not they place their order presently, in spite of having to wait.

Given that we have some measure of costs, the decision maker's goal is to design a servicing system that minimizes the total costs, i.e., the sum of the servicing and waiting costs. In order to effect change in the queueing process, there generally are two things that the decision maker can do. He can add or subtract facilities for service or, given that the facilities are fixed, he can alter the process by which customers reach the service point. The decision policy governing the order in which the customers will receive service is called the *queue discipline*. For example, service can be offered on a first-come, first-served basis, or service can be offered in a categorical fashion if more than one service point is available. We are all familiar with the express checkout counters in supermarkets that service only customers with small orders.

The two variables generally considered to be outside the decision maker's control, but which are at the heart of any queueing analysis, are the patterns of customer arrival times and customer service times.[1] If customer demand is regular and the time for service is fixed, the queueing problem is trivial. Consider the unrealistic situation where customers arrive exactly every five minutes and it takes exactly five minutes to service a customer. If we have one facility, the facility will always be working and no customer will

[1] In some cases the pattern of arrival times is under the decision maker's control, and the question of how to schedule arrivals is a decision variable.

be waiting. Now suppose that we consider the more realistic situation where customers arrive at irregular times but, on the average, one arrives every five minutes. We can determine what would happen if we were to treat the demand as regular and use the solution of one service facility. Suppose the first customer arrives at time 0. He receives service and ties up the service facility until $t = 5$. At $t = 7$, $t = 10$, and $t = 12$, three more customers arrive. The service facility is clear at $t = 5$ and remains idle for two minutes. It then services the next customer until $t = 12$. The customer arriving at $t = 10$ must wait two minutes. The customer arriving at $t = 12$ must wait a full five minutes. Moreover, since customers arrive on the average of one every five minutes, we can expect another customer to enter the queue before the last customer begins service. Extending this, we can envision the queue backing up indefinitely, or the queue choking up. The reason for this is that *facility time that is idle cannot be saved and used later to meet demand.* Idle facility time is lost, while excess demand remains in the system in a waiting line. It should be clear that if the queue is not to choke up, the expected number that can be serviced per period must be greater than the expected number of arrivals per period.

Terminology of Queueing Theory

Queueing theory, like almost all disciplines, has developed its own terminology. Thus, before discussing the queueing models in detail, let us first define the major terminology.

Queue discipline: the method of determining the order in which customers are serviced.

Service point: a facility that services only one customer at a time.

Line: a sequence of service points that sequentially serve a customer.

Channels: several service points or lines that simultaneously serve customers. All or some of the channels can be duplicated (i.e., can offer the identical service), or each or some of the channels may be specialized (i.e., offer different specialized services, such as an express line for small orders).

Queue: the line waiting for service. The number or time in the queue does not include the number or time at a service point or line being served.

System: the entire process of waiting and being served. The number or time in the system includes the number or time in the queue and at a service point or line.

QUEUEING ANALYSIS IN GENERAL

Modeling

In real life many queueing problems are handled without formal analysis. Managers familiar with the process in question, using past experience and their knowledge of the current situation, can often make reasonable decisions concerning the number and use of facilities. However, there is no guarantee that these decisions are in fact the best ones, and sometimes the process is so complex that intuition leads to costly errors. The alternative is formally to model the process through a system of equations and probability distributions describing the queue discipline and demand and service times, respectively. In theory such a complete queueing model could be built and evaluated to find the decision that minimizes total costs. This is usually a very ambitious and complex task. Because of the complexity, the main thrust of queueing theory is directed toward formulating a model which, when analyzed, will give a realistic description of a complex queueing process. Different alternative management strategies can be evaluated, and rational or optimal strategies (if costs are included and all relevant strategies evaluated) can be found.

There are a multitude of different queueing models that have been developed or could be developed. The choice of models depends on the properties of the process in question, although the basic components are the same for all models. The components of a queueing model are

1. The facilities available.
2. The queue discipline.
3. The pattern of arrival times to the system.
4. The pattern of customer service time.

The latter two represent patterns that are not regular; that is, there is uncertainty as to when customers will actually arrive and as to how long it will actually take to service each customer. The number of arrivals per time period and the time to service a customer can thus be considered random variables, and their patterns can be described by appropriate probability distributions. A crucial part of all queueing analysis is the choice of the probability distributions and the specification of the parameters of the distributions to describe the arrivals and service times. The usefulness of any queueing model, therefore, depends upon how realistically the chosen probability distributions (and their parameters) represent the actual process.

Moreover, since we must deal with randomness in the process, the results of any analysis can at best give us the expected outcomes or the probability of any outcome occurring. But it will never tell us exactly what will occur at any point in time. Thus decisions are optimal only in a long-run sense. They are not optimal necessarily for any single period of time.

Analysis

Developing or selecting the appropriate mathematical model to describe the process is the most crucial, and usually the most difficult, part of any queueing analysis. Once a model has been constructed, analysis of the model can be performed in either of two different ways: (a) through analytical solution or (b) through simulation. Both methods use mathematical models to represent the system and assume probability distributions for arrival times and for service times. They differ in that the analytical method approaches the problem by solving sets of equations derived to represent the mathematical properties of the process and finding probabilistic expected outcomes. In the simulation method, the process is experimentally repeated (in theory) a large number of times, the model being used to generate outcomes (usually by a computer), and the range and frequency of outcomes over the large number of trials is found. In this chapter we shall deal only with the analytical approach. Simulation in general, and simulation of a queueing problem in particular, is discussed in Chapter 16.

Regardless of the technique of solution, the outcome of the analysis is usually the same: (a) a summary description of the waiting of customers and (b) a summary description of usage (or nonusage) of the facilities. Although there are many possible ways of summarizing the waiting and servicing process, the five most common and usually most informative analytical outputs are

A. Waiting
  1. The expected number of customers in the system at any point in time.
  2. The expected number of customers waiting for service (in the queue) at any point in time.
  3. The expected time that a customer will spend in the system.
  4. The expected waiting time (in the queue) before being served.
B. Service
  5. The expected proportion of time that a service facility is idle.

SPECIFIC QUEUEING MODELS

In this chapter we shall discuss only the simplest model, a single-channel model[2] with Poisson arrival and exponential service distributions. We shall discuss in detail the structure and analysis of the single-channel and present a summary of results. This is done so as not to get bogged down in mathematical detail but to allow the reader, if he desires, to gain an understanding of the mathematical logic of queueing theory. The detailed discussion, however, requires some mathematical sophistication on the part of the reader and can be skipped by going directly to the summary of results without a loss in continuity.

POISSON-EXPONENTIAL SINGLE-CHANNEL MODEL

Arrivals and Service

In the Poisson-exponential model, the arrival of customers is assumed to follow the Poisson distribution with mean λt. That is, the average number of

[2] The term "single-channel model" refers to a system that contains only one service point or line, while a "multiple-channel system" contains at least two service points or lines.

arrivals per unit of time (minutes, hours, days, etc.) is λ. For the Poisson distribution to be appropriate, arrivals must occur randomly. That is, it must be equally likely for an arrival to occur at any point of time, and the arrivals must be independent of one another. Independence means that the time of the last arrival does not affect the time of the next arrival. The Poisson distribution for arrivals empirically seems to fit many situations; for instance, phone calls to a switchboard, cars at a tollbooth, and planes arriving at an airport tend to follow a Poisson distribution. The last example is especially interesting, because it represents arrivals that are actually scheduled. In many cases where arrivals are scheduled, the normal fluctuations from scheduled arrival times, due to varying causes, makes the sequence of arrivals appear random. In many situations the arrivals do not follow exactly the Poisson distributions, but the use of the Poisson still is a good approximation. There are two classes of arrivals, however, for which the Poisson distribution is likely to provide a poor fit. One is where the arrivals are scheduled and variation in the scheduled arrivals is slight compared to the scheduled time between arrivals. The other is where arrivals are the result of time passage. For example, if a store bills everyone at the end of the month, phone calls to the credit department are apt to bunch in the first week of the month; thus the assumption of equally likely arrivals at all times is unjustified.

If the number of arrivals follows the Poisson distribution, then the distribution of the time between arrivals[3] follows the exponential distribution with mean $1/\lambda$. On the average there is an arrival every $1/\lambda$ unit of time.

In considering servicing time, we assume that the time it takes to service an individual customer is exponential with mean $1/\mu$. It therefore follows that the average service rate, the average number of elements serviced per unit time of servicing, is μ. The distinction between "service" time and "arrival" time is important. "Arrival" time is continuous. The process of arrival goes on continuously. "Service" time, on the other hand, can take place only if at least one customer is in the system. Service time refers to the system's capacity to provide service. Thus when we say, for instance, that the service rate is 10 per hour we do *not* imply that every hour 10 customers will be serviced. Ten customers will be serviced if and only if there is no idle time in the system. As pointed out previously, however, the service rate must be greater than the arrival rate, or the queue will back up indefinitely; thus the existence of some idle time is a necessity. Therefore, the service rate represents the average number of customers serviced per unit of time if service is continuous.

Analysis

Now let us see how these probability distributions are used to analyze the queueing process of a single-channel system. First we shall calculate the probability that there will be n customers in the system at any given time. Consider an extremely small period of time Δt. During the period Δt, the

---

[3] See Chapter 2 for discussion of the Poisson and exponential distributions.

expected number of arrivals is $\lambda \, \Delta t$. If Δt is extremely small, then $\lambda \, \Delta t$ will be considerably less than one. For example, if on the average there are 12 arrivals per hour ($\lambda = 12$, $t =$ hours), then in a single second (Δt) the expected number of arrivals is $(12)(\frac{1}{360}) = 0.033$. Since the interval is so small, $\lambda \, \Delta t$ can be interpreted as the probability of an arrival in Δt if we assume that the probability of two arrivals is so small it can be considered zero. Conversely, $1 - \lambda \, \Delta t$ is the probability that there are no arrivals in Δt. Similarly, if on the average μ customers per hour can be serviced and leave the system, then in Δt we would expect $\mu \, \Delta t$ customers to be serviced and depart under continuous servicing. If we again assume that Δt is so small that no more than one customer will be serviced, $\mu \, \Delta t$ represents the probability that a customer will be serviced and leave the system. Conversely, $1 - \mu \, \Delta t$ is the probability that there are no departures during Δt.

Now let us consider the probability that at $t + \Delta t$ there will be *no customers in the system*. Let $P_t(n)$ represent the probability that in a given time t, there are n customers in the system. Then we are calculating $P_{t+\Delta t}(0)$. The event that there are to be no customers in the system at $t + \Delta t$ could result from two mutually exclusive possibilities. One possibility would be that no one was in the system at time t and there were no arrivals in Δt. The probability of this possibility is $P_t(0)(1 - \lambda \, \Delta t)$. The second possibility is that at time t there was one customer in the system and in Δt he is serviced and there are no new arrivals. The probability of this occurrence is $P_t(1)(\mu \, \Delta t)(1 - \lambda \, \Delta t)$. Thus

$$P_{t+\Delta t}(0) = P_t(0)(1 - \lambda \, \Delta t) + P_t(1)(\mu \, \Delta t)(1 - \lambda \, \Delta t)$$

Since we are interested in any time t, the time subscripts can be eliminated.[4] Algebraic manipulation of the above terms yields

$$P(1) = \frac{\lambda}{\mu} P(0) - P(1)\lambda(\Delta t)$$

Now if we consider Δt to be infinitesimally small, or approximately 0, we have[5]

$$P(1) = \frac{\lambda}{\mu} P(0)$$

Using the same approach, we can generate the general recursive relationship

$$P(n) = \left(\frac{\lambda}{\mu}\right)^n P(0) \tag{15–1}$$

It is worth noting that the above is a mathematical proof of what we saw intuitively before—that unless $\mu > \lambda$ the probability of the system choking up ($n \to \infty$) is 1.

---

[4] In effect we are dealing with the steady state of the system.

[5] Those familiar with calculus will recognize this as $dP(n)/dt$.

In order to use the recursive formula (15–1) we must know $P(0)$. To calculate $P(0)$ we need to recall that the sum of any probability distribution is 1. Thus

$$1 = \sum_{n=0}^{\infty} P(n) = \sum_{n=0}^{\infty} \left(\frac{\lambda}{\mu}\right)^n P(0)$$

Since $\lambda/\mu < 1$, we have the infinite sum of a geometric progression and

$$1 = \frac{P(0)}{1 - \lambda/\mu}$$

and

$$(15-2)$$

$$P(0) = 1 - \frac{\lambda}{\mu}$$

Hence the *proportion of time the facility will be idle is* $1 - \lambda/\mu$. Again since $\lambda/\mu < 1$, we have mathematical proof of what we intuitively concluded before, that there must be some idle service time in a system.

To calculate the expected or average number of customers in the system, we need only use the common expectation formula,

$$E(n) = \sum_{n=0}^{\infty} nP(n)$$

$$E(n) = \sum_{n=0}^{\infty} n \left(\frac{\lambda}{\mu}\right)^n P(0)$$

$$E(n) = P(0) \sum_{n=0}^{\infty} n \left(\frac{\lambda}{\mu}\right)^n$$

Using the known geometric progression sum $\sum_{x=0}^{\infty} xr^x = r/(1 - r)^2$, we have[6]

$$E(n) = P(0) \frac{(\lambda/\mu)}{(1 - (\lambda/\mu))^2}$$

$$(15-3)$$

$$E(n) = \frac{\lambda/\mu}{1 - \lambda/\mu}$$

Hence Eq. (15–3) *gives the average number of customers in the system.*

Now let us solve for the average time that a customer will spend in the system, $E(t)$. A customer arrives at some random point in time. On the average, the customer remains in the system W units of time, where $W = E(t)$. During the W units he is in the system, on the average λW additional arrivals

[6] For those who know calculus, $\sum_{x=0}^{\infty} xr^x = r \sum_{x=1}^{\infty} xr^{x-1} = r \sum dr^{x-1} = rd \sum r^{x-1} = rd(1/1 - r) = r(1/(1 - r)^2) = r/(1 - r)^2$.

will occur, since arrivals occur on the average at λ per unit time. Thus when the initial customer departs, there will be, on the average, λW customers in the system. Thus

$$E(n) = \lambda W$$

But from Eq. (15–3) we know $E(n)$. Hence

$$\frac{\lambda/\mu}{1 - \lambda/\mu} = \lambda W$$

and the *average time a customer spends in the system is*

$$W = E(t) = \frac{1}{\mu - \lambda} \tag{15–4}$$

So far we have dealt only with the complete system. It is often necessary, however, to consider only the queue. If the results for the system are given, the equivalent results for the queue are easily obtained. Equation (15–4) gives the average total time spent in the system. This total time consists of the expected time spent in the queue plus the expected time receiving service. Since the average service time is $1/\mu$, the *average waiting time in the queue is*

$$
\begin{aligned}
E(t_q) &= \frac{1}{\mu - \lambda} - \frac{1}{\mu} \\
&= \frac{\lambda}{\mu}\left(\frac{1}{\mu - \lambda}\right) \tag{15–5} \\
&= \frac{\lambda}{\mu} E(t)
\end{aligned}
$$

Similarly, if the average waiting time in a queue is $(\lambda/\mu)E(t)$ and arrivals occur at rate λ per unit time, the *expected number of customers in the queue is*

$$
\begin{aligned}
E(n_q) &= \frac{\lambda}{\mu} W\lambda \\
&= \frac{\lambda^2}{\mu} \frac{1}{\mu - \lambda} \\
&= \frac{(\lambda/\mu)(\lambda/\mu)}{1 - \lambda/\mu} \tag{15–6} \\
&= \frac{\lambda}{\mu} E(n)
\end{aligned}
$$

It should be noted that the waiting time and number in the queue can be calculated by multiplying the corresponding quantity in the system by λ/μ.

SUMMARY OF RESULTS OF SINGLE-CHANNEL POISSON EXPONENTIAL MODEL

In the Poisson exponential single-channel model, we assume that arrivals follow the Poisson probability distribution and servicing times follow the exponential probability distribution. Customers are serviced by one facility on a first-come, first-served basis. We define

λ = average number of arrivals per unit t of time.

μ = average number of customers that can be serviced per unit of time.

The process so described has the following characteristics:

1. The expected number of customers in the system

$$E(n) = \frac{\lambda/\mu}{1 - \lambda/\mu} \qquad (15\text{--}7)$$

2. The expected number of customers in the queue

$$E(n_q) = \left(\frac{\lambda}{\mu}\right) E(n) \qquad (15\text{--}8)$$

where $E(n)$ comes from Eq. (15–7).

3. The average waiting time in the system

$$E(t) = \frac{1}{\mu - \lambda} \qquad (15\text{--}9)$$

4. The average waiting time in the queue,

$$E(t_q) = \left(\frac{\lambda}{\mu}\right) E(t) \qquad (15\text{--}10)$$

where $E(t)$ comes from Eq. (15–9).

5. The expected proportion of time a facility will be idle

$$E(\text{idle}) = 1 - \frac{\lambda}{\mu} \qquad (15\text{--}11)$$

Example 1

A firm has a single machinist in a repair shop. He works eight hours a day, and on the average six machines break each day. It takes on the average one hour to repair a machine. Using the Poisson-exponential model, we have

$$\lambda = 0.75 \text{ machine per hour}$$

and

$$\mu = 1 \text{ machine per hour}$$

Thus, on the average, at any point in time the number of machines in the shop but not fixed will be [from Eq. (15–7)]

$$\frac{0.75/1}{1} - \frac{0.75}{1} = \frac{0.75}{0.25} = 3 \text{ machines}$$

The expected number of machines at any point in time in the shop on which he has not started to work is [from Eq. (15–8)] $(0.75/1)(3) = 2.25$ machines.[7] On the average, a machine will be down (i.e., waiting for repairs or undergoing repairs) $1/(1 - 0.75) = 4$ hours [from Eq. (15–9)] after failing. Of these four hours, the machine will be idle waiting for service on the average [from Eq. (15–10)] $(0.75/1)(4) = 3$ hours.

Finally, the repairman will, on the average, spend [from Eq. (15–11)] $(1 - 0.75/1) = 25$ percent of each working day idle waiting for a machine to come into the shop.

Scrutiny of these results illustrates the price of irregular demand on the system and the fact that idle time is lost. Despite the fact that the repairman is idle an average of two hours a day, and it takes only an hour to repair a machine, on the average a broken machine will be unproductive for four hours. This is primarily because the breakdown of machines will not be equally spaced. Breakdowns will at times occur in clusters, and at other times none may break down for a long period. Clearly, however, this above result represents a long-term average, and many machines will in fact be serviced immediately.[8]

Example 2

At a one-man barbershop, it takes on the average one-half hour ($\mu = 2$ per hour) to service a customer, and customers arrive at an average rate of one every 45 minutes ($\lambda = 1\frac{1}{3}$ per hour). If the Poisson-exponential model is assumed, it follows that at any point in time, on the average,

1. There are two $[(\frac{2}{3})(1 - \frac{2}{3})]$ customers in the shop.
2. A customer will spend one hour and 30 minutes $[1/\frac{2}{3}]$ in the shop, of which one hour $[(\frac{2}{3})(1\frac{1}{2})]$ will be spent waiting to be served.
3. The barber will be idle one-third of the day $[1 - \frac{2}{3}]$.

OTHER MODELS

The model presented is one of the simplest of all models to analyze. However, it is easy to conceive of numerous other models. Instead of one repair service we could consider two or three. Thus we would have a multiple-channel service process. We could change the queue discipline and instead of servicing on a first-come, first-served basis, do all the fast jobs first. Obviously in real life there are many configurations for servicing and determining the order of service. Also we could consider different patterns of arrival other than the Poisson and different service time distributions than the exponential.

[7] Note that this is a long-run average, since at any specific point in time there cannot actually be one-fourth of a machine in the shop.

[8] Specifically, the probability of this is $P(\text{idle}) \times P(\text{a customer arrives})$ or $P(\text{idle}) \times [1 - P(\text{no customer arrives})]$. Since customers arrive following the Poisson probability distribution with parameter $\lambda = 0.75$, from the Poisson tables, we find $P(\text{no customer}) = 0.47$ and hence the proportion of a machine will be serviced immediately is 0.12.

However, it should be known that as the complexity of the system increases the difficulty of analytical solution generally increases at a much faster rate. Most realistic problems therefore are solved through simulation with a great deal of the effort being spent on the initial stage of modeling satisfactorily a very complex real-life situation.

PROBLEMS

1. What is the objective of queueing models? What cost determinations must be made in order to solve queueing problems? What is meant by the term "queue discipline"?

2. In the solution of a queueing problem, why is it necessary for the expected number that could be serviced per period to be greater than the expected number of arrivals per period?

3. What is meant by "the analysis of a model through analytical solution"? What types of assumptions must be made when the analytical method is used to obtain a solution?

4. What information is provided by the analysis of a queueing problem?

5. The Towaway Company operates a garage which has the capacity of servicing 12 trucks per hour. A truck arrives every 6 minutes on the average assuming a Poisson exponential model.
   a. What is the average waiting time in line for each truck?
   b. At any given time, what is the average number of trucks waiting in line?
   c. What is the probability that there are three trucks waiting in line?
   d. What is the probability that there are four or more trucks in the system?
   e. What proportion of the time will the garage be idle?
   f. How is it possible that, on the average, there are trucks waiting in line, while some of the time the entire system is idle?

6. A community counselling clinic is staffed by a professional counsellor. Arrivals at the clinic average $1\frac{1}{2}$ per hour, and each counselling session is scheduled to take one-half hour assuming a Poisson exponential model:
   a. What is the expected waiting time for each arrival?
   b. What is the expected number of people waiting for counselling at any given time?
   c. What is the expected number of people in the system (i.e., waiting for or receiving counselling) at any given time?
   d. What proportion of the time is the counsellor idle?
   e. What is the probability that there is exactly one person in the queue at any given time?
   f. What is the probability that there are two or more people waiting in line?
   g. What is the probability that there are two or more people in the system at any given time?
   h. Compare your answers to f and g above.

7. A growing population has increased the average number of arrivals at the above counselling clinic to $5\frac{1}{2}$ per hour. Answer questions a through h in Problem 6. What has happened to the stability of the system? Why?

8. Assume that a further growth in population has increased the average number of arrivals in Problem 6 to $6\frac{1}{2}$ per hour. Now what has happened to the stability of the system? Why? Calculate the expected number of people in the queue after five hours; after eight hours.

9. A museum has a 10 minute slide presentation available to visitors for a cost of 25¢. Only one person can view the presentation at a time. Patrons arrive randomly following the Poisson distribution at the rate of 5 per hour.

a. An individual arrives. What is his expected waiting time?

b. What is the probability he will have no wait?

c. What proportion of time will the presentation not be in use?

d. What are the expected revenues from the presentation per 40 hour week?

16

simulation

The advent of high-speed computers has opened up vast new potential for quantitative analysis. The computer's ability to do a multitude of complex logic and arithmetic operations at extremely high speeds has made it possible to solve in minutes problems that are so large in scale that they would have taken months to solve manually. For example, the solution of a linear programming problem with 25 variables and 30 constraints can be obtained in minutes with a computer, whereas it would take weeks to solve the same problem by hand. Perhaps the greatest contribution made by computers to the area of quantitative analysis, however, is not the capability to handle large problems with incredible speed and accuracy but the fact that they make available an entirely new method for evaluating models, Monte Carlo simulation.

Before the computer appeared, solution to quantitative problems generally was conducted as follows: Develop a model that abstracts the problem and then analytically evaluate the model to obtain a solution.[1] All the models presented in this text are of this same basic type. It is the second aspect—analytical evaluation—which has been the tremendously limiting factor in the use of quantitative analysis. The term *analytical evaluation* refers to the process of obtaining a mathematical solution of the model. For example, given the single-channel, Poisson-exponential model presented in the preceding chapter, we were able to find the average time spent in the system to be $1/(\mu - \lambda)$ through the use of the mathematics of algebra, probability, and calculus. Even in this simplest of all queueing models, however, it was

[1] Actually, the ability to obtain a solution through computers stimulated the development of many of the techniques discussed in this book. Advances in both high speed computer technology and quantitative methods evolved from research conducted during World War II.

evident that mathematical evaluation is not always easily accomplished. It is not hard to conceive of situations so complex that analytical solution is in fact impossible (or at least extremely difficult and time-consuming), given the current state of mathematical development.

The constraint that a model has to be evaluated mathematically can lead to a tendency to sacrifice the realism of the model for the solvability of the model. How often have you heard the phrase "simplifying assumption" used in reference to the development of a mathematical model? "Simplifying assumption" often means that, although the model really should be in form *A*, we shall structure it in form *B* because we can analytically evaluate *B* but not *A*. Thus realism is sacrificed to make the model solvable. The assumption of linearity or the use of well-known probability distributions is often strongly influenced by the knowledge that assumptions of linearity, or the normal distribution, or the Poisson-exponential combination, lead to solutions while other assumptions, though more realistic, do not. In many cases, the solutions resulting from simplifying assumptions are more than adequate for the needs of the decision maker. Occasionally, however, they are not. Before high-speed computers there was no choice, because if a model could not be evaluated analytically, there was no other way to arrive at a solution (other than the imposing task of trial and error). If a model was to be useful, a solvable model had to be developed.

Currently, for many types of problems, there is an alternative to analytical evaluation of a model, the technique of Monte Carlo simulation. Simulation is not a perfect substitute, however, but rather an alternative procedure for evaluating a model. Analytical solution produces *the* optimal or correct answer, while Monte Carlo simulation yields a solution which should be very close to the optimal but not necessarily the exact correct solution. (In Monte Carlo simulation, the solution converges to the optimal or correct solution as the number of simulated trials goes to infinity. In actual practice, it is necessary to truncate the simulation process after a finite number of trials.)

CONCEPT OF MONTE CARLO SIMULATION

Monte Carlo simulation is a substitute for the mathematical evaluation of a model. Clearly, therefore, it does *not* eliminate the need for the development of a model that depicts the operation of the system under study. Hence, the first step, defining the problem and structuring it in a quantitative format, remains the same regardless of whether the solution is to be obtained by simulation or by analytical methods. Because the requirement of analytical solution is no longer a constraint, however, the model can be developed without concern about its mathematical solvability.

It should be emphasized that although the model developed still needs to be a complete and realistic representation of all important aspects of the system under study, it need only represent the essential aspects of the system. Being overly realistic results in spending a great deal of effort and computer time to obtain very small improvements in the over-all results. Moreover, the mass of trivial implications may obscure the significant results. There is sometimes a tendency to include irrelevant aspects of the system when solution is to be by simulation, perhaps as an overreaction to the "simplifying assumptions" made to obtain analytical solutions.

Not all models are amenable to Monte Carlo simulation solution. Only models under uncertainty can be evaluated via Monte Carlo methods. This is obvious because *the basic premise of Monte Carlo simulation is the continued observation of the system over a long period of experience.* This long history of the system's operation is, of course, a simulated rather than a real history. *Theoretically, we draw on a large number of samples from the model* and, through these observations, examine the behavior of the system. Without a random aspect to the model, all samples (or trials) would yield the same outcome.[2]

Random Numbers

The method used to simulate a sample is based on the use of random numbers. (The use of random number tables will be discussed later in the chapter.) Random numbers are numbers selected in such a fashion that every number has an equal probability of being drawn. Once we select a random number, we convert it into an observation drawn from the probability distribution specified by the model.

Let us consider a rather trivial example to illustrate the basic concept of Monte Carlo simulation. Suppose we build a model of a production line that produces on the average seven percent defective items. Defective items occur randomly. Items are packaged for sale in lots of five. We would like to know what percentage of the lots contains no defectives. Using analytical methods, we could easily arrive at the answer, $(0.93)^5 = 0.70$. However, for illustrative purposes, let us use Monte Carlo simulation to answer the same question.

The four-digit numbers 0000 to 9999 can be used, where the random numbers 0000 through 0699 represent a defective item and 0700 through 9999 represent a good item. This assignment of the numbers in effect represents the probability distribution associated with selecting a defective or good item. The random number selection procedure we shall use is called the *midsquare technique.*

This is only one of an abundance of methods that are used for generating random numbers. But no matter what method is used, careful attention must be paid to insuring that the numbers generated are in fact random and result in the observations following the probability distribution specified in the model. This is the crucial aspect of Monte Carlo simulation. If the random number generating process cycles or contains a bias, the results of simulation will be erroneous. Careful analysis of the samples drawn is necessary to insure that the simulated solution is valid.

[2] The term "Monte Carlo," generally associated with gambling, refers to the uncertain or random nature of a system to be evaluated by using the technique of simulation.

Midsquare Procedure

The midsquare procedure works as follows. Take a four-digit number, square it, and use the four digits starting with the third from the left. To get the second random number, start with the new four-digit number and repeat the process.[3] Such a procedure generally will produce 10^5 random numbers.[4] For our example, suppose that we start with the number 4261. The first random number is thus 1561 ($4261^2 = 18\underline{1561}21$), and the first item sampled is good. The second item (random number 3672) is also good. The third (4835), fourth (3772), and fifth (2279) are also good. The first randomly sampled lot is therefore good. Repeating this process so that we draw ten lots yields the results in Exhibit 16–1.

Exhibit 16–1 Simulated Lots Drawn

Lot	Random Numbers	Simulated Items	Defective Number in Lot
1	1561, 3672, 4835, 3772, 2279	G, G, G, G, G	0
2	9384, 0594, 2836, 4289, 3955	G, D, G, G, G	1
3	6420, 2164, 8289, 7075, 0556	G, G, G, G, D	1
4	9136, 4664, 7258, 6707, 9838	G, G, G, G, G	0
5	7862, 8110, 7721, 6138, 6750	G, G, G, G, G	0
6	5625, 6406, 0368, 5424, 4197	G, G, D, G, G	1
7	6148, 7979, 6644, 1427, 3632	G, G, G, G, G	0
8	1914, 6339, 1829, 4524, 4665	G, G, G, G, G	0
9	7622, 0948, 8704, 7596, 6992	G, G, G, G, G	0
10	8880, 8544, 9999, 9800, 0400	G, G, G, G, D	1

Simulation Results

On the basis of the simulated sample of ten lots, we would estimate the expected percentage of good lots as 0.60. Obviously, this does not equal the analytical answer of 0.70 found above. The analytical answer equals the true expected value, or the average number of good lots over the "long run,"[5] while the result from Exhibit 16–1 is based on only ten samples. With the aid of computers, however, we could increase the number of samples from 10 to 10,000 in a few minutes of computer time, and concurrently the accuracy of our answer should also increase. It should be recognized, however, that Monte Carlo simulation yields only an approximate answer. If the number of simulated replications is large and the model is good, the approximation should be excellent. Exact solutions come only from analytical solution, however, and hence are generally preferred where obtainable.

---

[3] This procedure breaks down, however, when the number zero appears since the square of zero is zero. In such cases we choose a new random value other than zero and continue.

[4] Generally between 10^4 and 10^5 sequential random numbers, the procedure returns to the initial number.

[5] The "long run" in statistics is an infinite period of experiences.

It should be pointed out that while we speak of the computer time necessary to perform a simulation in terms of minutes, the magnitude of the effort required to perform a simulation should not be underestimated. The time spent constructing the model and structuring the mechanics and computer programs for simulation is often measured in weeks and months. For very complex problems, years of effort are not uncommon, with the computer time being measured in days and weeks. This is especially so because, by the very nature of problems that often are solved by simulation, they are extremely complex.

Inventory Example

Now let us illustrate a somewhat more realistic simulation problem. A small firm intuitively feels that its casual approach to the problem of inventory control has led to substantial diseconomies. The bulk of the firm's business is concentrated in one item, and the formulation of an inventory policy would be concerned only with this item. The firm's management would like to determine (a) the optimal (or a near-optimal) inventory policy and (b) the extent to which deviations from this policy will result in increases in total inventory costs.

Investigation reveals that the pattern of daily demand is random and unstable (i.e., it varied from day to day in an unpredictable pattern), making the application of the economic order quantity model[6] inappropriate for this particular problem. Further investigation, however, discloses that the pattern of daily demand does conform to a fairly stable probability distribution, with no detectable seasonal or secular shifts. The probability distribution of daily demand, based on historical observations, is given in columns (1) and (2) of Exhibit 16–2. Notice that the distribution is not symmetric; it is skewed in the direction of high daily demand. (Thus, for example, the use of an optimization model based on the assumption of daily demand being normally distributed would not be appropriate.) The firm's management also finds that the lead time from placement of an order to receiving delivery varies randomly, but follows the probability distribution given in columns (4) and (5) of Exhibit 16–2. These historical data do not seem to fit the assumptions of any of the better-known inventory policy optimization models.

Exhibit 16–2   Data for Inventory Policy Example

(1) Daily Demand	(2) Probability	(3) Random Numbers	(4) Lead Time	(5) Probability	(6) Random Numbers
5 units	0.08	00–07	3 days	0.15	00–14
6	0.13	08–20	4 days	0.40	15–54
7	0.15	21–35	5 days	0.25	55–79
8	0.18	36–53	6 days	0.20	80–99
				1.00	
9	0.17	54–70			
10	0.12	71–82			
11	0.08	83–90			
12	0.06	91–96			
13	0.03	97–99			
	1.00				

[6] The derivation and use of the economic order quantity model were discussed in Chapter 11. The economic order quantity model is an optimization model.

This information—probability distributions of daily demand and lead time—culled from old sales and purchasing records is sufficient for some preliminary investigations of alternative inventory policies. An inventory policy is specified by two parameters, the order point and the order quantity. That is, the inventory policy will indicate at what level of existing inventory an order should be placed and the number of units that should be specified in that order.

A meeting of the firm's top management is called to discuss the problem of formulating an inventory policy. Someone suggests a policy of ordering 40 units whenever the inventory at the end of a day is 35 units or less. There are some murmurings of disagreement, but they contain varied opinions as to whether the order quantity and order point should be greater or less than the levels first suggested. After considerable discussion, it is agreed that they should evaluate the policy indicated above [denoted by (35, 40)].

They quickly agree that it could be an expensive lesson if they follow the (35, 40) policy for a year's time and it turns out to be a very inefficient policy. Given the availability of dependable data on daily demand and lead times, however, they decide that simulation is an appropriate technique for quickly and inexpensively evaluating the suggested (35, 40) inventory policy.

For the purpose of performing the simulation, the two-digit random numbers given in column (3) of Exhibit 16–2 are assigned to various levels of daily demand and the random numbers in column (6) are assigned to alternative lead times.[7] Notice that, from a long sequence of two-digit uniform random numbers,[8] a random number in the range 00–07 should occur about 8 percent of the time; a random number in the range 08–20 should occur about 13 percent of the time, and so on. Thus the random numbers are assigned in such a way that the occurrence of random numbers should conform to the probability distribution of daily demand. Similarly, random numbers are assigned to lead times so as to conform to the associated probability distribution.

The experience of 45 days under the (35, 40) inventory policy is simulated in Exhibit 16–3. A series of two-digit random numbers, used to indicate units of daily demand, is given in column (2). The random numbers are obtained from Appendix F–7, a table of uniform random numbers. The term "uniform" means that every n-digit random number has an equal probability of being encountered in the table. The table consists of seven columns of five-digit random numbers. A series of two-digit random numbers can be taken from any arbitrary starting point in the table. For purposes of simulating a pattern of daily demand for our current example, the first two digits in the second column of five-digit numbers is used. This procedure generates the sequence of numbers 80, 47, 59, 32, 01, 15, and so on. Simulated lead times are determined from the last two digits on the right-hand side of the table.

The inventory at the beginning of day 1 is arbitrarily assumed to be 70 units. From Exhibit 16–2, it is seen that the random number 80 represents daily demand of 10 units [as indicated in column (4) of Exhibit 16–3]. The inventory at the end of day 1 is 60 units [indicated in column (5)]. The random number for day 2 corresponds to daily demand of eight units, giving

---

[7] Random numbers can be obtained from tables of random numbers (see Exhibit F–7 in Appendix F), or they can be obtained by computers through the use of random number generating routines.

[8] Uniform random numbers are simply random numbers where all possible numbers have equal probabilities of being selected.

Exhibit 16–3 Simulation for Inventory Policy Example

(1) Day	(2) Random Number	(3) Beginning Inventory	(4) Daily Demand	(5) Ending Inventory	(6) Lost Sales	(7) Shipment Received	(8) Random Number	(9) Lead Time	(10) Order Quantity
1	80	70	10	60	0	0			
2	47	60	8	52	0	0			
3	59	52	9	43	0	0			
4	32	43	7	36	0	0			
5	01	36	5	31	0	0	15	4 days	44
6	15	31	6	25	0	0			
7	21	25	7	18	0	0			
8	49	18	8	10	0	0			
9	32	10	7	3	0	44			
10	13	47	6	41	0	0			
11	47	41	8	33	0	0	99	6 days	42
12	43	33	8	25	0	0			
13	54	25	9	16	0	0			
14	72	16	10	6	0	0			
15	82	6	10	0	4	0			
16	71	0	10	39	10	0			
17	54	6	9	31	9	42			
18	06	42	5	37	0	0			
19	83	37	11	26	0	0	34	4 days	49
20	68	26	9	17	0	0			
21	83	17	11	6	0	0			
22	71	6	10	0	4	0			
23	52	0	8	0	8	49			
24	76	49	10	39	0	0			
25	32	39	7	32	0	0	75	5 days	43
26	08	32	6	26	0	0			
27	96	26	12	14	0	0			
28	59	14	9	5	0	0			
29	47	5	8	0	3	0			
30	37	0	8	0	8	43			
31	30	43	7	36	0	0			
32	17	36	6	30	0	0	09	3 days	45
33	52	30	8	22	0	0			
34	18	22	6	16	0	0			
35	36	16	8	8	0	45			
36	86	53	11	42	0	0			
37	67	42	9	33	0	0	41	4 days	42
38	97	33·	13	20	0	0			
39	55	20	9	11	0	0			
40	61	11	9	2	0	0			
41	04	2	5	0	3	42			
42	93	42	12	30	0	0	47	4 days	45
43	42	30	8	22	0	0			
44	05	22	5	17	0	0			
45	63	17	9	8	0	0			

an ending inventory of 52 units. By the end of day 5, the inventory level is down to 31 units, for the first time falling below the order point of 35 units.

At the end of day 5, an order is made to replenish the inventory. Strict adherence to the stated inventory policy would call for ordering 40 units. It has generally been found, however, that a preferable policy is to order the specified order quantity plus enough additional units to bring the inventory up to the order point. Following this convention, an order for 44 units is placed at the end of day 5. The random number 15 in column (8) corresponds to a lead time of 4 days, as shown in column (9). This means that delivery will be received at the end of day 9, as indicated in column (7). Notice that the demand in day 15 exceeds the beginning inventory, resulting in unsatisfied demand. This unsatisfied demand is shown as lost sales in column (6).

This same procedure is continued for the 45 days' experience shown in Exhibit 16–3. (In actual practice, experience over a longer period of time would be simulated.) The next step would be to evaluate the results of the simulation. For this purpose, management would have to estimate ordering costs, inventory carrying costs, and the costs of unsatisfied demand. These estimated costs would then be applied to the inventory experience depicted in Exhibit 16–3 to get the total cost of the (35, 40) inventory policy.

Exhibit 16–3 shows lost sales in days 15, 16, 17, 22, 23, 29, 30, and 41. These frequent stockouts indicate that the order point should be raised. There were seven orders placed during the 45 days' experience. Unless inventory carrying costs are high relative to ordering costs, it probably would be advisable also to increase the order quantity. Thus a new simulation could be performed using an inventory policy of, perhaps, (50, 60). This policy could be simulated and evaluated and, on the basis of the results, could be modified and a new policy could be specified. Repeated refinement of the inventory policy would continue until management has determined the inventory policy that best meets their needs.

The implementation of the final policy would be accomplished readily if the item in question has a low inventory level or a high inventory turnover. It is easy to increase inventory levels. But if a large, slow moving inventory is on hand, implementation could be more difficult. The firm would have to decide if it will let normal attrition reduce the inventory level or whether it will temporarily lower the prices to make the inventory move more rapidly. A comparison of inventory carrying costs and the magnitude of the price reduction necessary to stimulate sales should indicate which policy would be preferable.

Queueing Example

Formulas for solving queueing problems were given in Chapter 15. Like the economic order quantity model, however, these formulas are based on specific assumptions about the statistical characteristics of the underlying process. To the extent that these assumptions are met, the use of these formulas is appropriate. But if the underlying assumptions are violated, the queueing theory formulas will not give useful or meaningful results. In these situations, Monte Carlo simulation provides an alternative method of analyzing the problem. The use of simulation in such a situation is illustrated in the following example.

Suppose that a small factory has one dock available to unload incoming railroad cars. The dock will accommodate only two cars at a time. Incoming cars arrive during the night and are positioned beside the dock before the unloading crew arrives in the morning. It takes half a day to unload a car, so the crew can unload up to two cars a day. If less than two cars are available for unloading, the crew has idle time. Nevertheless, the union contract requires that they receive a full day's pay. If more than two cars are available, the limited capacity of the dock and the unloading crew makes it necessary to postpone the unloading of some cars until a later day.

The plant manager is considering the construction of a second dock and the addition of a second unloading crew. This would increase the unloading capacity of the plant to four cars a day. The construction cost of a new dock would be $8000 and the weekly wages of the additional unloading crew would be $300. A one-day delay in unloading a railroad car costs the company $60.

The plant manager decides to use simulation to compare the total costs that would be incurred with one dock and with two docks. A probability distribution giving the number of cars arriving on a given night is presented in Exhibit 16–4. Random number assignments corresponding to the probability distribution are also shown.

Exhibit 16–4   Probability Distribution of Number of Railroad Cars Arriving per Night

Number of Arrivals	Probability	Random Numbers
0	0.16	00–15
1	0.24	16–39
2	0.32	40–71
3	0.19	72–90
4	0.06	91–96
5	0.03	97–99
	1.00	

The simulated experience for 45 working days (9 weeks) is given in Exhibit 16–5. The two-digit random numbers are taken from the first two left-hand columns on the second page of Appendix F–7. The simulation is started with the assumption that no cars have been delayed and are waiting from previous days.

The results show that, for the 45-day experience simulated in Exhibit 16–5, almost all delays would be eliminated with the addition of a second dock.[9] This elimination of 156 days in delayed unloading time, at a cost of $60 per day, would save 156($60) = $9360. The wages of the second unloading crew, over a nine-week period, would be 9($300) = $2700, however, resulting in a net savings of $6660. Given that the $8000 construction cost for a second dock could be spread over several years, the plant manager decided to expand his unloading capacity.

OTHER TYPES OF SIMULATION

In Monte Carlo simulation, solutions to the model are derived. Under the broad title of simulation, many other types of analysis of models, such as transitional analysis, sensitivity analysis, parameter estimation, and operational gaming can be accomplished. All four have the basic characteristic of simulation, manipulation of a model to produce a theoretical history of the system.

Transitional Analysis

Transitional analysis is nothing more than a normal byproduct of Monte Carlo simulation. When one is solving a model by simulation, the resultant

---

[9] Notice that with two docks, a delay would occur only when more than four cars arrived in one night. It can be seen in Exhibit 16–4 that this would occur only 3 percent of the time.

Exhibit 16–5 Simulation of Queueing Problem

Day	Random Number	Number of Arrivals	With One Dock			With Two Docks		
			Total Number	Number Unloaded	Number Delayed	Total Number	Number Unloaded	Number Delayed
1	48	2	2	2	0	2	2	0
2	78	3	3	2	1	3	3	0
3	19	1	2	2	0	1	1	0
4	51	2	2	2	0	2	2	0
5	55	2	2	2	0	2	2	0
6	77	3	3	2	1	3	3	0
7	77	3	4	2	2	3	3	0
8	15	0	2	2	0	0	0	0
9	14	0	0	0	0	0	0	0
10	68	2	2	2	0	2	2	0
11	93	4	4	2	2	4	4	0
12	09	0	2	2	0	0	0	0
13	93	4	4	2	2	4	4	0
14	04	0	2	2	0	0	0	0
15	86	3	3	2	1	3	3	0
16	65	2	3	2	1	2	2	0
17	90	3	4	2	2	3	3	0
18	97	5	7	2	5	5	4	1
19	21	1	6	2	4	2	2	0
20	41	2	6	2	4	2	2	0
21	23	1	5	2	3	1	1	0
22	59	2	5	2	3	2	2	0
23	82	3	6	2	4	3	3	0
24	83	3	7	2	5	3	3	0
25	61	2	7	2	5	2	2	0
26	99	5	10	2	8	5	4	1
27	48	2	10	2	8	3	3	0
28	33	1	9	2	7	1	1	0
29	06	0	7	2	5	0	0	0
30	32	1	6	2	4	1	1	0
31	82	3	7	2	5	3	3	0
32	51	2	7	2	5	2	2	0
33	54	2	7	2	5	2	2	0
34	66	2	7	2	5	2	2	0
35	55	2	7	2	5	2	2	0
36	69	2	7	2	5	2	2	0
37	64	2	7	2	5	2	2	0
38	80	3	8	2	6	3	3	0
39	39	1	7	2	5	1	1	0
40	90	3	8	2	6	3	3	0
41	78	3	9	2	7	3	3	0
42	87	3	10	2	8	3	3	0
43	08	0	8	2	6	0	0	0
44	39	1	7	2	5	1	1	0
45	21	1	6	2	4	1	1	0
Total number of days delayed					158			2

294

solution often represents the ultimate optimal solution. That is, when solving a complex inventory problem, we may find the optimal stocking levels for a multitude of items and the expected inventory investment. Such results are called *steady state results*, because they represent the final outcome which will occur a sufficient period of time after the appropriate policy changes are made. However, in many situations it is difficult to accomplish major changes in a short period of time. Even the apparently simple change of an inventory policy may require considerable time to bring about. Items understocked can quickly be corrected by additional purchases, but overstocked items can not so easily be brought to desired levels, since we do not have complete control over usage. The decision makers must then know what is going to occur during transition to the optimal policy and how long it will take. In our example, it may be important to know how high investment levels may reach in transition and how long it will take before our investment tapers off to optimal. With the use of simulation it is not only possible to find the solution but to trace the expected path to the solution. Even when analytical solution can be used to find the optimal steady state result, the use of transitional simulation to determine the intermediate states may be of great value to a decision maker.

Parameter Estimation and Sensitivity Analysis

In some situations we may be able to structure the model, but certain parameters in the model may be unknown because of lack of appropriate data or because it is impossible to estimate analytically the value of the parameters. In such a situation, if a good past history of outcomes exists, we can use simulation to try various possible values for the parameters to see which values fit the data best. For some cases, search algorithms have been developed to reduce the scope of the set of possible values that must be tested. This same type of simulation can be used to explore alternative forms of the model.

Sensitivity analysis is similar to parameter estimation in that we vary the parameter values, or functional form of the model, but rather than seeing which variations result in outcomes closest to past outcomes, we examine the impact on the optimal solution. This gives the decision maker valuable information to: (a) determine how sensitive the solution is to estimated parameters in the model (this is especially important for indicating those parameters that must be estimated precisely), (b) evaluate the impact of possible future changes in the uncontrolled variables in the model, and (c) evaluate the impact of changes in the basic environment of the problem resulting in structural changes in the model.

Operational Gaming

A simulation that has as an input the interactive input of one or more decision makers is called *operational gaming*. Essentially, gaming is simulated experimentation of the behavior of decision makers under controlled conditions and the interaction of decisions and outcomes. The military has long used gaming in the area of "war games." In this interactive, competitive, two-person game, simulation has offered a method for evaluating competitive strategies. This has been extended by psychologists to study the interactive pattern of competitive decision makers in order to understand better the concept of conflict, competition, and "optimal" resolution of conflict. The primary use of games today, however, has been as a teaching device. Management decision games are quite commonly found in business schools today. Operational gaming allows the participants instantly to evaluate decisions or courses of decisions in order to gain insight into the process and impact of decision making.

PROBLEMS

1. Discuss the impact of computer simulation on quantitative analysis.
2. What are the disadvantages of:
   a. Making too many simplifying assumptions in the mathematical model?
   b. Including unimportant aspects of the system in the mathematical model?
   c. Simulating too few events?
   d. Simulating too many events?
3. Why was simulation appropriate in the inventory example?
4. What types of models should Monte Carlo simulation be used for? What types should it not be used for?
5. In which of the following problems should simulation be used?
   a. Simulation of last year's sales to estimate the value of last year's total income.
   b. Simulation of traffic across an intersection to estimate the best time sequence for traffic lights.
   c. Simulation of the economy to predict the effect of different economic policy decisions.
6. What is the basic premise of Monte Carlo simulation?
7. What are random numbers? After a random number has been selected for a simulation experiment, what is it converted into?
8. How are samples simulated?
9. Give a brief theoretical explanation of Monte Carlo simulation.
10. Use the midsquare procedure and start with 2543. Determine two lots of size 3.
11. Suppose that the two lots of the previous problem each represent three tosses of an unbiased coin. Assign 0000–4999 to a head.
    a. How many of the tosses are heads?
    b. Why does the number of heads not equal 3?
12. If the coin tossing was simulated 200,000 times, would the number of heads equal 100,000?
13. Refer to Exhibit 16–2.
    a. The random number 45 represents a daily demand of how many units?
    b. A lead time of how many days?

14. Define transitional analysis and operations gaming. Give an example of where each could be used.

15. What are the advantages of sensitivity analysis?

16. If sensitivity analysis were used in the inventory example, what parameters could be varied?

17. A new gas station has one hydraulic lift for lubricating cars. The profit for each car serviced is approximately $1.50. The owner wants to decide how many parking spaces to provide for cars waiting to be lubricated. The cost of land for each parking space will be about $0.70 per day. Assume that only one customer can be turned away at a time; i.e., two customers cannot arrive at the same time. The following table has been simulated for 25 days.

**Number of Times One Customer
Has Been Turned Away**

Day	5 Parking Spaces	6 Parking Spaces
1	3	2
2	4	4
3	2	2
4	1	1
5	3	2
6	4	2
7	0	0
8	1	1
9	3	2
10	2	2
11	4	3
12	2	1
13	0	0
14	2	1
15	1	1
16	4	3
17	3	2
18	1	0
19	2	1
20	3	1
21	2	1
22	2	0
23	3	1
24	4	2
25	3	2

a. Which number of parking spaces should be provided, 5 or 6?

b. Would sensitivity analysis be used in analyzing this problem?

18. A retail store distributes catalogues and takes orders by telephone. Distributions for intervals between incoming calls and the length of time required to complete each call are given below. The store management has determined that they want a probability of no more than 5 percent that a caller will have to wait no longer than 10 seconds for the telephone to be answered. Use simulation to determine how many sales representatives should be available to answer incoming calls.

Interval Between Incoming Calls	Probability	Length of Call	Probability
10 seconds	.08	60 seconds	.07
12	.11	65	.12
14	.14	70	.18
16	.16	75	.16
18	.14	80	.15
20	.12	85	.12
22	.08	90	.08
24	.07	95	.06
26	.04	100	.06
28	.04		
30	.02		

IV
STATISTICAL TOOLS

17
forecasting

A key aspect of most decision-making processes is being able to predict the circumstances that surround that decision. Forecasting is the title that has been given to the problem of trying to predict the circumstances that will surround a decision or situation some time in the future. Forecasts are made daily in all phases of business operations: marketing, production, personnel, financial and accounting, and top management decisions usually require forecasts of future conditions that will affect the decision. The amount of detail and frequency of need for forecasts varies tremendously among specific users, reflecting the diversity of specific decision needs. Some general uses are described here. The discussion obviously will cover only a small set of the possible uses of forecasting.

Marketing departments clearly need forecasts of demand to plan sales strategies. Such forecasts may be made on the basis of total market, market regions, yearly, by month, by consumer characteristics, etc.

Production scheduling requires detailed estimates of demand by specific lines of production (i.e., color, style, etc.) and usually by the week or month. Moreover, forecasts of trends in availability and prices of raw materials are needed.

Financial planners need projections of cash flows in order to maintain company liquidity efficiently and of interest rates and money market conditions to plan new capital acquisitions and financing.

Personnel departments need forecasts of labor turnover, labor supply, absenteeism, and trends in wages.

Top management requires forecasts of technological change, economic conditions, and future company growth in order to plan capital expenditures for new plant and equipment, and for planning the long-term general future course of the company.

FORECASTING VERSUS DECISION MAKING

Forecasting must be distinguished from decision making. In decision making, we weigh all the information available and then often exercise personal judgment as well when evaluating alternative actions in terms of potential costs and payoffs. Forecasting simply predicts the future; it is in itself not a decision. It is, or should be, however, an important component of the decision-making process; the forecasted estimates should be key inputs in a decision model. In sum, forecasting is a means and not an end unto itself. Only the government and academicians can enjoy the luxury of forecasting for forecasting's sake. For the rest of the world, forecasts must ultimately be linked to the decision maker's needs. This means that forecasting must be initiated by decision makers' needs, must meet these needs, and consequently must be evaluated in the light of its ability to meet these needs.

Hence, the best forecasting technique is not necessarily the most sophisticated or accurate, but rather the one that meets the needs at a minimum cost and inconvenience. Since decision needs vary considerably in scope and importance, it should be evident that there is no magical single best forecasting technique. Not surprisingly, therefore, there are today numerous well-developed forecasting techniques, some better than others in given situations, and vice versa for other situations.

BASIC ELEMENTS OF FORECASTS

Although there is a wide diversity of types of forecasts and methodologies, all forecasts have in common three basic elements. First, they all deal with situations in the future, so time is directly and importantly involved. Every forecast must be made for a specific point in time. The point in time for which the forecast is made is called the *time frame* of the forecast. Generally, changing the time frame affects the whole forecasting process.

Second, all forecasts deal with a certain level of uncertainty. That is, we are never certain as to what the situation will actually be in the future. If we were, the forecasting problem would be trivial. Because of the uncertainty, it is necessary to make assumptions or judgments about relevant conditions in the future which underly the forecast; as a result, some error in forecasting must be expected.

Third, all forecasts must, to some extent, rely on information that is contained in historical data. As Patrick Henry stated, "I know of no way of judging the future but by the past." It is important to differentiate the term *data* from *information*. *Data* refer to any numbers or facts that may be available. *Information* refers to that portion of the data that is relevant to what will happen in the future. Thus, we can have tremendous amounts of data and little information and, conversely, relatively little data but a great amount of information. One of the most important and difficult tasks in forecasting is separating the information from the data.

All quantitative forecasting methods, as mentioned above, rely on the use of historical data. The basic assumption inherent in the use of these data is that some pattern or relationship exists that can be identified and extrapolated to prepare predictions. Therefore, the crux of any forecasting methodology is to find the technique that is appropriate for the time pattern of the data.

There are basically four common types of patterns. One is a *horizontal* or *random pattern*; that is, there is no real trend to the data. The data simply fluctuate randomly about a mean value. Horizontal patterns usually are important only when one is considering very short time frames. Some examples are short-run sales totals for a product or the percentage of defective items produced by a process over a short time span. In analyzing horizontal patterns, the prime task is separating out the random fluctuations in the historical data in order to determine the true effect.

The second pattern is *seasonal*. This represents fluctuations in the data that occur during some fixed time period of one year or less according to some seasonal factor; the pattern repeats itself over each consecutive time period. For example, department store sales vary by month; a firm's output may vary by day due to weekly production schedules; cash receipts may vary by week within a month due to billing cycles.

The third pattern, *cyclical*, is similar to the seasonal pattern, except that the time period exceeds one year. This corresponds to the general business cycle theory and could reflect cyclical patterns induced by the economy.

The final pattern is that of *trend*, which is the situation where the data follow a generally increasing or decreasing pattern over time. Trend is generally very significant when one is considering intermediate or long-term forecasts, although in some cases, where the trend is quite steep, it is also important in short-term forecasts. Most data, such as sales, GNP, stock prices, and so forth, exhibit a trend.

The four patterns outlined above need not necessarily occur alone. In many situations they can be found operating together. In classical forecasting, data are assumed to consist of a trend, a seasonal, a cyclical, and a random component. The methodology then focuses on decomposition of the data into each component, estimating each pattern separately and combining the projected impact of each component in the future to produce the final forecast.

It should be pointed out that analyzing historical data to determine the underlying pattern or patterns can yield quite useful management information aside from its use in forecasting. Such analysis allows the manager better to understand what has happened and hence to evaluate current management policies. For instance, the determination of whether a drop in sales is due to seasonal variation, cyclical variation, random fluctuation, or a trend of declining sales (or how much can be attributed to each) can be vitally important to management in evaluating its current policies and indicating needed action.

TYPES OF MODELS

As discussed previously, there are many different forecasting techniques. Nevertheless, techniques can be classified into two basic types. The first and most common is a *time series model*. In a time series model, the variable to be predicted is analyzed historically over time and the pattern or patterns are modeled and estimated. A time series model assumes that the time-sequenced pattern that has occurred in the past will continue into the future. The model thus can be identified solely from the historical pattern of the variable to be predicted. Consequently, any time series model will give the same forecast, no matter what management decisions are currently made. Thus, such models, while useful for forecasting when the status quo is prevalent, are not particularly useful for predicting what changes will occur from a change in such management policies as a price reduction or a new advertising campaign.

The second type of forecasting techniques uses what is called the *causal model*. In these techniques, other variables related to the entity to be predicted are delineated, and their predictive relationship to it is modeled and used to forecast. For example, sales can be related to advertising expenditures, sales efforts (number of man-hours of salesmen expended), price of the item, competitors' prices, and so forth. Sales would then be considered a function of these independent variables and the functional relationship would be estimated. Thus, using expected future values of the independent variables, one can predict the dependent variable. The advantage of such models is that they allow incorporation of changes in management policies or shifts in the environment. The disadvantages are that they are more difficult to develop, that they require much more historical data (i.e., data on various variables and not simply on the item to be predicted), and that the ability to predict requires knowledge or ability to predict accurately the future values of the independent variables. Such models generally are more useful in evaluating the impact of management policy than in simply predicting, especially for an intermediate or long-range prediction.

Exhibit 17–1 lists some of the most common quantitative forecasting methodologies and the types of patterns of data for which they can be used. In this chapter we shall discuss, for illustrative purposes, two of the simplest time series techniques–simple moving averages and simple exponential smoothing.[1] Both are called smoothing techniques.

For a complete discussion of the various forecasting methodologies the interested reader is referred to one of the many texts dealing exclusively with forecasting.[2]

---

[1] Two causal models, input-output, which has gained popularity recently, and regression, the most commonly used causal model, are discussed in some depth in Chapter 18.

[2] For example, Steven Wheelwright and Spyios Makridakis, *Forecasting Methods for Management* (New York: Wiley, 1973).

Exhibit 17–1   Quantitative Forecasting Techniques

Methods	Useful for Pattern			
	Horizontal	Trend	Seasonal	Cyclical
Time series				
Simple moving average	X			
Linear moving average		X		
Spencer's moving average	X	X		
Henderson's moving average	X	X		
Simple exponential smoothing	X			
Linear exponential smoothing		X		
Winter's exponential smoothing		X	X	
Classical decomposition		X	X	
Census II	X	X	X	X
Foran	X	X	X	X
Adaptive filtering	X	X	X	X
Box-jenkins	X	X	X	X
Life cycle curves		X		
Causal				
Simple regression		X		
Multiple regression		X		
Econometric models	X	X	X	X
Input-output models	X	X	X	X

SMOOTHING TECHNIQUES

Simple smoothing techniques are usually applied to data that follow a horizontal pattern. Hence, smoothing is used primarily for very short-term forecasts where the data indicate a fairly stable pattern over short-term horizons. Some common uses are for predicting monthly demand or weekly stock prices. Such techniques are easily and cheaply applied and are useful if there is no sharp trend to the data or significant short-term fluctuations due to seasonal or cyclical effects. The aim of these techniques is to remove from the observed data the random fluctuations and thus to uncover the basically stable underlying pattern. Once the smoothed historical data is found, the prediction is simply the last smoothed value.

Let us consider the data in Exhibit 17–2. If we assume that the true underlying data are stable, we can write each observation as $X_t = \bar{X} + e_t$, where X_t is the observed value in time period t, $\bar{X}$ is the true stable underlying value, and e_t is the purely random fluctuation. If we knew $\bar{X}$, that would be the best estimate of X_{t+1}. Since the e_t terms are random fluctuations, it is reasonable to assume that if the e values are averaged over time, they should average out to zero. To do this, of course, we actually average the observed values.

Exhibit 17–2   Moving Average Forecasts

Time Period	Observed Sales	Forecast	
		3-Period Moving Average	5-Period Moving Average
1	1500		
2	1725		
3	1510		
4	1720	1578	
5	1330	1652	
6	1535	1520	1557
7	1740	1528	1564
8	1810	1535	1567
9	1760	1695	1627
10	1930	1770	1635
11	2000	1834	1755
12	1850	1897	1848

Hence, we have the forecasting method:

$$\hat{X}_{t+1} = \sum_{i=0}^{N-1} \frac{X_{t-i}}{N} \qquad (17\text{--}1)$$

where the hat ($\hat{X}$) notation denotes the predicted value. Such an estimation procedure is called a *simple moving average*. The term "moving average" is used because as each new observation becomes available a new average is computed to estimate the next period. The choice of how many prior periods to include in the averaging process (N) must be made judgmentally. Any N (for which enough historical data exist) can be chosen. The larger the N, the more stable the forecast and, consequently, the less sensitive the prediction is to changes in the underlying values. The smaller the N, conversely, the more sensitive the forecast is to random movements and the more likely it is to be "deceived" by a large random occurrence into a too-high or too-low forecast. Generally, the choice of N is made on the basis of experimentation to see what N value seems to work best. Exhibit 17–2 contains the forecast values one would get using a three-period and a five-period moving average.

SIMPLE EXPONENTIAL SMOOTHING

In principle, *exponential smoothing* is analogous to a moving average in that it attempts to smooth out the randomness from the historical data. The procedure, however, is different. In exponential smoothing the observations are weighted, with more weight being given to the more recent observations. The weights used are α for the most recent observation, $\alpha(1 - \alpha)$ for the next most recent, $\alpha(1 - \alpha)^2$ for the next, and so forth. This weighting system can be written compactly as

$$\hat{X}_{t+1} = \alpha X_t + (1 - \alpha)\hat{X}_t \qquad (17\text{--}2)$$

The weight α is a number between 0 and 1. In order better to interpret α, Eq. (17–2) can be rewritten as

$$\hat{X}_{t+1} = \hat{X}_t + \alpha(X_t - \hat{X}_t)$$

Thus, we see that exponential smoothing is simply the old forecast plus α times the error in the old forecast. When α is set close to 0, the new forecast will be substantially similar to the old. This is analogous to choosing a large N for the moving average method. Conversely, if α is set close to one, the forecasts will make marked shifts reflecting any errors that occurred in the previous forecasts. This is analogous to choosing a small N for a moving average.

The choice of α generally is made on the basis of experimentation with various α values. Exhibit 17–3 presents forecasts using exponential smoothing with $\alpha = 0.1$ and $\alpha = 0.9$ for the data in Exhibit 17–2. It should be recognized that, to forecast using exponential smoothing, we need to know only the most recent observation and the most recent forecast. Because of the reduced data requirements compared to using the moving average method, most forecasters prefer exponential smoothing to moving averages.

Exhibit 17–3   Exponential Smoothing

Time Period	Observed Sales	Forecast	
		$\alpha = 0.1$	$\alpha = 0.9$
1	1500		
2	1725	1500	1500
3	1510	1523	1703
4	1720	1522	1529
5	1330	1542	1701
6	1535	1521	1367
7	1740	1522	1518
8	1810	1544	1718
9	1760	1571	1801
10	1930	1590	1764
11	2000	1624	1913
12	1850	1662	1991

ACCURACY OF FORECAST

As stated previously, to choose the constants α or N for exponential smoothing or moving averages, respectively, the most common technique is to try different values and see which works "best." Generally, to evaluate the predictive capabilities of any forecasting method, we need some way to gauge its accuracy. One approach may be simply to compute each error of forecast and sum over all the data. The problem with this, of course, is that if errors tend to be random, we shall find positive errors offsetting negative errors, and the sum will always be close to zero regardless of how close the forecasts really are. (However, examination of the pattern of errors over time can be most useful in seeing if some trend or cyclical pattern is being ignored.)

To avoid this problem, we can simply deal with the absolute value of the error terms. This measure is referred to as the absolute deviation, and the average of the absolute deviations of the forecasts is called *mean absolute deviation* (MAD). An alternative to this commonly used measure is the square of the error terms, which also eliminates the problem of differences in direction of the errors. This is referred to as the *squared error* (SE) and the average as the *mean squared error* (MSE). The major difference between the MSE and MAD measures is that the MSE, unlike the MAD, penalizes a forecast method relatively much more for extreme errors than it does for a small error (i.e., an error of 2 yields an SE of 4, while an error twice that of 4 yields an SE 4 times that, or 16). Thus, using MSE rather than MAD implies that we would rather have several small errors in forecasts than one large error.

It must be realized, however, that this type of evaluation is not sufficient in evaluating a forecasting technique or in comparing different techniques. Many other factors, such as costs, level of effort involved in preparing forecasts, data requirements, and so forth, must be considered. Moreover, in evaluating any error measurement some basic standard of comparison is needed to place the errors in perspective. A common practice is to consider various so-called "naive" models. A *naive model* is an extremely simple model that can be implemented cheaply and easily without formal statistical analysis and without the aid of a computer. For example, a naive model might be to forecast that the next value will equal the last observed value (i.e., $\hat{X}_{t+1} = X_t$).[3] This would be an appropriate naive model for a horizontal pattern of data. For data that show a trend, a naive model might be $\hat{X}_{t+1} = X_t + (X_t - X_{t-1})$; that is, the last observation is increased (or decreased) by the amount of the change from its previous observation to obtain a forecast of the next observation.[4] Normally an analysis of the problem and inspection of the data will suggest an appropriate naive model. Then the ease of applying the naive model can be compared against the greater reliability of a more sophisticated and complex model.

Exhibit 17–4 uses the data from Exhibit 17–3 to compare the exponential smoothing forecasts with $\alpha = 0.1$ and $\alpha = 0.9$ with the naive model $X_{t+1} = X_t$.

Examination of Exhibit 17–4 indicates that when one is using exponential smoothing on this set of data, an α of 0.9 works better than an α of 0.1. However, the increase in forecast accuracy of exponential smoothing compared to the naive model seems hardly to justify the use of exponential

---

[3] This naive model is a special case of exponential smoothing where $\alpha = 0$ and a special case of a moving average forecast where $N = 1$.

[4] This naive model is a special case of exponential smoothing where $\alpha = 1$.

smoothing. The failure of exponential smoothing, of course, does not mean that there is not a better alternative to a naive model for this set of data.

Finally, simple smoothing techniques presented herein are successful only for horizontal data patterns. When the data exhibit other patterns such as trend or cyclical or seasonal variations, other methods must be considered. Many alternative methods exist that will handle a variety of different patterns of data including very complex patterns.

Exhibit 17–4 Measurement of Error in Forecasts

Time Period	Actual	Predicted			Error		
		A	B	C	A	B	C
1	1500	—	—	—	—	—	—
2	1725	1500	1500	1500	225	225	225
3	1510	1523	1703	1725	− 13	−193	−215
4	1720	1522	1529	1510	198	191	+210
5	1330	1542	1701	1720	−188	−371	−390
6	1535	1521	1367	1330	14	168	+205
7	1740	1522	1518	1535	218	222	+205
8	1810	1544	1718	1740	366	92	+ 70
9	1760	1571	1801	1810	189	− 41	− 50
10	1930	1590	1764	1760	340	166	+170
11	2000	1624	1913	1930	376	87	+ 70
12	1850	1662	1991	2000	188	−141	−150
				SUM	1943	405	350

Time Period	Actual	Absolute Error			Squared Error		
		A	B	C	A	B	C
1	1500	—	—	—	—	—	—
2	1725	225	225	225	50,625	50,625	50,625
3	1510	13	193	215	169	37,249	46,225
4	1710	198	191	210	39,204	36,481	44,100
5	1330	188	371	390	35,344	137,641	152,100
6	1535	14	168	205	196	28,224	42,025
7	1740	218	222	205	47,524	49,284	42,025
8	1810	366	92	70	133,956	8,464	4,900
9	1760	189	41	50	35,721	1,681	2,500
10	1930	340	166	170	1,156	27,556	28,900
11	2000	376	87	70	141,376	7,569	4,900
12	1850	188	141	150	35,344	19,881	22,500
	SUM	2345	1901	1960	635,059	377,099	440,800
	MAD	213	173	178			
	MSE				57,733	34,282	40,073

A = Exponential smoothing $\alpha = 0.1$
B = Exponential smoothing $\alpha = 0.9$
C = Naive $\hat{X}_{t+1} = X_t$

So far we have dealt with the idea of finding the pattern present in the historical data. We have not considered the problem of what to do when no data are available or when the historical data are irrelevant because of technological change. For example, suppose that an urban planner wants to forecast the date when at least 75 percent of the people working in the central part of the city will commute to work using mass transportation. Does he have a third alternative to (a) making a stab in the dark or (b) throwing up his hands in despair? A technique was developed by the Rand Corporation around 1950 that is intended to allow qualitative forecasts, or forecasts on questions for which hard data do not currently exist or are irrelevant, to be made.

This technique of long-range forecasting, called Delphi,[5] is based on the premise that a group of experts can arrive at a consensus forecast of what some company, industry, etc., will be like at some point in the future. Although it is still too early to assess the reliability of this technique, the concept is interesting.

How would our urban planner use the Delphi technique to obtain forecasts on the use of mass transportation? The first step is to select a panel of experts—perhaps 30 or so—and ask each to make an anonymous forecast. Each panelist then receives composite feedback on the forecasts of the other members of the panel. He digests this information, and a second round of forecasting begins. (The importance of anonymity is now apparent—it allows the expert to weigh group opinion, alter his forecast if appropriate, and leave his ego intact.) This same process repeats itself two or three or more times, until finally the continued feedback begins to give some focus to the forecasts.

A series of experiments by the Rand Corporation has shown that the feedback techniques dramatically refine—and improve—the forecasts in successive rounds. Needless to say, the quality of the forecasts will be a function of the quality of the panel of experts. But a good panel, presented with innovative and well-structured questions, could make the time and expense of conducting a Delphi well worthwhile.[6]

Most of the early uses of Delphi's dealt with forecasting scientific, technological, and sociological accomplishments. Questions dealt with desalination of salt water and ocean farming, using drugs to control hereditary defects and to raise intelligence, controlled thermonuclear power, commercial production of synthetic protein for food, etc. More recently, Delphi has been put to a wide variety of business uses. For example, the following areas have been studied: the future of commercial air transportation; upcoming developments in the construction industry; the creation of development alternatives for state and even national economies; mapping the

---

[5] The name is derived from the Oracle at Delphi in ancient Greece.

[6] The process can be time-consuming, since each round is usually conducted by mail. Delivery time, plus the time for processing the results of each round and each panelist's natural tendencies to procrastinate, can add up to a substantial period of time.

development of employee fringe benefits; the use of plastics to replace paper-based packaging materials. Useful forecasts on these and related topics, where conventional quantitative forecasting methods could not be used, would have great utility to the businessman in the preparation of his long-range plans.

PROBLEMS

1. Why would forecasts be useful to government administrators when they are formulating future economic policies?

2. What is the difference between forecasting and decision making? How are the two concepts related?

3. Why must all forecasts contain an element of uncertainty? Why must forecasts rely at least partly on historical data?

4. What is meant by the statement that forecasting is a means and not an end unto itself?

5. Explain what is meant by horizontal, seasonal, cyclical, and trend patterns of data. Why is the identification of data patterns important in forecasting? Is pattern identification useful for other than forecasting purposes?

6. How does a time series forecasting model differ from a causal model? Which type of model has the greater simplicity? Which allows for greater flexibility? Explain your answers.

7. How is the accuracy of a forecasting technique determined? Is the most accurate technique always the best one to use?

8. Calculate a three-month moving average for the time series data given below; a five-month moving average.

Period	Value		Period	Value
1	10		1	27
2	12		2	30
3	13		3	32
4	14		4	31
5	13		5	28
6	14		6	27
7	17		7	30
8	17		8	33
9	16		9	33
10	19		10	31
11	20		11	32
12	23		12	34
13	22		13	32
14	25		14	30
15	26		15	31

9. Use exponential smoothing to compute forecasts for the data given in Problem 8 if $\alpha = 0.3$; if $\alpha = 0.7$.

10. Use the naive forecasting methods discussed in the text and compare the results with the forecasts obtained above, using a five-month moving average and exponential smoothing with $\alpha = 0.3$.

11. The daily volume of sales for a corner newsstand are given below for a recent ten-day period. Discuss various techniques—and their limitations—that could be used to forecast sales on the eleventh day. Also discuss how you would assess the reliability of your forecasts using these various techniques.

Day	1	2	3	4	5	6	7	8	9	10
Sales	67	65	72	69	70	65	67	62	68	75

12. Assume that you are working for a major dairy products company. Your company is considering a major capital investment in equipment to manufacture its own nonreturnable milk containers, but is concerned about when new biodegradable materials will be available for milk containers and whether the proposed equipment will be able to be reasonably converted to handle the new materials. Your assignment is to investigate the current and expected future state of the related technology and report back to management regarding the two questions above. Outline the procedure you would follow in conducting your investigation.

18

multivariate models regression and input-output analyses

SIMPLE LINEAR REGRESSION MODEL

Two alternative analysis and forecasting techniques will be presented in this chapter. The first, regression analysis, has been widely known and used for a long time. The second, input-output analysis, has been developed more recently and is not nearly as well known as regression analysis. Regression can be used in a wide variety of areas, whereas input-output analysis has been used essentially as an aid to economic planning and forecasting. Given the growing emphasis on economic planning and the apparent shortcomings of traditional economic forecasting techniques in recent years, it can be expected that input-output analysis will receive more attention in the future. Many managerial decisions require predictions or forecasts of future events. These predictions frequently are based on historically observed relationships between two variables. For example, a marketing manager may budget his advertising expenditures on the basis of the expected effect on total sales revenue of a change in the level of advertising expenditures. A personnel manager may screen job applicants on the basis of their aptitudes as measured by a test score. A banker could predict deposits on the basis of per capita income in the trading area of his bank. Similarly, a hospital administrator could project his need for beds on the basis of total population. The owner of a beach could predict the number of customers he would have on a given day, and, in turn, make staff assignments and establish inventory levels for refreshment stands, on the basis of temperature. Obviously, the variable upon which the prediction is to be based should be under the control of the manager, or it should be known or be able to be forecast with reasonable accuracy.

These predictions could be made by using regression analysis. This technique is widely used to determine the statistical relationship between two (or more) variables and to make predictions of one variable on the basis of the other(s). When regression analysis is used for making predictions, it is assumed that there is an actual relationship between the dependent and independent variables. For example, if advertising expenditures are increased in order to increase sales, a relationship between advertising expenditures and sales volume is obviously implied. Furthermore, we are also indicating the direction of the relationship; i.e., we are saying that advertising has an affect on sales, but we are not saying that sales has an affect on advertising. Stated somewhat more formally, sales volume is a function of the level of advertising expenditures. (It should be stressed, however, that an observed statistical relationship, regardless of how strong it is, does not in itself imply a causal relationship.)

In this section, we shall explain the basic concepts underlying regression, examine some of the important assumptions and limitations, and illustrate the use of this technique through several examples.

Initially, we shall limit our discussion to a consideration of simple regression analysis, where a single variable is used to predict another variable. The variable to be predicted is called the dependent variable. The variables on which the prediction is based are called the independent variables.

A simple regression model is in the form of $y_i = \alpha + \beta x_i + \varepsilon_i$, where y_i is the dependent variable and x_i is the associated independent variable. The ε_i term represents a random element that is unpredictable in the model. It is called a residual, disturbance, or error term. The model assumes that $E(\varepsilon_i) = 0$, $E(x_i \cdot \varepsilon_i) = 0$, and $E(\varepsilon_i/\varepsilon_j) = 0$, $i \neq j$. These assumptions mean in effect that ε_i is unpredictable. The first, $E(\varepsilon_i) = 0$, simply says that the random disturbance to the system averages out, or has an expected value of zero for any single observation.[1]

The second assumption means that the random disturbances are independent of the value of x_i. That is, the size of the disturbances are not related to the magnitude of the x's. If this were not true, then knowledge of x_i could be used to predict ε_i which, in turn, would help us predict y_i. Similarly, the last assumption states that the disturbances are independent of one another.[2] If this assumption is violated, we could use the value of one disturbance to predict the value of another. Since the ε_i terms are assumed to be unpredictable, we use $\alpha + \beta x_i$ to predict y_i.

The α represents the *intercept* and β represents the *slope* of the regression line. The intercept specifies the value of the dependent variable when the independent variable has a value of zero, although this term has practical meaning only if a zero value for the independent variable is possible. The

---

[1] Practically speaking, it is a necessary but meaningless assumption. Since $E(\varepsilon_i) \neq 0$, the average effect would simply be absorbed by the α term and estimated as part of α.

[2] When this assumption is untrue, i.e., $E(\varepsilon_i/\varepsilon_j) \neq 0$, we say we have a problem of auto-correlation.

315

Multivariate
Models:
Regression and
Input-Output
Analyses

slope, β, indicates the expected or predicted amount of change in the value of the dependent variable for a unit change in the independent variable. For example, if $\beta = 2$, we would predict that y would increase by 4 if x increases by 2; if $\beta = -\frac{7}{2}$ we would predict that y would decrease by 7 if x increases by 2 and that y would increase by 14 if x decreases by 4. In the first example, where $\beta = 2$, the slope is positive and y varies directly with x; when $\beta = -\frac{7}{2}$, the slope is negative and y varies inversely with x. Given an equation of the form $y_i = -2 + 3x_i + \varepsilon_i$, some values of x and the related (predicted) y values are given below.

x	−3	−2	−1	0	1	2	3
predicted y	−11	−8	−5	−2	1	4	7

Clearly, given that the model is correct and α and β are known, the accuracy of our prediction of y, denoted $\hat{y}$, depends on the magnitude of the values of ε_i. If the ε_i's (the unpredictable element) in the model tend to have very large positive and negative values, our estimates will not be very good. Conversely, if the ε_i's are relatively small, our predictions will tend to be very close to the true y_i values.

In addition to the basic objective of prediction, estimation of the relationship between the variables is of interest in its own right. Knowledge of α and, in particular, β can be useful for management decision-making purposes. For example, suppose that we are interested in evaluating the value of radio advertising for a certain product. We can estimate the parameters of the regression equation of sales as a function of advertising (as perhaps measured in minutes of time) and estimate β to have a value of $500. Thus the estimated expected increase in sales per minute of radio advertising is $500, and the estimated net return from radio advertising is positive if it costs less than $500 and negative if it costs more than $500.

Estimation of Model

Let us consider the problem of using aptitude test scores to predict actual job performance to illustrate the use of the simple linear regression model. Suppose that a sales manager, faced with the problem of hiring one new salesman from several applicants, wants to predict the total sales each would achieve during his first year on the job on the basis of a sales aptitude test score. He can obtain data on the relationship between test scores and first-year sales from the records of salesmen hired in the past. These data are presented in the scatter diagram shown in Illustration 18–1. Test scores are shown on the horizontal axis, and first-year sales are shown on the vertical axis. Each dot in the scatter diagram reflects the test score and first-year sales of an individual salesman. For example, the salesman corresponding to point A had a test score of 73 and generated sales of $450,000 during his first year on the job.

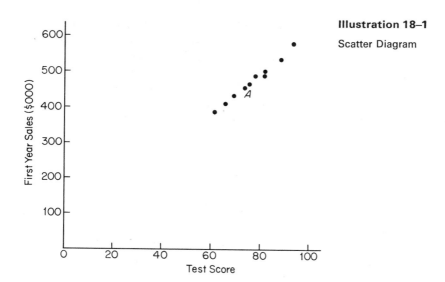

Illustration 18–1

Scatter Diagram

The scatter diagram indicates that there is a positive relationship that appears linear in form (i.e., the data form approximately a straight line) between aptitude as measured by a test score and actual performance for our simple data. The scatter diagram by itself, however, is not sufficient for predicting actual sales. Some formal expression of the relationship between a test score x and actual sales y is necessary for predictive purposes.

We might assume that the simple regression model of $y_i + \alpha = \beta x_i + \varepsilon_i$ is appropriate for describing the statistical relationship between y_i and x_i. Ideally we would like to know α and β, which would give the true statistical relationship between x and y. Unfortunately, α and β are population values that generally are unknown and therefore must be estimated from sample information. The estimates of α and β are denoted by a and b respectively. The estimate of y based on estimated values of α and β is denoted as $\hat{y}$. Thus $\hat{y} = a + bx_i$. It would be possible to simply take a ruler and draw a straight line through the points in the scatter diagram. The intercept and the slope of this straight line could be determined, and the resulting relationship could be expressed in the form $\hat{y} = a + bx$, where a and b are the estimates of α and β respectively. Once a and b are determined, this equation could be used to predict y, given a value of x.[3] There are several shortcomings to this approach, however. If ten different people each drew a line through the same scatter diagram, it is likely that ten different estimates of a and b would result (particularly if the points in the diagram were more dispersed). Furthermore, even if they all agreed on their estimates of a and b, they would have no way of knowing how much confidence to have in the resulting

---

[3] Notice that, as with sales and advertising, the analysis implies that predicted first year sales are a function of the aptitude test score, or $y = f(x)$.

317

Multivariate
Models:
Regression and
Input-Output
Analyses

predictions. Thus it would be desirable to have a systematic statistical procedure for estimating the intercept and slope of the predictive equation that would overcome these shortcomings.

Least Squares Method

The method that we shall use to fit a line through the scatter diagram is called the method of least squares. This method minimizes the sum of the squared vertical deviations from the fitted line; i.e., no other line, no matter how it is computed, will have a smaller sum of squared deviations. Notice in Illustration 18–2 that the vertical deviations measure the distances between actual and predicted values of the dependent variable.

The choice of minimizing the sum of the squared deviations needs some explanation. If we denote the deviation from the actual value, y_i, to the predicted value, $\hat{y}_i$, as e_i, it is logical that we would want the sum of the e's to be as small as possible. However, simply examining $\sum_{i=1}^{n} e_i$ is inappropriate, since any e_i can be positive or negative and large positive values, and large negative values could cancel one another out. Nevertheless, large values of e_i, regardless of sign, indicate a poor prediction. Hence it might seem reasonable to take the absolute value of e_i and minimize that sum, i.e., minimize $\sum_{i=1}^{n} |e_i|$. But the use of absolute values creates difficulties in the calculations of minimization, so the standard procedure is to eliminate the

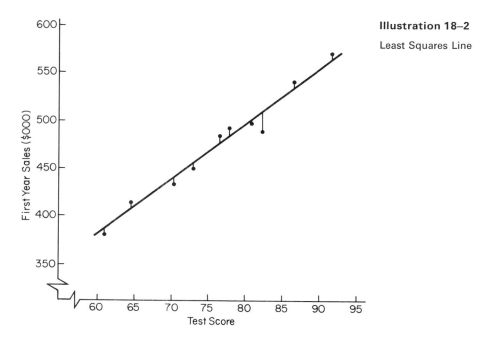

Illustration 18–2

Least Squares Line

effect of signs by squaring each observation. The choice of minimizing the squared sum of errors rather than the sum of the absolute values implies that we would rather make many small errors rather than a few large errors. By using the squared sum, we place a disproportionately large penalty for large errors compared to small errors. For example, Exhibit 18–1 gives two possible sets of errors. The first set has a larger average absolute error but smaller average squared error than the second.

Exhibit 18–1   Comparison of Minimizing Squared Error versus Absolute Error

	Data A			Data B		
	e	$|e|$	e^2	e	$|e|$	e^2
	2	2	4	4	4	16
	−3	3	9	0	0	0
	−2	2	4	0	0	0
	3	3	9	−4	4	16
Total	0	10	26	0	8	32
Average	0	2.5	6.5	0	2	8

Thus we get the least squares method of estimation, which selects as estimators of α and β those values which minimize the $\sum e_i^2$ for our data.[4] Mathematically, we select the values of a and b which minimize $\sum_{i=1}^{n}$ $(y_i - a - bx_i)^2$. The values of a and b that minimize the sum of the squared errors for a given set of data are obtained from the simulations solution of Eqs. (18–1) and (18–2), where n is the number of observations. These equations are called normal equations.[5]

$$\sum y = na + b\sum x \qquad (18\text{–}1)$$

$$\sum xy = a\sum x + b\sum x^2 \qquad (18\text{–}2)$$

These two equations can be rewritten so that the values of a and b can be obtained directly from the following equations:

$$b = \frac{n \sum xy - \sum x \cdot \sum y}{n \sum x^2 - (\sum x)^2} \qquad (18\text{–}3)$$

$$a = \frac{\sum y}{n} - b \cdot \frac{\sum x}{n} \qquad (18\text{–}4)$$

[4] It can be shown that the least square estimates are unbiased and the most reliable of all unbiased estimators if we assume the previously mentioned conditions for e_i and that they are identically distributed.

[5] These equations are derived through the use of calculus.

Example One

To illustrate the use of these equations in obtaining a least squares line, let us return to the problem of using test scores to predict sales performance. The sales manager has ten pairs of observations of test scores and actual sales with which to estimate the values of a and b. The necessary summations are presented in Exhibit 18–2 (the y^2 column is not needed immediately, but it is calculated here for future reference).

Exhibit 18–2 Summations for Regression Equation

Observation	x_i	y_i ($000)	$x_i y_i$	x_i^2	y_i^2
1	73	450	32,850	5329	202,500
2	78	490	38,220	6084	240,100
3	92	570	52,440	8464	324 900
4	61	380	23,180	3721	144,400
5	87	540	46,980	7569	291,600
6	81	500	40,500	6561	250,000
7	77	480	36,960	5929	230,400
8	70	430	30,100	4900	184 900
9	65	410	26,650	4225	168,100
10	82	490	40,180	6724	240,100
Sums	766	4740	368,060	59,506	2,277 000

Using the summations in Eqs. (18–3) and (18–4) yields the following results:

$$b = \frac{10(368,060) - (766)(4740)}{10(59,506) - (766)^2}$$

$$b = \frac{3,680,600 - 3,630,840}{595,060 - 586,756} = \frac{49,760}{8304} = 5.99$$

$$a = \frac{4740}{10} - (5.99)(766/10) = 474.0 - 459.0 = 15.0$$

The resulting estimated relationship between test scores and predicted sales is $\hat{y} = 15.0 + (5.99)x$, where $\hat{y}$ denotes the predicted first year sales given the test score x. Thus if a job applicant scores 75 on the aptitude test, his predicted first-year sales would be $\hat{y} = 15.0 + (5.99)(75) = 15.0 + 449.2 = 462.2$ thousands of dollars.

Residuals Of course, it is unlikely that the actual value of y_i will equal exactly its predicted level. It is possible that the actual y_i could be either above or below the predicted amount. There are three possible reasons why $\hat{y}_i$ may differ from y_i: (1) The model could be invalid. (2) Even if the model is correct, our estimates of α and β may be in error. (3) Even if the model and the estimates of α and β are correct, the random disturbance terms ε_i will cause $\hat{y}_i$ to differ from y_i.

While predicted y_i values are expressed as $\hat{y}_i = a + bx_i$, actual y_i values can be expressed with the equation $y_i = a + bx_i + e_i$. The e term accounts for the difference between the actual and predicted values of the dependent variable, and it is called a sample residual, disturbance, or error term and is our best estimate of ε_i. Notice that if $\hat{y}_i = a + bx_i$, then $y_i = \hat{y} + e_i$ or $e_i = y_i - \hat{y}_i$; i.e., e is equal to the actual minus the predicted value. Exhibit 18–3 presents the regression results, the predicted value of the dependent variable and the error term for the original data shown in Exhibit 18–2.

Exhibit 18–3   Error Terms from Regression Equation

Observation	x_i	y_i ($000)	$\hat{y}_i$ ($000)	e_i ($000)
1	73	450	452.3	−2.3
2	78	490	582.2	7.8
3	92	570	566.1	3.9
4	61	380	380.4	−0.4
5	87	540	536.1	3.9
6	81	500	500.2	−0.2
7	77	480	476.2	3.8
8	70	430	434.3	−4.3
9	65	410	404.4	5.6
10	82	490	506.2	−16.2

A great deal of information is contained in the e_i values about the correctness of the model, the reliability of our estimates of α and β, and the ability of the model to predict y.

Plot of Residuals   A graphical analysis of the residuals is a convenient way to spot any bias that might be contained in the estimated regression equation due to misspecification of the model. The residuals can be plotted against the actual values of the dependent variable.[6]

The absence of bias would be indicated by the random dispersion of the points in the residual plot. Since the points in Illustration 18–3 are fairly well distributed, we do not have to be too concerned about a bias systematically affecting our results. Suppose, however, that positive residuals tended to be associated with the lower values of the dependent variable and negative residuals tended to be associated with the higher values of the dependent variable. That is, in general, $e = y - \hat{y} > 0$ at the lower end of the range of y values and $e = y - \hat{y} < 0$ at the upper end of the range. Since $\hat{y} = y - e$, it follows that our equation would be underpredicting (or biased downward) for low values of y and overpredicting (or biased upward) for high value of y. When the residuals are not normally randomly distributed, it is an indication

[6] We might also graph the residuals against the independent variable to examine the assumption that x_i and e_i are independent.

Illustration 18–3

Plot of Residuals

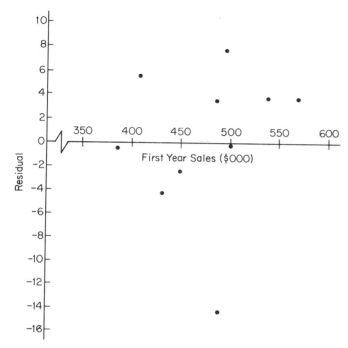

that ordinary regression analysis is not appropriate for analyzing the set of data.

Formal statistical procedures exist for analyzing residuals to test the appropriateness of the model for a given set of data, but these procedures are beyond the scope of this text.[7]

Standard Error of Estimate As noted previously, the key to how accurately a regression model can predict (assuming the model specified is appropriate) lies in the magnitudes of the ε_i terms. We can estimate the ε_i's by using the e_i's from our sample data. Hence examination of the e_i's will give us an estimate of the reliability of the regression model.

The e's are both positive and negative and the mathematics of estimating the regression assures that $\sum e = 0$. Hence the mean of the e's is useless as a measure of reliability, since it will always equal zero. We could use $\sum |e|/n$ but, as noted previously, absolute values complicate further mathematical analysis. Thus the dispersion of e, as measured by its variance, is the basic measure of reliability. The larger the variance, the more significant are the magnitudes of the e's and the less reliable is the regression analysis in predicting our sample data. To calculate the variance of e, we take the sum of the squared differences between the e's and their mean (which is 0)

[7] The interested reader is referred to any standard classical text on regression analysis, such as Draper and Smith, *Applied Regression Analysis* (New York: John Wiley and Sons, 1966).

and divide by $n - 2$.[8] Symbolically, $S_e^2 = \sum e^2/(n - 2)$. Computationally, the variance is best calculated by

$$S_e^2 = \frac{1}{n-2}\left(\sum y^2 - \frac{(\sum xy)^2}{\sum x^2}\right) \qquad (18\text{--}5)$$

The square root of this equation gives a quantity that is called the standard error of estimate, denoted S_e. Assuming the same variance for all the ε_i's, this expression estimates the standard deviation of the error terms ε_i and provides an estimate of the standard deviation of the observations around the regression line.

Coefficient of Determination, R^2 While the standard error gives us some indication of the reliability of our regression, in isolation it is not enough. Clearly the larger the S_e^2, the less reliably the model will predict. However, the question of "how reliable?" requires placing the magnitude of the errors in perspective. For example, an error of $10,000 is substantial if we are estimating the income of a professor, but is trivial if we are estimating the total annual sales of IBM. The measure that does this, which is the most commonly used measure of how well the regression line fits the sample data, is the *coefficient of determination*, denoted by R^2.[9]

With no information about the value of x, the best estimate of y is its mean, $\bar{y}$. Thus the dispersion about $\bar{y}$ represents the inaccuracy of $\bar{y}$ as an estimate of all y's. This dispersion is best represented for all the data by $\sum (y_i - \bar{y})^2$. If the x_i is known, the best estimate of y_i becomes the point on the regression line $\hat{y}_i = a + bx$. The difference in the estimate y_i and the $\bar{y}$ estimate can be attributed to knowledge about x and its relationship with y. Hence the dispersion of the regression estimates from the mean of y, $\sum (\hat{y}_i - \bar{y})^2$, is in a sense dispersion which can be explained by the relationship between x and y. Thus, for example, a predicted y value might be above $\bar{y}$ due to the fact that its corresponding x value is large. Conversely, the difference between an actual y_i value and the regression estimate $\hat{y}_i$ and the resultant dispersion $\sum (y_i - \hat{y}_i)^2$ cannot be explained by the relationship between x and y. Consequently it is useful to partition the total dispersion of y into two parts, one that can be attributed to the regression relationship and one that can not be explained by x's relationship with y. That is, $\sum (y_i - \bar{y})^2 = \sum (y_i - \hat{y}_i)^2 + \sum (\hat{y}_i - \bar{y})^2$. Dividing by the total dispersion and rearranging terms yields the coefficient of determination.

$$R^2 = \frac{\sum (\hat{y}_i - \bar{y})^2}{\sum (y_i - \bar{y})^2} = 1 - \frac{\sum (y_i - \hat{y}_i)^2}{\sum (y_i - \bar{y})^2} \qquad (18\text{--}6)$$

---

[8] We divide by $n - 2$ rather than n or $n - 1$ to get an unbiased estimate of σ_ε^2, the true variance of the error terms.

[9] In simple linear regression R^2 is the square of the correlation coefficient of x and y.

323

Multivariate
Models:
Regression and
Input-Output
Analyses

The coefficient of determination can assume values ranging from zero to one. A value of one can occur only if $\sum (y_i - \hat{y}_i)^2 = 0$ or, in other words, if every data point falls exactly on the regression line. For a zero value to occur, $\sum (y_i - \hat{y}_i)^2 = \sum (y_i - \bar{y})^2$, or $\hat{y}_i = a + bx = \bar{y}$. The only way for this to occur would be for $b = 0$ and $a = \bar{y}$, meaning that x tells us nothing about y and hence there is no regression relationship between x and y. Values between zero and one indicate the "goodness of fit" of the regression line to the sample data. The higher the value of R^2, the better the fit.

One way to interpret R^2 is as the percentage of the total variance of y in our sample data that can be statistically explained by the differences in the associated x values of the y's. Thus if R^2 is close to one, it indicates that the regression equation explains most of the variation in the dependent variable in our sample. For example, if $R^2 = 0.92$, 92 percent of the variance of the dependent variable is explained by the equation. In other words, only 8 percent of the variance of the dependent variable is unexplained by the equation.

Equation 18–6 can be used to calculate the R^2 value for our sales-test score problem. The preliminary computations are performed in Exhibit 18–4. Thus $R^2 = 1 - 423.4/30,240 = 1 - 0.014 = 0.986$. This result tells us that the regression has explained 98.6 percent of the variation in the performance of the ten salesmen. Or, less than 2 percent of the variation in the data on first year sales is statistically explained by factors other than the differing scores on the sales aptitude test.[10]

Exhibit 18–4 Calculation of Coefficient of Determination

Observation	$y_i - \hat{y}_i$	$(y_i - \hat{y}_i)^2$	$(y_i - \bar{y}_i)$	$(y_i - \bar{y})^2$
1	−2.3	5.3	−24	576
2	7.8	60.8	16	256
3	3.9	15.2	96	9216
4	−0.4	0.16	−94	8836
5	3.9	15.2	66	4356
6	−0.2	0.04	26	676
7	3.8	14.4	6	36
8	−4.3	18.5	−44	1936
9	5.6	31.4	−64	4096
10	−16.2	262.4	16	256
		423.4		30,240

Another Example

The data for another problem illustrating the use of regression analysis is presented below. The data are presented in Exhibit 18–5. The variable x

---

[10] The reader should not be misled by the high R^2 value found for this example. In practice, equations with R^2 values in the range of 0.60 to 0.80 could be very useful, particularly for cross-section samples, and in some cases even very small R^2 values can be useful.

Exhibit 18–5 Data for Regression Analysis

Attendance (x_i)	Gin Sales (y_i)	$x_i \cdot y_i$	x_i^2	y_i^2
31	30	930	961	900
24	47	1,128	576	2,999
27	41	1,107	729	1,681
25	42	1,050	625	1,764
29	34	986	841	1,156
30	32	960	900	1,024
22	48	1,056	484	2,304
28	38	1,064	784	1,444
29	35	1,015	841	1,225
26	40	1,040	676	1,600
271	387	10,336	7417	15,307

represents the average daily classroom attendance in the public school of a small rural community during ten selected days in May, and y represents the corresponding daily sales of gin at the local liquor store. The estimated regression line is found using Eqs. (18–3) and (18–4).

$$b = \frac{(10)(10,336) - (271)(387)}{(10)(7417) - (271)^2} = -2.08$$

$$a = \frac{387}{10} - (-2.08)\frac{271}{10} = 99.07$$

Hence

$$\hat{y}_i = 95,07 - 2.08x_i$$

Exhibit 18–6 presents the data and the calculation of R^2, which has a value of 0.956.

Exhibit 18–6 Calculation of R^2 for Gin/Attendance Problem

y_i	$\hat{y}_i$ (95.07 − 2.08x_i)	$y_i - \hat{y}_i$	$(y_i - \hat{y}_i)^2$	$(y_i - \bar{y})$	$(y_i - \bar{y})^2$
30	30.59	−0.59	0.35	−8.7	75.69
47	45.15	+1.85	3.42	8.3	68.89
41	38.91	+2.09	4.37	2.3	5.29
42	43.05	−1.05	1.10	3.3	10.89
34	34.75	−0.75	0.56	−4.7	22.09
32	32.67	−0.67	0.45	−6.7	44.89
48	49.31	−1.31	1.72	+9.3	86.59
38	36.83	+1.17	1.37	−0.7	0.49
35	34.75	+1.25	0.06	−3.7	13.69
40	40.99	−0.99	0.98	+1.3	1.69
387		0	14.38	0	330.10

$\bar{y} = 38.7$

$$R^2 = 1 - \frac{14.38}{330.10} = 0.956$$

What do these results tell us? The coefficient b is negative and R^2 is very high. The strong negative relationship tells us that, for our data, gin

325

Multivariate
Models:
Regression and
Input-Output
Analyses

sales go up when classroom attendance goes down. Does this mean that the community's public school students have a tendency to skip school and drink gin? Perhaps, but probably not. These results probably are attributable to a third unidentified factor that explains the apparent relationship between x and y.

Having grown up in a small town, one of the authors knows the joys of escaping into the countryside to engage in a little fishing during the first warm days of spring. Having reached adulthood, both authors known the joys of relaxing with a gin and tonic at the end of the first warm days of spring. Thus during the month of May, classroom attendance and gin sales could both be related to the weather. A warm spring day could drive classroom attendance down and gin sales up. Thus the weather is the third factor that would explain the strong negative statistical relationship between attendance and gin sales. This example illustrates the dangers in making inferences about cause and effect relationships based on the results of a regression analysis. However, for purely predictive purposes the regression using classroom attendance may be quite useful because of its relationship to weather.

Standard Error of b   We have seen how to measure how well the regression line fits the sample data. We must remember, however, that generally we are dealing with sample data and not with the complete population, so that we are estimating the regression model, and in particular the value of β. Thus it would be useful, especially if we use the value of b not only for prediction but also as a value upon which to measure the relationship between x and y for decision purposes, to have an indication of the reliability of the b estimate of β.[11]

This can be done by examining the standard error of the estimates. The larger the standard error, the less reliable is the estimate of β. An estimate of the standard error of the regression coefficient b can be calculated by the following equation

$$S_b = S_e \sqrt{\frac{1}{\sum x_i^2 - n\bar{x}^2}} \tag{18–7}$$

Using Eq. 18–5 to calculate S_e and Eq. 18–7 for S_b, the estimate of the standard error of b for the data in Exhibit 18–2 would be

$$S_e = \left[\frac{1}{10 - 2} \left(2{,}277{,}000 - \frac{(368{,}060)^2}{59{,}506} \right) \right]^{1/2}$$

$$S_e{}^{12} = [\tfrac{1}{8}(2{,}277{,}000 - 2{,}276{,}540)]^{1/2} = 7.53$$

$$S_b = 7.53 \sqrt{\frac{1}{59{,}506 - (10)(76.6)^2}} = 0.26$$

[11] It can be shown that b is an unbiased estimate of β if the model and the assumptions about ε_i are correct.

[12] This calculation varies slightly from that of $\sqrt{\sum e_i^2/(n-2)}$ (using the data in Exhibit 18–3) due to rounding errors.

Standard Error of Prediction Given an estimated simple linear regression model, the best estimate of y_i if x_i is known is $a + bx_i$. We know of course that usually $\hat{y}_i$ will differ from y_i, even assuming the model specified is correct, due to the fact that we are estimating α and β and the random error term ε_i. We have seen that we can get an estimate of the variability of ε_i and can estimate the variability of our estimate of the true regression coefficients. Thus, we can combine the two to arrive at an estimate of the standard error of prediction, i.e., the standard deviation of $\hat{y}_i$. Eq. 18–8 gives the method of calculating the estimate of the standard error of prediction.

$$S_{\hat{y}_i} = S_e \sqrt{1 + \frac{1}{n} + \frac{(x_i - \bar{x})^2}{\sum (x_i - \bar{x})^2}} \qquad (18\text{–}8)$$

Examination of Eq. 18–8 shows that the estimated standard error of prediction is different for each estimate of y based on a different x_i value. Note that the last term in the equation under the square root sign is

$$\frac{(x_i - \bar{x})^2}{\sum (x_i - \bar{x})^2}$$

and its value is dependent on the particular value of x_i. Obviously the estimated standard error is smallest when we are predicting y_i for $x_i = \bar{x}$ and increases the more a particular x_i observation varies from $\bar{x}$. This fact highlights the risk inherent in estimating y for a value of x which is not typical of the values from which the regression equation was estimated.

Exhibit 18–7 presents the standard error of prediction for each of the estimates for the aptitude test-first year sales example.

Exhibit 18–7 Estimate of Standard Error of Prediction for Aptitude Test/Sales Example $(S_e = 7.53; 1/n = 0.1)$

Observation*	x_i	$(x_i - \bar{x})$	$(x_i - \bar{x})^2$	$1 + \dfrac{1}{n} + \dfrac{(x_i - \bar{x})^2}{\sum (x_i - \bar{x})^2}$	$S_{\hat{y}_i}$
4	61	−15.6	243.36	1.18	8.89
9	65	−11.6	134.56	1.12	8.43
8	70	−6.6	43.56	1.07	8.06
1	73	−3.6	12.96	1.06	7.98
7	77	+0.4	0.16	1.04	7.83
2	78	+1.4	1.96	1.05	7.91
6	81	+4.4	19.36	1.06	7.98
10	82	+5.4	29.16	1.07	8.06
5	87	+10.4	108.16	1.11	8.36
3	92	+15.4	237.16	1.17	8.81
Sums	766		830.40		
	$(\bar{x} = 76.6)$				

* This refers to the original observation numbering of Exhibit 18–2. The observations have been re-ordered according to the magnitude of x_i to demonstrate the effect of $(x_i - \bar{x})$ on the estimated standard error.

327

Multivariate
Models:
Regression and
Input-Output
Analyses

Confidence Intervals While standard errors of prediction of the regression estimates and of the residual are useful measures of reliability, it must be remembered that they should be put in perspective.

The magnitude of the standard error must be interpreted in light of the magnitude of the variables we are dealing with. It would be useful to be able to relate the standard error of a variable to the estimate of the value of the variable in such a way as to be able to make statements about the range in which the true value lies. This can be done if we add the assumption that the ε_i's are normally distributed[13] with a statistical technique called confidence interval estimation.[14] A confidence interval gives a range which we estimate will include the true value with a given level of confidence in the correctness of the estimate. For example, we would estimate y_i, given a value of x_i, to be between 40.1 and 50.1 with 95 percent confidence; or that the true value of β is between 10 and 14 with confidence of 99 percent. The width of the intervals is derived through probability theory and basically depends on the magnitude of the appropriate standard error and the level of confidence desired, assuming the sample size is given. The larger the standard error, the larger the width, and vice versa. The higher the level of confidence desired in our interval estimate, the larger the width, and vice versa. Clearly, to the user, the larger the width for a given level of confidence, the more he should hedge his prediction of y_i or β.[15]

The Formula for Computing a 1 − α Level Confidence intervals for y_i and β are given in Eqs. (18–9) and (18–10) respectively.

$$\hat{y}_i \pm t_{n-2,\alpha} S_{y_i} \qquad (18\text{–}9)$$

and

$$b \pm t_{n-2,\alpha} S_{y_i} \qquad (18\text{–}10)$$

The term $t_{n-2,\alpha} S_{y_i}$ refers to the value of a t statistic with $n - 2$ degrees of freedom such that probability of exceeding it is $\alpha/2$.[16] This number can be obtained directly from a table of t statistics (see Exhibit F–11). To find the proper tabled t value we look down the column labeled Degrees of Freedom until we find the entry corresponding to $n - 2$. We then go across to the column headed by the α level we are using.

---

[13] Statistical procedures exist to test if this assumption is reasonable. Examining the plot of the residuals will also yield insight into the correctness of the assumption.

[14] For a discussion of the complete rationale of confidence intervals, the reader should refer to any standard statistical text.

[15] If we allow the sample size to vary, the larger the sample size the smaller the width will be of the confidence interval, all other things equal.

[16] Unfortunately, standard statistical nomenclature uses α to denote both the intercept of a regression equation and the level of significance of a confidence interval. The reader can usually tell from the context which of these two meanings is intended.

The choice of the α level must be made by the decision maker. Generally most people choose either a 90, 95, or 99 percent level of confidence or, equivalently, α values of 0.10, 0.05, or 0.01, respectively.

In examining the confidence interval for y_i, it should be evident that the band gets wider as we predict y_i for values of x_i further and further away from $\bar{x}$, since $S_{\hat{y}_i}$ increase. The shape of confidence bands for y_i values given different x_i values is shown in Illustration 18–4. The actual calculation of 95 percent confidence intervals for our aptitude test/sales data example is presented in Exhibit 18–8.

Exhibit 18–8 95 Percent Confidence Interval for y_i for Aptitude Test/Sales Example $(t_{8,0.05} = 2.306)$

Observation*	$\hat{y}_i$	$S\hat{y}_i$	Width of Interval	Upper Bound	Lower Bound
4	380.4	295.12	680.5	1060.9	−300.1
9	404.4	280.12	646.0	1050.4	−241.6
8	434.3	267.61	617.1	1051.4	−182.8
1	452.3	265.11	611.3	1063.6	−159.0
7	476.2	260.11	599.8	1072.4	−123.6
2	482.2	262.61	605.6	1087.8	−123.4
6	500.2	265.61	612.5	1112.7	−112.3
10	506.2	267.61	617.1	1123.3	−110.9
5	536.1	277.61	640.2	1176.3	−104.1
3	566.1	292.62	674.8	1240.9	−108.7

* This refers to the original observation numbering of Exhibit 18–2. The observations have been reordered to demonstrate the parabolic shape of the intervals as a function of $(x_i - \bar{x})$.

The confidence band for the true value of β is, of course, a single interval for a given confidence level. For example, a 95 percent confidence interval for β for the aptitude test/sales problem would be

$$5.99 \pm (2.306)(0.03) =$$

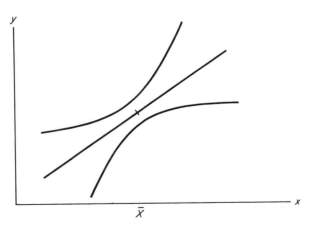

Illustration 18–4

Confidence Intervals for Y_i

329

Multivariate
Models:
Regression and
Input-Output
Analyses

or we could say with 95 percent confidence that the true β is between 6.06 and 5.92.

Test of Hypothesis of Over All Regression Of special interest is whether the value of β equal to zero is in the confidence interval. If it is, then in effect we are recognizing the possibility that the true β may be 0 and the reason our estimate b is not 0 may be due simply to chance variation in our estimation. Moreover, if $\beta = 0$, clearly there is no true statistical relationship between x and y and the regression model is useless. The question of deciding whether the sample regression line indicates a real relationship between x and y, or whether an apparent relationship occurred because of chance fluctuations in the data, can be addressed more directly by the calculation of a t statistic.[17] The t statistic is calculated as follows.

$$t = \frac{(n-2)r^2}{1-r^2} \tag{18-11}$$

The calculated t value is then compared with a value obtained from a table of t statistics (see Exhibit F-11). If the calculated t value exceeds the tabled t value, we can conclude that there is a real relationship between x and y, or that b has a value greater or less (depending on whether b is positive or negative) than zero. If it is less, we conclude that b may be equal to zero.

The value selected from the table depends on the risk that we are willing to take of concluding incorrectly that a relationship exists when it does not. Across the top of the t table is the probability of making such an error if the appropriate t value in that column is used to make the decision. This probability is called the level of significance. To find the properly tabled t value for comparison, we look down the column labeled Degrees of Freedom until we find the entry corresponding to $n-2$. We then go across to the column headed by the risk we are willing to take. The choice of the risk level must be made by the decision maker.

For example, in the previous illustration, $n = 10$ and $r^2 = 0.986$. Thus the calculated t value is

$$t = \frac{(10-2)(0.986)}{1-0.986} = 23.74$$

Assuming we are willing to assume a 0.01 probability of incorrectly deciding a real relationship exists, the tabled t value would be (8 d.f.; 0.01) 2.90. Since 23.74 is greater than 2.90, we would conclude that a relationship does exist between x and y, and thus that b is greater than zero.[18]

[17] For an explanation of the concept of statistical testing of hypothesis that is employed here, the interested reader is referred to any standard statistics text.

[18] It should be pointed out testing at a α level of significance is equivalent to constructing a $1-\alpha$ percent confidence interval for β and concluding there is no true relationship if the interval contains the value zero.

Common Mistakes

When regression is used for predictive purposes, two mistakes are frequently made that can lead to very bad predictions. The first is to use the regression equation to predict values outside the range for which it is valid. Consider the regression equation predicting earnings of MBA graduates five years after graduation, on the basis of their college grade-point average. Suppose our regression equation, based on data from previous graduates, is of the form $y = \$6,500 + 2500x$, where y is income and x is grade point average (assume a 4.0 represents straight A's and a 2.0 represents a C average). Suppose we try this equation to predict the income of a student who flunks out after failing all his courses the first term. His grade average would be 0 and the equation would lead to an estimate of $6,500 for his income. This estimate clearly would be low, even if the individual does not have a graduate degree. The poor estimate occurs because the model was constructed to predict the income of MBA *graduates*; thus the acceptable grade values (x) are between 2 and 4. Predictions based on grade averages outside this range would not be valid. Moreover, even in situations where we might assume that the relationship were to hold, the reliability of the estimate outside the range might be very poor because no corresponding observations were used to obtain the parameters of the regression equation.

The second common error is to not compensate for events that would alter the basic structure of the prediction model. When using a regression model, a basic underlying assumption is that the conditions that existed when the relationship between x and y was estimated by the regression are the same when the model is being used. For example, consider what would happen to our prediction of sales on the basis of aptitude test scores if the data for the model were gathered during a boom period for the company, and predictions are to be made in a period of recession. Most likely our estimates would be much too high. Similarly, using historical data to estimate the relationship between grade-point average and future income ignores the effects on salary levels of factors such as changing job-market conditions and inflation.

MULTIPLE REGRESSION ANALYSIS

Suppose a simple regression is run expressing sales as a function of advertising expenditures. Let us also suppose that the regression coefficient is significant and that the equation has an R^2 value of 0.63. This means that 37 percent of the variation in sales could be due to the influences of other variables besides advertising expenditures. For example, per capita income in the trading area could also have an influence on sales. Therefore, the results of the simple regression model, while useful, might be improved by adding per capita income as an explanatory variable. This extension of the simple regression technique (i.e., the use of two or more independent variables) is called multiple regression analysis.

331

Multivariate
Models:
Regression and
Input-Output
Analyses

The above example can be expressed in the multiple regression form

$$y = a + b_1 x_1 + b_2 x_2 \qquad (18\text{--}12)$$

where x_1 = advertising expenditures, x_2 = per capita income, and b_1 and b_2 are their respective regression coefficients. If appropriate, additional independent variables could be used in the regression equation. The technique for estimating the parameters of the regression equation are similar to those used for simple regressions. Rather than specifying an equation for a straight line, however, Eq. 18–12 specifies a plane. The statistical objective is still to obtain a set of parameters that minimizes the squared distances between the regression estimate and the individual observations.

Use of Multiple Regression

A multiple regression model is much more complicated to use than a simple regression model. Generally speaking, the assumptions about the statistical form of the data and the procedures used for assessing the reliability of the estimates are extensions of those associated with simple linear regression. There are more assumptions and more involved computational procedures, however, so that a thorough discussion of multiple regression would be lengthy and involved. Therefore we are going to present only a brief overview of the multiple regression technique and refer the interested reader to a text devoted to the topic of regression analysis.

Estimates of the intercept and regression coefficients are obtained from a set of normal equations, the same as for simple regression, although the normal equations become more complicated and laborious to solve as the number of independent variables increases. Since there are three unknowns to be solved for in Eq. 18–12, for example, three normal equations are required to solve for a, b_1, and b_2. The addition of another independent variable would require the addition of another normal equation, i.e., four equations would be required to solve for four unknowns.[19]

The interpretation of R^2 in a multiple regression model remains the same as in simple regression. The definition of the b's is very similar as well. Any particular b value, say b_1, gives the predicted change in y per unit change in x_1, *all other x's remaining constant.* In cases where the x values are under our control or are independent, this definition has clear meaning. When we simply observe the x's and they are interrelated, however, the b values must be interpreted much more carefully. In these situations, the constraint "all other x's remaining constant" might be infeasible or unrealistic. When this is the case, the overall regression and the b values must be viewed as a total system predicting y, and extreme caution must be taken in attempting to interpret any individual b value.

---

[19] In practice, these computations are seldom performed by hand. Several easy-to-use computer routines are available to do the required computations, although it is the responsibility of the user to correctly specify the model and interpret the results.

For example, ocassionally the b value for a particular x will not agree in sign with the simple correlation between that x and y. The reason is that the relationship between the x's themselves and y is taken into account so that the net effect of all the b's reflecting the joint movement of the x's predicts the y value. Individual b's viewed in isolation, however, can be misleading. In a multiple regression predicting hospital-bed usage, the coefficient of age was negative. This result, of course, contradicts the intuitive feeling that the probability of serious illness increases with age. The overall regression predicted very accurately, however, because the other b's in the equation took into consideration the relationship between age and the other independent variables. As a result, the net effect of increasing a person's age, after allowing for the corresponding increases in the other x values, led to an increase in the predicted value of y.

Nonlinear Relationships

The basic regression model is linear in form, although there are several nonlinear functions whose parameters can be estimated with multiple regression analysis. If a basic linear model is used, the data should fall along a straight line in a plot of y_i against x_i.[20] In practice, however, the relationship between x_i and y_i is often not linear. When these situations occur, it is frequently possible to transform the nonlinear relationships into linear functional expressions so that linear regression analysis can be conducted on the transformed values of x and y. In other cases, it may be possible to use the ordinary procedures on a nonlinear relationship.

Efforts directed toward choosing the best possible functional relationship should result in a regression equation that provides the best fit to the sample data; this specification of the form of the equation should also provide the most accurate predictions. It is good practice to plot the raw data before the form of the relationship to be used is decided. The pattern emerging from the points in the plot should indicate which functional form will best conform to the actual data. Four different nonlinear relationships are considered in this section.

Parabolic Relationship The parabola is a function that can be used to estimate many nonlinear relationships. The general form of a parabola can be expressed as

$$y = a + b_1 x_1 + b_2 x_1^2 \qquad (18\text{--}13)$$

The statistical procedures necessary to estimate the parameters of this equation are the same as those used for the more general multiple regression model discussed above. The major difference is that the coefficients b_1 and b_2 now relate to different forms of the same variable, although the X_1^2 term is treated as a second independent variable in the multiple regression equation.

---

[20] If all e_i values are exactly equal to zero, the data should fall exactly in a straight line.

333

Multivariate
Models:
Regression and
Input-Output
Analyses

This must be taken into consideration when the regression results are analyzed. The general form specified in Eq. (18–13) can be expanded to allow for multidimensional nonlinear relationships or to combine linear and nonlinear relationships. For example, the following equations could be used:

$$y = a + b_1x_1 + b_2x_1^2 + b_3x_1^3$$
$$y = a + b_1x_1 + b_2x_1^2 + b_3x_2 + b_4x_4$$

There is no limit to the number of terms that might be added, although in practice the number of sample observations imposes a very real constraint. An equation using eight variables could be used to obtain a very good fit to a sample of ten observations, but the equation might be useless for predicting the eleventh observation.[21]

Square Root Relationship Many economic relationships involve the concept of diminishing returns. Although there are other alternatives, one way to express this type of relationship is to use the square root of one of the variables. For example, suppose a simple regression of the form $y = f(x)$ is to be used to estimate the relationship between the x and y values given below. A simple linear relationship will provide a very poor fit, because the x values increase at a faster rate than do the y values.

x	3	4	5	6	7	8	9
y	1.7	2	2.2	2.5	2.6	2.8	3.0

A regression using the square root of x as the independent variable, however, would provide a very close fit to the data. As indicated above, a plot of the data should be sufficient to suggest the use of a square root relationship.

Power Function Relationship The square root relationship actually is a special case of the more general power function relationship. The basic power function relationship is given in Eq. (18–14) and is rewritten in logarithmic form in Eq. (18–14'). The nonlinear function shown in Eq. (18–14), when rewritten in logarithmic form, is a linear function.[22]

$$y = a \cdot x^b \qquad (18–14)$$
$$\log y = \log a + b \cdot \log x \qquad (18–14')$$

[21] As a rough rule of thumb, it is advisable to have at least six sample observations for every independent variable included in the regression equation.

[22] See Appendix B for a discussion of some of the functional relationships discussed in this section.

The data is read in the form of log y and log x. Notice that both the dependent variable and the independent variable are in logarithmic form. The least squares method estimates the parameters log a and b. Notice that Eq. (18–14′) is the square root relationship when $b = \frac{1}{2}$.

A more elaborate power function can be written in the form $y = ax_1^{b_1}x_2^{b_2}$ and can be rewritten in logarithmic form as log $y = $ log $a + b_1 \cdot$ log $x_1 + b_2 \cdot$ log x_2. The logarithmic form is linear and the parameters can again be estimated in the usual way.[23] Notice that, in their arithmetic form [as in Eq. (18–15)] these functions are hyperbolas. When transformed to logarithmic form, the regression coefficients are estimates of elasticity. For example, if $y = $ demand, $x_1 = $ price, and $x_2 = $ income, the equation $y = ax_1^{b_1}x_2^{b_2}$ is a demand equation in terms of price and income. The coefficient b_1 is an estimate of price elasticity of demand and b_2 is an estimate of income elasticity of demand.[24]

Exponential Relationship An equation of the general form shown in Eq. (18–15) is called an exponential function. It is rewritten in logarithmic form in Eq. (18–15′). Notice that the data is read in the form log y and x,

$$y = ab^x \qquad (18\text{–}15)$$

$$\log y = \log a + x \cdot \log b \qquad (18\text{–}15')$$

whereas both variables were read in logarithmic form for the linear representation of the power function. Both parameters in Eq. (18–15′) are estimated in logarithmic form.

Dummy Variables

Another very useful technique in regression analysis is the dummy variable. Dummy variables are used when qualitative observations are to be included in the data.

For example, suppose you were developing an equation to predict the number of units of some product an individual consumer might purchase in one year. You might use the individual's annual income, sex, and whether or not he or she graduated from college as independent variables. Income can be used in the usual manner and will be denoted by x_1. A dummy variable x_2 can be used to indicate the individual's sex, where $x_2 = 1$ indicates male and $x_2 = 0$ indicates female. The same scheme could be used to reflect

[23] Most of the available computer routines have the capability to transform variables to logarithmic form, so a power function relationship is really very convenient to work with.

[24] Hyperbolic demand functions have the same elasticities at all levels of price and income. It must be remembered, however, that a hyperbola is being used to estimate the demand equation and it probably will not be a perfect fit. The regression coefficients represent elasticity estimated at the geometric means of the sample observations. Therefore, there is particularly great danger in using the estimated equation to forecast at points far beyond the range of the sample data.

335

Multivariate
Models:
Regression and
Input-Output
Analyses

educational attainment, where $x_3 = 1$ indicates a college degree, and $x_3 = 0$ indicates no college degree. The regression equation could therefore be written

$$y = a + b_1 x_1 + b_2 x_2 + b_3 x_3.$$

This is a straightforward linear regression model and it is computed and interpreted in the same manner as before. The coefficients of dummy variables can be tested for significance just like any other variable. Notice that dummy variables exert their influence by, in effect, shifting the intercept. That is, if b_2 is positive, the equation is telling us that a male of a given income level will purchase more units in a year's time than a female of the same income level. Thus the use of dummy variables allows a shift or modification of the equation to be estimated.

The use of dummy variables is not restricted to observations with only two characteristics. For example, suppose it is desirable to distinguish between college graduates, high school graduates, and those who did not finish high school. Another dummy variable would have to be added, and the above equation could be rewritten as:

$$y = a + b_1 x_1 + b_2 x_2 + b_3 x_3 + b_4 x_4$$

where x_3 and x_4 indicate educational achievement. This could be accomplished using the following scheme:

Education	x_3	x_4
College	1	0
High school	0	1
Didn't finish high school	0	0

The effect of the dummy variables is again to shift the intercept. In general, when n different characteristics are to be accounted for with dummy variables, $n - 1$ dummy variables must be used. One variable will have a value of 1 and all the rest will have a value of 0 for $n - 1$ characteristics, while all the dummy variables will have a value of 0 for the nth characteristic.

INPUT-OUTPUT ANALYSIS

Recent innovations in forecasting methods have not been restricted to qualitative techniques (such as the Delphi Technique discussed in Chapter 17). Relatively new quantitative methods are also being used.[25] The traditional approach to forecasting using regression analysis is to relate the activities of a firm or industry to broad economic aggregates. Thus sales

[25] The development of the method to be described pre-dates its popular use by a few decades. Thus the use of the method, if not the development, is relatively recent.

might be expressed as functions of such variables as gross national product, population, per capita income, inventories, housing starts, demographic characteristics, etc. The alternative is to dissect these aggregates into fundamental component parts that account for the myriad of intricate interrelationships that exist within the economy. For example, the relationships among industries and among the corporate, private, and public sectors of the economy might be determined. Once these relationships are established, a few projections can be made on key variables (such as the rate of inflation, unemployment, and growth in gross national product) and forecasts for the individual components of the economy follow. This technique is called input-output analysis.

Input-output analysis is a technique that allows the analyst to follow the intra-industry and inter-industry flow of goods in the national economy. It allows examination of all transactions at all levels of production, from raw materials through semifinished to the final product. The basic tool is a table (also called a matrix or grid) which shows the output, or sales, made by each industry to each other industry and the inputs, or purchases, made by each industry from each other industry.

Input-output analysis was invented in the 1920's by Wasily Leontief, an economist at Harvard University, and its real impetus came with the development of electronic data processing. It is based on the concept that "there is a fundamental relationship between the volume of an output of an industry and the size of the inputs going into it."[26] Thus it really is a descriptive model of the structure of the economy which is based on the assumption of stability of these fundamental relationships.

Input-output tables are published every few years by the Commerce Department's Office of Business Economics. One of the obstacles to using the tables as a practical planning tool has been the long time-lag resulting from the mammoth job of collecting and analyzing the data. The 1963 version, however, which contained 370 industrial classifications (requiring 136,900 entries in a table), was completed in one year less than it took to produce the 1958 version, which contained only 82 industrial classifications (requiring 6724 entries in a table). As the scope of new tables increases and their production time decreases, the usefulness of input-output tables should increase considerably.

The results published by the Office of Business Economics consists of several sets of tables. The simplest table shows what each industry bought from and sold to each other industry during the base year. A more elaborate table shows how, for example, an increase in demand for consumer durables would ripple through the economy to create increased sales for steel companies and electronics manufacturers. An even more sophisticated table accounts for the feedback effects where an increase in the demand for steel would lead to an increased demand for iron ore, which would, in turn, require an even greater output of steel.

[26] W. W. Leontief, "Input-Output Economics," *Scientific American*, October 1951.

337

Multivariate
Models:
Regression and
Input-Output
Analyses

It obviously would be a demanding job to analyze a particular industry using the large and complicated Office of Business Economics tables. All of the basic concepts can be presented, however, by developing a set of input-output tables for a simplified hypothetical economy. We will develop tables for an economy consisting of industries X, Y, and Z (the corporate sector), consumers (the private sector), and government (the public sector).

The basic data are presented in the modified balance sheets shown in Exhibit 18–9. Notice that the total inputs equal the total outputs for each industry. These accounts show the capital labor inputs as well as the materials purchased from other industries. The outputs include sales to other industries as well as sales to consumers and government.

Exhibit 18–9   Input-Output Data for Industries X, Y, and Z

Industry X

Inputs		Outputs	
Purchases from industry Y	$50	Sales to industry Y	$30
Wages and salaries	40	Sales to industry Z	20
Depreciation	10	Sales to consumers	35
Profits	25	Sales to government	40
Total	$125	Total	$125

Industry Y

Inputs		Outputs	
Purchases from industry X	$30	Sales to industry X	$50
Purchases from industry Y	15	Sales to industry Y	15
Purchases from industry Z	40	Sales to industry Z	20
Wages and salaries	60	Sales to consumers	90
Depreciation	15	Sales to government	25
Profits	40	Total	$200
Total	$200		

Industry Z

Inputs		Outputs	
Purchases from industry X	$20	Sales to industry Y	$40
Purchases from industry Y	20	Sales to consumers	50
Wages and salaries	50	Sales to government	45
Depreciation	15	Total	$135
Profits	30		
Total	$135		

The purchases (inputs) of some industries represent the sales (outputs) of other industries. For example, industry X uses inputs representing purchases totaling $50 from industry Y. Industry Y, then, has outputs of $50 in the form of sales to industry X. Since one industry's purchases represent another's sales, and vice versa, these industry transfers must net out when totaled. They are not included in national income and product accounting since they would result in double counting. The gross national product of our hypothetical economy is calculated in Exhibit 18–10. The distribution of income is shown on one side of the balance sheet and expenditures by the consumer and government sectors are shown on the other side. As required, the two sides balance.

Exhibit 18–10 Gross National Product Accounts

Income		Expenditures	
Wages and salaries	$150	Consumers	$175
Depreciation	40	Government	110
Profits	95	GNP =	$285
GNP =	$285		

The data in Exhibit 18–9 can be assembled into a basic input-output flow table, as shown in Exhibit 18–11. This table shows all inter-industry flows while preserving the same information that is contained in the national income and product accounts. Notice that the Consumer and Government columns and the Wages and Salaries, Depreciation, and Profits rows give the same information as Exhibit 18–10; Exhibit 18–11, however, also shows all industry transfers.

Exhibit 18–11 Input-Output Flow Table

Inputs	Outputs					
	Industry X	Industry Y	Industry Z	Consumers	Government	Total
Industry X	$0	$30	$20	$35	$40	$125
Industry Y	50	15	20	90	25	200
Industry Z	0	40	0	50	45	135
Wages and salaries	40	60	50	—	—	150
Depreciation	10	15	15	—	—	40
Profits	25	40	30	—	—	95
Total	$125	$200	$135	$175	$110	

Each industry is represented by both a row and a column. The rows represent the inputs (purchases) of each industry and the columns represent the outputs (sales) of each industry. Thus, for example, the second row shows that industry Y has outputs totaling $50 to industry X, $15 to industry Y, $20 to industry Z, $90 to consumers, and $25 to government, for an aggregate total output of $200. Similarly, the third column shows that industry Z uses inputs totaling $20 from industry X, $20 from industry Y, and so on. The first three rows represent material inputs, and the last three

339

Multivariate
Models:
Regression and
Input-Output
Analyses

rows represent the value added by each industry. Value added consists of processing costs plus profits.

The information contained in the basic flow table presented above can be restated in other formats that are more useful for particular applications of the tables. One such modification would be the input requirements table (or direct requirements table, as it is called in the publications of the Office of Business Economics) shown in Exhibit 18–12. This table gives the inputs required to produce one dollar of output (or consumption) from each industry or sector of the economy.

Exhibit 18–12 Input Requirements Table

	Industry X	Industry Y	Industry Z	Consumers	Government
Industry X	0	0.150	0.15	0.20	0.36
Industry Y	0.40	0.075	0.15	0.51	0.23
Industry Z	0	0.200	0	0.29	0.41
Wages and salaries	0.32	0.300	0.37	0	0
Depreciation	0.08	0.075	0.11	0	0
Profits	0.20	0.200	0.22	0	0
Total	1.00	1.000	1.00	1.00	1.00

This table clearly shows the interdependencies existing in our hypothetical economy. Suppose the sales of industry Z increase by $500. The input requirements table tells us that, for the output of industry Z to increase by $500, the transfers from industry X to industry Z (i.e., the output of X and the input of Z) must increase by $500(0.15) = $75. Similarly, the input from industry Y must increase by $500(0.15) = $75, wages and salaries will increase by $500(0.37) = $185, depreciation will increase by $500(0.11) = $55, and profits will increase by $500(0.22) = $110. Thus the $500 increase in the output of industry Z consists of input increases of $150 in raw materials, $240 in processing, and $110 in profits.

If the sales of industry Y were to increase by $1000, the following increased inputs, as obtained from Exhibit 18–12, would be required: $150 from industry X; $75 from industry Y; $200 from industry Z; $300 in wages and salaries; $75 in depreciation; and $200 in profits. But these figures do not tell a complete story. In the first example above, the $500 increase in output from industry Z required, among other things, $75 in inputs from industry Y. In order to increase the output of industry Y by $75, however, inputs totaling $15 [equal to (75)(0.20)] are required from industry Z. Thus total output of $515 from industry Z is now required. The increased output of industry Z will further increase the required inputs from industry Y, and so on. Even in our highly simplified hypothetical economy, the interdependencies cause complications. The reader might now begin to appreciate the complexities of constructing a table involving 370 industrial classifications.

The second example presented above, where the sales of industry Y increased by $1000, is more involved than the first example. One of industry

Y's required inputs was an input of $75 from industry Y; i.e., industry Y must produce outputs for its own use. The amount of feedback required to find the ultimate total inputs is increased due to both inter-industry and intra-industry dependencies.

Fortunately, it is not necessary for the user of input-output tables to trace through the effects of all of these interdependencies for himself. These computations are performed in another type of table that we will discuss shortly.

First, however, let us look at the complement of the input requirements table, the output distribution table. The output distribution table, shown in Exhibit 18–13, gives the distribution of sales per dollar of output for each industry. For example, $100 of total sales from industry X is distributed as follows: $24 to industry Y; $16 to industry Z; $28 to consumers; $32 to government. This type of table could be very useful to a company's marketing director. The output distribution of the industry could be compared to the distribution of his firm to help identify the firm's strengths and weaknesses in various types of markets.

Exhibit 18–13 Output Distribution Table

	Industry X	Industry Y	Industry Z	Consumers	Government	Total
Industry X	0	0.24	0.16	0.28	0.32	1.00
Industry Y	0.25	0.08	0.10	0.45	0.12	1.00
Industry Z	0	0.30	0	0.37	0.33	1.00

The last table to be presented is called the total requirements table. This table accounts for all the interdependencies that we encountered when discussing the input requirements table. The total requirements table shows both the direct and indirect input requirements necessary to produce one dollar of final output in each industry. Thus it is possible to find the ultimate effect of a change in the sales of any industry listed in the table. The total requirements table for our hypothetical economy is given in Exhibit 18–14.

Exhibit 18–14 Total Requirements Table

	Industry X	Industry Y	Industry Z
Industry X	1.087	0.219	0.196
Industry Y	0.486	1.215	0.255
Industry Z	0.097	0.243	1.051

The sum of the fourth and fifth columns in Exhibit 18–12 give the total final demand from the non-corporate sectors from each of industries X, Y, and Z. Exhibit 18–14 can be used to calculate the effect on each industry of a change in final demand for one or more of them. For example, suppose final demand (total from consumers and government) for industry X is $1000.

341

Multivariate
Models:
Regression and
Input-Output
Analyses

This would require total outputs of $1087 from industry X, $486 from industry Y, and $97 from industry Z. The entries along the diagonal in Exhibit 18–14 must all be equal to or greater than one. The value would be exactly one if an industry produces exclusively for final demand. It would be greater than one if, in addition to producing for final demand, there were also intra-industry or inter-industry requirements.

Because the total requirements table accounts for both the direct (i.e., for final demand) and indirect (i.e., for intra-industry and inter-industry needs) requirements, the entries in the table must be at least equal to the corresponding entries in the direct requirements table. In our example, the industry interrelationships are extensive enough that all entries in the total requirements table exceed the corresponding entries in the direct requirements table.

The entries in the total requirements table could be obtained by tracing through the interactions in the direct requirements table resulting from a change in final demand. By accumulating the outputs required in successive cycles through the production feedback loops, the total effect on all industries could eventually be determined. In practice, however, this laborious procedure is not used. The procedure simply involves the inversion of a matrix, a task which is best accomplished by computer solution.[27]

As indicated near the beginning of this section, the use of input-output tables for planning purposes is based on the assumption that the structural coefficients will remain reasonably stable over time. It also must be assumed that industry interdependencies and production processes can be described by linear relationships. Of course, the analyst does not have to naively apply a set of derived coefficients in his planning. Coefficients frequently are adjusted, particularly if they are somewhat dated, to reflect technological innovations and structural changes in the economy. For example, as the steel industry converted from open-hearth furnaces to oxygen-generating

---

[27] An understanding of matrix algebra is necessary to follow the procedure used to obtain the total requirements table. The mechanics involve subtracting the matrix obtained from the industry related entries in the input requirements table from the identity matrix and inverting the difference. Thus, if T represents the total requirements matrix, I represents the identity matrix, and D represents the industry input requirements matrix, $T = [I - D]^{-1}$. When the appropriate entries are taken from the direct requirements table, we can solve:

$$T = \left\{ \begin{bmatrix} 1 & 0 & 0 \\ 0 & 1 & 0 \\ 0 & 0 & 1 \end{bmatrix} - \begin{bmatrix} 0 & 0.175 & 0.15 \\ 0.40 & 0.075 & 0.15 \\ 0 & 0.200 & 0 \end{bmatrix} \right\}^{-1}$$

$$T = \begin{bmatrix} 1 & -0.15 & -0.15 \\ -0.40 & 0.925 & -0.15 \\ 0 & -0.20 & 1 \end{bmatrix}^{-1} = \begin{bmatrix} 1.087 & 0.219 & 0.196 \\ 0.486 & 1.215 & 0.255 \\ 0.097 & 0.243 & 1.051 \end{bmatrix}$$

If O = total outputs matrix (the last column in Exhibit 18–10), F = final demand (the sum of the fourth and fifth columns of Exhibit 18–10), and I, D, and T are as defined above, we can use matrix notation to write

$$O = D \cdot O + F$$
$$F = [I - D]O$$
$$O = [I - D]^{-1}F = T \cdot F$$

equipment, the mix of required inputs also changed. If the tables are to produce useful predictions, they must be modified to show these changing relationships.

The analyst must beware of price changes that can cause shifts in coefficients that might appear to mean considerably more than they actually do. If an industry's prices have increased relative to its customers, its apparent market gain might be highly overstated. For example, the 1963 tables showed oil producers to be selling relatively more to refiners than did the 1958 tables. During that period, however, crude oil prices increased and final product prices fell.

Broad industry classifications also limit the usefulness of input-output tables for some companies, although this problem eased considerably when the 1963 tables expanded to 370 classifications from the 82 classifications used in the 1958 tables. There is still room, however, for further refinement of these classifications.

A firm is assigned to an industry classification according to its primary product. This produces some difficulty for the growing number of firms that produce a wide variety of products. Secondary products that would fall into another classification are treated as output of the industry of which the producing firm is a part. But then these secondary products are treated as inputs to the industry for which they would be primary products, whether they are actually sold or not. Finally, the sale of these products to the final purchaser is treated as output of the industry for which these products would be primary, again whether or not such transactions actually occur. Imports that are substitutes for domestic products receive similar treatment.

While in its infancy, input-output analysis has dealt with broad industry trends. That does not mean, however, that future applications must be so restrictive. Tables already have been developed for individual companies and even highly detailed product lines. These tables would have far greater utility to managers than tables based on broad industry classifications.

Other more novel applications also are possible. For example, Leontief has suggested that the tables be expanded "to quantify the byproducts with which the various industries pollute the atmosphere."[28] This could lead to a clearer understanding of the relationships between technological processes and the environment, and could "help solve what he [Leontief] considers the most pressing economic problem of the United States—the rapid deterioration in the quality of life."[29]

PROBLEMS

1. When an investment banking firm agrees to underwrite (guarantee the marketing of) a new bond issue, it retains a portion of the total amount received from the sale of the bonds. This difference, or spread, between the gross proceeds (the total amount that investors pay for the bonds) and the net proceeds (the amount

[28] "Forecasters Get Some Better Props," *Business Week* (November 22, 1969), p. 126.

[29] *Ibid.*

343

Multivariate
Models:
Regression and
Input-Output
Analyses

passed on from the investment banker to the corporation that issued the bonds) represents the investment banker's compensation. The gross proceeds and investment banker's spread for ten bond issues of comparable rating (quality) are given below.

Gross Proceeds ($ million)	Investment Banker's Spread ($ million)
100	2.9
120	3.5
90	2.6
50	1.8
75	2.2
20	1.2
60	1.7
150	4.2
35	1.5
80	2.2

a. Use regression analysis to express the investment banker's spread as a linear function of the gross proceeds.
b. Interpret the results obtained in a.
c. Calculate the coefficient of determination and the standard error of the regression coefficient.
d. Use the t-test to check the significance of the regression equation.
e. Compute the residuals and plot them. What do they indicate about the validity of the regression equation?
f. Assume that a new bond issue of $70 million is to be underwritten. What would be the predicted investment banker's spread? Calculate a 95 percent confidence interval.

2. As an aid to analyzing future acquisition candidates, the president of a multibank holding company wants to determine the relationship between bank deposits and population. He has collected data for ten different banks located in various parts of his state.

Deposits ($ million)	Population per Banking Office
33	3700
45	4000
42	4100
35	3600
38	4500
42	3600
47	4100
36	3700
40	4400
34	3800

a. Use regression analysis to determine the desired relationship.
b. How good a fit is obtained? How might the analysis be improved?

3. A suburban community is planning to build a hospital and is uncertain about the size that will be necessary. To get some idea of a bed size that would be adequate, data on hospital bed usage have been collected from other similar communities. These data are given below.

Average Daily Occupancy	Population (000)	Average Annual Family Income ($000)
325	12.0	9.6
350	13.2	10.8
280	8.5	10.5
680	27.6	9.3
450	18.3	9.2
275	9.5	10.2
435	18.1	9.5
730	33.9	9.2
550	21.5	10.4
480	17.4	10.2
420	16.8	10.0
310	10.7	10.6
480	19.6	9.2
230	7.6	9.8
450	17.2	9.7

a. Use simple regression to expression the demand for hospital beds as a function of (1) population and (2) income.
b. What are the effects on hospital utilization of population and income? On the basis of the data given above, which of the two variables appears to be most important?
c. How useful is the regression equation for predictive purposes?
d. Could the two separate models be improved by comβining them some way?

4. A corporation with a convertible bond issue outstanding would like to be able to anticipate the annual amount of voluntary conversion that will occur. The company feels that conversion should be related to (a) the income difference among dividends that would be received following conversion and interest currently being received and the bond and (b) the volatility of the market price of the company's common stock (a measure of the risk of holding the common). The company has collected data for 15 convertible bond issues. It was noticed that some issues had constant conversion terms, while others had scheduled periodic reductions in the attractiveness of the conversion terms. The data collected by the company are given below.

Percent Converted of Outstanding Bonds	Income Difference	Index of Stock Price Volatility	Periodic Reduction in Conversion Terms
25	24.50	1.25	No
10	16.25	1.08	No
75	33.00	0.95	No
5	−12.50	1.12	No
55	18.50	0.87	No
42	7.75	1.04	Yes
80	18.25	0.91	Yes
1	−22.50	0.88	No
70	37.50	0.97	No
75	28.75	1.05	Yes
20	7.50	0.85	No
35	−16.25	1.09	Yes
40	18.00	0.93	No
18	24.25	1.18	No
28	−13.50	1.09	Yes

345

Multivariate
Models:
Regression and
Input-Output
Analyses

a. Formulate a multiple regression model to explain the volume of voluntary conversion.

b. Explain how you might use the information dealing with periodic reductions in conversion terms.

5. The daily high temperature during a period in July and the number of ice cream sales by a corner vendor are listed below.

Daily High Temperature	Ice Cream Sales
78	86
82	95
91	125
86	109
81	90
87	116
77	81
83	97
88	115
85	105

a. Calculate the regression of ice cream sales as a function of temperature.

b. Construct a 95 percent confidence interval for the true β.

6. The manager of a new manufacturing facility kept records of labor hours and units of production to check for the possible existence of a learning curve (see Appendix B). The data he accumulated are given below, where x = the cumulative number of units produced and y = the average labor hours per unit.

x	1	5	10	15	20	40	60	80	100
y	100	77	64	58	53	43	37	33	31

a. Is there any evidence of a learning curve? If so, what is the learning rate?

b. According to your calculations, what should be the average labor hours per unit when x = 200 units?

7. Industry R is comprised of Companies A, B, and C. Input-output data for these three companies are given below.

Company A

Inputs		Outputs	
Purchases from Company B	$25	Sales to Company B	$40
Wages and salaries	40	Sales to Company C	20
Depreciation	20	Sales outside industry	40
Profits	15	Total	$100
Total	$100		

Company B

Inputs		Outputs	
Purchases from Company A	$40	Sales to Company A	$25
Purchases from Company B	30	Sales to Company B	30
Purchases from Company C	15	Sales to Company C	40
Wages and salaries	25	Sales outside industry	25
Depreciation	5	Total	$120
Profits	10		
Total	$125		

Company C

Inputs		Outputs	
Purchases from Company A	$20	Sales to Company B	$15
Purchases from Company B	40	Sales outside industry	145
Wages and salaries	50	Total	$160
Depreciation	30		
Profits	20		
Total	$160		

a. From the above data, prepare a statement showing the gross national product accounts.

b. Prepare an input-output flow table.

c. Prepare an input requirements table.

d. Prepare an output distribution table.

e. Prepare a total requirements table.

f. By citing numbers contained in the tables prepared above in questions b through e and explaining their meaning, indicate the interpretation of each of the tables.

19

selected
multivariate models:
discriminant
and cluster analysis

Two statistical techniques useful to decision makers will be discussed in this chapter—object[1] cluster analysis and linear discriminant analysis. Both tools fall into the broad statistical category of classification analysis. In both cases the objective is to classify or group an object or objects into one of two or more populations. In discriminant analysis the populations of interest are defined *a priori* on the basis of some categorical criterion variable. For example, all loan applicants can be categorized as belonging to one of two populations, either good credit risks or bad credit risks. The discriminant problem is: How do we best predict or assign an object whose population identity we do not know to one of the known populations of interest? In cluster analysis, on the other hand, there are no clearly defined populations. We simply have a group of objects that we assume are partially heterogeneous. That is, we assume that the objects actually are a collection of objects from various populations. The cluster analysis problem, then, is how best to separate the objects into clusters or populations so that each object is more like objects within the same cluster than like objects in other clusters.

Both techniques are mathematically and statistically complex, and to understand fully the subtleties and full scope of these tools is beyond the level of this text. A basic overview of the techniques is presented in this chapter to acquaint the student with the availability of these tools to decision makers.

---

[1] "Object" is used here without gender implication, since the objects in question can be persons or things.

OBJECT CLUSTER ANALYSIS[2]

Let us consider a few examples of the use of cluster analysis in business.

A marketing manager must select k test market sites from a group of n potential areas. Each potential area can be described by numerous socio-economic and demographic variables. In selecting test areas it makes sense to select diverse areas so that the product's success under varying market conditions can be estimated. Moreover, should the product succeed in some areas and fail in others, it would be useful to know what other areas are similar to those in which it failed and those in which it succeeded. In effect, the test market selection problem can be formulated as a cluster analysis problem of how to group n potential test areas into k clusters such that areas within each cluster are as similar as possible and areas in different clusters are as dissimilar as possible. Once the clusters have been defined, the marketing manager need only select one (or more) from each of the k clusters for his test sites.

An investment service summarizes the investment characteristics of each common stock on the New York Stock Exchange using price/earnings ratios and four indices: capital appreciation, income, positive capital appreciation risk, and negative capital appreciation risk. It then asks its customers to place a relative weight of importance on each characteristic. In turn the service provides a listing of all the stocks, grouped into clusters so that the profile of each stock in a cluster is similar and the profiles of stocks in different clusters are dissimilar. In addition, the "typical" profile of each cluster is presented. This investment service is another example of the use of cluster analysis.

Methodology of Cluster Analysis

Now let us turn our attention to the methodology of cluster analysis. The basic methodological questions raised by cluster analysis are:

1. What are the relevant n descriptive measures of an entity?
2. How do we measure the similarity between entities?
3. Given that we have a measure of similarity between entities, how do we form clusters?
4. How do we decide on how many clusters to form?

The first question is extremely important, but we cannot answer it, since no unique answer exists. The choice of what variables are relevant for describing an entity is basically one that must be made by the user. The

---

[2] The term "object cluster analysis" encompasses a variety of techniques for grouping objects. In this text we shall restrict our discussion to one such technique, the hierarchical method based on euclidean distance. For an overview of the different clustering techniques, the student should refer to R. E. Frank and P. E. Green, "Numerical Taxonomy in Marketing Analysis: A Review Article," *Journal of Marketing Research*, Vol. 5 (Feb. 1968), pp. 83–94.

349

Selected
Multivariate
Models:
Discriminant and
Cluster Analysis

decision maker must predetermine what variables are important and should be included in the analysis on the basis of his knowledge of the entities in question and the objectives to be met by clustering the objects.

Now let us address the question of how we measure similarity. Assume that the decision maker has defined the list of relevant variables for describing an entity. We then collect the data on each variable for each entity. If we have p variables of interest and n entities, the data can be presented in the form below.

$$
\begin{array}{c}
\\
\text{entity 1} \\
\text{entity 2} \\
\vdots \\
\text{entity } n
\end{array}
\begin{array}{ccc}
\text{Var. 1} & \text{Var. 2} & \cdots & \text{Var. } P \\
\left[\begin{array}{cccc}
X_{11} & X_{12} & \cdots & X_{1p} \\
X_{21} & X_{22} & \cdots & X_{2p} \\
\vdots & & & \\
X_{n1} & X_{n2} & \cdots & X_{np}
\end{array}\right]
\end{array}
$$

The question is how to determine how similar or dissimilar each row of data is from the others. This task is complicated by the fact that, in most cases, the data in its original form is measured in different units and/or scale. Hence comparisons between variables are difficult. Thus the initial step is to standardize each variable.[3] This procedure converts each variable to a pure number (no units such as dollars, pounds, etc.) and the scale is the same, standard deviations from the mean. The input variables having been standardized, the measure used to define similarity between two entities, i and j, is computed as

$$
d_{ij} = (X_{1j} - X_{1i})^2 + (X_{2j} - X_{2i})^2 + \cdots + (X_{nj} - X_{ni})^2
$$

The smaller the value of d_{ij}, the more similar the two entities.

Forming Clusters

The measure of similarity having been defined, the basic method of object clustering can easily be seen in the following illustration. Consider the simplified case where we have four market areas, each described by its per capita income and per capita expenditures. If we plot the two variables (standardized) for each of the four market areas, we might find the following:

Per Capita Expenditures / Per Capita Income

---

[3] To standardize a variable, subtract its mean and divide by its standard deviation. Thus $X^* = (X - \bar{X})/S$, where X^* is the standardized variable.

It is obvious that if we want two clusters, we should group entities one and two into one cluster and entities three and four into a second cluster, since that grouping produces the clusters for which the entities within each cluster are most similar. We often deal with a large number of variables of description, however. Thus this graphical approach is not very feasible, since we cannot visualize in a multitude of dimensions.

In order to develop a mathematical procedure for forming the clusters, we need a criterion upon which to judge alternative clustering patterns. This criterion defines the optimal cluster pattern as the one that has the minimum sum of the distances between entities within each cluster. The within-cluster distance is defined as the sum of all the distances between the entities in each cluster. That is, if the first cluster contains entities 1, 3, and 5, the within-group distance for that cluster is

$$d_{13} + d_{15} + d_{35} = \tilde{d}_1$$

or, generally, the within-group distance for the kth group is

$$\tilde{d}_k = \sum_{i<j} \sum d_{ij} \quad \text{for all } i, j \text{ in cluster } k$$

Then, the total within-group distance for k clusters is

$$\sum_{i=1}^{k} \tilde{d}_i$$

By minimizing the within-cluster distance we have found the cluster pattern that gives us the minimum average distance between the entities grouped together.

This procedure is equivalent to maximizing the distance between clusters. The distance between two clusters is

$$d^*_{pq} = \sum_i \sum_j d_{ij} \quad \begin{array}{l} \text{over all } i \text{ in cluster } p \\ \text{over all } j \text{ in cluster } q \\ p \neq q \end{array}$$

Thus, the total distance between clusters is:

$$\sum_{p<q} \sum d^*_{pq}$$

Since the total distance $\sum_{i<j} \sum d_{ij}$ between all entities is constant regardless of what clusters are formed, and since

$$\sum_{i<j} \sum d_{ij} = \sum_{i=1}^{k} d_i + \sum_{p<q} \sum d^*_{pq}$$

351

Selected
Multivariate
Models:
Discriminant and
Cluster Analysis

the objective of minimizing the sum of the within-group distances is clearly equivalent to maximizing the sum of the between group distances.

Consider the simple example where we have just three entities. The distance matrix might be as follows:

	1	2	3
1	0	5	10
2		0	8
3			0

The possible clusters and their respective distances would be

Group 1	Group 2	Distance within	Distance between	Distance Total
1	2–3	8	15	23
2	1–3	10	13	23
3	1–2	5	18	23

Thus, the best grouping would be to cluster entities 1 and 2 together. This would yield the minimum within cluster distance (5) and, conversely, the maximum between cluster distance (18).

Obviously, if the number of entities is large, it is a prohibitive task to construct every possible cluster pattern, compute each within-cluster distance sum, and select the pattern that yields the minimum. The computer time needed can be substantial even with the aid of high-speed computers, if the numbers of entities and dimensions are large. Consequently, various algorithms have been developed that bypass complete enumeration in the search process. Since the mathematics of these procedures is quite complex for our purposes, it will suffice to know that such computer packages are available.

Optimal Number of Clusters

The criterion of minimizing the within-cluster distances to determine the best possible grouping to form k clusters assumes that k clusters are to be formed. If the number of clusters to be formed is not *a priori* fixed, the criterion will not specify the optimal number of clusters. Clearly, to minimize the sum of the within-cluster distances if the number of clusters is free to vary, all we have to do is make each entity its own cluster and the sum of the within distances will be 0.[4] This is of no value to a decision maker. The question

---

[4] Clearly, the more clusters, the lower the sum of the within-cluster distances.

of what is the optimal number of clusters has yet to be solved. Hence the choice of the number of clusters to be formed must be made arbitrarily by the decision maker. Most computer routines will find the optimal clustering patterns for two clusters, then three, four, and so on, until all entities represent a cluster unto themselves (or an arbitrary defined limit on the number of clusters is reached). Such routines are called *hierarchical*. Some insight into a reasonable choice for the number of clusters can be gained by examining the amount of incremental decrease in the sum of within-cluster distances as the number of clusters is increased. However, the ultimate decision must rest upon the purpose for which the cluster analysis is undertaken.

Other Problems Related to Clustering

Are the clusters truly different?

The question of whether the clusters are statistically significantly different is often raised, sometimes justifiably and sometimes not justifiably. If the entities in the study are the population, then the question of statistical significance has no meaning. To ask if entity A is different from entity B, for example, can evoke only an answer of yes or no. However, if we consider each cluster as a sample from its respective population, then the question of statistical significance has meaning. The clustering technique, being basically a data analysis method rather than an inference technique, will not assure that the clusters will prove to be statistically significantly different, i.e., that the populations created are really different. Moreover, the problem of determining if they are statistically significant has yet to be technically resolved.

Differing Importance of Descriptive Variables

Often the decision maker, when developing the list of descriptive variables, may consider one variable more important in the decision process than another.

Cluster analysis allows for each variable to be weighted in importance. The weights are placed on each variable in the distance function; that is, the similarity measure would be

$$d_{ij} = [w_1(X_{1i} - X_{1j})]^2 + [w_2(X_{2i} - X_{2j})]^2 + \cdots + [w_n(X_{ni} - X_{nj})]^2$$

where w_i = weight on the ith descriptive variable. Therefore, the importance of each variable in affecting the distance function, and thus the clustering process, is in relationship to its importance as specified by the weights. The weights, however, must be exogenously determined by the decision maker to reflect the importance he wishes to place on each variable.

Describing the Cluster

After clusters are formed we may want to describe each cluster. The centroid of each cluster is a useful concept for this purpose. The centroid of a cluster is the mean of each cluster and represents the "typical value" of the cluster.

353

Selected
Multivariate
Models:
Discriminant and
Cluster Analysis

Moreover, using Cartesian distance, we can compare each entity in a cluster to the centroid of the cluster to determine which entities in a cluster are most typical and which are least typical. The distance of an entity i in a cluster j to the centroid of the cluster is computed as

$$d_{ic} = \sum_{i=1}^{n} (X_{ij} - \bar{X}_{cj})^2$$

where

$$\bar{X}_{cj} = \sum_{i=1}^{n} \frac{X_{ij}}{n^*}$$

and

n = number of entities in cluster.

DISCRIMINANT ANALYSIS

Unlike cluster analysis, where the objective is to create a system for grouping entities on the basis of the similarity of their characteristics, in discriminant analysis the appropriate populations are known *a priori*. For example, a loan customer belongs to one of two possible groups—those who meet their obligation or those who default; sales in a given area may be classified as either profitable or unprofitable; an item produced is either good or defective. In effect, the population of items can be classified categorically into groups on the basis of some clearly defined criterion variable. Moreover, the number of groups need not be limited to two, as given in the above examples. For instance, a loan customer can be classified as "good pay," "slow pay," or "no pay"; an individual can be classified as belonging to one of the twelve astrological signs.

The primary purpose of the discriminant problem is to develop a basis for predicting which group an entity belongs to on the basis of the characteristics of the entity. A byproduct of developing such a procedure is the ability to infer the relative importance of each of the characteristics used to discriminate between the different groups in the population. Such a byproduct is often more valuable to management than the actual ability to predict an entity's proper classification. Consider a study of banks, in which each bank can be classified as "growing," "stagnant," or "declining," and each bank can be described by a set of financial, demographic, and socioeconomic variables. If we are able to develop a discriminant analysis model that infers the relative importance of each financial, demographic, and socioeconomic characteristic to growth (or lack of growth) of a bank, we will have given bank planners invaluable guidance in developing strategies for growth and expansion.

Assumption and Concept

The minimum set of conditions necessary to conduct linear discriminant analysis are (a) there are k ($k \geq 2$) *a priori* groups or classifications of the population of entities; (b) a sample of entities known to belong to each group exists; (c) each entity can be described by a set of quantitative variables; (d) the variance and relationship among each of the variables are the same for each group. The last assumption is necessary for the prediction function to be linear. The term "minimum set" is used because these conditions allow the construction of the appropriate linear prediction function. However, in order to perform more sophisticated analysis, such as conducting statistical tests of hypothesis (e.g., testing the hypothesis that the mean values of the variable describing group 1 are really different from the mean values of the variables describing group 2), other assumptions about the data describing the variables must be satisfied.

The linear discriminant function was originally developed by R. A. Fisher. Given the above assumptions, he sought the function that would maximize the separation between the mean value of the function for each group standardized by the variance. It was subsequently shown that if the assumption that the two groups are multivariate normally distributed was added, the resultant function was optimal in that it minimized the probability of misclassification. The use of the function, however, has not been restricted to situations where data is assumed multivariate normal. In fact, for both real life examples presented later in this chapter, many of the variables are yes/no type variables which obviously are not normally distributed. In such situations the use of a linear discriminant function must be viewed simply as a method of prediction. The success of the procedure can be determined for the sample data and perhaps some test data, but proper statistical inferences about its true characteristics cannot be drawn.

For purposes of simplicity, let us restrict our attention to the situation where there are only two groups. Consider the situation where we have six entities, three known to belong to one group and three belonging to a second group. Suppose that each entity can be described by the two variables for which values are given in Exhibit 19–1.

Exhibit 19–1   Data for Discriminant Analysis Example

	Entity Number	Descriptive Variable	
		X	Y
Group 1	1	1	3
	2	1	2
	3	3	4
Group 2	4	2	1
	5	3	2
	6	3	1

The data for these six entities are in Illustration 19–1. Given the two-dimensional picture of the two groups, the problem is to find a mathematical

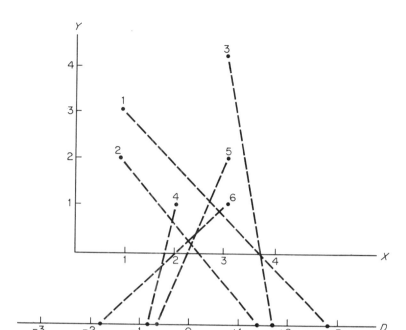

Illustration 19–1

Graphic Display of Two-
Group Linear Discriminant
Function

function of X and Y that will yield some single measure that will provide a means for separating the two populations into the correct groups. Under the assumption stated above, such a function will be a linear combination of the variables and is denoted as the *linear discriminant function*. Technically the function is formed by computing the coefficients for the variables X and Y which maximize the separation between the two groups relative to the variation of the variables within each group. The function developed projects from the two-dimensional X,Y axes to a single discriminant axis. If we have n variables, the function reduces the data from n-dimensions to a single dimension. This dimensional reduction is of tremendous value, since it is very difficult to graph or visualize an item's characteristics in more than three dimensions. We shall not concern ourselves with the actual method of calculating the linear discriminant function, since it is complex and beyond the scope of this text. Numerous computer programs exist that will construct the function for us. For our example the appropriate linear discriminant function is

$$-1X + 1.2Y = D$$

Looking at the discriminant axis in Illustration 19–1, we see that those items belonging to group 1 are clustered on the negative side of the axis, while those items belonging to group 2 are clustered on the positive side.

In this case the function is a perfect discriminator for the data, since all the entities from group 1 are on the right portion of the discriminant axis and those from group 2 are on the left portion. In realistic problems there generally is overlap so that certain entities, when projected onto the discriminant axis, appear to belong to the wrong group. The frequency of these incorrect assignments basically determines how accurate or useful the linear discriminant function will be.

Suppose now we draw a new entity whose group identity is unknown but whose characteristics are $X = 4$ and $Y = 6$. Using the discriminant function, we get a discriminant score of $+3.2$ $[-4 + 1.2(6)]$. We should, therefore, predict that the entity belongs to group 1. Suppose we draw another entity whose characteristics are $X = 1$ and $Y = 1$. We get a discriminant score of $+0.2$, and it is not so obvious to which group this entity should be assigned. What is needed, of course, is a cutoff score or decision rule concerning D. That is, if the discriminant score D is greater than or equal to some specified value, the observation should be assigned to group 1, and if the score is less than the specified value, the observation should be assigned to group 2. If we assume (a) the cost of misclassification of an entity from either group is the same and (b) there is equal probability *a priori* that the entity to be classified comes from either group, the expected cost of prediction error is minimized if we use $D = 0$ as the cutoff point for our decision rule.[5] Thus for $X = 1$, $Y = 1$, yielding $D = +0.2$, we should assign the entity to group 1.[6]

The linear discriminant function itself contains valuable information aside from its role in prediction. Examination of the coefficients of the function yields useful insights into the relationship between the characteristics of the entities and the entities' group identification. For instance, in our example the function infers that it is the difference in X and Y that seems to be related to grouping. If $Y \geq X$ the entity tends to belong to group 1, while if $X < Y$ it tends to belong to group 2.

Confusion Matrix

After we have developed a linear discriminant function, we need some method of evaluating its effectiveness. The most common method is through examination of how well it separates the sample data into the correct groups. As noted earlier, if there is greater overlapping on the discriminant axis, the function is not very effective. Such examination of its effectiveness is done through the presentation of a confusion matrix. A confusion matrix, shown in Exhibit 19–2, delineates the outcome of predicted classifications of the sample items from each group. It should be noted that since these are the data from which the linear discriminant function was derived, the error rate for these data almost always underestimates the error rate that will occur in actual future prediction.

[5] This technically is an asymptotic result as the sample size of entities from each group goes to infinity.

[6] If we assume unequal costs of misclassification and/or unequal *a priori* probabilities, there are statistical methods available for determining the D cutoff score for the decision rule that minimizes the expected cost of prediction error.

Exhibit 19–2   Confusion Matrix

<table>
<tr><td></td><td></td><td colspan="2" align="center">Actual</td></tr>
<tr><td></td><td></td><td align="center">Group 1</td><td align="center">Group 2</td></tr>
<tr><td rowspan="2">**Predicted**</td><td>Group 1</td><td align="center">N_1</td><td align="center">N_2</td></tr>
<tr><td>Group 2</td><td align="center">N_3</td><td align="center">N_4</td></tr>
</table>

Hits over-all: $N_1 + N_4$

Hit percentage over-all: $\dfrac{N_1 + N_4}{N_1 + N_2 + N_3 + N_4}$

Hit percentage, group 1: $\dfrac{N_1}{N_1 + N_3}$

Hit percentage, group 2: $\dfrac{N_2}{N_2 + N_4}$

The usual procedure for measuring how "good" the hit percentage (i.e., the percentage of correct assignments) is would be to compare it with either the rate you would expect from random guessing (50 percent) or the "best" rate you would expect to achieve without use of the characteristics of the entities. The "best" rate would be constructed by assuming that all entities belong to the group that contains the largest total number of entities. For example, suppose a linear discriminant function yielded the confusion matrix given below:

<table>
<tr><td></td><td></td><td colspan="2" align="center">Actual</td></tr>
<tr><td></td><td></td><td align="center">Group 1</td><td align="center">Group 2</td></tr>
<tr><td rowspan="2">**Predicted**</td><td>Group 1</td><td align="center">61</td><td align="center">19</td></tr>
<tr><td>Group 2</td><td align="center">37</td><td align="center">53</td></tr>
</table>

The over-all linear discriminant function hit rate would be $(61 + 53)/(61 + 37 + 19 + 53) = 67$ percent; for group 1 the hit rate would be $61/(61 + 37) = 62.2$ percent, and for group 2 it would be $53/(15 + 53) = 73.6$ percent. All these results are better than the random rate of 50 percent.

The "best" rate without knowledge of the characteristics would be obtained by assuming that all items are predicted to belong to group 1, since that group contains the largest number of entities. Thus we would assign group 1 entities correctly and all group 2 entities incorrectly, achieving an over-all hit rate of $98/(98 + 72) = 57.6$ percent. This result would still be lower than that achieved by use of the linear discriminant function. We must remember, however, not to be overly optimistic, since the hit percentage of future prediction will almost always be less than that calculated from the sample data.

EXAMPLES OF DISCRIMINANT ANALYSIS

Example 1

Consider the problem of trying to predict corporate bankruptcy.[7] A sample of 33 bankrupt and 33 nonbankrupt firms is selected for analysis, and the following data are collected from the firms' balance and income statements one year prior to the bankruptcy:

Exhibit 19–3 Variables Used in Discriminant Analysis of Bankruptcy

X_1 = working capital/total assets
X_2 = retained earnings/total assets
X_3 = earnings before interest and taxes/total assets
X_4 = market value equity/book value of total debt
X_5 = sales/total assets

A linear discriminant analysis yields the following discriminant function

$$D = -2.355 + 0.012X_1 + 0.014X_2 + 0.033X_3 + 0.006X_4 + 0.999X_5$$

which predicts correctly (using 0 as the cutoff, positive scores indicating non-bankrupt) 95 percent of the cases in the study. In this situation the relative importance of each of the variables in indicating bankruptcy is of equal interest with prediction. Standardizing the coefficients[8] yields the results given in Exhibit 19–4. The standardized coefficients clearly indicate the relative importance of each ratio as a warning sign for bankruptcy. The larger the standardized coefficient, the greater is the relative importance of the associated variable. Further financial analysis can relate each ratio back to the firm's policy and practices and possible trouble may be averted.

Exhibit 19–4 Standardized Discriminant Coefficients

Variable	Standardized Coefficient	Rank
X_1	3.29	5
X_2	6.04	4
X_3	9.89	1
X_4	7.42	3
X_5	8.41	2

Example 2

A standard problem facing all credit institutions is that of when or when not to extend credit. The profitability of such institutions often depends upon the proper

---

[7] This example comes from the article by Edward I. Altman, "Financial Ratios, Discriminant Analysis and the Prediction of Corporate Bankruptcy," *Journal of Finance*, Vol. XXIII (Sept. 1968), pp. 589–609.

[8] This is done by multiplying each coefficient by its standard deviation so that each coefficient is of the same scale; then they can be directly compared.

359

Selected
Multivariate
Models:
Discriminant and
Cluster Analysis

judgment of credit risk. Such judgment is normally based on the past credit experiences of the lending institution. Discriminant analysis can be of assistance in making these decisions. We can separate the loan applicant population into two distinct subpopulations, good accounts and bad accounts. In addition, through information contained on loan applications we can obtain various characteristics describing the potential loan applicants.

Consider the approach of a home mortgage firm[9] which from its files randomly selects 150 good accounts opened between January 1960 and October 1961 and 150 repossessions opened during January 1960 and repossessed by October 1961. From the loan applications, the data in Exhibit 19–5 were obtained about each account.

Exhibit 19–5   Variables Used in Discriminant Analysis of Loan Applicants

X_1 = Age
X_2 = Number of dependents
X_3 = Have phone (1 = yes, 0 = no)
X_4 = Occupation (5 = profession, 4 = self-employed, 3 = skilled,
          2 = semiskilled, 1 = unskilled)
X_5 = Total monthly income
X_6 = Time at present job
X_7 = Time at present address
X_8 = Savings account (1 = yes, 0 = no)
X_9 = Year of auto
X_{10} = Previous high credit amount
X_{11} = Number of unsatisfactory credit references
X_{12} = Number of satisfactory credit references
X_{13} = Amount of mortgage requested
X_{14} = Total outstanding debts
X_{15} = Total down payment
X_{16} = Assessed value of home
X_{17} = Total current assets
X_{18} = New or used home (1 = new, 0 = used)
X_{19} = Ratio of mortgage payment to monthly income

Using a discriminant analysis computer routine, a linear discriminant function of the form

$$D = a + b_1X_1 + b_2X_2 + \cdots + b_{19}X_{19}$$

was computed. The b's represent the respective coefficients of the variables in the discriminant function which correspond to the above attributes relating to the credit risk of the applicant. For this problem, the groups were labeled so that large values of D tended to be an indicator of a good account and small values indicated a bad or repossession account. The scale, or range, of D was from 0 to 51.

The cutoff score of D remains to be chosen. Clearly, the lower the cutoff score, the greater is the number of "bad" loans that will be made but, conversely, the lower is the number of "good" loans that will be rejected. For higher cutoff scores of D, the reverse will hold true. Exhibit 19–6 presents the resultant confusion matrix for various D cutoff scores.

[9] The following example is adapted from James H. Meyers and Edward W. Forgy, *Journal of the American Statistical Association*, 58, 303 (Sept. 1963), pp. 799–806.

Exhibit 19–6   Confusion Matrix for Credit Rating Example

$D = 20$

		Actual	
		Good	Repossession
Predicted	Good	149	120
	Repossessions	1	30

Hit percentage: 60 percent over-all

$D = 25$

		Actual	
		Good	Repossession
Predicted	Good	135	82
	Repossessions	15	63

Hit percentage: 66 percent over-all

$D = 30$

		Actual	
		Good	Repossession
Predicted	Good	85	43
	Repossessions	65	107

Hit percentage: 64 percent over-all

As the cutoff score is increased, the number of bad loans that would be made (i.e., incorrectly predicted good) decreases, but at the expense of passing up many good loan prospects (i.e., incorrectly predicting bad).

Cutoff	Number of Good Loans Rejected	Number of Bad Loans Made
20	1	120
25	15	82
30	65	43

Clearly, the final choice of the cutoff score will be made by the decision maker, who must weight the costs associated with rejecting good applicants versus making bad loans. Moreover, his decision may vary substantially over time as conditions and management policy changes. For example, in a tight money market, where the number of applicants is quite large compared to the funds available, a very high cutoff would be best. In a loose money market, where the number of applicants is small compared to the funds available, a loan company may not want to forego the lost income from rejecting good loan applicants and consequently may lower the cutoff score.

The linear discriminant function thus produces a credit rating system in which the b's represent the relative weights of each item of information and the resultant score gives the credit rating for decision purposes. In addition, if any b's are insignificantly small, that item can be eliminated, thereby simplifying the credit application.

Variables to be Used

The type of variables that can be used in a discriminant function is restricted to those which are continuous and/or have a natural ranking order. For

361

Selected
Multivariate
Models:
Discriminant and
Cluster Analysis

example, in the list in Exhibit 19–5 we find continuous variables, such as age and income, and classification variables, such as "have phone" and "occupation." In considering occupation, a ranking of the types of occupations is necessary for the variable to be used.

Often one of the most interesting and informative questions is what variables should go into the discriminant function and the importance or nonimportance of each variable. An initial list of all possible variables must be developed by the decision maker from his knowledge of the process under study. Mathematical techniques such as stepwise discriminant analysis exist which will select the subset of variables that best discriminate the populations, and statistical techniques exist to test the significance of each variable's input to the discriminant function. However, these techniques are statistically sophisticated and well beyond the scope of this text.

PROBLEMS

1. What is the purpose of object cluster analysis and linear discriminant analysis?

2. How does the population in discriminant analysis differ from that in cluster analysis?

3. What is the discriminant analysis problem? the cluster analysis problem?

4. How can the test market selection problem be formulated as a cluster analysis problem?

5. Suppose that stocks are characterized with two indices: predicted appreciation over the next year and predicted appreciation over the next decade.
   a. Form two clusters of stocks based on these indices.
   b. Describe each cluster.
   c. Describe the difference between the two clusters.

	Predicted Appreciation over Next Year	Predicted Appreciation over Next Decade
Stock A	$0.10	$0.80
B	$0.07	$1.00
C	$0.11	$0.85
D	$0.06	$1.05

6. What are the basic questions raised by cluster analysis?

7. Can the relevant n descriptors be determined quantitatively?

8. How is the similarity between entities measured in cluster analysis?

9. Consider the case where we have nine market areas, each described by the average number of hours per week spent watching television and the average number of hours per week spent listening to radio.

Avg. no. hours/wk.
listen to radio

Avg. no. hours/wk.
watch TV

Form three clusters, using the data from this graph.

10. How do the computer techniques discussed in this chapter form clusters?
11. What is the equation used to find the within-group distance?
12. What happens to the sum of the within group distance as the number of clusters increase?
13. Consider the following distance matrix.

	1	2	3
1	0	10	12
2		0	6
3			0

    a. List all possible clusters and their respective distances.
    b. If two clusters were desired, which groups would be selected?
14. How is the number of clusters determined?
15. Why might one want to place weights on the variables in the distance function?
16. What is meant by the centroid of a cluster? Why is this concept useful?
17. For which of the following problems would discriminant analysis be used?
    a. Grouping job applicants
    b. Rating insurance salesmen.
    c. Predicting political affiliation of a person.
18. What are the minimum conditions necessary to conduct linear discriminant analysis?
19. What is the criterion for forming the linear discriminant function?
20. Use Exhibit 19–1 and the corresponding discriminant function $-x + 1.2Y = D$. A new entity whose group identity is unknown and whose characteristics are $x = 5$ and $y = 4$ is selected. To which group should we assign the entity?
21. What can be learned by examining the coefficient of the linear discriminant function?
22. When is the linear discriminant function most accurate?
23. How is the effectiveness of the linear discriminant function evaluated?
24. What is meant by a confusion matrix?
25. A linear discriminant function results in the following confusion matrix:

		Actual	
		Group 1	**Group 2**
Predicted	Group 1	50	30
	Group 2	40	80

    a. Determine the over-all hit rate.
    b. What is the "best" rate without knowledge of the characteristics?
    c. Does the linear discriminant function give a better result than the "best" rate without knowledge of the characteristics?

363

Selected
Multivariate
Models:
Discriminant and
Cluster Analysis

d. Determine the hit rate for group 1.

e. Determine the hit rate for group 2.

26. Sales in a particular area are classified as highly profitable, moderately profitable, or unprofitable. It has been decided to use discriminant analysis for predicting to which group an area belongs.

a. What variables could be used to describe potential sales areas?

b. Discuss the advantages and disadvantages of high and low cutoff scores.

20
survey designs

The objective in the preceding chapters was to develop models that led to optimal decisions on the basis of given sets of data. In this chapter, we shall examine the question of how, given the model, do we best gather the data that the model needs to generate optimal decisions. The science of gathering sample information in a systematic way, so that the resulting inferences are unbiased and as precise as possible for a given cost, is called *sampling theory*. The procedures specified for collecting the data are called the *sample design*.

POPULATION

In any investigation there is some set of objects about which information is desired. The first step of any sample design is clearly to define that set of objects which is to be studied. This totality of items about which an inference is to be drawn is called a *population*. The specification of the particular population to be studied is dependent upon the problem. Besides the actual elements of the population, time and space limitations must also be clearly defined. For example, consider the problem of a bank trying to determine the profitability of a new type of savings account. One of the necessary inputs for the analysis might be the average savings deposit transaction. The elements of the population, savings deposit transactions, are obvious from the definition of the problem. However, the time and space limitations also need to be specified. Are we interested in the transactions of a specific bank branch, of all branches of the bank, or of all banks in a geographic area? Moreover, we must specify whether we are interested in the transactions for the month of December 1970, all of 1970, or possibly transactions in future years. Although it may seem that these questions can be answered readily, subtle and discerning errors can occur (as illustrated by the *Literary Digest* poll described later in the chapter). Thus careful thought must be given to the specification of the appropriate population.

If the population consists of a fixed number of elements so that it is possible to enumerate it in its totality, the population is finite. If we were actually to examine the total population, we would be taking a census rather than a sample. A sample is differentiated from a census by the fact that a sample consists of only a portion of the population. Obviously, a census can be conducted only if the population is finite, but even then it would seldom be undertaken because of cost and time constraints.

It is possible for a population to be infinite rather than finite. This phenomenon occurs when the data are generated by a process which may be thought of as continuing indefinitely. For example, the output from a machine can be viewed as a sample from the infinite population that would be produced by the machine over time. In these situations, moreover, it must be determined whether the process is stable over time (i.e., whether the characteristics of the population do not change over time).

SAMPLING FRAME

The population of interest having been defined, the second step in any sample design is to develop the sampling frame. The frame consists of a list of elements from which the sample is to be drawn. If the population is finite and the time frame is in the present or past, it is possible for the frame to be identical with the population. In most cases, however, they are not identical, since it is often impractical or impossible to draw a sample directly from the population.

Nevertheless, it is extremely important for the frame to be as representative of the population as possible. For example, the *Literary Digest* (now defunct) presidential poll of 1936 predicted that Alf Landon would defeat Franklin D. Roosevelt. The proper population consisted of all persons who would vote on election day. It obviously was impossible to construct, prior to the election, a list of all persons who would actually vote. The frame that the *Literary Digest* chose to use was based on telephone books and automobile registration lists. This frame represented a very poor selection, since only the relatively affluent could generally afford telephones or automobiles during the Depression. Thus the frame presented a very biased picture of the voting population and led to a fallacious inference.

A more appropriate frame would have been the voter registration lists, although even this frame would have had a serious time reference problem. The population in question was all individuals who would be voting on election day. Since it would have been infeasible to sample on election day, it was necessary to conduct the sampling on some prior date. Thus even if a sample was taken from a population of all eligible voters, it is doubtful that all of them would actually vote. Furthermore, even if it had been possible to sample from a frame of individuals who would actually vote on election day, bias might have occurred, since the percentage of voters who would vote for a certain candidate changes as election day approaches. Some instances of incorrect predictions of election outcomes have occurred simply because the sample was taken too far in advance of election day. In well-constructed election polls, repeated sampling is conducted, and the sampling is continued as close to election day as feasible so that trends in voting patterns can be observed.

Clearly, when the time frame of the population is in the future, there is no alternative but to use current or historical data to estimate future data. If the population is stationary with respect to time (i.e., if the characteristics in question do not change over time) there is no problem. However, if the population is not stable over time, extreme care and thought should be used. For example, to estimate savings transaction deposits in the future, it probably would be naive and misleading to use the average of a sample of the current year's transactions. Moreover, it would be unfortunate if data were gathered on this year's transactions only. In such a situation, data should be collected for a series of past years, and forecasting techniques could be used to determine the trend over time to provide a better estimate of the size of future transactions.

ERRORS IN SAMPLING

Once the population and the appropriate sampling frame have been specified, the final step is to determine the procedure for selecting the elements from the frame. In practice, this step and the selection of the frame are generally performed concurrently, since the choice of the frame often depends on the procedure to be used in selecting the sample. Before we look at some of the more common sampling selection procedures, let us first discuss criteria for selecting a procedure. In sampling theory, there are two costs that must be considered: (a) the cost of collecting the data and (b) the cost of an incorrect inference resulting from the data. There are two causes of incorrect inferences, systematic bias and random or sampling error.

Systematic Bias

A systematic bias results from errors in the sampling procedures. This bias cannot be reduced or eliminated by increasing the sample size, although the causes of these errors can usually be determined and corrected. Some of the more common causes of systematic bias are:

1. Inappropriate Frame The sampling frame can be a biased representation of the population. This bias may occur because the objects in the frame are a nonrepresentative subset of objects from the population (as in the *Literary Digest* poll) or because the time or space frame is incorrect.

2. *Natural Bias in the Reporting of Data* There is probably a downward bias in the figures presented for gross income based on data gathered by the Internal Revenue Service. On the other hand, estimating the average account balance of a group of individuals (for nontax purposes) by means of a telephone survey would very likely result in a high estimate if some individuals tend to overstate their balances in order to appear more successful or affluent than they really are. Incidences of this type of problem often occur in opinion or psychological surveys, where persons tend to give what they think is the "correct" or socially acceptable answer rather than reveal their true feelings. This bias is frequently easy to identify, but usually is difficult to correct.

3. *Indeterminancy Principle* Sometimes individuals under observation act differently than they do in nonobserved situations. Two instances where this may hold true are work study analysis and quality control inspection. In a work study analysis, workers are studied on the job to determine the average length of time required to complete a task, usually so that quotas can be set for piece work. It is generally found that workers tend to slow down so that quotas will be set low if they are aware that they are undergoing work-study. This tendency has led to the design of some elaborate methods, such as hidden cameras or one-way windows, to hide from individuals the fact that they are being observed.

Consider also an example where a firm institutes a quality control check system to monitor secretarial accuracy. If secretaries are aware that they are being monitored, they tend to be more careful and accurate, but their speed suffers as a result. Once the system is removed or gradually becomes commonplace, their speed tends to increase and their accuracy returns to normal. Hence, upward biased estimates of accuracy would have been gathered from the initial monitoring system.

4. *Nonrespondents* In surveys a common cause of systematic bias results from not being able to sample all the individuals initially included in the sample. This type of bias occurs because the likelihood of establishing contact or receiving a response from an individual is often correlated with the measure of what is to be estimated. For example, in a survey of individual savings account balances, a higher respondent rate might be expected from those who have larger savings account balances than from those who have smaller balances.

5. *Bias in the Instrument of Collection* This type of bias would occur if the physical measuring device is constantly in error, such as a scale being calibrated an ounce too light. Bias due to physical measurement error is probably the easiest to avoid if rigorous inspection and testing of all measuring devices are employed. In survey work, this error can result if the questionnaire or interviewer is biased. Questionnaires can be inadvertently or skillfully worded so as to increase the probability of eliciting a certain response. A survey worded, "This is a survey of the public's awareness of the nutritional value of breakfast food. Are you aware of the fact that brand K has twice the nutritional value as the leading brand?" will tend to invoke an inflated proportion of yes responses. The ordering of questions may also result in biased responses. The use of leading subjective adjectives, such as "high," "disproportionate," or "small," is also a common cause of bias in questionnaire responses. Moreover, studies have shown that, when a survey is conducted by an interviewer, results can be drastically altered by the emphasis that the interviewer places on certain words in the question or by the facial expressions of the interviewer. In survey work interviewers should be carefully trained to avoid biasing the results.

Sampling Errors

Random or sampling errors are random variations in the sample estimates around the true population values. Since they occur randomly and are equally likely to be in either direction, their expected value is zero and the term *bias* is inappropriate. Sampling errors result from a conglomeration of non-determinable effects and the fact that *the sample result will vary depending upon which particular set of observations is drawn.* The more homogeneous the population, the smaller the sampling error. As the sample size increases, the sampling error decreases. Random error is eliminated in a census, and only systematic error is possible.

A measure of the random sampling error can be calculated for a given sample design and size. This measure is called the *precision* of the sampling plan. Precision can always be improved by increasing the number of sample observations, but two practical constraints exist: (a) Increasing the number of observations increases the cost of obtaining the estimates, and (b) increasing the sample size may increase the systematic error. This last trade-off has prompted the observation that better estimates can be made by sampling rather than by census-taking. The most effective way to increase precision is often not to substantially increase the sample size but to use a "better" sampling design, i.e., a design which for a given sample size for a given cost has a smaller sampling error.

SAMPLE DESIGNS

The sample design specifies the procedures to be used in collecting the sample. There are many sample selection designs from which a researcher can choose. For certain sampling problems, certain designs are more precise and easier to apply than others. In theory, it makes sense to use that design which, for a given cost, yields the most precision. In practice, however, we sometimes use a less precise design because it is easier to administer. A less precise design can often be justified because the results can be gathered more efficiently and systematic errors can be better controlled.

The selection of sample elements can be based on either personal judgment or probability. Samples that are drawn on the basis of judgment are called *judgment samples*. In this type of sampling, items are systematically selected which are hopefully representative of the population. A marketing manager who wants to test-market a new product may select certain test areas which he feels are typical of the total market area. The results of these test areas can then be generalized to the total market area. In political polling, it is common for pollsters to base their predictions on certain selected areas where voting patterns are felt to be characteristic of the total voting area. In fact, one successful pollster predicts presidential election results on the basis of pre-election sampling of a few selected areas in Delaware. Clearly, the validity of any judgment sample hinges on the soundness of the judgment of whoever selects the sample. Furthermore, there is no objective way to compute the precision of such a sample and no assurance that increasing the sample size will actually increase the precision.

On the other hand, the precision of a probability sample (where sample elements are drawn on the basis of probability) can be determined and increased by increasing the sample size. Thus probability samples are generally preferred, and most of sampling theory concerns itself with different types of probability samples. It should not be inferred, however, that all judgment samples are bad. If the judgment is sound, judgment samples can often lead to better inferences at a lower cost than probability samples. But they are more risky in the sense that we cannot measure whether the judgment is sound or how precise our estimates are. Thus we have no objective measure of the degree of confidence that can be placed in our estimates. Let us now turn our attention to some of the more common probability sampling designs.

Simple Random Sampling

A simple random sample results from a sample design wherein every element in the population has an equal probability of being chosen. The precision of a simple random sample will depend upon the homogeneity of the population. The more uniform the population, the more appropriate is simple random sampling. If a simple random sample is to be drawn, assurances must be made that each element does in fact have an equal probability of being chosen. Mistakes are frequently made because the term "randomness" is confused with "haphazard."

Prudent forethought must be used to properly draw a random sample. For example, suppose that ten penlight batteries are to be drawn from a lot shipment of 100 for the purpose of estimating the average life of a battery from the lot. One method, seemingly random, would be to mix the batteries thoroughly and draw out ten batteries. This is a haphazard procedure, however, because it is extremely difficult to know when and if the items are thoroughly mixed. Suppose that defective batteries tend to settle toward the bottom of the lot; their probability of selection might be less than it should be under random selection. The result could be an upward bias in the estimation of the average life of the batteries.

A mixing procedure was used to select draft dates the first year the draft lottery was instituted. It was afterward generally concluded that the selection was not a random process, as intended. The method used—placing the dates in a cylinder and mixing them—led to higher than chance probabilities that the early and late months would be selected either early or late. The result was that 26 out of 31 December dates and 21 out of 30 November dates were selected in the first half of the lottery, while only 12 out of 31 January dates and 12 out of 29 February dates were selected in the first half.

The proper procedure for selecting a simple random sample is to use a table of random numbers (such as Exhibit F–7 in Appendix F) or a random number generator (a device, usually a computer routine, which generates random numbers). The procedure would be to first assign a number to each element in the sampling frame and then go to a table of random numbers or a random number generator to select a set of nonrepeated random numbers equal to the sample size. Each numbered element corresponding to a selected random number would be included in the sample. The random numbers can be selected from the table by any methodical manner decided on prior to the numbering of the population. Clearly, this simple random sampling procedure is feasible only for limited finite populations.

Systematic Sampling

Systematic sampling is an easier method of selecting a sample than simple random sampling. In systematic sampling every ith item on a list is selected. For example, if a 5 percent sample is desired, the first item would be selected randomly from the first twenty and thereafter every twentieth item would automatically be included in the sample. This method of selection has the advantage of not requiring the use of random numbers. More importantly, it is not necessary to number or actually count the population size. Thus it is very amenable to sampling a given percentage of a large population.

There are dangers inherent in using systematic sampling, however. If there is a hidden periodicity in the population, systematic sampling is an inefficient method of sampling. Suppose a sample is to be taken from an assembly line where every tenth item produced is defective. If we were to select a 10 percent systematic sample, we would either get 100 percent defective or zero percent defective, depending upon the random starting position.[1] If the population list is in random order in relation to what we are trying to measure, systematic sampling is equivalent to random sampling. If the list is in a monotonically increasing or decreasing relationship to the measured character, then systematic sampling is actually more precise than simple random sampling. In practice, when lists of the population are readily available but are of considerable length, systematic sampling tends to be used.

---

[1] Note, however, that the estimator is an unbiased predictor of P, since

$$(0.9)(0) + (0.1)(1.00) = 0.10.$$

Stratified Sampling

The precision of simple random sampling depends upon the homogeneity of the population and the sample size. If it is possible to divide the population into several subpopulations that are individually more homogeneous than the total population, stratified sampling is appropriate. The different subpopulations are called *strata*. The concept of stratified sampling is first to estimate the characteristics of each stratum separately and then combine them with proper weighting to estimate the characteristics of the total population. Since each stratum is more homogeneous than the total population, we are able to get more precise estimates for each stratum. By estimating more accurately each of the component parts we get a better estimate of the whole. For example, suppose that we are conducting a survey of market potential for a new product line. If we examine consumers with a broad range of incomes, we may expect to find a great disparity in opinions. Thus rather than simply select *n* potential consumers, it is more efficient to divide the sample frame into strata on the basis of income and then sample from within each income stratum. Besides yielding a better estimate of the population, stratified sampling results in more reliable detailed information, in this case a measure of the income effect on market potential.

Three problems remain to be resolved if a stratified sampling design is to be used: (a) How do we select the sample elements from each stratum? (b) How do we allocate the sample size to each stratum? (c) How do we select the strata? The first problem is easily resolved. The usual method for selection of elements is to select a simple random sample from each stratum. If systematic sampling is appropriate, it may be used instead of simple random selection.

The usual method of allocating the sample size is to sample proportionately from each stratum. That is, if P_i represents the proportion of the population included in stratum i, and n represents the total sample size, then the number of elements selected from stratum i is nP_i. Proportionate selection is most efficient when the cost of selecting an item is equal for each stratum, and the purpose of sampling is to estimate the population value of some characteristic. If the purpose of the stratified design is rather to compare the differences among the strata, then equal sample selection from each stratum would be more efficient even if the strata are of unequal sizes.

The third problem posed above is the most difficult to solve. The optimal division of the population would be to select strata which, in terms of precision, lead to elements being most homogeneous within each stratum and most heterogeneous between strata. Careful consideration, based on past experience and personal judgment, of the relationship between the characteristics of the population and the characteristics to be estimated are normally used to define the strata. In cases where it is not clear whether the choice of strata is appropriate, it is common to conduct a pilot study. The pilot study usually consists of taking small samples of equal size from each of the proposed strata and examining the variances within and among the possible stratifications to determine which, if any, stratification plan seems most efficient.

Cluster Sampling

In all the designs that we have discussed thus far, the elements selected were the individual elements to be studied. This requires the sampling frame to be a list of all the individual elements from which we could sample. However, it is often extremely expensive, time-consuming, or even impossible to construct such a list or to sample from such a list. It is sometimes more feasible to develop a sampling frame where the primary sampling units represent groups of elements rather than each individual element of the population. Selection of a primary sampling unit from such a frame, then, requires investigating all the elements clustered in that primary sampling unit. Such sample designs are called *cluster sampling*. The selection of clusters can be accomplished by either simple random sampling or systematic sampling. It is also common to use a stratified design, dividing the clustered primary sampling units into strata.

Consider the problem of estimating the percentage of switches in inventory that are defective. Assume that there currently are 10,000 switches in inventory, stored in 200 boxed lots of 50 each. Using a cluster sampling design, we would use the 200 boxes as the sample frame, and randomly select *n* boxes, the primary sampling units, and examine all the switches in each randomly selected box.

Another example of the use of cluster sampling would be for an investigation of banks in the United States. The individual element of interest would be a bank. It is conceivable that a population of all banks could be listed for a sampling frame and simple random sampling, systematic sampling, or stratified sampling could be undertaken. If the investigation involves only a short interview with each bank manager, however, it is quite likely that any of these designs would require a great amount of time for traveling between banks and allow relatively little time for interviewing. It would be more economical to build a sampling frame based on cities or some other geographic area, randomly to select areas, and then to interview all banks in the selected areas. Such cluster designs, where the primary sampling unit represents a cluster of units based on geographic area are distinguished as *area sampling*.

In general, cluster sampling is less precise than the previously mentioned sampling designs, because the elements within each cluster tend to be correlated and have about the same value. Thus there is not as much information in *n* observations within a cluster as there is in *n* randomly drawn observations. Because of the economic advantages of cluster sampling, however, it is often possible to more than offset this factor. For a given sampling cost, the number of observations that can be obtained if cluster sampling is used will normally be larger than if simple random sampling is used.

In general, the precision of cluster sampling can be increased by using a larger number of small clusters rather than a small number of large clusters. However, it usually is more economical to use the latter rather than the former, since more elements can be sampled for a given cost. Economics are especially large for area sampling. Hence, if we have a fixed dollar amount to spend on sampling, it is not always clear which will lead to better results.

Multistage Sampling

Let us return to the cluster sampling design discussed above for the selection of banks. Suppose that the primary sampling unit used in the sampling frame is states. After randomly selecting the initial primary units, rather than sample all banks in the state, we could construct a new sampling frame for each chosen state based on counties within the state. Then we could randomly select counties and interview all banks in the chosen counties. This would represent a two-stage sampling design with the ultimate sampling units being clusters of counties. If, instead of taking a census of all banks within the selected counties, we were randomly to sample banks from each selected county, we would have a three-stage sampling plan.

Multistage sampling is useful not only for area sampling. In drawing the sample of switches mentioned above, a two-stage plan could be used. That is, rather than examine all 50 switches in each selected box, a random or systematic sample could be drawn from each box initially selected.

There are two advantages of multistage sampling. First, it is easier to administer than most single-stage designs, since the sampling frame can be developed in partial units. For example, in the three-stage bank design, where we ultimately drew individual banks, it was necessary to construct a list of banks only for those counties that were selected in stage two. Moreover, we needed a list of counties only for those states that were selected in stage one. If we were to use a simple random design we would have had to compile a list of all banks in the United States and, if we used a cluster design with counties as primary sampling units, a list of all counties in the United States. Second, because of the sequential clustering, multistage sampling permits a larger number of units to be sampled for a given cost than do simple designs.

It is desirable for each of the cluster sampling units at each stage to have approximately the same number of elements. If they do not, it is appropriate to use a random selection process, where the probability of each cluster being included in the sample is proportional to the size of the cluster. Such a random selection process is discussed in the next section.

Sampling with Probability Proportional to Size

Suppose that we wish to select ten banks from 16 major cities. Exhibit 20–1 contains a hypothetical list of the 16 cities and the number of banks in each.

Exhibit 20–1 Hypothetical List of Selected Cities
and Sample of Ten with
Probability Proportional Size

City	Number of Banks	Cumulative Total	Sample	
New York	75	75	16	70
Philadelphia	38	113		
Boston	42	155	124	
Chicago	60	215	178	
Los Angeles	48	263	232	
Baltimore	18	281		
Pittsburgh	26	307	286	
Washington, D.C.	51	358	340	
Buffalo	13	371		
St. Louis	24	395	394	
New Orleans	16	411		
San Francisco	29	440	448	
Cleveland	23	463		
Milwaukee	20	483		
Detroit	31	514	502	
Dallas	28	542		

The first step in the procedure for sampling with probability proportional to cluster size is to list the number of elements in each cluster. Any method of ordering the cluster is acceptable. The next step is systematically to sample the appropriate number of elements from the cumulative totals. The actual numbers selected do not refer to individual elements, but rather indicate which clusters, and how many from the cluster, are to be selected by simple random or systematic sampling. In this illustration we have 542 banks, so the appropriate sampling interval is 54. Picking a random starting point, 16 in this case, we add successively increments of 54 until ten numbers have been selected. We next select randomly two banks from New York and one each from Boston, Chicago, Los Angeles, Pittsburgh, Washington, D.C., St. Louis, Cleveland, and Detroit. Often when we are using area sampling, rather than use the actual number of entities in each cluster, which may not be easily obtainable, population of the area is used.

The results of this method of sampling are equivalent to those of a simple random sample method, although it is clearly less cumbersome and less expensive to use.

THE SAMPLE SIZE PROBLEM

Probably the most frequent question asked of statisticians is, "What size sample should I take?" Unfortunately, this is also one of the most difficult questions to answer. There are two alternative approaches that can be taken to determine the sample size. The first is to specify the precision of estimation

374

desired and then to determine the sample size necessary to insure it. This is by far the most common procedure, chiefly because it is amenable to exact mathematical solution or approximation. This method has a serious defect, however, in that it does not rigorously analyze the cost of gathering the information or the expected value of the information. The second approach uses Bayesian statistics to weigh the cost of additional information against the expected value of the additional information. Though theoretically optimal, this approach is seldom used in practice because of the great difficulty in measuring the value of information.

The use of the specified precision method for two simple random sampling situations and an example of the Bayesian approach for a simplified situation are presented below.

Determining Sample Size when Estimating a Percentage

Suppose a simple random sample is to be drawn from a population of size N in order to estimate the percentage p of the population which has some characteristic. We could specify that we want the estimate of p to be within δ of the true value of p with probability α [i.e., $p(|\hat{p} - p| < \delta) \leq \alpha$, where $\hat{p}$ is the estimator of p]. The sample size n necessary to meet this constraint is

$$n = \frac{Z_\alpha^2 N p(1 - p)}{(N - 1)\delta^2 + Z_\alpha^2 p(1 - p)} \tag{20-1}$$

where Z_α represents that value such that the probability of a standard normal variable exceeding it is $(1 - \alpha)/2$. This value, for chosen α level, can be read directly from Exhibit F–6 in Appendix F.

A problem arises in using this formula, since n is a function of p, the unknown value we are trying to estimate. One conservative method of resolving the problem is to set $p = 0.5$, that value of p which maximizes n. Thus, regardless of the true value of p, the sample will yield at least the desired precision. A second approach is to make an initial estimate of p based on either personal judgment or the results of a pilot study. How much error is introduced by this procedure can not be determined, but it has been suggested that if the pilot study has a sample size of approximately 225 or more, the pilot values are a reasonable approximation of p for this purpose.

From Eq. (20–1), it follows that the necessary sample size increases as α increases and decreases as δ increases and as p varies from 0.5. If the population is infinite, Eq. (20–1) reduces to

$$n = \frac{Z_\alpha^2 p(1 - p)}{\delta^2} \tag{20-2}$$

Exhibit 20–2 presents the numerical results from Eq. (20–2) for selected values of δ and p for $\alpha = 95.5$ percent.

Exhibit 20–2 Minimum Sample Size n Required when Estimating p for Specified δ when the Population Is Infinite and α Is 95.5 Percent

δ	0.01 or 0.99	0.10 or 0.90	0.30 or 0.70	0.50
0.01	400	3600	8400	10,000
0.02	100	900	2100	2,500
0.03	44	400	934	1,112
0.04	25	225	525	625
0.05	16	144	336	400
0.10	4	36	84	100

Determining the Sample Size when Estimating an Average

Suppose that we are planning to select a simple random sample from a large population of size N in order to estimate the average value of some parameter of the population. Moreover, suppose that we specify that we desire the estimate of μ, the average parameter value, to be within δ of μ with probability α [i.e., $p(|\bar{x} - \mu| < \delta) \leq \alpha$]. The sample size necessary to do this is given by

$$n = \frac{Z_\alpha^2 N \sigma^2}{(N-1)\delta^2 + Z_\alpha^2 \sigma^2} \qquad (20\text{–}3)$$

Unfortunately, this formula requires knowledge of the variance of the population, which is never really known. Thus it is necessary to substitute for σ^2 an approximation based on either the results of a pilot study, past experience, or personal judgment.

If the population is infinite, Eq. (20–3) reduces to

$$n = \frac{Z_\alpha^2 \sigma^2}{\delta^2} \qquad (20\text{–}4)$$

Exhibit 20–3 presents the numerical results from Eq. (20–4) for selected values of δ and α. Since σ^2 equals 1 in the Exhibit, δ can be generalized to mean units of standard deviation.

Comments on Examples

It should be noted from Eqs. (20–2) and (20–4) that, in order to double the accuracy (half δ) for a fixed probability level, it is necessary to increase the sample size fourfold. Thus, extremely high levels of precision often require prohibitive sample sizes. In practice, an upper bound on the sample size is normally specified by the maximum amount of money available for the purpose of sampling.

Although the choice of α and δ in these procedures is arbitrary, it must be remembered that increasing the reliability of the estimates (i.e., increasing

Exhibit 20–3 Minimum Sample Size n Required when Estimating an Average for Specified α and δ when $\sigma^2 = 1$ (Infinite Population)

			α		
δ	99	97	95	92	90
0.1	656	480	384	310	272
0.2	164	120	96	76	68
0.3	78	52	43	34	30
0.4	41	30	24	19	17
0.5	26	19	15	12	11

α and/or δ) also increases the cost of obtaining the estimates and may not be justified. The ultimate purpose of using the estimates must be carefully considered to determine what level of precision is justifiable.

As a final warning, it is necessary to recall that we are only discussing control of sampling error. Although increasing n decreases the sampling error, it may also increase the systematic bias.

Determining the Sample Size Using the Bayesian Approach

Since precision of the sample estimate is an increasing function of the sample size, the expected value of the sample information, EVSI, is also an increasing function of n. Similarly, the cost of sampling is an increasing function of n. As demonstrated previously,[2] it is possible to compute the EVSI and ENG (expected net gain) for any given sample size. Moreover, in most cases the cost of taking a sample of a given size can be calculated (or reasonably approximated). Therefore, it follows that the optimal sample size, that value of n which maximizes the difference between the EVSI and the cost of the sample, can be determined.

Unfortunately, the usual procedure for finding the optimal value of n is to compute the EVSI for every possible n and compare it to the respective cost. This is normally a burdensome task and generally is feasible only with the aid of high-speed computers. Besides the difficulty of computation, a major stumbling block in using this approach is the inability (or lack of confidence) to formulate the opportunity loss table, which is necessary for calculating the EVSI.

[2] The groundwork for this analysis was laid in Chapter 4.

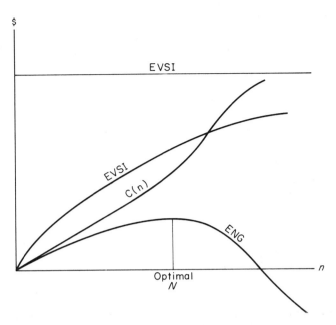

Illustration 20–1

Graphic Display of
Bayesian Sample Size
Selection

Illustration 20–1 shows graphically the general Bayesian approach for maximizing the ENG and thereby determining the optimal sample size.

PROBLEMS

1. What type of sampling might be used to estimate
   a. The weight of a group of men and women?
   b. Inventory losses due to breakage?
   (*Hint:* Are fragile items more likely to break than nonfragile?)
2. A sample of insurance executives is to be interviewed. It has been decided to use multistage sampling.
   a. What is the primary sampling unit?
   b. What is the second-stage unit?
3. What is the difference between systematic bias and random or sampling errors?
4. Identify the cause of systematic bias in the following three situations.
   a. A newspaper asks people to write letters expressing their attitude toward private industry.
   b. "I represent Silo's appliance store and want to ask you questions concerning the appliance store you prefer."
   c. "How well are you informed about politics?"
5. What is wrong with the wording of these two questions, specifically the choice of answers provided?
   a. "Profits are too high."
      (1) agree   (2) neutral   (3) disagree
   b. "During the last six months, in which department stores have you shopped?"
      (1) Gimbels   (2) Korvettes   (3) Wanamakers   (4) Strawbridge

6. Why are the following sampling frames inappropriate?
   a. The population is voters in the next election.
      The sampling frame consists of all people who voted in the last election.
   b. The population is people who watch Monday Night Football.
      The sampling frame consists of people attending professional football games.
   c. The population is people who use a certain detergent.
      The sampling frame consists of people who are shopping in Food Fair.

7. The following are the number of department stores in 12 cities: 33, 25, 22, 30, 40, 28, 32, 38, 27, 36, 20, and 29.
   a. If we want to select a sample of 20 stores using cities as clusters and selecting within clusters proportional to size, how many stores from each city should be chosen? (Use a starting point of 6.)
   b. If a simple random sample of size 3 is taken from the list, what is the probability that the city with 30 department stores will be included?

8. The following are an insurance company's claims for one day: $100, $500, $175, $900, $550, $1000, $125, $600, $150, and $950. List the possible systematic samples of size 3 that can be taken from this list. How many strata should there be?

9. We want to select 8 appliance stores from 10 major East Coast cities. Explain what sample design or designs might be used.

10. If we want to draw a simple random sample from a population of 4000 items, how large a sample do we need to draw if we desire to estimate the percent defective within 2 percent of the true value with 95.5 probability?

11. What would be the answer to Problem 10 if the population were infinite rather than 4000?

12. Suppose we plan to draw a simple random sample of cereal containers and estimate the true weight. In the past we have found the variance of weight to be 4 ounces. How large a sample should be drawn if we want our estimate to be within 0.8 ounces of the true average weight with probability 0.99.

APPENDICES

APPENDIX A

present value tables

It is a well-known fact that money has a time value; i.e., one would prefer a dollar today to a dollar a year from now. Therefore, if you are asked to forego the current use of your money (lend), you will expect to be paid for this sacrifice. Likewise, if you increase the amount of money you currently have at the expense of later periods (borrow), you will expect to have to pay for this privilege. The cost of money might be reflected through interest rates. If the demand for money is high relative to the supply, interest rates should be high and borrowing should become more expensive and lending more profitable. An alternative measure of the cost of money, however, and perhaps one more relevant to the individual firm, is the cost of capital. The cost of capital is discussed in Chapter 12.

Present value tables (Exhibits A–3 and A–4) are used to give decreasing weights to dollars to be received farther and farther in the future, so that cash flows that occur in different time periods can be put on a comparable basis. To better understand how present value tables are constructed and used, let us begin by first finding the future value of a sum of money to be invested today.

FUTURE VALUE OF A SINGLE SUM

If $100 is invested for one period at a return of 7 percent, we would have $107 after one period. This total is comprised of the initial $100 principal plus $7 in interest earned during the period. More generally, letting P_0 = amount initially invested, P_1 = accumulated amount after one period, and r = the rate of return earned during the period, we have

$$P_1 = P_0 + P_0 r = P_0(1 + r) \qquad (A\text{--}1)$$

Assuming that we let the investment ride for a second period, we have

$$P_2 = P_1(1 + r) = P_0(1 + r)^2 \qquad \text{(A-2)}$$

Likewise,

$$P_3 = P_2(1 + r) = P_0(1 + r)^3 \qquad \text{(A-3)}$$

and, more generally,

$$P_n = P_0(1 + r)^n \qquad \text{(A-4)}$$

Equation (A-4) gives the future value of an amount P_0 invested for n periods at a return of r per period. By dividing both sides by $(1 + r)^n$, we can rewrite Eq. (A-4) as

$$P_0 = \frac{P_n}{(1 + r)^n} = P_n \left[\frac{1}{(1 + r)^n} \right] \qquad \text{(A-5)}$$

PRESENT VALUE OF A SINGLE SUM

Equation (A-5) gives the *present value* of an amount P_n to be received n periods in the future discounted at a rate of r per period. The value of $1/(1 + r)^n$, the present value of one dollar to be received in n periods discounted at r percent, is given in Exhibit A-3. For example, the present value of $1.00 to be received in three periods discounted at 10 percent is $1.00[1/(1 + 0.10)^3] = 1.00(0.751) = 0.751$; the present value of $1.00 to be received in five periods discounted at 10 percent is $1.00[1/(1 + 0.10)^5] = 1.00(0.621) = 0.621$; the present value of $1.00 to be received in five periods discounted at 15 percent is $1.00[1/(1 + 0.15)^5] = 1.00(0.497) = 0.497$. It is seen that the present value decreases as (a) the time before the one dollar is to be received increases or (b) the discount rate increases.

The present value of any amount to be received in the future is simply the appropriate value from Exhibit A-3 times the amount. The present value of $100 to be received in three periods discounted at 10 percent is $100(0.751) = 75.10$; the present value of $500 to be received in five periods discounted at 10 percent is $500(0.621) = 310.50$; the present value of $200 to be received in five periods discounted at 15 percent is $200(0.497) = 99.40$.

PRESENT VALUE OF AN ANNUITY

Now suppose that $230 is to be received at the end of *each* of the next five periods. To find the present value of this stream of payments discounted at 8 percent, we could formulate the problem as shown in Exhibit A-1.

Exhibit A-1   Present Value Calculations

Year	Amount of Payment		Discount Factor		Present Value of Payment
1	$230	×	0.926	=	$212.98
2	230	×	0.857	=	197.11
3	230	×	0.794	=	182.62
4	230	×	0.735	=	169.05
5	230	×	0.681	=	156.63

Present value of stream of payments = $918.39

But the problem could alternatively have been set up as

$$\frac{230}{1 + 0.08} + \frac{230}{(1 + 0.08)^2} + \frac{230}{(1 + 0.08)^3} + \frac{230}{(1 + 0.08)^4} + \frac{230}{(1 + 0.08)^5}$$

$$= 230\left(\frac{1}{1 + 0.08} + \frac{1}{(1 + 0.08)^2} + \frac{1}{(1 + 0.08)^3} + \frac{1}{(1 + 0.08)^4} + \frac{1}{(1 + 0.08)^5}\right)$$

$$= 230 \sum_{i=1}^{5} \frac{1}{(1 + 0.08)^i}$$

$$= 230(0.926 + 0.857 + 0.794 + 0.735 + 0.681) = 230(3.993)$$

$$= \$918.39$$

Rather than perform five multiplications and one addition, it is more efficient to perform one addition and then one multiplication. This simplified procedure is possible because the stream of cash flows is an annuity—equal payments that occur at equal intervals of time. The present value of an annuity is given in Exhibit A-4. The table tells us that the present value of one dollar *per period* for five periods discounted at 8 percent is $3.993; the present value of $230 per period for five periods is $230 (3.993) = $918.39.

As illustrated in the above example, the values in Exhibit A-4 are obtained by the cumulative addition of the values in Exhibit A-3 (which give the present value of *single* payments). For example, the present value of an annuity of $1.00 per period for four periods discounted at 10 percent is, from Exhibit A-4, $3.170; i.e., $\sum_{i=1}^{4} 1/(1 + 0.10)^i = 3.170$. From Exhibit A-2, the present value of a single payment of $1.00 to be received at the end of five years discounted at 10 percent is $1/(1 + 0.10)^5 = 0.621$. Then the value of a five-year annuity must be

$$\sum_{i=1}^{5} \frac{1}{(1 + 0.10)^i} = \sum_{i=1}^{4} \frac{1}{(1 + 0.10)^i} + \frac{1}{(1 + 0.10)^5}$$

$$= 3.170 + 0.621 = 3.791$$

which is the value that can be read directly from Exhibit A-4.

The present value of a stream of payments of $120 per period for five periods discounted at 10 percent is $120(3.791) = $454.92. Alternatively, if $454.92 were invested now at an annual rate of return of 10 percent, we could withdraw $120 at the end of each of the next five periods and have a zero balance at the end. This example is illustrated in Exhibit A–2, where the final balance is $0.03 due to a small rounding error.

Exhibit A–2   Example of an Annuity

Period	1	2	3	4	5
Principal, beginning of period	$454.92	$380.41	$298.45	$208.29	$109.12
Interest earned during period	45.49	38.04	29.84	20.83	10.91
Value, end of period	500.41	418.45	328.29	229.12	120.03
Withdrawal	120.00	120.00	120.00	120.00	120.00
Principal, beginning of next period	380.41	298.45	208.29	109.12	0.03

As another example of the use of the present value tables, it should be seen that, if we use a discount rate of 12 percent, the present value of $125 per period in periods one through five, $200 per period in periods six through nine, and $500 in period ten can be alternatively set up as:

1. 125(3.605) + 200(5.328 − 3.605) + 500(0.322)

2. 125(5.328) + 75(5.328 − 3.605) + 500(0.322)

3. 200(5.650) − 75(3.605) + 300(0.322)

Other alternative formulations are also possible. All are numerically equivalent, and the choice of which formulation to use becomes largely a matter of convenience and personal preference.

Finally, suppose that a bond pays interest of $80 per year for 15 years and then returns a $1000 principal amount at the end of the fifteenth year. What bond price would give a yield to maturity of 10 percent? To find the price, both interest and principal payments have to be discounted at a 10 percent rate. Notice that the interest payments are an annuity and the principal payment is a single sum. Thus the bond price is $80(7.600) + $1000(0.239) = $847.48.[1] This is the price that an investor would pay to earn a yield of exactly 10 percent. If more than $847.48 is paid for the bond, the yield will be something less than 10 percent; if less than $847.48 is paid for the bond, the yield will be something more than 10 percent.

If a yield to maturity of only 6 percent is required, the bond price will be $80(9.712) + $1000(0.417) = $1193.96. Notice that as the required return (or discount rate) decreases, the bond price (or present value) increases.

[1] For simplicity, it is assumed that interest payments on the bond are made annually.

Exhibit A-3   Present Value of $1.00

Years Hence	1%	2%	4%	6%	8%	10%	12%	14%	15%	16%	18%	20%	22%	24%	25%	26%	28%	30%	35%	40%	45%	50%
1	0.990	0.980	0.962	0.943	0.926	0.909	0.893	0.877	0.870	0.862	0.847	0.833	0.820	0.806	0.800	0.794	0.781	0.769	0.741	0.714	0.690	0.667
2	0.980	0.961	0.925	0.890	0.857	0.826	0.797	0.769	0.756	0.743	0.718	0.694	0.672	0.650	0.640	0.630	0.610	0.592	0.549	0.510	0.476	0.444
3	0.971	0.942	0.889	0.840	0.794	0.751	0.712	0.675	0.658	0.641	0.609	0.579	0.551	0.524	0.512	0.500	0.477	0.455	0.406	0.364	0.328	0.296
4	0.961	0.924	0.855	0.792	0.735	0.683	0.636	0.592	0.572	0.552	0.516	0.482	0.451	0.423	0.410	0.397	0.373	0.350	0.301	0.260	0.226	0.198
5	0.951	0.906	0.822	0.747	0.681	0.621	0.567	0.519	0.497	0.476	0.437	0.402	0.370	0.341	0.328	0.315	0.291	0.269	0.223	0.186	0.156	0.132
6	0.942	0.888	0.790	0.705	0.630	0.564	0.507	0.456	0.432	0.410	0.370	0.335	0.303	0.275	0.262	0.250	0.227	0.207	0.165	0.133	0.108	0.088
7	0.933	0.871	0.760	0.665	0.583	0.513	0.452	0.400	0.376	0.354	0.314	0.279	0.249	0.222	0.210	0.198	0.178	0.159	0.122	0.095	0.074	0.059
8	0.923	0.853	0.731	0.627	0.540	0.467	0.404	0.351	0.327	0.305	0.266	0.233	0.204	0.179	0.168	0.157	0.139	0.123	0.091	0.068	0.051	0.039
9	0.914	0.837	0.703	0.592	0.500	0.424	0.361	0.308	0.284	0.263	0.225	0.194	0.167	0.144	0.134	0.125	0.108	0.094	0.067	0.048	0.035	0.026
10	0.905	0.820	0.676	0.558	0.463	0.386	0.322	0.270	0.247	0.227	0.191	0.162	0.137	0.116	0.107	0.099	0.085	0.073	0.050	0.035	0.024	0.017
11	0.896	0.804	0.650	0.527	0.429	0.350	0.287	0.237	0.215	0.195	0.162	0.135	0.112	0.094	0.086	0.079	0.066	0.056	0.037	0.025	0.017	0.012
12	0.887	0.788	0.625	0.497	0.397	0.319	0.257	0.208	0.187	0.168	0.137	0.112	0.092	0.076	0.069	0.062	0.052	0.043	0.027	0.018	0.012	0.008
13	0.879	0.773	0.601	0.469	0.368	0.290	0.229	0.182	0.163	0.145	0.116	0.093	0.075	0.061	0.055	0.050	0.040	0.033	0.020	0.013	0.008	0.005
14	0.870	0.758	0.577	0.442	0.340	0.263	0.205	0.160	0.141	0.125	0.099	0.078	0.062	0.049	0.044	0.039	0.032	0.025	0.015	0.009	0.006	0.003
15	0.861	0.743	0.555	0.417	0.315	0.239	0.183	0.140	0.123	0.108	0.084	0.065	0.051	0.040	0.035	0.031	0.025	0.020	0.011	0.006	0.004	0.002
16	0.853	0.728	0.534	0.394	0.292	0.218	0.163	0.123	0.107	0.093	0.071	0.054	0.042	0.032	0.028	0.025	0.019	0.015	0.008	0.005	0.003	0.002
17	0.844	0.714	0.513	0.371	0.270	0.198	0.146	0.108	0.093	0.080	0.060	0.045	0.034	0.026	0.023	0.020	0.015	0.012	0.006	0.003	0.002	0.001
18	0.836	0.700	0.494	0.350	0.250	0.180	0.130	0.095	0.081	0.069	0.051	0.038	0.028	0.021	0.018	0.016	0.012	0.009	0.005	0.002	0.001	0.001
19	0.828	0.686	0.475	0.331	0.232	0.164	0.116	0.083	0.070	0.060	0.043	0.031	0.023	0.017	0.014	0.012	0.009	0.007	0.003	0.002	0.001	
20	0.820	0.673	0.456	0.312	0.215	0.149	0.104	0.073	0.061	0.051	0.037	0.026	0.019	0.014	0.012	0.010	0.007	0.005	0.002	0.001	0.001	
21	0.811	0.660	0.439	0.294	0.199	0.135	0.093	0.064	0.053	0.044	0.031	0.022	0.015	0.011	0.009	0.008	0.006	0.004	0.002	0.001		
22	0.803	0.647	0.422	0.278	0.184	0.123	0.083	0.056	0.046	0.038	0.026	0.018	0.013	0.009	0.007	0.006	0.004	0.003	0.001	0.001		
23	0.795	0.634	0.406	0.262	0.170	0.112	0.074	0.049	0.040	0.033	0.022	0.015	0.010	0.007	0.006	0.005	0.003	0.002	0.001			
24	0.788	0.622	0.390	0.247	0.158	0.102	0.066	0.043	0.035	0.028	0.019	0.013	0.008	0.006	0.005	0.004	0.003	0.002	0.001			
25	0.780	0.610	0.375	0.233	0.146	0.092	0.059	0.038	0.030	0.024	0.016	0.010	0.007	0.005	0.004	0.003	0.002	0.001	0.001			
26	0.772	0.598	0.361	0.220	0.135	0.084	0.053	0.033	0.026	0.021	0.014	0.009	0.006	0.004	0.003	0.002	0.002	0.001				
27	0.764	0.586	0.347	0.207	0.125	0.076	0.047	0.029	0.023	0.018	0.011	0.007	0.005	0.003	0.002	0.002	0.001	0.001				
28	0.757	0.574	0.333	0.196	0.116	0.069	0.042	0.026	0.020	0.016	0.010	0.006	0.004	0.002	0.002	0.001	0.001	0.001				
29	0.749	0.563	0.321	0.185	0.107	0.063	0.037	0.022	0.017	0.014	0.008	0.005	0.003	0.002	0.002	0.001	0.001					
30	0.742	0.552	0.308	0.174	0.099	0.057	0.033	0.020	0.015	0.012	0.007	0.004	0.003	0.002	0.001	0.001	0.001					
40	0.672	0.453	0.208	0.097	0.046	0.022	0.011	0.005	0.004	0.003	0.001	0.001										
50	0.608	0.372	0.141	0.054	0.021	0.009	0.003	0.001	0.001	0.001												

Exhibit A–4 Present Value of $1.00 Received Annually for N Years

Years (N)	1%	2%	4%	6%	8%	10%	12%	14%	15%	16%	18%	20%	22%	24%	25%	26%	28%	30%	35%	40%	45%	50%
1	0.990	0.980	0.962	0.943	0.926	0.909	0.893	0.877	0.870	0.862	0.847	0.833	0.820	0.806	0.800	0.794	0.781	0.769	0.741	0.714	0.690	0.667
2	1.970	1.942	1.886	1.833	1.783	1.736	1.690	1.647	1.626	1.605	1.566	1.528	1.492	1.457	1.440	1.424	1.392	1.361	1.289	1.224	1.165	1.111
3	2.941	2.884	2.775	2.673	2.577	2.487	2.402	2.322	2.283	2.246	2.174	2.106	2.042	1.981	1.952	1.923	1.868	1.816	1.696	1.589	1.493	1.407
4	3.902	3.808	3.630	3.465	3.312	3.170	3.037	2.914	2.855	2.798	2.690	2.589	2.494	2.404	2.362	2.320	2.241	2.166	1.997	1.849	1.720	1.605
5	4.853	4.713	4.452	4.212	3.993	3.791	3.605	3.433	3.352	3.274	3.127	2.991	2.864	2.745	2.689	2.635	2.532	2.436	2.220	2.035	1.876	1.737
6	5.795	5.601	5.242	4.917	4.623	4.355	4.111	3.889	3.784	3.685	3.498	3.326	3.167	3.020	2.951	2.885	2.759	2.643	2.385	2.168	1.983	1.824
7	6.728	6.472	6.002	5.582	5.206	4.868	4.564	4.288	4.160	4.039	3.812	3.605	3.416	3.242	3.161	3.083	2.937	2.802	2.508	2.263	2.057	1.883
8	7.652	7.325	6.733	6.210	5.747	5.335	4.968	4.639	4.487	4.344	4.078	3.837	3.619	3.421	3.329	3.241	3.076	2.925	2.598	2.331	2.108	1.922
9	8.566	8.162	7.435	6.802	6.247	5.759	5.328	4.946	4.772	4.607	4.303	4.031	3.786	3.566	3.463	3.366	3.184	3.019	2.665	2.379	2.144	1.948
10	9.471	8.983	8.111	7.360	6.710	6.145	5.650	5.216	5.019	4.833	4.494	4.192	3.923	3.682	3.571	3.465	3.269	3.092	2.715	2.414	2.168	1.965
11	10.368	9.787	8.760	7.887	7.139	6.495	5.988	5.453	5.234	5.029	4.656	4.327	4.035	3.776	3.656	3.544	3.335	3.147	2.752	2.438	2.185	1.977
12	11.255	10.575	9.385	8.384	7.536	6.814	6.194	5.660	5.421	5.197	4.793	4.439	4.127	3.851	3.725	3.606	3.387	3.190	2.779	2.456	2.196	1.985
13	12.134	11.343	9.986	8.853	7.904	7.103	6.424	5.842	5.583	5.342	4.910	4.533	4.203	3.912	3.780	3.656	3.427	3.223	2.799	2.468	2.204	1.990
14	13.004	12.106	10.563	9.295	8.244	7.367	6.628	6.002	5.724	5.468	5.008	4.611	4.265	3.962	3.824	3.695	3.459	3.249	2.814	2.477	2.210	1.993
15	13.865	12.849	11.118	9.712	8.559	7.606	6.811	6.142	5.847	5.575	5.092	4.675	4.315	4.001	3.859	3.726	3.483	3.268	2.825	2.484	2.214	1.995
16	14.718	13.578	11.652	10.106	8.851	7.824	6.974	6.265	5.954	5.669	5.162	4.730	4.357	4.033	3.887	3.751	3.503	3.283	2.834	2.489	2.216	1.997
17	15.562	14.292	12.166	10.477	9.122	8.022	7.120	6.373	6.047	5.749	5.222	4.775	4.391	4.059	3.910	3.771	3.518	3.295	2.840	2.492	2.218	1.998
18	16.398	14.992	12.659	10.828	9.372	8.201	7.250	6.467	6.128	5.818	5.273	4.812	4.419	4.080	3.928	3.786	3.529	3.304	2.844	2.494	2.219	1.999
19	17.226	15.678	13.134	11.158	9.604	8.365	7.366	6.550	6.198	5.877	5.316	4.844	4.442	4.097	3.942	3.799	3.539	3.311	2.848	2.496	2.220	1.999
20	18.046	16.351	13.590	11.470	9.818	8.514	7.469	6.623	6.259	5.929	5.353	4.870	4.460	4.110	3.954	3.808	3.546	3.316	2.850	2.497	2.221	1.999
21	18.857	17.011	14.029	11.764	10.017	8.649	7.562	6.687	6.312	5.973	5.384	4.891	4.476	4.121	3.963	3.816	3.551	3.320	2.852	2.498	2.221	2.000
22	19.660	17.658	14.451	12.042	10.201	8.772	7.645	6.743	6.359	6.011	5.410	4.909	4.488	4.130	3.970	3.822	3.556	3.323	2.853	2.498	2.222	2.000
23	20.456	18.292	14.857	12.303	10.371	8.883	7.718	6.792	6.399	6.044	5.432	4.925	4.499	4.137	3.976	3.827	3.559	3.325	2.854	2.499	2.222	2.000
24	21.243	18.914	15.247	12.550	10.529	8.985	7.784	6.835	6.434	6.073	5.451	4.937	4.507	4.143	3.981	3.831	3.562	3.327	2.855	2.499	2.222	2.000
25	22.023	19.523	15.622	12.783	10.675	9.077	7.843	6.873	6.464	6.097	5.467	4.948	4.514	4.147	3.985	3.834	3.564	3.329	2.856	2.499	2.222	2.000
26	22.795	20.121	15.983	13.003	10.810	9.161	7.896	6.906	6.491	6.118	5.480	4.956	4.520	4.151	3.988	3.837	3.566	3.330	2.856	2.500	2.222	2.000
27	23.560	20.707	16.330	13.211	10.935	9.237	7.943	6.935	6.514	6.136	5.492	4.964	4.524	4.154	3.990	3.839	3.567	3.331	2.857	2.500	2.222	2.000
28	24.316	21.281	16.663	13.406	11.051	9.307	7.984	6.961	6.534	6.152	5.502	4.970	4.528	4.157	3.992	3.840	3.568	3.331	2.857	2.500	2.222	2.000
29	25.066	21.844	16.984	13.591	11.158	9.370	8.022	6.983	6.551	6.166	5.510	4.975	4.531	4.159	3.994	3.841	3.569	3.332	2.857	2.500	2.222	2.000
30	25.808	22.396	17.292	13.765	11.258	9.427	8.055	7.003	6.566	6.177	5.517	4.979	4.534	4.160	3.995	3.842	3.569	3.332	2.857	2.500	2.222	2.000
40	32.835	27.355	19.793	15.046	11.925	9.779	8.244	7.105	6.642	6.234	5.548	4.997	4.544	4.166	3.999	3.846	3.571	3.333	2.857	2.500	2.222	2.000
50	39.196	31.424	21.482	15.762	12.234	9.915	8.304	7.133	6.661	6.246	5.554	4.999	4.545	4.167	4.000	3.846	3.571	3.333	2.857	2.500	2.222	2.000

PROBLEMS

1. Find the present value of $825 (a) to be received in five years discounted at 8 percent; (b) to be received in three years discounted at 8 percent; (c) to be received in three years discounted at 6 percent.

2. Using Exhibit A–3, find the future value of (a) $100 to be invested for four years at 10 percent; (b) $250 to be invested for 10 years at 15 percent; (c) $75 to be invested for seven years at 12 percent.

3. Find the present value of $200 to be received in two years discounted at an annual rate of 8 percent, assuming that discounting is done (a) annually; (b) semi-annually; (c) quarterly. What generalization can you make from your results? What would you expect to find if you calculated the future value by compounding (a) annually; (b) semi-annually; (c) quarterly; (d) continuously?

4. Find the present value of the following cash flows, assuming that all payments are received at the end of each period and are discounted at 12 percent. Try setting the problems up in different ways.

	a	b	c	d	e
Year 1	$420	$400	$820	$1000	$1000
Year 2	420	400	820	1000	1000
Year 3	420	400	820	1000	1000
Year 4	420	400	820	1000	1000
Year 5	420	0	420	1000	1000
Year 6	420	0	420	600	1600
Year 7	420	0	420	600	1600
Year 8	420	0	420	600	1600

5. How would you find the present value of the cash flows in Problem 4 if payments are assumed to be received at the *beginning*, rather than the end, of each period?

6. Using a discount rate of 8 percent, find the present value of (a) $70 at the end of each of the next 12 years plus $1000 at the end of the twelfth year; (b) $70 at the end of each of the next 20 years plus $1000 at the end of the twentieth year. (c) Repeat (a) and (b), using $80 per year instead of $70; (d) Repeat (a) and (b), using $90 per year instead of $70. Discuss your results.

7. **a.** Assume that $750 is to be received in four years. What is the present value of this cash receipt if (i) a discount rate of 10 percent is used for years 1 and 2 while a discount rate of 15 percent is used for years 3 and 4; and if (ii) the 15 percent rate is used for the first two years and the 10 percent rate is used for the last two years? Compare your results.

   b. Assume that $570 is to be received at the end of *each* of the next four years. Repeat (i) and (ii) as above for this stream of payments and again compare your results.

APPENDIX B

exponential functions, power functions, and logarithms

EXPONENTIAL FUNCTIONS

An algebraic expression of the general form $y = f(x) = a^x$ is called an exponential function. In this expression, x is the independent variable, y is the dependent variable (i.e., the value of y is dependent upon the given value of x), and the base a is some constant. The numerical value of the base a must be positive and not equal to one. The value of x can assume any value from minus to plus infinity. Since a is positive, y will always be positive. If x equals zero, y will equal one regardless of the value of a (i.e., $a^0 = 1$). As shown in Illustration B–1, the value of y will increase as x increases if a is greater than one and will decrease as x increases if a is less than one.

Exponential expressions can be used to represent various kinds of relationships between x and y. A fractional exponent indicates that the functional relationship involves some root of the base number a. Thus $a^{1/2} = \sqrt{a}$, the square root of a; $a^{1/3} = \sqrt[3]{a}$, the cube root of a; and so on. A negative exponent indicates an inverse relationship. For example, $a^{-2} = 1/a^2$; $a^{-5} = 1/a^5$; $a^{-1/2} = 1/\sqrt{a}$.

An exponent clearly can be a convenient way of expressing a more complicated functional relationship. In general, the exponent simply tells the number of times the base number is multiplied by itself. Thus $a^4 = a \cdot a \cdot a \cdot a$. From this basic fact, many of the fundamental rules regarding exponential functions can be demonstrated.

While a can have any positive value other than one, by far the most commonly used base for exponential expressions is the irrational number denoted by e ($= 2.71828\ldots$), where $y = e^x$. In fact, general reference to an

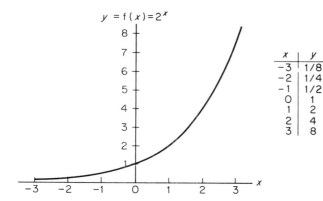

$y = f(x) = 2^x$

x	y
-3	1/8
-2	1/4
-1	1/2
0	1
1	2
2	4
3	8

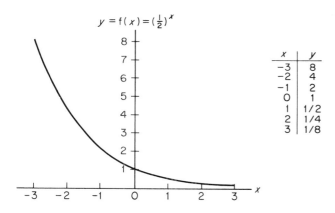

$y = f(x) = (\tfrac{1}{2})^x$

x	y
-3	8
-2	4
-1	2
0	1
1	1/2
2	1/4
3	1/8

General Rule	**Examples**
1. $a^x \cdot a^z = a^{x+z}$	1a. $a^2 \cdot a^3 = a^5$
	1b. $6^2 \cdot 6^3 = 6^5$
	1c. $(\tfrac{1}{3})^4 \cdot (\tfrac{1}{3})^2 = (\tfrac{1}{3})^6$
2. $a^x \cdot a^{-z} = a^{x-z}$	2a. $a^5 \cdot a^{-3} = a^5/a^3 = a^2$
	2b. $7^4 \cdot 7^{-7} = 7^{-3}$
	2c. $h^4 \cdot h^{-4} = h^4/h^4 = h^0 = 1$
3. $(a^x)^z = a^{xz}$	3a. $(a^3)^2 = (a \cdot a \cdot a)^2 = (a \cdot a \cdot a)(a \cdot a \cdot a) = a^6$
	3b. $(\sqrt{e})^3 = (e^{1/2})^3 = e^{3/2}$
	3c. $(10^{1/2})^2 = 10$

"exponential function" generally implies an exponential expression with base e. Despite the distress that sometimes accompanies an initial introduction to the irrational number e, it should not be any more mystifying than the more familiar irrational number π ($= 3.1416 \ldots$). By way of encouragement, e has several useful mathematical properties that more than compensate

391

for any temporary discomfort its introduction may cause. We shall use e later in this Appendix and again in Appendix E.[1]

Let us consider a very practical application of an exponential function. From Appendix A, we know that the present value of $100 to be received five years from now, discounted annually at 10 percent, is equal to $100/(1 + 0.10)^5 = 100(0.621) = \$62.10$. The present value of that same $100, discounted semi-annually, would be $100/(1 + 0.05)^{10} = 100(0.614) = \$61.40$. We see that discounting more frequently, at the same nominal *annual* rate, decreases the present value. In general, $PV = 100(1 + 0.10/n)^{5n}$, where n is the number of discounting periods per year. At the extreme, n could approach infinity so we would be approaching continuous discounting. While use of the above expression becomes impractical as n gets very large, continuous discounting can be performed using exponential expressions. The general notation is $PV = e^{-rt}$, where r is the periodic rate and t is the number of periods. (The negative exponent indicates discounting. A positive exponent, e^{rt}, indicates continuous compounding.) Thus the present value of $100 to be received in five years, discounted continuously at an annual rate of 10 percent, is $\$100 \cdot e^{-rt} = 100 \cdot e^{-0.10(5)} = 100e^{-0.5} = 100(0.6065) = \$60.65$.

Finally, exponential functions are not restricted to the simple form $y = a^x$. Other more complex relationships, such as $y = a^{3x}$, $y = b^{5x^2}$, and $y = d^{\log x}$ are also exponential functions.

POWER FUNCTIONS

An algebraic expression of the general form $y = f(x) = x^a$ is called a power function, where x is the independent variable and a can be any real number. A more complete variation of the above expression might be $y = ax^2 + bx + c$. This is the general form of the frequently encountered quadratic equation. It could also be called a second-degree equation. The degree of the equation specifies the highest exponent in the equation. Thus $y = ax^3 + bx^2 + cx + d$ is a third-degree equation. A first-degree equation, $y = ax + b$, is simply a linear equation.

Whereas y was restricted to positive values only in an exponential expression, it can assume either positive or negative values in a power function. Consider, for example, the quadratic equation $y = 2x^2 - 6x - 4$. y is negative for values of x close to zero and becomes positive for large positive or negative values of x. A few (x, y) values are given below.

x	-3	-2	-1	0	1	2	3	4	5	6
y	32	16	4	-4	-8	-8	-4	4	16	32

[1] For future reference, and for the curious, the mathematical definition of e is

$$e = \lim_{n \to \infty} \left(1 + \frac{1}{n}\right)^n$$

As an example of the use of power functions, suppose that the management of a small one-product plant is able to use historic data to determine an average daily cost curve of the approximate form $AC = 0.8Q^2 - 48Q + 1000$ (where AC = average daily cost and Q = number of units produced per day). Let us also suppose that this equation reasonably represents actual average costs only between 15 and 40 units. The equation will underestimate average costs below 15 units and overestimate above 40 units. The firm's daily volume is typically between 15 and 40 units, however. From this equation, the firm could determine that average cost per unit declines until 30 units are produced per day; beyond that point average cost will increase with each additional unit produced (see Appendix E). The firm could also find that, given that it has produced Q units, the marginal cost of producing one more unit would be $2.4Q^2 - 96Q + 1000$ (again see Appendix E).

Another use of power functions would be for learning curves, which are of the general form $y = ax^b$ (where $a > 0$ and $-1 \leq b \leq 0$). Learning curves are useful in industries that must frequently produce new or redesigned products, such as aerospace, durable goods, electronics, etc. They are based on past observations that, as a worker gains more experience on a job, he becomes more efficient. Learning curves are typically identified by the learning rate. An 80 percent learning curve means that when the number of units produced is doubled, the labor hours per unit should be 80 percent of the current level. That is, an 80 percent learning curve means that the second unit produced should require 80 percent as much labor cost as the first; the fourth should require 80 percent as much labor cost as the second, the eighth, 80 percent the cost of the fourth; and so on. Since the exponent b is the learning rate, it follows that $2^b = 0.8$. Solving, we obtain $b = -0.3219$. Hence, for an 80 percent learning curve, $y = ax^{-0.3219}$.

In the general learning curve $y = ax^b$, y is the average labor hours per unit given x, x is the cumulative number of units produced, a is the labor cost of producing the first unit, and the exponent b reflects the learning rate. Once the parameters of a learning curve are determined (and they tend to be fairly stable for given product classifications), the curve can be used for forecasting labor costs, scheduling and budgeting, control, etc.

LOGARITHMS

Let us return to our consideration of exponential functions. The expression $y = a^x$ can be rewritten $x = \log_a y$, which is read x = the log (short for logarithm) to the base a of y. Both conventions represent the same relationship and convey the same information.

Logarithms have the following basic properties.

1. The base a must be positive, and not equal to one.
2. Only positive numbers have logarithms; thus y can never equal zero or be negative.

3. If it is assumed that $a > 1$, as is generally, but not necessarily always, the case:
   a. $x > 1$ if $y > a$
   b. $x = 1$ if $y = a$
   c. $x < 1$ if $y < a$
   d. $x = 0$ if $y = 0$
   e. $x < 0$ if $y < 1$

In a logarithmic expression, x is the log to the base a of y if x is the power to which the number a must be raised so that $a^x = y$. In other words, given some positive number a, not equal to one, the unique number x associated with each positive number y such that $y = f(x) = a^x$ is called the logarithm of y. A logarithm, then, is nothing more than an exponent. Just as in exponential form $y = f(x) = a^x$, y is a function of x, so in logarithmic form $x = g(y) = \log_a y$, x is a function of y. A few examples follow: if $100 = 10^2$, $\log_{10} 100 = 2$; if $4^2 = 16$, $\log_4 16 = 2$; if $y = b^z$, $\log_b y = z$.

There are certain basic rules that apply to logarithmic relationships:

1. $\log_a (U \cdot V) = \log_a U + \log_a V$
2. $\log_a (U/V) = \log_a U - \log_a V$
3. $\log_a (U^k) = k \log_a U$
4. $\log_a (b^x) = x \log_a b$

Although a can take on an infinite number of values, the two most commonly used are 10 and e. Logarithms to the base 10 are called *common logarithms*. Logarithms to the base e are called *natural logarithms*. The natural log of y is generally indicated by $\ln y$. Tables of common and natural logarithm values (Exhibits B–1 and B–2) are generally included in any collection of mathematical tables.

The following examples illustrate the use of logarithms (and the importance of knowing how to work with exponents).

Example 1 Express $\log_{10} \left(\dfrac{x}{y} \right) = y - 3$ in terms of $x = f(y)$.

If $\log_{10} \dfrac{x}{y} = y - 3$, then

$$\frac{x}{y} = 10^{y-3} = (10^y)(10^{-3}) = \frac{10^y}{10^3}$$
$$y \cdot 10^y = 10^3 \cdot x = 1000x$$
$$x = \frac{y \cdot 10^y}{1000}$$

Example 2 Express $w = \dfrac{x^{1/2} z^3}{y^2}$ in terms of logs.

$$\log w = \tfrac{1}{2} \log x + 3 \log z - 2 \log y$$

Example 3 Given $\log y = \log u + \frac{1}{3}\log v + 2(\log x + \log v) - (\log 3 + 4\log w)$, express $y = f(u, v, w, x)$.

$$\log y = \log u + \log v^{1/3} + 2(\log xv) - \log 3w^4$$

$$y = \frac{u(v)^{1/3}(xv)^2}{3w^4}$$

Example 4 Express $y = (x + 4)^{3z}$ in terms of logs.

$$\log y = 3z \log (x + 4)$$

Example 5 Express $y = e^{3x}$ in terms of natural logs.

$$\ln y = 3x \ln e = 3x \quad (\ln e = 1)$$

A major advantage of working with logarithms is that it is sometimes possible to transform a nonlinear exponential function into linear logarithmic form. The exponential function $y = ab^x$ can be rewritten $\log y = \log a + x \log b$. Very simple power functions, such as $y = x^3$, can also be expressed linearly with logarithms ($\log y = 3 \log x$) if x is restricted to positive values.

Rewriting the general learning curve $y = ax^b$ in terms of logs, we get $\log y = \log a + b \log x$. From this linear form, and given previous values of x and y, we can easily obtain estimates of a and b. Suppose that a is 150 hours and $b = -0.3219$ ($y = 150x^{-0.3219}$) and we want to know the average labor hours per unit for $x = 100$ units. We want to find $y = 150(100)^{-0.3219}$, which is more easily solved by finding $\log y = \log 150 - 0.3219 \log 100 = 2.1761 - 0.3219(2) = 1.5323$. If $\log y = 1.5323$, we can find from Exhibit B–1 that $y = 34.1$.

The advantage of taking the logarithm of a simple power function is that a nonlinear, increasing rate of change can be expressed in linear form. For example, consider $y = x^3$ and its log transformation, $\log_2 y = 3 \log_2 x$. From the (x, y) and $(\log_2 x, \log_2 y)$ values given below, we see that y increases much more rapidly than x, while $\log_2 y$ increases proportionately with $\log_2 x$ by a factor of three.

x	1	2	4	8	16
y	1	8	64	512	4096
$\log_2 x$	0	1	2	3	4
$\log_2 y$	0	3	6	9	12

Exhibit B–1   Logarithms

N	0	1	2	3	4	5	6	7	8	9
10	0000	0043	0086	0128	0170	0212	0253	0294	0334	0374
11	0414	0453	0492	0531	0569	0607	0645	0682	0719	0755
12	0792	0828	0864	0899	0934	0969	1004	1038	1072	1106
13	1139	1173	1206	1239	1271	1303	1335	1367	1399	1430
14	1461	1492	1523	1553	1584	1614	1644	1673	1703	1732
15	1761	1790	1818	1847	1875	1903	1931	1959	1987	2014
16	2041	2068	2095	2122	2148	2175	2201	2227	2253	2279
17	2304	2330	2355	2380	2405	2430	2455	2480	2504	2529
18	2553	2577	2601	2625	2648	2672	2695	2718	2742	2765
19	2788	2810	2833	2856	2878	2900	2923	2945	2967	2989
20	3010	3032	3054	3075	3096	3118	3139	3160	3181	3201
21	3222	3243	3263	3284	3304	3324	3345	3365	3385	3404
22	3424	3444	3464	3483	3502	3522	3541	3560	3579	3598
23	3617	3636	3655	3674	3692	3711	3729	3747	3766	3784
24	3802	3820	3838	3856	3874	3892	3909	3927	3945	3962
25	3979	3997	4014	4031	4048	4065	4082	4099	4116	4133
26	4150	4166	4183	4200	4216	4232	4249	4265	4281	4298
27	4314	4330	4346	4362	4378	4393	4409	4425	4440	4456
28	4472	4487	4502	4518	4533	4548	4564	4579	4594	4609
29	4624	4639	4654	4669	4683	4698	4713	4728	4742	4757
30	4771	4786	4800	4814	4829	4843	4857	4871	4886	4900
31	4914	4928	4942	4955	4969	4983	4997	5011	5024	5038
32	5051	5065	5079	5092	5105	5119	5132	5145	5159	5172
33	5185	5198	5211	5224	5237	5250	5263	5276	5289	5302
34	5315	5328	5340	5353	5366	5378	5391	5403	5416	5428
35	5441	5453	5465	5478	5490	5502	5514	5527	5539	5551
36	5563	5575	5587	5599	5611	5623	5635	5647	5658	5670
37	5682	5694	5705	5717	5729	5740	5752	5763	5775	5786
38	5798	5809	5821	5832	5843	5855	5866	5877	5888	5899
39	5911	5922	5933	5944	5955	5966	5977	5988	5999	6010
40	6021	6031	6042	6053	6064	6075	6085	6096	6107	6117
41	6128	6138	6149	6160	6170	6180	6191	6201	6212	6222
42	6232	6243	6253	6263	6274	6284	6294	6304	6314	6325
43	6335	6345	6355	6365	6375	6385	6395	6405	6415	6425
44	6435	6444	6454	6464	6474	6484	6493	6503	6513	6522
45	6532	6542	6551	6561	6571	6580	6590	6599	6609	6618
46	6628	6637	6646	6656	6665	6675	6684	6693	6702	6712
47	6721	6730	6739	6749	6758	6767	6776	6785	6794	6803
48	6812	6821	6830	6839	6848	6857	6866	6875	6884	6893
49	6902	6911	6920	6928	6937	6946	6955	6964	6972	6981
50	6990	6998	7007	7016	7024	7033	7042	7050	7059	7067
51	7076	7084	7093	7101	7110	7118	7126	7135	7143	7152
52	7160	7168	7177	7185	7193	7202	7210	7218	7226	7235
53	7243	7251	7259	7267	7275	7284	7292	7300	7308	7316
54	7324	7332	7340	7348	7356	7364	7372	7380	7388	7396

From John E. Freund, *Modern Elementary Statistics*, 4th ed. (Englewood Cliffs, N.J.: Prentice-Hall, 1973). By permission of the publisher.

Exhibit B-2 Natural or Naperian Logarithms

N	0	1	2	3	4	5	6	7	8	9
0.00	− ∞	−6‡ .90776	−6 .21461	−5 .80914	−5 .52146	−5 .29832	−5 .11000	−4 .96185	−4 .82831	−4 .71053
.01	−4.60517	.50986	.42285	.34281	.26870	.19971	.13517	.07454	.01738	*.96332
.02	−3.91202	.86323	.81671	.77226	.72970	.68888	.64966	.61192	.57555	.54046
.03	.50656	.47377	.44202	.41125	.38139	.35241	.32424	.29684	.27017	.24419
.04	.21888	.19418	.17009	.14656	.12357	.10109	.07911	.05761	:03655	.01593
.05	−2.99573	.97593	.95651	.93746	.91877	.90042	.88240	.86470	.84731	.83022
.06	.81341	.79688	.78062	.76462	.74887	.73337	.71810	.70306	.68825	.67365
.07	.65926	.64508	.63109	.61730	.60369	.59027	.57702	.56395	.55105	.53831
.08	.52573	.51331	.50104	.48891	.47694	.46510	.45341	.44185	.43042	.41912
.09	.40795	.39690	.38597	.37516	.36446	.35388	.34341	.33304	.32279	.31264
0.10	−2.30259	.29263	.28278	.27303	.26336	.25379	.24432	.23493	.22562	.21641
.11	.20727	.19823	.18926	.18037	.17156	.16282	.15417	.14558	.13707	.12863
.12	.12026	.11196	.10373	.09557	.08747	.07944	.07147	.06357	.05573	.04794
.13	.04022	.03256	.02495	.01741	.00992	.00248	*.99510	*.98777	*.98050	*.97328
.14	−1.96611	.95900	.95193	.94491	.93794	.93102	.92415	.91732	.91054	.90381
.15	.89712	.89048	.88387	.87732	.87080	.86433	.85790	.85151	.84516	.83885
.16	.83258	.82635	.82016	.81401	.80789	.80181	.79577	.78976	.78379	.77786
.17	.77196	.76609	.76026	.75446	.74870	.74297	.73727	.73161	.72597	.72037
.18	.71480	.70926	.70375	.69827	.69282	.68740	.68201	.67665	.67131	.66601
.19	.66073	.65548	.65026	.64507	.63990	.63476	.62964	.62455	.61949	.61445
0.20	−1.60944	.60445	.59949	.59455	.58964	.58475	.57988	.57504	.57022	.56542
.21	.56065	.55590	.55117	.54646	.54178	.53712	.53248	.52786	.52326	.51868
.22	.51413	.50959	.50508	.50058	.49611	.49165	.48722	.48281	.47841	.47403
.23	.46968	.46534	.46102	.45672	.45243	.44817	.44392	.43970	.43548	.43129
.24	.42712	.42296	.41882	.41469	.41059	.40650	.40242	.39837	.39433	.39030
.25	.38629	.38230	.37833	.37437	.37042	.36649	.36258	.35868	.35480	.35093
.26	.34707	.34323	.33941	.33560	.33181	.32803	.32426	.32051	.31677	.31304
.27	.30933	.30564	.30195	.29828	.29463	.29098	.28735	.28374	.28013	.27654
.28	.27297	.26940	.26585	.26231	.25878	.25527	.25176	.24827	.24479	.24133
.29	.23787	.23443	.23100	.22758	.22418	.22078	.21740	.21402	.21066	.20731
0.30	−1.20397	.20065	.19733	.19402	.19073	.18744	.18417	.18091	.17766	.17441
.31	.17118	.16796	.16475	.16155	.15836	.15518	.15201	.14885	.14570	.14256
.32	.13943	.13631	.13320	.13010	.12701	.12393	.12086	.11780	.11474	.11170
.33	.10866	.10564	.10262	.09961	.09661	.09362	.09064	.08767	.08471	.08176
.34	.07881	.07587	.07294	.07002	.06711	.06421	.06132	.05843	.05555	.05268
.35	−1.04982	.04697	.04412	.04129	.03846	.03564	.03282	.03002	.02722	.02443
.36	.02165	.01888	.01611	.01335	.01060	.00786	.00512	.00239	*.99967	*.99696
.37	−0.99425	.99155	.98886	.98618	.98350	.98083	.97817	.97551	.97286	.97022
.38	.96758	.96496	.96233	.95972	.95711	.95451	.95192	.94933	.94675	.94418
.39	.94161	.93905	.93649	.93395	.93140	.92887	.92634	.92382	.92130	.91879
0.40	−0.91629	.91379	.91130	.90882	.90634	.90387	.90140	.89894	.89649	.89404
.41	.89160	.88916	.88673	.88431	.88189	.87948	.87707	.87467	.87227	.86988
.42	.86750	.86512	.86275	.86038	.85802	.85567	.85332	.85097	.84863	.84630
.43	.84397	.84165	.83933	.83702	.83471	.83241	.83011	.82782	.82554	.82326
.44	.82098	.81871	.81645	.81419	.81193	.80968	.80744	.80520	.80296	.80073
.45	.79851	.79629	.79407	.79186	.78966	.78746	.78526	.78307	.78089	.77871
.46	.77653	.77436	.77219	.77003	.76787	.76572	.76357	.76143	.75929	.75715
.47	.75502	.75290	.75078	.74866	.74655	.74444	.74234	.74024	.73814	.73605
.48	.73397	.73189	.72981	.72774	.72567	.72361	.72155	.71949	.71744	.71539
.49	.71335	.71131	.70928	.70725	.70522	.70320	.70118	.69917	.69716	.69515

From Robert L. Childress, *Calculus for Business and Economics* (Englewood Cliffs, N.J.: Prentice-Hall, 1972). By permission of the publisher.

N	0	1	2	3	4	5	6	7	8	9
0.50	−0.69315	.69115	.68916	.68717	.68518	.68320	.68122	.67924	.67727	.67531
.51	.67334	.67139	.66934	.66748	.66553	.66359	.66165	.65971	.65778	.65585
.52	.65393	.65201	.65009	.64817	.64626	.64436	.64245	.64055	.63866	.63677
.53	.63488	.63299	.63111	.62923	.62736	.62549	.62362	.62176	.61990	.61804
.54	.61619	.61434	.61249	.61065	.60881	.60697	.60514	.60331	.60148	.59966
.55	.59784	.59602	.59421	.59240	.59059	.58879	.58699	.58519	.58340	.58161
.56	.57982	.57803	.57625	.57448	.57270	.57093	.56916	.56740	.56563	.56387
.57	.56212	.56037	.55862	.55687	.55513	.55339	.55165	.54991	.54818	.54645
.58	.54473	.54300	.54128	.53957	.53785	.53614	.53444	.53273	.53103	.52933
.59	.52763	.52594	.52425	.52256	.52088	.51919	.51751	.51584	.51416	.51249
0.60	−0.51083	.50916	.50750	.50584	.50418	.50253	.50088	.49923	.49758	.49594
.61	.49430	.49266	.49102	.48939	.48776	.48613	.48451	.48289	.48127	.47965
.62	.47804	.47642	.47482	.47321	.47160	.47000	.46840	.46681	.46522	.46362
.63	.46204	.46045	.45887	.45728	.45571	.45413	.45256	.45099	.44942	.44785
.64	.44629	.44473	.44317	.44161	.44006	.43850	.43696	.43541	.43386	.43232
.65	.43078	.42925	.42771	.42618	.42465	.42312	.42159	.42007	.41855	.41703
.66	.41552	.41400	.41249	.41098	.40947	.40797	.40647	.40497	.40347	.40197
.67	.40048	.39899	.39750	.39601	.39453	.39304	.39156	.39008	.38861	.38713
.68	.38566	.38419	.38273	.38126	.37980	.37834	.37688	.37542	.37397	.37251
.69	.37106	.36962	.36817	.36673	.36528	.36384	.36241	.36097	.35954	.35810
0.70	−0.35667	.35525	.35382	.35240	.35098	.34956	.34814	.34672	.34531	.34390
.71	.34249	.34108	.33968	.33827	.33687	.33547	.33408	.33268	.33129	.32989
.72	.32850	.32712	.32573	.32435	.32296	.32158	.32021	.31883	.31745	.31608
.73	.31471	.31334	.31197	.31061	.30925	.30788	.30653	.30517	.30381	.30246
.74	.30111	.29975	.29841	.29706	.29571	.29437	.29303	.29169	.29035	.28902
.75	.28768	.28635	.28502	.28369	.28236	.28104	.27971	.27839	.27707	.27575
.76	.27444	.27312	.27181	.27050	.26919	.26788	.26657	.26527	.26397	.26266
.77	.26136	.26007	.25877	.25748	.25618	.25489	.25360	.25231	.25103	.24974
.78	.24846	.24718	.24590	.24462	.24335	.24207	.24080	.23953	.23826	.23699
.79	.23572	.23446	.23319	.23193	.23067	.22941	.22816	.22690	.22565	.22439
0.80	−0.22314	.22189	.22065	.21940	.21816	.21691	.21567	.21433	.21319	.21196
.81	.21072	.20949	.20825	.20702	.20579	.20457	.20334	.20212	.20089	.19967
.82	.19845	.19723	.19601	.19480	.19358	.19237	.19116	.18995	.18874	.18754
.83	.18633	.18513	.18392	.18272	.18152	.18032	.17913	.17793	.17674	.17554
.84	.17435	.17316	.17198	.17079	.16960	.16842	.16724	.16605	.16487	.16370
.85	−0.16252	.16134	.16017	.15900	.15782	.15665	.15548	.15432	.15315	.15199
.86	.15032	.14966	.14850	.14734	.14618	.14503	.14387	.14272	.14156	.14041
.87	.13926	.13811	.13697	.13582	.13467	.13353	.13239	.13125	.13011	.12897
.88	.12783	.12670	.12556	.12443	.12330	.12217	.12104	.11991	.11878	.11766
.89	.11653	.11541	.11429	.11317	.11205	.11093	.10981	.10870	.10759	.10647
0.90	−0.10536	.10425	.10314	.10203	.10093	.09982	.09872	.09761	.09651	.09541
.91	.09431	.09321	.09212	.09102	.08992	.08883	.08744	.08665	.08556	.08447
.92	.08338	.08230	.08121	.08013	.07904	.07796	.07688	.07580	.07472	.07365
.93	.07257	.07150	.07042	.06935	.06828	.06721	.06614	.06507	.06401	.06294
.94	.06!88	.06081	.05975	.05869	.05763	.05657	.05551	.05446	.05340	.05235
.95	.05129	.05024	.04919	.04814	.04709	.04604	.04500	.04395	.04291	.04186
.96	.04082	.03978	.03874	.03770	.03666	.03563	.03459	.03356	.03252	.03149
.97	.03046	.02943	.02840	.02737	.02634	.02532	.02429	.02327	.02225	.02122
.98	.02020	.01918	.01816	.01715	.01613	.01511	.01410	.01309	.01207	.01106
.99	.01005	.00904	.00803	.00702	.00602	.00501	.00401	.00300	.00200	.00100

Exhibit B–2 Natural or Naperian Logarithms (Continued)

N	0	1	2	3	4	5	6	7	8	9
0	− ∞	0.00000	0.69315	1.09861	.38629	60944	.79176	.94591	*.07944	*.19722
1	2.30259	.39790	.48491	.56495	.63906	.70805	.77259	.83321	.89037	.94444
2	.99573	*.04452	*.09104	*.13549	*.17805	*.21888	*.25810	*.29584	*.33220	*.36730
3	3.40120	.43399	.46574	.49651	.52636	.55535	.58352	.61092	.63759	.66356
4	.68888	.71357	.73767	.76120	.78419	.80666	.82864	.85015	.87120	.89182
5	.91202	.93183	.95124	.97029	.98898	*.00733	*.02535	*.04305	*.06044	*.07754
6	4.09434	.11087	.12713	.14313	.15888	.17439	.18965	.20469	.21951	.23411
7	.24850	.26268	.27667	.29046	.30407	.31749	.33073	.34381	.35671	.36945
8	.38203	.39445	.40672	.41884	.43082	.44265	.45435	.46591	.47734	.48864
9	.49981	.51086	.52179	.53260	.54329	.55388	.56435	.57471	.58497	.59512
10	4.60517	.61512	.62497	.63473	.64439	.65396	.66344	.67283	.68213	.69135
11	.70048	.70953	.71850	.72739	.73620	.74493	.75359	.76217	.77068	.77912
12	.78749	.79579	.80402	.81218	.82028	.82831	.83628	.84419	.85203	.85981
13	.86753	.87520	.88280	.89035	.89784	.90527	.91265	.91998	.92725	.93447
14	.94164	.94876	.95583	.96284	.96981	.97673	.98361	.99043	.99721	*.00395
15	5.01064	.01728	.02388	.03044	.03695	.04343	.04986	.05625	.06260	.06890
16	.07517	.08140	.08760	.09375	.09987	.10595	.11199	.11799	.12396	.12990
17	.13580	.14166	.14749	.15329	.15906	.16479	.17048	.17615	.18178	.18739
18	.19296	.19850	.20401	.20949	.21494	.22036	.22575	.23111	.23644	.24175
19	.24702	.25227	.25750	.26269	.26786	.27300	.27811	.28320	.28827	.29330
20	5.29832	.30330	.30827	.31321	.31812	.32301	.32788	.33272	.33754	.34233
21	.34711	.35186	.35659	.36129	.36598	.37064	.37528	.37990	.38450	.38907
22	.39363	.39816	.40268	.40717	.41165	.41610	.42053	.42495	.42935	.43372
23	.43808	.44242	.44674	.45104	.45532	.45959	.46383	.46806	.47227	.47646
24	.48064	.48480	.48894	.49306	.49717	.50126	.50533	.50939	.51343	.51745
25	.52146	.52545	.52943	.53339	.53733	.54126	.54518	.54908	.55296	.55683
26	.56068	.56452	.56834	.57215	.57595	.57973	.58350	.58725	.59099	.59471
27	.59842	.60212	.60580	.60947	.61313	.61677	.62040	.62402	.62762	.63121
28	.63479	.63835	.64191	.64545	.64897	.65249	.65599	.65948	.66296	.66643
29	.66988	.67332	.67675	.68017	.68358	.68698	.69036	.69373	.69709	.70044
30	5.70378	.70711	.71043	.71373	.71703	.72031	.72359	.72685	.73010	.73334
31	.73657	.73979	.74300	.74620	.74939	.75257	.75574	.75890	.76205	.76519
32	.76832	.77144	.77455	.77765	.78074	.78383	.78690	.78996	.79301	.79606
33	.79909	.80212	.80513	.80814	.81114	.81413	.81711	.82008	.82305	.82600
34	.82895	.83188	.83481	.83773	.84064	.84354	.84644	.84932	.85220	.85507
35	.85793	.86079	.86363	.86647	.86930	.87212	.87493	.87774	.88053	.88332
36	.88610	.88888	.89164	.89440	.89715	.89990	.90263	.90536	.90808	.91080
37	.91350	.91620	.91889	.92158	.92426	.92693	.92959	.93225	.93489	.93754
38	.94017	.94280	.94542	.94803	.95064	.95324	.95584	.95842	.96101	.96358
39	.96615	.96871	.97126	.97381	.97635	.97889	.98141	.98394	.98645	.98896
40	5.99146	.99396	.99645	.99894	*.00141	*.00389	*.00635	*.00881	*.01127	*.01372
41	6.01616	.01859	.02102	.02345	.02587	.02828	.03069	.03309	.03548	.03787
42	.04025	.04263	.04501	.04737	.04973	.05209	.05444	.05678	.05912	.06146
43	.06379	.06611	.06843	.07074	.07304	.07535	.07764	.07993	.08222	.08450
44	.08677	.08904	.09131	.09357	.09582	.09807	.10032	.10256	.10479	.10702
45	.10925	.11147	.11368	.11589	.11810	.12030	.12249	.12468	.12687	.12905
46	.13123	.13340	.13556	.13773	.13988	.14204	.14419	.14633	.14847	.15060
47	.15273	.15486	.15698	.15910	.16121	.16331	.16542	.16752	.16961	.17170
48	.17379	.17587	.17794	.18002	.18208	.18415	.18621	.18826	.19032	.19236
49	.19441	.19644	.19848	.20051	.20254	.20456	.20658	.20859	.21060	.21261

N	0	1	2	3	4	5	6	7	8	9
50	6.21461	.21661	.21860	.22059	.22258	.22456	.22654	.22851	.23048	.23245
51	.23441	.23637	.23832	.24028	.24222	.24417	.24611	.24804	.24998	.25190
52	.25383	.25575	.25767	.25958	.26149	.26340	.26530	.26720	.26910	.27099
53	.27288	.27476	.27664	.27852	.28040	.28227	.28413	.28600	.28786	.28972
54	.29157	.29342	.29527	.29711	.29895	.30079	.30262	.30445	.30628	.30810
55	.30992	.31173	.31355	.31536	.31716	.31897	.32077	.32257	.32436	.32615
56	.32794	.32972	.33150	.33328	.33505	.33683	.33859	.34036	.34212	.34388
57	.34564	.34739	.34914	.35089	.35263	.35437	.35611	.35784	.35957	.36130
58	.36303	.36475	.36647	.36819	.36990	.37161	.37332	.37502	.37673	.37843
59	.38012	.38182	.38351	.38519	.38688	.38856	.39024	.39192	.39359	.39526
60	6.30693	.39859	.40026	.40192	.40357	.40523	.40688	.40853	.41017	.41182
61	.41346	.41510	.41673	.41836	.41999	.42162	.42325	.42487	.42649	.42811
62	.42972	.43133	.43294	.43455	.43615	.43775	.43935	.44095	.44254	.44413
63	.44572	.44731	.44889	.45047	.45205	.45362	.45520	.45677	.45834	.45990
64	.46147	.46303	.46459	.46614	.46770	.46925	.47080	.47235	.47389	.47543
65	.47697	.47851	.48004	.48158	.48311	.48464	.48616	.48768	.48920	.49072
66	.49224	.49375	.49527	.49677	.49828	.49979	.50129	.50279	.50429	.50578
67	.50728	.50877	.51026	.51175	.51323	.51471	.51619	.51767	.51915	.52062
68	.52209	.52356	.52503	.52649	.52796	.52942	.53088	.53233	.53379	.53524
69	.53669	.53814	.53959	.54103	.54247	.54391	.54535	.54679	.54822	.54965
70	6.55108	.55251	.55393	.55536	.55678	.55820	.55962	.56103	.56244	.56386
71	.56526	.56667	.56808	.56948	.57088	.57228	.57368	.57508	.57647	.57786
72	.57925	.58064	.58203	.58341	.58479	.58617	.58755	.58893	.59030	.59167
73	.59304	.59441	.59578	.59715	.59851	.59987	.60123	.60259	.60394	.60530
74	.60665	.60800	.60935	.61070	.61204	.61338	.61473	.61607	.61740	.61874
75	.62007	.62141	.62274	.62407	.62539	.62672	.62804	.62936	.63068	.63200
76	.63332	.63463	.63595	.63726	.63857	.63988	.64118	.64249	.64379	.64509
77	.64639	.64769	.64898	.65028	.65157	.65286	.65415	.65544	.65673	.65801
78	.65929	.66058	.66185	.66313	.66441	.66568	.66696	.66823	.66950	.67077
79	.67203	.67330	.67456	.67582	.67708	.67834	.67960	.68085	.68211	.68336
80	6.68461	.68586	.68711	.68835	.68960	.69084	.69208	.69332	.69456	.69580
81	.69703	.69827	.69950	.70073	.70196	.70319	.70441	.70564	.70686	.70808
82	.70930	.71052	.71174	.71296	.71417	.71538	.71659	.71780	.71901	.72022
83	.72143	.72263	.72383	.72503	.72623	.72743	.72863	.72982	.73102	.73221
84	.73340	.73459	.73578	.73697	.73815	.73934	.74052	.74170	.74288	.74406
85	.74524	.74641	.74759	.74876	.74993	.75110	.75227	.75344	.75460	.75577
86	.75693	.75809	.75925	.76041	.76157	.76273	.76388	.76504	.76619	.76734
87	.76849	.76964	.77079	.77194	.77308	.77422	.77537	.77651	.77765	.77878
88	.77992	.78106	.78219	.78333	.78446	.78559	.78672	.78784	.78897	.79010
89	.79122	.79234	.79347	.79459	.79571	.79682	.79794	.79906	.80017	.80128
90	6.80239	.80351	.80461	.80572	.80683	.80793	.80904	.81014	.81124	.81235
91	.81344	.81454	.81564	.81674	.81783	.81892	.82002	.82111	.82220	.82329
92	.82437	.82546	.82655	.82763	.82871	.82979	.83087	.83195	.83303	.83411
93	.83518	.83626	.83733	.83841	.83948	.84055	.84162	.84268	.84375	.84482
94	.84588	.84694	.84801	.84907	.85013	.85118	.85224	.85330	.85435	.85541
95	.85646	.85751	.85857	.85961	.86066	.86171	.86276	.86380	.86485	.86589
96	.86693	.86797	.86901	.87005	.87109	.87213	.87316	.87420	.87523	.87626
97	.87730	.87833	.87936	.88038	.88141	.88244	.88346	.88449	.88551	.88653
98	.88755	.88857	.88959	.89061	.89163	.89264	.89366	.89467	.89568	.89669
99	.89770	.89871	.89972	.90073	.90174	.90274	.90375	.90475	.90575	.90675

PROBLEMS

1. In the exponential function $y = a^x$, why cannot a have negative values? (*Hint:* graph $y = a^x$ for $a = -z$ and $x = -3, -2, -1, 0, 1, 2, 3$.)

2. What is the y-intercept for a plot of $y = a^x$?

3. Calculate the following:
   a. $8^{2/3}$;   **b.** $4^{1/2}$;   **c.** 2^{-3};   **d.** $9^{3/2}$

4. Graph (a) $y = x^2 + x - 20$; (b) $y = -x^2 + 9x + 10$; (c) $y = x^3 + 2x^2 - x - 2$. What general observations can you make?

5. Find the following:
   a. $\log_2 8$;   **b.** $\log_4 2$;   **c.** $\log_9 27$;   **d.** $\log_5 (5^3)$

6. Express in terms of logs:
   a. $y = a^2 b^3 c^{1/2}$ **b.** $y = \dfrac{d^2 h^3}{g}$ **c.** $y = \dfrac{4xe^{2x}}{z + 2}$ **d.** $y = \dfrac{U(V)^{3/2}(VW)^3}{4(x + 1)^2}$

7. Prove that $\log_a y = \dfrac{\log_b y}{\log_b a}$.

APPENDIX C
rules of counting

The basic rule of counting is: If there are a ways to do one thing and b ways to do another, then there are $a \times b$ ways to do both. For example, if there is a choice of obtaining any of three cars and cars can be obtained by either buying or leasing, then there are six (3×2) different decisions that can be made. The basic rule of counting can be generalized to n events. If there are A_1 outcomes for event one, A_2 outcomes for event two, and A_n outcomes for event n, events one through n can occur together in $A_1 \times A_2 \times \cdots \times A_n$ ways. Hence, if we are going to flip a coin four times, there are sixteen ($2 \times 2 \times 2 \times 2$) possible outcomes.

Now let us consider the question of how many different ways we can order n distinct objects. The solution to this problem follows directly from the basic rule of counting. Suppose, for example, we have five letters, A, B, C, D, and E. Conceptually, the problem of ordering is that of filling five blank slots _ _ _ _ _. There are five ways to fill the first slot, four ways to fill the second slot (since one letter is already used), three ways to fill the third slot, and so forth. Thus there are $5 \times 4 \times 3 \times 2 \times 1$ ways to order the five letters. The descending string of multiplications indicated by the answer can be written 5! and pronounced "five factorial."[1] Generalizing, we say that the number of ways n distinct objects can be ordered is $n!$.

Suppose that we had only $r (r \leq n)$ slots instead of n slots for the n objects. The problem would then be: How many ways can we select and order r items from n distinct items? Such problems are called *permutation problems* and are denoted as $_nP_r$, the permutation of n things taken r at a time. The solution to these problems also follows directly from the basic rule of counting. Suppose that we have a group of eight people from which to

402   [1] 0! is defined as 1.

select a president, a vice-president, and a treasurer. There are three slots to fill with eight ways to fill the first, seven ways to fill the second, and six ways to fill the third. Thus there are 186 ($8 \times 7 \times 6$) ways to fill all three positions. In general, therefore,

$$_nP_r = \underset{[1]}{n} \times \underset{[2]}{(n-1)} \times \cdots \times \underset{[r]}{(n-r+1)} \qquad \text{(C-1)}$$

The numbers in brackets represent the cumulative number of slots filled and are given for illustrative purposes; they are not part of the formula. Equation (C-1) is often rewritten in more compact factorial form. We can multiply the equation by $(n-r)!/(n-r)!$ (multiplication by 1 does not change its value). However, $(n-r)!$ multiplied by the decreasing multiplicative string from n given in (C-1) completes the factorial so that the equation can be rewritten

$$_nP_r = \frac{n!}{(n-r)!}$$

In the above discussion, the order of the objects has been accounted for, and we have differentiated sets containing the same entries if they appeared in different sequences. That is, we considered the outcome ABC different from ACB. There are many situations, however, where we are not interested in order but only in how many different groups of r objects can be selected from n objects ($r \leq n$). In such a case the outcomes ABC and ACB would be considered as one outcome consisting of the selection of the three letters A, B, and C. Such problems are called *combinations* and are denoted as $\binom{n}{r}$: the combination of n things taken r at a time, or the combination of n above r. In order to calculate $\binom{n}{r}$ let us put all the rules of counting into perspective.

Suppose we have four letters, A, B, C, and D. Now let us examine the following matrix:

$$\binom{4}{2}\left[\binom{n}{r}\right] \quad \begin{array}{|ll} \multicolumn{2}{l}{2! \, [r\,!]} \\ \hline AB & BA \\ AC & CA \\ AD & DA \\ BC & CB \\ BD & DB \\ CD & DC \end{array} \quad {}_4P_2[{}_nP_r]$$

The total number of items in the matrix represents the number of ways of selecting two letters from four and ordering them, or $_4P_2$. Each row represents a unique selection of two items from the four, or the number of rows $= \binom{4}{2}$. The number of columns represents the number of different orders of the two items, or 2!. Now since the number of rows times the number of columns equals the total number of entries

$$\binom{4}{2}(2!) = {_4}P_2$$

and

$$\binom{4}{2} = \frac{{_4}P_2}{2!} = \frac{4!}{(4-2)!\,2!}$$

we can find

$$\binom{n}{r} = \frac{{_n}P_r}{r!} = \frac{n!}{(n-r)!\,r!} \tag{C–2}$$

The following example illustrates the use of Eq. (C–2). We have a list of ten stocks recommended by an investment service, and we want to select three to purchase. How many options do we have to consider? The answer is

$$\binom{10}{3} = \frac{10!}{3!\,7!} = 120$$

It must be realized, of course, that all the above rules of counting can be used in combination to solve certain problems.

PROBLEMS

1. A manager has selected nine players to start a baseball game. How many different batting orders could he devise if he wanted the pitcher to bat ninth?
2. If there are 25 players on the baseball team, how many batting orders could the manager make up? How many groups of nine players could he specify to start the game, irrespective of batting order?
3. A restaurant's menu lists four appetizers, six entrees, three vegetables, and four desserts. How many dinner combinations could be ordered?
4. An investor is studying a list of ten stocks. How many groups of three stocks could he select from the list of ten? How many groups of five stocks? How many groups of seven stocks? Explain the differences in your answers.
5. Suppose the investor in the above problem also has a list of seven bonds. How many groups of eight securities could he select from the combined lists? If the chosen securities must include five stocks and three bonds, how many groups could be selected? How many if three stocks and five bonds must be included? Explain the differences in your answers.
6. How many bridge hands could be dealt from a standard deck of 52 cards? Four bridge hands are dealt and are to be distributed randomly to the four players. In how many different ways could the four hands be distributed?

APPENDIX D

index numbers

Index numbers are sets of numbers that indicate the relative values of some variable over time. They relate the value of the variable during the period of interest to the value of the same variable during some base period. The base period can be either a point or interval of time, depending on whether the variable is a stock or flow variable.[1] For example, asset values or bond prices are measured at a particular point in time, while sales or profit figures must be measured over some interval of time.

There are many types of index numbers, and they are used for many purposes. The consumer price index and the wholesale price index reflect changes in the cost of living or doing business. There is a wide variety of stock price indexes. They vary not only by the stocks they include, but also by their methods of computation. There are sales volume indexes, indexes of industrial activity and capacity utilization, sales price indexes, and so on. Almost all businesses and government agencies use index numbers for evaluation, planning, and control purposes. Some they construct for their own individual use. Others are supplied by public agencies. In addition to the widely known price and stock market indexes, the reader should be familiar with the index numbers reported in the *Federal Reserve Bulletin*, a monthly publication of the Board of Governors of the Federal Reserve System, or, perhaps of more general interest, the *Survey of Current Business*, a monthly publication of the United States Department of Commerce. Regardless of his particular area of interest, a businessman can benefit from following the common index number series relevant to his field.

---

[1] In many cases the base period for a stock variable is an interval where the base period value is determined by averaging the values of the variable over the interval.

Some series of index numbers are general, simply constructed, and easy to interpret. Others are highly specialized and are computed by using complicated weighting and averaging techniques. It is not the purpose of this appendix to delve into all the complexities and variations of index number construction. The intent is to provide some general insights into the more common methods of computation so that the reader may better appreciate the significance of index numbers, at the same time gaining some awareness of their limitations.

The computation of index numbers from time series data can be illustrated by using the annual sales figures for the Fairmount Corporation given in Exhibit D–1. The raw data give annual sales for each year during the decade of the 1960's. The index number for each year is obtained by dividing the sales for that year by the sales for the base year and then multiplying the quotient by 100. (Notice that the procedure is the same as for calculating percentages.) Thus the index number for the base year is 100. The sales index for 1964 is $(68.7/49.3)(100) = 139.4$, as shown in the third column of Exhibit D–1. This figure tells us that sales for 1964 were 39.4 percent greater than sales for the base year 1960. Index numbers specify only relative values, however; the index alone would not enable the absolute sales for 1964 to be determined unless the sales for the base year were also known.

Exhibit D–1 Construction of Index Numbers

Year	Sales ($ million)	Index Numbers (base = 1960)	Index Numbers (base = 1960–62)
1960	$49.3	100.0	91.8
1961	57.1	115.8	106.3
1962	54.7	111.0	101.9
1963	61.5	124.7	114.5
1964	68.7	139.4	127.9
1965	70.2	142.4	130.7
1966	73.4	148.9	136.7
1967	72.1	146.2	134.3
1968	76.3	154.8	142.1
1969	81.2	164.7	151.2

In some cases, particularly for a cyclical time series, it is not desirable to use a single year as the base period. An average value over a period of a few years may be used instead. Suppose that we want to use the base period 1960–62, as shown in the fourth column of Exhibit D–1. The average value over the base period would be $(\frac{1}{3})(49.3 + 57.1 + 54.7) = 53.7$. Then the index number for 1960 is $(49.3/53.7)(100) = 91.8$, the index number for 1964 is $(68.7/53.7)(100) = 127.9$, and so on.

There is little difficulty in computing, understanding, and using index numbers such as the ones calculated above. The problems are not so simple, however, when an index must be constructed from an aggregation of time series data. For example, suppose that an industry-related composite price index is to be calculated for the 1960's by the Fairmount Corporation. The desired index should take into account the prices of all major commodities relevant to the industry. If we assume that the problems of measuring prices and identifying those items to be included in the index have been taken care of, the next step is to combine, or weight, the various prices.[2] One obvious choice of weights for use in a price index would be the quantity of units used or sold. Possible distortions that could be caused by fluctuations in quantity can be avoided by using constant weights. For example, the quantities observed during the base period could be used as constant weights throughout the life of the index. If p denotes price and q denotes quantity, and there are n items to be included in the index, the value of the index for period t would be computed as follows:

$$I_t = \frac{\sum_{i=1}^{n} (p_{t,i})(q_{0,i})}{\sum_{i=1}^{n} (p_{0,i})(q_{0,i})} \tag{D-1}$$

where $p_{t,i}$ represents the price of the ith item included in the index for period t.

The construction of an aggregate index is illustrated in Exhibit D–2. It is assumed in the illustration that eight different items are used in the construction of the index. The sums of the last two columns of Exhibit D–2 are, respectively, the denominator and the numerator of Eq. (D–1). From these two sums, the price index for period t, I_t, is found to be

$$534.75/499.50(100) = 107.1$$

This result tells us that the same quantity of merchandise cost 1.071 times as much in period t as it did in the base period.

Exhibit D–2   Construction of Aggregate Index with Constant Weights

Item Number	p_0	q_0	p_t	$p_0 \cdot q_0$	$p_t \cdot q_0$
1	1.80	20	2.00	36.00	40.00
2	2.10	10	2.25	21.00	22.50
3	0.95	50	1.05	47.50	52.50
4	1.30	35	1.40	45.50	49.00
5	5.25	20	5.50	105.00	110.00
6	3.85	15	4.10	57.75	61.50
7	2.70	40	2.95	108.00	118.00
8	3.15	25	3.25	78.75	81.25
			Totals	499.50	534.75

[2] Notice that price is a stock variable. The price used in the index may be the price observed at the mid-point or the end of the period, or it may be an average of prices observed over the period, such as an average of the prices at the end of each month.

Equation (D–1) can be modified so that the quantities vary and the prices are used as weights. Thus Eq. (D–2) can be used to calculate a quantity index.

$$I_t = \frac{\sum_{i=1}^{n}(p_{0,i})(q_{t,i})}{\sum_{i=1}^{n}(p_{0,i})(q_{0,i})} \tag{D–2}$$

This type of index indicates relative changes in aggregate quantity over time.

An index calculated according to Eq. (D–1) or Eq. (D–2) is called Laspeyre's Index. Two other commonly used indexes are Paasche's Index, given by Eq. (D–3), and Fisher's Index, given by Eq. (D–4). Both of these equations can also be modified to obtain quantity indexes.

$$P_t = \frac{\sum_{i=1}^{n}(p_{t,i})(q_{t,i})}{\sum_{i=1}^{n}(p_{0,i})(q_{t,i})} \tag{D–3}$$

$$F_t = (I_t \times P_t)^{1/2} \tag{D–4}$$

In Eq. (D–2), I_t fails to reflect important shifts that might have taken place in the relative usage of different items. For many purposes, alloys are now used in place of cast iron. Similarly, cotton fabric has lost much of its market to new synthetics. An index based on constant weights fails to indicate changing patterns of materials and technology over time. Paasche's Index changes the weights assigned to each item every period to reflect current rates of usage; i.e., the weights are $q_{t,i}$ rather than $q_{0,i}$.

These two methods use weighting procedures that are at opposite extremes. In fact, under certain assumptions, it can be shown that I_t represents the lower level and P_t the upper level of the "true" value of an index. Fisher's Index, which is a geometric mean of I_t and P_t, is an attempt to approximate the "true" index that lies between the extremes.

To illustrate the effect changes in quantities can have on the index value, the preliminary computations for calculating P_t are given in Exhibit D–3. The numbers are the same as those in Exhibit D–2, except that it is assumed that the usage of items 1 and 3 has increased and the usage of items 5 and 8 has decreased. The value of P_t is $(505.50/465.50)(100) = 108.6$. This value is greater than I_t, which was 107.1. The difference results from the fact that the items with increased usage increased more in price than the items with decreased usage.

Index numbers have important uses other than portraying relative fluctuations or trends in some variable over time. One common use of index numbers is to deflate economic time series. Many time series are affected by inflation, so the data are deflated, or adjusted for inflation, before being used for forecasting purposes (see Chapter 18). The deflated values are called

Construction of Aggregate Index with Varying Weights

Item Number	p_0	p_t	q_t	$p_0 \cdot q_t$	$p_t \cdot q_t$
1	1.80	2.00	50	90.00	100.00
2	2.10	2.25	10	21.00	22.50
3	0.95	1.05	90	85.50	94.50
4	1.30	1.40	35	45.50	49.00
5	5.25	5.50	5	26.25	27.50
6	3.85	4.10	15	57.75	61.50
7	2.70	2.95	40	108.00	118.00
8	3.15	3.25	10	31.50	32.50
				Totals 465.50	505.50

"real," or constant dollar values. Thus if your income went up by 5 percent but the cost of living as measured by some price index also went up by 5 percent, your "real" income did not change. Changes in real income, then, represent changes in actual purchasing power as measured by the quantity of goods that could be acquired.

Suppose that Fairmount Corporation wants to know how much of its growth in total sales has been due to "real" growth and how much has resulted simply from inflation. The sales index numbers calculated in Exhibit D–1 can be deflated by an appropriate price index to give a series of sales index numbers that have been adjusted to remove the influences of inflation. The necessary computations are performed in Exhibit D–4. A price index, using 1960 as the base year, is given in the third column.

Exhibit D–4   Computation of Deflated Sales Index

Year	Sales ($ million)	Price Index	Sales Index	Deflated Sales Index	Deflated Sales	Deflated Sales Index
1960	49.3	100.0	100.0	100.0	49.3	100.0
1961	57.1	104.5	115.8	110.8	54.6	110.8
1962	54.7	107.9	111.0	102.9	50.7	102.8*
1963	61.5	111.2	124.7	112.1	55.3	112.2*
1964	68.7	114.9	139.4	121.3	59.8	121.3
1965	70.2	118.3	142.4	120.4	59.3	120.3*
1966	73.4	121.4	148.9	122.7	60.5	122.7
1967	72.1	124.7	146.2	117.2	57.8	117.2
1968	76.3	128.6	154.8	120.4	59.3	120.3*
1969	81.2	132.8	164.6	124.0	61.1	123.9*

* Index values in Columns 5 and 7 differ because of rounding.

Two different methods are presented for calculating the deflated sales index series, although both yield the same results. One method is to divide the sales index by the corresponding price index of the same year; i.e., divide Column 4 by Column 3 to get Column 5, the deflated sales index values. The alternative method is to calculate deflated annual sales (Column 6) by dividing total sales (Column 2) by the price index (Column 3). The deflated sales figures can then be used to obtain the deflated sales index series shown in Column 7.

The deflated sales and deflated sales index figures show that a large portion of the growth in undeflated sales (as given in Column 4) was attributable to inflation. Undeflated sales grew by 64.7 percent from 1960 to 1969, while deflated sales increased by only 24.0 percent (from Column 5). The results also show that, while total dollar sales increased, real dollar sales actually decreased from 1964 to 1965. Furthermore, there was no growth in real sales from 1965 to 1968, even though total dollar sales increased by $6.1 million. This dollar increase was due solely to inflation.

A comparison of Columns 4 and 5 should tell the management of Fairmount Corporation that their performance during the latter half of the 1960's was rather flat. While dollar sales gave the illusion of reasonable growth, we can see from Column 5 that there was little real growth from 1964 to 1969. Certainly the firm's performance during the first half of the 1960's was far superior to that of the second half.

These examples should illustrate the difference between dollar values and real values. Index numbers clearly can be useful when one is analyzing economic data. The significance attached to index numbers should be conditioned, however, by an awareness of their composition and method of computation.

PROBLEMS

1. Recalculate the index numbers in Exhibit D–1, using 1965 as a base year; using 1964–1966 as a base period.
2. Given the data below, calculate price indexes using (a) Laspeyre's Index, (b) Paasche's Index, and (c) Fisher's Index. Compare your results.

Item Number	p_0	q_0	p_t	q_t
1	18.75	50	20.55	50
2	5.30	40	5.80	40
3	7.70	35	10.00	70
4	10.50	40	11.60	40
5	9.85	120	10.25	50
6	6.25	90	6.85	90
7	12.45	70	13.15	30
8	20.65	20	25.30	60
9	18.20	25	21.40	25
10	15.40	60	17.10	60

3. Repeat Problem 2, but calculate quantity indexes.
4. Assume that price levels change at various rates in different regions of the country. You are sitting in the national headquarters reviewing the cost efficiency performance of plant managers who are widely dispersed throughout the country. Explain how you would use index numbers to help make more meaningful evaluations.

5. Professor Swanick's annual income over a period of years and a cost of living index series are given below. Calculate Professor Swanick's real income each year and construct both undeflated and deflated income indexes. What has happened to Professor Swanick's standard of living over the 10-year period? How might he use the two income index series when he next discusses his annual salary with his department chairman?

Year	Income	Cost of Living Index
1	$8,000	100.0
2	8,400	105.5
3	8,700	110.2
4	9,100	116.3
5	9,700	122.5
6	10,200	128.7
7	10,500	135.9
8	11,000	143.2
9	11,400	149.5
10	11,800	155.3

6. How would a manufacturer use index numbers to justify a price increase to his customers? What particular index number series would he find most helpful? If you were a customer, what questions might you raise about the index used by the manufacturer?

APPENDIX E

differential calculus

The objective of this appendix is to provide a basic understanding of what a derivative is and to show how it can be applied to business and economic problems. We shall present a few formulas for finding derivatives of relatively simple functions and discuss a few examples illustrating the use of derivatives.

In very simple terms, a derivative indicates the effect of a change in the independent variable x on the dependent variable y. Consider the linear equation $y = a + bx$. Assume that x changes by some amount Δx, causing a change in y of Δy. We could thus write $y + \Delta y = a + b(x + \Delta x) = a + bx + b\,\Delta x$. Subtracting the first equation from the second, we get

$$
\begin{aligned}
y + \Delta y &= a + bx + b\,\Delta x \\
- (y\quad\;\; &= a + bx) \\
\hline
\Delta y &= \qquad\quad b\,\Delta x
\end{aligned}
$$

or $\Delta y / \Delta x = b$. We know that b is the slope of a linear equation, so $\Delta y / \Delta x$ must also be the slope. Finally, just as $y = f(x)$, so does $y + \Delta y = f(x + \Delta x)$. Therefore, $\Delta y = f(x + \Delta x) - y = f(x + \Delta x) - f(x)$, and we can represent the slope of our linear equation as

$$
\frac{f(x + \Delta x) - f(x)}{\Delta x}
$$

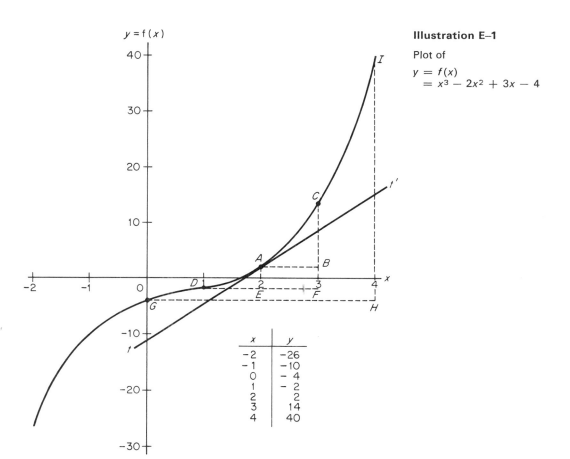

$y = f(x)$

40

30

20

10

-2   -1   O

-10

-20

-30

Plot of

$y = f(x)$
$= x^3 - 2x^2 + 3x - 4$

x	y
-2	-26
-1	-10
0	-4
1	-2
2	2
3	14
4	40

The slope of the linear equation $y = a + bx$ can be readily obtained by checking the value of the coefficient b. Furthermore, the slope is constant for all values of x. However, consider a function such as $y = f(x) = x^3 - 2x^2 + 3x - 4$. This equation is plotted in Illustration E-1 for a few values of x. Suppose we want to determine the slope of this curve when $x = 2$. The slope of a nonlinear function is defined to be the slope of a line tangent to the curve at the point where we want to measure the slope. Thus the slope of the curve when $x = 2$ is the slope of the tangency line tt'. (Notice that, unlike a nonlinear function, the slope of a function changes as the point of measurement changes; i.e., as the value of x changes.) Our problem, then, is to find a way to measure the slope of tt'. We might try to approximate the slope of tt' by selecting some Δx, finding the corresponding value of Δy, and then computing $\Delta y/\Delta x$. We could let $\Delta x = 3 - 2$, for example. (We obviously want to take a Δx close to $x = 2$.) This is shown by the line segment AB in Illustration E-1. The corresponding Δy (shown by line

413

segment BC) is $14 - 2 = 12$, so $\Delta y/\Delta x = BC/AB = \frac{12}{1} = 12$. Suppose, however, that we had chosen to let $\Delta x = 2 - 1$ (segment DE), where the corresponding $\Delta y = 2 - (-2) = 4$ (segment AE). Then $\Delta y/\Delta x = AE/DE = \frac{4}{1} = 4$. We might reasonably feel that Δx should extend to either side of $x = 2$. Letting $\Delta x = 3 - 1$, we could find

$$\frac{\Delta y}{\Delta x} = \frac{CF}{DF} = \frac{14 - (-2)}{3 - 1} = \frac{16}{2} = 8$$

Finally, assume that we select $\Delta x = 4 - 0$. Then

$$\frac{\Delta y}{\Delta x} = \frac{HI}{GH} = \frac{40 - (-4)}{4 - 0} = \frac{44}{4} = 11$$

We have used four measures to approximate the slope of tt', and have obtained four widely different results. We thus see the need for a systematic procedure for finding the slope of tt'. We can intuitively see from our above results that we would get the best approximation by keeping Δx as small and as close to $x = 2$ as possible. Ideally, Δx would be infinitesimally small, which roughly means as close to zero as possible. We could also say that we want to measure $\Delta y/\Delta x$ as Δx approaches zero. How do we perform such a measurement? This is the job of the derivative. The derivative of some function $y = f(x)$ is defined as follows (it is assumed that the limit exists and the function is continuous):

$$f'(x) = \lim_{\Delta x \to 0} \frac{\Delta y}{\Delta x} = \lim_{\Delta x \to 0} \frac{f(x + \Delta x) - f(x)}{\Delta x} \qquad \text{(E–1)}$$

The notation $f'(x)$ is used to denote the derivative of $f(x)$. The alternate notation dy/dx, read "the derivative of y with respect to x," is also frequently used. The definition of the derivative satisfies our requirements of the ideal measure of slope. The expression $\lim_{\Delta x \to 0} (\Delta y/\Delta x)$ means that we are finding the limit (value) that $\Delta y/\Delta x$ approaches as Δx approaches 0. Thus the derivative provides us with a means of finding the slope of a nonlinear function, or, more elegantly, a means for finding the *instantaneous* rate of change.

Let us apply the definition to find the derivative of a few functions. Notice that, once obtained, the derivative provides us with an equation to find the slope (or rate of change). Since the slope of a nonlinear curve changes continuously, we must then specify the value of x at which we want to measure the slope. Now to some examples.

Example 1 Find the slope of $y = f(x) = x^2 - 4$ when $x = 2$.

Step 1 Find the derivative of $f(x)$.

$$f'(x) = \lim_{\Delta x \to 0} \frac{f(x + \Delta x) - f(x)}{\Delta x}$$

$$f'(x) = \lim_{\Delta x \to 0} \frac{[(x + \Delta x)^2 - 4] - [x^2 - 4]}{\Delta x}$$

$$f'(x) = \lim_{\Delta x \to 0} \frac{[x^2 + 2x\,\Delta x + \Delta x^2 - 4] - x^2 + 4}{\Delta x}$$

$$f'(x) = \lim_{\Delta x \to 0} \frac{2x\,\Delta x + \Delta x^2}{\Delta x} = \lim_{\Delta x \to 0} (2x + \Delta x)$$

The limit of $(2x + \Delta x)$, as Δx approaches zero, is simply $2x$. Therefore,

$$f'(x) = \lim_{\Delta x \to 0} (2x + \Delta x) = 2x$$

Step 2 Since $f'(x) = 2x$, and we want the slope when $x = 2$, the slope is $2x = 2(2) = 4$.

Example 2 Find the slope of $y = f(x) = 3x^2 - 2x + 1$ when $x = 0$ and again when $x = 1$.

Step 1

$$f'(x) = \lim_{\Delta x \to 0} \frac{[3(x + \Delta x)^2 - 2(x + \Delta x) + 1] - [3x^2 - 2x + 1]}{\Delta x}$$

$$f'(x) = \lim_{\Delta x \to 0} \frac{[3(x^2 + 2x\,\Delta x + \Delta x^2) - 2x - 2\,\Delta x + 1] - 3x^2 + 2x - 1}{\Delta x}$$

$$f'(x) = \lim_{\Delta x \to 0} \frac{6x\,\Delta x + 3\,\Delta x^2 - 2\,\Delta x}{\Delta x} = \lim_{\Delta x \to 0} (6x + 3\,\Delta x - 2) = 6x - 2$$

Step 2

(a) Slope when $x = 0$ is $6(0) - 2 = -2$.
(b) Slope when $x = 1$ is $6(1) - 2 = 4$.

Example 3 Let us return to our original problem and find the slope of $y = f(x) = x^3 - 2x^2 + 3x - 4$ when $x = 2$.

Step 1

$$f'(x) = \lim_{\Delta x \to 0} \frac{[(x + \Delta x)^3 - 2(x + \Delta x)^2 + 3(x + \Delta x) - 4]}{\Delta x}$$

$$f'(x) = \lim_{\Delta x \to 0} \frac{[(x^3 + 3x^2 \Delta x + 3x \Delta x^2 + \Delta x^3) - 2(x^2 + 2x \Delta x + \Delta x^2)}{+ 3(x + \Delta x) - 4] - x^3 + 2x^2 - 3x + 4}$$

$$= \lim_{\Delta x \to 0} \frac{3x^2 \Delta x + 3x \Delta x^2 + \Delta x^3 - 4x \Delta x - 2 \Delta x^2 + 3 \Delta x}{\Delta x}$$

$$= \lim_{\Delta x \to 0} (3x^2 + 3x \Delta x + \Delta x^2 - 4x - 2 \Delta x + 3) = 3x^2 - 4x + 3$$

Step 2 Slope when $x = 2$ is $3(2)^2 - 4(2) + 3 = 12 - 8 + 3 = 7$.

While a derivative can always be obtained by working from the definition, Example 3 indicates that it becomes quite cumbersome for fairly complex functions. You may have already begun to recognize certain consistent patterns in our results, however, that can greatly facilitate the task of finding a derivative. Let us present (without proofs) the following general rules of differentiation.

1. If $y = k, \dfrac{dy}{dx} = 0$

2. If $y = f(x) = ax, \dfrac{dy}{dx} = a$

3. If $y = f(x) = ax^n, \dfrac{dy}{dx} = n \cdot ax^{n-1}$

4. If $y = f(x) \pm g(x), \dfrac{dy}{dx} = f'(x) \pm g'(x)$

5. If $y = f(x) \cdot g(x), \dfrac{dy}{dx} = f'(x) \cdot g(x) + f(x) \cdot g'(x)$

6. If $y = \dfrac{f(x)}{g(x)}, \dfrac{dy}{dx} = \dfrac{f'(x) \cdot g(x) - f(x) \cdot g'(x)}{[g(x)]^2}$

7. If $y = f(z)$ and $z = g(x), \dfrac{dy}{dx} = f'(z) \cdot g'(x) = \dfrac{dy}{dz} \cdot \dfrac{dz}{dx}$ [1]

8. If $y = e^{f(x)}, \dfrac{dy}{dx} = e^{f(x)} \cdot f'(x)$

[1] This particular rule is commonly known as the *chain rule*.

9. If $y = a^{f(x)}$, $\dfrac{dy}{dx} = e^{f(x)} \cdot f'(x) \cdot \ln a$

10. If $y = f(x) = \ln x$, $\dfrac{dy}{dx} = \dfrac{1}{x}$

11. If $y = f(x) = \ln g(x)$, $\dfrac{dy}{dx} = \dfrac{1}{g(x)} \cdot g'(x)$

Let us apply these rules to some actual functions, including the three worked out above.

Example 1 $\quad y = f(x) = x^2 - 4$
$$f'(x) = 2x^{(2-1)} - 0 = 2x$$

Example 2 $\quad y = f(x) = 3x^2 - 2x + 1$
$$f'(x) = 2 \cdot 3x^{(2-1)} - 2x^{(1-1)} + 0 = 6x - 2$$

Example 3 $\quad y = f(x) = x^3 - 2x^2 + 3x - 4$
$$f'(x) = 3x^{(3-1)} - 2 \cdot 2x^{(2-1)} + 3x^{(1-1)} - 4 = 3x^2 - 4x + 3$$

Example 4 $\quad y = f(x) \cdot g(x) = (x^2 - 4)(x^2 - 2x + 1)$

$$\frac{dy}{dx} = f'(x) \cdot g(x) + f(x)g'(x) = 2x(x^2 - 2x + 1) + (x^2 - 4)(2x - 2)$$

Example 5 $\quad y = \dfrac{f(x)}{g(x)} = \dfrac{x^3 - x + 3}{x - 7}$

$$\frac{dy}{dx} = \frac{f'(x) \cdot g(x) - f(x)g'(x)}{[g(x)]^2} = \frac{(3x^2 - 1)(x - 7) - (x^3 - x + 3)(1)}{(x - 7)^2}$$

Example 6 $\quad y = f(x) = 6e^{2x}$
$$f'(x) = 6e^{2x}(2) = 12e^{2x}$$

Example 7 $\quad y = f(x) = 6a^{2x}$
$$f'(x) = 6a^{2x}(2) \ln a = 12a^{2x} \ln a$$

Example 8 $\quad y = f(x) = (x^2 - 2)^3$; let $u = x^2 - 2$, so $y = u^3$ then $y = f(u)$, $u = f(x)$

$$\frac{dy}{dx} = \frac{dy}{dx} \cdot \frac{du}{dx} = 3u^2 \cdot 2x = 3(x^2 - 2)^2(2x) = 6x(x^2 - 2)^2$$

Example 9 $\quad y = f(x) = \ln (2x^3 + 3x)$

$$f'(x) = \frac{6x^2 + 3}{2x^3 + 3x}$$

Once we know how to find a derivative, and what the result means, we can proceed with some examples of practical applications. Most business and economic uses of derivatives fall into one of three broad classifications. Perhaps the simplest applications would consist of checking the sign of the derivative to see the sign of the associated slope. The derivative of sales revenue R with respect to advertising expenditures A should hopefully be positive ($dR/dA > 0$). In a model of the over-all economy, we might find the derivative of the rate of unemployment with respect to the money supply to be negative while the derivative of the rate of inflation with respect to the money supply is positive. Thus the sign of the slope indicates the direction of change.

A second major use of derivatives may be broadly classified as marginal analysis. The derivative provides a measure of the instantaneous, or marginal, rate of change. We can illustrate this use of derivatives with two of the examples presented in Appendix B in the section on power functions.

In one example, we were given an average cost curve of the form $AC = 0.8Q^2 - 48Q + 1000$ (AC = average cost, Q = quantity). Given the average cost, we can multiply it by quantity to obtain total cost. Thus $TC = 0.8Q^3 - 48Q^2 + 1000Q$. Marginal cost is defined as the change in total cost resulting from a unit change in quantity produced, or $MC = \Delta TC/\Delta Q$. But since the total cost curve is nonlinear, we again have the problem of how to measure $\Delta TC/\Delta Q$. The obvious answer is to use the derivative, so $MC = dTC/dQ = 2.4Q^2 - 96Q + 1000$. We now find that, when $Q = 30$, $MC = 2.4(30)^2 - 96(30) + 1000 = \$280$.

Similarly, suppose that we know the total revenue curve is $TR = 520Q - 2.10Q^2$. We might take the derivative of the total revenue to get marginal revenue and obtain $MR = 520 - 4.20Q$. Since we know from our basic economics that profits are maximized when $MR = MC$, we could equate our MR and MC equations and solve for the value of Q that would maximize profits. Solving the equation $520 - 4.20Q = 2.4Q^2 - 96Q + 1000$ for Q, we find $Q = 32$. This means that when 32 units are produced, $MR = MC$ and total profit is maximized.[2] If more or less than 32 units are produced, total profits will decline.

As a second example, consider a learning curve (see Appendix B) of the general form $y = ax^b$, where y = average labor hours per unit, x = the cumulative number of units produced, a = the number of hours required for the first unit, and b = the learning rate. If y is the *average* hours per unit, then $x \cdot y$ is the *total* cumulative number of hours. Thus total hours $TH = x \cdot ax^b = ax^{b+1}$, and the marginal number of hours required to produce the xth unit is given by dTH/dx. Solving, we get $dTH/dx = (b + 1)ax^b = (b + 1)y$ (remember that $0 \leq b \leq 1$). The marginal labor time can therefore be readily obtained from the original learning curve. In fact, the term $(b + 1)$ is sometimes referred to as the *conversion factor*.

The third major application of derivatives is for optimization problems. Derivatives are especially useful for this type of problem. For example,

---

[2] $Q = 6.25$ units also satisfies the equation where $MR = MC$. We were told in Appendix B, however, that the AC equation was not valid for Q less than 15. We will, therefore, disregard this second solution.

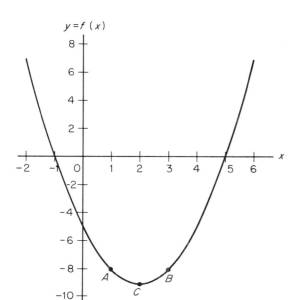

y = f (x)

Plot of

x	y	f'(x)
-2	7	-8
-1	0	-6
0	-5	-4
1	-8	-2
2	-9	0
3	-8	2
4	-5	4
5	0	6
6	7	8

$y = f(x)$
$\quad = x^2 - 4x - 5$

consider the curve $y = f(x) = x^2 - 4x - 5$, which is plotted in Illustration E–2. $f'(x) = 2x - 4$. Thus we can find the slope at point A (where $x = 1$) to be $2(1) - 4 = -2$. The slope at point B (where $x = 3$) is $2(3) - 4 = 2$. The direction of the curve shifts from point A to B, and the slope changes from negative to positive. In making this change, we pass through point C, where the slope goes from negative to zero to positive. Right at point C, the slope is exactly equal to zero. This will be true at any turning point. The slope is equal to zero at a maximum or minimum point on the curve.[3] We can, therefore, optimize (minimize or maximize) a function such as the above by setting the first derivative equal to zero and solving for x.

Suppose that we wanted to minimize the function $y = f(x) = 2x^2 - 10x + 7$. We set the first derivative equal to zero, $f'(x) = 4x - 10 = 0$, and, solving, we find $x = 2.5$. The function $y = f(x) = 2x^2 - 10x + 7$ is, therefore, minimized (y has its lowest possible value) when $x = 2.5$.

One nagging question may be bothering some readers at this point. How do we know if we have solved for a maximum or minimum point? We can quickly tell by checking the sign of the second derivative. The second derivative is the derivative of the first derivative, and is denoted by $f''(x)$ or d^2y/dx^2. Thus if $f(x) = 2x^2 - 10x + 7$, $f'(x) = 4x - 10$, and $f''(x) = 4$. Notice in Illustration E–2 that the slope of the curve was changing from negative to positive, or generally increasing, as it passed through the minimum point. Just as the first derivative gives the slope of the original function, the second derivative gives the *direction* of the change in slope. The slope

---

[3] For third-degree and higher curves, we would find only "local" maximum and minimum points. Thus it would also be necessary to examine the boundaries of the range of values being considered.

should be increasing with x around a minimum, and the second derivative should, therefore, be positive. For similar reasons, a maximum point would be indicated if the second derivative is negative.

Let us now reconsider the problem where we obtained a total cost curve $= TC = 0.8Q^3 - 48Q^3 + 1000Q$ and a total revenue curve $= TR = 520Q - 2.10Q^2$. Since profit equals total revenue minus total cost, we can obtain a profit function $P = TR - TC = 520Q - 2.10Q^2 - 0.8Q^3 + 48Q^2 - 1000Q = -0.8Q^3 + 45.90Q^2 - 480Q$. We can maximize profits by setting dP/dQ equal to zero and solving for Q. We have $dP/dQ = -2.4Q^2 + 91.80Q - 480 = 0$; solving, we obtain $Q = 32.$[4] The second derivative is $d^2P/dQ^2 = -4.8Q + 91.80$ which, for $Q = 32$, is equal to $-4.8(32) + 91.80 = -153.60 + 91.80 - 61.80$. The second derivative is negative, so we can, indeed, maximize profits by operating where $Q = 32$.

Let us make one final observation. Since $P = TR - TC$, $dP/dQ = dTR/dQ - dTC/dQ = 0$ to maximize P. But $dTR/dQ - dTC/dQ = MR - MC$. Again we have maximized profits by equating marginal revenue and marginal cost.

PROBLEMS

1. Using Eq. (E–1), the definition of a derivative, find the first derivative of the following functions:
   a. $y = f(x) = 5x - 3$ **b.** $y = f(x) = x^2 - 2x + 7$
   c. $y = f(x) = -x^2 + 4x + 1$ **d.** $y = f(x) = 2x^3 - 3x^2 + x + 8$
2. Find the slope of the four functions in Problem 1 when (a) $x = 0$; (b) $x = -3$; (c) $x = 2$.
3. Using the general rules of differentiation, find the first derivative of the following functions:
   a. $y = f(x) = 2x^3 + 6x - 3$
   b. $y = f(x) = (2x^2 - 3x + 1)(4x^3 - 7x^2 + 2x - 1)$
   c. $y = f(x) = (2x^3 - 4x^2 + x)/(4x^2 - 3x + 1)$
   d. $y = f(x) = (x^2 - 7x)^4$

   e. $y = f(x) = \dfrac{1}{(x^2 + 2x + 3)^2}$

   f. $y = f(x) = 4e^{2x} + 5$
   g. $y = f(x) = 2 \cdot (10)^{3x}$
   h. $y = f(x) = \ln (2x^2)$
4. Find the second derivative of the eight functions in Problem 3.
5. Find the maximum and/or minimum points of the following functions. Indicate for each solution you find whether it corresponds to a maximum or a minimum.
   a. $y = f(x) = 2x^2 - 7x + 3$
   b. $y = f(x) = -x^2 - 4x + 8$
   c. $y = f(x) = x^3 - x^2 - x + 4$
   d. $y = f(x) = -2x^3 - x^2 + 4x + 1$
   e. $y = f(x) = 2x^4 - 8x^3 - x^2 + 6x - 7$

[4] With, again, a second solution of $Q = 6.25$, which we shall disregard.

APPENDIX F

tables

Exhibit F–1   Binomial Distribution*

$$b(x|n, p) = \binom{n}{x} p^x (1 - p)^{n-x}$$

						p						
n	*x*	0.05	0.1	0.2	0.3	0.4	0.5	0.6	0.7	0.8	0.9	0.95
2	0	0.902	0.810	0.640	0.490	0.360	0.250	0.160	0.090	0.040	0.010	0.002
	1	0.095	0.180	0.320	0.420	0.480	0.500	0.480	0.420	0.320	0.180	0.095
	2	0.002	0.010	0.040	0.090	0.160	0.250	0.360	0.490	0.640	0.810	0.902
3	0	0.857	0.729	0.512	0.343	0.216	0.125	0.064	0.027	0.008	0.001	
	1	0.135	0.243	0.384	0.441	0.432	0.375	0.288	0.189	0.096	0.027	0.007
	2	0.007	0.027	0.096	0.189	0.288	0.375	0.432	0.441	0.384	0.243	0.135
	3		0.001	0.008	0.027	0.064	0.125	0.216	0.343	0.512	0.729	0.857
4	0	0.815	0.656	0.410	0.240	0.130	0.062	0.026	0.008	0.002		
	1	0.171	0.292	0.410	0.412	0.346	0.250	0.154	0.076	0.026	0.004	
	2	0.014	0.049	0.154	0.265	0.346	0.375	0.346	0.265	0.154	0.049	0.014
	3		0.004	0.026	0.076	0.154	0.250	0.346	0.412	0.410	0.292	0.171
	4			0.002	0.008	0.026	0.062	0.130	0.240	0.410	0.656	0.815
5	0	0.774	0.590	0.328	0.168	0.078	0.031	0.010	0.002			
	1	0.204	0.328	0.410	0.360	0.259	0.156	0.077	0.028	0.006		
	2	0.021	0.073	0.205	0.309	0.346	0.312	0.230	0.132	0.051	0.008	0.001
	3	0.001	0.008	0.051	0.132	0.230	0.312	0.346	0.309	0.205	0.073	0.021
	4			0.006	0.028	0.077	0.156	0.259	0.360	0.410	0.328	0.204
	5				0.002	0.010	0.031	0.078	0.168	0.328	0.590	0.774
6	0	0.735	0.531	0.262	0.118	0.047	0.016	0.004	0.001			
	1	0.232	0.354	0.393	0.303	0.187	0.094	0.037	0.010	0.002		
	2	0.031	0.098	0.246	0.324	0.311	0.234	0.138	0.060	0.015	0.001	
	3	0.002	0.015	0.082	0.185	0.276	0.312	0.276	0.185	0.082	0.015	0.002
	4		0.001	0.015	0.060	0.138	0.234	0.311	0.324	0.246	0.098	0.031
	5			0.002	0.010	0.037	0.094	0.187	0.303	0.393	0.354	0.232
	6				0.001	0.004	0.016	0.047	0.118	0.262	0.531	0.735
7	0	0.698	0.478	0.210	0.082	0.028	0.008	0.002				
	1	0.257	0.372	0.367	0.247	0.131	0.055	0.017	0.004			
	2	0.041	0.124	0.275	0.318	0.261	0.164	0.077	0.025	0.004		
	3	0.004	0.023	0.115	0.227	0.290	0.273	0.194	0.097	0.029	0.003	
	4		0.003	0.029	0.097	0.194	0.273	0.290	0.227	0.115	0.023	0.004

From John E. Freund, *Modern Elementary Statistics*, 4th ed. (Englewood Cliffs, N.J.: Prentice-Hall, 1973). By permission of the publisher.

* All values omitted in this table are 0.0005 or less.

							p					
n	x	0.05	0.1	0.2	0.3	0.4	0.5	0.6	0.7	0.8	0.9	0.95
7	5			0.004	0.025	0.077	0.164	0.261	0.318	0.275	0.124	0.041
	6				0.004	0.017	0.055	0.131	0.247	0.367	0.372	0.257
	7					0.002	0.008	0.028	0.082	0.210	0.478	0.698
8	0	0.663	0.430	0.168	0.058	0.017	0.004	0.001				
	1	0.279	0.383	0.336	0.198	0.090	0.031	0.008	0.001			
	2	0.051	0.149	0.294	0.296	0.209	0.109	0.041	0.010	0.001		
	3	0.005	0.033	0.147	0.254	0.279	0.219	0.124	0.047	0.009		
	4		0.005	0.046	0.136	0.232	0.273	0.232	0.136	0.046	0.005	
	5			0.009	0.047	0.124	0.219	0.279	0.254	0.147	0.033	0.005
	6			0.001	0.010	0.041	0.109	0.209	0.296	0.294	0.149	0.051
	7				0.001	0.008	0.031	0.090	0.198	0.336	0.383	0.279
	8					0.001	0.004	0.017	0.058	0.168	0.430	0.663
9	0	0.630	0.387	0.134	0.040	0.010	0.002					
	1	0.299	0.387	0.302	0.156	0.060	0.018	0.004				
	2	0.063	0.172	0.302	0.267	0.161	0.070	0.021	0.004			
	3	0.008	0.045	0.176	0.267	0.251	0.164	0.074	0.021	0.003		
	4	0.001	0.007	0.066	0.172	0.251	0.246	0.167	0.074	0.017	0.001	
	5		0.001	0.017	0.074	0.167	0.246	0.251	0.172	0.066	0.007	0.001
	6			0.003	0.021	0.074	0.164	0.251	0.267	0.176	0.045	0.008
	7				0.004	0.021	0.070	0.161	0.267	0.302	0.172	0.063
	8					0.004	0.018	0.060	0.156	0.302	0.387	0.299
	9						0.002	0.010	0.040	0.134	0.387	0.630
10	0	0.599	0.349	0.107	0.028	0.006	0.001					
	1	0.315	0.387	0.268	0.121	0.040	0.010	0.002				
	2	0.075	0.194	0.302	0.233	0.121	0.044	0.011	0.001			
	3	0.010	0.057	0.201	0.267	0.215	0.117	0.042	0.009	0.001		
	4	0.001	0.011	0.088	0.200	0.251	0.205	0.111	0.037	0.006		
	5		0.001	0.026	0.103	0.201	0.246	0.201	0.103	0.026	0.001	
	6			0.006	0.037	0.111	0.205	0.251	0.200	0.088	0.011	0.001
	7			0.001	0.009	0.042	0.117	0.215	0.267	0.201	0.057	0.010
	8				0.001	0.011	0.044	0.121	0.233	0.302	0.194	0.075
	9					0.002	0.010	0.040	0.121	0.268	0.387	0.315
	10						0.001	0.006	0.028	0.107	0.349	0.599

Exhibit F–1   Binomial Distribution (Continued)

n	x	0.05	0.1	0.2	0.3	0.4	0.5	0.6	0.7	0.8	0.9	0.95
11	0	0.569	0.314	0.086	0.020	0.004						
	1	0.329	0.384	0.236	0.093	0.027	0.005	0.001				
	2	0.087	0.213	0.295	0.200	0.089	0.027	0.005	0.001			
	3	0.014	0.071	0.221	0.257	0.177	0.081	0.023	0.004			
	4	0.001	0.016	0.111	0.220	0.236	0.161	0.070	0.017	0.002		
	5		0.002	0.039	0.132	0.221	0.226	0.147	0.057	0.010		
	6			0.010	0.057	0.147	0.226	0.221	0.132	0.039	0.002	
	7			0.002	0.017	0.070	0.161	0.236	0.220	0.111	0.016	0.001
	8				0.004	0.023	0.081	0.177	0.257	0.221	0.071	0.014
	9				0.001	0.005	0.027	0.089	0.200	0.295	0.213	0.087
	10					0.001	0.005	0.027	0.093	0.236	0.384	0.329
	11						0.004	0.020	0.086	0.314	0.569	
12	0	0.540	0.282	0.069	0.014	0.002						
	1	0.341	0.377	0.206	0.071	0.017	0.003					
	2	0.099	0.230	0.283	0.168	0.064	0.016	0.002				
	3	0.017	0.085	0.236	0.240	0.142	0.054	0.012	0.001			
	4	0.002	0.021	0.133	0.231	0.213	0.121	0.042	0.008	0.001		
	5		0.004	0.053	0.158	0.227	0.193	0.101	0.029	0.003		
	6			0.016	0.079	0.177	0.226	0.177	0.079	0.016		
	7			0.003	0.029	0.101	0.193	0.227	0.158	0.053	0.004	
	8			0.001	0.008	0.042	0.121	0.213	0.231	0.133	0.021	0.002
	9				0.001	0.012	0.054	0.142	0.240	0.236	0.085	0.017
	10					0.002	0.016	0.064	0.168	0.283	0.230	0.099
	11						0.003	0.017	0.071	0.206	0.377	0.341
	12							0.002	0.014	0.069	0.282	0.540
13	0	0.513	0.254	0.055	0.010	0.001						
	1	0.351	0.367	0.179	0.054	0.011	0.002					
	2	0.111	0.245	0.268	0.139	0.045	0.010	0.001				
	3	0.021	0.100	0.246	0.218	0.111	0.035	0.006	0.001			
	4	0.003	0.028	0.154	0.234	0.184	0.087	0.024	0.003			
	5		0.006	0.069	0.180	0.221	0.157	0.066	0.014	0.001		
	6		0.001	0.023	0.103	0.197	0.209	0.131	0.044	0.006		
	7			0.006	0.044	0.131	0.209	0.197	0.103	0.023	0.001	

n	x	0.05	0.1	0.2	0.3	0.4	0.5	0.6	0.7	0.8	0.9	0.95
13	8			0.001	0.014	0.066	0.157	0.221	0.180	0.069	0.006	
	9				0.003	0.024	0.087	0.184	0.234	0.154	0.028	0.003
	10				0.001	0.006	0.035	0.111	0.218	0.246	0.100	0.021
	11					0.001	0.010	0.045	0.139	0.268	0.245	0.111
	12						0.002	0.011	0.054	0.179	0.367	0.351
	13							0.001	0.010	0.055	0.254	0.513
14	0	0.488	0.229	0.044	0.007	0.001						
	1	0.359	0.356	0.154	0.041	0.007	0.001					
	2	0.123	0.257	0.250	0.113	0.032	0.006	0.001				
	3	0.026	0.114	0.250	0.194	0.085	0.022	0.003				
	4	0.004	0.035	0.172	0.229	0.155	0.061	0.014	0.001			
	5		0.008	0.086	0.196	0.207	0.122	0.041	0.007			
	6		0.001	0.032	0.126	0.207	0.183	0.092	0.023	0.002		
	7			0.009	0.062	0.157	0.209	0.157	0.062	0.009		
	8			0.002	0.023	0.092	0.183	0.207	0.126	0.032	0.001	
	9				0.007	0.041	0.122	0.207	0.196	0.086	0.008	
	10				0.001	0.014	0.061	0.155	0.229	0.172	0.035	0.004
	11					0.003	0.022	0.085	0.194	0.250	0.114	0.026
	12					0.001	0.006	0.032	0.113	0.250	0.257	0.123
	13						0.001	0.007	0.041	0.154	0.356	0.359
	14							0.001	0.007	0.044	0.229	0.488
15	0	0.463	0.206	0.035	0.005							
	1	0.366	0.343	0.132	0.031	0.005						
	2	0.135	0.267	0.231	0.092	0.022	0.003					
	3	0.031	0.129	0.250	0.170	0.063	0.014	0.002				
	4	0.005	0.043	0.188	0.219	0.127	0.042	0.007	0.001			
	5	0.001	0.010	0.103	0.206	0.186	0.092	0.024	0.003			
	6		0.002	0.043	0.147	0.207	0.153	0.061	0.012	0.001		
	7			0.014	0.081	0.177	0.196	0.118	0.035	0.003		
	8			0.003	0.035	0.118	0.196	0.177	0.081	0.014		
	9			0.001	0.012	0.061	0.153	0.207	0.147	0.043	0.002	
	10				0.003	0.024	0.092	0.186	0.206	0.103	0.010	0.001
	11				0.001	0.007	0.042	0.127	0.219	0.188	0.043	0.005
	12					0.002	0.014	0.063	0.170	0.250	0.129	0.031
	13						0.003	0.022	0.092	0.231	0.267	0.135
	14							0.005	0.031	0.132	0.343	0.366
	15								0.005	0.035	0.206	0.463

Exhibit F–2   Cumulative Binomial Probability Distribution

$$P(r \geq r \mid n, p)$$

$$n = 1$$

	p	01	02	03	04	05	06	07	08	09	10
r	1	0100	0200	0300	0400	0500	0600	0700	0800	0900	1000
	p	11	12	13	14	15	16	17	18	19	20
r	1	1100	1200	1300	1400	1500	1600	1700	1800	1900	2000
	p	21	22	23	24	25	26	27	28	29	30
r	1	2100	2200	2300	2400	2500	2600	2700	2800	2900	3000
	p	31	32	33	34	35	36	37	38	39	40
r	1	3100	3200	3300	3400	3500	3600	3700	3800	3900	4000
	p	41	42	43	44	45	46	47	48	49	50
r	1	4100	4200	4300	4400	4500	4600	4700	4800	4900	5000

$$n = 2$$

	p	01	02	03	04	05	06	07	08	09	10
r	1	0199	0396	0591	0784	0975	1164	1351	1536	1719	1900
	2	0001	0004	0009	0016	0025	0036	0049	0064	0081	0100
	p	11	12	13	14	15	16	17	18	19	20
r	1	2079	2256	2431	2604	2775	2944	3111	3276	3439	3600
	2	0121	0144	0169	0196	0225	0256	0289	0324	0361	0400
	p	21	22	23	24	25	26	27	28	29	30
r	1	3759	3916	4071	4224	4375	4524	4671	4816	4959	5100
	2	0441	0484	0529	0576	0625	0676	0729	0784	0841	0900
	p	31	32	33	34	35	36	37	38	39	40
r	1	5239	5376	5511	5644	5775	5904	6031	6156	6279	6400
	2	0961	1024	1089	1156	1225	1296	1369	1444	1521	1600
	p	41	42	43	44	45	46	47	48	49	50
r	1	6519	6636	6751	6864	6975	7084	7191	7296	7399	7500
	2	1681	1764	1849	1936	2025	2116	2209	2304	2401	2500

$$n = 3$$

	p	01	02	03	04	05	06	07	08	09	10
r	1	0297	0588	0873	1153	1426	1694	1956	2213	2464	2710
	2	0003	0012	0026	0047	0073	0104	0140	0182	0228	0280
	3				0001	0001	0002	0003	0005	0007	0010
	p	11	12	13	14	15	16	17	18	19	20
r	1	2950	3185	3415	3639	3859	4073	4282	4486	4686	4880
	2	0336	0397	0463	0533	0608	0686	0769	0855	0946	1040
	3	0013	0017	0022	0027	0034	0041	0049	0058	0069	0080
	p	21	22	23	24	25	26	27	28	29	30
r	1	5070	5254	5435	5610	5781	5948	6110	6268	6421	6570
	2	1138	1239	1344	1452	1563	1676	1793	1913	2035	2160
	3	0093	0106	0122	0138	0156	0176	0197	0220	0244	0270
	p	31	32	33	34	35	36	37	38	39	40
r	1	6715	6856	6992	7125	7254	7379	7500	7617	7730	7840
	2	2287	2417	2548	2682	2818	2955	3094	3235	3377	3520
	3	0298	0328	0359	0393	0429	0467	0507	0549	0593	0640

$n = 3$

p	41	42	43	44	45	46	47	48	49	50
r 1	7946	8049	8148	8244	8336	8425	8511	8594	8673	8750
2	3665	3810	3957	4104	4253	4401	4551	4700	4850	5000
3	0689	0741	0795	0852	0911	0973	1038	1106	1176	1250

$n = 4$

p	01	02	03	04	05	06	07	08	09	10
r 1	0394	0776	1147	1507	1855	2193	2519	2836	3143	3439
2	0006	0023	0052	0091	0140	0199	0267	0344	0430	0523
3			0001	0002	0005	0008	0013	0019	0027	0037
4									0001	0001

p	11	12	13	14	15	16	17	18	19	20
1	3726	4003	4271	4530	4780	5021	5254	5479	5695	5904
2	0624	0732	0847	0968	1095	1228	1366	1509	1656	1808
3	0049	0063	0079	0098	0120	0144	0171	0202	0235	0272
4	0001	0002	0003	0004	0005	0007	0008	0010	0013	0016

p	21	22	23	24	25	26	27	28	29	30
1	6105	6298	6485	6664	6836	7001	7160	7313	7459	7599
2	1963	2122	2285	2450	2617	2787	2959	3132	3307	3483
3	0312	0356	0403	0453	0508	0566	0628	0694	0763	0837
4	0019	0023	0028	0033	0039	0046	0053	0061	0071	0081

p	31	32	33	34	35	36	37	38	39	40
1	7733	7862	7985	8103	8215	8322	8425	8522	8615	8704
2	3660	3837	4015	4193	4370	4547	4724	4900	5075	5248
3	0915	0996	1082	1171	1265	1362	1464	1569	1679	1792
4	0092	0105	0119	0134	0150	0168	0187	0209	0231	0256

p	41	42	43	44	45	46	47	48	49	50
1	8788	8868	8944	9017	9085	9150	9211	9269	9323	9375
2	5420	5590	5759	5926	6090	6252	6412	6569	6724	6875
3	1909	2030	2155	2283	2415	2550	2689	2831	2977	3125
4	0283	0311	0342	0375	0410	0448	0488	0531	0576	0625

$n = 5$

p	01	02	03	04	05	06	07	08	09	10
r 1	0490	0961	1413	1846	2262	2661	3043	3409	3760	4095
2	0010	0038	0085	0148	0226	0319	0425	0544	0674	0815
3		0001	0003	0006	0012	0020	0031	0045	0063	0086
4						0001	0001	0002	0003	0005

p	11	12	13	14	15	16	17	18	19	20
r 1	4416	4723	5016	5296	5563	5818	6061	6293	6513	6723
2	0965	1125	1292	1467	1648	1835	2027	2224	2424	2627
3	0112	0143	0179	0220	0266	0318	0375	0437	0505	0579
4	0007	0009	0013	0017	0022	0029	0036	0045	0055	0067
5				0001	0001	0001	0001	0002	0002	0003

p	21	22	23	24	25	26	27	28	29	30
r 1	6923	7113	7293	7464	7627	7781	7927	8065	8196	8319
2	2833	3041	3251	3461	3672	3883	4093	4303	4511	4718
3	0659	0744	0836	0933	1035	1143	1257	1376	1501	1631
4	0081	0097	0114	0134	0156	0181	0208	0238	0272	0308
5	0004	0005	0006	0008	0010	0012	0014	0017	0021	0024

Exhibit F–2   Cumulative Binomial Probability Distribution (Continued)

$n = 5$

p	31	32	33	34	35	36	37	38	39	40
r 1	8436	8546	8650	8748	8840	8926	9008	9084	9155	9222
2	4923	5125	5325	5522	5716	5906	6093	6276	6455	6630
3	1766	1905	2050	2199	2352	2509	2670	2835	3003	3174
4	0347	0390	0436	0486	0540	0598	0660	0726	0796	0870
5	0029	0034	0039	0045	0053	0060	0069	0079	0090	0102

p	41	42	43	44	45	46	47	48	49	50
r 1	9285	9344	9398	9449	9497	9541	9582	9620	9655	9688
2	6801	6967	7129	7286	7438	7585	7728	7865	7998	8125
3	3349	3525	3705	3886	4069	4253	4439	4625	4813	5000
4	0949	1033	1121	1214	1312	1415	1522	1635	1753	1875
5	0116	0131	0147	0165	0185	0206	0229	0255	0282	0313

$n = 6$

p	01	02	03	04	05	06	07	08	09	10
r 1	0585	1142	1670	2172	2649	3101	3530	3936	4321	4686
2	0015	0057	0125	0216	0328	0459	0608	0773	0952	1143
3		0002	0005	0012	0022	0038	0058	0085	0118	0159
4				0001	0002	0003	0005	0008	0013
5										0001

p	11	12	13	14	15	16	17	18	19	20
r 1	5030	5356	5664	5954	6229	6487	6731	6960	7176	7379
2	1345	1556	1776	2003	2235	2472	2713	2956	3201	3446
3	0206	0261	0324	0395	0473	0560	0655	0759	0870	0989
4	0018	0025	0034	0045	0059	0075	0094	0116	0141	0170
5	0001	0001	0002	0003	0004	0005	0007	0010	0013	0016
6										0001

p	21	22	23	24	25	26	27	28	29	30
r 1	7569	7748	7916	8073	8220	8358	8487	8607	8719	8824
2	3692	3937	4180	4422	4661	4896	5128	5356	5580	5798
3	1115	1250	1391	1539	1694	1856	2023	2196	2374	2557
4	0202	0239	0280	0326	0376	0431	0492	0557	0628	0705
5	0020	0025	0031	0038	0046	0056	0067	0079	0093	0109
6	0001	0001	0001	0002	0002	0003	0004	0005	0006	0007

p	31	32	33	34	35	36	37	38	39	40
r 1	8921	9011	9095	9173	9246	9313	9375	9432	9485	9533
2	6012	6220	6422	6619	6809	6994	7172	7343	7508	7667
3	2744	2936	3130	3328	3529	3732	3937	4143	4350	4557
4	0787	0875	0969	1069	1174	1286	1404	1527	1657	1792
5	0127	0148	0170	0195	0223	0254	0288	0325	0365	0410
6	0009	0011	0013	0015	0018	0022	0026	0030	0035	0041

p	41	42	43	44	45	46	47	48	49	50
r 1	9578	9619	9657	9692	9723	9752	9778	9802	9824	9844
2	7819	7965	8105	8238	8364	8485	8599	8707	8810	8906
3	4764	4971	5177	5382	5585	5786	5985	6180	6373	6563
4	1933	2080	2232	2390	2553	2721	2893	3070	3252	3438
5	0458	0510	0566	0627	0692	0762	0837	0917	1003	1094
6	0048	0055	0063	0073	0083	0095	0108	0122	0138	0156

$n = 7$

$n = 7$									

p	01	02	03	04	05	06	07	08	09	10
r 1	0679	1319	1920	2486	3017	3515	3983	4422	4832	5217
2	0020	0079	0171	0294	0444	0618	0813	1026	1255	1497
3		0003	0009	0020	0038	0063	0097	0140	0193	0257
4				0001	0002	0004	0007	0012	0018	0027
5								0001	0001	0002

p	11	12	13	14	15	16	17	18	19	20
r 1	5577	5913	6227	6521	6794	7049	7286	7507	7712	7903
2	1750	2012	2281	2556	2834	3115	3396	3677	3956	4233
3	0331	0416	0513	0620	0738	0866	1005	1154	1313	1480
4	0039	0054	0072	0094	0121	0153	0189	0231	0279	0333
5	0003	0004	0006	0009	0012	0017	0022	0029	0037	0047
6					0001	0001	0001	0002	0003	0004

p	21	22	23	24	25	26	27	28	29	30
r 1	8080	8243	8395	8535	8665	8785	8895	8997	9090	9176
2	4506	4775	5040	5298	5551	5796	6035	6266	6490	6706
3	1657	1841	2033	2231	2436	2646	2861	3081	3304	3529
4	0394	0461	0536	0617	0706	0802	0905	1016	1134	1260
5	0058	0072	0088	0107	0129	0153	0181	0213	0248	0288
6	0005	0006	0008	0011	0013	0017	0021	0026	0031	0038
7					0001	0001	0001	0001	0002	0002

p	31	32	33	34	35	36	37	38	39	40
r 1	9255	9328	9394	9454	9510	9560	9606	9648	9686	9720
2	6914	7113	7304	7487	7662	7828	7987	8137	8279	8414
3	3757	3987	4217	4447	4677	4906	5134	5359	5581	5801
4	1394	1534	1682	1837	1998	2167	2341	2521	2707	2898
5	0332	0380	0434	0492	0556	0625	0701	0782	0869	0963
6	0046	0055	0065	0077	0090	0105	0123	0142	0164	0188
7	0003	0003	0004	0005	0006	0008	0009	0011	0014	0016

p	41	42	43	44	45	46	47	48	49	50
r 1	9751	9779	9805	9827	9848	9866	9883	9897	9910	9922
2	8541	8660	8772	8877	8976	9068	9153	9233	9307	9375
3	6017	6229	6436	6638	6836	7027	7213	7393	7567	7734
4	3094	3294	3498	3706	3917	4131	4346	4563	4781	5000
5	1063	1169	1282	1402	1529	1663	1803	1951	2105	2266
6	0216	0246	0279	0316	0357	0402	0451	0504	0562	0625
7	0019	0023	0027	0032	0037	0044	0051	0059	0068	0078

$n = 8$

p	01	02	03	04	05	06	07	08	09	10
r 1	0773	1492	2163	2786	3366	3904	4404	4868	5297	5695
2	0027	0103	0223	0381	0572	0792	1035	1298	1577	1869
3	0001	0004	0013	0031	0058	0096	0147	0211	0289	0381
4			0001	0002	0004	0007	0013	0022	0034	0050
5							0001	0001	0003	0004

Exhibit F–2 Cumulative Binomial Probability Distribution (Continued)

$n = 8$

	p	11	12	13	14	15	16	17	18	19	20
r	1	6063	6404	6718	7008	7275	7521	7748	7956	8147	8322
	2	2171	2480	2794	3111	3428	3744	4057	4366	4670	4967
	3	0487	0608	0743	0891	1052	1226	1412	1608	1815	2031
	4	0071	0097	0129	0168	0214	0267	0328	0397	0476	0563
	5	0007	0010	0015	0021	0029	0038	0050	0065	0083	0104
	6		0001	0001	0002	0002	0003	0005	0007	0009	0012
	7									0001	0001

	p	21	22	23	24	25	26	27	28	29	30
r	1	8483	8630	8764	8887	8999	9101	9194	9278	9354	9424
	2	5257	5538	5811	6075	6329	6573	6807	7031	7244	7447
	3	2255	2486	2724	2967	3215	3465	3718	3973	4228	4482
	4	0659	0765	0880	1004	1138	1281	1433	1594	1763	1941
	5	0129	0158	0191	0230	0273	0322	0377	0438	0505	0580
	6	0016	0021	0027	0034	0042	0052	0064	0078	0094	0113
	7	0001	0002	0002	0003	0004	0005	0006	0008	0010	0013
	8									0001	0001

	p	31	32	33	34	35	36	37	38	39	40
r	1	9486	9543	9594	9640	9681	9719	9752	9782	9808	9832
	2	7640	7822	7994	8156	8309	8452	8586	8711	8828	8936
	3	4736	4987	5236	5481	5722	5958	6189	6415	6634	6846
	4	2126	2319	2519	2724	2936	3153	3374	3599	3828	4059
	5	0661	0750	0846	0949	1061	1180	1307	1443	1586	1737
	6	0134	0159	0187	0218	0253	0293	0336	0385	0439	0498
	7	0016	0020	0024	0030	0036	0043	0051	0061	0072	0085
	8	0001	0001	0001	0002	0002	0003	0004	0004	0005	0007

	p	41	42	43	44	45	46	47	48	49	50
r	1	9853	9872	9889	9903	9916	9928	9938	9947	9954	9961
	2	9037	9130	9216	9295	9368	9435	9496	9552	9602	9648
	3	7052	7250	7440	7624	7799	7966	8125	8276	8419	8555
	4	4292	4527	4762	4996	5230	5463	5694	5922	6146	6367
	5	1895	2062	2235	2416	2604	2798	2999	3205	3416	3633
	6	0563	0634	0711	0794	0885	0982	1086	1198	1318	1445
	7	0100	0117	0136	0157	0181	0208	0239	0272	0310	0352
	8	0008	0010	0012	0014	0017	0020	0024	0028	0033	0039

$n = 9$

	p	01	02	03	04	05	06	07	08	09	10
r	1	0865	1663	2398	3075	3698	4270	4796	5278	5721	6126
	2	0034	0131	0282	0478	0712	0978	1271	1583	1912	2252
	3	0001	0006	0020	0045	0084	0138	0209	0298	0405	0530
	4			0001	0003	0006	0013	0023	0037	0057	0083
	5						0001	0002	0003	0005	0009
	6										0001

Exhibit F–2   Cumulative Binomial Probability Distribution (Continued)

$n = 9$

p	11	12	13	14	15	16	17	18	19	20
r 1	6496	6835	7145	7427	7684	7918	8131	8324	8499	8658
2	2599	2951	3304	3657	4005	4348	4685	5012	5330	5638
3	0672	0833	1009	1202	1409	1629	1861	2105	2357	2618
4	0117	0158	0209	0269	0339	0420	0512	0615	0730	0856
5	0014	0021	0030	0041	0056	0075	0098	0125	0158	0196
6	0001	0002	0003	0004	0006	0009	0013	0017	0023	0031
7						0001	0001	0002	0002	0003

p	21	22	23	24	25	26	27	28	29	30
r 1	8801	8931	9048	9154	9249	9335	9411	9480	9542	9596
2	5934	6218	6491	6750	6997	7230	7452	7660	7856	8040
3	2885	3158	3434	3713	3993	4273	4552	4829	5102	5372
4	0994	1144	1304	1475	1657	1849	2050	2260	2478	2703
5	0240	0291	0350	0416	0489	0571	0662	0762	0870	0988
6	0040	0051	0065	0081	0100	0122	0149	0179	0213	0253
7	0004	0006	0008	0010	0013	0017	0022	0028	0035	0043
8			0001	0001	0001	0001	0002	0003	0003	0004

p	31	32	33	34	35	36	37	38	39	40
r 1	9645	9689	9728	9762	9793	9820	9844	9865	9883	9899
2	8212	8372	8522	8661	8789	8908	9017	9118	9210	9295
3	5636	5894	6146	6390	6627	6856	7076	7287	7489	7682
4	2935	3173	3415	3662	3911	4163	4416	4669	4922	5174
5	1115	1252	1398	1553	1717	1890	2072	2262	2460	2666
6	0298	0348	0404	0467	0536	0612	0696	0787	0886	0994
7	0053	0064	0078	0094	0112	0133	0157	0184	0215	0250
8	0006	0007	0009	0011	0014	0017	0021	0026	0031	0038
9				0001	0001	0001	0001	0002	0002	0003

p	41	42	43	44	45	46	47	48	49	50
r 1	9913	9926	9936	9946	9954	9961	9967	9972	9977	9980
2	9372	9442	9505	9563	9615	9662	9704	9741	9775	9805
3	7866	8039	8204	8359	8505	8642	8769	8889	8999	9102
4	5424	5670	5913	6152	6386	6614	6836	7052	7260	7461
5	2878	3097	3322	3551	3786	4024	4265	4509	4754	5000
6	1109	1233	1366	1508	1658	1817	1985	2161	2346	2539
7	0290	0334	0383	0437	0498	0564	0637	0717	0804	0898
8	0046	0055	0065	0077	0091	0107	0125	0145	0169	0195
9	0003	0004	0005	0006	0008	0009	0011	0014	0016	0020

$n = 10$

p	01	02	03	04	05	06	07	08	09	10
r 1	0956	1829	2626	3352	4013	4614	5160	5656	6106	6513
2	0043	0162	0345	0582	0861	1176	1517	1879	2254	2639
3	0001	0009	0028	0062	0115	0188	0283	0401	0540	0702
4			0001	0004	0010	0020	0036	0058	0088	0128
5					0001	0002	0003	0006	0010	0016
6									0001	0001

$n = 10$

r	p	11	12	13	14	15	16	17	18	19	20
	1	6882	7215	7516	7787	8031	8251	8448	8626	8784	8926
	2	3028	3417	3804	4184	4557	4920	5270	5608	5932	6242
	3	0884	1087	1308	1545	1798	2064	2341	2628	2922	3222
	4	0178	0239	0313	0400	0500	0614	0741	0883	1039	1209
	5	0025	0037	0053	0073	0099	0130	0168	0213	0266	0328
	6	0003	0004	0006	0010	0014	0020	0027	0037	0049	0064
	7			0001	0001	0001	0002	0003	0004	0006	0009
	8									0001	0001

r	p	21	22	23	24	25	26	27	28	29	30
	1	9053	9166	9267	9357	9437	9508	9570	9626	9674	9718
	2	6536	6815	7079	7327	7560	7778	7981	8170	8345	8507
	3	3526	3831	4137	4442	4744	5042	5335	5622	5901	6172
	4	1391	1587	1794	2012	2241	2479	2726	2979	3239	3504
	5	0399	0479	0569	0670	0781	0904	1037	1181	1337	1503
	6	0082	0104	0130	0161	0197	0239	0287	0342	0404	0473
	7	0012	0016	0021	0027	0035	0045	0056	0070	0087	0106
	8	0001	0002	0002	0003	0004	0006	0007	0010	0012	0016
	9							0001	0001	0001	0001

r	p	31	32	33	34	35	36	37	38	39	40
	1	9755	9789	9818	9843	9865	9885	9902	9916	9929	9940
	2	8656	8794	8920	9035	9140	9236	9323	9402	9473	9536
	3	6434	6687	6930	7162	7384	7595	7794	7983	8160	8327
	4	3772	4044	4316	4589	4862	5132	5400	5664	5923	6177
	5	1679	1867	2064	2270	2485	2708	2939	3177	3420	3669
	6	0551	0637	0732	0836	0949	1072	1205	1348	1500	1662
	7	0129	0155	0185	0220	0260	0305	0356	0413	0477	0548
	8	0020	0025	0032	0039	0048	0059	0071	0086	0103	0123
	9	0002	0003	0003	0004	0005	0007	0009	0011	0014	0017
	10								0001	0001	0001

r	p	41	42	43	44	45	46	47	48	49	50
	1	9949	9957	9964	9970	9975	9979	9983	9986	9988	9990
	2	9594	9645	9691	9731	9767	9799	9827	9852	9874	9893
	3	8483	8628	8764	8889	9004	9111	9209	9298	9379	9453
	4	6425	6665	6898	7123	7340	7547	7745	7933	8112	8281
	5	3922	4178	4436	4696	4956	5216	5474	5730	5982	6230
	6	1834	2016	2207	2407	2616	2832	3057	3288	3526	3770
	7	0626	0712	0806	0908	1020	1141	1271	1410	1560	1719
	8	0146	0172	0202	0236	0274	0317	0366	0420	0480	0547
	9	0021	0025	0031	0037	0045	0054	0065	0077	0091	0107
	10	0001	0002	0002	0003	0003	0004	0005	0006	0008	0010

$n = 11$

$n = 11$

p / r	01	02	03	04	05	06	07	08	09	10
1	1047	1993	2847	3618	4312	4937	5499	6004	6456	6862
2	0052	0195	0413	0692	1019	1382	1772	2181	2601	3026
3	0002	0012	0037	0083	0152	0248	0370	0519	0695	0896
4			0002	0007	0016	0030	0053	0085	0129	0185
5					0001	0003	0005	0010	0017	0028
6								0001	0002	0003

p / r	11	12	13	14	15	16	17	18	19	20
1	7225	7549	7839	8097	8327	8531	8712	8873	9015	9141
2	3452	3873	4286	4689	5078	5453	5811	6151	6474	6779
3	1120	1366	1632	1915	2212	2521	2839	3164	3494	3826
4	0256	0341	0442	0560	0694	0846	1013	1197	1397	1611
5	0042	0061	0087	0119	0159	0207	0266	0334	0413	0504
6	0005	0008	0012	0018	0027	0037	0051	0068	0090	0117
7		0001	0001	0002	0003	0005	0007	0010	0014	0020
8							0001	0001	0002	0002

p / r	21	22	23	24	25	26	27	28	29	30
1	9252	9350	9436	9511	9578	9636	9686	9730	9769	9802
2	7065	7333	7582	7814	8029	8227	8410	8577	8730	8870
3	4158	4488	4814	5134	5448	5753	6049	6335	6610	6873
4	1840	2081	2333	2596	2867	3146	3430	3719	4011	4304
5	0607	0723	0851	0992	1146	1313	1493	1685	1888	2103
6	0148	0186	0231	0283	0343	0412	0490	0577	0674	0782
7	0027	0035	0046	0059	0076	0095	0119	0146	0179	0216
8	0003	0005	0007	0009	0012	0016	0021	0027	0034	0043
9			0001	0001	0001	0002	0002	0003	0004	0006

p / r	31	32	33	34	35	36	37	38	39	40
1	9831	9856	9878	9896	9912	9926	9938	9948	9956	9964
2	8997	9112	9216	9310	9394	9470	9537	9597	9650	9698
3	7123	7361	7587	7799	7999	8186	8360	8522	8672	8811
4	4598	4890	5179	5464	5744	6019	6286	6545	6796	7037
5	2328	2563	2807	3059	3317	3581	3850	4122	4397	4672
6	0901	1031	1171	1324	1487	1661	1847	2043	2249	2465
7	0260	0309	0366	04.0	0501	0581	0670	0768	0876	0994
8	0054	0067	0082	0101	0122	0148	0177	0210	0249	0293
9	0008	0010	0013	0016	0020	0026	0032	0039	0048	0059
10	0001	0001	0001	0002	0002	0003	0004	0005	0006	0007

$n = 11$

p	41	42	43	44	45	46	47	48	49	50
r 1	9970	9975	9979	9983	9986	9989	9991	9992	9994	9995
2	9739	9776	9808	9836	9861	9882	9900	9916	9930	9941
3	8938	9055	9162	9260	9348	9428	9499	9564	9622	9673
4	7269	7490	7700	7900	8089	8266	8433	8588	8733	8867
5	4948	5223	5495	5764	6029	6288	6541	6787	7026	7256
6	2690	2924	3166	3414	3669	3929	4193	4460	4729	5000
7	1121	1260	1408	1568	1738	1919	2110	2312	2523	2744
8	0343	0399	0461	0532	0610	0696	0791	0895	1009	1133
9	0072	0087	0104	0125	0148	0175	0206	0241	0282	0327
10	0009	0012	0014	0018	0022	0027	0033	0040	0049	0059
11	0001	0001	0001	0001	0002	0002	0002	0003	0004	0005

$n = 12$

p	01	02	03	04	05	06	07	08	09	10
r 1	1136	2153	3062	3873	4596	5241	5814	6323	6775	7176
2	0062	0231	0486	0809	1184	1595	2033	2487	2948	3410
3	0002	0015	0048	0107	0196	0316	0468	0652	0866	1109
4		0001	0003	0010	0022	0043	0075	0120	0180	0256
5				0001	0002	0004	0009	0016	0027	0043
6							0001	0002	0003	0005
7										0001

p	11	12	13	14	15	16	17	18	19	20
r 1	7530	7843	8120	8363	8578	8766	8931	9076	9202	9313
2	3867	4314	4748	5166	5565	5945	6304	6641	6957	7251
3	1377	1667	1977	2303	2642	2990	3344	3702	4060	4417
4	0351	0464	0597	0750	0922	1114	1324	1552	1795	2054
5	0065	0095	0133	0181	0239	0310	0393	0489	0600	0726
6	0009	0014	0022	0033	0046	0065	0088	0116	0151	0194
7	0001	0002	0003	0004	0007	0010	0015	0021	0029	0039
8					0001	0001	0002	0003	0004	0006
9										0001

p	21	22	23	24	25	26	27	28	29	30
r 1	9409	9493	9566	9629	9683	9730	9771	9806	9836	9862
2	7524	7776	8009	8222	8416	8594	8755	8900	9032	9150
3	4768	5114	5450	5778	6093	6397	6687	6963	7225	7472
4	2326	2610	2904	3205	3512	3824	4137	4452	4765	5075
5	0866	1021	1192	1377	1576	1790	2016	2254	2504	2763
6	0245	0304	0374	0453	0544	0646	0760	0887	1026	1178
7	0052	0068	0089	0113	0143	0178	0219	0267	0322	0386
8	0008	0011	0016	0021	0028	0036	0047	0060	0076	0095
9	0001	0001	0002	0003	0004	0005	0007	0010	0013	0017
10						0001	0001	0001	0002	0002

Exhibit F-2   Cumulative Binomial Probability Distribution (Continued)

$n = 12$

p	31	32	33	34	35	36	37	38	39	40
r 1	9884	9902	9918	9932	9943	9953	9961	9968	9973	9978
2	9256	9350	9435	9509	9576	9634	9685	9730	9770	9804
3	7704	7922	8124	8313	8487	8648	8795	8931	9054	9166
4	5381	5681	5973	6258	6533	6799	7053	7296	7528	7747
5	3032	3308	3590	3876	4167	4459	4751	5043	5332	5618
6	1343	1521	1711	1913	2127	2352	2588	2833	3087	3348
7	0458	0540	0632	0734	0846	0970	1106	1253	1411	1582
8	0118	0144	0176	0213	0255	0304	0359	0422	0493	0573
9	0022	0028	0036	0045	0056	0070	0086	0104	0127	0153
10	0003	0004	0005	0007	0008	0011	0014	0018	0022	0028
11				0001	0001	0001	0001	0002	0002	0003

p	41	42	43	44	45	46	47	48	49	50
r 1	9982	9986	9988	9990	9992	9994	9995	9996	9997	9998
2	9834	9860	9882	9901	9917	9931	9943	9953	9961	9968
3	9267	9358	9440	9513	9579	9637	9688	9733	9773	9807
4	7953	8147	8329	8498	8655	8801	8934	9057	9168	9270
5	5899	6175	6443	6704	6956	7198	7430	7652	7862	8062
6	3616	3889	4167	4448	4731	5014	5297	5577	5855	6128
7	1765	1959	2164	2380	2607	2843	3089	3343	3604	3872
8	0662	0760	0869	0988	1117	1258	1411	1575	1751	1938
9	0183	0218	0258	0304	0356	0415	0481	0555	0638	0730
10	0035	0043	0053	0065	0079	0095	0114	0137	0163	0193
11	0004	0005	0007	0009	0011	0014	0017	0021	0026	0032
12				0001	0001	0001	0001	0001	0002	0002

$n = 13$

p	01	02	03	04	05	06	07	08	09	10
r 1	1225	2310	3270	4118	4867	5526	6107	6617	7065	7458
2	0072	0270	0564	0932	1354	1814	2298	2794	3293	3787
3	0003	0020	0062	0135	0245	0392	0578	0799	1054	1339
4		0001	0005	0014	0031	0060	0103	0163	0242	0342
5				0001	0003	0007	0013	0024	0041	0065
6						0001	0001	0003	0005	0009
7									0001	0001

p	11	12	13	14	15	16	17	18	19	20
r 1	7802	8102	8364	8592	8791	8963	9113	9242	9354	9450
2	4270	4738	5186	5614	6017	6396	6751	7080	7384	7664
3	1651	1985	2337	2704	3080	3463	3848	4231	4611	4983
4	0464	0609	0776	0967	1180	1414	1667	1939	2226	2527
5	0097	0139	0193	0260	0342	0438	0551	0681	0827	0991
6	0015	0024	0036	0053	0075	0104	0139	0183	0237	0300
7	0002	0003	0005	0008	0013	0019	0027	0038	0052	0070
8			0001	0001	0002	0003	0004	0006	0009	0012
9								0001	0001	0002

$n = 13$

p / r	21	22	23	24	25	26	27	28	29	30
1	9533	9604	9666	9718	9762	9800	9833	9860	9883	9903
2	7920	8154	8367	8559	8733	8889	9029	9154	9265	9363
3	5347	5699	6039	6364	6674	6968	7245	7505	7749	7975
4	2839	3161	3489	3822	4157	4493	4826	5155	5478	5794
5	1173	1371	1585	1816	2060	2319	2589	2870	3160	3457
6	0375	0462	0562	0675	0802	0944	1099	1270	1455	1654
7	0093	0120	0154	0195	0243	0299	0365	0440	0527	0624
8	0017	0024	0032	0043	0056	0073	0093	0118	0147	0182
9	0002	0004	0005	0007	0010	0013	0018	0024	0031	0040
10			0001	0001	0001	0002	0003	0004	0005	0007
11									0001	0001

p / r	31	32	33	34	35	36	37	38	39	40
1	9920	9934	9945	9955	9963	9970	9975	9980	9984	9987
2	9450	9527	9594	9653	9704	9749	9787	9821	9849	9874
3	8185	8379	8557	8720	8868	9003	9125	9235	9333	9421
4	6101	6398	6683	6957	7217	7464	7698	7917	8123	8314
5	3760	4067	4376	4686	4995	5301	5603	5899	6188	6470
6	1867	2093	2331	2581	2841	3111	3388	3673	3962	4256
7	0733	0854	0988	1135	1295	1468	1654	1853	2065	2288
8	0223	0271	0326	0390	0462	0544	0635	0738	0851	0977
9	0052	0065	0082	0102	0126	0154	0187	0225	0270	0321
10	0009	0012	0015	0020	0025	0032	0040	0051	0063	0078
11	0001	0001	0002	0003	0003	0005	0006	0008	0010	0013
12							0001	0001	0001	0001

p / r	41	42	43	44	45	46	47	48	49	50
1	9990	9992	9993	9995	9996	9997	9997	9998	9998	9999
2	9895	9912	9928	9940	9951	9960	9967	9974	9979	9983
3	9499	9569	9630	9684	9731	9772	9808	9838	9865	9888
4	8492	8656	8807	8945	9071	9185	9288	9381	9464	9539
5	6742	7003	7254	7493	7721	7935	8137	8326	8502	8666
6	4552	4849	5146	5441	5732	6019	6299	6573	6838	7095
7	2524	2770	3025	3290	3563	3842	4127	4415	4707	5000
8	1114	1264	1426	1600	1788	1988	2200	2424	2659	2905
9	0379	0446	0520	0605	0698	0803	0918	1045	1183	1334
10	0096	0117	0141	0170	0203	0242	0287	0338	0396	0461
11	0017	0021	0027	0033	0041	0051	0063	0077	0093	0112
12	0002	0002	0003	0004	0005	0007	0009	0011	0014	0017
13							0001	0001	0001	0001

$n = 14$

p / r	01	02	03	04	05	06	07	08	09	10
1	1313	2464	3472	4353	5123	5795	6380	6888	7330	7712
2	0084	0310	0645	1059	1530	2037	2564	3100	3632	4154
3	0003	0025	0077	0167	0301	0478	0698	0958	1255	1584
4		0001	0006	0019	0042	0080	0136	0214	0315	0441
5				0002	0004	0010	0020	0035	0059	0092
6						0001	0002	0004	0008	0015
7									0001	0002

$n = 14$

p	11	12	13	14	15	16	17	18	19	20
r 1	8044	8330	8577	8789	8972	9129	9264	9379	9477	9560
2	4658	5141	5599	6031	6433	6807	7152	7469	7758	8021
3	1939	2315	2708	3111	3521	3932	4341	4744	5138	5519
4	0594	0774	0979	1210	1465	1742	2038	2351	2679	3018
5	0137	0196	0269	0359	0467	0594	0741	0907	1093	1298
6	0024	0038	0057	0082	0115	0157	0209	0273	0349	0439
7	0003	0006	0009	0015	0022	0032	0046	0064	0087	0116
8		0001	0001	0002	0003	0005	0008	0012	0017	0024
9						0001	0001	0002	0003	0004

p	21	22	23	24	25	26	27	28	29	30
r 1	9631	9691	9742	9786	9822	9852	9878	9899	9917	9932
2	8259	8473	8665	8837	8990	9126	9246	9352	9444	9525
3	5887	6239	6574	6891	7189	7467	7727	7967	8188	8392
4	3366	3719	4076	4432	4787	5136	5479	5813	6137	6448
5	1523	1765	2023	2297	2585	2884	3193	3509	3832	4158
6	0543	0662	0797	0949	1117	1301	1502	1718	1949	2195
7	0152	0196	0248	0310	0383	0467	0563	0673	0796	0933
8	0033	0045	0060	0079	0103	0132	0167	0208	0257	0315
9	0006	0008	0011	0016	0022	0029	0038	0050	0065	0083
10	0001	0001	0002	0002	0003	0005	0007	0009	0012	0017
11						0001	0001	0001	0002	0002

p	31	32	33	34	35	36	37	38	39	40
r 1	9945	9955	9963	9970	9976	9981	9984	9988	9990	9992
2	9596	9657	9710	9756	9795	9828	9857	9881	9902	9919
3	8577	8746	8899	9037	9161	9271	9370	9457	9534	9602
4	6747	7032	7301	7556	7795	8018	8226	8418	8595	8757
5	4486	4813	5138	5458	5773	6080	6378	6666	6943	7207
6	2454	2724	3006	3297	3595	3899	4208	4519	4831	5141
7	1084	1250	1431	1626	1836	2059	2296	2545	2805	3075
8	0381	0458	0545	0643	0753	0876	1012	1162	1325	1501
9	0105	0131	0163	0200	0243	0294	0353	0420	0497	0583
10	0022	0029	0037	0048	0060	0076	0095	0117	0144	0175
11	0003	0005	0006	0008	0011	0014	0019	0024	0031	0039
12		0001	0001	0001	0001	0002	0003	0003	0005	0006
13										0001

p	41	42	43	44	45	46	47	48	49	50
r 1	9994	9995	9996	9997	9998	9998	9999	9999	9999	9999
2	9934	9946	9956	9964	9971	9977	9981	9985	9988	9991
3	9661	9713	9758	9797	9830	9858	9883	9903	9921	9935
4	8905	9039	9161	9270	9368	9455	9532	9601	9661	9713
5	7459	7697	7922	8132	8328	8510	8678	8833	8974	9102
6	5450	5754	6052	6344	6627	6900	7163	7415	7654	7880
7	3355	3643	3937	4236	4539	4843	5148	5451	5751	6047
8	1692	1896	2113	2344	2586	2840	3105	3380	3663	3953
9	0680	0789	0910	1043	1189	1348	1520	1707	1906	2120
10	0212	0255	0304	0361	0426	0500	0583	0677	0782	0898
11	0049	0061	0076	0093	0114	0139	0168	0202	0241	0287
12	0008	0010	0013	0017	0022	0027	0034	0042	0053	0065
13	0001	0001	0001	0002	0003	0003	0004	0006	0007	0009
14										0001

$n = 15$

P	01	02	03	04	05	06	07	08	09	10
r 1	1399	2614	3667	4579	5367	6047	6633	7137	7570	7941
2	0096	0353	0730	1191	1710	2262	2832	3403	3965	4510
3	0004	0030	0094	0203	0362	0571	0829	1130	1469	1841
4		0002	0008	0024	0055	0104	0175	0273	0399	0556
5			0001	0002	0006	0014	0028	0050	0082	0127
6					0001	0001	0003	0007	0013	0022
7								0001	0002	0003

P	11	12	13	14	15	16	17	18	19	20
r 1	8259	8530	8762	8959	9126	9269	9389	9490	9576	9648
2	5031	5524	5987	6417	6814	7179	7511	7813	8085	8329
3	2238	2654	3084	3520	3958	4392	4819	5234	5635	6020
4	0742	0959	1204	1476	1773	2092	2429	2782	3146	3518
5	0187	0265	0361	0478	0617	0778	0961	1167	1394	1642
6	0037	0057	0084	0121	0168	0227	0300	0387	0490	0611
7	0006	0010	0015	0024	0036	0052	0074	0102	0137	0181
8	0001	0001	0002	0004	0006	0010	0014	0021	0030	0042
9					0001	0001	0002	0003	0005	0008
10									0001	0001

P	21	22	23	24	25	26	27	28	29	30
r 1	9709	9759	9802	9837	9866	9891	9911	9928	9941	9953
2	8547	8741	8913	9065	9198	9315	9417	9505	9581	9647
3	6385	6731	7055	7358	7639	7899	8137	8355	8553	8732
4	3895	4274	4650	5022	5387	5742	6086	6416	6732	7031
5	1910	2195	2495	2810	3135	3469	3810	4154	4500	4845
6	0748	0905	1079	1272	1484	1713	1958	2220	2495	2784
7	0234	0298	0374	0463	0566	0684	0817	0965	1130	1311
8	0058	0078	0104	0135	0173	0219	0274	0338	0413	0500
9	0011	0016	0023	0031	0042	0056	0073	0094	0121	0152
10	0002	0003	0004	0006	0008	0011	0015	0021	0028	0037
11			0001	0001	0001	0002	0002	0003	0005	0007
12									0001	0001

P	31	32	33	34	35	36	37	38	39	40
r 1	9962	9969	9975	9980	9984	9988	9990	9992	9994	9995
2	9704	9752	9794	9829	9858	9883	9904	9922	9936	9948
3	8893	9038	9167	9281	9383	9472	9550	9618	9678	9729
4	7314	7580	7829	8060	8273	8469	8649	8813	8961	9095
5	5187	5523	5852	6171	6481	6778	7062	7332	7587	7827
6	3084	3393	3709	4032	4357	4684	5011	5335	5654	5968
7	1509	1722	1951	2194	2452	2722	3003	3295	3595	3902
8	0599	0711	0837	0977	1132	1302	1487	1687	1902	2131
9	0190	0236	0289	0351	0422	0504	0597	0702	0820	0950
10	0048	0062	0079	0099	0124	0154	0190	0232	0281	0338
11	0009	0012	0016	0022	0028	0037	0047	0059	0075	0093
12	0001	0002	0003	0004	0005	0006	0009	0011	0015	0019
13					0001	0001	0001	0002	0002	0003

Exhibit F–2   Cumulative Binomial Probability Distribution (Continued)

$n = 15$

p \ r	41	42	43	44	45	46	47	48	49	50
1	9996	9997	9998	9998	9999	9999	9999	9999	10000	10000
2	9958	9966	9973	9979	9983	9987	9990	9992	9994	9995
3	9773	9811	9843	9870	9893	9913	9929	9943	9954	9963
4	9215	9322	9417	9502	9576	9641	9697	9746	9788	9824
5	8052	8261	8454	8633	8796	8945	9080	9201	9310	9408
6	6274	6570	6856	7131	7392	7641	7875	8095	8301	8491
7	4214	4530	4847	5164	5478	5789	6095	6394	6684	6964
8	2374	2630	2898	3176	3465	3762	4065	4374	4686	5000
9	1095	1254	1427	1615	1818	2034	2265	2510	2767	3036
10	0404	0479	0565	0661	0769	0890	1024	1171	1333	1509
11	0116	0143	0174	0211	0255	0305	0363	0430	0506	0592
12	0025	0032	0040	0051	0063	0079	0097	0119	0145	0176
13	0004	0005	0007	0009	0011	0014	0018	0023	0029	0037
14			0001	0001	0001	0002	0002	0003	0004	0005

$n = 16$

p \ r	01	02	03	04	05	06	07	08	09	10
1	1485	2762	3857	4796	5599	6284	6869	7366	7789	8147
2	0109	0399	0818	1327	1892	2489	3098	3701	4289	4853
3	0005	0037	0113	0242	0429	0673	0969	1311	1694	2108
4		0002	0011	0032	0070	0132	0221	0342	0496	0684
5			0001	0003	0009	0019	0038	0068	0111	0170
6					0001	0002	0005	0010	0019	0033
7							0001	0001	0003	0005
8										0001

p \ r	11	12	13	14	15	16	17	18	19	20
1	8450	8707	8923	9105	9257	9386	9493	9582	9657	9719
2	5386	5885	6347	6773	7161	7513	7830	8115	8368	8593
3	2545	2999	3461	3926	4386	4838	5277	5698	6101	6482
4	0907	1162	1448	1763	2101	2460	2836	3223	3619	4019
5	0248	0348	0471	0618	0791	0988	1211	1458	1727	2018
6	0053	0082	0120	0171	0235	0315	0412	0527	0662	0817
7	0009	0015	0024	0038	0056	0080	0112	0153	0204	0267
8	0001	0002	0004	0007	0011	0016	0024	0036	0051	0070
9			0001	0001	0002	0003	0004	0007	0010	0015
10							0001	0001	0002	0002

p \ r	21	22	23	24	25	26	27	28	29	30
1	9770	9812	9847	9876	9900	9919	9935	9948	9958	9967
2	8791	8965	9117	9250	9365	9465	9550	9623	9686	9739
3	6839	7173	7483	7768	8029	8267	8482	8677	8851	9006
4	4418	4814	5203	5583	5950	6303	6640	6959	7260	7541
5	2327	2652	2991	3341	3698	4060	4425	4788	5147	5501
6	0992	1188	1405	1641	1897	2169	2458	2761	3077	3402
7	0342	0432	0536	0657	0796	0951	1125	1317	1526	1753
8	0095	0127	0166	0214	0271	0340	0420	0514	0621	0744
9	0021	0030	0041	0056	0075	0098	0127	0163	0206	0257
10	0004	0006	0008	0012	0016	0023	0031	0041	0055	0071
11	0001	0001	0001	0002	0003	0004	0006	0008	0011	0016
12						0001	0001	0001	0002	0003

Exhibit F–2 Cumulative Binomial Probability Distribution (Continued)

$n = 16$

p r	31	32	33	34	35	36	37	38	39	40
1	9974	9979	9984	9987	9990	9992	9994	9995	9996	9997
2	9784	9822	9854	9880	9902	9921	9936	9948	9959	9967
3	9144	9266	9374	9467	9549	9620	9681	9734	9778	9817
4	7804	8047	8270	8475	8661	8830	8982	9119	9241	9349
5	5846	6181	6504	6813	7108	7387	7649	7895	8123	8334
6	3736	4074	4416	4759	5100	5438	5770	6094	6408	6712
7	1997	2257	2531	2819	3119	3428	3746	4070	4398	4728
8	0881	1035	1205	1391	1594	1813	2048	2298	2562	2839
9	0317	0388	0470	0564	0671	0791	0926	1076	1242	1423
10	0092	0117	0148	0185	0229	0280	0341	0411	0491	0583
11	0021	0028	0037	0048	0062	0079	0100	0125	0155	0191
12	0004	0005	0007	0010	0013	0017	0023	0030	0038	0049
13		0001	0001	0001	0002	0003	0004	0005	0007	0009
14								0001	0001	0001

p r	41	42	43	44	45	46	47	48	49	50
1	9998	9998	9999	9999	9999	9999	10000	10000	10000	10000
2	9974	9979	9984	9987	9990	9992	9994	9995	9997	9997
3	9849	9876	9899	9918	9934	9947	9958	9966	9973	9979
4	9444	9527	9600	9664	9719	9766	9806	9840	9869	9894
5	8529	8707	8869	9015	9147	9265	9370	9463	9544	9616
6	7003	7280	7543	7792	8024	8241	8441	8626	8795	8949
7	5058	5387	5711	6029	6340	6641	6932	7210	7476	7728
8	3128	3428	3736	4051	4371	4694	5019	5343	5665	5982
9	1619	1832	2060	2302	2559	2829	3111	3405	3707	4018
10	0687	0805	0936	1081	1241	1416	1607	1814	2036	2272
11	0234	0284	0342	0409	0486	0574	0674	0786	0911	1051
12	0062	0078	0098	0121	0149	0183	0222	0268	0322	0384
13	0012	0016	0021	0027	0035	0044	0055	0069	0086	0106
14	0002	0002	0003	0004	0006	0007	0010	0013	0016	0021
15					0001	0001	0001	0001	0002	0003

$n = 17$

p r	01	02	03	04	05	06	07	08	09	10
1	1571	2907	4042	5004	5819	6507	7088	7577	7988	8332
2	0123	0446	0909	1465	2078	2717	3362	3995	4604	5182
3	0006	0044	0134	0286	0503	0782	1118	1503	1927	2382
4		0003	0014	0040	0088	0164	0273	0419	0603	0826
5			0001	0004	0012	0026	0051	0089	0145	0221
6					0001	0003	0007	0015	0027	0047
7							0001	0002	0004	0008
8										0001

p r	11	12	13	14	15	16	17	18	19	20
1	8621	8862	9063	9230	9369	9484	9579	9657	9722	9775
2	5723	6223	6682	7099	7475	7813	8113	8379	8613	8818
3	2858	3345	3836	4324	4802	5266	5711	6133	6532	6904
4	1087	1383	1710	2065	2444	2841	3251	3669	4091	4511
5	0321	0446	0598	0778	0987	1224	1487	1775	2087	2418

$n = 17$

p r	11	12	13	14	15	16	17	18	19	20
6	0075	0114	0166	0234	0319	0423	0548	0695	0864	1057
7	0014	0023	0037	0056	0083	0118	0163	0220	0291	0377
8	0002	0004	0007	0011	0017	0027	0039	0057	0080	0109
9		0001	0001	0002	0003	0005	0008	0012	0018	0026
10						0001	0001	0002	0003	0005
11										0001

p r	21	22	23	24	25	26	27	28	29	30
1	9818	9854	9882	9906	9925	9940	9953	9962	9970	9977
2	8996	9152	9285	9400	9499	9583	9654	9714	9765	9807
3	7249	7567	7859	8123	8363	8578	8771	8942	9093	9226
4	4927	5333	5728	6107	6470	6814	7137	7440	7721	7981
5	2766	3128	3500	3879	4261	4643	5023	5396	5760	6113
6	1273	1510	1770	2049	2347	2661	2989	3329	3677	4032
7	0479	0598	0736	0894	1071	1268	1485	1721	1976	2248
8	0147	0194	0251	0320	0402	0499	0611	0739	0884	1046
9	0037	0051	0070	0094	0124	0161	0206	0261	0326	0403
10	0007	0011	0016	0022	0031	0042	0057	0075	0098	0127
11	0001	0002	0003	0004	0006	0009	0013	0018	0024	0032
12				0001	0001	0002	0002	0003	0005	0007
13									0001	0001

p r	31	32	33	34	35	36	37	38	39	40
1	9982	9986	9989	9991	9993	9995	9996	9997	9998	9998
2	9843	9872	9896	9917	9933	9946	9957	9966	9973	9979
3	9343	9444	9532	9608	9673	9728	9775	9815	9849	9877
4	8219	8437	8634	8812	8972	9115	9241	9353	9450	9536
5	6453	6778	7087	7378	7652	7906	8142	8360	8559	8740
6	4390	4749	5105	5458	5803	6139	6465	6778	7077	7361
7	2536	2838	3153	3479	3812	4152	4495	4839	5182	5522
8	1227	1426	1642	1877	2128	2395	2676	2971	3278	3595
9	0492	0595	0712	0845	0994	1159	1341	1541	1757	1989
10	0162	0204	0254	0314	0383	0464	0557	0664	0784	0919
11	0043	0057	0074	0095	0120	0151	0189	0234	0286	0348
12	0009	0013	0017	0023	0030	0040	0051	0066	0084	0106
13	0002	0002	0003	0004	0006	0008	0011	0015	0019	0025
14				0001	0001	0001	0002	0002	0003	0005
15										0001

p r	41	42	43	44	45	46	47	48	49	50
1	9999	9999	9999	9999	10000	10000	10000	10000	10000	10000
2	9984	9987	9990	9992	9994	9996	9997	9998	9998	9999
3	9900	9920	9935	9948	9959	9968	9975	9980	9985	9988
4	9610	9674	9729	9776	9816	9849	9877	9901	9920	9936
5	8904	9051	9183	9301	9404	9495	9575	9644	9704	9755
6	7628	7879	8113	8330	8529	8712	8878	9028	9162	9283
7	5856	6182	6499	6805	7098	7377	7641	7890	8122	8338
8	3920	4250	4585	4921	5257	5590	5918	6239	6552	6855

$n = 17$

p	41	42	43	44	45	46	47	48	49	50
r 9	2238	2502	2780	3072	3374	3687	4008	4335	4667	5000
10	1070	1236	1419	1618	1834	2066	2314	2577	2855	3145
11	0420	0503	0597	0705	0826	0962	1112	1279	1462	1662
12	0133	0165	0203	0248	0301	0363	0434	0517	0611	0717
13	0033	0042	0054	0069	0086	0108	0134	0165	0202	0245
14	0006	0008	0011	0014	0019	0024	0031	0040	0050	0064
15	0001	0001	0002	0002	0003	0004	0005	0007	0009	0012
16							0001	0001	0001	0001

$n = 18$

p	01	02	03	04	05	06	07	08	09	10
r 1	1655	3049	4220	5204	6028	6717	7292	7771	8169	8499
2	0138	0495	1003	1607	2265	2945	3622	4281	4909	5497
3	0007	0052	0157	0333	0581	0898	1275	1702	2168	2662
4		0004	0018	0050	0109	0201	0333	0506	0723	0982
5			0002	0006	0015	0034	0067	0116	0186	0282
6				0001	0002	0005	0010	0021	0038	0064
7							0001	0003	0006	0012
8									0001	0002

p	11	12	13	14	15	16	17	18	19	20
r 1	8773	8998	9185	9338	9464	9566	9651	9719	9775	9820
2	6042	6540	6992	7398	7759	8080	8362	8609	8824	9009
3	3173	3690	4206	4713	5203	5673	6119	6538	6927	7287
4	1282	1618	1986	2382	2798	3229	3669	4112	4554	4990
5	0405	0558	0743	0959	1206	1482	1787	2116	2467	2836
6	0102	0154	0222	0310	0419	0551	0708	0889	1097	1329
7	0021	0034	0054	0081	0118	0167	0229	0306	0400	0513
8	0003	0006	0011	0017	0027	0041	0060	0086	0120	0163
9		0001	0002	0003	0005	0008	0013	0020	0029	0043
10					0001	0001	0002	0004	0006	0009
11								0001	0001	0002

p	21	22	23	24	25	26	27	28	29	30
r 1	9856	9886	9909	9928	9944	9956	9965	9973	9979	9984
2	9169	9306	9423	9522	9605	9676	9735	9784	9824	9858
3	7616	7916	8187	8430	8647	8839	9009	9158	9288	9400
4	5414	5825	6218	6591	6943	7272	7578	7860	8119	8354
5	3220	3613	4012	4414	4813	5208	5594	5968	6329	6673
6	1586	1866	2168	2488	2825	3176	3538	3907	4281	4656
7	0645	0799	0974	1171	1390	1630	1891	2171	2469	2783
8	0217	0283	0363	0458	0569	0699	0847	1014	1200	1407
9	0060	0083	0112	0148	0193	0249	0316	0395	0488	0596
10	0014	0020	0028	0039	0054	0073	0097	0127	0164	0210
11	0003	0004	0006	0009	0012	0018	0025	0034	0046	0061
12		0001	0001	0002	0002	0003	0005	0007	0010	0014
13						0001	0001	0001	0002	0003

Exhibit F-2 Cumulative Binomial Probability Distribution (Continued)

$n = 18$

P r	31	32	33	34	35	36	37	38	39	40
1	9987	9990	9993	9994	9996	9997	9998	9998	9999	9999
2	9886	9908	9927	9942	9954	9964	9972	9978	9983	9987
3	9498	9581	9652	9713	9764	9807	9843	9873	9897	9918
4	8568	8759	8931	9083	9217	9335	9439	9528	9606	9672
5	7001	7309	7598	7866	8114	8341	8549	8737	8907	9058
6	5029	5398	5759	6111	6450	6776	7086	7379	7655	7912
7	3111	3450	3797	4151	4509	4867	5224	5576	5921	6257
8	1633	1878	2141	2421	2717	3027	3349	3681	4021	4366
9	0720	0861	1019	1196	1391	1604	1835	2084	2350	2632
10	0264	0329	0405	0494	0597	0714	0847	0997	1163	1347
11	0080	0104	0133	0169	0212	0264	0325	0397	0480	0576
12	0020	0027	0036	0047	0062	0080	0102	0130	0163	0203
13	0004	0005	0008	0011	0014	0019	0026	0034	0044	0058
14	0001	0001	0001	0002	0003	0004	0005	0007	0010	0013
15						0001	0001	0001	0002	0002

P r	41	42	43	44	45	46	47	48	49	50
1	9999	9999	10000	10000	10000	10000	10000	10000	10000	10000
2	9990	9992	9994	9996	9997	9998	9998	9999	9999	9999
3	9934	9948	9959	9968	9975	9981	9985	9989	9991	9993
4	9729	9777	9818	9852	9880	9904	9923	9939	9952	9962
5	9193	9313	9418	9510	9589	9658	9717	9767	9810	9846
6	8151	8372	8573	8757	8923	9072	9205	9324	9428	9519
7	6582	6895	7193	7476	7742	7991	8222	8436	8632	8811
8	4713	5062	5408	5750	6085	6412	6728	7032	7322	7597
9	2928	3236	3556	3885	4222	4562	4906	5249	5591	5927
10	1549	1768	2004	2258	2527	2812	3110	3421	3742	4073
11	0686	0811	0951	1107	1280	1470	1677	1902	2144	2403
12	0250	0307	0372	0449	0537	0638	0753	0883	1028	1189
13	0074	0094	0118	0147	0183	0225	0275	0334	0402	0481
14	0017	0022	0029	0038	0049	0063	0079	0100	0125	0154
15	0003	0004	0006	0007	0010	0013	0017	0023	0029	0038
16		0001	0001	0001	0001	0002	0003	0004	0005	0007
17									0001	0001

$n = 19$

P r	01	02	03	04	05	06	07	08	09	10
1	1738	3188	4394	5396	6226	6914	7481	7949	8334	8649
2	0153	0546	1100	1751	2453	3171	3879	4560	5202	5797
3	0009	0061	0183	0384	0665	1021	1439	1908	2415	2946
4		0005	0022	0061	0132	0243	0398	0602	0853	1150
5			0002	0007	0020	0044	0085	0147	0235	0352
6				0001	0002	0006	0014	0029	0051	0086
7						0001	0002	0004	0009	0017
8								0001	0001	0003

Exhibit F–3 Poisson Distribution*

λ

x	0.1	0.2	0.3	0.4	0.5	0.6	0.7	0.8	0.9	1.0
0	.9048	.8187	.7408	.6703	.6065	.5488	.4966	.4493	.4066	.3679
1	.0905	.1637	.2222	.2681	.3033	.3293	.3476	.3595	.3659	.3679
2	.0045	.0164	.0333	.0536	.0758	.0988	.1217	.1438	.1647	.1839
3	.0002	.0011	.0033	.0072	.0126	.0198	.0284	.0383	.0494	.0613
4	.0000	.0001	.0002	.0007	.0016	.0030	.0050	.0077	.0111	.0153
5	.0000	.0000	.0000	.0001	.0002	.0004	.0007	.0012	.0020	.0031
6	.0000	.0000	.0000	.0000	.0000	.0000	.0001	.0002	.0003	.0005
7	.0000	.0000	.0000	.0000	.0000	.0000	.0000	.0000	.0000	.0001

λ

x	1.1	1.2	1.3	1.4	1.5	1.6	1.7	1.8	1.9	2.0
0	.3329	.3012	.2725	.2466	.2231	.2019	.1827	.1653	.1496	.1353
1	.3662	.3614	.3543	.3452	.3347	.3230	.3106	.2975	.2842	.2707
2	.2014	.2169	.2303	.2417	.2510	.2584	.2640	.2678	ʻ.2700	.2707
3	.0738	.0867	.0998	.1128	.1255	.1378	.1496	.1607	.1710	.1804
4	.0203	.0260	.0324	.0395	.0471	.0551	.0636	.0723	.0812	.0902
5	.0045	.0062	.0084	.0111	.0141	.0176	.0216	.0260	.0309	.0361
6	.0008	.0012	.0018	.0026	.0035	.0047	.0061	.0078	.0098	.0120
7	.0001	.0002	.0003	.0005	.0008	.0011	.0015	.0020	.0027	.0034
8	.0000	.0000	.0001	.0001	.0001	.0002	.0003	.0005	.0006	.0009
9	.0000	.0000	.0000	.0000	.0000	.0000	.0001	.0001	.0001	.0002

λ

x	2.1	2.2	2.3	2.4	2.5	2.6	2.7	2.8	2.9	3.0
0	.1225	.1108	.1003	.0907	.0821	.0743	.0672	.0608	.0550	.0498
1	.2572	.2438	.2306	.2177	.2052	.1931	.1815	.1703	.1596	.1494
2	.2700	.2681	.2652	.2613	.2565	.2510	.2450	.2384	.2314	.2240
3	.1890	.1966	.2033	.2090	.2138	.2176	.2205	.2225	.2237	.2240
4	.0992	.1082	.1169	.1254	.1336	.1414	.1488	.1557	.1622	.1680
5	.0417	.0476	.0538	.0602	.0668	.0735	.0804	.0872	.0940	.1008
6	.0146	.0174	.0206	.0241	.0278	.0319	.0362	.0407	.0455	.0504
7	.0044	.0055	.0068	.0083	.0099	.0118	.0139	.0163	.0188	.0216
8	.0011	.0015	.0019	.0025	.0031	.0038	.0047	.0057	.0068	.0081
9	.0003	.0004	.0005	.0007	.0009	.0011	.0014	.0018	.0022	.0027
10	.0001	.0001	.0001	.0002	.0002	.0003	.0004	.0005	.0006	.0008
11	.0000	.0000	.0000	.0000	.0000	.0001	.0001	.0001	.0002	.0002
12	.0000	.0000	.0000	.0000	.0000	.0000	.0000	.0000	.0000	.0001

From *Handbook of Probability and Statistics with Tables* by Burington and May. Copyright © 1953, by McGraw-Hill Book Company.

* Entries in this table are values of $(e^{-\lambda}\lambda^x/x!)$ for the indicated values of x and λ.

Exhibit F–3   Poisson Distribution (Continued)

λ

x	3.1	3.2	3.3	3.4	3.5	3.6	3.7	3.8	3.9	4.0
0	.0450	.0408	.0369	.0334	.0302	.0273	.0247	.0224	.0202	.0183
1	.1397	.1304	.1217	.1135	.1057	.0984	.0915	.0850	.0789	.0733
2	.2165	.2087	.2008	.1929	.1850	.1771	.1692	.1615	.1539	.1465
3	.2237	.2226	.2209	.2186	.2158	.2125	.2087	.2046	.2001	.1954
4	.1734	.1781	.1823	.1858	.1888	.1912	.1931	.1944	.1951	.1954
5	.1075	.1140	.1203	.1264	.1322	.1377	.1429	.1477	.1522	.1563
6	.0555	.0608	.0662	.0716	.0771	.0826	.0881	.0936	.0989	.1042
7	.0246	.0278	.0312	.0348	.0385	.0425	.0466	.0508	.0551	.0595
8	.0095	.0111	.0129	.0148	.0169	.0191	.0215	.0241	.0269	.0298
9	.0033	.0040	.0047	.0056	.0066	.0076	.0089	.0102	.0116	.0132
10	.0010	.0013	.0016	.0019	.0023	.0028	.0033	.0039	.0045	.0053
11	.0003	.0004	.0005	.0006	.0007	.0009	.0011	.0013	.0016	.0019
12	.0001	.0001	.0001	.0002	.0002	.0003	.0003	.0004	.0005	.0006
13	.0000	.0000	.0000	.0000	.0001	.0001	.0001	.0001	.0002	.0002
14	.0000	.0000	.0000	.0000	.0000	.0000	.0000	.0000	.0000	.0001

λ

x	4.1	4.2	4.3	4.4	4.5	4.6	4.7	4.8	4.9	5.0
0	.0166	.0150	.0136	.0123	.0111	.0101	.0091	.0082	.0074	.0067
1	.0679	.0630	.0583	.0540	.0500	.0462	.0427	.0395	.0365	.0337
2	.1393	.1323	.1254	.1188	.1125	.1063	.1005	.0948	.0894	.0842
3	.1904	.1852	.1798	.1743	.1687	.1631	.1574	.1517	.1460	.1404
4	.1951	.1944	.1933	.1917	.1898	.1875	.1849	.1820	.1789	.1755
5	.1600	.1633	.1662	.1687	.1708	.1725	.1738	.1747	.1753	.1755
6	.1093	.1143	.1191	.1237	.1281	.1323	.1362	.1398	.1432	.1462
7	.0640	.0686	.0732	.0778	.0824	.0869	.0914	.0959	.1002	.1044
8	.0328	.0360	.0393	.0428	.0463	.0500	.0537	.0575	.0614	.0653
9	.0150	.0168	.0188	.0209	.0232	.0255	.0280	.0307	.0334	.0363
10	.0061	.0071	.0081	.0092	.0104	.0118	.0132	.0147	.0164	.0181
11	.0023	.0027	.0032	.0037	.0043	.0049	.0056	.0064	.0073	.0082
12	.0008	.0009	.0011	.0014	.0016	.0019	.0022	.0026	.0030	.0034
13	.0002	.0003	.0004	.0005	.0006	.0007	.0008	.0009	.0011	.0013
14	.0001	.0001	.0001	.0001	.0002	.0002	.0003	.0003	.0004	.0005
15	.0000	.0000	.0000	.0000	.0001	.0001	.0001	.0001	.0001	.0002

λ

x	5.1	5.2	5.3	5.4	5.5	5.6	5.7	5.8	5.9	6.0
0	.0061	.0055	.0050	.0045	.0041	.0037	.0033	.0030	.0027	.0025
1	.0311	.0287	.0265	.0244	.0225	.0207	.0191	.0176	.0162	.0149
2	.0793	.0746	.0701	.0659	.0618	.0580	.0544	.0509	.0477	.0446
3	.1348	.1293	.1239	.1185	.1133	.1082	.1033	.0985	.0938	.0892
4	.1719	.1681	.1641	.1600	.1558	.1515	.1472	.1428	.1383	.1339

444

					λ					
x	5.1	5.2	5.3	5.4	5.5	5.6	5.7	5.8	5.9	6.0
5	.1753	.1748	.1740	.1728	.1714	.1697	.1678	.1656	.1632	.1606
6	.1490	.1515	.1537	.1555	.1571	.1584	.1594	.1601	.1605	.1606
7	.1086	.1125	.1163	.1200	.1234	.1267	.1298	.1326	.1353	.1377
8	.0692	.0731	.0771	.0810	.0849	.0887	.0925	.0962	.0998	.1033
9	.0392	.0423	.0454	.0486	.0519	.0552	.0586	.0620	.0654	.0688
10	.0200	.0220	.0241	.0262	.0285	.0309	.0334	.0359	.0386	.0413
11	.0093	.0104	.0116	.0129	.0143	.0157	.0173	.0190	.0207	.0225
12	.0039	.0045	.0051	.0058	.0065	.0073	.0082	.0092	.0102	.0113
13	.0015	.0018	.0021	.0024	.0028	.0032	.0036	.0041	.0046	.0052
14	.0006	.0007	.0008	.0009	.0011	.0013	.0015	.0017	.0019	.0022
15	.0002	.0002	.0003	.0003	.0004	.0005	.0006	.0007	.0008	.0009
16	.0001	.0001	.0001	.0001	.0001	.0002	.0002	.0002	.0003	.0003
17	.0000	.0000	.0000	.0000	.0000	.0001	.0001	.0001	.0001	.0001

					λ					
x	6.1	6.2	6.3	6.4	6.5	6.6	6.7	6.8	6.9	7.0
0	.0022	.0020	.0018	.0017	.0015	.0014	.0012	.0011	.0010	.0009
1	.0137	.0126	.0116	.0106	.0098	.0090	.0082	.0076	.0070	.0064
2	.0417	.0390	.0364	.0340	.0318	.0296	.0276	.0258	.0240	.0223
3	.0848	.0806	.0765	.0726	.0688	.0652	.0617	.0584	.0552	.0521
4	.1294	.1249	.1205	.1162	.1118	.1076	.1034	.0992	.0952	.0912
5	.1579	.1549	.1519	.1487	.1454	.1420	.1385	.1349	.1314	.1277
6	.1605	.1601	.1595	.1586	.1575	.1562	.1546	.1529	.1511	.1490
7	.1399	.1418	.1435	.1450	.1462	.1472	.1480	.1486	.1489	.1490
8	.1066	.1099	.1130	.1160	.1188	.1215	.1240	.1263	.1284	.1304
9	.0723	.0757	.0791	.0825	.0858	.0891	.0923	.0954	.0985	.1014
10	.0441	.0469	.0498	.0528	.0558	.0588	.0618	.0649	.0679	.0710
11	.0245	.0265	.0285	.0307	.0330	.0353	.0377	.0401	.0426	.0452
12	.0124	.0137	.0150	.0164	.0179	.0194	.0210	.0227	.0245	.0264
13	.0058	.0065	.0073	.0081	.0089	.0098	.0108	.0119	.0130	.0142
14	.0025	.0029	.0033	.0037	.0041	.0046	.0052	.0058	.0064	.0071
15	.0010	.0012	.0014	.0016	.0018	.0020	.0023	.0026	.0029	.0033
16	.0004	.0005	.0005	.0006	.0007	.0008	.0010	.0011	.0013	.0014
17	.0001	.0002	.0002	.0002	.0003	.0003	.0004	.0004	.0005	.0006
18	.0000	.0001	.0001	.0001	.0001	.0001	.0001	.0002	.0002	.0002
19	.0000	.0000	.0000	.0000	.0000	.0000	.0000	.0001	.0001	.0001

					λ					
x	7.1	7.2	7.3	7.4	7.5	7.6	7.7	7.8	7.9	8.0
0	.0008	.0007	.0007	.0006	.0006	.0005	.0005	.0004	.0004	.0003
1	.0059	.0054	.0049	.0045	.0041	.0038	.0035	.0032	.0029	.0027
2	.0208	.0194	.0180	.0167	.0156	.0145	.0134	.0125	.0116	.0107
3	.0492	.0464	.0438	.0413	.0389	.0366	.0345	.0324	.0305	.0286
4	.0874	.0836	.0799	.0764	.0729	.0696	.0663	.0632	.0602	.0573
5	.1241	.1204	.1167	.1130	.1094	.1057	.1021	.0986	.0951	.0916
6	.1468	.1445	.1420	.1394	.1367	.1339	.1311	.1282	.1252	.1221
7	.1489	.1486	.1481	.1474	.1465	.1454	.1442	.1428	.1413	.1396
8	.1321	.1337	.1351	.1363	.1373	.1382	.1388	.1392	.1395	.1396
9	.1042	.1070	.1096	.1121	.1144	.1167	.1187	.1207	.1224	.1241

λ

x	7.1	7.2	7.3	7.4	7.5	7.6	7.7	7.8	7.9	8.0
10	.0740	.0770	.0800	.0829	.0858	.0887	.0914	.0941	.0967	.0993
11	.0478	.0504	.0531	.0558	.0585	.0613	.0640	.0667	.0695	.0722
12	.0283	.0303	.0323	.0344	.0366	.0388	.0411	.0434	.0457	.0481
13	.0154	.0168	.0181	.0196	.0211	.0227	.0243	.0260	.0278	.0296
14	.0078	.0086	.0095	.0104	.0113	.0123	.0134	.0145	.0157	.0169
15	.0037	.0041	.0046	.0051	.0057	.0062	.0069	.0075	.0083	.0090
16	.0016	.0019	.0021	.0024	.0026	.0030	.0033	.0037	.0041	.0045
17	.0007	.0008	.0009	.0010	.0012	.0013	.0015	.0017	.0019	.0021
18	.0003	.0003	.0004	.0004	.0005	.0006	.0006	.0007	.0008	.0009
19	.0001	.0001	.0001	.0002	.0002	.0002	.0003	.0003	.0003	.0004
20	.0000	.0000	.0001	.0001	.0001	.0001	.0001	.0001	.0001	.0002
21	.0000	.0000	.0000	.0000	.0000	.0000	.0000	.0000	.0001	.0001

λ

x	8.1	8.2	8.3	8.4	8.5	8.6	8.7	8.8	8.9	9.0
0	.0003	.0003	.0002	.0002	.0002	.0002	.0002	.0002	.0001	.0001
1	.0025	.0023	.0021	.0019	.0017	.0016	.0014	.0013	.0012	.0011
2	.0100	.0092	.0086	.0079	.0074	.0068	.0063	.0058	.0054	.0050
3	.0269	.0252	.0237	.0222	.0208	.0195	.0183	.0171	.0160	.0150
4	.0544	.0517	.0491	.0466	.0443	.0420	.0398	.0377	.0357	.0337
5	.0882	.0849	.0816	.0784	.0752	.0722	.0692	.0663	.0635	.0607
6	.1191	.1160	.1128	.1097	.1066	.1034	.1003	.0972	.0941	.0911
7	.1378	.1358	.1338	.1317	.1294	.1271	.1247	.1222	.1197	.1171
8	.1395	.1392	.1388	.1382	.1375	.1366	.1356	.1344	.1332	.1318
9	.1256	.1269	.1280	.1290	.1299	.1306	.1311	.1315	.1317	.1318
10	.1017	.1040	.1063	.1084	.1104	.1123	.1140	.1157	.1172	.1186
11	.0749	.0776	.0802	.0828	.0853	.0878	.0902	.0925	.0948	.0970
12	.0505	.0530	.0555	.0579	.0604	.0629	.0654	.0679	.0703	.0728
13	.0315	.0334	.0354	.0374	.0395	.0416	.0438	.0459	.0481	.0504
14	.0182	.0196	.0210	.0225	.0240	.0256	.0272	.0289	.0306	.0324
15	.0098	.0107	.0116	.0126	.0136	.0147	.0158	.0169	.0182	.0194
16	.0050	.0055	.0060	.0066	.0072	.0079	.0086	.0093	.0101	.0109
17	.0024	.0026	.0029	.0033	.0036	.0040	.0044	.0048	.0053	.0058
18	.0011	.0012	.0014	.0015	.0017	.0019	.0021	.0024	.0026	.0029
19	.0005	.0005	.0006	.0007	.0008	.0009	.0010	.0011	.0012	.0014
20	.0002	.0002	.0002	.0003	.0003	.0004	.0004	.0005	.0005	.0006
21	.0001	.0001	.0001	.0001	.0001	.0002	.0002	.0002	.0002	.0003
22	.0000	.0000	.0000	.0000	.0001	.0001	.0001	.0001	.0001	.0001

λ

x	9.1	9.2	9.3	9.4	9.5	9.6	9.7	9.8	9.9	10
0	.0001	.0001	.0001	.0001	.0001	.0001	.0001	.0001	.0001	.0000
1	.0010	.0009	.0009	.0008	.0007	.0007	.0006	.0005	.0005	.0005
2	.0046	.0043	.0040	.0037	.0034	.0031	.0029	.0027	.0025	.0023
3	.0140	.0131	.0123	.0115	.0107	.0100	.0093	.0087	.0081	.0076
4	.0319	.0302	.0285	.0269	.0254	.0240	.0226	.0213	.0201	.0189

Exhibit F–3   Poisson Distribution (Continued)

λ

x	9.1	9.2	9.3	9.4	9.5	9.6	9.7	9.8	9.9	10
5	.0581	.0555	.0530	.0506	.0483	.0460	.0439	.0418	.0398	.0378
6	.0881	.0851	.0822	.0793	.0764	.0736	.0709	.0682	.0656	.0631
7	.1145	.1118	.1091	.1064	.1037	.1010	.0982	.0955	.0928	.0901
8	.1302	.1286	.1269	.1251	.1232	.1212	.1191	.1170	.1148	.1126
9	.1317	.1315	.1311	.1306	.1300	.1293	.1284	.1274	.1263	.1251
10	.1198	.1210	.1219	.1228	.1235	.1241	.1245	.1249	.1250	.1251
11	.0991	.1012	.1031	.1049	.1067	.1083	.1098	.1112	.1125	.1137
12	.0752	.0776	.0799	.0822	.0844	.0866	.0888	.0908	.0928	.0948
13	.0526	.0549	.0572	.0594	.0617	.0640	.0662	.0685	.0707	.0729
14	.0342	.0361	.0380	.0399	.0419	.0439	.0459	.0479	.0500	.0521
15	.0208	.0221	.0235	.0250	.0265	.0281	.0297	.0313	.0330	.0347
16	.0118	.0127	.0137	.0147	.0157	.0168	.0180	.0192	.0204	.0217
17	.0063	.0069	.0075	.0081	.0088	.0095	.0103	.0111	.0119	.0128
18	.0032	.0035	.0039	.0042	.0046	.0051	.0055	.0060	.0065	.0071
19	.0015	.0017	.0019	.0021	.0023	.0026	.0028	.0031	.0034	.0037
20	.0007	.0008	.0009	.0010	.0011	.0012	.0014	.0015	.0017	.0019
21	.0003	.0003	.0004	.0004	.0005	.0006	.0006	.0007	.0008	.0009
22	.0001	.0001	.0002	.0002	.0002	.0002	.0003	.0003	.0004	.0004
23	.0000	.0001	.0001	.0001	.0001	.0001	.0001	.0001	.0002	.0002
24	.0000	.0000	.0000	.0000	.0000	.0000	.0000	.0001	.0001	.0001

λ

x	11	12	13	14	15	16	17	18	19	20
0	.0000	.0000	.0000	.0000	.0000	.0000	.0000	.0000	.0000	.0000
1	.0002	.0001	.0000	.0000	.0000	.0000	.0000	.0000	.0000	.0000
2	.0010	.0004	.0002	.0001	.0000	.0000	.0000	.0000	.0000	.0000
3	.0037	.0018	.0008	.0004	.0002	.0001	.0000	.0000	.0000	.0000
4	.0102	.0053	.0027	.0013	.0006	.0003	.0001	.0001	.0000	.0000
5	.0224	.0127	.0070	.0037	.0019	.0010	.0005	.0002	.0001	.0001
6	.0411	.0255	.0152	.0087	.0048	.0026	.0014	.0007	.0004	.0002
7	.0646	.0437	.0281	.0174	.0104	.0060	.0034	.0018	.0010	.0005
8	.0888	.0655	.0457	.0304	.0194	.0120	.0072	.0042	.0024	.0013
9	.1085	.0874	.0661	.0473	.0324	.0213	.0135	.0083	.0050	.0029
10	.1194	.1048	.0859	.0663	.0486	.0341	.0230	.0150	.0095	.0058
11	.1194	.1144	.1015	.0844	.0663	.0496	.0355	.0245	.0164	.0106
12	.1094	.1144	.1099	.0984	.0829	.0661	.0504	.0368	.0259	.0176
13	.0926	.1056	.1099	.1060	.0956	.0814	.0658	.0509	.0378	.0271
14	.0728	.0905	.1021	.1060	.1024	.0930	.0800	.0655	.0514	.0387
15	.0534	.0724	.0885	.0989	.1024	.0992	.0906	.0786	.0650	.0516
16	.0367	.0543	.0719	.0866	.0960	.0992	.0963	.0884	.0772	.0646
17	.0237	.0383	.0550	.0713	.0847	.0934	.0963	.0936	.0863	.0760
18	.0145	.0256	.0397	.0554	.0706	.0830	.0909	.0936	.0911	.0844
19	.0084	.0161	.0272	.0409	.0557	.0699	.0814	.0887	.0911	.0888
20	.0046	.0097	.0177	.0286	.0418	.0559	.0692	.0798	.0866	.0888
21	.0024	.0055	.0109	.0191	.0299	.0426	.0560	.0684	.0783	.0846
22	.0012	.0030	.0065	.0121	.0204	.0310	.0433	.0560	.0676	.0769
23	.0006	.0016	.0037	.0074	.0133	.0216	.0320	.0438	.0559	.0669
24	.0003	.0008	.0020	.0043	.0083	.0144	.0226	.0328	.0442	.0557

λ

x	11	12	13	14	15	16	17	18	19	20
25	.0001	.0004	.0010	.0024	.0050	.0092	.0154	.0237	.0336	.0446
26	.0000	.0002	.0005	.0013	.0029	.0057	.0101	.0164	.0246	.0343
27	.0000	.0001	.0002	.0007	.0016	.0034	.0063	.0109	.0173	.0254
28	.0000	.0000	.0001	.0003	.0009	.0019	.0038	.0070	.0117	.0181
29	.0000	.0000	.0001	.0002	.0004	.0011	.0023	.0044	.0077	.0125
30	.0000	.0000	.0000	.0001	.0002	.0006	.0013	.0026	.0049	.0083
31	.0000	.0000	.0000	.0000	.0001	.0003	.0007	.0015	.0030	.0054
32	.0000	.0000	.0000	.0000	.0001	.0001	.0004	.0009	.0018	.0034
33	.0000	.0000	.0000	.0000	.0000	.0001	.0002	.0005	.0010	.0020
34	.0000	.0000	.0000	.0000	.0000	.0000	.0001	.0002	.0006	.0012
35	.0000	.0000	.0000	.0000	.0000	.0000	.0000	.0001	.0003	.0007
36	.0000	.0000	.0000	.0000	.0000	.0000	.0000	.0001	.0002	.0004
37	.0000	.0000	.0000	.0000	.0000	.0000	.0000	.0000	.0001	.0002
38	.0000	.0000	.0000	.0000	.0000	.0000	.0000	.0000	.0000	.0001
39	.0000	.0000	.0000	.0000	.0000	.0000	.0000	.0000	.0000	.0001

Exhibit F–4 Summed Poisson Distribution

$$P(r \le r_0 \mid \mu)$$

μ \ r_0	0	1	2	3	4	5	6	7	8	9
0.02	980	1000								
0.04	961	999	1000							
0.06	942	998	1000							
0.08	923	997	1000							
0.10	905	995	1000							
0.15	861	990	999	1000						
0.20	819	982	999	1000						
0.25	779	974	998	1000						
0.30	741	963	996	1000						
0.35	705	951	994	1000						
0.40	670	938	992	999	1000					
0.45	638	925	989	999	1000					
0.50	607	910	986	998	1000					
0.55	577	894	982	998	1000					
0.60	549	878	977	997	1000					
0.65	522	861	972	996	999	1000				
0.70	497	844	966	994	999	1000				
0.75	472	827	959	993	999	1000				
0.80	449	809	953	991	999	1000				
0.85	427	791	945	989	998	1000				
0.90	407	772	937	987	998	1000				
0.95	387	754	929	984	997	1000				
1.00	368	736	920	981	996	999	1000			
1.1	333	699	900	974	995	999	1000			
1.2	301	663	879	966	992	998	1000			
1.3	273	627	857	957	989	998	1000			
1.4	247	592	833	946	986	997	999	1000		
1.5	223	558	809	934	981	996	999	1000		
1.6	202	525	783	921	976	994	999	1000		
1.7	183	493	757	907	970	992	998	1000		
1.8	165	463	731	891	964	990	997	999	1000	
1.9	150	434	704	875	956	987	997	999	1000	
2.0	135	406	677	857	947	983	995	999	1000	
2.2	111	355	623	819	928	975	993	998	1000	
2.4	091	308	570	779	904	964	988	997	999	1000
2.6	074	267	518	736	877	951	983	995	999	1000
2.8	061	231	469	692	848	935	976	992	998	999
3.0	050	199	423	647	815	916	966	988	996	999

μ	10
2.8	1000
3.0	1000

μ \ r_0	0	1	2	3	4	5	6	7	8	9
3.2	041	171	380	603	781	895	955	983	994	998
3.4	033	147	340	558	744	871	942	977	992	997
3.6	027	126	303	515	706	844	927	969	988	996
3.8	022	107	269	473	668	816	909	960	984	994
4.0	018	092	238	433	629	785	889	949	979	992
4.2	015	078	210	395	590	753	867	936	972	989
4.4	012	066	185	359	551	720	844	921	964	985
4.6	010	056	163	326	513	686	818	905	955	980
4.8	008	048	143	294	476	651	791	887	944	975
5.0	007	040	125	265	440	616	762	867	932	968
5.2	006	034	109	238	406	581	732	845	918	960
5.4	005	029	095	213	373	546	702	822	903	951
5.6	004	024	082	191	342	512	670	797	886	941
5.8	003	021	072	170	313	478	638	771	867	929
6.0	002	017	062	151	285	446	606	744	847	916
6.2	002	015	054	134	259	414	574	716	826	902
6.4	002	012	046	119	235	384	542	687	803	886
6.6	001	010	040	105	213	355	511	658	780	869
6.8	001	009	034	093	192	327	480	628	755	850
7.0	001	007	030	082	173	301	450	599	729	830

μ	10	11	12	13	14	15	16	17
3.2	1000							
3.4	999	1000						
3.6	999	1000						
3.8	998	999	1000					
4.0	997	999	1000					
4.2	996	999	1000					
4.4	994	998	999	1000				
4.6	992	997	999	1000				
4.8	990	996	999	1000				
5.0	986	995	998	999	1000			
5.2	982	993	997	999	1000			
5.4	977	990	996	999	1000			
5.6	972	988	995	998	999	1000		
5.8	965	984	993	997	999	1000		
6.0	957	980	991	996	999	999	1000	
6.2	949	975	989	995	998	999	1000	
6.4	939	969	986	994	997	999	1000	
6.6	927	963	982	992	997	999	999	1000
6.8	915	955	978	990	996	998	999	1000
7.0	901	947	973	987	994	998	999	1000

μ \ r_0	0	1	2	3	4	5	6	7	8	9
7.2	001	006	025	072	156	276	420	569	703	810
7.4	001	005	022	063	140	253	392	539	676	788
7.6	001	004	019	055	125	231	365	510	648	765
7.8	000	004	016	048	112	210	338	481	620	741
8.0	000	003	014	042	100	191	313	453	593	717
8.5	000	002	009	030	074	150	256	386	523	653
9.0	000	001	006	021	055	116	207	324	456	587
9.5	000	001	004	015	040	089	165	269	392	522
10.0	000	000	003	010	029	067	130	220	333	458
10.5	000	000	002	007	021	050	102	179	279	397
11.0	000	000	001	005	015	038	079	143	232	341
11.5	000	000	001	003	011	028	060	114	191	289
12.0	000	000	001	002	008	020	046	090	155	242
12.5	000	000	000	002	005	015	035	070	125	201

μ	10	11	12	13	14	15	16	17	18	19
7.2	887	937	967	984	993	997	999	999	1000	
7.4	871	926	961	980	991	996	998	999	1000	
7.6	854	915	954	976	989	995	998	999	1000	
7.8	835	902	945	971	986	993	997	999	1000	
8.0	816	888	936	966	983	992	996	998	999	1000
8.5	763	849	909	949	973	986	993	997	999	999
9.0	706	803	876	926	959	978	989	995	998	999
9.5	645	752	836	898	940	967	982	991	996	998
10.0	583	697	792	864	917	951	973	986	993	997
10.5	521	639	742	825	888	932	960	978	988	994
11.0	460	579	689	781	854	907	944	968	982	991
11.5	402	520	633	733	815	878	924	954	974	986
12.0	347	462	576	682	772	844	899	937	963	979
12.5	297	406	519	628	725	806	869	916	948	969

μ	20	21	22	23	24	25	26
8.5	1000						
9.0	1000						
9.5	999	1000					
10.0	998	999	1000				
10.5	997	999	999	1000			
11.0	995	998	999	1000			
11.5	992	996	998	999	1000		
12.0	988	994	997	999	999	1000	
12.5	983	991	995	998	999	999	1000

μ \ r_0	0	1	2	3	4	5	6	7	8	9
13.0	000	000	000	001	004	011	026	054	100	166
13.5	000	000	000	001	003	008	019	041	079	135
14.0	000	000	000	000	002	006	014	032	062	109
14.5	000	000	000	000	001	004	010	024	048	088
15.0	000	000	000	000	001	003	008	018	037	070

	10	11	12	13	14	15	16	17	18	19
13.0	252	353	463	573	675	764	835	890	930	957
13.5	211	304	409	518	623	718	798	861	908	942
14.0	176	260	358	464	570	669	756	827	883	923
14.5	145	220	311	413	518	619	711	790	853	901
15.0	118	185	268	363	466	568	664	749	819	875

	20	21	22	23	24	25	26	27	28	29
13.0	975	986	992	996	998	999	1000			
13.5	965	980	989	994	997	998	999	1000		
14.0	952	971	983	991	995	997	999	999	1000	
14.5	936	960	976	986	992	996	998	999	999	1000
15.0	917	947	967	981	989	994	997	998	999	1000

μ \ r_0	4	5	6	7	8	9	10	11	12	13
16	000	001	004	010	022	043	077	127	193	275
17	000	001	002	005	013	026	049	085	135	201
18	000	000	001	003	007	015	030	055	092	143
19	000	000	001	002	004	009	018	035	061	098
20	000	000	000	001	002	005	011	021	039	066
21	000	000	000	000	001	003	006	013	025	043
22	000	000	000	000	001	002	004	008	015	028
23	000	000	000	000	000	001	002	004	009	017
24	000	000	000	000	000	000	001	003	005	011
25	000	000	000	000	000	000	001	001	003	006

μ	14	15	16	17	18	19	20	21	22	23
16	368	467	566	659	742	812	868	911	942	963
17	281	371	468	564	655	736	805	861	905	937
18	208	287	375	469	562	651	731	799	855	899
19	150	215	292	378	469	561	647	725	793	849
20	105	157	221	297	381	470	559	644	721	787
21	072	111	163	227	302	384	471	558	640	716
22	048	077	117	169	232	306	387	472	556	637
23	031	052	082	123	175	238	310	389	472	555
24	020	034	056	087	128	180	243	314	392	473
25	012	022	038	060	092	134	185	247	318	394

μ	24	25	26	27	28	29	30	31	32	33
16	978	987	993	996	998	999	999	1000		
17	959	975	985	991	995	997	999	999	1000	
18	932	955	972	983	990	994	997	998	999	1000
19	893	927	951	969	980	988	993	996	998	999
20	843	888	922	948	966	978	987	992	995	997
21	782	838	883	917	944	963	976	985	991	994
22	712	777	832	877	913	940	959	973	983	989
23	635	708	772	827	873	908	936	956	971	981
24	554	632	704	768	823	868	904	932	953	969
25	473	553	629	700	763	818	863	900	929	950

μ	34	35	36	37	38	39	40	41	42	43
19	999	1000								
20	999	999	1000							
21	997	998	999	999	1000					
22	994	996	998	999	999	1000				
23	988	993	996	997	999	999	1000			
24	979	987	992	995	997	998	999	999	1000	
25	966	978	985	991	994	997	998	999	999	1000

Exhibit F–5   Exponential Functions

x	e^x	e^{-x}	x	e^x	e^{-x}
0.0	1.000	1.000	5.0	148.4	0.0067
0.1	1.105	0.905	5.1	164.0	0.0061
0.2	1.221	0.819	5.2	181.3	0.0055
0.3	1.350	0.741	5.3	200.3	0.0050
0.4	1.492	0.670	5.4	221.4	0.0045
0.5	1.649	0.607	5.5	244.7	0.0041
0.6	1.822	0.549	5.6	270.4	0.0037
0.7	2.014	0.497	5.7	298.9	0.0033
0.8	2.226	0.449	5.8	330.3	0.0030
0.9	2.460	0.407	5.9	365.0	0.0027
1.0	2.718	0.368	6.0	403.4	0.0025
1.1	3.004	0.333	6.1	445.9	0.0022
1.2	3.320	0.301	6.2	492.8	0.0020
1.3	3.669	0.273	6.3	544.6	0.0018
1.4	4.055	0.247	6.4	601.8	0.0017
1.5	4.482	0.223	6.5	665.1	0.0015
1.6	4.953	0.202	6.6	735.1	0.0014
1.7	5.474	0.183	6.7	812.4	0.0012
1.8	6.050	0.165	6.8	897.8	0.0011
1.9	6.686	0.150	6.9	992.3	0.0010
2.0	7.389	0.135	7.0	1,096.6	0.0009
2.1	8.166	0.122	7.1	1,212.0	0.0008
2.2	9.025	0.111	7.2	1,339.4	0.0007
2.3	9.974	0.100	7.3	1,480.3	0.0007
2.4	11.023	0.091	7.4	1,636.0	0.0006
2.5	12.18	0.082	7.5	1,808.0	0.00055
2.6	13.46	0.074	7.6	1,998.2	0.00050
2.7	14.88	0.067	7.7	2,208.3	0.00045
2.8	16.44	0.061	7.8	2,440.6	0.00041
2.9	18.17	0.055	7.9	2,697.3	0.00037
3.0	20.09	0.050	8.0	2,981.0	0.00034
3.1	22.20	0.045	8.1	3,294.5	0.00030
3.2	24.53	0.041	8.2	3,641.0	0.00027
3.3	27.11	0.037	8.3	4,023.9	0.00025
3.4	29.96	0.033	8.4	4,447.1	0.00022
3.5	33.12	0.030	8.5	4,914.8	0.00020
3.6	36.60	0.027	8.6	5,431.7	0.00018
3.7	40.45	0.025	8.7	6,002.9	0.00017
3.8	44.70	0.022	8.8	6,634.2	0.00015
3.9	49.40	0.020	8.9	7,332.0	0.00014
4.0	54.60	0.018	9.0	8,103.1	0.00012
4.1	60.34	0.017	9.1	8,955.3	0.00011
4.2	66.69	0.015	9.2	9,897.1	0.00010
4.3	73.70	0.014	9.3	10,938	0.00009
4.4	81.45	0.012	9.4	12,088	0.00008
4.5	90.02	0.011	9.5	13,360	0.00007
4.6	99.48	0.010	9.6	14,765	0.00007
4.7	109.95	0.009	9.7	16,318	0.00006
4.8	121.51	0.008	9.8	18,034	0.00006
4.9	134.29	0.007	9.9	19,930	0.00005

From Robert L. Childress, *Calculus for Business and Economics* (Englewood Cliffs, N.J.: Prentice-Hall, 1972). By permission of the publisher.

Exhibit F–6   The Standard Normal Distribution

z	.00	.01	.02	.03	.04	.05	.06	.07	.08	.09
0.0	.0000	.0040	.0080	.0120	.0160	.0199	.0239	.0279	.0319	.0359
0.1	.0398	.0438	.0478	.0517	.0557	.0596	.0636	.0675	.0714	.0753
0.2	.0793	.0832	.0871	.0910	.0948	.0987	.1026	.1064	.1103	.1141
0.3	.1179	.1217	.1255	.1293	.1331	.1368	.1406	.1443	.1480	.1517
0.4	.1554	.1591	.1628	.1664	.1700	.1736	.1772	.1808	.1844	.1879
0.5	.1915	.1950	.1985	.2019	.2054	.2088	.2123	.2157	.2190	.2224
0.6	.2257	.2291	.2324	.2357	.2389	.2422	.2454	.2486	.2517	.2549
0.7	.2580	.2611	.2642	.2673	.2704	.2734	.2764	.2794	.2823	.2852
0.8	.2881	.2910	.2939	.2967	.2995	.3023	.3051	.3078	.3106	.3133
0.9	.3159	.3186	.3212	.3238	.3264	.3289	.3315	.3340	.3365	.3389
1.0	.3413	.3438	.3461	.3485	.3508	.3531	.3554	.3577	.3599	.3621
1.1	.3643	.3665	.3686	.3708	.3729	.3749	.3770	.3790	.3810	.3830
1.2	.3849	.3869	.3888	.3907	.3925	.3944	.3962	.3980	.3997	.4015
1.3	.4032	.4049	.4066	.4082	.4099	.4115	.4131	.4147	.4162	.4177
1.4	.4192	.4207	.4222	.4236	.4251	.4265	.4279	.4292	.4306	.4319
1.5	.4332	.4345	.4357	.4370	.4382	.4394	.4406	.4418	.4429	.4441
1.6	.4452	.4463	.4474	.4484	.4495	.4505	.4515	.4525	.4535	.4545
1.7	.4554	.4564	.4573	.4582	.4591	.4599	.4608	.4616	.4625	.4633
1.8	.4641	.4649	.4656	.4664	.4671	.4678	.4686	.4693	.4699	.4706
1.9	.4713	.4719	.4726	.4732	.4738	.4744	.4750	.4756	.4761	.4767
2.0	.4772	.4778	.4783	.4788	.4793	.4798	.4803	.4808	.4812	.4817
2.1	.4821	.4826	.4830	.4834	.4838	.4842	.4846	.4850	.4854	.4857
2.2	.4861	.4864	.4868	.4871	.4875	.4878	.4881	.4884	.4887	.4890
2.3	.4893	.4896	.4898	.4901	.4904	.4906	.4909	.4911	.4913	.4916
2.4	.4918	.4920	.4922	.4925	.4927	.4929	.4931	.4932	.4934	.4936
2.5	.4938	.4940	.4941	.4943	.4945	.4946	.4948	.4949	.4951	.4952
2.6	.4953	.4955	.4956	.4957	.4959	.4960	.4961	.4962	.4963	.4964
2.7	.4965	.4966	.4967	.4968	.4969	.4970	.4971	.4972	.4973	.4974
2.8	.4974	.4975	.4976	.4977	.4977	.4978	.4979	.4979	.4980	.4981
2.9	.4981	.4982	.4982	.4983	.4984	.4984	.4985	.4985	.4986	.4986
3.0	.4987	.4987	.4987	.4988	.4988	.4989	.4989	.4989	.4990	.4990

From John E. Freund, *Modern Elementary Statistics*, 4th ed. (Englewood Cliffs, N.J.: Prentice Hall, 1973). By permission of the publisher.

RANDOM NUMBERS*

04433	80674	24520	18222	10610	05794	37515
60298	47829	72648	37414	75755	04717	29899
67884	59651	67533	68123	17730	95862	08034
89512	32155	51906	61662	64130	16688	37275
32653	01895	12506	88535	36553	23757	34209
95913	15405	13772	76638	48423	25018	99041
55864	21694	13122	44115	01601	50541	00147
35334	49810	91601	40617	72876	33967	73830
57729	32196	76487	11622	96297	24160	09903
86648	13697	63677	70119	94739	25875	38829
30574	47609	07967	32422	76791	39725	53711
81307	43694	835ö0	79974	45929	85113	72268
02410	54905	79007	54939	21410	86980	91772
18969	75274	52233	62319	08598	09066	95288
87863	82384	66860	62297	80198	19347	73234
68397	71708	15438	62311	72844	60203	46412
28529	54447	58729	10854	99058	18260	38765
44285	06372	15867	70418	57012	72122	36634
86299	83430	33571	23309	57040	29285	67870
84842	68668	90894	61658	15001	94055	36308
56970	83609	52098	04184	54967	72938	56834
83125	71257	60490	44369	66130	72936	69848
55503	52423	02464	26141	68779	66388	75242
47019	76273	33203	29608	54553	25971	69573
84828	32592	79526	29554	84580	37859	28504
68921	08141	79227	05748	51276	57143	31926
36458	96045	30424	98420	72925	40729	22337
95752	59445	36847	87729	81679	59126	59437
26768	47323	58454	56958	20575	76746	49878
42613	37056	43636	58085	06766	60227	96414
95457	30566	65482	25596	02678	54592	63607
95276	17894	63564	95958	39750	64379	46059
66954	52324	64776	92345	95110	59448	77249
17457	18481	14113	62462	02798	54977	48349
03704	36872	83214	59337	01695	60666	97410
21538	86497	33210	60337	27976	70661	08250
57178	67619	98310	70348	11317	71623	55510
31048	97558	94953	55866	96283	46620	52087
69799	55380	16498	80733	96422	58078	99643
90595	61867	59231	17772	67831	33317	00520
33570	04981	98939	78784	09977	29398	93896
15340	93460	57477	13898	48431	72936	78160
64079	42483	36512	56186	99098	48850	72527
63491	05546	67118	62063	74958	20946	28147
92003	63868	41034	28260	79708	00770	88643
52360	46658	66511	04172	73085	11795	52594
74622	12142	68355	65635	21828	39539	1898?
04157	50079	61343	64315	70836	82857	35335
86003	60070	66241	32836	27573	11479	94114
41268	80187	20351	09636	84668	42486	71303

Based on parts of *Table of 105,000 Random Decimal Digits*, Interstate Commerce Commission, Bureau of Transport Economics and Statistics, Washington, D.C. From John E. Freund, *Modern Elementary Statistics*, 4th ed. (Englewood Cliffs, N.J.: Prentice-Hall, 1973). By permission of the publisher.

RANDOM NUMBERS *(Continued)*

48611	62866	33963	14045	79451	04934	45576
78812	03509	78673	73181	29973	18664	04555
19472	63971	37271	31445	49019	49405	46925
51266	11569	08697	91120	64156	40365	74297
55806	96275	26130	47949	14877	69594	83041
77527	81360	18180	97421	55541	90275	18213
77680	58788	33016	61173	93049	04694	43534
15404	96554	88265	34537	38526	67924	40474
14045	22917	60718	66487	46346	30949	03173
68376	43918	77653	04127	69930	43283	35766
93385	13421	67957	20384	58731	53396	59723
09858	52104	32014	53115	03727	98624	84616
93307	34140	49516	42148	57740	31198	70336
04794	01534	92058	03157	91758	80611	45357
86265	49096	97021	92582	61422	75890	86442
65943	79232	45702	67055	39024	57383	44424
90038	94209	04055	27393	61517	23002	96560
97283	95943	78363	36498	40662	94188	18202
21913	72958	75637	99936	58715	07943	23748
41161	37341	81838	19389	80336	46346	91895
23777	98392	31417	98547	92058	02277	50315
59973	08144	61070	73094	27059	69181	55623
82690	74099	77885	23813	10054	11900	44353
83854	24715	48866	65745	31131	47636	45137
61980	34997	41825	11623	07320	15003	56774
99915	45821	97702	87125	44488	77613	56823
48293	86847	43186	42951	37804	85129	28993
33225	31280	41232	34750	91097	60752	69783
06846	32828	24425	30249	78801	26977	92074
32671	45587	79620	84531	38156	74211	82752
82096	21913	75544	55228	89796	05694	91552
51666	10433	10945	55306	78562	89630	41230
54044	67942	24145	42294	27427	84875	37022
66738	60184	75679	38120	17640	36242	99357
55064	17427	89180	74018	44865	53197	74810
69599	60264	84549	78007	88450	06488	72274
64756	87759	92354	78694	63638	80939	98644
80817	74533	68407	55862	32476	19326	95558
39847	96884	84657	33697	39578	90197	80532
90401	41700	95510	61166	33757	23279	85523
78227	90110	81378	96659	37008	04050	04228
87240	52716	87697	79433	16336	52862	69149
08486	10951	26832	39763	02485	71688	90936
39338	32169	03713	93510	61244	73774	01245
21188	01850	69689	49426	49128	14660	14143
13287	82531	04388	64693	11934	35051	68576
53609	04001	19648	14053	49623	10840	31915
87900	36194	31567	53506	34304	39910	79630
81641	00496	36058	75899	46620	70024	88753
19512	50277	71508	20116	79520	06269	74173

RANDOM NUMBERS *(Continued)*

24418	23508	91507	76455	54941	72711	39406
57404	73678	08272	62941	02349	71389	45605
77644	98489	86268	73652	98210	44546	27174
68366	65614	01443	07607	11826	91326	29664
64472	72294	95432	53555	96810	17100	35066
88205	37913	98633	81009	81060	33449	68055
98455	78685	71250	10329	56135	80647	51404
48977	36794	56054	59243	57361	65304	93258
93077	72941	92779	23581	24548	56415	61927
84533	26564	91583	83411	66504	02036	02922
11338	12903	14514	27585	45068	05520	56321
23853	68500	92274	87026	99717	01542	72090
94096	74920	25822	98026	05394	61840	83089
83160	82362	09350	98536	38155	42661	02363
97425	47335	69709	01386	74319	04318	99387
83951	11954	24317	20345	18134	90062	10761
93085	35203	05740	03206	92012	42710	34650
33762	83193	58045	89880	78101	44392	53767
49665	85397	85137	30496	23469	42846	94810
37541	82627	80051	72521	35342	56119	97190
22145	85304	35348	82854	55846	18076	12415
27153	08662	61078	52433	22184	33998	87436
00301	49425	66682	25442	83668	66236	79655
43815	43272	73778	63469	50083	70696	13558
14689	86482	74157	46012	97765	27552	49617
16680	55936	82453	19532	49988	13176	94219
86938	60429	01137	86168	78257	86249	46134
33944	29219	73161	46061	30946	22210	79302
16045	67736	18608	18198	19468	76358	69203
37044	52523	25627	63107	30806	80857	84383
61471	45322	35340	35132	42163	60332	98851
47422	21296	16785	66393	39240	51463	95963
24133	39719	14484	58613	88717	29289	77360
67253	67064	10748	16006	16767	57345	42285
62382	76941	01635	35829	77516	98468	51686
98011	16503	09201	03523	87192	66483	55649
37366	24386	20654	85117	74078	64120	04643
73587	83993	54176	05221	94119	20108	78101
33583	68291	50547	96085	62180	27453	18567
02878	33223	39109	49536	56199	05993	71201
91498	41673	17195	33175	04994	09879	70337
91127	19815	30219	55591	21725	43827	78862
12997	55013	18662	81724	24305	37661	18956
96098	13651	15393	69995	14762	69734	89150
97627	17837	10472	18983	28387	99781	52977
40064	47981	31484	76603	54088	91095	00010
16239	68743	71374	55863	22672	91609	51514
58354	24913	20435	30965	17453	65623	93058
52567	65085	60220	84641	18273	49604	47418
06236	29052	91392	07551	83532	68130	56970

RANDOM NUMBERS *(Continued)*

94620	27963	96478	21559	19246	88097	44926
60947	60775	73181	43264	56895	04232	59604
27499	53523	63110	57106	20865	91683	80688
01603	23156	89223	43429	95353	44662	59433
00815	01552	06392	31437	70385	45863	75971
83844	90942	74857	52419	68723	47830	63010
06626	10042	93629	37609	57215	08409	81906
56760	63348	24949	11859	29793	37457	59377
64416	29934	00755	09418	14230	62887	92683
63569	17906	38076	32135	19090	96970	75917
22693	35089	72994	04252	23791	60249	83010
43413	59744	01275	71326	91382	45114	20245
09224	78530	50566	49965	04851	18280	14039
67625	34683	03142	74733	63558	09665	22610
86874	12549	98699	54952	91579	26023	81076
54548	49505	62515	63903	13193	33905	66936
73236	66167	49728	03581	40699	10396	81827
15220	66319	13543	14071	59148	95154	72852
16151	08029	36954	03891	38313	34016	18671
43635	84249	88984	80993	55431	90793	62603
30193	42776	85611	57635	51362	79907	77364
37430	45246	11400	20986	43996	73122	88474
88312	93047	12088	86937	70794	01041	74867
98995	58159	04700	90443	13168	31553	67891
51734	20849	70198	67906	00880	82899	66065
88698	41755	56216	66852	17748	04963	54859
51865	09836	73966	65711	41699	11732	17173
40300	08852	27528	84648	79589	95295	72895
02760	28625	70476	76410	32988	10194	94917
78450	26245	91763	73117	33047	03577	62599
50252	56911	62693	73817	98693	18728	94741
07929	66728	47761	81472	44806	15592	71357
09030	39605	87507	85446	51257	89555	75520
56670	88445	85799	76200	21795	38894	58070
48140	13583	94911	13318	64741	64336	95103
36764	86132	12463	28385	94242	32063	45233
14351	71381	28133	68269	65145	28152	39087
81276	00835	63835	87174	42446	08882	27067
55524	86088	00069	59254	24654	77371	26409
78852	65889	32719	13758	23937	90740	16866
11861	69032	51915	23510	32050	52052	24004
67699	01009	07050	73324	06732	27510	33761
50064	39500	17450	18030	63124	48061	59412
93126	17700	94400	76075	08317	27324	72723
01657	92602	41043	05686	15650	29970	95877
13800	76690	75133	60456	28491	03845	11507
98135	42870	48578	29036	69876	86563	61729
08313	99293	00990	13595	77457	79969	11339
90974	83965	62732	85161	54330	22406	86253
33273	61993	88407	69399	17301	70975	99129

Exhibit F–8 Squares and Square Roots

n	n^2	$\sqrt{n}$	$\sqrt{10n}$	n	n^2	$\sqrt{n}$	$\sqrt{10n}$
1.00	1.0000	1.000000	3.162278	1.50	2.2500	1.224745	3.872983
1.01	1.0201	1.004988	3.178050	1.51	2.2801	1.228821	3.885872
1.02	1.0404	1.009950	3.193744	1.52	2.3104	1.232883	3.898718
1.03	1.0609	1.014889	3.209361	1.53	2.3409	1.236932	3.911521
1.04	1.0816	1.019804	3.224903	1.54	2.3716	1.240967	3.924283
1.05	1.1025	1.024695	3.240370	1.55	2.4025	1.244990	3.937004
1.06	1.1236	1.029563	3.255764	1.56	2.4336	1.249000	3.949684
1.07	1.1449	1.034408	3.271085	1.57	2.4649	1.252996	3.962323
1.08	1.1664	1.039230	3.286335	1.58	2.4964	1.256981	3.974921
1.09	1.1881	1.044031	3.301515	1.59	2.5281	1.260952	3.987480
1.10	1.2100	1.048809	3.316625	1.60	2.5600	1.264911	4.000000
1.11	1.2321	1.053565	3.331666	1.61	2.5921	1.268858	4.012481
1.12	1.2544	1.058301	3.346640	1.62	2.6244	1.272792	4.024922
1.13	1.2769	1.063015	3.361547	1.63	2.6569	1.276715	4.037326
1.14	1.2996	1.067708	3.376389	1.64	2.6896	1.280625	4.049691
1.15	1.3225	1.072381	3.391165	1.65	2.7225	1.284523	4.062019
1.16	1.3456	1.077033	3.405877	1.66	2.7556	1.288410	4.074310
1.17	1.3689	1.081665	3.420526	1.67	2.7889	1.292285	4.086563
1.18	1.3924	1.086278	3.435113	1.68	2.8224	1.296148	4.098780
1.19	1.4161	1.090871	3.449638	1.69	2.8561	1.300000	4.110961
1.20	1.4400	1.095445	3.464102	1.70	2.8900	1.303840	4.123106
1.21	1.4641	1.100000	3.478505	1.71	2.9241	1.307670	4.135215
1.22	1.4884	1.104536	3.492850	1.72	2.9584	1.311488	4.147288
1.23	1.5129	1.109054	3.507136	1.73	2.9929	1.315295	4.159327
1.24	1.5376	1.113553	3.521363	1.74	3.0276	1.319091	4.171331
1.25	1.5625	1.118034	3.535534	1.75	3.0625	1.322876	4.183300
1.26	1.5876	1.122497	3.549648	1.76	3.0976	1.326650	4.195235
1.27	1.6129	1.126943	3.563706	1.77	3.1329	1.330413	4.207137
1.28	1.6384	1.131371	3.577709	1.78	3.1684	1.334166	4.219005
1.29	1.6641	1.135782	3.591657	1.79	3.2041	1.337909	4.230839
1.30	1.6900	1.140175	3.605551	1.80	3.2400	1.341641	4.242641
1.31	1.7161	1.144552	3.619392	1.81	3.2761	1.345362	4.254409
1.32	1.7424	1.148913	3.633180	1.82	3.3124	1.349074	4.266146
1.33	1.7689	1.153256	3.646917	1.83	3.3489	1.352775	4.277850
1.34	1.7956	1.157584	3.660601	1.84	3.3856	1.356466	4.289522
1.35	1.8225	1.161895	3.674235	1.85	3.4225	1.360147	4.301163
1.36	1.8496	1.166190	3.687818	1.86	3.4596	1.363818	4.312772
1.37	1.8769	1.170470	3.701351	1.87	3.4969	1.367479	4.324350
1.38	1.9044	1.174734	3.714835	1.88	3.5344	1.371131	4.335897
1.39	1.9321	1.178983	3.728270	1.89	3.5721	1.374773	4.347413
1.40	1.9600	1.183216	3.741657	1.90	3.6100	1.378405	4.358899
1.41	1.9881	1.187434	3.754997	1.91	3.6481	1.382027	4.370355
1.42	2.0164	1.191638	3.768289	1.92	3.6864	1.385641	4.381780
1.43	2.0449	1.195826	3.781534	1.93	3.7249	1.389244	4.393177
1.44	2.0736	1.200000	3.794733	1.94	3.7636	1.392839	4.404543
1.45	2.1025	1.204159	3.807887	1.95	3.8025	1.396424	4.415880
1.46	2.1316	1.208305	3.820995	1.96	3.8416	1.400000	4.427189
1.47	2.1609	1.212436	3.834058	1.97	3.8809	1.403567	4.438468
1.48	2.1904	1.216553	3.847077	1.98	3.9204	1.407125	4.449719
1.49	2.2201	1.220656	3.860052	1.99	3.9601	1.410674	4.460942

From John E. Freund, *Modern Elementary Statistics*, 4th ed. (Englewood Cliffs, N.J.: Prentice-Hall, 1973). By permission of the publisher.

n	n^2	$\sqrt{n}$	$\sqrt{10n}$	n	n^2	$\sqrt{n}$	$\sqrt{10n}$
2.00	4.0000	1.414214	4.472136	2.50	6.2500	1.581139	5.000000
2.01	4.0401	1.417745	4.483302	2.51	6.3001	1.584298	5.009990
2.02	4.0804	1.421267	4.494441	2.52	6.3504	1.587451	5.019960
2.03	4.1209	1.424781	4.505552	2.53	6.4009	1.590597	5.029911
2.04	4.1616	1.428286	4.516636	2.54	6.4516	1.593738	5.039841
2.05	4.2025	1.431782	4.527693	2.55	6.5025	1.596872	5.049752
2.06	4.2436	1.435270	4.538722	2.56	6.5536	1.600000	5.059644
2.07	4.2849	1.438749	4.549725	2.57	6.6049	1.603122	5.069517
2.08	4.3264	1.442221	4.560702	2.58	6.6564	1.606238	5.079370
2.09	4.3681	1.445683	4.571652	2.59	6.7081	1.609348	5.089204
2.10	4.4100	1.449138	4.582576	2.60	6.7600	1.612452	5.099020
2.11	4.4521	1.452584	4.593474	2.61	6.8121	1.615549	5.108816
2.12	4.4944	1.456022	4.604346	2.62	6.8644	1.618641	5.118594
2.13	4.5369	1.459452	4.615192	2.63	6.9169	1.621727	5.128353
2.14	4.5796	1.462874	4.626013	2.64	6.9696	1.624808	5.138093
2.15	4.6225	1.466288	4.636809	2.65	7.0225	1.627882	5.147815
2.16	4.6656	1.469694	4.647580	2.66	7.0756	1.630951	5.157519
2.17	4.7089	1.473092	4.658326	2.67	7.1289	1.634013	5.167204
2.18	4.7524	1.476482	4.669047	2.68	7.1824	1.637071	5.176872
2.19	4.7961	1.479865	4.679744	2.69	7.2361	1.640122	5.186521
2.20	4.8400	1.483240	4.690416	2.70	7.2900	1.643168	5.196152
2.21	4.8841	1.486607	4.701064	2.71	7.3441	1.646208	5.205766
2.22	4.9284	1.489966	4.711688	2.72	7.3984	1.649242	5.215362
2.23	4.9729	1.493318	4.722288	2.73	7.4529	1.652271	5.224940
2.24	5.0176	1.496663	4.732864	2.74	7.5076	1.655295	5.234501
2.25	5.0625	1.500000	4.743416	2.75	7.5625	1.658312	5.244044
2.26	5.1076	1.503330	4.753946	2.76	7.6176	1.661325	5.253570
2.27	5.1529	1.506652	4.764452	2.77	7.6729	1.664332	5.263079
2.28	5.1984	1.509967	4.774935	2.78	7.7284	1.667333	5.272571
2.29	5.2441	1.513275	4.785394	2.79	7.7841	1.670329	5.282045
2.30	5.2900	1.516575	4.795832	2.80	7.8400	1.673320	5.291503
2.31	5.3361	1.519868	4.806246	2.81	7.8961	1.676305	5.300943
2.32	5.3824	1.523155	4.816638	2.82	7.9524	1.679286	5.310367
2.33	5.4289	1.526434	4.827007	2.83	8.0089	1.682260	5.319774
2.34	5.4756	1.529706	4.837355	2.84	8.0656	1.685230	5.329165
2.35	5.5225	1.532971	4.847680	2.85	8.1225	1.688194	5.338539
2.36	5.5696	1.536229	4.857983	2.86	8.1796	1.691153	5.347897
2.37	5.6169	1.539480	4.868265	2.87	8.2369	1.694107	5.357238
2.38	5.6644	1.542725	4.878524	2.88	8.2944	1.697056	5.366563
2.39	5.7121	1.545962	4.888763	2.89	8.3521	1.700000	5.375872
2.40	5.7600	1.549193	4.898979	2.90	8.4100	1.702939	5.385165
2.41	5.8081	1.552417	4.909175	2.91	8.4681	1.705872	5.394442
2.42	5.8564	1.555635	4.919350	2.92	8.5264	1.708801	5.403702
2.43	5.9049	1.558846	4.929503	2.93	8.5849	1.711724	5.412947
2.44	5.9536	1.562050	4.939636	2.94	8.6436	1.714643	5.422177
2.45	6.0025	1.565248	4.949747	2.95	8.7025	1.717556	5.431390
2.46	6.0516	1.568439	4.959839	2.96	8.7616	1.720465	5.440588
2.47	6.1009	1.571623	4.969909	2.97	8.8209	1.723369	5.449771
2.48	6.1504	1.574802	4.979960	2.98	8.8804	1.726268	5.458938
2.49	6.2001	1.577973	4.989990	2.99	8.9401	1.729162	5.468089

n	n^2	$\sqrt{n}$	$\sqrt{10n}$	n	n^2	$\sqrt{n}$	$\sqrt{10n}$
3.00	9.0000	1.732051	5.477226	3.50	12.2500	1.870829	5.916080
3.01	9.0601	1.734935	5.486347	3.51	12.3201	1.873499	5.924525
3.02	9.1204	1.737815	5.495453	3.52	12.3904	1.876166	5.932959
3.03	9.1809	1.740690	5.504544	3.53	12.4609	1.878829	5.941380
3.04	9.2416	1.743560	5.513620	3.54	12.5316	1.881489	5.949790
3.05	9.3025	1.746425	5.522681	3.55	12.6025	1.884144	5.958188
3.06	9.3636	1.749286	5.531727	3.56	12.6736	1.886796	5.966574
3.07	9.4249	1.752142	5.540758	3.57	12.7449	1.889444	5.974948
3.08	9.4864	1.754993	5.549775	3.58	12.8164	1.892089	5.983310
3.09	9.5481	1.757840	5.558777	3.59	12.8881	1.894730	5.991661
3.10	9.6100	1.760682	5.567764	3.60	12.9600	1.897367	6.000000
3.11	9.6721	1.763519	5.576737	3.61	13.0321	1.900000	6.008328
3.12	9.7344	1.766352	5.585696	3.62	13.1044	1.902630	6.016644
3.13	9.7969	1.769181	5.594640	3.63	13.1769	1.905256	6.024948
3.14	9.8596	1.772005	5.603570	3.64	13.2496	1.907878	6.033241
3.15	9.9225	1.774824	5.612486	3.65	13.3225	1.910497	6.041523
3.16	9.9856	1.777639	5.621388	3.66	13.3956	1.913113	6.049793
3.17	10.0489	1.780449	5.630275	3.67	13.4689	1.915724	6.058052
3.18	10.1124	1.783255	5.639149	3.68	13.5424	1.918333	6.066300
3.19	10.1761	1.786057	5.648008	3.69	13.6161	1.920937	6.074537
3.20	10.2400	1.788854	5.656854	3.70	13.6900	1.923538	6.082763
3.21	10.3041	1.791647	5.665686	3.71	13.7641	1.926136	6.090977
3.22	10.3684	1.794436	5.674504	3.72	13.8384	1.928730	6.099180
3.23	10.4329	1.797220	5.683309	3.73	13.9129	1.931321	6.107373
3.24	10.4976	1.800000	5.692100	3.74	13.9876	1.933908	6.115554
3.25	10.5625	1.802776	5.700877	3.75	14.0625	1.936492	6.123724
3.26	10.6276	1.805547	5.709641	3.76	14.1376	1.939072	6.131884
3.27	10.6929	1.808314	5.718391	3.77	14.2129	1.941649	6.140033
3.28	10.7584	1.811077	5.727128	3.78	14.2884	1.944222	6.148170
3.29	10.8241	1.813836	5.735852	3.79	14.3641	1.946792	6.156298
3.30	10.8900	1.816590	5.744563	3.80	14.4400	1.949359	6.164414
3.31	10.9561	1.819341	5.753260	3.81	14.5161	1.951922	6.172520
3.32	11.0224	1.822087	5.761944	3.82	14.5924	1.954483	6.180615
3.33	11.0889	1.824829	5.770615	3.83	14.6689	1.957039	6.188699
3.34	11.1556	1.827567	5.779273	3.84	14.7456	1.959592	6.196773
3.35	11.2225	1.830301	5.787918	3.85	14.8225	1.962142	6.204837
3.36	11.2896	1.833030	5.796551	3.86	14.8996	1.964688	6.212890
3.37	11.3569	1.835756	5.805170	3.87	14.9769	1.967232	6.220932
3.38	11.4244	1.838478	5.813777	3.88	15.0544	1.969772	6.228965
3.39	11.4921	1.841195	5.822371	3.89	15.1321	1.972308	6.236986
3.40	11.5600	1.843909	5.830952	3.90	15.2100	1.974842	6.244998
3.41	11.6281	1.846619	5.839521	3.91	15.2881	1.977372	6.252999
3.42	11.6964	1.849324	5.848077	3.92	15.3664	1.979899	5.260990
3.43	11.7649	1.852026	5.856620	3.93	15.4449	1.982423	6.268971
3.44	11.8336	1.854724	5.865151	3.94	15.5236	1.984943	6.276942
3.45	11.9025	1.857418	5.873670	3.95	15.6025	1.987461	6.284903
3.46	11.9716	1.860108	5.882176	3.96	15.6816	1.989975	6.292853
3.47	12.0409	1.862794	5.890671	3.97	15.7609	1.992486	6.300794
3.48	12.1104	1.865476	5.899152	3.98	15.8404	1.994994	6.308724
3.49	12.1801	1.868154	5.907622	3.99	15.9201	1.997498	6.316645

n	n^2	$\sqrt{n}$	$\sqrt{10n}$	n	n^2	$\sqrt{n}$	$\sqrt{10n}$
4.00	16.0000	2.000000	6.324555	4.50	20.2500	2.121320	6.708204
4.01	16.0801	2.002498	6.332456	4.51	20.3401	2.123676	6.715653
4.02	16.1604	2.004994	6.340347	4.52	20.4304	2.126029	6.723095
4.03	16.2409	2.007486	6.348228	4.53	20.5209	2.128380	6.730527
4.04	16.3216	2.009975	6.356099	4.54	20.6116	2.130728	6.737952
4.05	16.4025	2.012461	6.363961	4.55	20.7025	2.133073	6.745369
4.06	16.4836	2.014944	6.371813	4.56	20.7936	2.135416	6.752777
4.07	16.5649	2.017424	6.379655	4.57	20.8849	2.137756	6.760178
4.08	16.6464	2.019901	6.387488	4.58	20.9764	2.140093	6.767570
4.09	16.7281	2.022375	6.395311	4.59	21.0681	2.142429	6.774954
4.10	16.8100	2.024846	6.403124	4.60	21.1600	2.144761	6.782330
4.11	16.8921	20.27313	6.410928	4.61	21.2521	2.147091	6.789698
4.12	16.9744	2.029778	6.418723	4.62	21.3444	2.149419	6.797058
4.13	17.0569	2.032240	6.426508	4.63	21.4369	2.151743	6.804410
4.14	17.1396	2.034699	6.434283	4.64	21.5296	2.154066	6.811755
4.15	17.2225	2.037155	6.442049	4.65	21.6225	2.156386	6.819091
4.16	17.3056	2.039608	6.449806	4.66	21.7156	2.158703	6.826419
4.17	17.3889	2.042058	6.457554	4.67	21.8089	2.161018	6.833740
4.18	17.4724	2.044505	6.465292	4.68	21.9024	2.163331	6.841053
4.19	17.5561	2.046949	6.473021	4.69	21.9961	2.165641	6.848357
4.20	17.6400	2.049390	6.480741	4.70	22.0900	2.167948	6.855655
4.21	17.7241	2.051828	6.488451	4.71	22.1841	2.170253	6.862944
4.22	17.8084	2.054264	6.496153	4.72	22.2784	2.172556	6.870226
4.23	17.8929	2.056696	6.503845	4.73	22.3729	2.174856	6.877500
4.24	17.9776	2.059126	6.511528	4.74	22.4676	2.177154	6.884766
4.25	18.0625	2.061553	6.519202	4.75	22.5625	2.179449	6.892024
4.26	18.1476	2.063977	6.526868	4.76	22.6576	2.181742	6.899275
4.27	18.2329	2.066398	6.534524	4.77	22.7529	2.184033	6.906519
4.28	18.3184	2.068816	6.542171	4.78	22.8484	2.186321	6.913754
4.29	18.4041	2.071232	6.549809	4.79	22.9441	2.188607	6.920983
4.30	18.4900	2.073644	6.557439	4.80	23.0400	2.190890	6.928203
4.31	18.5761	2.076054	6.565059	4.81	23.1361	2.193171	6.935416
4.32	18.6624	2.078461	6.572671	4.82	23.2324	2.195450	6.942622
4.33	18.7489	2.080865	6.580274	4.83	23.3289	2.197726	6.949820
4.34	18.8356	2.083267	6.587868	4.84	23.4256	2.200000	6.957011
4.35	18.9225	2.085665	6.595453	4.85	23.5225	2.202272	6.964194
4.36	19.0096	2.088061	6.603030	4.86	23.6096	2.204541	6.971370
4.37	19.0969	2.090454	6.610598	4.87	23.7169	2.206808	6.978539
4.38	19.1844	2.092845	6.618157	4.88	23.8144	2.209072	6.985700
4.39	19.2721	2.095233	6.625708	4.89	23.9121	2.211334	6.992853
4.40	19.3600	2.097618	6.633250	4.90	24.0100	2.213594	7.000000
4.41	19.4481	2.100000	6.640783	4.91	24.1081	2.215852	7.007139
4.42	19.5364	2.102380	6.648308	4.92	24.2064	2.218107	7.014271
4.43	19.6249	2.104757	6.655825	4.93	24.3049	2.220360	7.021396
4.44	19.7136	2.107131	6.663332	4.94	24.4036	2.222611	7.028513
4.45	19.8025	2.109502	6.670832	4.95	24.5025	2.224860	7.035624
4.46	19.8916	2.111871	6.678323	4.96	24.6016	2.227106	7.042727
4.47	19.9809	2.114237	6.685806	4.97	24.7009	2.229350	7.049823
4.48	20.0704	2.116601	6.693280	4.98	24.8004	2.231591	7.056912
4.49	20.1601	2.118962	6.700746	4.99	24.9001	2.233831	7.063993

n	n^2	$\sqrt{n}$	$\sqrt{10n}$	n	n^2	$\sqrt{n}$	$\sqrt{10n}$
5.00	25.0000	2.236068	7.071068	5.50	30.2500	2.345208	7.416198
5.01	25.1001	2.238303	7.078135	5.51	30.3601	2.347339	7.422937
5.02	25.2004	2.240536	7.085196	5.52	30.4704	2.349468	7.429670
5.03	25.3009	2.242766	7.092249	5.53	30.5809	2.351595	7.436397
5.04	25.4016	2.244994	7.099296	5.54	30.6916	2.353720	7.443118
5.05	25.5025	2.247221	7.106335	5.55	30.8025	2.355844	7.449832
5 06	25.6036	2.249444	7.113368	5.56	30.9136	2.357965	7.456541
5.07	25.7049	2.251666	7.120393	5.57	31.0249	2.360085	7.463243
5.08	25.8064	2.253886	7.127412	5.58	31.1364	2.362202	7.469940
5.09	25.9081	2.256103	7.134424	5.59	31.2481	2.364318	7.476630
5.10	26.0100	2.258318	7.141428	5.60	31.3600	2.366432	7.483315
5.11	26.1121	2.260531	7.148426	5.61	31.4721	2.368544	7.489993
5.12	26.2144	2.262742	7.155418	5.62	31.5844	2.370654	7.496666
5.13	26.3169	2.264950	7.162402	5.63	31.6969	2.372762	7.503333
5.14	26.4196	2.267157	7.169379	5.64	31.8096	2.374868	7.509993
5.15	26.5225	2.269361	7.176350	5.65	31.9225	2.376973	7.516648
5.16	26.6256	2.271563	7.183314	5.66	32.0356	2.379075	7.523297
5.17	26.7289	2.273763	7.190271	5.67	32.1489	2.381176	7.529940
5.18	26.8324	2.275961	7.197222	5.68	32.2624	2.383275	7.536577
5.19	26.9361	2.278157	7.204165	5.69	32.3761	2.385372	7.543209
5.20	27.0400	2.280351	7.211103	5.70	32.4900	2.387467	7.549834
5.21	27.1441	2.282542	7.218033	5.71	32.6041	2.389561	7.556454
5.22	27.2484	2.284732	7.224957	5.72	32.7184	2.391652	7.563068
5.23	27.3529	2.286919	7.231874	5.73	32.8329	2.393742	7.569676
5.24	27.4576	2.289105	7.238784	5.74	32.9476	2.395830	7.576279
5.25	27.5625	2.291288	7.245688	5.75	33.0625	2.397916	7.582875
5.26	27.6676	2.293469	7.252586	5.76	33.1776	2.400000	7.589466
5.27	27.7729	2.295648	7.259477	5.77	33.2929	2.402082	7.596052
5.28	27.8784	2.297825	7.266361	5.78	33.4084	2.404163	7.602631
5.29	27.9841	2.300000	7.273239	5.79	33.5241	2.406242	7.609205
5.30	28.0900	2.302173	7.280110	5.80	33.6400	2.408319	7.615773
5.31	28.1961	2.304344	7.286975	5.81	33.7561	2.410394	7.622336
5.32	28.3024	2.306513	7.293833	5.82	33.8724	2.412468	7.628892
5.33	28.4089	2.308679	7.300685	5.83	33.9889	2.414539	7.635444
5.34	28.5156	2.310844	7.307530	5.84	34.1056	2.416609	7.641989
5.35	28.6225	2.313007	7.314369	5.85	34.2225	2.418677	7.648529
5.36	28.7296	2.315167	7.321202	5.86	34.3396	2.420744	7.655064
5.37	28.8369	2.317326	7.328028	5.87	34.4569	2.422808	7.661593
5.38	28.9444	2.319483	7.334848	5.88	34.5744	2.424871	7.668116
5.39	29.0521	2.321637	7.341662	5.89	34.6921	2.426932	7.674634
5.40	29.1600	2.323790	7.348469	5.90	34.8100	2.428992	7.681146
5.41	29.2681	2.325941	7.355270	5.91	34.9281	2.431049	7.687652
5.42	29.3764	2.328089	7.362065	5.92	35.0464	2.433105	7.694154
5.43	29.4849	2.330236	7.368853	5.93	35.1649	2.435159	7.700649
5.44	29.5936	2.332381	7.357636	5.94	35.2836	2.437212	7.707140
5.45	29.7025	2.334524	7.382412	5.95	35.4025	2.439262	7.713624
5.46	29.8116	2.336664	7.389181	5.96	35.5216	2.441311	7.720104
5.47	29.9209	2.338803	7.395945	5.97	35.6409	2.443358	7.726578
5.48	30.0304	2.340940	7.402702	5.98	35.7604	2.445404	7.733046
5.49	30.1401	2.343075	7.409453	5.99	35.8801	2.447448	7.739509

n	n^2	$\sqrt{n}$	$\sqrt{10n}$	n	n^2	$\sqrt{n}$	$\sqrt{10n}$
6.00	36.0000	2.449490	7.745967	6.50	42.2500	2.549510	8.062258
6.01	36.1201	2.451530	7.752419	6.51	42.3801	2.551470	8.068457
6.02	36.2404	2.453569	7.758866	6.52	42.5104	2.553429	8.074652
6.03	36.3609	2.455606	7.765307	6.53	42.6409	2.555386	8.080842
6.04	36.4816	2.457641	7.771744	6.54	42.7716	2.557342	8.087027
6.05	36.6025	2.459675	7.778175	6.55	42.9025	2.559297	8.093207
6.06	36.7236	2.461707	7.784600	6.56	43.0336	2.561250	8.099383
6.07	36.8449	2.463737	7.791020	6.57	43.1649	2.563201	8.105554
6.08	36.9664	2.465766	7.797435	6.58	43.2964	2.565151	8.111720
6.09	37.0881	2.467793	7.803845	6.59	43.4281	2.567100	8.117881
6.10	37.2100	2.469818	7.810250	6.60	43.5600	2.569047	8.124038
6.11	37.3321	2.471841	7.816649	6.61	43.6921	2.570992	8.130191
6.12	37.4544	2.473863	7.823043	6.62	43.8244	2.572936	8.136338
6.13	37.5769	2.475884	7.829432	6.63	43.9569	2.574879	8.142481
6.14	37.6996	2.477902	7.835815	6.64	44.0896	2.576820	8.148620
6.15	37.8225	2.479919	7.842194	6.65	44.2225	2.578759	8.154753
6.16	37.9456	2.481935	7.848567	6.66	44.3556	2.580698	8.160882
6.17	38.0689	2.483948	7.854935	6.67	44.4889	2.582634	8.167007
6.18	38.1924	2.485961	7.861298	6.68	44.6224	2.584570	8.173127
6.19	38.3161	2.487971	7.867655	6.69	44.7561	2.586503	8.179242
6.20	38.4400	2.489980	7.874008	6.70	44.8900	2.588436	8.185353
6.21	38.5641	2.491987	7.880355	6.71	45.0241	2.590367	8.191459
6.22	38.6884	2.493993	7.886698	6.72	45.1584	2.592296	8.197561
6.23	38.8129	2.495997	7.893035	6.73	45.2929	2.594224	8.203658
6.24	38.9376	2.497999	7.899367	6.74	45.4276	2.596151	8.209750
6.25	39.0625	2.500000	7.905694	6.75	45.5625	2.598076	8.215838
6.26	39.1876	2.501999	7.912016	6.76	45.6976	2.600000	8.221922
6.27	39.3129	2.503997	7.918333	6.77	45.8329	2.601922	8.228001
6.28	39.4384	2.505993	7.924645	6.78	45.9684	2.603843	8.234076
6.29	39.5641	2.507987	7.930952	6.79	46.1041	2.605763	8.240146
6.30	39.6900	2.509980	7.937254	6.80	46.2400	2.607681	8.246211
6.31	39.8161	2.511971	7.943551	6.81	46.3761	2.609598	8.242272
6.32	39.9424	2.513961	7.949843	6.82	46.5124	2.611513	8.258329
6.33	40.0689	2.515949	7.956130	6.83	46.6489	2.613427	8.264381
6.34	40.1956	2.517936	7.962412	6.84	46.7856	2.615339	8.270429
6.35	40.3225	2.519921	7.968689	6.85	46.9225	2.617250	8.276473
6.36	40.4496	2.521904	7.974961	6.86	47.0596	2.619160	8.282512
6.37	40.5769	2.523886	7.981228	6.87	47.1969	2.621068	8.288546
6.38	40.7044	2.525866	7.987490	6.88	47.3344	2.622975	8.294577
6.39	40.8321	2.527845	7.993748	6.89	47.4721	2.624881	8.300602
6.40	40.9600	2.529822	8.000000	6.90	47.6100	2.626785	8.306624
6.41	41.0881	2.531798	8.006248	6.91	47.7481	2.628688	8.312641
6.42	41.2164	2.533772	8.012490	6.92	47.8864	2.630589	8.318654
6.43	41.3449	2.535744	8.018728	6.93	48.0249	2.632489	8.324662
6.44	41.4736	2.537716	8.024961	6.94	48.1636	2.634388	8.330666
6.45	41.6025	2.539685	8.031189	6.95	48.3025	2.636285	8.336666
6.46	41.7316	2.541653	8.037413	6.96	48.4416	2.638181	8.342661
6.47	41.8609	2.543619	8.043631	6.97	48.5809	2.640076	8.348653
6.48	41.9904	2.545584	8.049845	6.98	48.7204	2.641969	8.354639
6.49	42.1201	2.547548	8.056054	6.99	48.8601	2.643861	8.360622

n	n^2	$\sqrt{n}$	$\sqrt{10n}$	n	n^2	$\sqrt{n}$	$\sqrt{10n}$
7.00	49.0000	2.645751	8.366600	7.50	56.2500	2.738613	8.660254
7.01	49.1401	2.647640	8.372574	7.51	56.4001	2.740438	8.660026
7.02	49.2804	2.649528	8.378544	7.52	56.5504	2.742262	8.671793
7.03	49.4209	2.651415	8.384510	7.53	56.7009	2.744085	8.677557
7.04	49.5616	2.653300	8.390471	7.54	56.8516	2.745906	8.683317
7.05	49.7025	2.655184	8.396428	7.55	57.0025	2.747726	8.689074
7.06	49.8436	2.657066	8.402381	7.56	57.1536	2.749545	8.694826
7.07	49.9849	2.658947	8.408329	7.57	57.3049	2.751363	8.700575
7.08	50.1264	2.660827	8.414274	7.58	57.4564	2.753180	8.706320
7.09	50.2681	2.662705	8.420214	7.59	57.6081	2.754995	8.712061
7.10	50.4100	2.664583	8.426150	7.60	57.7600	2.756810	8.717798
7.11	50.5521	2.666458	8.432082	7.61	57.9121	2.758623	8.723531
7.12	50.6944	2.668333	8.438009	7.62	58.0644	2.760435	8.729261
7.13	50.8369	2.670206	8.443933	7.63	58.2169	2.762245	8.734987
7.14	50.9796	2.672078	8.449852	7.64	58.3696	2.764055	8.740709
7.15	51.1225	2.673948	8.455767	7.65	58.5225	2.765863	8.746428
7.16	51.2656	2.675818	8.461678	7.66	58.6756	2.767671	8.752143
7.17	51.4089	2.677686	8.467585	7.67	58.8289	2.769476	8.757854
7.18	51.5524	2.679552	8.473488	7.68	58.9824	2.771281	8.763561
7.19	51.6961	2.681418	8.479387	7.69	59.1361	2.773085	8.769265
7.20	51.8400	2.683282	8.485281	7.70	59.2900	2.774887	8.774964
7.21	51.9841	2.685144	8.491172	7.71	59.4441	2.776689	8.780661
7.22	52.1284	2.687006	8.497058	7.72	59.5984	2.778489	8.786353
7.23	52.2729	2.688866	8.502941	7.73	59.7529	2.780288	8.792042
7.24	52.4176	2.690725	8.508819	7.74	59.9076	2.782086	8.797727
7.25	52.5625	2.692582	8.514693	7.75	60.0625	2.783882	8.803408
7.26	52.7076	2.694439	8.520563	7.76	60.2176	2.785678	8.809086
7.27	52.8529	2.696294	8.526429	7.77	60.3729	2.787472	8.814760
7.28	52.9984	2.698148	8.532292	7.78	60.5284	2.789265	8.820431
7.29	53.1441	2.700000	8.538150	7.79	60.6841	2.791057	8.826098
7.30	53.2900	2.701851	8.544004	7.80	60.8400	2.792848	8.831761
7.31	53.4361	2.703701	8.549854	7.81	60.9961	2.794638	8.837420
7.32	53.5824	2.705550	8.555700	7.82	61.1524	2.796426	8.843076
7.33	53.7289	2.707397	8.561542	7.83	61.3089	2.798214	8.848729
7.34	53.8756	2.709243	8.567380	7.84	61.4656	2.800000	8.854377
7.35	54.0225	2.711088	8.573214	7.85	61.6225	2.801785	8.860023
7.36	54.1696	2.712932	8.579044	7.86	61.7796	2.803569	8.865664
7.37	54.3169	2.714774	8.584870	7.87	61.9369	2.805352	8.871302
7.38	54.4644	2.716616	8.590693	7.88	62.0944	2.807134	8.876936
7.39	54.6121	2.718455	8.596511	7.89	62.2521	2.808914	8.882567
7.40	54.7600	2.720294	8.602325	7.90	62.4100	2.810694	8.888194
7.41	54.9081	2.722132	8.608136	7.91	62.5681	2.812472	8.893818
7.42	55.0564	2.723968	8.613942	7.92	62.7264	2.814249	8.899438
7.43	55.2049	2.725803	8.619745	7.93	62.8849	2.816026	8.905055
7.44	55.3536	2.727636	8.625543	7.94	63.0436	2.817801	8.910668
7.45	55.5025	2.729469	8.631338	7.95	63.2025	2.819574	8.916277
7.46	55.6516	2.731300	8.637129	7.96	63.3616	2.821347	8.921883
7.47	55.8009	2.733130	8.642916	7.97	63.5209	2.823119	8.927486
7.48	55.9504	2.734959	8.648699	7.98	63.6804	2.824889	8.933085
7.49	56.1001	2.736786	8.654479	7.99	63.8401	2.826659	8.938680

n	n^2	$\sqrt{n}$	$\sqrt{10n}$	n	n^2	$\sqrt{n}$	$\sqrt{10n}$
8.00	64.0000	2.828427	8.944272	8.50	72.2500	2.915476	9.219544
8.01	64.1601	2.830194	8.949860	8.51	72.4201	2.917190	9.224966
8.02	64.3204	2.831960	8.955445	8.52	72.5904	2.918904	9.230385
8.03	64.4809	2.833725	8.961027	8.53	72.7609	2.920616	9.235800
8.04	64.6416	2.835489	8.966605	8.54	72.9316	2.922328	9.241212
8.05	64.8025	2.837252	8.972179	8.55	73.1025	2.924038	9.246621
8.06	64.9636	2.839014	8.977750	8.56	73.2736	2.925748	9.252027
8.07	65.1249	2.840775	8.983318	8.57	73.4449	2.927456	9.257429
8.08	65.2864	2.842534	8.988882	8.58	73.6164	2.929164	9.262829
8.09	65.4481	2.844293	8.994443	8.59	73.7881	2.930870	9.268225
8.10	65.6100	2.846050	9.000000	8.60	73.9600	2.932576	9.273618
8.11	65.7721	2.847806	9.005554	8.61	74.1321	2.934280	9.279009
8.12	65.9344	2.849561	9.011104	8.62	74.3044	2.935984	9.284396
8.13	66.0969	2.851315	9.016651	8.63	74.4769	2.937686	9.289779
8.14	66.2596	2.853069	9.022195	8.64	74.6496	2.939388	9.295160
8.15	66.4225	2.854820	9.027735	8.65	74.8225	2.941088	9.300538
8.16	66.5856	2.856571	9.033272	8.66	74.9956	2.942788	9.305912
8.17	66.7489	2.858321	9.038805	8.67	75.1689	2.944486	9.311283
8.18	66.9124	2.860070	9.044335	8.68	75.3424	2.946184	9.316652
8.19	67.0761	2.861818	9.049862	8.69	75.5161	2.947881	9.322017
8.20	67.2400	2.863564	9.055385	8.70	75.6900	2.949576	9.327379
8.21	67.4041	2.865310	9.060905	8.71	75.8641	2.951271	9.332738
8.22	67.5684	2.867054	9.066422	8.72	76.0384	2.952965	9.338094
8.23	67.7329	2.868798	9.071935	8.73	76.2129	2.954657	9.343447
8.24	67.8976	2.870540	9.077445	8.74	76.3876	2.956349	9.348797
8.25	68.0625	2.872281	9.082951	8.75	76.5625	2.958040	9.354143
8.26	68.2276	2.874022	9.088454	8.76	76.7376	2.959730	9.359487
8.27	68.3929	2.875761	9.093954	8.77	76.9129	2.961419	9.364828
8.28	68.5584	2.877499	9.099451	8.78	77.0884	2.963106	9.370165
8.29	68.7241	2.879236	9.104944	8.79	77.2641	2.964793	9.375500
8.30	68.8900	2.880972	9.110434	8.80	77.4400	2.966479	9.380832
8.31	69.0561	2.882707	9.115920	8.81	77.6161	2.968164	9.386160
8.32	69.2224	2.884441	9.121403	8.82	77.7924	2.969848	9.391486
8.33	69.3889	2.886174	9.126883	8.83	77.9689	2.971532	9.396808
8.34	69.5556	2.887906	9.132360	8.84	78.1456	2.973214	9.402127
8.35	69.7225	2.889637	9.137833	8.85	78.3225	2.974895	9.407444
8.36	69.8896	2.891366	9.143304	8.86	78.4996	2.976575	9.412757
8.37	7.00569	2.893095	9.148770	8.87	78.6769	2.978255	9.418068
8.38	70.2244	2.894823	9.154234	8.88	78.8544	2.979933	9.423375
8.39	70.3921	2.896550	9.159694	8.89	79.0321	2.981610	9.428680
8.40	70.5600	2.898275	9.165151	8.90	79.2100	2.983287	9.433981
8.41	70.7281	2.900000	9.170605	8.91	79.3881	2.984962	9.439280
8.42	70.8964	2.901724	9.176056	8.92	79.5664	2.986637	9.444575
8.43	71.0649	2.903446	9.181503	8.93	79.7449	2.988311	9.449868
8.44	71.2336	2.905168	9.186947	8.94	79.9236	2.989983	9.455157
8.45	71.4025	2.906888	9.192388	8.95	80.1025	2.991655	9.460444
8.46	71.5716	2.908608	9.197826	8.96	80.2816	2.993326	9.465728
8.47	71.7409	2.910326	9.203260	8.97	80.4609	2.994996	9.471008
8.48	71.9104	2.912044	9.208692	8.98	80.6404	2.996665	9.476286
8.49	72.0801	2.913760	9.214120	8.99	80.8201	2.998333	9.481561

n	n^2	$\sqrt{n}$	$\sqrt{10n}$	n	n^2	$\sqrt{n}$	$\sqrt{10n}$
9.00	81.0000	3.000000	9.486833	9.50	90.2500	3.082207	9.746794
9.01	81.1801	3.001666	9.492102	9.51	90.4401	3.083829	9.751923
9.02	81.3604	3.003331	9.497368	9.52	90.6304	3.085450	9.757049
9.03	81.5409	3.004996	9.502631	9.53	90.8209	3.087070	9.762172
9.04	81.7216	3.006659	9.507891	9.54	91.0116	3.088689	9.767292
9.05	81.9025	3.008322	9.513149	9.55	91.2025	3.090307	9.772410
9.06	82.0836	3.009983	9.518403	9.56	91.3936	3.091925	9.777525
9.07	82.2649	3.011644	9.523655	9.57	91.5849	3.093542	9.782638
9.08	82.4464	3.013304	9.528903	9.58	91.7764	3.095158	9.787747
9.09	82.6281	3.014963	9.534149	9.59	91.9681	3.096773	9.792855
9.10	82.8100	3.016621	9.539392	9.60	92.1600	3.098387	9.797959
9.11	82.9921	3.018278	9.544632	9.61	92.3521	3.100000	9.803061
9.12	83.1744	3.019934	9.549869	9.62	92.5444	3.101612	9.808160
9.13	83.3569	3.021589	9.555103	9.63	92.7369	3.103224	9.813256
9.14	83.5396	3.023243	9.560335	9.64	92.9296	3.104835	9.818350
9.15	83.7225	3.024897	9.565563	9.65	93.1225	3.106445	9.823441
9.16	83.9056	3.026549	9.570789	9.66	93.3156	3.108054	9.828530
9.17	84.0889	3.028201	9.576012	9.67	93.5089	3.109662	9.833616
9.18	84.2724	3.029851	9.581232	9.68	93.7024	3.111270	9.838699
9.19	84.4561	3.031501	9.586449	9.69	93.8961	3.112876	9.843780
9.20	84.6400	3.033150	9.591663	9.70	94.0900	3.114482	9.848858
9.21	84.8241	3.034798	9.596874	9.71	94.2841	3.116087	9.853933
9.22	85.0084	3.036445	9.602083	9.72	94.4784	3.117691	9.859006
9.23	85.1929	3.038092	9.607289	9.73	94.6729	3.119295	9.864076
9.24	85.3776	3.039737	9.612492	9.74	94.8676	3.120897	9.869144
9.25	85.5625	3.041381	9.617692	9.75	95.0625	3.122499	9.874209
9.26	85.7476	3.043025	9.622889	9.76	95.2576	3.124100	9.879271
9.27	85.9329	3.044667	9.628084	9.77	95.4529	3.125700	9.884331
9.28	86.1184	3.046309	9.633276	9.78	95.6484	3.127299	9.889388
9.29	86.3041	3.047950	9.638465	9.79	95.8441	3.128898	9.894443
9.30	86.4900	3.049590	9.643651	9.80	96.0400	3.130495	9.899495
9.31	86.6761	3.051229	9.648834	9.81	96.2361	3.132092	9.904544
9.32	86.8624	3.052868	9.654015	9.82	96.4324	3.133688	9.909591
9.33	87.0489	3.054505	9.659193	9.83	96.6289	3.135283	9.914636
9.34	87.2356	3.056141	9.664368	9.84	96.8256	3.136877	9.919677
9.35	87.4225	3.057777	9.669540	9.85	97.0225	3.138471	9.924717
9.36	87.6096	3.059412	9.674709	9.86	97.2196	3.140064	9.929753
9.37	87.7969	3.061046	9.679876	9.87	97.4169	3.141656	9.934787
9.38	87.9844	3.062679	9.685040	9.88	97.6144	3.143247	9.939819
9.39	88.1721	3.064311	9.690201	9.89	97.8121	3.144837	9.944848
9.40	88.3600	3.065942	9.695360	9.90	98.0100	3.146427	9.949874
9.41	88.5481	3.067572	9.700515	9.91	98.2081	3.148015	9.954898
9.42	88.7364	3.069202	9.705668	9.92	98.4064	3.149603	9.959920
9.43	88.9249	3.070831	9.710819	9.93	98.6049	3.151190	9.964939
9.44	89.1136	3.072458	9.715966	9.94	98.8036	3.152777	9.969955
9.45	89.3025	3.074085	9.721111	9.95	99.0025	3.154362	9.974969
9.46	89.4916	3.075711	9.726253	9.96	99.2016	3.155947	9.979980
9.47	89.6809	3.077337	9.731393	9.97	99.4009	3.157531	9.984989
9.48	89.8704	3.078961	9.736529	9.98	99.6004	3.159114	9.989995
9.49	90.0601	3.080584	9.741663	9.99	99.8001	3.160696	9.994999

Exhibit F–9 The F Distribution (Values of $F_{.05}$)

Degrees of freedom for numerator

	1	2	3	4	5	6	7	8	9	10	12	15	20	24	30	40	60	120	∞
1	161	200	216	225	230	234	237	239	241	242	244	246	248	249	250	251	252	253	254
2	18.5	19.0	19.2	19.2	19.3	19.3	19.4	19.4	19.4	19.4	19.4	19.4	19.4	19.5	19.5	19.5	19.5	19.5	19.5
3	10.1	9.55	9.28	9.12	9.01	8.94	8.89	8.85	8.81	8.79	8.74	8.70	8.66	8.64	8.62	8.59	8.57	8.55	8.53
4	7.71	6.94	6.59	6.39	6.26	6.16	6.09	6.04	6.00	5.96	5.91	5.86	5.80	5.77	5.75	5.72	5.69	5.66	5.63
5	6.61	5.79	5.41	5.19	5.05	4.95	4.88	4.82	4.77	4.74	4.68	4.62	4.56	4.53	4.50	4.46	4.43	4.40	4.37
6	5.99	5.14	4.76	4.53	4.39	4.28	4.21	4.15	4.10	4.06	4.00	3.94	3.87	3.84	3.81	3.77	3.74	3.70	3.67
7	5.59	4.74	4.35	4.12	3.97	3.87	3.79	3.73	3.68	3.64	3.57	3.51	3.44	3.41	3.38	3.34	3.30	3.27	3.23
8	5.32	4.46	4.07	3.84	3.69	3.58	3.50	3.44	3.39	3.35	3.28	3.22	3.15	3.12	3.08	3.04	3.01	2.97	2.93
9	5.12	4.26	3.86	3.63	3.48	3.37	3.29	3.23	3.18	3.14	3.07	3.01	2.94	2.90	2.86	2.83	2.79	2.75	2.71
10	4.96	4.10	3.71	3.48	3.33	3.22	3.14	3.07	3.02	2.98	2.91	2.85	2.77	2.74	2.70	2.66	2.62	2.58	2.54
11	4.84	3.98	3.59	3.36	3.20	3.09	3.01	2.95	2.90	2.85	2.79	2.72	2.65	2.61	2.57	2.53	2.49	2.45	2.40
12	4.75	3.89	3.49	3.26	3.11	3.00	2.91	2.85	2.80	2.75	2.69	2.62	2.54	2.51	2.47	2.43	2.38	2.34	2.30
13	4.67	3.81	3.41	3.18	3.03	2.92	2.83	2.77	2.71	2.67	2.60	2.53	2.46	2.42	2.38	2.34	2.30	2.25	2.21
14	4.60	3.74	3.34	3.11	2.96	2.85	2.76	2.70	2.65	2.60	2.53	2.46	2.39	2.35	2.31	2.27	2.22	2.18	2.13
15	4.54	3.68	3.29	3.06	2.90	2.79	2.71	2.64	2.59	2.54	2.48	2.40	2.33	2.29	2.25	2.20	2.16	2.11	2.07
16	4.49	3.63	3.24	3.01	2.85	2.74	2.66	2.59	2.54	2.49	2.42	2.35	2.28	2.24	2.19	2.15	2.11	2.06	2.01
17	4.45	3.59	3.20	2.96	2.81	2.70	2.61	2.55	2.49	2.45	2.38	2.31	2.23	2.19	2.15	2.10	2.06	2.01	1.96
18	4.41	3.55	3.16	2.93	2.77	2.66	2.58	2.51	2.46	2.41	2.34	2.27	2.19	2.15	2.11	2.06	2.02	1.97	1.92
19	4.38	3.52	3.13	2.90	2.74	2.63	2.54	2.48	2.42	2.38	2.31	2.23	2.16	2.11	2.07	2.03	1.98	1.93	1.88
20	4.35	3.49	3.10	2.87	2.71	2.60	2.51	2.45	2.39	2.35	2.28	2.20	2.12	2.08	2.04	1.99	1.95	1.90	1.84
21	4.32	3.47	3.07	2.84	2.68	2.57	2.49	2.42	2.37	2.32	2.25	2.18	2.10	2.05	2.01	1.96	1.92	1.87	1.81
22	4.30	3.44	3.05	2.82	2.66	2.55	2.46	2.40	2.34	2.30	2.23	2.15	2.07	2.03	1.98	1.94	1.89	1.84	1.78
23	4.28	3.42	3.03	2.80	2.64	2.53	2.44	2.37	2.32	2.27	2.20	2.13	2.05	2.01	1.96	1.91	1.86	1.81	1.76
24	4.26	3.40	3.01	2.78	2.62	2.51	2.42	2.36	2.30	2.25	2.18	2.11	2.03	1.98	1.94	1.89	1.84	1.79	1.73
25	4.24	3.39	2.99	2.76	2.60	2.49	2.40	2.34	2.28	2.24	2.16	2.09	2.01	1.96	1.92	1.87	1.82	1.77	1.71
30	4.17	3.32	2.92	2.69	2.53	2.42	2.33	2.27	2.21	2.16	2.09	2.01	1.93	1.89	1.84	1.79	1.74	1.68	1.62
40	4.08	3.23	2.84	2.61	2.45	2.34	2.25	2.18	2.12	2.08	2.00	1.92	1.84	1.79	1.74	1.69	1.64	1.58	1.51
60	4.00	3.15	2.76	2.53	2.37	2.25	2.17	2.10	2.04	1.99	1.92	1.84	1.75	1.70	1.65	1.59	1.53	1.47	1.39
120	3.92	3.07	2.68	2.45	2.29	2.18	2.09	2.02	1.96	1.91	1.83	1.75	1.66	1.61	1.55	1.50	1.43	1.35	1.25
∞	3.84	3.00	2.60	2.37	2.21	2.10	2.01	1.94	1.88	1.83	1.75	1.67	1.57	1.52	1.46	1.39	1.32	1.22	1.00

Degrees of freedom for denominator

This table is reproduced from M. Merrington and C. M. Thompson, "Tables of percentage points of the inverted beta (F) distribution," Biometrika, vol. 33, 1943, by permission of the Biometrika trustees.

469

Exhibit F–9   The F Distribution (Values of $F_{.01}$)

Degrees of freedom for numerator

Degrees of freedom for denominator	1	2	3	4	5	6	7	8	9	10	12	15	20	24	30	40	60	120	∞
1	4,052	5,000	5,403	5,625	5,764	5,859	5,928	5,982	6,023	6,056	6,106	6,157	6,209	6,235	6,261	6,287	6,313	6,339	6,366
2	98.5	99.0	99.2	99.2	99.3	99.3	99.4	99.4	99.4	99.4	99.4	99.4	99.4	99.5	99.5	99.5	99.5	99.5	99.5
3	34.1	30.8	29.5	28.7	28.2	27.9	27.7	27.5	27.3	27.2	27.1	26.9	26.7	26.6	26.5	26.4	26.3	26.2	26.1
4	21.2	18.0	16.7	16.0	15.5	15.2	15.0	14.8	14.7	14.5	14.4	14.2	14.0	13.9	13.8	13.7	13.7	13.6	13.5
5	16.3	13.3	12.1	11.4	11.0	10.7	10.5	10.3	10.2	10.1	9.89	9.72	9.55	9.47	9.38	9.29	9.20	9.11	9.02
6	13.7	10.9	9.78	9.15	8.75	8.47	8.26	8.10	7.98	7.87	7.72	7.56	7.40	7.31	7.23	7.14	7.06	6.97	6.88
7	12.2	9.55	8.45	7.85	7.46	7.19	6.99	6.84	6.72	6.62	6.47	6.31	6.16	6.07	5.99	5.91	5.82	5.74	5.65
8	11.3	8.65	7.59	7.01	6.63	6.37	6.18	6.03	5.91	5.81	5.67	5.52	5.36	5.28	5.20	5.12	5.03	4.95	4.86
9	10.6	8.02	6.99	6.42	6.06	5.80	5.61	5.47	5.35	5.26	5.11	4.96	4.81	4.73	4.65	4.57	4.48	4.40	4.31
10	10.0	7.56	6.55	5.99	5.64	5.39	5.20	5.06	4.94	4.85	4.71	4.56	4.41	4.33	4.25	4.17	4.08	4.00	3.91
11	9.65	7.21	6.22	5.67	5.32	5.07	4.89	4.74	4.63	4.54	4.40	4.25	4.10	4.02	3.94	3.86	3.78	3.69	3.60
12	9.33	6.93	5.95	5.41	5.06	4.82	4.64	4.50	4.39	4.30	4.16	4.01	3.86	3.78	3.70	3.62	3.54	3.45	3.36
13	9.07	6.70	5.74	5.21	4.86	4.62	4.44	4.30	4.19	4.10	3.96	3.82	3.66	3.59	3.51	3.43	3.34	3.25	3.17
14	8.86	6.51	5.56	5.04	4.70	4.46	4.28	4.14	4.03	3.94	3.80	3.66	3.51	3.43	3.35	3.27	3.18	3.09	3.00
15	8.68	6.36	5.42	4.89	4.56	4.32	4.14	4.00	3.89	3.80	3.67	3.52	3.37	3.29	3.21	3.13	3.05	2.96	2.87
16	8.53	6.23	5.29	4.77	4.44	4.20	4.03	3.89	3.78	3.69	3.55	3.41	3.26	3.18	3.10	3.02	2.93	2.84	2.75
17	8.40	6.11	5.19	4.67	4.34	4.10	3.93	3.79	3.68	3.59	3.46	3.31	3.16	3.08	3.00	2.92	2.83	2.75	2.65
18	8.29	6.01	5.09	4.58	4.25	4.01	3.84	3.71	3.60	3.51	3.37	3.23	3.08	3.00	2.92	2.84	2.75	2.66	2.57
19	8.19	5.93	5.01	4.50	4.17	3.94	3.77	3.63	3.52	3.43	3.30	3.15	3.00	2.92	2.84	2.76	2.67	2.58	2.49
20	8.10	5.85	4.94	4.43	4.10	3.87	3.70	3.56	3.46	3.37	3.23	3.09	2.94	2.86	2.78	2.69	2.61	2.52	2.42
21	8.02	5.78	4.87	4.37	4.04	3.81	3.64	3.51	3.40	3.31	3.17	3.03	2.88	2.80	2.72	2.64	2.55	2.46	2.36
22	7.95	5.72	4.82	4.31	3.99	3.76	3.59	3.45	3.35	3.26	3.12	2.98	2.83	2.75	2.67	2.58	2.50	2.40	2.31
23	7.88	5.66	4.76	4.26	3.94	3.71	3.54	3.41	3.30	3.21	3.07	2.93	2.78	2.70	2.62	2.54	2.45	2.35	2.26
24	7.82	5.61	4.72	4.22	3.90	3.67	3.50	3.36	3.26	3.17	3.03	2.89	2.74	2.66	2.58	2.49	2.40	2.31	2.21
25	7.77	5.57	4.68	4.18	3.86	3.63	3.46	3.32	3.22	3.13	2.99	2.85	2.70	2.62	2.53	2.45	2.36	2.27	2.17
30	7.56	5.39	4.51	4.02	3.70	3.47	3.30	3.17	3.07	2.98	2.84	2.70	2.55	2.47	2.39	2.30	2.21	2.11	2.01
40	7.31	5.18	4.31	3.83	3.51	3.29	3.12	2.99	2.89	2.80	2.66	2.52	2.37	2.29	2.20	2.11	2.02	1.92	1.80
60	7.08	4.98	4.13	3.65	3.34	3.12	2.95	2.82	2.72	2.63	2.50	2.35	2.20	2.12	2.03	1.94	1.84	1.73	1.60
120	6.85	4.79	3.95	3.48	3.17	2.96	2.79	2.66	2.56	2.47	2.34	2.19	2.03	1.95	1.86	1.76	1.66	1.53	1.38
∞	6.63	4.61	3.78	3.32	3.02	2.80	2.64	2.51	2.41	2.32	2.18	2.04	1.88	1.79	1.70	1.59	1.47	1.32	1.00

* This table is reproduced from M. Merrington and C. M. Thompson, "Tables of percentage points of the inverted beta (F) distribution," *Biometrika*, vol. 33 (1943), by permission of the *Biometrika* trustees.

Exhibit F–10 Percentiles of the F Distribution

$F_{.90}(m_1, m_2)$

$\alpha = 0.1$

m_1 = degrees of freedom for numerator

m_2 \ m_1	1	2	3	4	5	6	7	8	9	10	12	15	20	24	30	40	60	120	∞
1	39.86	49.50	53.59	55.83	57.24	58.20	58.91	59.44	59.86	60.19	60.71	61.22	61.74	62.00	62.26	62.53	62.79	63.06	63.33
2	8.53	9.00	9.16	9.24	9.29	9.33	9.35	9.37	9.38	9.39	9.41	9.42	9.44	9.45	9.46	9.47	9.47	9.48	9.49
3	5.54	5.46	5.39	5.34	5.31	5.28	5.27	5.25	5.24	5.23	5.22	5.20	5.18	5.18	5.17	5.16	5.15	5.14	5.13
4	4.54	4.32	4.19	4.11	4.05	4.01	3.98	3.95	3.94	3.92	3.90	3.87	3.84	3.83	3.82	3.80	3.79	3.78	3.76
5	4.06	3.78	3.62	3.52	3.45	3.40	3.37	3.34	3.32	3.30	3.27	3.24	3.21	3.19	3.17	3.16	3.14	3.12	3.10
6	3.78	3.46	3.29	3.18	3.11	3.05	3.01	2.98	2.96	2.94	2.90	2.87	2.84	2.82	2.80	2.78	2.76	2.74	2.72
7	3.59	3.26	3.07	2.96	2.88	2.83	2.78	2.75	2.72	2.70	2.67	2.63	2.59	2.58	2.56	2.54	2.51	2.49	2.47
8	3.46	3.11	2.92	2.81	2.73	2.67	2.62	2.59	2.56	2.54	2.50	2.46	2.42	2.40	2.38	2.36	2.34	2.32	2.29
9	3.36	3.01	2.81	2.69	2.61	2.55	2.51	2.47	2.44	2.42	2.38	2.34	2.30	2.28	2.25	2.23	2.21	2.18	2.16
10	3.29	2.92	2.73	2.61	2.52	2.46	2.41	2.38	2.35	2.32	2.28	2.24	2.20	2.18	2.16	2.13	2.11	2.08	2.06
11	3.23	2.86	2.66	2.54	2.45	2.39	2.34	2.30	2.27	2.25	2.21	2.17	2.12	2.10	2.08	2.05	2.03	2.00	1.97
12	3.18	2.81	2.61	2.48	2.39	2.33	2.28	2.24	2.21	2.19	2.15	2.10	2.06	2.04	2.01	1.99	1.96	1.93	1.90
13	3.14	2.76	2.56	2.43	2.35	2.28	2.23	2.20	2.16	2.14	2.10	2.05	2.01	1.98	1.96	1.93	1.90	1.88	1.85
14	3.10	2.73	2.52	2.39	2.31	2.24	2.19	2.15	2.12	2.10	2.05	2.01	1.96	1.94	1.91	1.89	1.86	1.83	1.80
15	3.07	2.70	2.49	2.36	2.27	2.21	2.16	2.12	2.09	2.06	2.02	1.97	1.92	1.90	1.87	1.85	1.82	1.79	1.76
16	3.05	2.67	2.46	2.33	2.24	2.18	2.13	2.09	2.06	2.03	1.99	1.94	1.89	1.87	1.84	1.81	1.78	1.75	1.72
17	3.03	2.64	2.44	2.31	2.22	2.15	2.10	2.06	2.03	2.00	1.96	1.91	1.86	1.84	1.81	1.78	1.75	1.72	1.69
18	3.01	2.62	2.42	2.29	2.20	2.13	2.08	2.04	2.00	1.98	1.93	1.89	1.84	1.81	1.78	1.75	1.72	1.69	1.66
19	2.99	2.61	2.40	2.27	2.18	2.11	2.06	2.02	1.98	1.96	1.91	1.86	1.81	1.79	1.76	1.73	1.70	1.67	1.63

m_2 = degrees of freedom for denominator

Reproduced from "Tables of Percentage Points of the Inverted Beta (F) Distribution," computed by M. Merrington and C. M. Thompson, *Biometrika*, Vol. 33, 1943, by permission of the *Biometrika* trustees.

Exhibit F–10 Percentiles of the F Distribution (Continued)

$F_{.90}(m_1 m_2)$

$a = 0.1$

m_1 = degrees of freedom for numerator

m_2 = degrees of freedom

m_2 \ m_1	1	2	3	4	5	6	7	8	9	10	12	15	20	24	30	40	60	120	∞
20	2.97	2.59	2.38	2.25	2.16	2.09	2.04	2.00	1.96	1.94	1.89	1.84	1.79	1.77	1.74	1.71	1.68	1.64	1.61
21	2.96	2.57	2.36	2.23	2.14	2.08	2.02	1.98	1.95	1.92	1.87	1.83	1.78	1.75	1.72	1.69	1.66	1.62	1.59
22	2.95	2.56	2.35	2.22	2.13	2.06	2.01	1.97	1.93	1.90	1.86	1.81	1.76	1.73	1.70	1.67	1.64	1.60	1.57
23	2.94	2.55	2.34	2.21	2.11	2.05	1.99	1.95	1.92	1.89	1.84	1.80	1.74	1.72	1.69	1.66	1.62	1.59	1.55
24	2.93	2.54	2.33	2.19	2.10	2.04	1.98	1.94	1.91	1.88	1.83	1.78	1.73	1.70	1.67	1.64	1.61	1.57	1.53
25	2.92	2.53	2.32	2.18	2.09	2.02	1.97	1.93	1.89	1.87	1.82	1.77	1.72	1.69	1.66	1.63	1.59	1.56	1.52
26	2.91	2.52	2.31	2.17	2.08	2.01	1.96	1.92	1.88	1.86	1.81	1.76	1.71	1.68	1.65	1.61	1.58	1.54	1.50
27	2.90	2.51	2.30	2.17	2.07	2.00	1.95	1.91	1.87	1.85	1.80	1.75	1.70	1.67	1.64	1.60	1.57	1.53	1.49
28	2.89	2.50	2.29	2.16	2.06	2.00	1.94	1.90	1.87	1.84	1.79	1.74	1.69	1.66	1.63	1.59	1.56	1.52	1.48
29	2.89	2.50	2.28	2.15	2.06	1.99	1.93	1.89	1.86	1.83	1.78	1.73	1.68	1.65	1.62	1.58	1.55	1.51	1.47
30	2.88	2.49	2.28	2.14	2.05	1.98	1.93	1.88	1.85	1.82	1.77	1.72	1.67	1.64	1.61	1.57	1.54	1.50	1.46
40	2.84	2.44	2.23	2.09	2.00	1.93	1.87	1.83	1.79	1.76	1.71	1.66	1.61	1.57	1.54	1.51	1.47	1.42	1.38
60	2.79	2.39	2.18	2.04	1.95	1.87	1.82	1.77	1.74	1.71	1.66	1.60	1.54	1.51	1.48	1.44	1.40	1.35	1.29
120	2.75	2.35	2.13	1.99	1.90	1.82	1.77	1.72	1.68	1.65	1.60	1.55	1.48	1.45	1.41	1.37	1.32	1.26	1.19
∞	2.71	2.30	2.08	1.94	1.85	1.77	1.72	1.67	1.63	1.60	1.55	1.49	1.42	1.38	1.34	1.30	1.24	1.17	1.00

Note: This table does not give lower tail percentage points of F. To find a lower percentile of F, take the reciprocal of the complementary upper percentile of F with the numerator and denominator degrees of freedom reversed. For example, $F_{.05}$, $m_1 = 6$, $m_2 = 12 = 1/F_{.95}$, $m_1 = 12$, $m_2 = 6 = 1/4.00 = 0.25$. In testing quality of variances, one may routinely treat the larger estimated variance as the numerator variance. In so doing $F_{.90}$ corresponds to an alpha level of .20, $F_{.95}$ to an alpha level of .10, $F_{.975}$ to an alpha level of .05, and $F_{.99}$ to an alpha level of .02. However, in analysis of variance tests where the denominator variance is pre-assigned, the alpha levels indicated in the table hold.

Exhibit F–10   Percentiles of the F Distribution (Continued)

$F_{.95}(m_1, m_2)$

$a = 0.05$

m_1 = degrees of freedom for numerator

m_2 \ m_1	1	2	3	4	5	6	7	8	9	10	12	15	20	24	30	40	60	120	∞
1	161.4	199.5	215.7	224.6	230.2	234.0	236.8	238.9	240.5	241.9	243.9	245.9	248.0	249.1	250.1	251.1	252.2	253.3	254.3
2	18.51	19.00	19.16	19.25	19.30	19.33	19.35	19.37	19.38	19.40	19.41	19.43	19.45	19.45	19.46	19.47	19.48	19.49	19.50
3	10.13	9.55	9.28	9.12	9.01	8.94	8.89	8.85	8.81	8.79	8.74	8.70	8.66	8.64	8.62	8.59	8.57	8.55	8.53
4	7.71	6.94	6.59	6.39	6.26	6.16	6.09	6.04	6.00	5.96	5.91	5.86	5.80	5.77	5.75	5.72	5.69	5.66	5.63
5	6.61	5.79	5.41	5.19	5.05	4.95	4.88	4.82	4.77	4.74	4.68	4.62	4.56	4.53	4.50	4.46	4.43	4.40	4.36
6	5.99	5.14	4.76	4.53	4.39	4.28	4.21	4.15	4.10	4.06	4.00	3.94	3.87	3.84	3.81	3.77	3.74	3.70	3.67
7	5.59	4.74	4.35	4.12	3.97	3.87	3.79	3.73	3.68	3.64	3.57	3.51	3.44	3.41	3.38	3.34	3.30	3.27	3.23
8	5.32	4.46	4.07	3.84	3.69	3.58	3.50	3.44	3.39	3.35	3.28	3.22	3.15	3.12	3.08	3.04	3.01	2.97	2.93
9	5.12	4.26	3.86	3.63	3.48	3.37	3.29	3.23	3.18	3.14	3.07	3.01	2.94	2.90	2.86	2.83	2.79	2.75	2.71
10	4.96	4.10	3.71	3.48	3.33	3.22	3.14	3.07	3.02	2.98	2.91	2.85	2.77	2.74	2.70	2.66	2.62	2.58	2.54
11	4.84	3.98	3.59	3.36	3.20	3.09	3.01	2.95	2.90	2.85	2.79	2.72	2.65	2.61	2.57	2.53	2.49	2.45	2.40
12	4.75	3.89	3.49	3.26	3.11	3.00	2.91	2.85	2.80	2.75	2.69	2.62	2.54	2.51	2.47	2.43	2.38	2.34	2.30
13	4.67	3.81	3.41	3.18	3.03	2.92	2.83	2.77	2.71	2.67	2.60	2.53	2.46	2.42	2.38	2.34	2.30	2.25	2.21
14	4.60	3.74	3.34	3.11	2.96	2.85	2.76	2.70	2.65	2.60	2.53	2.46	2.39	2.35	2.31	2.27	2.22	2.18	2.13
15	4.54	3.68	3.29	3.06	2.90	2.79	2.71	2.64	2.59	2.54	2.48	2.40	2.33	2.29	2.25	2.20	2.16	2.11	2.07
16	4.49	3.63	3.24	3.01	2.85	2.74	2.66	2.59	2.54	2.49	2.42	2.35	2.28	2.24	2.19	2.15	2.11	2.06	2.01
17	4.45	3.59	3.20	2.96	2.81	2.70	2.61	2.55	2.49	2.45	2.38	2.31	2.23	2.19	2.15	2.10	2.06	2.01	1.96
18	4.41	3.55	3.16	2.93	2.77	2.66	2.58	2.51	2.46	2.41	2.34	2.27	2.19	2.15	2.11	2.06	2.02	1.97	1.92
19	4.38	3.52	3.13	2.90	2.74	2.63	2.54	2.48	2.42	2.38	2.31	2.23	2.16	2.11	2.07	2.03	1.98	1.93	1.88

m_2 = degrees of freedom for denominator

Exhibit F–10   Percentiles of the F Distribution (Continued)

$F_{.95}(m_1, m_2)$

$\alpha = 0.05$

m_1 = degrees of freedom for numerator

m_2 \ m_1	1	2	3	4	5	6	7	8	9	10	12	15	20	24	30	40	60	120	∞
20	4.35	3.49	3.10	2.87	2.71	2.60	2.51	2.45	2.39	2.35	2.28	2.20	2.12	2.08	2.04	1.99	1.95	1.90	1.84
21	4.32	3.47	3.07	2.84	2.68	2.57	2.49	2.42	2.37	2.32	2.25	2.18	2.10	2.05	2.01	1.96	1.92	1.87	1.81
22	4.30	3.44	3.05	2.82	2.66	2.55	2.46	2.40	2.34	2.30	2.23	2.15	2.07	2.03	1.98	1.94	1.89	1.84	1.78
23	4.28	3.42	3.03	2.80	2.64	2.53	2.44	2.37	2.32	2.27	2.20	2.13	2.05	2.01	1.96	1.91	1.86	1.81	1.76
24	4.26	3.40	3.01	2.78	2.62	2.51	2.42	2.36	2.30	2.25	2.18	2.11	2.03	1.98	1.94	1.89	1.84	1.79	1.73
25	4.24	3.39	2.99	2.76	2.60	2.49	2.40	2.34	2.28	2.24	2.16	2.09	2.01	1.96	1.92	1.87	1.82	1.77	1.71
26	4.23	3.37	2.98	2.74	2.59	2.47	2.39	2.32	2.27	2.22	2.15	2.07	1.99	1.95	1.90	1.85	1.80	1.75	1.69
27	4.21	3.35	2.96	2.73	2.57	2.46	2.37	2.31	2.25	2.20	2.13	2.06	1.97	1.93	1.88	1.84	1.79	1.73	1.67
28	4.20	3.34	2.95	2.71	2.56	2.45	2.36	2.29	2.24	2.19	2.12	2.04	1.96	1.91	1.87	1.82	1.77	1.71	1.65
29	4.18	3.33	2.93	2.70	2.55	2.43	2.35	2.28	2.22	2.18	2.10	2.03	1.94	1.90	1.85	1.81	1.75	1.70	1.64
30	4.17	3.32	2.92	2.69	2.53	2.42	2.33	2.27	2.21	2.16	2.09	2.01	1.93	1.89	1.84	1.79	1.74	1.68	1.62
40	4.08	3.23	2.84	2.61	2.45	2.34	2.25	2.18	2.12	2.08	2.00	1.92	1.84	1.79	1.74	1.69	1.64	1.58	1.51
60	4.00	3.15	2.76	2.53	2.37	2.25	2.17	2.10	2.04	1.99	1.92	1.84	1.75	1.70	1.65	1.59	1.53	1.47	1.39
120	3.92	3.07	2.68	2.45	2.29	2.17	2.09	2.02	1.96	1.91	1.83	1.75	1.66	1.61	1.55	1.50	1.43	1.35	1.25
∞	3.84	3.00	2.60	2.37	2.21	2.10	2.01	1.94	1.88	1.83	1.75	1.67	1.57	1.52	1.46	1.39	1.32	1.22	1.00

m_2 = degrees of freedom for denominator

Exhibit F–10 Percentiles of the F Distribution (Continued)

$F_{.975}(m_1 m_2)$

$\alpha = 0.025$

$m_1 =$ degrees of freedom for numerator

m_2 \ m_1	1	2	3	4	5	6	7	8	9	10	12	15	20	24	30	40	60	120	∞
1	647.8	799.5	864.2	899.6	921.8	937.1	948.2	956.7	963.3	968.6	976.7	984.9	993.1	997.2	1001	1006	1010	1014	1018
2	38.51	39.00	39.17	39.25	39.30	39.33	39.36	39.37	39.39	39.40	39.41	39.43	39.45	39.46	39.46	39.47	39.48	39.49	39.50
3	17.44	16.04	15.44	15.10	14.88	14.73	14.62	14.54	14.47	14.42	14.34	14.25	14.17	14.12	14.08	14.04	13.99	13.95	13.90
4	12.22	10.65	9.98	9.60	9.36	9.20	9.07	8.98	8.90	8.84	8.75	8.66	8.56	8.51	8.46	8.41	8.36	8.31	8.26
5	10.01	8.43	7.76	7.39	7.15	6.98	6.85	6.76	6.68	6.62	6.52	6.43	6.33	6.28	6.23	6.18	6.12	6.07	6.02
6	8.81	7.26	6.60	6.23	5.99	5.82	5.70	5.60	5.52	5.46	5.37	5.27	5.17	5.12	5.07	5.01	4.96	4.90	4.85
7	8.07	6.54	5.89	5.52	5.29	5.12	4.99	4.90	4.82	4.76	4.67	4.57	4.47	4.42	4.36	4.31	4.25	4.20	4.14
8	7.57	6.06	5.42	5.05	4.82	4.65	4.53	4.43	4.36	4.30	4.20	4.10	4.00	3.95	3.89	3.84	3.78	3.73	3.67
9	7.21	5.71	5.08	4.72	4.48	4.32	4.20	4.10	4.03	3.96	3.87	3.77	3.67	3.61	3.56	3.51	3.45	3.39	3.33
10	6.94	5.46	4.83	4.47	4.24	4.07	3.95	3.85	3.78	3.72	3.62	3.52	3.42	3.37	3.31	3.26	3.20	3.14	3.08
11	6.72	5.26	4.63	4.28	4.04	3.88	3.76	3.66	3.59	3.53	3.43	3.33	3.23	3.17	3.12	3.06	3.00	2.94	2.88
12	6.55	5.10	4.47	4.12	3.89	3.73	3.61	3.51	3.44	3.37	3.28	3.18	3.07	3.02	2.96	2.91	2.85	2.79	2.72
13	6.41	4.97	4.35	4.00	3.77	3.60	3.48	3.39	3.31	3.25	3.15	3.05	2.95	2.89	2.84	2.78	2.72	2.66	2.60
14	6.30	4.86	4.24	3.89	3.66	3.50	3.38	3.29	3.21	3.15	3.05	2.95	2.84	2.79	2.73	2.67	2.61	2.55	2.49
15	6.20	4.77	4.15	3.80	3.58	3.41	3.29	3.20	3.12	3.06	2.96	2.86	2.76	2.70	2.64	2.59	2.52	2.46	2.40
16	6.12	4.69	4.08	3.73	3.50	3.34	3.22	3.12	3.05	2.99	2.89	2.79	2.68	2.63	2.57	2.51	2.45	2.38	2.32
17	6.04	4.62	4.01	3.66	3.44	3.28	3.16	3.06	2.98	2.92	2.82	2.72	2.62	2.56	2.50	2.44	2.38	2.32	2.25
18	5.98	4.56	3.95	3.61	3.38	3.22	3.10	3.01	2.93	2.87	2.77	2.67	2.56	2.50	2.44	2.38	2.32	2.26	2.19
19	5.92	4.51	3.90	3.56	3.33	3.17	3.05	2.96	2.88	2.82	2.72	2.62	2.51	2.45	2.39	2.33	2.27	2.20	2.13

$m_2 =$ freedom for denominator

Exhibit F-10   Percentiles of the F Distribution (Continued)

$F_{.975}(m_1 m_2)$

$a = 0.025$

m_1 = degrees of freedom for numerator

m_2 = degrees of freedom

m_2 \ m_1	1	2	3	4	5	6	7	8	9	10	12	15	20	24	30	40	60	120	∞
20	5.87	4.46	3.86	3.51	3.29	3.13	3.01	2.91	2.84	2.77	2.68	2.57	2.46	2.41	2.35	2.29	2.22	2.16	2.09
21	5.83	4.42	3.82	3.48	3.25	3.09	2.97	2.87	2.80	2.73	2.64	2.53	2.42	2.37	2.31	2.25	2.18	2.11	2.04
22	5.79	4.38	3.78	3.44	3.22	3.05	2.93	2.84	2.76	2.70	2.60	2.50	2.39	2.33	2.27	2.21	2.14	2.08	2.00
23	5.75	4.35	3.75	3.41	3.18	3.02	2.90	2.81	2.73	2.67	2.57	2.47	2.36	2.30	2.24	2.18	2.11	2.04	1.97
24	5.72	4.32	3.72	3.38	3.15	2.99	2.87	2.78	2.70	2.64	2.54	2.44	2.33	2.27	2.21	2.15	2.08	2.01	1.94
25	5.69	4.29	3.69	3.35	3.13	2.97	2.85	2.75	2.68	2.61	2.51	2.41	2.30	2.24	2.18	2.12	2.05	1.98	1.91
26	5.66	4.27	3.67	3.33	3.10	2.94	2.82	2.73	2.65	2.59	2.49	2.39	2.28	2.22	2.16	2.09	2.03	1.95	1.88
27	5.63	4.24	3.65	3.31	3.08	2.92	2.80	2.71	2.63	2.57	2.47	2.36	2.25	2.19	2.13	2.07	2.00	1.93	1.85
28	5.61	4.22	3.63	3.29	3.06	2.90	2.78	2.69	2.61	2.55	2.45	2.34	2.23	2.17	2.11	2.05	1.98	1.91	1.83
29	5.59	4.20	3.61	3.27	3.04	2.88	2.76	2.67	2.59	2.53	2.43	2.32	2.21	2.15	2.09	2.03	1.96	1.89	1.81
30	5.57	4.18	3.59	3.25	3.03	2.87	2.75	2.65	2.57	2.51	2.41	2.31	2.20	2.14	2.07	2.01	1.94	1.87	1.79
40	5.42	4.05	3.46	3.13	2.90	2.74	2.62	2.53	2.45	2.39	2.29	2.18	2.07	2.01	1.94	1.88	1.80	1.72	1.64
60	5.29	3.93	3.34	3.01	2.79	2.63	2.51	2.41	2.33	2.27	2.17	2.06	1.94	1.88	1.82	1.74	1.67	1.58	1.48
120	5.15	3.80	3.23	2.89	2.67	2.52	2.39	2.30	2.22	2.16	2.05	1.94	1.82	1.76	1.69	1.61	1.53	1.43	1.31
∞	5.02	3.69	3.12	2.79	2.57	2.41	2.29	2.19	2.11	2.05	1.94	1.83	1.71	1.64	1.57	1.48	1.39	1.27	1.00

Exhibit F–10 Percentiles of the F Distribution (Continued)

$F_{.99}(m_1m_2)$

$a = 0.01$

m_1 = degrees of freedom for numerator

m_2 \ m_1	1	2	3	4	5	6	7	8	9	10	12	15	20	24	30	40	60	120	∞
1	4052	4999.5	5403	5625	5764	5859	5928	5982	6022	6056	6106	6157	6209	6235	6261	6287	6313	6339	6366
2	98.50	99.00	99.17	99.25	99.30	99.33	99.36	99.37	99.39	99.40	99.42	99.43	99.45	99.46	99.47	99.47	99.48	99.49	99.50
3	34.12	30.82	29.46	28.71	28.24	27.91	27.67	27.49	27.35	27.23	27.05	26.87	26.69	26.60	26.50	26.41	26.32	26.22	26.13
4	21.20	18.00	16.69	15.98	15.52	15.21	14.98	14.80	14.66	14.55	14.37	14.20	14.02	13.93	13.84	13.75	13.65	13.56	13.46
5	16.26	13.27	12.06	11.39	10.97	10.67	10.46	10.29	10.16	10.05	9.89	9.72	9.55	9.47	9.38	9.29	9.20	9.11	9.02
6	13.75	10.92	9.78	9.15	8.75	8.47	8.26	8.10	7.98	7.87	7.72	7.56	7.40	7.31	7.23	7.14	7.06	6.97	6.88
7	12.25	9.55	8.45	7.85	7.46	7.19	6.99	6.84	6.72	6.62	6.47	6.31	6.16	6.07	5.99	5.91	5.82	5.74	5.65
8	11.26	8.65	7.59	7.01	6.63	6.37	6.18	6.03	5.91	5.81	5.67	5.52	5.36	5.28	5.20	5.12	5.03	4.95	4.86
9	10.56	8.02	6.99	6.42	6.06	5.80	5.61	5.47	5.35	5.26	5.11	4.96	4.81	4.73	4.65	4.57	4.48	4.40	4.31
10	10.04	7.56	6.55	5.99	5.64	5.39	5.20	5.06	4.94	4.85	4.71	4.56	4.41	4.33	4.25	4.17	4.08	4.00	3.91
11	9.65	7.21	6.22	5.67	5.32	5.07	4.89	4.74	4.63	4.54	4.40	4.25	4.10	4.02	3.94	3.86	3.78	3.69	3.60
12	9.33	6.93	5.95	5.41	5.06	4.82	4.64	4.50	4.39	4.30	4.16	4.01	3.86	3.78	3.70	3.62	3.54	3.45	3.36
13	9.07	6.70	5.74	5.21	4.86	4.62	4.44	4.30	4.19	4.10	3.96	3.82	3.66	3.59	3.51	3.43	3.34	3.25	3.17
14	8.86	6.51	5.56	5.04	4.69	4.46	4.28	4.14	4.03	3.94	3.80	3.66	3.51	3.43	3.35	3.27	3.18	3.09	3.00
15	8.68	6.36	5.42	4.89	4.56	4.32	4.14	4.00	3.89	3.80	3.67	3.52	3.37	3.29	3.21	3.13	3.05	2.96	2.87
16	8.53	6.23	5.29	4.77	4.44	4.20	4.03	3.89	3.78	3.69	3.55	3.41	3.26	3.18	3.10	3.02	2.93	2.84	2.75
17	8.40	6.11	5.18	4.67	4.34	4.10	3.93	3.79	3.68	3.59	3.46	3.31	3.16	3.08	3.00	2.92	2.83	2.75	2.65
18	8.29	6.01	5.09	4.58	4.25	4.01	3.84	3.71	3.60	3.51	3.37	3.23	3.08	3.00	2.92	2.84	2.75	2.66	2.57
19	8.18	5.93	5.01	4.50	4.17	3.94	3.77	3.63	3.52	3.43	3.30	3.15	3.00	2.92	2.84	2.76	2.67	2.58	2.49

freedom for denominator

Exhibit F-10   Percentiles of the F Distribution (Continued)

$F_{.99}(m_1 m_2)$

$a = 0.01$

m_1 = degrees of freedom for numerator

m_2 \ m_1	1	2	3	4	5	6	7	8	9	10	12	15	20	24	30	40	60	120	∞
20	8.10	5.85	4.94	4.43	4.10	3.87	3.70	3.56	3.46	3.37	3.23	3.09	2.94	2.86	2.78	2.69	2.61	2.52	2.42
21	8.02	5.78	4.87	4.37	4.04	3.81	3.64	3.51	3.40	3.31	3.17	3.03	2.88	2.80	2.72	2.64	2.55	2.46	2.36
22	7.95	5.72	4.82	4.31	3.99	3.76	3.59	3.45	3.35	3.26	3.12	2.98	2.83	2.75	2.67	2.58	2.50	2.40	2.31
23	7.88	5.66	4.76	4.26	3.94	3.71	3.54	3.41	3.30	3.21	3.07	2.93	2.78	2.70	2.62	2.54	2.45	2.35	2.26
24	7.82	5.61	4.72	4.22	3.90	3.67	3.50	3.36	3.26	3.17	3.03	2.89	2.74	2.66	2.58	2.49	2.40	2.31	2.21
25	7.77	5.57	4.68	4.18	3.85	3.63	3.46	3.32	3.22	3.13	2.99	2.85	2.70	2.62	2.54	2.45	2.36	2.27	2.17
26	7.72	5.53	4.64	4.14	3.82	3.59	3.42	3.29	3.18	3.09	2.96	2.81	2.66	2.58	2.50	2.42	2.33	2.23	2.13
27	7.68	5.49	4.60	4.11	3.78	3.56	3.39	3.26	3.15	3.06	2.93	2.78	2.63	2.55	2.47	2.38	2.29	2.20	2.10
28	7.64	5.45	4.57	4.07	3.75	3.53	3.36	3.23	3.12	3.03	2.90	2.75	2.60	2.52	2.44	2.35	2.26	2.17	2.06
29	7.60	5.42	4.54	4.04	3.73	3.50	3.33	3.20	3.09	3.00	2.87	2.73	2.57	2.49	2.41	2.33	2.23	2.14	2.03
30	7.56	5.39	4.51	4.02	3.70	3.47	3.30	3.17	3.07	2.98	2.84	2.70	2.55	2.47	2.39	2.30	2.21	2.11	2.01
40	7.31	5.18	4.31	3.83	3.51	3.29	3.12	2.99	2.89	2.80	2.66	2.52	2.37	2.29	2.20	2.11	2.02	1.92	1.80
60	7.08	4.98	4.13	3.65	3.34	3.12	2.95	2.82	2.72	2.63	2.50	2.35	2.20	2.12	2.03	1.94	1.84	1.73	1.60
120	6.85	4.79	3.95	3.48	3.17	2.96	2.79	2.66	2.56	2.47	2.34	2.19	2.03	1.95	1.86	1.76	1.66	1.53	1.38
∞	6.63	4.61	3.78	3.32	3.02	2.80	2.64	2.51	2.41	2.32	2.18	2.04	1.88	1.79	1.70	1.59	1.47	1.32	1.00

m_2 = degrees of freedom

Exhibit F-11 Percentiles of the t Distribution*

m	$t_{.60}$	$t_{.70}$	$t_{.80}$	$t_{.90}$	$t_{.95}$	$t_{.975}$	$t_{.99}$	$t_{.995}$
1	.325	.727	1.376	3.078	6.314	12.706	31.821	63.657
2	.289	.617	1.061	1.886	2.920	4.303	6.965	9.925
3	.277	.584	.978	1.638	2.353	3.182	4.541	5.841
4	.271	.569	.941	1.533	2.132	2.776	3.747	4.604
5	.267	.559	.920	1.476	2.015	2.571	3.365	4.032
6	.265	.553	.906	1.440	1.943	2.447	3.143	3.707
7	.263	.549	.896	1.415	1.895	2.365	2.998	3.499
8	.262	.546	.889	1.397	1.860	2.306	2.896	3.355
9	.261	.543	.883	1.383	1.833	2.262	2.821	3.250
10	.260	.542	.879	1.372	1.812	2.228	2.764	3.169
11	.260	.540	.876	1.363	1.796	2.201	2.718	3.106
12	.259	.539	.873	1.356	1.782	2.179	2.681	3.055
13	.259	.538	.870	1.350	1.771	2.160	2.650	3.012
14	.258	.537	.868	1.345	1.761	2.145	2.624	2.977
15	.258	.536	.866	1.341	1.753	2.131	2.602	2.947
16	.258	.535	.865	1.337	1.746	2.120	2.583	2.921
17	.257	.534	.863	1.333	1.740	2.110	2.567	2.898
18	.257	.534	.862	1.330	1.734	2.101	2.552	2.878
19	.257	.533	.861	1.328	1.729	2.093	2.539	2.861
20	.257	.533	.860	1.325	1.725	2.086	2.528	2.845
21	.257	.532	.859	1.323	1.721	2.080	2.518	2.831
22	.256	.532	.858	1.321	1.717	2.074	2.508	2.819
23	.256	.532	.858	1.319	1.714	2.069	2.500	2.807
24	.256	.531	.857	1.318	1.711	2.064	2.492	2.797
25	.256	.531	.856	1.316	1.708	2.060	2.485	2.787

Exhibit F-11   Percentiles of the t Distribution (Continued)

m	$t_{.60}$	$t_{.70}$	$t_{.80}$	$t_{.90}$	$t_{.95}$	$t_{.975}$	$t_{.99}$	$t_{.995}$
26	.256	.531	.856	1.315	1.706	2.056	2.479	2.779
27	.256	.531	.855	1.314	1.703	2.052	2.473	2.771
28	.256	.530	.855	1.313	1.701	2.048	2.467	2.763
29	.256	.530	.854	1.311	1.699	2.045	2.462	2.756
30	.256	.530	.854	1.310	1.697	2.042	2.457	2.750
40	.255	.529	.851	1.303	1.684	2.021	2.423	2.704
60	.254	.527	.848	1.296	1.671	2.000	2.390	2.660
120	.254	.526	.845	1.289	1.658	1.980	2.358	2.617
∞	.253	.524	.842	1.282	1.645	1.960	2.326	2.576
m	$t_{.40}$	$t_{.30}$	$t_{.20}$	$t_{.10}$	$t_{.05}$	$t_{.025}$	$t_{.01}$	$t_{.005}$

Taken from Table III of R. A. Fisher and F. Yates, *Statistical Tables for Biological, Agricultural, and Medical Research*, published by Oliver and Boyd, Ltd., Edinburgh, 1938. By permission of the authors and publishers.

* When the table is read from the foot, the tabled values are to be prefixed with a negative sign.

index